REFLECTIONS ON ETHICS,

FREEDOM, WELFARE ECONOMICS,

POLICY, AND THE LEGACY OF

AUSTRIAN ECONOMICS

THE COLLECTED WORKS OF ISRAEL M. KIRZNER

Austrian Subjectivism and the Emergence of Entrepreneurship Theory

Competition, Economic Planning, and the Knowledge Problem

Competition and Entrepreneurship

Discovery, Capitalism, and Distributive Justice

The Economic Point of View

Essays on Capital and Interest

The Essence of Entrepreneurship and the Nature and Significance of Market Process

Ludwig von Mises: The Man and His Economics

Market Theory and the Price System

Reflections on Ethics, Freedom, Welfare Economics, Policy, and the Legacy of Austrian Economics

ISRAEL M. KIRZNER

Reflections on Ethics, Freedom, Welfare Economics, Policy, and the Legacy of Austrian Economics

Edited and with an Introduction by

PETER J. BOETTKE and FRÉDÉRIC SAUTET

LIBERTY FUND

Introduction and index © 2018 by Liberty Fund, Inc.

All articles are reprinted by permission.

All rights reserved

Printed in the United States of America

22 21 20 19 18 C 5 4 3 2 1
22 21 20 19 18 P 5 4 3 2 1

Library of Congress Cataloging-in-Publication Data

Names: Kirzner, Israel M., author. | Boettke, Peter J., author. | Sautet, Frederic E., author.

Title: Reflections on ethics, freedom, welfare economics, policy, and the legacy of Austrian economics / Israel M. Kirzner, Frederic Sautet, Peter J. Boettke.

Description: Carmel : Liberty Fund Inc., 2018. | Series: The collected works of Israel M. Kirzner ; 9 | Includes bibliographical references and index.

Identifiers: LCCN 2018018397 | ISBN 9780865978683 (hardback) | ISBN 9780865978690 (paperback)

Subjects: LCSH: Austrian school of economics. | Welfare economics. | Economic policy. | Economics—Moral and ethical aspects.

Classification: LCC HB98 .K575 2018 | DDC 330.15/7—dc23

LC record available at https://lccn.loc.gov/2018018397

LIBERTY FUND, INC.

11301 North Meridian Street

Carmel, Indiana 46032-4564

B'EZRAS HASHEM

CONTENTS

This volume in Israel Kirzner's *Collected Works* comprises a series of subjects that modern-day economists do not often explore. Indeed, this volume is largely dedicated to the normative aspect of Kirzner's research. The Austrian school of economics is well known for its free market approach; Kirzner's work is no exception. Throughout his career, he has consistently argued in favor of the free market as a desirable social system and has never been shy to defend his normative views against attacks. While many modern economists are reluctant to be known for their policy stance, especially one favoring the free enterprise system and private property, Kirzner's position is a reminder of the attitude of most economists before World War II.

Indeed, from the days of Adam Smith in eighteenth-century Scotland to those of Friedrich Hayek, Arnold Plant, and Lionel Robbins at the London School of Economics in the 1930s, most economists have been staunch defenders of economic freedom. The sect of economists, as it was called in continental Europe at the time of Frédéric Bastiat in the mid-nineteenth century, was known for its fierce opposition to government encroachments in the daily lives of citizens and its support for free trade, low taxes, and a fair administration of justice. That state of affairs changed, however, at the turn of the twentieth century with the rise of Fabian socialism in England and of the progressive movement in the United States. The economist's role in society evolved further in the 1930s with the Keynesian transformation.

In the wake of the Great Depression, mainstream economic thinking abandoned the traditional economists' defense of the market economy and instead developed varying recommendations for an "economics of control," justifying government regulation to curb microeconomic inefficiency on the one hand and government management of aggregate demand to ensure full employment and economic growth on the other. Moreover, economists began to advocate a variety of public policies that would produce a more equitable distribution of income. The age of economic laissez-faire gave way to one of progressive politics and economic management. These policies were supposed to mend the social ills of capitalism and correctly balance the trade-offs between equity and efficiency, stability and creative destruction, and security and prosperity. The New Deal gave way to the Fair Deal and eventually to the Great Society. It was in that intellectual climate of post–World War II that Israel Kirzner developed his approach to economic science and policy analysis.

Kirzner has applied his thinking to ethics, political philosophy, and public policy for a large part of his career. Friedrich Hayek, Ludwig von Mises, Max Weber, and Philip Wicksteed, among others, have shaped his intellectual path. Fundamentally Kirzner contends that in order to make ethical judgments about a social system, one must first understand the science behind it. In other words, having good knowledge of the principles that govern markets is a prerequisite for ethical statements about them. It is only through a clear grasp of the fundamental concepts of economic science, such as profit, interest, and entrepreneurship, that one can make true statements about welfare economics, the morality of market transactions, and policy issues. This places economics at the heart of most discussions on social systems.

While he has taken normative positions, Kirzner, following Mises, has also continuously affirmed the *Wertfrei* character of economics. Economics per se is concerned with establishing causes and effects, not with judging whether certain outcomes are desirable. This leaves economists the freedom to explain the consequences of minimum wage laws without sacrificing the value-free aspect of economics. Rejecting minimum wage laws because they cannot achieve full employment does not mean that one sacrifices *Wertfreiheit*.

Fundamentally Kirzner's work on ethics, political philosophy, and public policy has consisted in applying the insights he gained from his work on the market process to those fields. In Kirzner's view, the justifications for many public policies are based on various claims amounting to government omniscience. Instead, policy makers should rely on the entrepreneurial process, as it is the only way opportunities for the betterment of individuals can be eventually discovered and seized. As Kirzner explained many years ago in *Competition and Entrepreneurship*, "The crucial question for government-market comparisons [as alternative social devices for allocating resources] must concern the capacity of each of the two systems *to bring available opportunities to the attention of decision-makers.*"[1] In the absence of the profit and loss mechanism, there is no reason to expect that socially desirable opportunities will be discovered.

It is also through the consistent application of his insights on the role of the entrepreneurial function that Kirzner established the crucial difference between the notion of entrepreneurial discovery on the one hand and that of the entrepreneurial process on the other. The latter refers to the continual and simultaneous entrepreneurial discoveries that create a systematic process of adjustment in the allocation of resources in society. The existence of entrepreneurial discoveries does not imply the presence of an entrepreneurial process. This distinction is crucial to Kirzner's view of (a) the emergence of institutions and (b) the extent to which economics can be applied to non-market cases.

Overall, the implications of Kirzner's stance for public policy can be devastating, as "one is surely entitled to question the appropriateness of labeling *inefficient* an allocation of resources whose inefficiency no one, including the welfare theorist, has been able to discover."[2] Kirzner's approach questions the validity of many conclusions of popular policy views, such as the presence of widespread market failures and the effects of knowledge spillovers. Kirzner's insights reinforce the skeptical view of public policy that economists such as Ronald Coase, Armen Alchian, and Yale Brozen have developed since the 1960s.

This volume contains nine sections. The first eight sections offer Kirzner's reflections on the role of individual freedom, the nature of economic science, welfare economics, ethics and morality, institutions, public policy, economic education, and the legacy of Austrian economics. These sections are extremely rich in reflections. The welfare economics section comprises Kirzner's papers on coordination as a welfare criterion. The section on policy contains Kirzner's work on taxation and regulation in which he applies his market process perspective to age-old questions of economic policy. This section also includes a paper on anti-trust policy that was originally published in Spanish and is now presented in its

---

1. Israel M. Kirzner, *Competition and Entrepreneurship* (Chicago: University of Chicago Press, 1973; repr. Indianapolis: Liberty Fund, 2013), p. 184 (italics in the original). Citations refer to the Liberty Fund edition.

2. *Competition and Entrepreneurship*, p. 188.

original English version for the first time.[3] Note also that the section on the legacy of Austrian economics includes eulogies of Friedrich Hayek and Ludwig Lachmann.

The last section contains three long interviews of Kirzner. Stephen Boehm conducted the first interview in 1989. The Ludwig von Mises Institute published Kirzner's second interview in 1997. Finally, the editors of this volume conducted their own interview with the author in 2006.

ACKNOWLEDGMENTS

We would first like to thank wholeheartedly Israel Kirzner for his unparalleled contribution to economic science. Kirzner's research program has deeply enriched the discipline and has shed light on some of economics' most difficult puzzles. Economists owe him an immense intellectual debt.

The publication of *The Collected Works of Israel M. Kirzner* would not be a reality without the participation of Liberty Fund, Inc. We are extremely grateful to Liberty Fund, and especially Emilio Pacheco, for making this project possible. To republish Kirzner's unique œuvre has been on our minds since our time spent at New York University in the 1990s—where one of us was a professor (Peter) and the other a post-doc student (Frédéric). We are thrilled at the idea that current and future generations of economists and other scholars will have easy access to Kirzner's works.

Finally, we wish to thank Emily Washington for her invaluable help in the publication of this volume.

Peter J. Boettke and Frédéric Sautet

---

3. The title is "The Goals of Anti-Trust: A Critique."

ECONOMICS, MARKETS, AND INDIVIDUAL FREEDOM

ENTREPRENEURSHIP, CHOICE, AND FREEDOM

The concept of freedom is notoriously difficult to pin down. Philosophers and social scientists have exercised extraordinary ingenuity and subtlety in identifying the slight variations in meaning separating the many writers who have attempted to define freedom. Economists, perhaps more than others, have been subject to strong temptation to altogether overlook what should surely be considered an important, if not the essential, aspect of human freedom. The task of pointing out the source of this possible confusion presents, it will turn out, an opportunity worthwhile not only for its own sake, but also for its help in understanding the role of freedom in achieving social efficiency and in assessing the consequences for society of its curtailment. Stigler has recently challenged those who see the growth of the modern state as a danger to liberty to specify concretely the liberties that have been, in fact, impaired by this growth.[1] I shall argue that a proper understanding of liberty suggests that, in the very nature of things, such specification cannot be expected; moreover such proper understanding, it can be shown, reveals the loss of liberty that results from the growth of government in a manner so convincing as to render such specification hardly necessary.

FREEDOM, CHOICE, AND ECONOMICS

Among the multitude of meanings attached to the notion of freedom, it is widely held to pertain to some or other aspect of choice. And this circumstance seems responsible for what I shall argue to be the overly narrow perception of individual freedom that holds peculiar temptation for economists. Choice is, after all, very much a matter of concern to the economist. Efficiency—the norm for economic discussion—has everything to do with correct choice; rationality in choice is the assumption basic to the main body of economic theory, and economics itself is

Presented at a meeting of the Southern Economic Association, Washington, D.C., November 1978. From *Perception, Opportunity, and Profit: Studies in the Theory of Entrepreneurship* (Chicago and London: University of Chicago Press, 1979), 225–39. Reprinted by permission of Lucius & Lucius Verlagsgesellschaft mbH; the original source is *ORDO: Jahrbuch für die Ordnung von Wirtschaft und Gesellschaft*, 1979.

defined in terms of the choices people make concerning the allocation of scarce means to satisfy multiple competing ends. But this preoccupation by the economist with choice, one may argue, is responsible for the incomplete appreciation of freedom that seems to pervade much economic literature.

The problem is easily presented. Choice, for the economist, has come to mean the solution of a maximization problem. The economist sees the decision maker, whether consumer, producer, or resource owner, as allocating given means in such a way as to maximize the value of ends attained, with the relative rankings of the various ends seen as given. Freedom of choice refers to agent's liberty to select those courses of action he sees as maximizing his utility (or profit, or whatever else is seen as being maximized). Limitations on freedom take the form of prohibitions or constraints that prevent one's attaining goals that might otherwise be selected.

Basic to choice for the economist, then, is the *given* character of both ends and means.[2] The hierarchy of ends worthy of attainment is given; the constellation of means capable of achieving the various ends is also given. The act of choice is seen as occurring within the framework of this given ranking of ends and constellation of means. Freedom of choice, as well as limitations on such freedom, then, is viewed only as it impinges on the situation of the economizing individual *facing his given ends-means framework*. No matter what constraints, limitations, or prohibitions may be imposed on the economizing individual, they touch his freedom of choice not at all, for the economist, so long as they do not affect his ability to achieve the optimum position *relevant to and implicit in the given ends-means environment*.

It is here that confusion is found. No matter how important the problem of efficient decision making against the background of given ends and means may be, it represents only one narrow aspect of the human condition. As Mises,[3] Shackle,[4] and Lachmann[5] have again and again reminded us, the economist's view of the decision abstracts from elements that are crucial to the true character of human choice. The notion of given ends and means may be useful for certain purposes, but it does serious violence to the full reality of choice. The acting person never approaches the moment of decision *already* equipped with a clear, given picture of the relevant ends and means. It is only *at the moment of decision itself* that man is compelled to bring to some kind of focus all his doubts and conjectures concerning what goals are worth pursuing and what resources and technologies are available. The choices of people subject to unexplainable whims and taste changes—operating in a world whose realities are by no means immediately apparent and moreover character-ized by continuous, kaleidic change—can hardly be subsumed, without serious strain, under the heading of maximizing calculations.

Once this broader view of choice is recognized, the notion of freedom of choice is surely seen to mean far more than the ability to realize a cal-culated optimum position. Freedom of choice can now be seen to encom-pass the liberty *to make up one's own mind as to the ranking of the ends to be pursued and the means judged available for the purpose.* Once a given ends-means framework has been adopted, freedom can only mean the freedom to achieve what one has already announced that one wishes to achieve. It is this narrow view of freedom that many economists seem to have adopted. But, with the acting man seen as approaching choice without having firmly adopted any one framework of ends and means, freedom of choice is at once seen as freedom to announce (i.e., to choose) what it is one wishes to achieve.

We may, to put it more bluntly, say that the narrow view of freedom we have attributed to the standard economist's conception of choice turns out to involve no choice at all. One has, in this conception of choice, in effect already chosen *before* the moment of decision. With given ranking of ends and with given means, the optimum position is fully implied in the data. Freedom, as well as its curtailment, can in such assumed cir-cumstances refer only to the ability to achieve a given goal (or to its cur-tailment).[6] On the other hand, the wider view of freedom recognizes that, when people refer to the freedom to choose, they have in mind liberty to select among a wide range of moral and value frameworks, of ethical sys-tems, of tastes; to make their own guesses concerning present realities and future uncertainties; to determine for themselves what opportunities they are in fact confronted with.

The above discussion can be stated concisely using the contrast I have elsewhere drawn between the Robbinsian allocation, maximizing view of the economizing decision and the Misesian entrepreneurial view of human action.[7] For the Robbinsian decision maker freedom means free-dom to proceed to where one (already) wishes to be; for the Misesian entrepreneurial human agent, freedom means freedom to discover and to determine for oneself where it is that one wishes to be.[8]

FREEDOM AND POWER

The foregoing may throw light on the much-discussed confusion between *freedom* and *power*. Economists have tended to succumb to the temptation to define freedom so as to make it indistinguishable from power. For these writers, freedom means simply the ability to attain what one wishes to attain.[9] A small number of writers, among economists notably Hayek[10] and Machlup,[11] have emphatically denounced the blurring of the distinction between freedom and power. A number of writers (perhaps Knight is the most notable)[12] while recognizing that freedom is not the same as power, have somehow offered formulations of the concept of freedom that turn out to substantially identify it with power after all. Our earlier discussion can be helpful in clarifying the issues. Let us consider what has changed when a particular option, hitherto available to a decision maker, is somehow removed from the list of possibilities. In particular, let us ask what this change may possibly have done to the freedom of choice of that decision maker.

Now, from a Robbinsian point of view—that is, seeing the decision maker as having *already*, before the act of choice, become fully aware of the options available to him, and having *already* determined his ranking of conceivable outcomes—it should be apparent that the removal of an option that had hitherto been available may mean one of two things. If the option in question was one the Robbinsian decision maker would *not* have adopted, then its removal has no effect whatsoever. Since, even before his moment of decision, the decision maker had already adopted a well-defined ends-means framework, courses of action dominated by the optimal solution are simply irrelevant; they have been inexorably declared irrelevant by the structure of the ends-means framework taken as a datum. On the other hand, should the option that has been removed be the optimal one, then of course its removal affects our decision maker in a very significant way. But it is important for us not to misinterpret in what this effect consists. What has occurred is that a course of action the decision maker wished to adopt has been denied him. He may well be bitterly disappointed at having an anticipated desirable experience pulled out of his reach. If this option was removed by human design, he may well be outraged by its loss. He may denounce the loss as a violation of a commitment made to him, or as a violation of a right he possessed, or as sheer robbery, *but he will not be able to describe it as having affected his freedom to choose.* To be sure, his maximizing decision must now be recalculated from among those other courses of action he had hitherto rejected as suboptimal. The second-best solution now steps up into first place. But this does not constitute a restriction on freedom of choice. If there is a line of standby passengers, ranged in order of priority, hoping to get onto a particular flight, and only one seat is available, the person at the head of the line will get on the plane. If, just before he is permitted to enter the aircraft this individual is suddenly removed from the line, for whatever reason, the passenger second in line now steps up to the head of the line. The relative positions of the individuals in line has *already* marked out their priority ranking, and no selection needs to be made of who is to be admitted. The removal of the first passenger does not, therefore, create any new need to choose. It would not be correct to say that the removal of the first passenger has restricted freedom of choice with respect to who is permitted on the plane, because the line of hopeful passengers is now shorter. So, for Robbinsian decision making, the removal of a preferred option does not interfere with the decision maker's freedom of choice. In fact, the Robbinsian decision maker never does have to choose, in the true sense of the word. If, nonetheless, the removal of a preferred option does, in some crude use of language, come to be described as somehow cramping the freedom of choice of the decision maker, this can be understood only as consisting in the restriction imposed on the decision maker's ability to achieve definite goals. *Freedom has, in the Robbinsian framework, come inevitably to be merged with the concept of power to achieve goals.*

On the other hand, from the perspective of the acting person as an entrepreneur for whom the task of deciding embraces the very identification and ranking of ends and recognition of means, the matter seems altogether different. From this perspective, the removal of an option does indeed interfere with the decision maker's freedom of choice. For the human agent, seen as entrepreneur, *each* available course of action is, quite possibly, the optimal one. In fact, it is the essence of choice, in this context, *to choose* the optimal course of action, not in the sense of figuring out the solution to a maximization problem where the solution is already determined by the rankings assumed in the data, but in the sense of choosing the ranking itself. So the removal of an option does indeed affect freedom of choice. This is so not because its removal denies the decision maker something he wishes to attain; before the act of choice it has not yet been determined which option he does in fact wish to attain. The removal of an option restrictively alters the range from which choice may be made. Even if the lost option would, in some not well-defined sense, have been a *rejected* course of action, its removal nonetheless still constitutes an interference with freedom of choice. At the moment of choice, this option *was a possible option;* it had not yet been rejected either explicitly through choice, or implicitly through the given structure of some already-adopted ends-means framework.

FREEDOM AND THE RANGE OF ALTERNATIVES

Is freedom increased by the addition of options that the decision maker will not adopt because he prefers one of the existing options? Is freedom restricted by the removal of options the decision maker would have rejected anyway? The preceding discussion can throw light on these questions that have been raised from time to time in the literature on freedom.

Locke maintained that even if a prisoner does not wish to leave his cell, he is nonetheless not a free man because the option of leaving his cell is not available to him. If the action voluntarily taken by a man is the only one available to him, "he is not free, though perhaps the action is voluntary."[13] Knight, on the other hand, argued that a fence along the edge of a ravine does not restrict the freedom of hikers, since they would not wish to fall over the edge anyway.[14] As we have seen, the issue appears to revolve around the distinction between Robbinsian maximizing decisions and Misesian entrepreneurial choice.

If Locke's prisoner, who loves his cell beyond any other place he can imagine, is to be seen as not free, this can only mean that one considers what the prisoner would be at liberty to do *were he to change his mind.* Clearly, this is relevant only if one admits the possibility of escaping from a given Robbinsian framework in which one has one's mind already fully made up except for the chore of calculation. Knight's fence may be declared innocent of interfering with the freedom of hikers only because one views them as having already adopted a framework of ends that, however tentative and fluid, is yet seen as definitely ranking suicide below all other conceivable options.

Machlup, who insists strongly on maintaining the sharp distinction between freedom and power, has drawn attention to the possibility that an increment of freedom may itself inspire the acquisition of power. "In other words, certain freedoms may be of great importance for individuals and for society when no knowledge, no opportunity, and no power exist as yet to make use of presumably 'empty' freedoms. Their importance lies in the aspirations and ambitions which they arouse and which may lead to the search for the knowledge, opportunity, and power that are required to exercise the previously unused freedoms."[15] Machlup has in mind a potential option that the decision maker lacks the physical power to attain. So long as he is barred by human restrictions from exercising this option, even if he *had* the physical power to do so, he will not expend the effort or search for the knowledge required to win this physical power. The acquisition of freedom from human restrictions may inspire him to discover ways of overcoming the physical obstacles to exercising the option. This very interesting possibility provides an excellent example to illustrate my position.

On the face of it Machlup's case appears difficult to understand. There is, we take it, some course of action whose implementation requires certain inputs. These inputs may be physical, or they may take the form of knowledge or services of various kinds. Now, either the individual under consideration already has these inputs—or other inputs able to produce these inputs—available to him, or he does not. If he already had them available to him, then it is not clear how the acquisition of the freedom to pursue this particular course of action can be credited with inspiring the power to do so; this power was already possessed. On the other hand, if the inputs were not available until the moment when this freedom was acquired, then it is not clear how, merely through acquiring this freedom, our individual suddenly becomes endowed with inputs previously unavailable to him. Machlup uses the example of a bicycle rider able to pedal at no more than 20 mph who did not find it worthwhile to work harder to earn money to buy a car because of a law limiting all vehicles to a maximum of 25 mph. The abolition of the legal speed limit increases his desire for a car, and he works harder to earn the money to buy it. Thus the freedom to drive at 60 mph, while ineffective to one not owning a car, is effective, nonetheless, in arousing the ambition to achieve the power to exercise the previously unused freedom (to acquire a car).

But surely this example is one in which the *power* to acquire a car (and to drive at 60 mph) *was* possessed all the time. This individual always had open to him, physically, the option of working harder to earn money to buy the car; he did not exercise this option because of the existence of the speed limit which made this option not worthwhile. Machlup uses this example to show that actual capacity may be "created only after the freedom is established." It is true that the individual, until the lifting of the speed limit, had no car and thus lacked the "actual capacity" to drive at 60 mph immediately, but he certainly did not lack the actual capacity to acquire the car and thus, indirectly, to drive at 60 mph. It is true that the freedom acquired to drive at 60 mph converted the potential of owning a car into a reality. It is not, however, clear how this constitutes an expansion of power in any sense relevant to economic discussion.

What Machlup has noticed for us, it appears, is something highly significant, though his example, or his exposition of it, does not seem sufficiently clear. The point concerns the acquisition of freedom to pursue a particular course of action for which the individual indeed possessed the necessary inputs, but the very possibility of which has escaped his entrepreneurial attention. So long as the law limits all vehicles to 25 mph, a worker *may not see the acquisition of a car as being within his reach at all.* Opportunities one is unable to take advantage of tend not to be noticed at all. It is only when the speed limit has been lifted that an already feasible course of action comes into the decision maker's field of vision. The acquisition of freedom may indeed be credited with inspiring the determination to achieve a specific goal. As Machlup has noticed, freedom is fertile in creating actual (perceived) opportunities. A potential opportunity not yet noticed, may, through the addition of an increment of freedom, become an actual one. The process by which potential opportunities can, in this sense, be converted into actual ones is certainly of utmost importance for economists.

What I wish to point out here is that this *fertility of freedom,* to which Machlup has so valuably drawn our attention, can be discussed only within the context of what we have called the broader, entrepreneurial concept of freedom. An increment of freedom, in this sense, may be responsible for a decision maker's identifying a perceived ends-means framework otherwise hidden from him. This fertility of freedom is completely excluded from the purview of the narrower, "Robbinsian" conception of freedom. Within the Robbinsian given ends-means framework, freedom means the freedom to pursue perceived, chosen courses of action. The essence of this concept of freedom is that all opportunities have already been given to the decision maker in a manner that ensures his awareness of them. Under such conditions, an increment of freedom can hardly inspire new opportunities. Opportunities that may be physically possible *with* this increment of freedom are opportunities that would have been equally physically feasible without it. All opportunities of which the decision maker will be aware *after* acquiring an increment of freedom were opportunities of which, by the rules of the Robbinsian framework, he was aware *before* the increment of freedom was acquired. There is no room, within this framework, for any fertility in freedom.

ON NOT KNOWING WHAT ONE LACKS

So long as freedom is perceived from what we call the Robbinsian perspective, it becomes inevitable for it to become identified with the power to achieve chosen goals. Loss of freedom quite similarly, comes to be identified with thwarted desires. Freedom comes, from such a perspective, to be something whose curtailment triggers immediate pain. One cannot lose freedom, in this view, without feeling its loss. The matter is seen quite differently from the entrepreneurial perspective on freedom.

The entrepreneurial view of freedom permits us to see how freedom to choose may inspire the discovery of opportunities that may be invisible to those to whom this freedom is denied. Those to whom the freedom to choose has been denied will, in such cases, have no inkling that they are being denied an otherwise attainable goal. One denied the right to choose to enter college may never realize that he possesses the intellectual potential to be admitted to college. Denial of freedom to choose, from this perspective, does not necessarily inflict the pain of thwarted desires. In fact, *one may lack freedom and be convinced that one's well-being is wholly unaffected by its lack.*

All this appears directly relevant to Stigler's challenge. He asked for concrete specification of what liberties have, in fact, been impaired by the growth of the modern state. If "we canvass the population," Stigler claims, "we shall find few people who feel that their range of actions is seriously curtailed by the state."[16] Such a challenge takes it for granted that each impairment of liberty removes out of the reach of an individual some perceived and desired opportunity. To speak vaguely about loss of liberty without being able to specify precisely what opportunities have been closed off would, by such an understanding, indeed raise serious questions concerning the reality of the loss. But a broader understanding of the meaning of freedom, and of its loss, makes it entirely plausible that abrogations of freedom may indeed affect individuals without their being aware or for that matter without the awareness of anyone else, observing social scientists included, that their welfare has been damaged by this abrogation. It is no longer a necessary condition for the existence of loss of freedom that the loss be a felt one. It is true that Stigler himself seems not entirely unaware of the point here being made. He recognizes that "the most exploited of individuals probably does not feel the least bit exploited," citing the example of the complaisant slave. But the point as Stigler sees it appears to rest on naive ignorance of the very existence of limitations of freedom, and clearly assumes only the slightest importance in his view. For us, the point arises peculiarly from the entrepreneurial perspective on freedom, and is of much greater significance. I shall return later to the further implications of this insight.

THE PARADOX OF FREEDOM

Our discussion of the entrepreneurial view of the nature of freedom may throw some light on the riddle to which philosophers have drawn our attention in their discussions of the relation between freedom and reason. On the one hand, human choice is declared to be free, at least in the sense that people *feel* free to choose what they may. On the other hand, in the very exercise of their free choice, people discover themselves to be searching for the "correct" course of action, so that in fact their choice is in some sense *dictated* by that "correct" option. From this perspective, "when people . . . understand that in moral questions they are free to form their own opinions, they feel this freedom not as an emancipation but as a burden."[17] At least some philosophers have argued that no inconsistency is involved in this apparent paradox. "For a moral agent to choose that good which in the light of reflection approves itself as intrinsically greatest is to exercise the only freedom worth having. . . . To choose most responsibly is to see alternative goods with full clearness and to find the greatest of them tipping the beam."[18] No doubt these classic philosophic issues entail considerations far more profound than those raised here. Nonetheless our discussion does appear to hold some relevance for these issues.

In the course of arriving at a decision on any question, people *simultaneously* (1) fix the ends-means framework relevant to their situation, and (2) calculate the optimal course of action relevant to that framework. The latter task is one to which freedom of choice is, in a definite sense, irrelevant; the correct answer is given; one is merely searching for it. Freedom to choose, at this level, consists entirely of the burden of calculating correctly, of avoiding mistakes. Nonetheless, because this second task of calculation is never in fact divorced from the first step—that of identifying the ends-means framework—acts of choice are never possible without a genuine sense of freedom, without the unconstrained freedom to select whatever ranking of ends one may wish to uphold or whatever set of means one may wish to recognize as available. Now there may well be deeper levels of rationality that moral philosophers may wish to consider relevant to the very selection of a ranking of ends, but, at least at the superficial level appropriate to the economist, one source of the apparent paradox between one's sense of freedom and one's sense of the burden imposed by the rationality postulate seems to be illuminated by this discussion.

We now realize that in the course of the act of choice people freely identify the *criteria* for what will *now* be considered correct calculation of the optimal course of action. Ex post, one understands the course of action chosen by an individual as having been *constrained* by these criteria. In the calculations that are part of their actions, individuals seek the answer dictated by these criteria. But, at the same time, the very act of choice that encompasses these calculations encompasses also the free, undictated identification of what criteria are to be considered relevant. The sense of emancipation and the sense of burden and responsibility thus simultaneously have their places in free choice.

THE SOCIAL IMPORTANCE OF FREEDOM

The insights provided by the entrepreneurial view of freedom enable us to understand the social implications of individual freedom in a manner more profound than otherwise possible. Moreover, these insights enable us to understand how such a limited view of the social significance of freedom has in fact come to be adopted by so many economists.

For most economists, individual freedom is held to carry social significance, if indeed it is so held at all, only insofar as it permits the simultaneous achievement by each market participant of an optimal course of action within a framework of given ends and means. With given technological opportunity sets, with given resource endowments, and with given consumer preference functions, individual freedom allows market participants under specified assumptions to achieve the Paretian optimum embodied in the relevant general equilibrium solution. Restrictions on freedom by the state are therefore seen as bringing about suboptimal market outcomes, from the standpoint of the data. A free market in housing, it is understood, generates an equilibrium configuration of construction and of housing prices that may be, in some sense, optimal. Rent control, it is therefore shown, by restricting individual choices, generates suboptimal levels of prices and production. And so forth.

All this is no doubt correct and important. But it should be clear that it fails entirely to exhaust the full significance for society of an environment of freedom. This view rests entirely on the assumption that available opportunities are somehow instantaneously and costlessly known to market participants. But in the real world this is not the case. It is here that the full significance of freedom can be glimpsed. A free society is one in which individuals are free *to discover for themselves the available range of alternatives*. In his masterly critiques of the theory of central planning, Hayek directed attention to the circumstance that the information available in an economy is always scattered among countless individuals, never concentrated in the mind of a single central planner. Hayek pointed to the need for a social institutional structure capable of organizing the scattered scraps of available information so they can be used for the efficient allocation of society's resources.[19] The competitive market, Hayek showed us, is a discovery process, one in which society discovers what options are feasible and how important they are. Freedom, Hayek has shown in his more recent work, is of social significence precisely because no single mind can know in advance what will be discovered by social cooperation within a free environment. The "case for freedom," Hayek pointed out, "rests chiefly on the recognition of the inevitable ignorance of all of us concerning a great many of the factors on which the achievement of our ends and welfare depends. . . . Liberty is essential in order to leave room for the unforseeable and unpredictable. . . . It is . . . because we rarely know which of us knows best that we trust the independent and competitive efforts of many to induce the emergence of what we shall want when we see it."[20] "If we knew how freedom would be used, the case for it would largely disappear."[21] Our discussion approaches very similar conclusions from a somewhat different angle.

For us, individual freedom emerges as significant for society because it inspires each individual to discover what opportunities confront him. It is not only the case, that is, that society—or its central planners—do not know all the scattered information held by individuals in a society. In addition, at any given moment each individual does not know the information costlessly available to him. An environment of freedom encourages individuals to discover what opportunities each of them faces. If a market economy is believed to possess powerful equilibrating tendencies, these tendencies depend on freedom not only to permit, as Hayek showed, the social deployment of existing information, but also to permit (through the very same Hayekian market processes) the discovery by individuals of those opportunities made available by the attitudes and the knowledge of fellow market participants as well as by the technological possibilities existing in nature, the grasping of which constitutes the steps in the equilibrating process.

Restrictions on economic freedom hurt society, therefore, in ways far more serious than recognized by most economists. I have drawn attention to the circumstance that, from the entrepreneurial view of freedom, an individual may suffer loss of freedom without realizing any loss in his welfare. We now see that an analogous situation pertains to society as a whole. Restriction of economic freedom restrains society from reaching what would have been Pareto-optimal equilibrium situations. As Hayek showed, this in effect means that society would not know what losses in social welfare have been suffered as a result of the restricted freedom, since no one can know what the market might have discovered. Our own discussion shows us that restriction of economic freedom restrains society from achieving its full potential in yet another sense, again a sense in which it may never be known that any loss of welfare has occurred. As we have seen in our discussion (following Machlup) of the fertility of freedom, the restriction of economic freedom may inhibit individuals from discovering opportunities they might have noticed had they been free to exploit them. Loss of freedom may thus lower individual and social achievement without anyone's realizing what has been lost or not achieved. A free society is fertile and creative in the sense that its freedom generates alertness to possibilities that may be of use to society; a restriction on the freedom of a society numbs such alertness and blinds society to possibilities of social improvement. By the very nature of the damage such restriction wreaks, its harmful effects on social welfare may not be able to be noticed, measured, or specified. For the understanding of these profoundly important social consequences of economic freedom, I have argued, economists must in turn deepen their understanding of the nature of freedom itself.

NOTES

1. G. J. Stigler, "Reflections on Liberty," in *The Citizen and the State* (Chicago: University of Chicago Press, 1975), p. 14.

2. This was very clearly recognized in the earliest writings in which the economist's view of choice was spelled out. See L. Robbins, *The Nature and Significance of Economic Science*, 2d ed. (London: Macmillan, 1935), pp. 12, 24, 33, 46; F. H. Knight, "The Nature of Economic Science in Some Recent Discussion," *American Economic Review* 24 (June 1934): 229.

3. See, on this, I. M. Kirzner, *The Economic Point of View* (Princeton: Van Nostrand, 1960), pp. 161 ff.; idem, *Competition and Entrepreneurship* (Chicago: University of Chicago Press, 1973), pp. 33 ff.

4. See, e.g., G. L. S. Shackle, *Epistemics and Economics: A Critique of Economic Doctrines* (Cambridge: Cambridge University Press, 1972), for countless observations on this matter (many of them indexed under "choice").

5. L. M. Lachmann, "From Mises to Shackle: An Essay on Austrian Economics and the Kaleidic Society," *Journal of Economic Literature* 14 (March 1976): 54–62.

6. It is true that the given framework of ends and means is seen as that of the decision maker himself—the goal referred to in the text is the agent's "own" goal—but freedom is not, in the narrow view, referred back to the choice process by which that framework came to have been adopted as the relevant one.

7. See Kirzner, *Competition and Entrepreneurship*, pp. 33 ff.

8. The distinction drawn here between the narrow economist's view on freedom, and the broader entrepreneurial view has not, to my knowledge, been made in the literature. In the philosophical literature, it seems rather clear, many writers had the broader view in mind, apparently without dreaming of the possibility of the narrower view. Many of the writers cited by Mortimer J. Adler in chapter 24 of his *Idea of Freedom* (Garden City, N.Y.: Doubleday, 1958), "Creativity through Choice as an Element in the Meaning of Self-Determination," appear to fall into this class. Among economists, F. H. Knight, whose writings on freedom have been the most voluminous, complex, and difficult, appeared possibly to have at least glimpsed the broader view in a number of passages. "In economic discussion liberty means the right of the individual to choose his own ends and the means or procedure most effective for realizing them" (F. H. Knight, *Freedom and Reform* [New York: Harper, 1947], p. 377). "In practical application, the doctrine of maximum individual freedom necessitates . . . that the individual is the final judge of the *means* to his own happiness, as well as of the result" (ibid., p. 2). Isaiah Berlin has explored J. S. Mill's views on human freedom in terms that perhaps suggest the importance of the distinction argued in this paper. Berlin attributes to Mill a view of freedom that sees man as "The seeker of ends, . . . with the corollary that . . . the larger the field of interplay between individuals, the greater the opportunities of the new and the unexpected; the more numerous the possibilities for altering his own character in some fresh or unexplored direction" (I. Berlin, "John Stu-

art Mill and the Ends of Life," in *Four Essays on Liberty* [New York: Oxford University Press, 1969], p. 178). "Mill believes," Berlin maintains, "that man is spontaneous, that he has freedom of choice, that he moulds his own character. . . . Mill's entire view of human nature turns out to rest not on the notion of the repetition of an identical pattern, but on his perception of human lives as subject to perpetual incompleteness, self-transformation, and novelty" (ibid., p. 189).

9. A clear example is that offered by T. G. Moore's interesting suggestion for measuring the degree of freedom in a society. Moore's thesis is "that freedom can be defined in terms of welfare. A change in the cost of action . . . can be considered to be a movement toward freedom if it increases welfare. . . . If the cost to the individual of performing some action is lowered without affecting the cost to others, then we will consider that a movement toward a freer society" (T. G. Moore, "An Economic Analysis of the Concept of Freedom," *Journal of Political Economy* 77 [July/August 1969], pp. 532 ff.).

10. F. A. Hayek, *The Constitution of Liberty* (Chicago: University of Chicago Press, 1960), pp. 16 ff.

11. F. Machlup, "Liberalism and the Choice of Freedoms," in *Roads to Freedom: Essays in Honor of Friedrich A. von Hayek*, ed. E. Streissler (London: Routledge and Kegan Paul, 1969), pp. 124 ff.

12. On some of the difficulties in Knight's discussions of freedom, see Machlup, ibid., pp. 129 ff.; Hayek, *Constitution of Liberty*, p. 422, n. 7.

13. J. Locke, *Essay concerning Human Understanding*, vol. 1, book 2, chap. 21, sec. 8. See the discussion of Locke's view in M. J. Adler, *The Idea of Freedom*, pp. 115 ff.

14. F. H. Knight, "The Meaning of Freedom," in *The Philosophy of American Democracy*, ed. C. M. Perry (Chicago: University of Chicago Press, 1943), p. 65.

15. Machlup, "Liberalism and the Choice of Freedoms," p. 130.

16. Stigler, "Reflections on Liberty."

17. R. M. Hare, *Freedom and Reason* (Oxford: Clarendon Press, 1963), p. 3.

18. B. Blanshard, *Reason and Analysis* (LaSalle, Ill.: Open Court, 1973), p. 493.

19. F. A. Hayek, "The Use of Knowledge in Society," *American Economic Review* 35 (September 1945): 519–30.

20. Hayek, *Constitution of Liberty*, p. 29.

21. Ibid., p. 31.

DIVERGENT APPROACHES IN LIBERTARIAN ECONOMIC THOUGHT

The writings of the great majority of economists over the past thirty years have supported the powerful currents that sweep the modern world toward centralized authority, interventionism, and statism. The teachings of these economists led generations of students and laymen to believe uncritically that an economy based on unhampered individual enterprise and the institution of private property must breed unemployment, instability, resource misallocation, stagnation and an unjust distribution of income. And yet, there has consistently been a dissenting minority whose voices are not completely drowned out by the teachings of their colleagues.

These economists, arguing on strictly technical grounds, defend the efficiency of the unhampered market economy, and point out again and again how measures put into effect by governments must lead to consequences worse than the evils that they seek to avoid. Apart from the strictly technical questions involved, these writers also point to the value judgments implicit in many of the conclusions of their colleagues. They show how many of the welfare proposals offered in the name of economics merely reflect arbitrary opinions concerning such matters as the ethical status of private property, the ability of an individual to choose for himself, and the like.

In recent years this minority view among economists has gained considerable strength. Our younger economists are no longer persuaded that the old interventionist dogmas are beyond criticism. The benefits arising from the free interplay of market forces are more and more coming to be recognized. The views of free-market economists are becoming less and less easy for the still-dominant "mixed-economy" exponents to ignore.

This change in climate is being felt by the more inquiring of our undergraduate students around the country. Ten or fifteen years ago it was commonplace for an intelligent student to complete his undergraduate

This essay was delivered as an ISI-sponsored lecture at the University of Virginia, February 21, 1966. From *Intercollegiate Review* 3 (January–February 1967): 101–8. Reprinted by permission of Intercollegiate Studies Institute.

studies—often with even a major in economics—and yet gain no inkling of the very existence of a respectable minority free-market view in the contemporary economic literature. This has changed; the existence of an economic literature that formulates policy recommendations with full consciousness of the relevant market consequences and their implications for individual welfare and freedom of choice is now a matter of common knowledge.

The economists who have contributed to this literature in the United States have written as individuals, not as members of a single "school," and there have been significant differences of opinion among them, both on theoretical questions and on policy issues. It is, of course, always a hazardous undertaking to classify independent writers. However, it seems widely recognized that most of the economists who have emphasized the efficiency and other advantages of the free market can be associated with either one or the other of two intellectual sources. On the one hand there is an academic tradition strongly associated with the University of Chicago, embracing in particular the work of the late Henry Simons, of F. H. Knight, and of younger scholars such as Milton Friedman, Yale Brozen, and George J. Stigler. On the other hand there has since the 1940s been felt in this country an expanding, well-articulated influence that clearly traces back to the Austrian subjectivist school. This influence is almost synonymous with the work of Ludwig von Mises, and has inspired significant similar work by others in the same tradition. It is idle to speculate on the appropriateness of the term "schools" to describe these two intellectual sources. While the term school is widely applied to Chicago economists,[1] it would probably be inaccurate to refer to the writers most strongly influenced by Professor Mises as a "school."[2] Nonetheless, it remains a fact that there exist significant differences between the "Austrian" literature in which the works of Mises are the most important and influential, and the writings of the economists whom we will, for the sake of brevity and convenience, call the "Chicago" economists.

1. For an academic discussion of this usage, see *Journal of Political Economy*, February, 1962.
2. And, despite the fact that Professor Mises teaches at New York University, it would be quite incorrect to talk of a Misesist "New York University School."

It is, of course, important not to exaggerate the differences between the two streams of writing, the Misesist and the "Chicago." While, as we shall discover, there exist sharp differences in methodology and in perspective between the two trends, there is an almost surprising coincidence between their views on most important policy questions. This is especially true with respect to issues having to do more narrowly with the operation of the price system. The truth is that whatever differences exist between the two approaches, both have basically the same sound understanding of how a market operates, and this is responsible for the healthy respect which both approaches share in common for its achievements. It is this common denominator which provides the rationale of this essay, the purpose of which is to describe clearly the more important points of distinction that set apart their two approaches to the market. And for this reason this essay does not take up some important differences between these two streams of thought that occur in monetary economics and business cycle policy—areas in which the basic denominator common to both trends has far less direct relevance.

But whatever the similarities displayed in these two approaches, it does seem a useful task to enunciate with some care the more fundamental matters of method and perspective upon which agreement is absent. In what follows the writer presents the controversial issues as he understands them; he makes no claim to represent the distilled "official" views of any particular writers.

One way of presenting the difference between the two approaches under consideration might be as follows: The price theory that underlies the contributions of the "Chicago" writers is not fundamentally different from that accepted by American economists generally, including those holding the efficiency and justice of the market system in deep mistrust. It is merely that the "Chicago" economists apply their price theory more consistently and more resolutely, assigning to it a scope of relevance far wider than that granted by others. On the other hand the Misesist approach involves a theory of price that differs in important respects from that taught and applied by others.

This admittedly oversimplified way of stating the difference between the two approaches, among other advantages, enables us to perceive the intellectual roots of their divergence from one another. "Chicago" price theory, like that taught in most United States economics departments, is solidly in the Anglo-American neoclassical tradition associated most importantly with Alfred Marshall. The profound influence exercised by Marshall upon American price theory, in spite of its modification at the hands of Edward H. Chamberlin (a modification that is, from the point of view of this essay, yet on Marshallian lines), is clearly visible as the central thread in "Chicago"-type textbooks on price theory.[3]

On the other hand the price theory associated with Mises, nourished from the stream of Austrian thought going back to Carl Menger, has entered American economics as a distinctly alien element. (The only comparable influence, and that a rather muted one, is that deriving from the writings of Philip H. Wicksteed.) While Walrasian general equilibrium ideas made their strong impact early on American economics in the 'thirties and 'forties with the growing vogue of mathematical economics, it was not until much later, when Mises's writings came to be known in their American editions, that his ideas were seriously discussed in this country.

While there are numerous smaller points of difference that separate the two approaches—the dominant neo-Marshallian microeconomics of "Chicago," and the Austrian-type theory of the Misesist—it will prove convenient to concentrate on three rather major sources of disagreement. We will discuss in turn the following: (1) the role of equilibrium; (2) the role of empirical investigations; and (3) the concept of monopoly. A clear understanding of these matters will go a long way toward an understanding of what sets the two approaches apart, and the degree of the separation.

THE ROLE OF EQUILIBRIUM

In Marshallian economics, as in Walrasian, the concept of equilibrium plays a major, if not a permanent, role. Considering the various forces at work in a market, the price theorist asks himself what conditions would have to be fulfilled before one can pronounce these forces to be in balance. The initial data governing a situation determines the conditions needed to reach equilibrium. Since a situation in which these conditions are absent is not in balance, it cannot be assumed to be a lasting situation: market forces will bring about change. Because the direction of motion

---

3. The dissatisfactions with the theory of monopolistic competition that have been voiced by "Chicago" economists do not affect the validity of the statements in the text.

of a disequilibrium market was more or less uncritically assumed to lead toward the fulfillment of the conditions for equilibrium, the latter situation came to be looked upon as "the solution." In other words, whenever one is provided with a list of existing conditions, and is asked to use price theory to explain "what will happen" as a result of these initial conditions, the answer is seen to be provided by *the description of the equilibrium situation appropriate to the initial data.* This procedure of equilibrium analysis has become, through the method of "comparative statics," the principal means of analyzing the consequences of changes in the data. One simply compares the equilibrium conditions appropriate to the new set of data with those appropriate to the older set. The change in data can then be said to bring about a change in the market situation from the "old" equilibrium configuration to the new one.

The concept of equilibrium is one which has been applied, *mutatis mutandis,* to different market structures. In particular, the changes in neo-Marshallian price theory that resulted from the work of Harvard's Professor Chamberlin in the 'thirties did not affect the use of the equilibrium method. For Chamberlinian theory as for that of his predecessors, the important objective is the description of the equilibrium situation corresponding to the postulated data. Whereas pre-Chamberlinian theory had operated in a world in which only two patterns of market structure could occur, Chamberlin argued for a view of the market that should accommodate an entire spectrum of different structures. With respect to each kind of market structure there will then be sought the corresponding equilibrium configuration.

The equilibrium notion as applied to the market refers to the particular pattern of decisions on the part of the market participants that permits all the decisions to be successfully carried out. The particular market structure prevailing in a given situation determines the range of possible decisions open to each participant. The theorist's insight into how an individual participant reaches his decisions enables explanation of which possible decision will be selected as the best opportunity in given circumstances. It is thus possible to list the set of decisions that will have to be made by the various participants in a given market situation if one is to be able to say simultaneously (a) that each participant is making the best decision possible from his point of view; and (b) that all the decisions can be carried out at the same time.

As a result of this emphasis on the situation at equilibrium, consideration of the neo-Marshallian approach led naturally to a rather special view by economists of the method appropriate to their task, and this tendency was reinforced by the strong influences of Leon Walras. This methodological view emphasized the strictly formal character of the search for the equilibrium conditions. Given the structural conditions assumed for the market, the tastes of the consumers and the technological constraints governing production, we find that discovering the set of price offers and bids, the set of product quantities and qualities, and the set of inputs to be employed in production assumes a character amenable to mathematical attack. It became easy for price theorists to set up the appropriate equations that would have to be satisfied simultaneously in order to pronounce the market to be in equilibrium; it became easy to emphasize the task of examining the conditions under which a solution of these equations is formally possible.

In addition, the stress on equilibrium situations facilitated yet a further tendency (one that was reinforced by the work of Chamberlin), that is, a persistent pattern of analyzing markets on the assumption that *the structure of the market is a datum*. While this tendency has begun to wane in recent years, the more traditional approach, including that followed by "Chicago" economists, has been to specify the particular character of competition or monopoly believed to be relevant to a particular market, and to seek the corresponding equilibrium solution. Little attempt was made to understand how the relevant competitive structure of the market has been itself forged out of the dynamic process of the market, and how out of the continued operation of this process there may be expected, perhaps, an evolving market structure.[4]

Before turning to consider how different a role is assigned to the equilibrium notion in the Misesist system, it will be useful to notice one further implication of the dominant neo-Marshallian approach shared by "Chicago" economists. This is the seriousness with which the perfectly competitive model is treated. In the 'thirties the hitherto widespread use of this model by economists generally came under sharp attack on the grounds it lacked realism, but not in terms of its internal formal adequacy. ("Chicago" economists, in fact, have tended to defend continued

---

4. For a perceptive discussion of this point see J. M. Buchanan, "What Should Economists Do?," *Southern Economic Journal*, January, 1964.

wide use of the perfectly competitive model, arguing that it provides a workable approximation to the real world.)

And yet, as F. A. Hayek has pointed out, the perfectly competitive model suffers from the severe defect that it *is restricted to a situation that already satisfies the conditions for equilibrium.*[5] The perfectly competitive market is one in which conditions exist that by definition assume that no decision made need be disappointed. Each buyer and each seller in the perfectly competitive market is assured of being able to buy or to sell as much as he wishes at the going price; no possibility exists for analysis of a perfectly competitive market that is *not* in equilibrium. The astonishing willingness of economists to restrict so much of their work to analysis of a model that from the start rules out consideration of disequilibrium possibilities can clearly be ascribed only to the prevalent exclusive concern with equilibrium situations. With little interest attached to any but equilibrium solutions, with no awareness of the dynamics of market structure, there need be little compunction in raising the perfectly competitive model to a paramount position.

All this contrasts very starkly indeed with the role assigned to the equilibrium notion in the Misesist system. Here the emphasis is *not* on the configuration of decisions necessary to ensure that all of them can be carried out. The emphasis is, instead, on the *process* generated by the forces of the market. The focus is not on the set of prices, output and input quantities, that must prevail if a market is to be in equilibrium. Instead it is upon the manner in which prices, outputs, and inputs *change* from one period to the next as the logic of the market forces adjustments to be made in the decisions of the participants.

To the Misesist the problem to be solved is not the specification of equilibrium conditions corresponding to different market structures. The economist is called for, instead, to understand how one disequilibrium situation generates the pressures that lead toward a new situation in which disequilibrium maladjustments have, to some degree, been corrected.

Of course for Mises too the position of equilibrium is a unique one. But its uniqueness consists not in its providing the solution, the outcome determined by the data. Its uniqueness is simply that the equilibrium

5. Cf F. A. Hayek, *Individualism and Economic Order* (Chicago: Univ. of Chicago Press, 1948), pp. 92–106.

position, were it to prevail, would be characterized by the *cessation* of the market process, all relevant market forces having successfully spent themselves. Analysis of equilibrium conditions provides a useful *contrast* to the process of market agitation that marks a state of disequilibrium, but it is this agitation itself which is the focus of analytical attention.

It follows that for the Misesist view, the enumeration of the equations whose simultaneous solution is required for equilibrium, the examination of the possibilities for such a solution to exist, are activities of profoundly subsidiary importance. These activities do not provide the answers the Misesist economist is seeking. For this reason the elaborate techniques marshalled by the mathematical economists leave the Misesist totally unimpressed. Not only are they not addressing themselves to the problems the Misesist considers important, but they are confining themselves to analysis of conditions in which the market has nothing further to contribute.

For similar reasons the Misesist has little patience for the elaborate consideration of the perfectly competitive model. He objects to this model, not primarily on the Chamberlinian grounds of realism, but on account of the model's irrelevance to the market *process* set in motion by disequilibrium conditions. The perfectly competitive model has nothing to say about such a process; by definition such a process can occur only in the *absence* of perfectly competitive conditions.

In fact the entire concept of market structure has little relevance for the Misesist. From his point of view competition is not a condition of the market that indicates a certain pattern of decisions as being an equilibrium pattern. Rather, competition is seen as the driving force behind the adjustment process taking place in the market. Since only competition provides this driving force, analysis of different market structures boils down, in this view, to analysis of the strength of this drive. And since market structures are themselves *produced* by the process of market adjustment, it is hardly useful to take them as given, as data that independently determine the course of the market process.

One further implication of the Misesist approach may be mentioned in concluding this section, and that is the role of the entrepreneur. For a theory of price concerned primarily with states of equilibrium, the entrepreneur is a somewhat peripheral figure. He has no role at all in the central scheme of things, at least until we are ready to postulate changes in the data. Despite the careful attention which so original a "Chicagoan" as

Professor Knight has devoted to the theory of uncertainty and profit, the entrepreneur hardly occupies the center of attention in "Chicago" economics. It is otherwise in the Misesist approach. Here the entrepreneur, the initiator of change, searching for the profit opportunities spawned by disequilibrium conditions, performs the most essential role of all. It is his competitive pursuit of profits which sets the market process in motion. It is he who occupies the center of analytical attention.

THE ROLE OF EMPIRICAL INVESTIGATIONS

The contemporary dominant view of economics is one in which important roles are assigned both to the theorist and to the empirical research worker. The general attitude is somewhat as follows: In earlier days, when economics was rather primitive, there was disagreement on the method appropriate to the discipline. At the close of the last century there were those who stressed theory to the exclusion of empirical investigation, and there were others who believed it possible to acquire economic knowledge only through the methods of historical research. In the enlightened present we have come to realize that both kinds of investigation are required and that they complement one another. Theory and empirical research, in this dominant view, are closely intertwined. One is willing to deplore contemporary institutionalist attacks on theory; one is equally willing to deprecate armchair theorists who disdain to muddy their hands with down-to-earth statistics.

"Chicago" economists are in general strongly in agreement with the mixed approach. While they vigorously emphasize the power and usefulness of theory, they subscribe to the requirement that theory be "operational," and watch for "implications" of theory that can be tested against empirical data. Because "Chicago" economists have *more* faith in the power of theory than other (non-Misesist) economists, and because, as a result, they apply theory to many neglected facets of economic activity (e.g. many kinds of non-pecuniary motivations), they are in fact frequently engaged in a *wider* range of empirical investigations than other economists are. In this kind of approach a theory is a tentative "guess" whose validity must await confirmation by the evidence. While "Chicago" economists are probably more aware than other econometricians of the subtle difficulties of extracting watertight confirmations, or even refutations, of theories from observational data, they nonetheless tend to look upon these difficulties as merely a need for more refined statistical, observational and computational techniques, rather than as a problem ineradicably inherent in the nature of the material under investigation.

In this view, the investigator writing down market prices, measuring output volume, or describing the degree of concentration in industry, may be engaged in exactly the same kind of activity—that of helping to acquire economic knowledge—as is the theorist whose models suggest the particular sets of statistics to be collected.

The view is rather different when considered from the Misesist perspective, however, and some of the most extreme literary disagreements between the two approaches have to do with this issue. In the Misesist view the role of empirical investigation is an altogether different one, and knowledge obtained by the empirical investigator is of an altogether different character from that discovered by the theorist. In this view empirical confirmation of the theorems obtained by abstract logic is neither possible nor necessary. It is not possible, because there are no constants in the realm of human actions, it is therefore impossible to investigate the consequences of changes in one variable with assurance that no disturbance is at the same time being caused by changes in other variables. On the other hand confirmation of economic theorems is not necessary, because the theorems themselves describe relationships logically implied by hypothesized conditions. The validity of these relationships can be tested by examining the reasoning employed to establish them.

Empirical work, in the Misesist system, has the function of establishing the *applicability* of particular theorems, and thus of *illustrating* their operation. Factual measurement and description provide information which can be used in applying theory. Economic theory postulates certain relationships under specific conditions. Only concrete observation, therefore, can tell the applied economist which particular theorem is of relevance in a given situation. But the discovery that the facts fit perfectly with the predictions of a theory does not provide the economist with knowledge that he did not possess before; nor would the failure of the facts to fit with theory cause him to abandon a valid theorem—this might merely indicate inapplicability of the theorem. The world of facts is too complex to permit simple hypothetical relationships to be directly perceived or refuted; with only variables to be observed, the real world market can only be understood with the help of theory, not the reverse. Direct observation does indeed provide knowledge, possibly important knowledge, but of a different kind from that embodied in an economic theorem. Observation provides the material to be understood by applying the appropriate theory.

The skillful theorist well-acquainted with real market phenomena may be in an ideal position to illustrate the validity of theory by reference to well-chosen concrete facts. He may in this way convince laymen of the far-reaching truth of price theory far more powerfully than by direct teaching of the theory itself. But this is a matter of pedagogy, not of establishing the substantive truth of the theory in a manner satisfactory for science.

It will be seen that we have here a fundamental and profound difference in outlook between the two approaches being examined in this essay.

THE CONCEPT OF MONOPOLY

The last example of disagreement between the "Chicago" and Misesist views we shall consider here concerns the notion of monopoly. We have had occasion earlier in this essay to draw attention to the different concepts of competition that characterize the two approaches. The disagreement about monopoly that we shall consider here is not unconnected with the different outlooks noted earlier.

In the dominant Anglo-American tradition in price theory, monopoly is invariably associated with a particular pattern of decision possibilities seen facing the *firm*. In technical jargon the firm enjoying some degree of monopoly power faces a downward-sloping demand curve, i.e. it can sell any of a wide range of different volumes of output, but can sell the larger outputs only by charging lower prices. This is contrasted with the "perfectly competitive" firm, which is able to sell the amount it wishes, within reason, without having to lower its price.

This view of monopoly is the one upon which the Chamberlinian theory of monopolistic competition is predicated; it is the view upon which economic analysis of anti-trust policy is almost invariably based. The distinguishing features of this monopoly concept are first that monopoly power is possessed by the producing firm, and second, that it is evidenced by the power of the firm to raise its price by being willing to sell smaller quantities of output. This is the monopoly concept used as a matter of course by "Chicago" economists.

In the Misesist system, however, the term monopoly is used to denote a quite different concept. And there is in this system little significance attached altogether to the downward-sloping demand curve that faces a firm. In this system, with its utter disinterest in the perfectly competitive model mentioned earlier, the demand curve facing *any* firm is understood—at least in disequilibrium—to be more or less downward-sloping. This is not seen as in any way interfering with the dynamic process of competition which we earlier found to be central to the Misesist view of the market.

Moreover, in the Misesist emphasis on the process rather than on the result, the concept of monopoly is inseparable from the explanation of the source of monopoly power. To contend that a firm enjoys monopoly power one must be able to account for the existence of this power. Since a firm is merely the interim resource complex assembled by the entrepreneur, its possession of exclusive selling power can only be ascribed to possession of unique resources. Entrepreneurship is viewed as being by definition competitive in a free unhampered market. With no restriction on buying or selling, no one entrepreneur is able, without having already captured unique resources, to control any one branch of production. Clearly in the long-run view, monopolistic control over production cannot be ascribed to firms as such, but only to the fortunate owners of unique resources.

This is not the occasion to examine more thoroughly the implications of this view of monopoly for judgments on the efficiency of resource allocation, or for one's opinions on antitrust policy. It is not difficult to see that these implications must be considerable. We return to appraise very briefly the significance of the distinctions which we have drawn between the "Chicago" and Misesist approaches.

With such deep-seated differences separating the foundations of Misesist economics from that of "Chicago," it is, for the libertarian, reassuring to discover that so many policy questions seem to lead to the same answers in both approaches. Clearly there is some common ground possessed by the two, on which the cited differences do not make a great deal of direct practical difference. For the pragmatic policy-maker, less concerned with philosophical underpinnings than with ready-to-use conclusions, the distinctions setting apart the two approaches may not seem of great moment. On the other hand, for the student and scientist, these differences will seem of far greater importance. For the student of the history of ideas, the matters of disagreement are similarly of considerable interest. While there are, as we have seen, many policy questions on which both are in agreement, there can clearly be no guarantee that this will always be the case. Only careful, dispassionate study of both approaches can enable one to choose intelligently between them, and to be able to perceive the truth where the two views do in fact lead to divergent conclusions.

MUST CAPITALISM YIELD TO SOCIALISM?

Joseph A. Schumpeter was a world-famous, celebrated economist in his lifetime, but his reputation somehow diminished within the economics profession in the decades following his death in 1950. (Today's graduate students seem to know him principally as the author of a massive history of economic analysis, rather than as the brilliantly original economist he was in his own right.) The recent centenary of his birth in 1883, however, set in motion a revival of interest in Schumpeter's own system, an interest that expressed itself in the organisation of several conferences (and resulting volumes of papers, some by leading economists).

This article seeks, in view of this new interest in Schumpeter, to convey a sense of Schumpeter's economic vision, and to assess that vision—from an "Austrian" perspective—both sympathetically and critically, especially in the light of a number of paradoxes that lend his work a peculiar fascination. In writing this essay I have benefitted substantially by the fairly extensive literature on Schumpeter that has grown up since his death (including the papers generated by the centenary of his birth). We shall discover (and here the paradoxes begin) that, although Schumpeter himself strongly resisted the idea that scientific work be seen as leading directly to the exercise of influence upon policy-makers, his own system does hold considerable relevance for contemporary policy discussion.

PARADOX UPON PARADOX

(i) Schumpeter was, of course, an Austrian-born, Austrian-trained economist, who retained throughout his life a genuine admiration for the work of his teacher, the famed Austrian economist Eugen von Böhm-Bawerk. Yet, throughout his career, he seemed to endorse just about every doctrine, every major economist, whom his own teachers had emphatically rejected. Thus his very first (1908) book upheld the positivist approach to economics, (which held that the economic environment determines human action) in the teeth of the Mengerian subjectivist

From *Economic Affairs* (April–June 1985): 35–37. Copyright of *Economic Affairs* is the property of Blackwell Publishing Limited. Reprinted by permission of John Wiley and Sons, publisher.

tradition, which emphasised the importance of the individual in the economic process. The student of Böhm-Bawerk considered Walras the greatest of economic theorists, and considered Karl Marx to have possessed the grandest vision among all economists. The heir of Menger and Böhm-Bawerk, for whom mathematics was an inappropriate tool for economic analysis, spent a lifetime seeking (vainly according to his own students) to master the techniques of mathematical economics and of econometrics, and was at least indirectly responsible for the post–World War II mathematicisation of economic theory. I shall argue here that this paradox in regard to Schumpeter's Austrianism carries with it even more interesting ironies.

(ii) Despite Schumpeter's enthusiasm for mathematics and econometrics, and his role in turning the profession in the direction of more sophisticated techniques, it can be claimed with little fear of contradiction that the outcome of these developments in contemporary economics has not brought economists at all closer to Schumpeter's own economic vision. On the contrary, it appears to have generated a trend to analysis of the "small" questions, rather than the grand issues that captured Schumpeter's own attention; it appears to have reinforced the exclusive emphasis in economics on equilibrium, a recurrent, stable, static condition, where supply and demand are always equal, and with which Schumpeter himself was so impatient.

(iii) Again, despite Schumpeter's enormous admiration for Walras, Walrasian economics has come to be identified, in the economics profession, with the theory of general equilibrium, and is credited with pioneering the modern developments in this field. Yet it is precisely with this direction taken by modern economic theory that Schumpeter became impatient. His own vision of capitalism stressed the dynamic, entrepreneurially inspired features of capitalism—the very features for which the Walrasian vision of static equilibrium has no room whatever.

(iv) Schumpeter's no less ardent admiration for Marx, and his own style of thought have, indeed, often led him to be compared to Marx. Moreover, his conviction—like Marx's—that capitalism is doomed to destruction and to replacement by socialism ("dying of a psychosomatic ailment . . . neurosis . . . self-hate . . ." is how Samuelson has encapsulated this Schumpeterian view of capitalism's dim future), has often led to his being seen as a socialist. Yet, as a number of writers have documented, Schumpeter was no friend of socialism. His own heart was in capitalism, which he held to have been tremendously effective in serving the human race.

For Schumpeter the essence of capitalism is the dynamic process ("creative destruction") that it represents—in which new products, new methods of production, new markets are continually emerging to replace and displace earlier ones. This process of incessant change is driven by spurts of entrepreneurial vision and energy that continually disrupt the powerful equilibriating tendencies that would, in the absence of entre-preneurial innovation, bring the economy into the even state of "circular flow," i.e., into the state of Walrasian general equilibrium. (Samuelson has used here the metaphor of the violin string plucked into vibrant res-onance by entrepreneurial innovation: "without innovation it dies down to stationariness." The point is that the essence of capitalism is its ability to generate an incessant series of varied musical notes.) Schumpeter's view of capitalism cannot be grasped without perceiving the continual see-saw that he believed to exist between two opposing sets of power-ful forces: the Walrasian forces that, in the absence of innovation would generate the placid state of general equilibrium; and the Schumpe-terian forces of incessant, entrepreneurial, disruption of equilibrium that make up the essence of the visible, dynamic features of capitalism over the years.

The end result of this capitalist process has, for Schumpeter, been a spectacular record of growth that has brought enormous improvement in the conditions of the masses. It is in this that Schumpeter can be seen as a partisan of capitalism.

Schumpeter's understanding of the dynamism of capitalism also led him to some disturbing conclusions.

Schumpeter devoted extraordinary labours to his theoretical and empirical analysis of business cycles. His theory depended very much on the paramount of entrepreneurial innovation, on the forces likely to generate the appearance of such innovations in swarms, on the role of financial credit in making such innovations possible. Yet, although Schumpeter himself saw his own scientific contribution to consist per-haps most importantly in this work, on cycles there are grounds for believing that the longer-run significance of his work is likely to stem from the more general features of this overall vision. In this respect, the widespread interest in (even the fascination with) Schumpeter's predic-tion of the demise of capitalism is probably closer to the mark.

Schumpeter believed that the very success of capitalism in stimulating growth and innovation was likely to generate problems for its long-run survival. On the one hand its successes are likely to spawn large business firms—a development that threatens both to "routinise" (even bureaucratise) the innovative process and to displace the vigorous individual entrepreneurs who might have defended the system. On the other hand the successes of capitalism are likely to nourish anti-capitalist social attitudes, particularly within the class of intellectuals (whose social standing under capitalism is likely to be below what they believe to be appropriate to their own "superior," purely intellectual attainments, which have not been exposed to evaluation in the market). With widening antipathy toward the capitalist system, with the disappearance of vigorous entrepreneurial individuals who might have had an interest in defending the system, capitalism appeared, in Schumpeter's view, to be doomed to be replaced by socialism. Schumpeter did *not* accept the view (expounded by his fellow-Austrians, Mises and Hayek) that a socialist system suffers from fatal weaknesses in efficient economic calculation. Thus the future held forth the prospect of an economy reasonably well and efficiently coordinated in terms of established products and technology—but lacking the dynamism required to propel the economy to higher and higher standards of well-being.

Schumpeter's economic vision places him sharply at odds with the view that has dominated economics for several decades. In this dominant ("neo-classical") view the role of the equilibrium state (Schumpeter's circular flow) has been paramount. Virtually no scope was recognised in this dominant view for the entrepreneurial dynamism that Schumpeter saw continually disrupting the placidity of the state of circular flow and which for him signified the essential character of capitalism.

This dissonance between Schumpeterian economics and the contemporary mainstream is perhaps most sharply apparent in the contrasting roles the two approaches assign to *competition.* For mainstream economics competition has, for many decades, been understood as *a state of affairs,* most completely captured by the notion of "perfect competition." Economic agents are assumed to be confronted by prices (for products or resource services) at which each is free to buy or to sell whatever he chooses, in whatever quantities he pleases, without having to worry about not being able to carry out his buying or selling plans successfully, and with assurance that the respective prices will not depend on his own buying or selling plan. For mainstream economics this model holds extraordinary significance. Attempts made by economists (best known among them being the late Joan Robinson in England and Edward Chamberlin in the US) to modify the competitive model in the direction of more realism were, in the dominant view, held to involve "less perfect" notions of competition.

For Schumpeter (as indeed, for Austrian economists in general) the notion of competition always involved the dynamic thrust and counter-thrust of an active market process. Competition meant, not an already co-ordinated state of affairs, in which prices are already fully adjusted to consistency with the decisions they will themselves stimulate—but rather a process of give-and-take during which prices are continually buffeted by entrepreneurial impetuosity and activity.

This disparity between Schumpeter's view and that of contemporary orthodoxy has profound implications for any normative, policy-oriented appraisal of the economic benefits to be anticipated from real-world capitalism. For the orthodox view, it turns out, the features of real-world capitalism most significant for Schumpeter's vision happen to be the very features that render capitalism suspect, in the orthodox view, in terms of its ability to achieve social efficiency. For the orthodox view efficiency is inextricably bound up with the state of perfect competition. Departures from perfect competition are seen as potentially serious threats to the successful attainment of an efficient allocation of resources. For Schumpeter, on the other hand, it is precisely these dynamic aspects of the competitive process that have rendered capitalism so spectacularly successful in achieving rapid growth in the well-being enjoyed by the masses.

Thus indeed Schumpeter's vision implies an approach to economic policy radically at variance with that associated with the mainstream theory. For standard theory, if capitalism is to be rendered an efficient economic system, policy must be geared toward somehow bringing it closer to the perfectly competitive ideal—which for Schumpeter lacks the very essence of the capitalist system. From the mainstream perspective, thus idealising the perfectly competitive state, measures such as anti-trust legislation may appear to make sound sense. But it is not difficult to understand why Schumpeter considered this view to be absurdly wrong. For him such legislation can only hamper the entrepreneurial competition to which we must look for the real strengths of capitalism.

Despite the irony that Schumpeter's admiration for the economics of Walras helped steer modern economics *away* from Schumpeter's own concern for entrepreneurial processes, and his appreciation of the achievements of thinkers from other streams of thought in economics (for he found the Austrian economics tradition within which he had been trained too confining), what finally sets Schumpeter's system apart from the mainstream is precisely that aspect of his system that can be pronounced characteristically Austrian. Moreover, the current resurgence of interest in Schumpeter and in Schumpeterian economics may well be associated with the reserve, the coolness that has crept into the profession toward the hitherto dominant paradigm of Walrasian general equilibrium. At a time when economists are seeking to come to grips with the realities of a capitalism that seems less and less able to be compressed within general-equilibrium-type of explanatory frameworks the Schumpeterian dynamic vision is likely to be discovered to hold a definite appeal.

What then is likely to be the future status of Schumpeterian economics? Does the current flurry of interest in Schumpeter hold promise of a significant change in the focus and direction of modern economic thought, toward appreciation for the dynamic forces that constitute a vibrant capitalism? Will Schumpeter's own reputation and stature as a seminal economic thinker grow in the decades ahead, or will it continue to suffer the erosion of the past decades?

I certainly do not claim to know the answers to these questions. But I do have a suggestion to offer any contemporary economists who may wish to give the current history of economics a nudge in the Schumpeterian direction.

My suggestion has to do with the scope to be assigned to the entrepreneurial process. For Schumpeter the entrepreneurial process is seen as pushing the economy out of one state of circular flow, permitting the economy to gravitate upwards toward a higher state of circular flow. But the gravitation toward the state of circular flow was itself seen by Schumpeter as unrelated to the activity of entrepreneurs. One could rely on the host of "imitators" to bring about the placid, even state of the circular flow of economic activity. What has to be emphasised, to widen the appeal of the Schumpeterian "dynamic" vision, is the circumstance that *any* systematic market tendencies, those ordinarily considered co-ordinating and equilibrating, fully as much as those innovations that Schumpeter considered disruptive of equilibrium, depend crucially on entrepreneurial alertness and adjustment to changed conditions. Once this possibility is acknowledged, the Schumpeterian dynamic vision will be seen to embrace virtually the *whole* of the economic process, relegating mainstream models of circular flow to a far more modest role within the economic analysis of capitalism.

Such an extension of the Schumpeterian vision would emphasise the Austrian roots of Schumpeter's own thought, to an extent that he himself was unable or unwilling to do. Moreover, such a widened Schumpeterian view would indeed confirm those general normative (policy) implications cited earlier as flowing out of Schumpeter's system. It would achieve this by disengaging that system from its long-standing commitment to the Walrasian system, a commitment that has not only generated paradox upon paradox, but has also significantly obscured appreciation for the full potential of Schumpeter's brilliant, but arguably incomplete, vision of the capitalist process.

Much interest has been stirred in recent years by the modest but vigorous revival of the "Austrian" tradition in economics. Only a short while ago, the ideas of Mises, who died aged 92 in 1973, and of Hayek, who is intellectually vigorous at 82, were routinely dismissed—or simply ignored—within the economics profession. Today many economists, especially younger economists, and especially in the USA but also in Britain, are rediscovering their work. They are pursuing the implications of Austrian insights (such that expectations are subjective), the nature of the market as an entrepreneurial process, and the like.

But what does the Austrian approach say about *policy*? How is the "Austrianism" of Mises and Hayek related to their generally favourable assessments of free-market arrangement? Exactly how does this linkage between Austrian and free-market economics arise? As an "Austrian" economist this is how I see it.

Austrian economics is different from the standard or mainstream approach still generally taught as the core of modern economics in British and American universities. For the mainstream approach the market is a social institution with some effectiveness in computing the solution to the task of allocating scarce resources. Without central direction the market somehow steers resources—yes, as if led by an invisible hand—substantially toward those productive activities in which they can be most valuable. For Austrian economics, on the other hand, the market is seen as a social institution that is remarkably effective in *discovering* where existing resource utilisation falls short of the "best"—most valuable—pattern conceivable. At any moment, that is, ghastly errors are doubtless being made in allocating resources. The market, in Austrian view, is extraordinarily effective in spotting these errors, and in creating inducements that will tend to replace them by improved, less "faulty," more valuable, patterns of use. Here, for Austrian economics, lies the magic of the invisible hand. This is the fundamental difference between the mainstream and the Austrian views of what the market achieves in real, everyday life and it indicates the sharp difference in *attitude* toward perceived economic tasks, problems or difficulties.

For the mainstream view, a perceived economic difficulty—or the theoretical demonstration of less than optimal allocation (for example, through less than perfect composition, or through the existence of externalities)—is immediate apparent cause for corrective state intervention. If the invisible hand has, for whatever reason, faltered, clearly the error, in this mainstream view, must be corrected by the powerful, wise, benevolent hand of the state. It is true, first, that in recent years mainstream economists and others have come to question the power, the wisdom and the benevolence of the state. [This is a reference to the study of "the economics of politics" (including government, democracy and bureaucracy) which arrives at defects that could be described as "government failure"—in contrast to the "market failure" that economists have long diagnosed in their study of free markets.—Ed. (of *Economic Affairs*)] And, secondly, it has come to be recognised that the costs of intervention may be so substantial as to render the market outcome, flawed though it may be, the preferable option. But, despite these salutary caveats, mainstream economic policy begins from the view that a sub-optimal market allocation is *prima facie* reason for corrective, central action. The implications of the Austrian view are very different.

In the Austrian approach a sub-optimal pattern in the use of resources is not at all evidence of market *failure*. It is rather the result of unavoidable, "only-to-be-expected" error, which is precisely *the normal function of the market to discover and to correct*. From this perspective, state corrective action must be viewed with suspicion. Even if the diagnosis of sub-optimal market allocation is correct, intervention may

(a) unhelpfully frustrate or impede more comprehensive or more speedy spontaneous corrective market responses; and

(b) itself unintentionally set in motion perversely responsive market reactions.

Not only may the market—as recognised in mainstream economics—know things that the best intentioned of government officials does not know. The market process, in the Austrian view, is a sensitive, subtle *discovery procedure* (Hayek's phrase). Attempts to improve upon its results—whether in industrial concentration, or of environmental pollution, or monetary instability—may seriously hamper and distort that delicate process of discovering both unavoidable error in using resources and the solution.

The essence is not that market prices offer spontaneously developed "signals," able faultlessly to co-ordinate millions of independently made decisions. (This would occur only in equilibrium; in disequilibrium the market prices which prevail would *not* so perfectly co-ordinate decisions.) It is rather that it is in disequilibrium—when prices do not offer the correct signals—that entrepreneurs are offered the required incentives—in the form of profits—for the discrepancies to be noticed and corrected. New products may be introduced, new qualities of existing products may be developed, new methods of production may be ventured, new forms of industrial organisation, financing, marketing or tackling risk may be developed. All the ceaseless churning and agitation of the market is to be understood as the consequences of its never-ending discovery process.

LIBERALISM AND LIMITED GOVERNMENT

At first glance the role of limited government in [Ludwig von] Mises's system of classical liberalism appears as a somewhat uneasy compromise between two conflicting goals: on the one hand to achieve the advantages of a free market; on the other hand to benefit, in certain respects, by coordinated central direction. Indeed this compromise might appear to differ only in degree from the kind of compromise enshrined in those "mixed economic systems" that have become so dear to the hearts of the economists and politicians of our time. But such a view of the role of limited government in Misesian liberalism would be utterly incorrect. For Mises, limited government is in no sense a compromise; and the possibility of any viable, stable kind of "mixed" system was categorically rejected by Mises: "There is simply no other choice than this: either to abstain from interference in the free play of the market, or to delegate the entire management of production and distribution to the government . . . there exists no middle way." (*Liberalism*, p. 79)

The truth is that for Mises's liberalism the appropriate and important functions of government, as well as the severely circumscribed limits to government are *both* directly and consistently implied by the very essence of liberalism itself. "The program of liberalism . . . if condensed into a single word, would have to read: *property*, that is, private ownership of the means of production. . . ." (p. 19) It is the preservation of the institution of private property that most emphatically renders government a necessity for the liberal society; it is the preservation of precisely that same institution that makes it essential to prescribe strict and definite limits to government.

That government is necessary for liberalism was forthrightly emphasized by Mises. Government is defined as "the organs charged with the responsibility of administering the apparatus of compulsion." (p. 35) And "the liberal understands quite clearly that without resort to compulsion,

From *The Freeman / Ideas on Liberty:* http://www.thefreemanonline.org. © 2008 *The Freeman / Ideas on Liberty.* All rights reserved. Reprinted by permission of the Foundation for Economic Education. Originally appeared in print in *The Freeman* 35, no. 11 (1985): 38–40.

the existence of society would be endangered . . . One must be in a position to compel the person who will not respect the lives, health, personal freedom, or private property of others to acquiesce in the rules of life in society." (p. 37) And, again, "For the liberal, the state is an absolute necessity, since the most important tasks are incumbent upon it: the protection not only of private property, but also of peace, for in the absence of the latter the full benefits of private property cannot be reaped." (p. 39)

Recognition of the necessity of the state apparatus of compulsion does not, however, lead the liberal to ascribe special nobility, virtue, or esteem to the exercise of state functions. On the contrary, the liberal is thoroughly sensitive to the enormous potential for evil and corruption that inheres in the exercise of government. "Nothing corrupts a man so much as being an arm of the law and making men suffer. The lot of the subject is anxiety, a spirit of servility and fawning adulation; but the pharisaical self-righteousness, conceit, and arrogance of the master are no better." (p. 58)

It is because for Mises the exercise of state functions carries with it no inherent nobility or dignity, that he sees the merits of democracy in a manner entirely free of the mystique with which it is invested in current political ideology. There is, for the liberal, no special glory attached to the task of governing, and no indignity attached to being subject to (limited) governmental rule. The rule of government is a practical necessity; that is all. Division of labor then exercises its claims. "One cannot be an engineer and a policeman at the same time. It in no way detracts from my dignity, my well-being, or my freedom that I am not myself a policeman."

It then follows that there is nothing particularly glorious about a system that seeks to replace government by the few by self-government by the whole people—even were such a goal in fact a possible one. The only reason for endorsing democracy for the liberal society is a pragmatic one. "Democracy is that form of political constitution which makes possible the adaptation of the government to the wishes of the governed without violent struggles . . . By means of elections and parliamentary arrangements, the change of government is executed smoothly and without friction, violence, or bloodshed." (p. 42)

But if the preservation of private property was the basis for liberal acknowledgment of a vitally important role to government, that same essential element in liberalism implies a severely circumscribed set of functions for government. Liberalism reflects the teachings of economics concerning the enormous benefits that society reaps from the institution of private property in the means of production. But the very concept of private ownership involves "for the individual a sphere in which he is free of the state. It sets limits to the operation of the authoritarian will." Every attempt by the state to go beyond its function of "guaranteeing life, health, liberty and private property against violent attacks" is then seen by the liberal as "evil." (p. 52) No matter how well-meaning paternalistic acts of government may be, such acts necessarily invade the domain of private property. Consistent paternalism cannot but lead to complete authoritarianism, stifling all progress and innovation. "The wielding of powers of this kind even by men imbued with the best of intentions must needs reduce the world to a graveyard of the spirit." (p. 54)

Here then we have the *single* goal and raison d'etre of limited government in the Misesian system: The pragmatic lessons of economic science, joined with a passionate regard for individual freedom, point unequivocally to the liberal system of private ownership of the means of production. Preservation of this fundamental framework of individual rights calls for government that protects these rights against potential enemies; the concern that such protection emphatically refrain from itself invading those very rights is not the expression of any kind of compromise—it is merely the other side of the very same coin, the essentiality to liberalism of a protected, inviolate sphere of individual rights.

INDIVIDUALISTIC CAPITALISM

I would like to imagine us all in this magnificent library transferred into a space ship, with all this gorgeous paneling and the old books, taking us to another planet. The purpose of our trip in space is to settle a new world, a new planet. And we are debating among ourselves the best form of institutional organization that might serve our purposes. I take it as my task tonight, as we rush through space, oblivious to everything that is outside us, to spell out a case on behalf of one particular form of organization—that of capitalism, individualistic capitalism.

By individualistic capitalism we would mean that we propose, when we arrive at our destination, to assign property rights to each individual. Now, these rights should be assigned on the basis of the best ethical and legal expertise, and once these rights have been assigned they shall be inviolate. Further, each individual shall be entirely free to exercise these rights. Each shall be free to exchange rights with other mutually consenting parties. There should be absolutely no outside control other than that necessary to protect and preserve the assigned rights.

Such a system is, of course, the ideal of individualistic capitalism, a completely laissez-faire market in which the role of the state has been reduced to that of guaranteeing the inviolability of individual rights. Now, I see my contribution to this debate not merely to present an economist's case for individualistic capitalism, but particularly to state the perspective of *Austrian* economics. This means that my case will first of all be restricted in that it is an economic case, not a complete case. It is not a case that settles all aspects of the question. There are moral aspects of the choice between alternative institutional systems that an economist is not equipped and has no expertise to address. Although I will be saying something about some moral implications of the system, I certainly will not claim to have exhausted all moral aspects of the question. As an economist, then, I will be restricting myself to those issues surrounding our choice among institutional arrangements that have particularly to do with the question of whether we are achieving the goals at which we

From Israel M. Kirzner, "Individualistic Capitalism," in Donna C. Charron, editor, *Views on Individualism* (St. Louis: St. Louis Humanities Forum, 1986), 5–27.

aim in the most effective possible way, given what we are able to do. And the particular angle that I will add in terms of Austrian economics will, I think, become apparent as I go through some of the arguments on behalf of individualistic capitalism. I will try to develop Austrian insights that perhaps have not received emphasis in standard economic discussions of these questions.

My charge, then, is to present an economist's case for a laissez-faire capitalism. In the course of our discussion in space, allow me to bring up this hypothetical situation: supposing there are two individuals in our new world, one of whom has a house that needs painting very badly, and one of whom is very hungry, but is quite able to work hard at painting houses. Individualistic capitalism would argue that each individual should be free to enter into an agreement to trade labor services on the one hand for bread on the other. The owner of the house will provide bread in return for having his house painted. The owner of the house will be better off because he prefers having his house painted than retaining the bread and an unpainted house. The painter will be better off because he prefers working and receiving bread rather than sitting in outer space hungry. Now this is, of course, a simple exchange situation illustrating that individualistic capitalism, a system based on free exchange, can indeed benefit both parties. I think that at a very simple level a case for capitalism can be built on this simple insight—that *acts of exchange do benefit both parties to the exchange in their best prospective judgment.* I emphasize "in their best prospective judgment" because individuals may find later on that they've made mistakes. The house painter may later discover that he wasn't all that hungry after all. The house owner may have discovered that perhaps the latest rage is to leave houses unpainted for centuries. At any rate, at the time when the deal is entered into, each party believes himself in his best prospective judgment to be a gainer from the act of exchange.

We have discovered a phenomenon: both parties can gain, neither at the expense of the other. Something has been created out of nothing, *ex nihilo.* This is the remarkable aspect of free exchange. A market permits all potential acts of free exchange to be consummated.

Now having pointed this out, however, doesn't convince one surely that permitting people to exercise their own rights in their own individualistic way is necessarily the only way or even the best way of achieving the same results. After all the other side of the debate might argue we need not assign rights to individuals. We could instead just assign power to a central authority, a wise benevolent central authority, that could arrange exactly the same kind of transfer. That central authority will know that Mr. A needs his house painted and that Mr. B, who is able to provide painting services, needs bread. And the transfer will be made without free exchange. Perhaps free exchange is not the best way by which to achieve the advantages of exchange, as the preceding arguments seem to claim. So let us move on to a second stage in the discussion.

The first stage has shown that free exchange can indeed benefit both parties as far as it goes, but perhaps this does not constitute yet an airtight case for individualistic capitalism. A second stage in the argument might proceed as follows: To be sure, a central, powerful, wise, benevolent public authority could in principle be imagined to arrange these same transfers without individualistic exchange. But after all, who knows better than that individual what is good for that individual. The central authority, no matter how powerful, no matter how wise, no matter how benevolent, can never really know what the house owner really wants. He can never really know as thoroughly, as spontaneously, and as definitely as the house owner himself, say, what color the house owner really wants. Consequently the case for individualistic capitalism comes to be built on a second leg, namely that *each individual knows better than anyone else what is in that individual's best interest.* Now the case for capitalism does indeed depend to a large extent on this insight. That by assigning individuals their own rights, and permitting them to pursue these rights and to exercise these rights and to exploit these rights in what they consider to be their own best interests, they are far more likely to achieve what is indeed in their interest than by permitting any others, benevolent though they may be, wise though they may be, to make decisions on behalf of and affecting other individuals.

I set great store by this argument. But I must admit that this too is not entirely an airtight argument. There are cases, the opposing side will suggest, where individuals may not know what is in their best interest. Individuals may make mistakes. Other individuals may know better, and others wiser than they ought to be assigned responsibility and power to make decisions that will affect other individuals where those other individuals may mistakenly pursue goals and items which perhaps are not in their own ultimate best interest. Now this argument for paternalism is one which I view on the one hand with a great deal of scepticism and

fear, but on the other hand with a certain amount of reluctant, and grudg-
ing respect. I fear this argument because I don't know where it will stop.
What happens if someone says you must wear a seat belt because this is
in your best interest, and you are foolish when you don't buy a car with
a seat belt? What happens when one extends that argument to say that a
wise man may tell me: you shall read this good book once a week, or once
a day, or three times a day, because this is good for your soul? Where does
one stop when one considers the possibility that others may know better
than I what is in my ultimate best interest? On the other hand, fearful
though I am of this argument—and I think it obvious that this argument
leads to absurdity—it is difficult to reject it out of hand. It is difficult to
deny *possible* moral merit to an argument that individualistic capitalism
leaves each person a prey to his or her own weaknesses.

Let us consider further arguments that might be raised surrounding the issue of individualistic capitalism. I made reference to a central
authority, powerful, wise and benevolent. Well, a good deal of the case
for individualistic capitalism rests on the claim that to imagine a central authority both powerful and benevolent is almost a contradiction in
terms. Power corrupts! There is a school of thought that has developed
a high degree of scepticism about the very possibility of benevolence in
the minds and hearts of those who wield state power. Professor Stigler
at the University of Chicago, who is our most recent Nobel prize winner
in economics, has in recent years dwelt a great deal on arguments along
these lines that suggest that acts by regulators, by interveners, have never
tended to reflect the best interest of the public as such. Well this, too, provides a powerful basis for scepticism with regard to an institutional system that should deny to individuals the right to make decisions on their
own behalf. But I think one must beware of following Professor Stigler
or some economists of related schools to the ultimate to suggest that it is
out of the question to imagine central state authorities that should indeed
work for the public interest. I suspect that it would be somewhat too
cynical to adopt a position of that kind, and I suppose that one ought to
consider the possibility, at least, that ingenious political scientists might
devise political systems with rules that might constrain public authorities
to act, if not out of benevolence, at least along patterns that would be congruent with benevolence. So. I am not prepared to rest the case for capitalism on this particular argument that central authorities will inherently
and inevitably be corrupt and self-seeking.

Well then, where do we stand in our space ship with respect to developing the argument for individualistic capitalism? An argument is often advanced—and I think that this, too, carries with it a great deal of weight—that individualistic capitalism, permitting as it does each individual to seek his or her own gain without outside constraints, is a remarkably powerful force harnessing the motivation of individuals to better and improve their own situations. A society of free persons, it is pointed out, is a society of persons who are aware that what they get, they get for themselves; and consequently they are motivated and inspired to work hard. A colleague of mine, an eminent colleague, Professor Leontief, another Nobel prize winner, has likened this incentive force of individualism to a powerful wind that can provide the propulsion to a sail ship. The profit motive, the motive for individual gain which drives capitalism is indeed a powerful force. The material success that capitalist countries have demonstrated over the past two centuries is certainly in large measure to be ascribed to the powerful force of this incentive. However, Leontief, who is no strong supporter of capitalism, has argued that the wind that drives a ship in the right direction can under other circumstances drive a vessel on the rocks. Indeed he claims, I think erroneously, that individualistic capitalism, while it does harness this powerful force of self-interest, may very well turn out to harness this force in destructive, socially deleterious directions. So the question, then, is not whether capitalism does indeed harness the powerful force of self-interest, but what kind of social outcomes result from this harnessing of the incentive force of gain, this unleashing of the powerful inspiration of the profit motive?

One thinks here of Adam Smith's "invisible hand" principle. Ultimately, all arguments for laissez-faire individualistic capitalism return to this great insight that this wise Scottish economist, Adam Smith, had when he argued that in a free market, as if by an invisible hand, individuals are motivated to act in the general interest. In other words, that motive which Leontief identified as possibly leading to the rocks was declared by Adam Smith to lead to social gain. Standard economic theory has elaborated on the inner meaning and content of Adam Smith's invisible hand doctrine. Basically, the doctrine shows that under fairly plausible circumstances, individual self-interest can lead toward a social pattern of decision making, which, in the economists' jargon, is described as Pareto optimal. That is to say, the final outcome of a market in which individuals are free to act does, under specific assumptions, lead toward a state in which it would not be possible to benefit any members of the system without imposing costs on others. This result has satisfied economists that a capitalistic system tends to exhaust all opportunities for potential mutual gain. In other words, coming back to our simple two person example of a half an hour ago—the house owner and the hungry painter—what the doctrine suggests is that each and every potential opportunity will tend to be exhausted, will tend to be exploited, to be consummated, under individualistic capitalism.

There are problems. The invisible hand doctrine has, ever since the days of Pigou in Great Britain some eighty years ago, come under systematic attack. The basic doctrine upon which the invisible hand thesis depends requires that each participant in the market make decisions that fully take into account all consequences. But, of course, many decisions do not quite do that. Consider our two person example. The house owner who decides to paint his house has done so perhaps after a long period during which his neighbors have been disgusted by the unsightly condition of the house. His decision not to paint the house until today did not take into account their misery. Consider a somewhat different possibility. The house owner directs the painter to paint the house a color such that the neighbors immediately begin to sell their houses. The value of property in the neighborhood immediately drops as a result of the new style of painting introduced by this house owner. In other words, decisions affect others. The decision to paint the house or not to paint the house is a decision in which others are vitally interested, but over which they have no control. Now this question of externalities has been thoroughly analyzed in recent years. At this time I would simply draw attention to certain insights that ought not to be lost sight of. What the neighbors who object to the color of the house may do, of course, is to offer to pay the house owner a price to paint his house a decent color. You may offer to pay me anything you wish in order to persuade me to paint my house, or not to paint my house, or to paint it whatever color you want. But I have the right to do as I wish. Remember, we assign property rights, inviolate property rights. My house is my house. If you offer me a price, I will take that into account. And if I value my choice of color over your choice of color to the extent that I am willing to forego the price you wish to offer me not to paint my house the offending color, it is my right to do so. In so choosing, I will have taken into account the full consequences of my decision on everybody else. So in principle, it should be clear that the market could internalize what might superficially appear to be an externality. The market would permit me, in fact compel me, the house owner, to consider how heavily my decision disturbs others, because, after all, the degree to which they are disturbed will be reflected and expressed in the amount of money they offer me not to paint my house this offending color.

Up until now, most of the considerations that I've advanced on behalf of individualistic capitalism are considerations that I believe most economists in general would appreciate. But I would like to introduce some insights from a particularly Austrian perspective, Austrian in the sense of deriving from a tradition in economics that goes back to a school of economic thought begun by Carl Menger in 1871, in Vienna, and carried forth in our own time particularly by my own teacher the late Ludwig von Mises, and Professor Friedrich von Hayek. Let me briefly outline some considerations that the Austrian perspective introduces. The standard economic problem that is considered by most economists to confront an economic system, and in terms of which capitalism is itself judged, involves, in the Austrian view, a serious misunderstanding. The standard view perceives the economic problem for society as not being very different from the economic problem that you or I as individuals face in our daily lives. We receive a salary check and this has to last us for a month. We have to allocate, we have to budget, we have to plan. And, since the task of planning can be carried out efficiently or inefficiently, at the end of the month, we may find ourselves hungry because we unwisely spent too much in the first part of the month. We may regret at the end of the period having spent too much on one item and consequently having too little left for a second item. And clearly, we don't want to put ourselves in those situations of having to regret what we've done. We want to do what we believe is in our best interest to do. We wish to allocate our resources efficiently. Well, then, the standard idea is that society should do exactly as the individual seeks to do. The view is that society, too, is posed with a similar kind of economic problem. Society has its resources, society has its goals—whether these goals are individual goals or supra-individual goals. And the economic problem facing any economic system is seen as ensuring that society should not find itself in the position where it has allocated too much of its resources to one particular kind of goal, leaving too little for other worthwhile goals.

Now in the Austrian view, this way of looking at things misstates the true nature of the social and economic problem facing society. The analogy between the individual and society is flawed. It is an imperfect analogy. It is a misleading analogy. And the basic difference is the following. For an individual the economic problem is a clear cut one. It is a clearly defined one. Each individual has his or her goals. The resources are similarly clearly defined. I know my goals. I know the amount of my pay check. I know the resources at my disposal. I must allocate the resources in a fashion consistent with the hierarchy of goals in order not to be in contradiction to myself. To be inefficient is, in a sense, to act in contradiction to oneself. One announces that a certain goal is important and yet one spends one's resources on other less important goals. This kind of economizing, this kind of allocation, is a relatively simple matter at the individual level. It is a matter of calculation with the problem presenting itself in a manner ready for the calculation to be undertaken. The situation with respect to society, however, is totally different in this respect. No single mind in society possesses the information necessary for this kind of economic problem to be set up even conceptually. There is no such thing as a unified set of goals for society either in individualistic terms or in any other set of terms. I know what I want. You know what you want. In no sense can the urgency with which you want your goals and with which I want my goals be directly compared. But more seriously than that, in no sense is it possible for the wants of the members of society to be set up as constituting a framework within which allocation can be carried on. No one has all the necessary information. What is needed in order to set up the very notion of this kind of social economic problem is a logically prior process of discovery, a process of communication of knowledge which must not be taken for granted. We must not beg the question of mutual discovery by assuming that it has already taken place. Often, the market is assumed, particularly by the defenders of capitalism, as having successfully solved the economic problem, of having achieved desired Pareto-optimality. Well, the question that must not be begged in pursuing such discussion is the issue of how indeed separate goals are somehow brought into contact with each other. Separate awareness of needs, separate awareness of resources are somehow brought to bear on decision making. How can one consider individuals somehow fused together to constitute a social whole other than by a process of mutual discovery.

This is where, pursuing the Austrian perspective, the full strength of the case for individualistic capitalism can begin to be sensed. What individualistic capitalism sets in motion is entrepreneurial discovery, an alertness to what might improve situations. The idea that the profit incentive may blow the system on the rocks misunderstands the role of entrepreneurial discovery. Entrepreneurs discover where resources have been misallocated, where others have made mistakes, where opportunities exist. Entrepreneurial discovery, the sense for profit opportunities, directs individuals to feel where other people's desires could be better satisfied with available resources. This process brings people together, brings means and goals together in a manner which can only be imagined in the absence of capitalism. What motivates this process of discovery is the circumstance that individualistic capitalism permits individuals to gain by their discoveries. I think there is a profoundly important psychological insight here: people tend to see that which it is in their interest to discover. People overlook that which has no concern to them. Two people walk down the street, and they see different things. Each one sees that which is of interest to him. The market permits individuals to gain by profiting from the errors of others. In this way, by this discovery procedure, the market tends to harness the potential alertness of market participants for achieving a greater degree of coordination, a greater degree of interpersonal adjustment than could be imagined under any centralized system. I do indeed believe that there is a great deal to be said for individualistic capitalism in terms of the knowledge which individuals have of their own good, in terms of the incentive which individuals have to work for their own concerns. Remember, when we talk about the self-interest of individuals, we do not mean necessarily crassly selfish interest. Self-interest can certainly include one's own interest in benefiting one's neighbors, in benefiting the needy, in engaging in philanthropic endeavor. It must be noted that these altruistic activities are as self-interested as any others. Certainly, individualistic capitalism enables individuals to pursue their own goals without interference by others who may be less than fully benevolent. But ultimately I believe the case for capitalism requires us to perceive that under no other system can one imagine a systematic institutional procedure that will bring into view those errors that may have been committed or may be about to be committed which no one has suspected. Remember, a mistake that no one has suspected is not something that one can look up in the library, not even as good a library as this one.

If one does not know that there is anything to be looked for, then one will overlook the existence of the library. One will not know that any source exists for the information. We are likely to be ignorant of the fact that we are ignorant. And when one is ignorant of the fact that one is ignorant, there is no way in which one can deliberately seek to discover how to overcome one's ignorance. Capitalism permits one to notice where one has been ignorant. And it is upon the insight that capitalism is a systematic discovery procedure that, in my opinion, the case for individualistic capitalism—whether in outer space or here on earth—can be rested.

EDWARD McCLENNEN*: It seems to me that economists in general have a very interesting and powerful argument when they suggest that if we had a very thorough assignment of rights to individuals, and if we then allowed a market to operate, presumably people could trade themselves amongst each other the various rights they have, resulting in an optimal state. However, I am bothered about two features of that particular argument. First of all, as many people have pointed out, an optimal state is simply a state in which it is impossible to move from there to another state in which no one is worse off and at least some people are better off. That is a very technical sense of optimal, and one needs to be reminded of the fact that a state in which the "haves" have a great deal and the "have nots" have very little indeed can also be an optimal state. I think that a careful statement of optimality suggests that although it is an important criterion of value, or a way of evaluating social states, it is an incomplete one. The point about saying that the "haves" may have a great deal and that the "have nots" have nothing can be an optimal state, is a way of reminding ourselves that that particular virtue of markets does not speak to the question of justice or to the distribution of benefits throughout a society. A very maldistributed arrangement can nonetheless satisfy the economist's criterion of optimality. Although I spend a great deal of time thinking about economics these days, as a philosopher, I am bothered by the way that economists talk about a system of assigning rights as if that were nonproblematic. I would hope I would strike a responsive note here to lawyers in the audience. It seems to me that the business of assigning

---

* Edward F. McClennen is an ethics and decision theoretic philosopher at Washington University, St. Louis. He is co-editor of the two-volume work, *Foundations and Applications of Decision Theory*, Reidel Publishing Company, 1978.

rights is unbelievably complicated. It is a devilish business. There are rights, as it were, that we have yet to realize that we have, and we do not even know what the proper assignment of them would be. Moreover lawyers seem to tell you that they would like very much not to have some scheme whereby all rights are assigned in advance, completely accounted for. What they prefer is to make some assignments, cross our fingers, and then deal with things as the problems arise, deal with the cases as they come up. Suppose you plant your factory down on property next to mine, and it influences the life activities of myself and my friends. Who has the rights here? Our style of life has been damaged. If we have the rights, then the factory has to withdraw or has to pay some sort of money to improve things. Out of that arises one kind of litigation. If the factory has the rights, then the shoe is on the other foot, and we have to go to court or try to band together and buy out the factory and so on.

Now I would suggest the following as an argument that would perhaps open up some discussion. I am very sympathetic, Professor Kirzner, to what you have to say about trying to work toward a laissez-faire system and deregulation, but it does seem to me that it requires a great increase in the activities of courts. If I can borrow a phrase from the economists, I think there is in this case no such thing as a free lunch. If you want to cut back on the amount of governmental control, and specifically, legislative control of economic activities, you must greatly increase the opportunity for what is called in legal terms, standing. That is, people should have more access to courts so that when their rights, as they conceive them, are being infringed upon by the economic activities of others, they have some recourse. If we follow your prescription, as we dismantle the legislative branch of the government, we have to reexamine whether the judicial branch of the government ought to be more actively involved in adjudicating rights amongst people in society.

HOMER E. SAYAD*: I would like to raise the issue of global influence in the framework of the economy that we have today. No one particular country, say the United States, is independent. We have socialism in part of the world, the communist world. What they do, how they think impacts what we do, how we think in this country. Ten years ago, suddenly, there

---

* Homer E. Sayad studied Marshallian economics at Cambridge. After retiring as partner in charge of the St. Louis office of Deloitte Haskins and Sells, public accounting, he served as president of the Board of Police Commissioners of the City of St. Louis.

was an oil embargo that tremendously influenced the industrial world. How do you reconcile individualistic capitalism with the capitalism that we know today and with socialism.

KIRZNER: Professor McClennen and Mr. Sayad have drawn our attention to several important issues and questions. Professor McClennen is concerned particularly with distributional problems. I must state that Professor McClennen overlooked something that I did say in my talk that might have affected this point. You may remember that in the space ship that we were on we agreed that there would be an assignment of individual rights that shall be based upon the best legal and ethical advice we can get. In other words, I fully agree that the important task of assigning rights, which economists mention in passing, is in fact a complex and challengingly intricate task. I confess I do not know how to perform this task. Economists believe in division of labour, and we are delighted to farm that problem out to the jurists and the able in law schools and the philosophy departments without deluding ourselves that we can expect simple answers. And I admit that to the extent that we are dodging an important issue, we are guilty. But we do recognize the issue. The issue of assigning rights is a very difficult one. I suspect, though, that Professor McClennen is perhaps erring in the opposite direction when he suggests that avoiding capitalism somehow avoids this problem. There is no way of avoiding the problem of how to assign rights. In noncapitalistic systems, rights have to be assigned too. So it is not so much a question whether one shall assign rights, whether one shall engage in this complex decision making. It is a question of what, in fact, is the appropriate ethical and legal basis upon which to ground such an assignment of rights. I should point out that once rights *have* been assigned, distributional problems have by definition been taken care of. The problems of the "haves" and the "have-nots," the problems of economic justice, these problems evaporate once one is able in principle to rely on the expertise of the jurists and the ethicists in giving us a proper assignment of rights. If one is aesthetically and ethically disturbed by inequality, then, rights can be assigned equally. What one should of course remember is that even if we start out by assigning rights "equally," they may not remain equally distributed forever. We may start out by dividing the planet upon which we land into equal numbers of square miles. We should not be surprised when one visits that planet five years later, after five years of individualistic capitalism, to discover that there are "haves" and "have-nots." This fact should not disturb one in the least. The initial assignment of rights was strictly ethical; the subsequent reassignment of rights was based entirely on voluntary agreements on the part of the individual right-holders. I believe that the case for capitalism is inseparable from such an entitlement theory of rights assignment. To the extent that there may be philosophical and other objections to entitlement system, then the case for capitalism is correspondingly under a question mark, certainly. I would, moreover, draw Professor McClennen's attention to the fact that the task of determining the assignment of rights on this space ship, difficult as it is, is in a way not very important at all. The likelihood is that under a wide variety of different patterns of right assignments, the final outcome after five, ten or fifteen years of capitalistic activity would not show a great deal of difference between different original distributions of rights patterns. So while certainly we would want our rights system to be consistent with ethical norms, and there is no reason why we should not start out doing it correctly; nonetheless, the perceived distributional "problems" that are often associated with capitalism could not really be avoided by a more careful application of those very norms. I fully agree with Professor McClennen when he points out the need for a vastly increased volume of court activity in order to replace regulatory action by the state. I certainly agree with that, and I think that is a price well worth paying. Whether that price is to be paid through a state governed system of courts or through a private court system is a matter upon which reasonable exponents of capitalism debate.

Turning to Mr. Sayad's observations about the complexity of capitalism in a modern world, and of the great questions of international impact, events across the seas, upon our own economic system, I must agree. Yes, we are living in an interdependent world, and it is all too easy for the economist to set out in his space ship to ignore the nitty-gritty hard problems of the every day world. Nonetheless, I think the case has to be made that the complexities of the world in which we live can only begin to be understood by processes of simplification, abstraction. By initial abstraction followed by the successive introduction of more and more realistic aspects of the world, one can hope perhaps to understand the world. One can perhaps hope to be able to provide useful advice for the making of marginal adjustments in the institutions of society. Let me point out, perhaps provocatively, the interesting possibility that in a world of socialist countries, you would have capitalism at the international level. What you would have is a society of socialist countries between which there would occur international trade. Each socialist country would be buying and selling with other socialist countries in an international market. You would have international capitalism while you would have socialism at the level of each country. In fact the only way in which capitalism internationally could be imagined away would be to think of a world in which there was a world government with complete power over individual states which would, of course, have had to surrender their sovereignty. I do not think that an oil embargo is the kind of event which need compromise the possibility of capitalism within a nation. It seems to me that an oil embargo which is the result of a free association of oil sellers, oil resource owners, is perfectly consistent with individualistic capitalism. It is perfectly legitimate for owners of resources to get together and charge a higher price just as it is perfectly legitimate within a system of capitalism for buyers to seek to break the cartel, as they are usually successful in doing, and to operate on the self-interest of participants in the cartel as to make it worth their while to unravel the cartel agreement. I think the existence of an oil cartel is not something that is inherently inconsistent with capitalism. Whether it is successful or not need not seriously affect the validity of the arguments for capitalism.

SAYAD: How can you say that the oil embargo is not in violation of free market? The price we pay today for oil is not based on a free market?

KIRZNER: Well, the price for oil in this country is, you are probably right, not a free market price because we have many internal controls within the country. My claim simply is that the existence of an international cartel is by itself not inconsistent with a free market. Let me just step back a little bit and discuss in brief detail the effect of competition and monopoly on the capitalism and markets. Sometimes the case for a free market is stated in terms of competition. Indeed the argument often is that if monopolies were to exist, then the monopoly would introduce distortions in the market which would interfere with the ability of the market to achieve optimality conditions. The problem with the position that the existence of monopoly in fact compromises the case for capitalism is that it is likely to be based on an interpretation of competition that many economists have adopted, but that in fact is totally inconsistent with the meaning of competition as applied in every day business life.

These economists have used the notion of perfect competition, by which they have meant a system where each buyer and each seller is infinitesimally small as compared to the market as a whole, so that as a consequence each buyer and each seller is absolutely powerless to affect price. Now I submit that in business life that is not what competition means. Competition does not mean that you must passively accept a given price. Competition means that you get on your toes and cut price, it means that you get on your toes and offer a higher price if you are on the buying side. You get what you want, if necessary for a higher price; you sell what you are able to produce, if necessary you cut price. It is the change in price which vigorous competition brings about. Vigorous competition in its everyday sense is something quite different from the textbook notion of perfect competition. And when it is argued that the mere absence of perfect competition is inconsistent with the success of a market, one is reminded of the important work of Josef Schumpeter, a great economist who in his early years had been trained in the Austrian tradition. What Schumpeter argued was that perfect competition would be a state of affairs where capitalism would simply atrophy. Capitalism is a system of continual creativity, continual innovation, continual change. It is a system which depends upon the absence of perfect competition. The only sense in which capitalism depends on competition is that involving the notion called *absence of privilege*. No individual should be given privileges in the sense of interfering with the potential entry of any other individual for any amount. Competition means freedom of entry. So long as entry is free the market operates. The market operates precisely as Schumpeter showed us, precisely by the possibility of someone moving into the market, lowering the price, introducing a new commodity, innovating a new form of production, introducing a new form of business organization. Now in this sense the size of a firm, or the number of resource owners who have banded together ostensibly to keep up price, should not cause great alarm or concern. It is true that under such circumstances we will not be in a state of Pareto optimality, but the case for the market does not, at least from an Austrian perspective, depend on the end state achieved by a market process. Rather that case rests on the character of the *process* itself. And in a world of continual change, if people get together to set up a cartel for a particular resource, this is part of the competitive market process with freedom of entry. The market is still free to discover a substitute. Entrepreneurial ingenuity invariably comes up with a substitute.

That is what has happened in the past, and that is what will happen in the future. As a rule, cartels tend to break down. Where they continue to exist, substitutes come into the picture. This is a world of churning change. Capitalism depends upon such change. So in that sense, I believe a cartel is consistent with capitalism.

MCCLENNEN: I take it that Mr. Sayad is interested in the impact on the ordinary person of the oil cartel or any other number of vicissitudes that affect us in the economic world. It does not have to be a monopoly, it can be the result of the competition by a very effective competitor, let us say Japan damaging domestic production. The problem for most people is that when these things happen there is a real shock value to them. People lose their jobs. People's income is drastically altered. People's prospects in life are changed. Whereas they thought they had secure jobs which they had trained into they now suddenly discover that they don't. It seems to me that comes back to the issue of justice. Austrians keep reminding the rest of us that we ought to be much more interested in the dynamics of a capitalistic system, much more interested in process and less in the static picture of the neo-classical economy. Mr. Sayad's point is that things do change in the world, and as they change our rights and entitlements also drastically change. My prospects in life are seriously altered. And those become matters that people want to discuss and argue about and want to see if there is some way that they can control the change. Now it is true that over the long run cartels work their way out. Competition over the long run is supposed to benefit all of us. The trouble is that we do not lead our lives in the long run. In the long run we are all dead. What we're interested in is what happens in the next ten, twenty, thirty years. And in that period, your life and mine and everyone's in this room could be astoundingly altered by certain international economic events, which if we followed the ideology of the free market, we would simply be powerless to do anything about.

QUESTIONS AND ANSWERS

QUESTION: Both speakers have referred to the need of justice in allotting rights and entitlements, and both, to my surprise, at least, assume that it is a much better project for the courts than the legislature. And they expect us lawyers to find more clients, to get more standing, to bring more cases. The judges do make law, but they have to deny that they are making law. Is not the legislature the closest thing we have to sovereignty. People are bitterly complaining about the courts overruling the legislature. What's so terrible about letting the legislature handle these entitlements and rights?

MCCLENNEN: I want to tell you an anecdote here. This summer I attended a libertarian conference in Indiana. For about five days we were closeted in the beautiful little campus in Crawfordsville, at Wabash College. It was a marvel to behold. There were two bands of libertarians there. One came armed to say that the trouble with the United States is that the courts were taking over the country and the judges were making law. They had this elaborate set of programs for how we should dismantle the courts. The other group of libertarians arrived and said the trouble with the country is that the legislature is taking over control. They had an elaborate set of prescriptions as to how we should dismantle the legislature. But of course each intended to use the other branch in order to do the dismantling. So if you put their two sets of recommendations together, you were indeed in deep trouble. Now, as I understand Professor Kirzner, he escapes that dilemma. I don't think that he is trying to use one branch of the government against the other.

KIRZNER: My only reservation about using the legislature is that this would tend to permit rights to be changed every session of congress. That would be entirely unfortunate for any system. Presumably, the rights assigned are the bases upon which people engage in their transactions. What is extremely important is that rights should be secure and should be known, in so far as this is possible. If people are aware that their rights can be abrogated by an act of congress arbitrarily, anytime, then, in effect, they don't have rights. People will not act, people will not produce, people will not participate in markets if there is a strong likelihood that the proceeds of their activity will be confiscated by a nominal change of rights. However, beware of a problem here. The argument is sometimes made that those who are hurt by a particular catastrophe ought by that very fact to be entitled to have the entire rights system of the society changed in order to accommodate the particular situation at which they find themselves at a particular point in time. That I submit is extremely dangerous. To give everyone a right to have his economic situation protected against unforeseen catastrophe, economic, natural, or otherwise, is in fact to deny others secure rights to what they might otherwise have been entitled to. Now this does get to the question of justice and the question of ethics, which I'm perfectly willing to leave to the philosophers and jurists to discuss among themselves. All I can point out is that from the economic point of view, the inviolability of rights is something that would be an absolute prerequisite for an effectively operating capitalism. If rights are to be able to be abrogated and changed arbitrarily, then the notion of capitalism under such a system of rights would be totally out of the question.

QUESTION: Are there any rights under the Austrian school that are retained by the state?

KIRZNER: From the perspective that I was pursuing, the state would not exist as an entity possessing rights. The state would have a function, certainly. The function, as I see it, of the state, under the kind of capitalism I am envisioning would be the extremely important function of monitoring the assignment and the protection of the rights of individuals. Now the volume of activity that such a state function would involve would depend on the nature of the society. If the individuals in society had few disagreements and very limited criminal propensities, the function of the state could be quite limited. If the character of the individuals in the state were such that they had many disagreements and strong criminal propensities, then the function of the state would have to be correspondingly expanded.

SPONTANEOUS ORDER AND
THE CASE FOR THE FREE MARKET

The case for the free society, it has widely and correctly been understood, rests in large measure on its economic achievements. It is demonstrated, through reference to history and by economic reasoning, that the free market has enormous potential for stimulating economic growth and prosperity. The proponents of classical liberalism can therefore argue that their idea not only respects the dignity, humanity, and moral worth of the individuals who make up society—it also promotes their economic well-being. Were it the case—as the enemies of freedom have again and again erroneously claimed—that absence of central economic planning constitutes a sure recipe for economic chaos and failure, it would be much more difficult to argue persuasively for the classical liberal society.

Many thoughtful observers might conclude that such supposed economic failings add up to too high a price to pay for the moral virtues of freedom. So it is eminently understandable that classical liberals have seen economic science, with its demonstrations of the economic advantages of free markets, as an important element in the intellectual struggle on behalf of the free society. While economic science itself may be value-free and quite independent of its role in the case for freedom, the ideology of freedom is fully justified in deploying the teachings of economics in promoting its cause.

To a considerable extent, the relevant lessons from economics revolve around the concept of *spontaneous order*. Whereas the untutored view of society is likely to assume that absence of central control must inevitably generate hopeless discoordination and frustration—economics shows how the opposite of this view is in fact the truth. Economics shows how, from the independent decisions of many market participants, there emerges a systematic process of learning and coordination. The outcome of this process is the spontaneous order of the market economy. It is upon

From *Ideas on Liberty: Essays in Honor of Paul L. Poirot* (Irvington-on-Hudson: Foundation for Economic Education, 1987), 45–50. Reprinted by permission of the Foundation for Economic Education.

this spontaneous order that the unprecedented prosperity of market economies rests. In recent years, particularly under the influence of Hayek's writings, a good deal of emphasis has come to be placed in the literature of liberty on this specific doctrine, the doctrine of spontaneous order.

The purpose of the present essay is to draw cautionary attention to a tendency to treat *all* examples of spontaneous order uncritically as equally powerful intellectual ammunition in developing the classical liberal case. I shall argue that this tendency is based on a serious misunderstanding. While it is emphatically true that the economic rationale for the free society rests largely on the notion of spontaneous order, it is *not* the case, I shall maintain, that every example of spontaneous order represents a useful weapon in the arsenal of freedom. In particular, I shall claim, a number of recent demonstrations that benign social conventions and institutions may have evolved organically and spontaneously have been thought to represent useful lessons pointing unequivocally toward the appreciation of the virtues of freedom. My position will be that it would be hazardous for proponents of freedom to rest their case substantially on such demonstrations. The critical policy issues facing modern societies are likely to be such, I believe, as at best to render quite irrelevant the lessons of social science concerning the long-run spontaneous emergence of benign social conventions. Proponents of freedom, it seems, would be well-advised to distinguish sharply between the kinds of spontaneous order that are generated in markets (against a given institutional background) and those other kinds of spontaneous order that may operate benignly to modify the institutional framework itself.

A prefatory word of clarification is perhaps called for. Nothing in what follows should be read as in any way critical of theories of long-run spontaneous order themselves. Such theories are highly stimulating, and a number of them may well be thoroughly valid and important. They may go far to illuminate significant aspects of human history. Our purpose here is to point out that reference to such studies may weaken, rather than strengthen, the economic argument for liberty. The economic argument for liberty rests on the propensity of markets to coordinate decisions and activities. The extraordinary power of arguments rooted in market theory should not be compromised by well-meaning but unhelpful reference to other kinds of spontaneous order. To point all this out is in no way to denigrate the profound scientific and human value of the long-run spontaneous order studies.[1]

SPONTANEOUS ORDER: THE LONG RUN AND THE SHORT

It is first necessary to articulate more sharply the distinction we wish to draw between two levels of, or dimensions for, spontaneous order. Traditional spontaneous order theorists from Ferguson and Smith onwards, generally assumed a society of individuals acting independently *within a given institutional framework*. That framework provided them with a relatively fixed background against which to operate. Economics then teaches that, under such conditions, a learning and discovery process is likely to be set in motion such as spontaneously to coordinate the independent actions of the participants. Without central control, participating individuals are led to anticipate each other's decisions correctly, yielding an orderly situation in which mutually advantageous exchange opportunities tend to become discovered and exploited for mutual benefit. The prime example of this kind of spontaneous order is the ability of a market to generate a tendency toward the market-clearing price. Clearly, the demonstration that such a tendency toward spontaneous order exists is of great significance for a society contemplating the avoidance of central economic planning.

What has been emphasized, on the other hand, in an important recent strand of literature, is the plausibility of long-run social processes— proceeding by and large *without* a fixed given institutional background— generating the gradual emergence of beneficial social conventions and institutions. Here, too, the outcome of these spontaneous processes is a state of affairs in which individuals correctly and confidently anticipate the actions and responses of other members of society. (It is this confidence that individuals have concerning what others will do that constitutes the conventions and institutions that are the spontaneous outcomes of these social processes.) In this sense, therefore, these long-run processes are "orderly"—they generate coordinated outcomes. Standard examples of such spontaneously achieved social conventions are language, standards of weights and measures, and codes of behavior among members of social groups.

These two kinds of spontaneous coordination process are, despite their shared features, fundamentally different from one another. The emergence within society of a common language, a common set of standards for weight and measurement, and common codes of social behavior, differs sharply from the emergence of a market-clearing price for wheat or for unskilled labor in competitive markets. The former are the results of long-run processes, lasting centuries, during the course of which we can presume many long periods of discoordination. The latter are relatively rapid processes. The former generate institutions—social signposts which facilitate subsequent social intercourse, but which do not themselves fulfill the final goals of individuals; these long-run processes result in the fulfillment of intermediate objectives only. The shorter-run process of spontaneous coordination may apply to the actions taken directly to fulfill final consumption objectives. The former, longer-run processes generate coordinated actions and responses which do not constitute interpersonal exchange transactions. (That different market participants use common conventions concerning quality, units of measure, and even the use of a common medium of exchange may indeed *facilitate* exchanges, but are themselves merely ancillary to such exchanges.) The shorter-run processes are processes generating mutually gainful exchanges between participants.

We shall argue that, from the perspective of defenders of the free society, these important differences point to vitally significant normative implications separating long-run processes of spontaneous coordination from the short-run processes: The former do not, while the latter do, in general lend support to the case for a free society.

SPONTANEOUS ORDER AND SOCIAL WELFARE

The term "spontaneous order" is almost invariably taken to connote an outcome that is socially benign. There is indeed a sense in which this is likely to be true, but this sense is a quite limited one. No doubt it is in general desirable that individuals be able to arrive at confidently accurate anticipations concerning the actions and reactions of others. This avoids much disappointment and frustration on all sides. So that it is indeed useful that the language my children learn at home overlaps with the language learned by other children in *their* homes. This permits social intercourse and facilitates education. But there is hardly—in the insight that such institutions emerge spontaneously—any implication that the emerging institutions are the *best conceivable* such institutions. There is no guarantee that the English language my children learn at their mother's knee will be a "better" language for purposes of social intercourse than, say, French—or Esperanto. The demonstration that widely accepted social conventions can emerge without central authoritarian imposition does not necessarily point to any *optimality* in the resulting conventions.

What is demonstrated, on the other hand, by short-run spontaneous coordination theory (i.e., by the theory of the free market economy) is that there does exist a spontaneous tendency toward social optimality under the relevant conditions. The price that comes to be expected by all is not merely *any* price, but the *market-clearing* price, i.e., the price that stimulates the exploitation of the greatest possible volume of exchange opportunities. What is spontaneously tended to be achieved in these processes is not merely the avoidance of unrealizable anticipations, but the stimulation of anticipations that take advantage of conceivable opportunities.

SPONTANEOUS ORDER AND THE CASE FOR THE FREE SOCIETY

As noted at the outset of this essay, spontaneous order theory offers valuable ammunition for the proponent of the free society. Careful consideration of long-run processes of spontaneous coordination strongly suggests, however, that *these* processes not be cited as prime examples of what freedom can achieve. Awareness of these processes may indeed afford salutary refutation of naive prejudices concerning the chaos believed inevitably to ensue from the absence of central control. But such awareness is quite inadequate for building a general case for absence of centralized control. These processes cast much light on human history; but they offer little guidance for policy makers or social theorists pondering the foreseeable future. This is so for several reasons.

First, as noted in the preceding section, long-run spontaneous theory does not, in general, argue that evolved institutions are the best that might have come about. Second, long-run spontaneous theory does not, in general—there *are* exceptions—argue that deliberate centralized planning *could* not have arrived at equally benign (or better) social institutions. Third, because these processes are long-run in character, the benign character of the outcome may fall far short of justifying the process as a whole. After all, during the course of a centuries-long spontaneous process, there may occur (*conceivably* as a result of the absence of central control) a vast multitude of situations filled with human suffering and misery. It could be that the positive features of the resulting institution simply fail (no matter from *whose* perspective) to be judged worth these sacrifices.

Short-run processes of spontaneous coordination are far less vulnerable to such reservations. First, as noted, market processes tend, in general, to eliminate sub-optimalities. The relevance of Pareto-optimality to market processes is a systematic one. Second, market process theory not only shows how market coordination can be achieved spontaneously; it shows (as in the socialist calculation literature and related work) how such coordination could hardly be simulated by deliberate, central design. Third, because of the relative rapidity of market processes it is much more plausible to conclude that the optimality achieved by their outcomes justifies any sub-optimalities suffered (as a result of absence of control) during the process. (It must be recognized, however, that some of the institutions generated during long-run processes may continue to provide useful social services for a far longer period of time than can the market-clearing price achieved in a short-run market process.)

To recognize the limited relevance of long-run spontaneous processes for the theory of a free society is not to confess skepticism concerning the worthwhileness of such a society. After all, the traditional economic case for liberty rests not on possible long-term improvements in social institutions, but on the demonstrated advantages of liberty within a given institutional framework. A free society is prosperous, not because it generates a benign evolution in its laws, but because its given rule of law promotes innovative production and exchange. The classical case for freedom does not require that long-run spontaneous processes lead necessarily to better and better arrays of social institutions. In fact, for many proponents of the free society, its advantages depend on the fulfillment of limited but very definite assigned governmental functions. These governmental functions may well be assigned through explicit design. If the advantages of freedom *require* a framework of limited government, then one's assessment of the advantages of a centuries-long Nozickian process of freedom *without* a government may well be distinctly unfavorable—even if that process can be expected eventually to generate such limited governmental institutions.

But if all this is granted, then it should be pointed out that emphasis by proponents of classical liberalism on long-run spontaneous processes not only constitutes a weak reed on which to support their case—but in addition may itself *weaken* that case. Classical liberalism assumes an array of given institutions. To conflate classical liberalism with ideologies that call for no such given institutional framework is to sow confusion and misunderstanding. Out of such confusion and misunderstanding may emerge, not sympathy and appreciation for the free market society, but profound and unjustified skepticism of it. Efforts to broaden public understanding of the economic virtues of classical liberalism should, it very much appears, be undertaken with well-nigh exclusive emphasis of market processes with a given institutional framework. Reference to the possible spontaneous emergence of social institutions, where appropriate, should be made with careful clarification of their limited relevance for the economic case for the free society.

NOTE

1. Among the works dealing with the spontaneous emergence or evolution of social norms and institutions see especially: Edina Ullmann-Margalit, "Invisible-Hand Explanations," *Synthese* 39, No. 2 (October, 1978), pp. 263–91; A. Schotter, *The Economic Theory of Social Institutions* (Cambridge: Cambridge University Press, 1981); R. Axelrod, *The Evolution of Cooperation* (New York: Basic Books, 1984); R. Sugden, *The Economics of Rights, Co-operation and Welfare* (Oxford: Basil Blackwell, 1986). A good deal of Hayek's more recent work, especially his *Law, Legislation and Liberty*, 3 volumes (Chicago: University of Chicago Press, 1973, 1976, 1979), is steeped in this evolutionary perspective (and is probably partly responsible for the tendency being cautioned against in this essay).

THE "POWER" PROBLEM ON CAMPUS:
AN ECONOMIST'S VIEW

Much of the current crisis atmosphere in the universities revolves around the question of the locus of power—student power and faculty power. From all sides, one hears the opinion expressed that students and faculty, who have until now languished passively under authoritarian college administrations and boards of trustees, are entitled to share in the running of their university. A democratic university—one which permits faculty and students to participate in the host of administrative decisions which affect their lives—requires, we hear, a massive structural revision in the direction of greater direct student and faculty power. And there is no doubt that a feverish rush toward "democratization" is already under way on the part of college and university trustees and administrations fearful of campus disruptions by students and even by faculty.

In this writer's opinion, this tendency is—quite apart from the issue of disruptive and violent tactics—a most unfortunate one, the result of badly confused thinking on the role of the university in society, and likely to be responsible for serious deterioration in the quality of higher education in this country. Let it be emphasized that what is being criticized here is not at all the very sensible opinion that student and faculty views should help determine university decisions in a meaningful way. The error, as we will discover, lies instead in the naïve demands for a sharing of the *ultimate* responsibility for the university with faculty and students.

The attitude underlying the contemporary cries for greater student and faculty power is something like the following. The university is seen as a kind of self-governing community—comprised of administrative, faculty, and student members. However, the government of this community has until now been concentrated almost exclusively in the hands of the first of these groups: the administration—a group which is, in turn, answerable to the trustees or a similar body. Students and faculty, although they spend years of their lives in this community, have until recently been treated, in effect, as children, with the most important aspects of university life legislated upon without their being consulted in any meaningful way.

From *Intercollegiate Review* 6 (Spring 1970): 99–103. Reprinted by permission of Intercollegiate Studies Institute.

Democracy requires a change that will replace government by trustees and administrators with a government in which all the member groups of the community will participate. Campus stability requires that university rules be formulated on a procedure that ensures that student and faculty views be taken into direct account. (More extreme versions of this attitude would relegate administrators to an even more insignificant role.)

But this attitude completely misunderstands the economic relationship between the university and society in general. This attitude might be an appropriate one if a university were an economically independent entity, that is to say, if its ability to support its activities were unrelated to the character of these activities. If this were the case, arguments in favor of "democracy" within the university might perhaps carry weight. But, of course, the reality is quite a different one. The university, in order to carry on its activities, must compete for economic resources with alternative social purposes. It must, therefore, like other enterprises, win support for its activities by virtue of the importance of these activities *to others.*

Ultimate responsibility for the university, then, does not and cannot mean merely the responsibility to act as steward over *given* resources—which responsibility might then, at least in principle, be shared jointly with faculty and students. *Ultimate* responsibility for the university must mean the responsibility both to *marshall the resources necessary* to carry out the declared purposes for which the university is intended, and to *deploy these resources* in a manner faithful to the declared purposes. To fail to see this simple truth is to be hopelessly unrealistic. That this simple truth may be an unpalatable one is not surprising. The economist is accustomed to reactions of outraged shock whenever he points out that some noble and lofty goal competes for resources with other important purposes—and must justify its claim to these resources. But to the eyes of the economist, a refusal to recognize the importance of calling attention to such mundance matters as the need for justifying resources used, is worse than to be airily unrealistic and naïve; it borders on an arrogant conviction that all the other purposes of people in society must bow unconditionally to the needs of the university, no matter how or what the university turns out to be.

Who *should* bear the ultimate responsibility of marshalling and administering the resources needed for the university? In a free society this question is an inappropriate one. In a free society *anyone* may, if he chooses, act as an "entrepreneur." Anyone may, if he believes himself able to undertake the task, set out to build the institution he chooses. To do so he must convince owners of resources that it is worth their while to entrust their resources to his stewardship. He may conceivably, be able to do this on a strictly businesslike basis. He may be able to produce a saleable brand of education for which students are willing to pay sums sufficiently high to return a profit to investors. In this situation what is chosen to be produced and sold is a brand of schooling, carefully attuned to the needs of the prospective employers (reflected by the salaries that prospective graduates can expect to command), to the tastes of the immediate consumers—the students (as reflecting their willingness to undergo the rigors of the course of training being offered), and to the attitudes of the teachers (as reflected in the salaries and working conditions for which they are willing to sell their teaching skills). In such cases the paramount importance of paying careful attention to student and faculty opinions is abundantly clear—without, of course, the slightest need to share ultimate responsibility with anyone.

Or the "entrepreneur" may, on the other hand, persuade owners of resources to invest in an institution which cannot promise to return a pecuniary profit on investment. To do this he must convince philanthropic resource owners that his institution will fill a social need which these philanthropists are prepared to support. In this situation what is chosen to be produced by the entrepreneur will be a brand of schooling which not only reflects, in part, the attitudes of prospective employers, students, and faculty, but reflects also the philanthropic goals of the resource owners.

Of course, the "entrepreneur" may well be one of the resource owners or one of the consumers. He may be a teacher or a student, or a group of teachers and/or students. Who the "entrepreneur" is does not affect the basic relationship between the individual responsible for the institution and all those affected by its activities. Ultimate responsibility for the university, as for any enterprise or institution, will, in a free society, inevitably tend to come to rest in the hands of those able to choose successfully a mix of educational inputs and a mix of outputs that yields a return—whether in the form of pecuniary yield, or in the form of the psychic satisfaction to the philanthropist (who "enjoys" contributing to what he considers to be the betterment of society, or to the advancement of what he considers to be significant knowledge). It may well be that the successful "entrepreneur" of the university will be he who knows how much power to delegate to faculty and to students. But the ultimate responsibility must be his who is able to convince "investors" that he can secure them a return.

The possibility of state-supported universities does *not* alter the picture. The state may act as "entrepreneur" for the universities, raising the necessary support by taxation. Presumably taxpayers exercise, through their representatives, control over the purposes which they are supporting with their tax dollars. In a democratic society, the justification for the taxation must lie in the quality of the institutions supported.

No matter, then, how a university happens to be run—whether as a profitable business, a philanthropically supported institution, or a state-supported institution—decision making must relate output to the mobilization of the resources necessary for input. As far as prospective new institutions are concerned, anyone—not excepting prospective faculty, students, or janitorial staff for that matter—may seek to set up institutions which they believe can justify support. Their convictions can then be tested against competition in the relevant markets—the market for teachers, for graduates, for students, for philanthropic support, or in the competitive arena of those seeking government subsidies.

For anyone to attempt to control, or to share in the control, of an *existing* institution, is, however, quite another matter. Anyone may, of course, seek to persuade the present entrepreneurs—be they trustees, administrators, or whatever—of his own eligibility and suitability to run the institution. Times change, the tastes of students, teachers, and philanthropists change, and it may be entirely in order for an existing institution to change its direction. But such a bid, for a change in the pattern of control, cannot rest on grounds of "democracy"—which simply have no relevance in this context (except as a possible tool to be used by the entrepreneur to further the purposes of his institution). Such persuasion must rest on the ability to achieve, with superior efficiency, those goals selected by the entrepreneur as feasible in the light of the market constraints that are operative.

To demand that control over an existing institution be surrendered, in whole or in part, is to demand that one set of entrepreneurs arbitrarily—that is, without reference to the degree of success with which the "investors" can be assured a "return" on their investments—hand over their enterprise to another set. The ironic tragedy of such a demand does not lie, perhaps, so much in its trampling upon existing property and other rights as in its threat to the very future of the relevant institution. As soon as the direct entrepreneurial link between the supporters of the university and the university itself is severed, the university is in jeopardy.

It is not difficult to understand the reasons why the demands for student and faculty power have gained currency despite the above considerations. The naïve observer is not fully aware of the necessary link between the institution and its supporters. Very often an atmosphere is deliberately fostered to mask the dependency of the university as an institution upon outside, private or government support. Faculty and researchers are extremely jealous—and rightly so—of their independence from trustee, donor, or government interference with their work. But the wholly justified insistence that the supporters of education understand and respect the intellectual integrity of those whose educational endeavors they sponsor, has become transformed into the spurious notion that the supporters of education do not (and certainly should not) exercise ultimate responsibility for the uses to which their resources are put.

The illusion has resulted that the university is costless, or at least, that its activities, whatever they may be, can somehow be carried on regardless of cost. But the basic economic fact of life remains that in a free society ultimate control over the university *does* inevitably rest in the hands of those able to convince supporters of the worth of their final educational product. Only in an atmosphere in which a conceptual gulf separates the need for support on the one hand, from the substantive activities of the university on the other hand, could the current view of the university as an insulated island, an isolated community of scholars and students, arise.

Continued efforts to treat the university as an economically independent entity can only tend to bring about results that must be described as disastrous. To the extent that the power changes forced by student or faculty pressure result in an institution out of line with the goals of its supporters (private or government), the outcome must inevitably be a tendency toward the erosion of their support. A university, the control of which is the issue between competing power groups, is *not* a given asset being contested for by rival claimants. An asset's existence does *not* depend on the identity or the motives of its possessor; a university's existence depends on the availability of support—which cannot be expected to be provided without regard to the purposes of those under whose steward-ship the university rests.

In a free society the erosion of the support for a given existing insti-tution does not necessarily mean a long term net loss from the view of society. Support withdrawn from one institution may be available for the support of other, or new institutions. But to the extent that established institutions suffer decay and decline, society itself suffers "short-run" losses (which may, by the by, persist for a long time). And of course to friends of existing institutions the prospect that eventually new institu-tions will emerge to replace the old, is small comfort. It is not merely the past supporters of the established institutions who suffer losses when they discover that their investments in these institutions have gone sour. The erosion of such support represents a social loss, to the extent that the capital sunk into these existing institutions obtained its value from the expectation of continued support.

The point being made here is not that the supporters of a university, philanthropic or governmental, *should* have the power to control the uni-versity. The point is simply that the economic facts of life mean, ulti-mately that they *do* have this power. (And let it be noticed that from the neutral perspective of the economist, this ultimate control is not at all inefficient. With a given distribution of resources, a society "should"—as a matter not of ethical rightness, but of efficiency—get the universities which are desired by those willing to make the sacrifices needed for them. And this does not prevent the economist from recognizing that what donors desire *may* be quite "wrong" from the educational and cul-tural point of view.) Moreover, recognition of this ultimate economic con-trol does not, at all, necessarily spell the impossibility of free academic inquiry. Hopefully, supporters will deliberately seek to shape an insti-tuition designed to promote free inquiry and to respect the intellectual integrity of its faculty and students. But we must recognize that this is a hope which depends on the *willingness* to do so on the part of those whose resources support the university. (An entirely appropriate question in this regard is that touched on briefly by Professor Stigler in his well-known essay, "The Intellectual and the Market Place," of whether state support is more or less likely to conduce to an atmosphere of academic freedom than private philanthropic support.)

And once again, let it be stressed that supporters may well elect to delegate wide powers to faculty and to students. To differing extents this is, indeed, the almost universal practice. And it may be an entirely desirable policy to extend this practice further. The point being made here has nothing to do with this possibility. It deals only with the demands and procedures for power shifts within the university that rest upon the call for the *surrender* (partial or total) of the *ultimate* responsibility and power that rest on the supporters of the university. It is the calls for this kind of surrender which are both economically unrealistic and socially harmful.

THE NATURE OF
ECONOMIC
SCIENCE

The doctrine of *Wertfreiheit* (of which the term "value-freedom" is the literal translation) prescribes for the social scientist a methodological stance aimed at carefully separating and insulating scientific work from the personal ("unscientific") preferences of the researcher. (A standard work on the meaning and history of the doctrine is Hutchison, 1964.) The doctrine rests on several premises, each of which has been subjected to debate. First, the doctrine affirms a sharp qualitative distinction between scientific statements presenting empirical or theoretical assertions, on the one hand, and "unscientific" expressions of personal preference, on the other. The latter, "judgements of value," are in fact in *Wertfreiheit* discussions often held to be inherently incapable of being established on objective, scientific grounds that might convince an impartial observer insisting on proof. Second, the doctrine of *Wertfreiheit* assumes the possibility of in fact being able to engage in scientific work in a manner ensuring that personal value judgements are in no way expressed in the substantive content of the science. It *is* possible, that is, to enunciate scientific propositions the validity of which can be equally apparent to detached scientific observers holding opposing judgements of value. Third, the *Wertfreiheit* doctrine maintains that, both in order to maintain the integrity of the scientific enterprise and in order to ensure widespread confidence in the validity of the conclusions reached by scientists, it is necessary to insist on *Wertfreiheit*, and to ensure that the public be convinced that science is not simply an elaborate facade expressing the personal interests and preferences of scientists. *Wertfreiheit* is a tenet to be adhered to, in other words, not only in order to guard the integrity of science, but also in order to ensure that its integrity be recognized and appreciated.

The doctrine has had, of course, particular reference to economics, where the pronouncements of economists have often (justifiably) been dismissed as simply expressing the political or ideological positions of the economists or of those whom the economists are supporting. *Wertfreiheit* has often been urged as the only way to correct this unfortunate situation. In particular, Austrian economists have traditionally been outspoken on

From *The Elgar Companion to Austrian Economics*, ed. Peter J. Boettke (Aldershot, U.K.: Edward Elgar Publishing, 1994), 313–19. Reprinted by permission.

the need for *Wertfreiheit* in economics. Despite certain murmurings of apparent dissent on this matter within the ranks of contemporary Austrian economists, as we shall see, *Wertfreiheit* is still stoutly upheld as an ideal within the mainstream of contemporary Austrian economics (for examples, see Rizzo, 1992; White, 1992).

In what follows we shall (1) draw brief attention to well-known major pronouncements by important figures in the Austrian tradition which have argued for *Wertfreiheit* in economics; (2) refer briefly to some recent statements on the part of some Austrian economists which appear, at first glance, to challenge some of the assumptions upon which the *Wertfreiheit* doctrine must rest; and (3) explore the thesis that, for economists steeped in the Austrian tradition in economics, the doctrine is likely to seem especially plausible and, indeed, well-nigh essential to the methodological underpinnings of that tradition.

VALUE-FREEDOM IN THE AUSTRIAN TRADITION

The Austrian tradition was, of course, born into a struggle with the German historical school of economics. The outstanding figures in that school tended to fuse their economics with their personal ethical views on social justice and morality, sometimes addressing their lecture classes almost as if they were political rallies. It was against this style of economics that Max Weber was, at the start of the present century, to rebel vigorously in his call for an austere *Wertfreiheit* in scientific economic research and discussion. It is no surprise, therefore, to discover that the first statement on the *Wertfreiheit* issue made within the Austrian tradition was indeed directed—years before Max Weber—against the German historical school. In his 1883 *Untersuchungen* (in which he threw down the methodological gauntlet in his criticisms of the historical method), Carl Menger wrote an appendix in which he briefly but emphatically criticized the tendency of the German economists to confuse ethical positions with the conclusions of economics.

The next prominent statement arising out of the Austrian tradition that should be cited is that of Robbins. Lionel Robbins wrote his classic *An Essay on the Nature and Significance of Economic Science* under strong Austrian influence (see, for example, Robbins, 1935, pp. xv–xvi). It can be persuasively argued that it is due to Robbins that the early Austrian commitment to *Wertfreiheit* came to be routinely accepted within mainstream neoclassical post–Second World War economics. An important element in Robbins's position in his *Essay* was his enthusiastic adoption of Max

Weber's position on *Wertfreiheit*: "Economics is neutral as between ends. Economics cannot pronounce on the validity of ultimate judgments of value. . . . Between the generalizations of positive and normative studies there is a logical gulf fixed which no ingenuity can disguise and no juxtaposition in space or time bridge over . . . [Economic Science] is fundamentally distinct from Ethics" (ibid., pp. 147–52). What is distinctive in Robbins's statement of the *Wertfreiheit* doctrine is the fact that the doctrine emerges organically from Robbins's conception of the very nature of economic science (we shall take up this feature of his work in a later section of this essay). Robbins's "positivism" was sharply attacked by his critics, who denounced his refusal to accord the name "science" to normative disciplines, but Robbins stood his ground in the second edition of his book, emphasizing his continued acceptance of Max Weber's position (ibid., pp. xif).

Since Robbins, the most emphatic voice within Austrian economics on the issue of *Wertfreiheit* has certainly been that of Ludwig von Mises. It seems fair to say that it is due to Mises's insistence on this matter that Austrian economics is today widely recognized as endorsing the Weberian doctrine. The theme seems to have been foremost in Mises's mind over the last several decades of his scientific career. In 1933, Mises dwelt at length on the obligation of the economic scientist to maintain objectivity and neutrality in regard to judgements of value: "What is impermissible . . . is the obliteration of the boundary between scientific explanation and political value judgement" (Mises, 1933, p. 37). Mises had no doubt that this boundary can be clearly drawn: "The objectivity of bacteriology . . . is not in the least vitiated by the fact that the researchers in this field regard their task as a struggle against the viruses responsible for conditions harmful to the human organism" (p. 36). In his 1949 magnum opus, *Human Action,* Mises again carefully addressed this issue, concluding that economics "is perfectly neutral with regards to all judgments of value, as it refers always to means and never to the choice of ultimate ends." The fact that this discussion comes in the very last chapter of the book is surely significant. It serves to highlight Mises's concluding sentence in the book, in which he calmly declares that disregard of the warnings of the neutral science of economics must "stamp out society and the human race" (Mises, 1949, p. 881). Mises returned to the *Wertfreiheit* theme in one of his last books, *Theory and History* (1957). Here the discussion does not conclude the book, but is in fact the substance of the first chapter and generally pervades the whole of Part One of the book. It serves as a prelude to a trenchant dismissal of Marxist (and other) charges that the teachings of economics are the product of bias.

Of course the *Wertfreiheit* doctrine is not peculiar to the Austrian tradition. In a comprehensive critique of the doctrine, Subroto Roy links the doctrine to Hume's insistence upon a categorical distinction between "ought" statements and "is" statements (with the concomitant denial of the possibility of deducing the former from the latter). Roy cites close to twenty of the most renowned figures in nineteenth and twentieth-century economics as having subscribed to some form of this doctrine (Roy, 1989, p. 17, and p. 194, note 1). Yet, despite the apparent near-universal acceptance of the doctrine among both mainstream and Austrian economists, a case does appear to be able to be made that Austrian economics tends to support the *Wertfreiheit* doctrine in a peculiarly characteristic way. We shall take up this argument in a later section of this essay. Here we pause to take brief note of certain intimations of apparent dissent concerning the *Wertfreiheit* doctrine, which might at first suggest a possible incompleteness in the unanimity of contemporary support for the doctrine.

DISSENT WITHIN THE AUSTRIAN CAMP?

Although several statements by Austrian economists during recent decades seem to point in a direction opposite to that taken by the proponents of *Wertfreiheit,* careful examination of them reveals that the disagreements involved (with the traditional Austrian position on the matter) are relatively minor. In several papers, Murray Rothbard has challenged, not so much the *Wertfreiheit* doctrine itself, as the claim that economic policy pronouncements can be made without violating the doctrine. Whereas Mises and other Austrians have appealed to *Wertfreiheit* as the basis for the possibility of economic policy pronouncements being made independently of any ethical presuppositions, Rothbard flatly denies any such possibility. While Misesian "economic theory is extremely useful in providing data and knowledge for framing economic policy, it cannot be sufficient by itself . . . to advocate any public policy whatsoever" (Rothbard, 1976, p. 109). Economic policy, Rothbard argues, necessarily involves some ethical foundation. Although this conclusion of Rothbard's *appears* diametrically opposed to Mises's claims that the objectivity of value-free economic science ensures the unbiased character of implied policy pronouncements, one may question the extent of the substantive disagreement between Mises and Rothbard. Rothbard, too, insists that sciences, including economics, are in themselves value-free; he merely claims that policy prescriptions by economists cannot fail to transcend such value-freedom. Although there is room for differences in nuance between the Misesian and Rothbardian approaches to economic policy advice, it seems that they share a basic commitment to the Weberian ideals.

Jack High (1985) sharply criticizes the thesis that economics is "independent of ethics." High argues that in fact the very definitions of basic entities crucial to economic inquiry must necessarily implicitly rely upon ethical norms for their very meaning. We cannot sensibly distinguish between market and government without resort to ethical standards (needed in order to assign meaning to the concepts of "voluntary," "coercive" and "ownership"). It might seem, on a first reading, that High is attacking that separation between economics and ethics which served Menger and Weber as the foundation of the *Wertfreiheit* doctrine. Indeed, High cites critically those very observations of Menger on the subject which we saw earlier to be the foundation of *Wertfreiheit* in the Austrian tradition. Yet it becomes clear, upon further study, that High does *not* wish to challenge the doctrine itself. In fact he concludes his paper by assuring the reader that his central thesis leaves "the much-cherished 'value-freedom' of economic science" untouched. In other words, what High has argued is not at all that economic science is committed to a *particular* set of values, but that *some* set of values must be supplied before the propositions of economic science can be applied to concrete situations. For example, High writes, we can characterize the market economy as "acquisition and use of resources that respect natural rights" without endorsing the ethical correctness of natural rights. So that High accepts, after all, the central foundation of the *Wertfreiheit* doctrine, that any ethical content implied in substantive economic propositions *can* be disentangled and separated from the non-ethical components in such propositions.

It is true that Rothbard's (and perhaps High's) position expresses disagreement with the thesis (central to at least many statements of the *Wertfreiheit* doctrine) which declares the correctness of value-judgements to be incapable of scientific demonstration. (In this they are concurring with a number of recent philosophical contributions.) But their position is nonetheless entirely consistent with traditional Austrian emphasis on

the desirability of pursuing economic analysis in a way which protects
it from dependency upon any particular ethical norms whatsoever. We
conclude, therefore, that, while the degree of enthusiastic support for
the centrality of the *Wertfreiheit* doctrine may vary among at least some
Austrian economists, it yet remains valid to assert that acceptance of the
doctrine remains characteristic of the Austrian tradition. Let us further
explore this connection.

WERTFREIHEIT AND THE AUSTRIAN APPROACH

Although, as noted, the *Wertfreiheit* doctrine has been accorded general
acceptance by many schools of modern economic thought, it may be
argued that its affinity to Austrian economics is an especially natural and
organic one. It may be argued, that is, that the very way in which Austrian
economics has conceived of its subject-matter entails a methodological
stance which can hardly fail to be highly sympathetic to the *Wertfreiheit*
doctrine.

No doubt the initial thrust of the Austrian tradition, its affirmation of
the independence of theory from historical context, helped crystallize the
ideas which were to mature into the *Wertfreiheit* doctrine. To declare the
validity of propositions showing chains of causation which apply across
widely differing institutional and historical backgrounds must certainly
help promote understanding of the objectivity of such causation chains
and their independence of the analyst's ethical evaluation of any of the
specific situations in which they may manifest themselves. But Austrian
economics, of course, was not the only school of modern economics to
reject the position of the German historical school.

More to the point, perhaps, has been the Austrian focus on *individual
choice* as the analytical unit in economics. The implications for *wertfreiheit* are perhaps most clearly seen in Robbins. Because economics is the
logic of choice, the working out of the systematic consequences of the
circumstance that man's actions are dictated by the configuration of his
scarce *given* means and multiple, ranked, *given* ends, it follows that the
propositions of economics depend not one whit on the ethics underlying the choice of ends or the morality of the distributive system responsible for the given means. For Robbins, writing under Austrian influence,
the independence of economic science from ethics was explicitly seen
as flowing out of his definition of the science. To be sure, Robbins's
ideas on economics as the logic of choice have become the foundation

for mainstream (non-Austrian) treatments of microeconomics, yet we should not lose sight of the characteristically Austrian influences which appear to have helped shape Robbins's *Wertfreiheit* commitment.

Mises's own commitment to *Wertfreiheit* appears to have emerged in a manner parallel to (although not quite identical with) that which we have seen in Robbins. As is well known, Mises saw economics as praxeology, the pure science of human action. Because Mises saw praxeology as consisting of propositions developed a priori from economic reasoning, and applying in the real world wherever the relevant circumstances pertain, it followed that the positive truths of economics will manifest themselves whether we like them or not, whether we approve of the ethics of any particular set of circumstances (in which these truths manifest themselves) or not. Through appropriate demonstration, it is then possible to hope, these truths can appear as reasonable and persuasive to open-minded students of economics, regardless of any ethical prejudgements which they may hold.

The notion of human action, central to the very idea of Misesian praxeology, appeared to have confirmed, for Mises, the underpinnings of the *Wertfreiheit* doctrine: "The significance of value judgments consists precisely in the fact they are the springs of human action. Guided by his valuations, man is intent upon substituting conditions that please him better for conditions which he deems less satisfactory. He employs means in order to attain ends sought" (Mises, 1957, p. 20). Mises sees this as the basis for asserting a sharp distinction between ultimate judgements of value and the propositions of economics: "As soon as we start to refute by arguments an ultimate judgment of value, we look upon it as a means to attain definite ends. But then we merely shift the discussion to another plane. We no longer view the principle concerned as an ultimate value but as a means to attain an ultimate value" (Mises, 1957, pp. 22–23).

It seems to follow that Mises's commitment to the doctrine of *Wertfreiheit* does not depend on the assertion that the correctness of value judgements can never be demonstrated or disproved by scientific methods. His commitment to the doctrine rests merely on the contention that, in the context of any economic problem, the correctness of the relevant judgements of value is not itself the issue. In this respect Mises and Robbins appear to concur in every significant respect.

Austrian economics has often been understood to support the free market political program. What we have seen is that, despite the fact that many Austrian economists (Mises in particular!) were indeed emphatic in their belief that economic science lends support to proponents of the free enterprise system, they have consistently maintained that the theoretical basis of such support is by itself politically neutral. Precisely because the support by economists for free market institutional arrangements has often been sharply attacked as the product of bias, Austrian economists have felt it necessary to emphasize the need for their science to be absolutely untainted by such bias. They have, we have seen, found the basis for such a possible "purity," unstained by judgements of value, in the most fundamental of their conceptions of what makes a science of economics possible. It is because of their conviction of the soundness of this possibility, and their lively awareness of the need to escape unfair charges of pro-market bias, that Austrians have again and again felt impelled to uphold the doctrine of value-freedom.

BIBLIOGRAPHY

High, J. (1985), "Is Economics Independent of Ethics?" *Reason Papers*, No. 10, spring.

Hutchison, T. W. (1964), *"Positive" Economics and Policy Objectives*, Cambridge, Mass.: Harvard University Press.

Mises, L. von (1933), *Grundprobleme der Nationalökonomie*, translated as *Epistemological Problems of Economics*, Princeton, N.J.: Van Nostrand, 1960.

Mises, L. von (1949), *Human Action*, New Haven: Yale University Press.

Mises, L. von. (1957), *Theory and History*, New Haven: Yale University Press.

Rizzo, M. J. (1992), "Afterword: Austrian Economics for the Twenty-First Century," in Bruce J. Caldwell and Stephen Böhm (eds), *Austrian Economics: Tensions and New Directions*, Boston: Kluwer Academic.

Robbins, L. (1935), *An Essay on the Nature and Significance of Economic Science*, 2nd edn, London: Macmillan.

Rothbard, M. N. (1976), "Praxeology, Value Judgments, and Public Policy," in E. Dolan (ed.), *The Foundations of Modern Austrian Economics*, Kansas City: Sheed and Ward.

Roy, S. (1989), *Philosophy of Economics*, London/New York: Routledge.

White, L. M. (1992), "Afterword: Appraising Austrian Economics—Contentions and Misdirections," in Bruce J. Caldwell and Stephen Böhm (eds), *Austrian Economics: Tensions and New Directions*, Boston: Kluwer Academic.

PHILOSOPHICAL AND ETHICAL IMPLICATIONS
OF AUSTRIAN ECONOMICS

The title of this paper contains an apparent paradox: it assumes that Austrian economic theory *can* have philosophical and ethical implications, while the tradition within Austrian economics has been strongly in support of *Wertfreiheit* as a cardinal precept of scientific propriety. A good deal of what I have to say in this paper relates to the resolution of this paradox. Let us first rapidly review the history of the doctrine of value-freedom in economics.

WERTFREIHEIT: A THUMBNAIL SKETCH

In his 1884 *Untersuchungen* Carl Menger included an appendix that briefly but very clearly criticized the tendency of the German "historical" economists to confuse ethical positions with the conclusions of economics.[1] At that time holders of chairs of economics at the German universities considered themselves social reformers. They fused their economics with their personal views on social justice and morality. In their lectures they reportedly permitted their emotions free rein. Adolf Wagner, for example, would shake his fist at imaginary opponents of his proposals. Other professors would lecture as if addressing preelection meetings, to the cheers of their students.[2] It was with this style of economic discussion that Menger was expressing his disenchantment.

In subsequent decades the figure to mount a vigorous campaign for *Wertfreiheit* in the social sciences was, of course, Max Weber. He described the fusion of ethical and scientific statements as "the work of the devil."[3] The issue was heatedly debated at the 1909 meeting of the *Verein für Sozialpolitik* in what Schumpeter described as almost amounting to a row.[4] In Weber's opinion, when a scientist combines his scientific conclusions with his ethical views, he may mislead the layman into supposing that these views carry with them the authority of science. For science to be interpersonally valid, it must not depend on the personal views of any one scholar. Any departure from an austere neutrality on the part

From *The Foundations of Modern Austrian Economics,* ed. Edwin G. Dolan (Kansas City: Sheed & Ward, 1976), 75–88. Reprinted by permission of the Institute for Humane Studies.

of the scientist qua scientist with respect to judgments of value must be denounced. Weber not only stated value-freedom to be a canon of scientific procedure to be jealously guarded but also defended the possibility of pursuing this procedure in economics. Others argued that since economics and social science in general deal with material permeated with ethical content—values, interests, and motives—it is impossible to engage in value-free research in these areas. Weber's contribution was to point out that the investigator's own value judgments need not (and also should not) color the conclusions that he reaches concerning the admittedly value-laden activities and phenomena with which his research deals.

Writing in the early 1930s, Lionel Robbins pursued the Weber doctrine still further. Under the influence of Austrian thought, Robbins offered a definition of economics with the incidental property of establishing that the economist's value judgments have nothing at all to do with his concerns as a scientific investigator.[5] Robbins defined economics as the science concerned with the implications of the insight that men are economizing individuals who seek to allocate given scarce resources among given competing ends. Because both the ends and the means are given, what is being investigated is strictly the patterns of behavior generated by the particular configuration of ends and means that happen to be given. The concrete content of the ends does not determine these patterns of behavior. An ends-means configuration applicable to a specific factual situation may also be applicable to an entirely different situation in which the concrete content of both ends and means is entirely different. Economic science, therefore, is value-free in the sense that the *particular* ends being pursued are not essential to the economic analysis of a given situation. The purposes being aimed at in the economizing aspects of men's activities may be lofty or mundane. The generalizations economic science develops concerning economizing behavior are equally valid in both situations. Thus Robbins was able to show that *Wertfreiheit* emerges as an implication of this definition of economics.

In the writings of Ludwig von Mises the *Wertfreiheit* tradition was vigorously upheld. Mises was deeply concerned with insuring that the scientific truths embodied in economics be perceived as such, that they should not be disparaged as partisan propaganda. Accordingly, it was essential to guard jealously against any lapses from *Wertfreiheit*—lapses that might lay economics open to the charge of being the expression of someone's vested interests. As is well known, Mises firmly rejected all suggestions (such as those contained in Marxist literature and in the literature on the sociology of knowledge) that science is subject to a relativism in logic, that its conclusions must inevitably reflect the class consciousness or interests of the scientists.[6] Logic, Mises insisted, is universally and interpersonally valid; so is economic science. To surrender *Wertfreiheit* will unnecessarily and tragically jeopardize the acceptance of scientific conclusions by those not sharing the values revealed by the non-*wertfrei* scientist.

THE CRITICS OF *WERTFREIHEIT*

The *Wertfreiheit* doctrine had come under attack in a number of different ways. One episode of particular interest involves the evolution of Gunnar Myrdal's attitude toward the doctrine. In *The Political Element in the Development of Economic Theory*, published in 1929 when he was still a young man and not translated into English until 1954, he charged that economists have consistently violated the *Wertfreiheit* ideal. From the beginning of economic science until our own times, economists have consciously or unconsciously—possibly quite innocently—permitted their value judgments and ethical positions to color their analyses and help determine their normative conclusions. He saw his task as being to complete Weber's work by criticizing, from the perspective of the *Wertfreiheit* doctrine, "the political speculation in classical and neoclassical economic theory."[7] This task required him to expose the errors introduced into economic doctrines by "the insertion of valuations."[8] Both from his 1929 preface and from the 1953 preface to the English translation, it is clear that what stimulated his research was his wish to protest the "uncompromising laissez-faire doctrine" that "dominated the teaching of economics in Sweden" in the late 1920s. By exposing the valuations that must be smuggled into economic analysis before such a normative doctrine as laissez-faire can be extracted, he hoped to discredit the dominant "economic liberalism" of his time.[9]

Thus, in this early work, Myrdal had no quarrel with Weberian *Wertfreiheit* as a scientific ideal. He was merely pointing out how seriously, in his view, this ideal has been trampled on in the course of the history of economics. But in his later writings he drastically shifted his point of view. As he himself put it, "Throughout [this early work] there lurks the idea that when all metaphysical elements are radically cut away, a healthy body of positive economic theory will remain, which is altogether independent of valuations."[10] This idea he later emphatically rejected. Such an idea, as a

> belief in the existence of a body of scientific knowledge acquired independently of all valuations is . . . naive empiricism. Facts do not organize themselves into concepts and theories just by being looked at;

indeed, except within the framework of concepts and theories, there are no scientific facts but only chaos. . . . Questions must be asked before answers can be given. The questions are an expression of our interest in the world, they are at bottom valuations.[11]

Nor does Myrdal shy away from the rejection of the *Wertfreiheit* doctrine that his later views entail. "I have therefore arrived at the belief in the necessity of working always, from the beginning to the end, with explicit value premises."[12] This position—emphasizing the *impossibility* of *wertfrei* social science—Myrdal vigorously pursued in a series of writings, the most important of which have been collected under the title *Value in Social Theory* (London: Routledge and Kegan Paul, 1958).

Myrdal was not, of course, alone in this rejection of *Wertfreiheit*. It will perhaps suffice, for my purpose in this article, merely to refer to the excellent history of the debate concerning *Wertfreiheit* contained in T. W. Hutchison's *"Positive" Economics and Policy Objectives* (Cambridge: Harvard University Press, 1964). We should, however, also note that after the publication of Hutchison's book Myrdal's skepticism concerning the possibility of *Wertfreiheit* in the social sciences came to characterize the position often taken by scholars on the New Left. Throughout the various branches of the social sciences, these writers denounced all claims of *Wertfreiheit* to be either examples of downright fraud or else evidence of naiveté.

It is against this Myrdal tradition, which denies the possibility and/or desirability of *Wertfreiheit* in economics, that we must contrast the mainstream perspective of Austrian economics from Menger down to Mises as outlined earlier. Furthermore, this Austrian perspective forces us to confront certain apparent inconsistencies in the Austrian (and particularly the Misesian) position.

MISES, *WERTFREIHEIT*, AND POLICY PRESCRIPTIONS

In his 1929 book Myrdal gave Austrian economics relatively good marks for disinterested objectivity:

In Austria, economics has never had direct political aims in spite of the close connection of the Austrian marginal utility theory with utilitarian philosophy. The Austrians were preoccupied with value theory and never elaborated a detailed theory of welfare economics.[13]

It is interesting to note that Fritz Machlup, in his review of the English translation of Myrdal's book, asked with amazement whether Myrdal was not familiar with Mises's strongly anti-interventionist writings.[14] Misesian economics, it is implied in Machlup's question, can hardly qualify as being free of "direct political aims." Again, we find Hutchison in a footnote rather clearly implying that Mises was guilty of this inconsistency.[15] He juxtaposed two positions taken by Mises, which, it appears, Hutchison considered to be mutually incompatible. On the one hand, Mises vigorously defended the *Wertfreiheit* doctrine; on the other hand, he made strong normative statements concerning the desirability of the free market. Here then is the apparent difficulty that we must confront: can we reconcile Mises's strong normative position in economics with his declared insistence on *Wertfreiheit?* I believe that we can. I believe moreover that such a reconciliation bears a definite relationship to the specifically Austrian character of Misesian economics.

In arguing that a reconciliation is possible in this way, it is necessary for me to modify to some extent a position I defended a short while ago. In an eloquent article in *Intercollegiate Review,* John Davenport advocated a closer relationship between economics and philosophy.[16] Davenport deplored the gap in communication between the economists, concerned only with pure (i.e., abstract) efficiency, and those scholars in philosophy and ethics, concerned with the concrete nature of the goals and ends of efficient action. If we are to achieve a good society, Davenport argued, discussions of efficiency cannot remain divorced from philosophical concepts of the good and the bad, the beautiful and the ugly, the true and the untrue. In pursuing his critique of economics from this point of view, Davenport referred approvingly to Robbins and to Mises as having to some extent "humanized" economics. The emphasis that both Robbins and Mises placed on human choice and purpose made it inevitable, Davenport explained, that attention be paid to the *nature* of choice and purpose. To this extent, therefore, Davenport credited Robbins and Mises with having "made a beginning at least of rebuilding the bridge that connects [economics] with philosophy."[17]

Commenting recently on Davenport's paper, I took issue with this last point and argued that the subjectivism of Robbins and Mises in no way requires or implies the possibility of a synthesis between ethical values and the value-free propositions of economic science.[18] The tradition of *Wertfreiheit,* so stoutly upheld by both Robbins and Mises, was not at all inconsistent—even by implication—with their emphasis on purposeful decision making. It would, it seemed to me, be a distortion of both the Robbinsian and the Misesian points of view to perceive either of them as uniquely capable of initiating the kind of bridge building between economics and ethics that Davenport advocated.[19]

It now appears necessary for me to modify this position. While I would still insist that Misesian purposefulness in no way implies the need to surrender the ideal of *Wertfreiheit*, Davenport's observation regarding Mises may embody an insight I previously missed. Furthermore, it is by means of this insight that I hope to reconcile the apparent inconsistency between Mises's pronouncements concerning the economic advantages of the free market and his insistence on *Wertfreiheit* in economics.

The Misesian emphasis on purposeful choice enables us to avoid discussions of efficiency that depend on such notions as utility and welfare. Efficiency, in the Misesian framework, does not mean welfare maximization (not individual welfare maximization nor social welfare); it means instead the fulfillment of the purposes deemed most important rather than the fulfillment of less important purposes. It is impossible therefore to speak of efficiency in terms other than those of the purposes of specific individuals under discussion. Nothing in the concept of Misesian efficiency is consistent with the belief that an economist's approval of, say, a specific policy reflects his own approval of the ends of that policy, or even his belief that the ends will command general approval. For Mises, professional approval by an economist of a specific policy proposal merely means that the economist believes the policy will enhance the fulfillment of the purposes of those interested in the economist's professional opinion. (By contrast, other approaches to economic welfare that do not place this emphasis on individual purposes—even though it is acknowledged that welfare depends on individual tastes—tend to jeopardize their *Wertfreiheit* when making policy pronouncements. It is now a well-established conclusion of welfare economics that such policy pronouncements, insofar as they imply a maximization of social welfare, cannot escape arbitrary, and thus value-laden, assignments of weights to individuals.)

And, indeed, when one examines Mises's many statements about economic policy, whether they be about price controls, tariffs, antitrust policy, or anything else, one invariably discovers that his conclusions do not at all reflect his own personal valuations. They reflect only his opinions concerning the degree of success with which others are pursuing *their* purposes. Sometimes Mises made clear whose purposes he had in mind. Sometimes it is taken for granted that the reader will be aware of whose purposes are being used as a frame of reference, and that the general nature of the preferences expressed in these purposes is also well known. One may on occasion question such an assumption; one may on occasion find language superficially implying that a certain policy is simply wrong or bad. But a careful reading of Mises will support the interpretation we are placing here on his policy pronouncements. This was made very clear indeed in Mises's oral presentations. He would emphasize again and again that interventionist policies are "wrong," not from the point of view of the economist himself, but from the point of view of those initiating these policies (or at least from the point of view of those whose well-being the policies are supposed to enhance).

SOME FURTHER REMARKS ON VALUE-FREE ECONOMICS

In discussions concerning *Wertfreiheit* in economics, analogies have often been drawn with medical research. Almost a century and a half ago Archbishop Whately used such an analogy in responding to criticism directed against the study of economics. The critics felt that the "science of wealth" was too mundane a discipline, concerned with too sinful a subject matter, to be the proper concern of moral persons. Whately's defense was to point to medical research as a model. The critics, identifying wealth as sinful, saw the economist as promoting sin. Not so, argued Whately. The researcher investigating the causes of disease surely cannot be accused of promoting disease. If wealth be sinful, then it behooves us to encourage the study of political economy in order most effectively to eliminate the offensive immoral affluence.[20]

To put Whately's defense in other words, we may say that pure research itself is *wertfrei*. If a scientist searches for and identifies the factors that foster a specific phenomenon, we are unable without additional information to determine whether his motivation has been fueled by pure curiosity, by a desire to promote the phenomenon in question, or by a desire to eliminate it. In Misesian context the phenomenon in question turns out to be the fulfillment of individual purposes. Economic analysis is able to provide insight into the circumstances and policies that foster or frustrate the fulfillment of individual purposes. Without further information one is unable to identify any specific valuations as being implied in an economist's policy conclusions; he may be in favor of these purposes, he may abhor them, or he may be indifferent about them. Value judgments are simply not prerequisites for policy conclusions.

It has sometimes been argued that, in providing a client with policy advice, the economist is after all making a moral judgment to the effect that the client's purposes are worthy of support. Surely, it is pointed out, an economist should not as a moral being offer a prospective mass murderer *wertfrei* advice on how to achieve his purposes most effectively.[21] Apparently, economic policy advice turns out inevitably to reflect and endorse the values of those to whom advice is being proffered. This reasoning does not, it should be clear, invalidate our claim that the policy conclusions of economics can be entirely consistent with the ideals of *wertfrei* science. Here again Whately's analogy is helpful.

Research into the causes of a dread disease can, we have seen, be entirely *wertfrei*. Nonetheless, we recognize that what motivates a scientist to dedicate his life to such research may be his wish to free mankind from the scourge. Or, again, a malevolent individual intent on harming his enemies may be interested in the results of this research for sinister reasons. The *Wertfreiheit* of the research itself and the objectivity of its conclusions are not affected in the least by our recognition that the researcher should not as a moral being divulge these conclusions to the man of malevolence. The choice of his clients must indeed be governed by the scientist's moral values; policy advice can indeed be given only to those whose purposes are not repugnant to the professional; but the objectivity and *Wertfreiheit* of the analysis that led to these policy conclusions are not one whit compromised by these considerations.

To pursue this argument one step further, in many cases the economist discovers policy conclusions that are applicable to situations in which a wide variety of quite different purposes may be involved. A policy statement pointing out that voluntary exchange benefits both participants (in their own prospective estimation) may after all be made without regard to what is being exchanged or the purposes to which the exchanged items will be put. In publishing such a general policy conclusion the economist can, therefore, hardly be accused of seeking personally out of his own sense of moral worth to promote any *specific* purposes that may in fact turn out to be served by free exchange.

POLICY STATEMENTS, INTERPERSONAL
COMPARISONS, AND COORDINATION

Implicit in our discussion of Mises's *wertfrei* approach to economic policy and in our argument that it is the peculiarly Austrian aspect of the Misesian approach that makes it possible is an insight to which we have briefly referred. This insight is important and deserves to be spelled out more fully.

Statements by non-Austrian economists on economic policy are made against the background of the theory of welfare economics. Crucial to this theory is the attempt to aggregate, in some sense, the tastes, the purposes, or the satisfactions of individuals into an entity that it is the ideal of economic policy to maximize. The principal conceptual difficulties involved in this procedure are two. The first is well known: the problem of interpersonal comparisons of welfare inevitably stands in the way of any kind of aggregation. The second difficulty, less well known but no less serious, was pointed out by Hayek many years ago: welfare economics, in discussing efficiency at the aggregate level, is compelled to make the illegitimate assumption that the bits of information scattered throughout society concerning individual tastes (and everything else) can somehow be spontaneously integrated and fed into a single mind in order for the notion of aggregate welfare maximization to be meaningful.[22] These difficulties make it clear that, for policy statements to be made without these embarrassments, an analytical framework is needed *that preserves the individuality of individual purposes.* If policies or institutions can be judged on the extent to which they permit individual purposes—seen simply as the unaggregated preference structures of individuals—to be fulfilled, then both of the aforementioned difficulties can be avoided. Such an approach has been found, on Austrian lines, in the notion of *coordination.*[23]

In the coordination approach to normative economics it is made clear that the ideal is not the maximization of aggregate social welfare or any such entity. Instead, the far more modest, but meaningful, criterion of success in social economic arrangements is the degree to which the purposes of separate individuals can be harmonized through coordination of decision making and action. The obvious example of coordinated action is voluntary interpersonal exchange in which each participant acts to improve his position, with such improvement possible only because each participant's action is coordinated precisely with that of his trading partner. In using the coordination criterion as the theoretical basis for evaluating social efficiency, the individuality of purposes is not lost sight of; on the contrary, the very notion of coordination prohibits submersion of these purposes into any social aggregate.

The thesis advanced in this paper, that Misesian policy pronouncements are entirely consistent with *Wertfreiheit*, depends crucially on the nonaggregation of individual purposes. What we have been at pains to emphasize is that this Austrian feature of Misesian economics may be exploited—through the cognate notion of coordination—to escape those pitfalls that other approaches have characteristically been unable to avoid.

WERTFREIHEIT: A CONCLUDING REMARK

Mises the defender of the free market and Mises the economic scientist were indeed one and the same individual. It was not necessary for Mises, in order to extol the market and condemn intervention, to remove his value-free scientist's cap and don a political one. To extol and to condemn were for Mises so circumscribed as to be strictly within the limits of *Wertfreiheit*. It remains for his followers to subject themselves to similar self-imposed restraints, not only because of Weberian ideals of scientific propriety, but also because explicitly value-laden perspectives are frequently found consorting with Austrian economics.

There is, of course, nothing improper about the proponent of a value-laden political position seeking support in the *wertfrei* conclusions of science. One who values the preservation of life and crusades against cigarette smoking is acting quite properly in citing the conclusions of medical research to the effect that smoking is dangerous to health. Similarly, one who wishes to promote a free society with unhampered markets may legitimately cite the conclusions of economic science with respect to the coordinative-allocative properties of competitive markets. What is essential, however, if such scientific support is to be persuasive, is that the scientific research not only be conducted with strict objectivity but also be widely recognized as having been so conducted. Any suspicion that the conclusions of the economic theorist depend upon the perception of particular goals as being more valid than others will only jeopardize the acceptance of those conclusions as objectively determined truths. At every stage of the process of economic reasoning, *Wertfreiheit* thus becomes a crucially important element in scientific procedure. Until the stage where scientific conclusions come to be marshalled as fuel for explicitly political-persuasive positions, any surrender of *Wertfreiheit* carries with it, therefore and in fact, the altogether unwholesome prospect that such positions will necessarily be taken without the benefit of scientific information at all. Surely, if one is imbued with the value judgment that scientific truth is worth pursuing and disseminating, one can be expected to be prepared to exercise the restraint necessary to prevent that truth from being dismissed in the eyes of the public as mere propaganda.

NOTES

1. Carl Menger, *Problems of Economics and Sociology,* trans. F. J. Nock, ed. L. Schneider (Urbana: University of Illinois Press, 1963), pp. 235–37; see above p. 51, note 5 [in original].

2. Joseph A. Schumpeter, *History of Economic Analysis* (New York: Oxford University Press, 1954), p. 802.

3. See T. W. Hutchison, *"Positive" Economics and Policy Objectives* (Cambridge: Harvard University Press, 1964), p. 43.

4. Schumpeter, *History,* p. 805.

5. See Lionel Robbins, *An Essay on the Nature and Significance of Economic Science,* 2d ed. (London: Macmillan & Co., 1935), pp. xv–xvi.

6. Ludwig von Mises, *Human Action: A Treatise on Economics* (New Haven: Yale University Press, 1949), pp. 72–91.

7. Gunnar Myrdal, *The Political Element in the Development of Economic Theory* (Cambridge: Harvard University Press, 1954), p. 12.

8. Ibid., p. 18.

9. Ibid., pp. 56–76.

10. Ibid., p. vii.

11. Ibid.

12. Ibid., p. viii.

13. Ibid., p. 128.

14. Fritz Machlup, "Review of G. Myrdal, *The Political Element in the Development of Economic Theory," American Economic Review* 45 (December 1955): 950.

15. Hutchison, *"Positive" Economics,* p. 42.

16. John Davenport, "From a Western Window: Economics and Philosophy Have Need of Each Other," *Intercollegiate Review* 8 (Spring 1973): 147–58.

17. Ibid., p. 151.

18. Israel M. Kirzner, "Letter to the Editor," *Intercollegiate Review* 9 (Winter 1973–74): pp. 59–60.

19. This disagreement with Davenport does not imply that I am unwilling to endorse his principal theme, that is, the need for economists to speak out not merely as *wertfrei* professionals but also as concerned citizens. Professionals must be concerned with moral as well as scientific truth.

20. See Richard Whately, *Introductory Lectures on Political Economy, Delivered at Oxford in Easter Term,* 1831, 4th ed. (London: John W. Parker, 1855), p. 25.

21. See Murray N. Rothbard, "Value Implications of Economic Theory," *American Economist* 17 (Spring 1973): 35–39; see also Clarence E. Philbrook, "'Realism' in Policy Espousal," *American Economic Review* 43 (December 1953): 379–82.

22. See Israel M. Kirzner, *Competition and Entrepreneurship* (Chicago: University of Chicago Press, 1973), pp. 213–22. Hayek's critique of welfare economics was presented in "The Use of Knowledge in Society," *American Economic Review* 35 (September 1945): 519–30.

23. Kirzner, *Competition and Entrepreneurship,* pp. 212–42.

SELF-INTEREST AND THE NEW BASHING
OF ECONOMICS: A FRESH OPPORTUNITY
IN THE PERENNIAL DEBATE?

A spate of recent attacks on the rationality assumption in economic theory is noticed. Some of these attacks are fresh and, in many ways, original, but the central ideas underlying them are not new. They appear to have been provoked by the direction in which much of mainstream economics has been moving in recent years. On the other hand, it is suggested here, certain developments in contemporary economics, associated particularly with the revival of interest in the Austrian paradigm, offer a fresh understanding of the way in which the rationality assumption, its role in economics properly understood, is able to meet these old-new attacks.

The self-interest assumption in economic theory has aroused passionate debate again and again in the history of the discipline. The passions were first ignited in reaction to classical economics, which appeared to assume not only a world of self-interested persons but one in which they were intent on nothing else except material satisfaction. For a John Ruskin all this meant that classical economists and those who could read their work with acceptance "must have got into" an "entirely damned state of soul" (Ruskin 1934: 14n.). As the nineteenth century advanced, the tone of the criticism of the role of *homo oeconomicus* in economics shifted from indignation to methodological outrage. Both on the Continent and in England, and very soon in the United States, critics of economics, in both its classical and neoclassical versions, denounced as irredeemably flawed those cardinal assumptions upon which economic theory seemed to rest. From Cliffe Leslie in the United Kingdom to Thorstein Veblen in the United States, historicist and institutionalist critics demanded a reformed economics that should recognize the complexity of human

From *The Meaning of Market Process: Essays in the Development of Modern Austrian Economics* (New York and London: Routledge, 1992), 195–208. Reprinted by permission of Taylor and Francis Ltd., www.tandfonline.com, on behalf of Critical Review Foundation; the original source is "Self-Interest and the New Bashing of Economics: A Fresh Opportunity in the Perennial Debate?" *Critical Review* 4, 1–2 (1990): 27–40. Copyright Critical Review Foundation.

nature, the variety of human goals and motives, and the degree to which sociological and psychological forces are intertwined with (or even swallow up entirely) those singled out by economic theorists. An entire literature burgeoned around these controversial issues, with the same charges and rebuttals being raised again and again.

A spate of recent books—by Robert Frank (1988), Gregg and Paul Davidson (1988) and Amitai Etzioni (1988)—has once more injected these hoary issues into current debate. These volumes are not simply rehashes of the old outcries of the moralists or historicists; each of them attacks mainstream, late-twentieth-century economics in a fresh way. Yet basically the points of substance from which these attacks derive their force are, with some notable exceptions, the very same points which nourished the attacks on economics over a century ago. Although the authors display scant interest in possible intellectual predecessors, their fundamental disagreements with mainstream economics boil down to a few key, classic, objections—in fact objections that have been debated repeatedly. Although at certain places in these books reference is made to standard responses that can be anticipated to be forthcoming from the defenders of mainstream economics, these defences are dismissed as insufficiently serious.

Our purpose in these pages is not to review these books but to reflect once again on the venerable issues of which they remind us. In particular, the circumstance that these book-length critiques of standard economics have appeared at this time is itself worthy of attention. What have today's mainstream economists done to arouse once again the old passionate denunciations of their science? Or, to take a different tack, can the economics of the 1990s perhaps lay these criticisms to rest in a more definitive manner than the economics of the 1890s—or the 1930s—was able to do? We shall in fact argue that (a) some modern developments in mainstream economics may indeed have played a role in provoking these criticisms, but (b) that (not entirely coincidentally) other modern developments in economics, developments which have themselves emerged out of a separate strand of critical analysis of mainstream economics, can help show how the classic defences of economics against the kind of criticisms raised in these new books can be appreciated, and extended, in a new way. Thus it is perhaps just possible that the complicated state of modern economics, while provoking renewals of the old critiques in ever more aggressive forms, can also point the way to deeper appreciation of the ultimate irrelevance of these critiques.

SELFISHNESS AND ECONOMICS

An only slightly unfair caricature of the ancient criticisms levelled against economics would be to portray these criticisms as understanding economics to be the theory of a society in which all individuals are strictly selfish and coldly logical, with not an iota of morality or ounce of emotion in their veins. The economic man which these criticisms perceive to be central to economic theory is unattractively intent, in the first place, only on more and more wealth, motivated exclusively by the urge to enjoy those pleasures which money can buy. His character is unredeemed by any altruistic sympathies; his drive to satisfy his appetites is unrestrained by any moral reservations. His actions are governed by steel-trap-like logic, never softened or dislodged by emotion or weakness of will. From the perspective of the critics, economic theory is able to reach firm conclusions, and in particular to ascribe benign properties to the free market economy, only by developing models populated exclusively by such economic men. The three books cited above begin with roughly this perception of mainstream economics. Each of them attacks this economics from a slightly different point of departure.

Robert Frank's critique is, in a sense, the mildest, and the least "dangerous" for the practitioners of mainstream economics. There is no need, Professor Frank argues, for economics to assume exclusive rationality, understood as complete freedom from emotion and passion. The validity of economics is therefore not threatened by pervasive real world examples of passionate behaviour. It can be shown, by ingenious theorizing and striking hypothetical examples, that it may, in the long run, be entirely useful to permit one's decisions to be shaped by moral sympathy, by the urge for revenge, by the prick of conscience, by trust and the like, even where cooler reasoning might at first glance appear to point to different courses of action. Building on earlier work by Thomas Schelling and others, Frank shows how the practice of moral behaviour, for example, may not only be good for society, it may also be materially beneficial to the practising individuals themselves. Clearly, while all this would permit the economists' models to encompass kinds of behaviour traditionally excluded, the overall perspective attributed to economics need not be substantially altered. So far from calling for severely restricted scope for the models of economists, Professor Frank's work can in fact be construed as demonstrating the relevance of these models for rationalizing behaviour once thought to be beyond their scope. Highly original in many ways, this work can in no way be dismissed as merely rediscovering nineteenth-century criticisms of economics.

The Davidsons certainly do not come to extend the applicability of the models of the economists. They construe economics as lauding the social usefulness of exclusively self-regarding behaviour. Economics arrives at theorems demonstrating the social optimality of strictly individualistic behaviour. Not only does economics appear to frown on the civic virtues, it is seen as promoting technical efficiency for its own sake (even where such efficiency may be sought to promote genocidal goals!) and of measuring social worth only in so far as it can be captured by a market price in dollars. For the Davidsons the world explicated by economic theory is a most repulsive place; a civilized society, they argue, requires a totally different economics. The moral and scientific blindness of economists, the Davidsons feel, is not only responsible for their promotion of this repulsive, uncivilized society. This blindness prevents the economists from realizing that even the material well-being upon which they focus such exclusive attention must suffer in a world bereft of civilized values. Without trust and civic virtue markets cannot work. The cynicism concerning moral values which pervades mainstream economics is ultimately inconsistent with the prosperity which is being sought. Much of the Davidsons' critique is strongly reminiscent of mid-nineteenth-century condemnations of economics, particularly those of Carlyle and Ruskin.

Professor Etzioni's attack on economics is the most ambitious. The focus of his criticism is on the validity of economic theory in explaining the phenomena of the real world, rather than on the moral (or other) desirability of a world built according to the specifications of the economists' models. For Etzioni economics is simply not good social science; its assumptions are false and its conclusions invalid. The falsity of the assumptions of the economists relates, in particular, (a) to the nature of the consumer (whom economists falsely assume to be in pursuit only of pleasure) and (b) to the decisions made by economic agents (which economists falsely believe to be made entirely rationally and without any distortion arising from passion and emotion). Although it is impossible here to do justice to the richness of Etzioni's exhaustive critical survey of modern economics, it should be pointed out that his critique is, at base, entirely similar to the late-nineteenth-century appeals for a reformed science of economics. Just like earlier critics, Etzioni is asking for an economics (he calls it "socioeconomics") which should in fact be a kind of economic sociology. In fact his objections to economics, like those of his century-old predecessors, attack the very concept of a pure science of economics. Indeed, this line of criticism has consistently maintained that economics can be rescued only by abandoning the traditional boundaries of the discipline. For explanations of social phenomena which, for analytical purposes, begin by postulating a separate field of strictly economic action are fatally flawed from their very beginning.

THE STANDARD DEFENCES AND THE STANDARD REBUTTALS

Traditionally, economists have defended themselves against attacks on the unrealisticness of economic man along one or other of two possible lines of reasoning.

One line of defence has been to argue that the rationality assumption (or the assumption of selfishness, or whichever version of the fundamental assumption of economizing activity is under attack) is never meant as *more than a useful first approximation*. The assumption is held to be roughly valid for much of human activity, so that the models of economic theory provide indispensable guidance in understanding the real world. This guidance must, admittedly, be supplemented by careful consideration of actual behaviour in specific situations; none the less it would be folly to reject out of hand the guidance of the pure economic models. The inclusion of all relevant sociological and/or psychological features of real world situations can only obscure those powerful chains of cause and effect which arise from the significant extent to which the economist's assumptions *are* empirically relevant to those situations.[1]

The critics of economics (including, in particular, Professor Etzioni) have, in one way or another, rejected this line of defence. They have denied the empirical usefulness of the economists' assumptions. They have accused economists of ignoring, at least in their policy recommendations, their own fine-print lip-service to the limited actual relevance of their models. In fact, the critics maintain, economists have permitted their models to run away with them, so that they are simply unable to shake off their adherence to these suspect assumptions. This rebuttal has been sharpened by the contemporary work of economists such as Gary Becker, who has applied the models of economics to areas of human life (such as marriage and the family) in which (the critics believe) the economists' assumptions are, even more than usual, egregiously unrealistic. These critics are deeply offended by the economists' insistence, not merely on barring the insights of sociology from their explanations for economic phenomena, but on in fact "imperialistically" laying claim, on behalf of their own caricature-like models of human behaviour, to territory traditionally recognized as the preserve of the other social sciences.

The second of the two traditional defences of economics has been to argue for a highly refined version of the assumption of economic man. It is argued that economics does not need, and never has needed, the cruder assumptions sometimes employed in the characterization of *homo oeconomicus*. Economic man does not need to be materialistic, or selfish; he does not even have to be efficient in any objective sense. *He merely has to pursue goals purposefully,* in the light of his own perceptions of relevant possibilities and constraints. Ever since, in 1932, Lionel Robbins built on the ideas of Philip Wicksteed in the United Kingdom and a number of Austrian economists of the 1920s and early 1930s to formulate this rarefied depiction of the economizing agent (Robbins 1935), economists have felt justified in brushing aside much of the standard criticism. As Mises (one of the Austrians on whose ideas Robbins had drawn) had explained as early as 1922, there is nothing in the economist's approach which implies absence of moral restraints. There is nothing amoral or "uncivilized" in the economist's perspective. Truly sensitive natures, Mises pointed out, need not be dismayed by the economist's way of putting things. "Called upon to choose between bread and honour, [such truly sensitive natures] will never be at a loss how to act. If honour cannot be eaten, eating can at least be foregone for honour" (Mises 1936).

The critics have not accepted this line of defence. As Etzioni (1988: 21) points out (with regard to the more modern version of the Wicksteed–Mises–Robbins line of defence, which treats utility as a "strictly formal concept, as the common denominator of all human preferences"), this defence involves first the reduction of utility theory to a tautology. Second, it suppresses important substantive differences which separate human actions designed to pursue pleasure from those taken in response to moral imperatives (Etzioni 1988: 23–50). To insist on the "mono-utilitarian" paradigm is both to offer theories empty of empirical content and relevance and to obscure significant and easily understandable differences in behaviour patterns.

Our position in what follows will be generally on the side of the defenders of economics, especially those employing the Mises–Robbins approach. But we shall argue that the full significance of this reply to the sociological and historicist critics has not yet been properly articulated. Our elaboration of the Mises–Robbins argument will require us to reject (as the critics of economics reject) the first line of defence referred to earlier. Our defence of the "rationality" assumption—using the quotation marks in order to avoid becoming embroiled in definitional debates concerning precisely which concept of rationality undergirds economics—will emphasize the significance of this assumption, not for the theory of decision making, but for the theory of *market process*.

"RATIONALITY" AND THE MARKET PROCESS:
TOWARD A FRESH ARTICULATION

We shall maintain, somewhat dogmatically perhaps, that the core of economic theory is the theory of markets. Even the harshest of the critics of economics is unlikely to deny that at least some markets work systematically at least some of the time. The explication of the responsible systematic forces, we assert, constitutes the central idea in economic theory. For us the existence of systematic market forces means the existence of *a spontaneous process of learning*. What economic theory essentially sets out to explain, therefore, is how a spontaneous learning process can be set in motion by the interaction of exchanging individuals. To assert that markets work systematically is to assert that market participants tend spontaneously to become better informed about each other, as a result of initial market experiences based on earlier erroneous perceptions about one another's abilities, attitudes and degrees of eagerness. *The great contribution of economic science to social understanding has been to discern and explain this kind of spontaneous learning process—in all kinds of specific contexts.* There is nothing, in the economic theory which explicates this process, which depends on any specific context in which it may manifest itself. There is nothing in economic theory which confines it to individuals pursuing strictly material satisfactions or which excludes the operation of moral imperatives and restraints. Perhaps more to the point for present purposes, strictly speaking, *nothing in economic theory purports to explain how individuals, with given information, make their decisions; it relates exclusively to the spontaneously changing patterns of information in the light of which these decisions are made during the course of the market process.* Our defence of the "rationality" assumption in economics boils down to the claim that the only essential role played by this assumption relates not to the way in which decisions are made but instead to the manner in which hitherto overlooked opportunities for market gains come to be perceived. All this calls for some elaboration; it represents, admittedly, a highly unorthodox understanding of the role of the "rationality" principle.

MICROECONOMICS AND ECONOMIC THEORY

The generally perceived role of the "rationality" assumption in modern economic theory—in our view a somewhat misperceived role—arises from the way in which microeconomics is generally perceived. It is recognized (of course correctly) that the central elements in economic theory are those which make up microeconomics. That is, these elements are understood analytically as proceeding from the decisions made by individual market participants. From this sound starting point there has developed, however, the unfortunate perception that a central task of economic theory is *to explain the individual decision,* in the sense of providing, in principle, a way of predicting what a given individual consumer, resource owner or owner of a firm will decide to do under given circumstances. For this explanation, it is generally understood, the "rationality" assumption provides the controlling principle. In the modern criticism of economics it is the validity of this controlling principle which is under attack. We believe this perception of microeconomics, and thus the criticism of economics on the basis of perceived weaknesses in the "rationality" assumption, to be fundamentally imprecise.

In our view the central element in microeconomic theory is its explication of the manner in which systematic market tendencies arise. These tendencies arise out of the interplay of individual decisions; it is this which makes microeconomics central to economic theory. But the prime focus of microeconomics should, in our view, be the process through which this interplay of individual decisions systematically generates greater mutual awareness. The central role of "rationality," we shall see, concerns this process of learning. In fact, in our view, it is not the function of economics to explain decision making at all, in any except the most formal ("tautological") sense. The function of microeconomics is to explain how, in the course of the market process, decisions tend to change—spontaneously but systematically—from patterns which are initially based on more erroneously assumed information (concerning the attitudes of one's fellow market participants) toward patterns which are based on more correct information. We recognize, of course, that it is certainly important, in developing such a microeconomics, to work out a formal framework within which to envisage decisions being made. It is, after all, only in this way that we can focus carefully and precisely on the ways in which erroneous assumptions on the part of market participants tend to be systematically replaced by more correct assumptions. But the working out of such formal frameworks never has the function of providing operational theories concerning individual decisions. The role of the "rationality" assumption in the microeconomic theory of the individual decision ought therefore to appear totally innocuous *precisely because of* its empirical emptiness. We thus fully endorse the Mises–Robbins defence of the role of the "rationality" assumption, which emphasizes the complete *generality* of the utility toward which individuals are assumed to be purposefully aiming. But we wish to make two relevant observations. First, we shall argue that this defence is only the beginning of the full story. Second, it should be clear from our discussion that the standard rebuttals offered against the Mises–Robbins defence, denouncing it as turning the micro-theory of the decision into a tissue of tautologies, incapable of explaining important, obvious distinctions between classes of decisions under a variety of circumstances, totally miss the mark. This is because the function of the microeconomic theory of the decision is *precisely* that of providing the tautologous framework required for the subsequent theory of the market process. The usefulness and the validity of the "rationality" assumption must, in our view, be judged most crucially in terms of its success in explicating the market process.

SELF-INTEREST AND DISCOVERY

The learning process which drives the forces of the market is made up primarily of disappointments and discoveries. Individuals are, perhaps, initially over-optimistic in regard to what they believe others will be prepared to pay for what they wish to buy, or in regard to what they believe others will be prepared to accept for what they wish to sell. Over-optimism generates disappointments. The cold realities drive home the truth. Subsequent buying and selling plans tend to be made on the basis of more realistic assessments. Price tends toward the market clearing level, at which no one need be disappointed. So runs the stuff of market equilibration theory.

Or again, individuals may be unnecessarily pessimistic regarding the interest of others in trading. They may believe that prospective buyers are only very slightly interested, that they will not buy except at very low prices (or that prospective sellers will not sell except at very high prices). Such excessive pessimism means that market participants may be over-looking valuable opportunities for mutual gain through exchange. Such opportunities for (what amounts to) pure profit tend to stimulate discovery. As discoveries are made, prices for a given commodity, or productive service or whatever, converge; input prices and output prices converge; pure profit is squeezed out until, in equilibrium, it is entirely absent. So runs the stuff of general equilibrium theory.

These processes of learning are spontaneous, not deliberate. They are driven, not by planning for the acquisition of costly knowledge, but by the spontaneous realization (resulting from experience) of earlier error. In particular they are driven by *the alertness of individuals intent on achieving their purposes.* Persons with no interests or goals will not tend to discover the changes in external conditions that favour or threaten the realization of interests or goals. Alertness without some degree of purposefulness is simply and totally implausible. Self-interest (in the rarefied Mises–Robbins sense of purposefulness) switches on one's awareness to hitherto unnoticed disappointing conditions, or hitherto unnoticed opportunities for gain. Without the "rationality" assumption tending to assure gradual spontaneous discovery of relevant market truths, economists would have no basis upon which to account for the systematic character of market processes.

The self-interest, the purposefulness, postulated here need in no way deny either man's moral concerns or his susceptibility to blind passions. The theory does not, recall, postulate *specific* patterns of concrete decision making; it merely asks that we recognize *some* role, in human action, for "rationality." *To the extent that* "rationality" plays a role in human decisions, we are entitled to demonstrate how it may generate systematic patterns of mutual learning on the part of participating individuals. To reject the scientific demonstration of the power of such systematic learning patterns, on the grounds of occasional or frequent human "irrationality," is to refuse to see a powerful tendency which manifests itself in regard to *all* the interests of human beings. The "laws of supply and demand" really do explicate a host of matters; they do rely on the powerful effects of human purposefulness—without in the least obscuring the influence of moral concerns, altruistic concerns or other concerns which may be expressed *through* those purposes, and without in the least presuming the total absence of passionate and emotional obstacles to the discoveries which might be made by pure reason alone.

Nothing in the explication of the laws of supply and demand denies the possible existence of other laws ("non-economic" laws) relevant to human behaviour. There is nothing in economic theory which need displace other disciplines (sociology, psychology, whatever) from exploring the possibility of such other regularities. But, at the same time, the insights of economic theory cannot be grasped without perceiving the role of the "self-interested" pursuit of possibly altruistic or other purposes in generating processes of mutual discovery.

INADEQUATE AND INEPT DEFENCES OF ECONOMICS

Those defending economics on the grounds of the approximate accuracy of specific assumptions concerning the absence of altruistic or other moral concerns, or concerning the absence of passionate and emotional elements in human action, are, from the perspective here articulated, in the last analysis doing economics a disservice. To the extent that their defence proposes that economics displace other social sciences in accounting for the specifics of human behaviour, they render valid all the criticisms of those challenging the realism of selfish, calculating and ruthlessly amoral economic man. Whatever occasional usefulness, in understanding specific social or economic phenomena, may be derived from the application of such narrowly conceived, highly specific models of human behaviour is surely outweighed by the attendant costs. These costs include, in particular, the unfortunate expectations raised in many lay—and even professional—observers that economics, by itself, can account for and in principle predict what people will do under specific circumstances. A related cost is the diversion of attention from what economics does in fact uniquely provide: a satisfying explanation of why and how markets work.

One particularly unfortunate cost of this ineffective line of defence has been to perpetuate the myth that the normative implications of standard economic theory stand or fall with the validity of this narrowly defined *homo oeconomicus*. It is largely by pointing to the presence in real world human beings of moral impulses and of powerful passions directly influencing decisions that critics of economics feel free to reject the insights to be learned from economics concerning the socially benign consequences of free markets. Such rejection has, of course, often been the major motive inspiring the methodological criticisms made against economics, ever since the 1870s.

But once it is recognized that it is the Mises–Robbins line of defence which accurately comprehends the role of the "rationality" assumption, matters appear decidedly differently. The Mises–Robbins line of defence points, as discussed, to the paramountcy of the "rationality" assumption not so much in the theory of decision making as in the theory of spontaneous learning. The "rationality" assumption permits us to recognize that markets encourage people spontaneously to discover opportunities to gain—in terms of whatever they happen to be interested in. With the emphasis shifted from the particular decision made, to the *changing frameworks of information and perceptions within which decisions can be made* (whether under the inspiration of logic, emotion, passion or whatever), the alleged implausibility of the role of "rationality" in economics becomes an accusation more and more difficult to take seriously. It is true that the postulation of equilibrating tendencies requires a role for deliberate purposefulness, but it by no means requires an exclusive role. The theorems showing how processes of mutual learning can develop spontaneously can be seen as relevant to all kinds of human interests, and retain validity so long as human purposefulness is at least one element in the psychological make-up of market participants. Admittedly, facile deployment of the theory of markets to account for developments in particular historical circumstances is a highly treacherous enterprise. Where moral or personal concerns complicate business decisions, it may turn out to be hazardous to attempt to identify empirically the particular "commodities" in regard to which economics is supposed somehow to postulate the existence of spontaneous processes of learning. But the general thrust of economics surely remains sound: the market is understood as a seething ocean of interacting decisions continually tending, subject to continual buffetings of "external changes," toward systematic mutual discovery by all pairs of individuals between whom (given *their* interests) exchange (of *something*) might be mutually beneficial. This tendency is never completed, neither is it ever suspended. It is frequently interrupted, often possibly distorted, but it never ceases to exert its influence.

SELF-INTEREST AND LATE-TWENTIETH-CENTURY ECONOMICS

It may be useful to conclude briefly with some thoughts about the timeliness of this new round of debate on the role of the "rationality" assumption in economics. These thoughts centre on two themes: why modern economics has, at this particular time, provoked this new outburst of attacks on the "rationality" assumption; and how the contemporary revival of the Austrian tradition (the same tradition which nurtured the Mises–Robbins defence cited earlier) has made it possible to outline a fresh (and even more effective) aspect of the classic Mises–Robbins defence of the "rationality" assumption in economics.

That modern mainstream economics has provoked the renewed spate of attacks revolving round the "rationality" assumption is eminently understandable. It is in our time that microeconomics has once again assumed the controlling paradigmatic role in economic theory. It has done so in a manner which has emphasized the concrete contributions which, it is claimed, the "rationality" assumption can make to empirical social science. Modern microeconomics has proceeded to "invade" the territories of other social sciences, placing ever more weight on the crucial character of the constrained maximization behaviour which the "rationality" assumption sees as so central. It has turned out to be those economists (associated very often with the University of Chicago) who have been understood to be the most enthusiastic supporters of free markets (as a consequence of their economics) whose economics appears most heavily indebted to the narrowest formulations of the "rationality" assumption. It was a George Stigler who suggested (1984) that dollars and liberty are, for relevant purposes, entirely synonymous. It was a Richard Posner (1983) whose work on law and economics seemed to make the maximization of market value the sole criterion for human happiness. In other words, modern economists have seemed to permit the narrowest of formulations of the rationality assumption to dictate social policy in what critics could easily perceive to be a highly dangerous fashion. It is not surprising that all this has stimulated sharply critical reactions.

Yet at the same time as mainstream economics has been formulated on narrower and narrower conceptions of rationality, at the same time as rationality came perilously close to being seen as virtually synonymous with universal omniscience, the revival of the Austrian tradition has enabled us to extend the classic Mises–Robbins defence with renewed vigour. Developments within the Austrian tradition have emphasized the centrality, not of states of equilibrium generated by completely rational (i.e. omniscient) market participants, but of market processes of spontaneous learning sparked by entrepreneurial alertness (Kirzner 1973, 1985a).

In these processes, self-interest is indeed a central element, but this self-interest must, as we have seen, be understood with a certain subtlety. Properly understood self-interest does not exclude altruistic motivation; it depends on purposefulness, but not on any selfishness of purpose. The point to be stressed is that it is one's *own* purposes which inspire one's actions and excite one's alertness. One's purposes may be altruistic or otherwise; one's interest in achieving one's (possibly altruistic) goals switches on one's alertness to opportunities for advancing those goals. One may appear to be acting selfishly in amassing profits in market activities; but if this drive to win profits is inspired solely by a dream of endowing a research effort to fight a dread disease that threatens mankind, we would hardly label it as selfish. It is human dreams and goals which provide the motive force for market processes. Economics depends, for its understanding of market processes, upon the alert purposefulness, the purposeful alertness, of human beings. In these processes the controlling principle is goal-motivated discovery. And it is the emphasis on these disequilibrium processes of mutual discovery which has led us to underscore the relevance of the classic Mises–Robbins insistence on the utter generality of human motives.

NOTE

1. Probably the most sophisticated and careful restatement of this line of defence is that of Machlup (1972).

REFERENCES

Davidson, G. and Davidson, P. (1988) *Economics for a Civilized Society*, New York: W. W. Norton.

Etzioni, A. (1988) *The Moral Dimension: Toward a New Economics*, New York: Free Press.

Frank, R. H. (1988) *Passions within Reason: The Strategic Role of the Emotions*, New York: W. W. Norton.

Kirzner, I. M. (1973) *Competition and Entrepreneurship*, Chicago, IL: University of Chicago Press.

Kirzner, I. M. (1985a) *Discovery and the Capitalist Process*, Chicago, IL: University of Chicago Press.

Machlup, F. (1972) "The universal bogey: economic man," in M. Peston and B. Corry (eds) *Essays in Honour of Lord Robbins*, London: Weidenfeld & Nicolson.

Mises, L. von (1936) *Socialism: An Economic and Sociological Analysis*, London: Jonathan Cape (translation from the German of *Die Gemeinwirtschaft*, 1st edn 1922, 2nd edn 1932).

Posner, R. A. (1983) "Utilitarianism, economics and social theory," *The Economics of Justice*, Cambridge, MA: Harvard University Press.

Robbins, L. (1935) *An Essay on the Nature and Significance of Economic Science*, 2nd edn, London: Macmillan (1st edn 1932).

Ruskin, J. (1934) *Unto This Last*, Oxford: Humphrey Milford, Oxford University Press.

Stigler, G. J. (1984) "Wealth, and possibly liberty," *The Intellectual and the Marketplace*, Cambridge, MA: Harvard University Press.

HUMAN ATTITUDES AND ECONOMIC GROWTH

Peter Bauer was very much concerned with the question of how attitudes may affect the potential for economic development in underdeveloped countries. He was forced to deal with it because much of the conventional wisdom on development, which he was contending, denied the relevance of basic economic theory to developing countries.

THE RELEVANCE OF ECONOMIC
THEORY TO DEVELOPING COUNTRIES

In *Economic Analysis and Policy in Underdeveloped Countries*, Bauer (1957: 15–16) wrote:

> Those who dispute the relevance of the propositions of economics to underdeveloped countries usually base their arguments on the differences in attitudes and institutions between the underdeveloped world and the western countries. . . . A few years ago in the Gold Coast a highly placed civil servant told me that his experience had convinced him that economics was irrelevant in Africa, because the African simply did not respond to economic motives.

But Bauer was thoroughly convinced that basic economics, in particular, supply and demand theory, was emphatically relevant to underdeveloped countries. As he and Basil Yamey noted in their classic *The Economics of Under-developed Countries:*

> Although many of the differences between the different parts of the under-developed world are very deep-seated, some of the basic tools and concepts of economics apply widely to under-developed countries. This is true, for example, of the basic elements of supply and demand analysis [Bauer and Yamey 1957: 8].

Moreover, from his own extensive study and direct observation in Asia and Africa, Bauer (1957: 15) concluded:

> I am now convinced of the very wide applicability to underdeveloped countries of the basic methods and approach of economics. . . . I am

From *Cato Journal*, vol. 25, no. 3 (Fall 2005): 465–69. Cato Institute. Reprinted by permission.

thinking especially of the elements of supply and demand analysis and its simpler conclusions, the tendency of people to seek activities and occupations which yield the highest net advantage within the opportunities open to them.

In a 1967 paper, Bauer emphasized the importance of elementary economic principles. He criticized sophisticated economic models "in which the abstraction and aggregation involved render them irrelevant . . . they become travesties which divert attention from the essentials and obscure the issues." He pointed out that "the necessity of emphasizing the importance of apparently trite elementary propositions is that in the last 20 years or so economists themselves have ignored them." Among these "elementary propositions" are those of supply and demand theory, with particular emphasis on "supply, demand and price as functional relationships" (Bauer [1967] 1976: 285–87).

It was for this reason that Bauer pleaded for direct observation of conditions in developing countries. In this emphasis his point was precisely the opposite of what many other economists who, throughout the history of economic thought have emphasized observation, have had in mind. Throughout the history of economics, critics of economic theory, particularly critics of supply and demand theory, have argued that economics should be based not on theory but on empirically established relationships. Bauer's point was precisely the opposite. In order to be able to apply simple economic propositions to widely disparate real-world contexts, it is necessary to recognize the particularities of these disparate contexts—otherwise the relevance of these simple propositions of economic theory will be overlooked or denied.

Bauer's conviction of the universal relevance of supply and demand analysis was based on his insight that despite the differences in "the values which people cherish and thus in the objectives they wish to attain, and in the various social and technical obstacles which circumscribe their activities"—human beings share a basically "economic" attitude (Bauer 1957: 17–18). In the words of Lord Desai (2002: 62), Bauer believed "that the driving force of self-interest in pursuit of well-being is of universal application."

I will seek to push Bauer's approach a little further than his recognition of the powerful, universal force of simple economic self-interest. My focus will be not so much on the insight, central to Bauer's position, that self-interest ensures that demand curves slope down and that supply curves slope up, thus ensuring the relevance of simple supply-demand analysis. Rather, my focus will be on the entrepreneurial process of dynamic market competition, upon which we depend for our conviction that markets do indeed tend to gravitate toward the prices and quantities marked out by the supply-demand intersection.

BEYOND PECUNIARY SELF-INTEREST

Critics of economic theory have traditionally focused their attacks on the model of *homo oeconomicus,* with its emphasis on maximizing net pecuniary gain. They believed it was this model of the economic agent that underlies economic theory. The economists whom Bauer cites as denying the relevance of economic theory to developing countries were arguing that the attitudes of economic agents in developing countries were so different from the attitude of *homo oeconomicus* that supply-demand analysis was no longer of relevance. Bauer was defending this relevance by challenging the critics' understanding of the attitudes of economic agents in developing countries.

I will take issue with the critics' arguments not by claiming the universal presence of strong pecuniary self-interest, but by denying that the crucial theorems of economics in fact depend on such pecuniary self-interest at all. Instead, I will claim, the economists' view of the market process and of the so-called law of supply and demand rests on the insight that economic agents are *purposeful.* In this I am following a tradition (associated with the names of Philip Wicksteed, Lionel Robbins, and Ludwig von Mises) that does not see economic theory as resting on the assumption of narrow selfishness, but on the human propensity to manipulate scarce means consistently toward the achievement of adopted goals.

In fact, I have argued that the same kind of competitive market processes that underlie the conclusions of elementary economic theory can be expected even in an imaginary society peopled only by altruists. Even if each economic agent has no other goal but that of benefiting his or her fellow citizens in some particular way, we should expect, in a society permitting freedom for market activities, the kinds of market activity and market phenomena with which we are familiar in our own world, in which altruism is *not* the prime universal goal of members of society (see Kirzner 1990, 2004).

In such an imaginary altruistic world one person, intent on healing the sick, might seek to maximize his profits in manufacturing, say, cheese, in order to support hospitals in their healing and in their medical research. He will pay no more than market wages (and provide no more than the absolutely necessary perks and amenities) in order to secure the labor he requires. In so doing he is not being selfish at all, he is being altruistic toward the sick.

A second industrialist may be producing bicycles in order to feed the hungry. He, too, will act in accordance with the profit-maximizing theory of the firm, competing vigorously with other market participants.

More important, both the cheese manufacturer and the bicycle manufacturer—precisely because they are the altruists that they are—will be on the lookout for pure profit opportunities. As entrepreneurs they will be not merely "maximizing profits" (more accurately, maximizing quasi-rents) as in the theory of the firm in equilibrium markets. They will be continually alert to opportunities to buy inputs (including labor) at lower than most prevailing prices. They will be continually alert to opportunities to sell their cheese or their bicycles at higher prices in newly discovered markets. And they will be alert to possibilities of switching from the production of cheese or of bicycles to that of sweaters or of golf lessons—all, of course, with the overpowering objective of in some way channeling pecuniary profits to the altruistic improvement of the human condition.

THE RELEVANCE OF MARKET PROCESS THEORY

My point, of course, is not to suggest that in our world, even in non-urban, nonindustrialized societies, selfishness is replaced by altruism. Rather, my point is to show that the relevance of market process theory, of entrepreneurial theory, of the theory of dynamic competition in the Mises-Hayek sense, does not depend on the assumption of pecuniary self-interest in the sense of selfishness, as usually understood.[1]

Consequently, Bauer was correct in arguing that "differences in attitudes" of economic agents in underdeveloped countries do not cast into doubt the relevance of simple economic theory. That relevance holds across

---

1. I am deliberately refraining from using language that would describe as "selfish" the attitude of an individual who insists on assigning a higher ranking of urgency to some altruistic objective than others would.

a wide variety of possible "attitudes" and cultures—not because pecuniary selfishness holds across all cultures (it may), but because all that is necessary for simple economic theory to be relevant is *human purposefulness.*

Such human purposefulness is characterized by (a) chosen objectives, which may vary widely among different cultures, as Bauer recognized; (b) consistency in the pursuit of those objectives, which does not mean constancy in the pattern of choice but rather systematic manipulation of available scarce means in order to achieve chosen ends; and (c) human alertness to new possibilities of achieving objectives, which is what constitutes the entrepreneurial element in human behavior. Indeed, it is this entrepreneurial element in human behavior that separates Mises's "human action" from standard microtheorizing, in which individuals are simply assumed to maximize some objective function within the constraints of resource limitations.

CONCLUSION

One may, of course, describe human purposefulness (and especially entrepreneurial alertness) as an "attitude." And one would then say that economic development in underdeveloped countries (as was the case in the history of western economies) does indeed depend on an "attitude."

However, I believe that Peter Bauer would agree that our discussion shows that economic development does not depend on any *particular* attitudes. Instead, I believe he would agree that economic development depends on the humanity shared by all members of the human race—not on the attitudes of *homo oeconomicus,* but on the attitude of *homo sapiens.*

REFERENCES

Bauer, P. T. (1957) *Economic Analysis and Policy in Underdeveloped Countries.* Durham, N.C.: Duke University Press.

——— ([1967] 1976) "Economics as a Form of Technical Assistance." In *Dissent on Development,* chap. 7. Revised ed. Cambridge, Mass.: Harvard University Press.

Bauer, P. T., and Yamey, B. S. (1957) *The Economics of Under-developed Countries.* Chicago: University of Chicago Press.

Desai, M. (2002) "Peter Bauer and the Observation of Economic Life." In *A Tribute to Peter Bauer,* chap. 4. London: Institute of Economic Affairs.

Kirzner, I. M. (1990) "Self-interest and the New Bashing of Economics: A Fresh Opportunity in the Perennial Debate?" *Critical Review* 4 (Winter/Spring): 27–40.

——— (2004) "Economic Science and the Morality of Capitalism." In *Economy and Virtue: Essays on the Theme of Markets and Morality.* London: Institute of Economic Affairs.

WHAT ECONOMISTS DO

In his recent exciting presidential address "What Should Economists Do?"[1] Professor Buchanan demands that economists abandon their preoccupation with the problem of efficient resource allocation, and turn, instead, toward a positive study of "catallactics"—the consequences of the human propensity to trade. The stress on allocation, Buchanan charges, has tended to turn the discipline into a branch of applied mathematics, concerned with the *computation* of efficient solutions to allocation problems. It has, moreover, facilitated the uncritical acceptance and continued analysis of the notion of the existence of social or group allocation problems, when this notion "prejudges the central issue that has been debated in theoretical welfare economics."

There is, Buchanan argues, a profound difference between the kind of "economic" problem solved in a Crusoe economy on the one hand, and the achievements of a market economy on the other. Crusoe's problem is one of choosing efficiently; it is essentially computational, i.e., it consists in calculating the allocation pattern, at the level of means, that corresponds to a given ordering of ends. The "solution" is thus "mechanically" obtainable from the data. The currently fashionable view of economics sees the market, too, as merely a computational device with respect to the "social" allocation of resources. The "correct" solution to the "problem" relevant to the market can, in principle, be obtained by computation from the data. But, this view, argues Buchanan, completely overlooks the significant aspect of the market consisting in its embodiment of voluntary exchange processes. This currently misplaced emphasis is, in Buchanan's view, apparent in the likewise misplaced preoccupation with the perfectly competitive model. In this model the "individual responds to a set of externally-determined, exogenous variables, and his choice problem again becomes purely mechanical." This view of the market is faulty primarily in "its conversion of individual choice behavior from a social-institutional context to a physical-computational one." By contrast, Buchanan's own economics, focusing on exchange as its central idea, "draws attention to

From *Southern Economic Journal* 31, 3 (1965): 257–61. Reproduced by permission of Southern Economic Association.

1. *Southern Economic Journal,* January 1964, pp. 213–22.

a unique sort of relationship, that which involves the cooperative association of individuals, one with another, even when individual interests are different." It concentrates on the profound social importance of the mutuality of advantage that can be secured by cooperative arrangements.

This note, while concurring wholeheartedly with most of Buchanan's criticisms of the currently fashionable allocation economics, will seek 1) to emphasize that the fault does not lie with the concern with the allocation concept itself (or, at least, not with that allocation that makes up the formal structure of the *individual* act of choice); 2) to show that most of Buchanan's objections have, in fact, already been raised by a group of writers who happen to emphasize—more than any other economists— the role of individual planning, allocation, and choice; 3) to show that the view supported by this last group of writers, while broad enough to encompass the catallactic view of economics that Buchanan is espousing, embodies at the same time fundamental insights which the more limited catallactic view is unable to exploit.

I

It will be helpful, at the outset, to clarify the relationship between that view of economics which Buchanan tries to demote, and the view of the nature and the scope of economics that has been made famous by Lord Robbins. Buchanan's paper tends to convey the suggestion that these are identical, that the currently fashionable stress on allocative computation derives directly from the definition of economics as the science "which studies human behaviour as a relationship between ends and scarce means which have alternative uses."[2] Buchanan's objections to economics seen as an exercise in allocative computation, might thus seem at the same time to apply to Robbins's view of economic science. But this is, in fact, by no means the case.

Buchanan is of course correct in ascribing the historical source of the current interest in allocative computation to Robbins's clear statement of the allocative nature of the "economic problem." But it must at the same time be pointed out—something that Buchanan's discussion fails to do— that Robbins's view of the nature of economics does *not* itself in any way see the task of economic science as that of *solving* such allocation problems, whether for an individual or for a society. Robbinsian economics

2. L. Robbins, *The Nature and Significance of Economic Science,* 2nd ed. (London: Macmillan & Co., 1935), p. 16.

studies the activities of men engaged in solving their economic problems. It is not its task to compute efficient solutions to anybody's allocative problems; its task is to explain the phenomena (including interpersonal exchange processes) which result from the circumstance that men are, in fact, engaged in seeking efficient solutions to their allocative problems.

It follows then, that Buchanan's quarrel is not, or ought not to be, with Robbins's own emphasis on allocation and choice at all, but is properly to be restricted to that literature that is concerned, in the name of economics, with the *attainment* of efficient solutions, and that evaluates the market primarily with respect to its efficiency as an "allocative mechanism." In fact it is obvious that Buchanan's own characterization of economics as concerned with the implications of the human propensity to truck, can, without strain, be subsumed under Robbins's economics. After all men *do* seek out exchange opportunities in the course of their attempts to avoid "wasting" their resources. Buchanan's understandable enthusiasm for the unique features that are present in a process of voluntary exchange, need not preclude him from recognizing these features as the logical implications of the fact that men do choose courses of action that exploit all discoverable opportunities of avoiding waste.

In brief the kernel of the Robbins allocation-formula is a methodological one. It focuses analytical attention upon a particular aspect of human activity. This makes possible the extraction of laws that permit an understanding, at a specified level of abstraction, of regularities that characterize social (and in particular, market) phenomena. The relevant aspect of human activity is that common to all action undertaken subject to scarcity, viz. the planful, allocative aspect. From the fundamental necessity imposed upon human beings to plan, to allocate, to choose, to compute, there derives a body of propositions that explain the phenomena of the market. Nothing in the Robbins formulation requires that the scientific excogitation of these propositions itself take the form of computing efficient solutions to any postulated economic problem.[3] In other words the

3. Buchanan is on firm ground when he questions the fundamentality of the Mayer-Robbins distinction between economic and technological activity that depends on the multiplicity of ends involved in the former. See my *The Economic Point of View* (Princeton, N.J.: D. Van Nostrand, 1960), pp. 127, 133–36, for a discussion of the similar objections raised by Knight and Rivett. It must be observed, however, that the broader concept of economic choice embraced by the writers to be cited below, does not rely at all on this distinction.

theorems of Robbins's economics are not "mechanical" in the sense in which the solution of a maximization problem can be mechanically computed from the relevant data. They do explain the emergence of those very market phenomena to which Buchanan properly and instructively wishes to draw attention. The theorems of Robbinsian economics do, in other words, explain how from the *individual* actions of market participants there emerge *social* phenomena; and how these social phenomena are completely different in significance from the separate ("computational") economic problems of the individuals. Of course Buchanan is at liberty to choose these social exchange processes themselves as being the primary focus of attention. But, if he so chooses, his implied rejection of the view of economics as an extended logic of choice must clearly rest on different, and far narrower grounds than those powerful objections which support Buchanan's rejection of the current allocation-economics.

II

But we may go further than this. It is not sufficient merely to show that the Robbins stress on the individual plan is not vulnerable to these objections of Buchanan. In fact we will discover that, on the contrary, it is precisely this stress on the individual plan that is able to lend force to these very objections. This can be seen most clearly by observing the striking similarity which Buchanan's objections bear to those of a group of writers, including Mises and Hayek, who emphasize the individual plan in economics even more vigorously than Robbins does.[4]

It is indeed significant that it is the still fashionable stress on the perfectly competitive model that typifies for Buchanan that which he finds objectionable in allocation-economics. It is remarkable that many of the strictures of writers such as Mises, Hayek and others of like methodological viewpoints—strictures that parallel those of Buchanan—became crystallized out of their extreme dissatisfaction with this same competitive model.

(a) These writers have consistently objected to a theory of price which, at each instant, assumes *that each participant in the market is powerless to bring about price changes*. Such a theory can merely enumerate the

---

4. On the relation between the praxeological view of economics expounded by the writers cited, and the allocation-of-scarce-means formulation of Robbins, see my *The Economic Point of View,* chapters 6 and 7.

conditions mathematically required for each individual to have reached his "equilibrium" with respect to given market prices. These writers have stressed that the very concept of a perfectly competitive market assumes that market equilibrium has already been attained, that the market process has already been fully carried out. The description of the competitive solution consists, therefore, merely in the listing of the conditions mathematically required in order that all of the market participants be simultaneously in positions of individual "equilibrium" with respect to a common set of market prices.[5]

(b) It is, as a consequence, only to be expected that *the market has come to be viewed merely as a computing device*—one of a number of conceivable similar devices—able to discover the set of actual prices and quantities that can satisfy these conditions. And the above cited writers have pointed this out forcefully.[6]

(c) In the same line of thought, these writers have, again similarly to Buchanan, vigorously rebelled against the theories which ignore the market *process,* and which concentrate on equilibrium *positions.* They stress, as Buchanan would have economists stress, the fact that markets *become* competitive; that it is the task of price theory to analyze the course of this process; that the degree of competitiveness is something to be explained, not something to be taken as data.[7]

(d) Moreover in the writings of the same group of economists is to be found recognition of the staggering theoretical difficulties that are calmly ignored when economists speak glibly about a nation solving "its" economic problem, of an efficient "social" allocation of resources, and the like. Almost inevitably habits of thought such as these are associated, as

5. See L. Mises, *Human Action* (New Haven, Conn.: Yale University Press, 1949), pp. 278, 375; F. A. Hayek, *Individualism and Economic Order* (London: Routledge & Kegan Paul, 1949), pp. 92–106; M. N. Rothbard, *Man, Economy, and State* (Princeton, N.J.: D. Van Nostrand, 1962), pp. 632f; see also the writer's "Rational Action and Economic Theory," *Journal of Political Economy,* August 1962, especially pp. 383–84, and *Market Theory and the Price System* (Princeton, N.J.: D. Van Nostrand, 1963), pp. 289–91.

6. Cf. L. Mises, *op. cit.* pp. 706f; M. Rothbard, *op. cit.* pp. 549f; see especially F. A. Hayek, "The Use of Knowledge in Society," *American Economic Review,* September 1945 (reprinted in *Individualism and Economic Order,* pp. 77–91).

7. L. Mises, *op. cit.* pp. 250–51; F. A. Hayek, *Individualism and Economic Order,* pp. 44f, 94f.

Buchanan penetratingly points out, with a failure to see the market as the embodiment of voluntary individual exchange processes.[8]

III

But, by following Buchanan away from the emphasis on individual choice, we would not only not be gaining the advantage that he offers to us (since we already possess that advantage), we would, on the contrary, be *sacrificing* an important advantage.

This advantage possessed by the Mises–Robbins view of economics as concerned primarily with the consequences of individual choice (an advantage not possessed by Buchanan's catallactics) is that *it relates economic theory to (what this writer believes to be) its appropriate epistemological underpinnings.* The final section of this paper will now very briefly spell out the nature of this advantage.

Much attention has been paid to the nature of the knowledge that is provided by economic analysis. For immediate purposes, a highly sophisticated debate in an extensive literature can be crudely summarized as follows: There are two views on the matter. The one view, by far the more popular one, sees economics as fundamentally an empirical science. Observation suggests certain regularities in economic phenomena; deductive logic then derives implications from these regularities. These derived propositions may then be tested against experience, leading to possible revisions in the assumptions originally adopted, or the incorporation of new postulates. In this view, therefore, economics provides knowledge obtained with broadly the same methods employed by the physical sciences.

The second, far less popular view, sees economics as providing knowledge of a fundamentally different character from that comprising the physical sciences. Economics, on this second view, provides knowledge concerning the real world, that is derived by considering the logical implications of human purposefulness, under various possible sets of circumstances. Insight into the purposefulness of human action provides economists with a tool for the acquisition of knowledge that is not

---

8. Cf. L. Mises, *op. cit.* pp. 691–93; F. A. Hayek, *The Counter-Revolution of Science* (Glencoe, Ill.: Free Press, 1952), p. 209, note 20; see especially the writer's *Market Theory and the Price System,* chapters 3, 13.

available to those who work in the physical sciences. The place of empirical observation in economics is reduced from a source of substantive knowledge to that of establishing the circumstances relevant to the analysis of the implications of human purposefulness. No assertion concerning economic matters can be made, according to this view, that does not take account of the fact that men seek to attain goals.

The writer has elsewhere set forth his opinion that this second view is by far the more fruitful of the two approaches and reflects most faithfully the nature of the theorems of price theory as traditionally developed.[9] For present purposes we note that this "praxeological" view implies adherence to a characteristic methodological approach. Economics is seen as a subjective, a priori, discipline with the individual *plan*—purposeful and allocative—the focal point of analysis.

The outstanding merit of the Mises–Robbins conception of economic science in terms of purposeful, allocative human choice, is thus its provision of an immediate link to what we have stated to be the true (praxeological) epistemological foundations of the discipline. It is true that Buchanan's catallactics might too (although of course not necessarily) be pursued as a praxeological discipline. But an enormous intellectual economy is achieved by couching the statement of the scope of a science in terms that identify directly the method of investigation proper to it. And it is this advantage which Buchanan's catallactics lacks. The purpose of this note has been to show that the exploitation by the Mises–Robbins conception of economic science of this advantage, by no means entails those objectionable features in current economics to which Buchanan so valuably draws our attention. On the contrary, we have tried to indicate, consistent exploitation of this advantage itself induces immunity against the aberrations that Buchanan criticizes.

9. See the writer's *The Economic Point of View*, chapters 6, 7; also *Market Theory and the Price System*, chapter 1.

The tragedy of "mainstream" economic theory is that its present crisis-like situation appears as the natural outcome of an intellectual process that was, perversely, set in motion by a series of significant theoretical advances. Somehow the dynamics of this history has produced, out of basically sound insights, an elaborate structure of theory, dazzling in its technical sophistication, inspiring in the architectonic quality of its intellectual edifice—but seriously deficient in any genuine understanding of the workings of market capitalism. Such, at any rate, is the "Austrian" perspective on the current state of the dominant Anglo-American "neoclassical" orthodoxy in economic theory.*

Several important aspects of this unique Austrian perspective need to be noted. First, this perspective sees the edifice of modern neoclassical economics as built upon essentially sound foundations. (This is certainly the case insofar as these foundations are compared with the general world view expressed in the classical economics which neoclassical economics replaced.) The required task of reconstruction does not, in the Austrian view, call for a radically different set of *fundamental* insights (as would be required, for example, by a Marxist view). On the contrary, the task of reconstruction calls, in part, for consistent attention to precisely those fundamental insights to which the dominant neoclassical tradition owes its beginnings—insights to which its proponents still, on occasion, pay lip service. Indeed, part of the difficulty encountered by Austrians in persuading their colleagues of the need for reconstruction arises out of the circumstance that many of these orthodox colleagues believe themselves to be *already* thoroughly in sympathy with what (to Austrians at least) appear to be the revolutionary insights which form the basis for Austrian economics.

From *The Crisis in Economic Theory*, ed. D. Bell and I. Kristol (New York: Basic Books, 1981), 111–22. Reprinted by permission of Perseus Books Group.

* The term "Austrian" economics has been used with a number of different meanings. For our purposes the term refers to the work now being done in this country by a group of younger economists who have rediscovered, especially through the work of Mises and Hayek, the value and fruitfulness of certain insights basic to the earlier school of Austrian economics, originating in the 1870s with Karl Menger in Vienna.

Second, the task of Austrian reconstruction is one which calls for a good deal of attention to the history of economic ideas, especially in the early years of modern economics. If the essentially healthy elements in modern neoclassical economics are to be preserved, if the basically sound ideas fundamental to it are to serve as the inspiration for a hoped-for reconstruction of the edifice, reconstruction dare not be undertaken without thorough familiarity with the sources of earlier mistakes. It is necessary to know where, in its earliest development, neoclassical economics went wrong. Only in this way may we hope to make over the shape of modern economics in a radical manner—yet without sacrificing its positive features.

Third, despite our remarks on the healthy roots of modern neoclassical economics, there should be no doubt about the gulf which separates the mainstream view of market capitalism from that with which Austrian economics proposes to replace it. *In the Austrian view, a thorough training in neoclassical economics simply does not equip one with a sensitive understanding of how the market economy works.* It is this very disturbing circumstance which has spurred the current resurgence of interest in the Austrian tradition.

THE EMERGENCE OF NEOCLASSICAL ECONOMICS

During the last three decades of the nineteenth century, mainstream economics underwent a series of drastic alterations. In 1870 a frayed and battered classical orthodoxy, represented typically by John Stuart Mill's *Principles of Political Economy* (1848), still struggled—in the face of widespread undercurrents of skepticism and incipient rebellion—to maintain its position of dominance. By 1900 fresh winds had conclusively swept out the old orthodoxy and had firmly installed its successor—a body of thought by no means homogeneous or monolithic, but one nonetheless often referred to generically as "neoclassical economics," in the broadest possible interpretation of that term. Mainstream historians of economic thought tend to see the various separate schools which made up the neoclassical revolution as having made their separate contributions within a broadly shared consensus. Before World War I, the various schools pursued their work with relatively little international cross-fertilization. Marshall in Cambridge, England; Walras, and later Pareto, in Lausanne, Switzerland; Menger and Böhm-Bawerk in Vienna, Austria; J. B. Clark in the United States, carried on their work, each in his own way, within the broadly shared neoclassical world view. It has come to be held that between the two World Wars the various strands of neoclassicism merged naturally, as a result of more vigorous international flows of ideas, into the body of thought which has, since World War II, dominated Anglo-American thought. Thus, in this view, the current orthodoxy has beneficially absorbed the special strengths of all these various schools. The "subjectivism" of the early Austrians, the "general equilibrium" system of Lausanne, joined the mainline of Marshallian and Clarkian economics to produce what is today taught on both sides of the Atlantic. From this historical perspective the Keynesian attack on neoclassical orthodoxy appears now, in retrospect, to have had relatively little permanent *revolutionary* impact. Although Keynesian macroeconomics successfully dominated the stage during the immediate postwar decades, it has since then come to be significantly assimilated to neoclassical orthodoxy, first through Samuelson's "neoclassical synthesis," and more recently as a result of sustained growth of interest in the "micro-foundations" of macro theory.

The Austrian perspective on the same historical period in the development of modern economics sees the picture somewhat differently. Careful study of the various schools at work before World War I reveals that the differences which separated them probably exceed in significance the elements generally held to justify grouping these schools together under the neoclassical umbrella. It is true that all the great post-1870 economists were attempting to recast economics along lines which (in contrast to classical economics) recognized the role of the consumer, of marginal utility, and of the demand side of markets. But, except for the Austrians in Vienna, this emphasis came to be subordinated to other, more dominant, themes. For both the Walrasians and the Marshallians, economic theory came more and more to point primarily toward the derivation of the conditions for market equilibrium. In these treatments the role of the entrepreneur came to be lost sight of, the dynamics of the market process came to be overlooked or misunderstood, and the role of competition came to be recast until its meaning for technical economics was almost the exact opposite of what it had meant to Adam Smith (and still means to the layman).

From this Austrian historical perspective, the absorption into Anglo-American orthodoxy of the ideas developed by the various separate pre–World War I schools assumes a different aspect. It was not that the various schools made their contributions to the development of an already commonly shared body of understanding. Rather it was a case of the dominant Marshallian neoclassical strand assimilating important features of Walrasian economics, as well as, in some degree, certain insights from other traditions. The confluence of Walrasian and Marshallian traditions had the consequence, it is now clear in retrospect, of decisively turning modern economics away from an appreciation of capitalism as a market *process*. It is in a number of respects ironic that the very injection of certain fundamental Austrian ideas into the Anglo-American orthodoxy (as occurred, for example, in 1932 with the appearance of Lord Robbins's justly celebrated *Nature and Significance of Economic Science*) seems to have helped crystallize the new direction taken by neoclassical thought.

As a result of the dominance achieved by this new direction, the older Austrian tradition came to be almost completely submerged. By the mid-1940s the dynamic view of the competitive market process shared (despite their differences!) by Austrians, such as Schumpeter, Mises, and Hayek, had become a view completely alien to the mainstream perspective. The success achieved during this period by Keynesianism contributed still further to the eclipse of the Austrian tradition. To an observer of the profession in the mid-1950s, the Misesian view appeared as one thoroughly discredited—or at least ignominiously ignored—by the mainstream of economic thought. That mainstream, by contrast, was enormously busy in developing sophisticated mathematical models, elaborate econometric techniques, and massive programs of empirical studies.

It is only in recent years that the younger members of the economics profession, in the United States, in Great Britain, and elsewhere, are finding it no longer possible to ignore the major flaws in the dominant view. A small but growing group of scholars has rediscovered the Austrian tradition and are engaged in a broad effort toward the restatement of economics along lines embodying the brilliant, neglected insights developed by the modern exponents of that tradition, Mises and Hayek. In what follows, I examine briefly the nature of the principal flaws in modern economics as seen from the Austrian perspective. This perspective is that which particularly emphasizes: the purposefulness of individual action; the role of knowledge in economic choice; the subjectivity of the phenomena that interest economists; the competitive-entrepreneurial character of the market process; and the *ex ante* role in which time affects economic activity.

SOME FLAWS IN NEOCLASSICAL ECONOMICS

Although Austrian critics of the modern neoclassical tradition often refer critically to the excessive technical sophistication affected by the present-day exponents of that tradition, such criticism should not be misunderstood. It is not so much that Austrians are driven to question the relevance, even in principle, of the mathematics and the econometric techniques which today fill the pages of the professional economic journals, nor is it even the conviction (often shared by non-Austrians) that the sheer bulk of the technical baggage is too massive and too abstract to be fruitfully applied in explaining the real world with which we wish to deal. Rather, Austrian skepticism of the technical sophistication that pervades modern economics stems from painful awareness that the attention paid to the formal apparatus has been responsible for failure to appreciate a number of insights crucially important for economic understanding. As a result, modern mainstream economics displays a number of related features which, for Austrians, appear as serious flaws. These features include especially: a) an excessive preoccupation with the state of *equilibrium*; b) an unfortunate perspective on the nature and role of *competition* in markets; c) grossly insufficient attention to the role (and subjective character) of *knowledge, expectations,* and *learning* in market processes; and, d) a normative approach heavily dependent on questionable *aggregation* concepts and thus insensitive to the idea of *plan coordination* among market participants. Together these flaws represent very serious distortions, at best, in the understanding of the market process in capitalist economies which modern neoclassical economics is able to provide.

Equilibrium

Probably the central notion in modern neoclassical economics is that of market equilibrium. A very large part of economics is concerned with working out the mathematical conditions which must be satisfied in order for particular markets to have achieved equilibrium—i.e., the state of affairs in which all plans are successfully carried out without disappointment and without reason for subsequent regret. A very large part of applied economic theory proceeds by assuming that market data can be treated as consistent with the hypothesis of markets being *already* in equilibrium. To a large extent the mathematicization of economics, as well as the disappearance of the entrepreneur from the theory of markets, can be attributed to the central role of equilibrium theory. For Austrians this pre-occupation with equilibrium represents a serious shortcoming. Without in any way denying the usefulness of the equilibrium concept as a tool of analysis, Austrians see the neoclassical emphasis on equilibrium as a failure to recognize the really important aspects of a market economy—namely, those which relate to the nature of market *processes*. Equilibrium economics has tended simply to take these processes for granted, treating them in effect as working so rapidly, and as being so definitely equilibrat-ing in their character, as to permit the analyst to assume instantaneous attainment of equilibrium. This is not only unrealistic; it leads to a totally false perception of the social usefulness of the market.

The inadequacies of equilibrium theory have not escaped the attention of contemporary theorists. I will a little later comment on the attempts being made, within the neoclassical framework, to address these inad-equacies. For our present purpose it is sufficient to point out that, despite these well-meaning attempts, the corpus of mainstream economics is still heavily dependent on the equilibrium assumption. It is precisely the widespread awareness of this crippling handicap which contributes to the crisis-like atmosphere surrounding contemporary discussion of eco-nomic theory.

Competition
Economists have always emphasized the beneficial role of competition in market processes. Sad to say, neoclassical economics long ago developed a technical notion of *static* competition which is not only antithetical to that used in everyday layman's speech, but which, more seriously, fails entirely to appreciate the nature and enormous importance of dynamic competition. Not only did neoclassical economics introduce a meaning to the term "competition" which is almost the opposite of its ordinary meaning, but, in so doing, it diverted attention from market *processes*.

For neoclassical economics a "perfectly" competitive market means a market already in full equilibrium, in which individual buyers and sellers have no discretion with respect to price whatsoever—price having been already somehow set at the level such that utility-maximizing buyers and profit-maximizing sellers make the set of decisions which will clear the market. Competition is thus a state of affairs in which there is no need and no opportunity to "compete," in the everyday sense of striving to outdo one's competitors.

This notion of competition is so obviously bizarre, unrealistic, and unhelpful in understanding markets, that it long ago led to attempts within the neoclassical paradigm to replace it with more realistic models, notably that of "monopolistic competition." In the 1930s and 1940s Joseph A. Schumpeter (who in this respect, at least, was thoroughly Austrian) ridiculed the standard competitive models. Unfortunately, the attempts to replace the unrealistic economists' notion of competition by and large failed. On the one hand, the substitutes that were offered suffered from serious limitations of their own. On the other, the mainstream of economics still proceeded to use—almost without compunction—the standard, unrealistic, static concept of competition.

For Austrians, an economics built around this unfortunate notion of perfect competition is seriously inadequate. Not only does it reinforce the regrettable preoccupation with equilibrium, it has also been responsible for a disastrous failure to understand the requirements for, and benefits of, the dynamic kind of competition (in which the conditions of the economists' static view of perfect competition are in fact *necessarily violated*). The results of this failure include, among other matters, a misunderstanding of the role of advertising in modern economics, as well as an approach to the economics of anti-trust which has seriously threatened the efficiency and vitality of American industry. Instead of recognizing the critical importance for dynamic competition of *freedom of entry* (and of the harmfulness of all the well-meaning governmental regulatory actions which have eroded this freedom in modern times), mainstream economics has supported the view that sheer size is *per se* anti-competitive, and that the presence of any discretion to a firm, with respect to price, is essentially sinister.

The work of industrial-organization theorists has also come to recognize the harm wrought by the dominance of the perfectly competitive model in mainstream economics. A good portion of the widespread dissatisfaction with contemporary theory must indeed be laid at the door of this model.

Knowledge, Expectations, and Learning

The shortcomings associated with neoclassical preoccupation with equilibrium and "perfect" competition, can be traced to a deeper flaw—a failure to recognize the role of knowledge in the face of radical uncertainty, and of learning processes in dynamically competitive markets. For mainstream economics, objective data are viewed as somehow able instantly to determine the decisions of market participants. Until quite recently the main body of neoclassical theory was entirely comfortable with the assumption of perfect knowledge. No attention was paid to the extent to which buying and selling decisions must express the expectations being held with respect to *other* people's buying and selling decisions. No attention was paid to Hayek's demonstration that market equilibrium means the possession by market participants of sets of mutually sustaining expectations with respect to one another's actions.

This neoclassical lack of appreciation for the role of knowledge and expectations has gone hand in hand with failure to recognize the nature and significance of *entrepreneurial discovery* in an uncertain world. In particular it has been responsible for misunderstanding the nature of competitive market processes, and for failure to ask the relevant questions with respect to whether or not the *learning* sequences, of which such processes consist, are likely to be equilibrating. For Austrians, sensitized to awareness of these matters, all this adds up to a powerful indictment of mainstream economics.

Allocation, Aggregation, and Social Welfare
Economic theory has always been pursued not only for the light of understanding which it promises, but also for the fruit of improvement in the well-being of society for which such understanding might be deployed. The neoclassical framework within which mainstream economics has pursued these latter ("normative") interests, contains certain key features which, in the opinion of Austrians, compound the faulty perception of market capitalism which that tradition represents.

First, normative economics is conducted in terms of a notion of *social allocational efficiency* which begs the very essence of the normative problem. Second, the economic well-being of society has (partly under the impact of macroeconomic thinking popularized by Lord Keynes) come to be identified with such deeply flawed *aggregate* notions as gross national product and the like.

For Austrians, to see the economic problem of society as one of efficiently allocating scarce social resources for the attainment of social goals, is not only to extend misleadingly the notion of choice from the level of the individual (where it properly belongs) to that of society as a whole (where it can only apply as a metaphor). Far worse, it is in effect to assume away essential elements of the question. For the notion of social allocation of resources must assume that *somehow it can already be known* (how? to whom?) exactly what the available resources of society are, and exactly what is to be the relevant priority ranking of social goals. As Hayek has shown, it is the essence of the social-economic problem to grapple with the obvious circumstance that these matters are in fact *not* known to any single mind at all. Indeed, from the Austrian perspective the social relevance of the market process lies precisely in the extent to which it facilitates the way in which scattered (and even as yet entirely undiscovered) information is mobilized and brought to bear upon decision making.

Austrian criticisms of *aggregate* notions of social economic welfare derive both from the methodological individualism and from the subjectivism embedded in the Austrian tradition. Aggregate notions of welfare imply that there is some objective entity such as "output" which can be aggregated across individuals for purposes of welfare comparisons. For Austrians this raises well-nigh insuperable conceptual problems. The circumstance that such aggregates rely on market prices to achieve value homogenization of physically heterogeneous products only compounds Austrian unhappiness.

The truth, as seen by Austrians, is that economic welfare—consisting as it does of nothing but the subjective sense of well-being of separate *individuals*—displays an interpersonal incommensurability which simply defies aggregation. Moreover, market prices at any given time are sure to be *dis*equilibrium prices, and thus wholly inappropriate for purposes of aggregation (even if aggregation were unconcerned with welfare aspects of output). More fundamentally, perhaps, the Austrian emphasis on the individuality of choice and on the crucial significance of mutual expectations, on the basis of which choices are made in society, focuses attention on normative issues that have been wholly neglected by mainstream economics. For Austrians such questions as the coordination of plans, the extent to which decisions of different individuals can be systematically modified by market experience to more correctly anticipate each other's preferences, and the degree to which disequilibrium prices contribute to such improved anticipation through generating opportunities for entrepreneurial discovery, are all at the heart of normative discussion. But they are nowhere to be found in mainstream normative economics.

THE MONETARY FRAMEWORK: FURTHER FLAWS

For market capitalism to work smoothly and effectively in the coordination of the plans of market participants, a reasonably stable monetary framework is an important requirement. For Austrians one of the gravest consequences of mainstream economics during the present century has been persistent mismanagement by governmental monetary authorities—mismanagement that has again and again brought in its train inflationary booms followed by bouts of depression. Mainstream Keynesian economics, it is now fairly widely felt (by non-Austrians as well as by Austrians), has failed miserably to live up to its presumptuous claims of having rendered economic instability obsolete. Contemporary disillusionment with the Keynesian mainstream has in large measure arisen from a shrewd suspicion that Keynesian policies are not only inadequate to ensure stability, but have in fact been to blame for its disappearance. For today's intelligent layman to put the mainstream economist in his place, it is only necessary for him to ask the now well-known and troublesome questions about inflation and stagnation.

To Austrians these mainstream failures appear as natural consequences of neoclassical misunderstanding of market processes and of its blindness toward the critical importance of plan coordination. The decades of Keynesian ascendancy emerge as a period during which it was somehow blithely believed possible to analyze the interaction of various "macro" variables without any examination of the micro-underpinnings of these aggregate entities. It was held possible, for example, to examine the impact of changes in the money supply without considering their structural consequences, as manifested through the market interplay of individual transactions. To put it somewhat differently, it was held possible to talk, say, of "price level" changes consequent upon increases in the supply of money, in a manner assuming that possible changes in *relative* prices (and the consequences of such changes) may be safely ignored. It was held possible to talk, say, of changes in aggregate "investment" without regard to the delicate web of plans governing the social structure of capital utilization, and the role of relative prices in achieving and modifying this structure of production. The insight that market forces—with all the scope they provide for action based on erroneous information, and for the incentives they offer for the entrepreneurial discovery of such errors—govern monetary phenomena as well as "real" phenomena, was missed. The tragic result of all this has been that mainstream economics has, to its shame, come to appear to endorse the popular and dangerous folklore that in order to stimulate economic activity and to avoid depression, it is necessary merely to inflate the money supply. That such inflation may induce serious distortions in the economy, that it may systematically foster failures of coordination among the decisions of individual market participants, are concerns that have tended not to disturb mainstream economists.

RESCUE AND RECONSTRUCTION

Contemporary mainstream theorists have not remained entirely unaware of all the shortcomings that have been briefly noted here. A good deal of work appearing in current journals is in fact directed at extending mainstream economics to deal with such matters as market processes during disequilibrium, the role of uncertainty, and the search for information. The need to provide "micro foundations" for macroeconomics is by now almost universally conceded, and considerable work in this direction has been achieved, much of it involving careful attention to the role of individual expectations in market responses to macro policy. These efforts are most encouraging, as far as they go. Nevertheless, to Austrians these efforts seem unlikely to effect the radical repairs so sorely needed by the leaky structure of contemporary neoclassical theory.

The fact is that these efforts at improvement are directed at specific perceived limitations of existing theory. Unfortunately, they appear generally not to recognize the extent to which the entire theoretical structure needs reconstruction. Instead of dismantling the elaborate equilibrium models of which neoclassical economics consists—and appreciating the subtle processes of spontaneous learning made possible by market interaction under imperfect knowledge—the new work seeks to address the problems by constructing even more complicated equilibrium models. Instead of recognizing the high price (in fundamental economic understanding) paid in order to deploy sophisticated technical tools of dubious practical value, the new work has largely taken the form of pouring still more intellectual investment into the technical tool kit. Instead of seeking to escape the mechanical quality which neoclassical theory has imparted to economic analysis, much of the new work (notably that centered around the "economics of search") has tended to extend that mechanical quality to areas (such as those of knowledge and discovery) which had, until recently, mercifully escaped it. The Austrian economist is compelled to conclude that the new work is being conducted along lines that, unfortunately, simply do not point in the required direction.

For Austrians the present state of economics is seen to stem naturally from its historical development. Consideration of this background appears to identify very clearly the direction of required reconstruction. Neoclassical mainstream economics possesses great virtues. With all its faults, it does perceive the market economy as an interlocking array of individual decisions. It perceives the pattern in which decisions at the level of production are inextricably linked with expected decisions of resource suppliers and of prospective consumers. What is required is to retain these fundamental insights, and to begin to explore, with a humility which sophisticated model building is somehow unsuited to generate, the way in which individual decisions are likely to be modified by the discovery of error, by the awareness of radical uncertainty, and by the awareness of the *futurity* of the perceived time dimension within which decisions must be made. Economic theory needs to be reconstructed so as to recognize at each stage the manner in which changes in external phenomena modify economic activity strictly *through the filter of the human mind.* Economic consequences, that is, dare not be linked functionally and mechanically to external changes, as if the consequences emerge independently of the way in which the external changes are *perceived,* of the way in which these changes affect expectations, and of the way in which these changes are discovered at all.

Of course, these are very "Austrian" prescriptions. Contemporary Austrian economists indeed believe that the tradition which they have rediscovered offers the strongest hope for economics in its present time of crisis.

LIONEL ROBBINS'S *NATURE AND SIGNIFICANCE*, FIFTY YEARS LATER

Time is likely to lend helpful perspective to the appreciation of any classic work. The passage of years is likely to have produced more sensitive understanding of the currents of thought that led up to the work in question; and, again, that passage of time permits the identification of currents of ideas to which the work in question may have itself made decisive contribution. All this seems particularly relevant to the consideration of Lord Robbins's *An Essay on the Nature and Significance of Economic Science,* a remarkable book that has been a classic, now, for a full half century since its first edition was published in 1932. I shall argue in this paper that Robbins's book occupies a less-than-fully understood place in the history of twentieth-century economic thought.[1] This reappraisal, it turns out, could hardly have been possible without insights provided by recent developments in economic discussion. These developments, we shall maintain, permit us to understand more adequately in what Robbins's contribution consisted, and how that contribution impinged upon the course of ideas in this century. In particular, we can now perceive (a) how the Robbinsian contribution of 1932[2] represented a turning point in the history of modern economics; (b) how this contribution consisted of the injection, into English-language economics, of insights central to the Austrian tradition stemming from Menger, but also how (c) the specific turn subsequently taken by economics came, as a result of the particular formulation embraced by Robbins, to proceed in a direction not at all consistent with that toward which the Mengerian tradition was itself to lead. Let us see how this rather confusing sequence of intellectual events came to pass. The clue is to be found in what must strike many as a puzzling aspect of some extremely sharp, early criticisms which Robbins's book had to encounter.

ROBBINS, THE AUSTRIANS, AND POSITIVISM

In May 1933 R. W. Souter published a bitter attack on Robbins's book in a lengthy article in the *Quarterly Journal of Economics.*[3] Souter began his critique by drawing attention to the book's Austrian character and

A paper delivered at the annual meeting of the History of Economics Society, Duke University, May 25, 1982, C. V. Starr Center for Applied Economics, Economic Research Report R.R. 82–12. Reprinted by permission of C. V. Starr Center for Applied Economics, New York University.

to the novelty of this character to English-speaking economics. The work, Souter wrote, "provides English and American students with an able, scholarly and succinct account of the main tenets of 'the Austrian School' (it is Professor Robbins's *credo* as an adherent of that school)." That Souter is correct in this judgment of the extent of Austrian influence is hardly subject to dispute. Robbins's book is simply studded with references to and quotations from Austrian writers, especially Menger, Mayer, Mises, Strigl and Hayek—as well as to that "British Austrian," Philip Wicksteed. And in the 1932 preface, the only two sources of influence to be identified are "Professor Ludwig von Mises and . . . the late Philip Wicksteed," to whose works "especial indebtedness" is acknowledged.

But then, having thus identified the Austrian background of Robbins's work, Souter proceeded to attack its major propositions in terms both vehement and bitter. It will be useful to refer to Talcott Parsons's report of Souter's attack: "The principal terms of opprobrium which Souter freely applies to Robbins and his ilk are 'atomism,' 'exclusionist positivism,' and 'static formalism.' In these are implied five interrelated concepts. . . . The one of most general bearing and hence the natural starting point is 'positivism.'"[4] It should be observed that, while Parsons couched his own critique of Robbins in terms far less intemperate than those employed by Souter, he nonetheless concurs with Souter in finding Robbins "continually being pressed into a radically positivistic position,"[5] and points out further that by opening "the door wide open . . . to radical rationalistic positivism" Robbins is in effect rendering the "subjective aspect" of actions merely an "epiphenomenon."

Here surely the present-day reader must feel inclined to rub his eyes. In the same breath, it seems, the work of Robbins is being identified as Austrian and is being criticized for radical positivism and for insufficient appreciation for the subjective character of economic phenomena! For most economists, surely, the Austrian School, (and especially Ludwig von Mises, through whose work the school evidently influenced Robbins most decisively) are best known for the thoroughgoing extent of their subjectivist approach; and many economists are surely aware of Mises's lifelong crusade against the influence of "positivists" (of all kinds) upon economics. The spectacle of Robbins, the acknowledged Austrian, being pilloried for insufficient subjectivism and for "radical positivism," seems, at first glance, to be puzzling indeed.

Souter (and to a lesser extent Parsons) built their case in regard to their allegations of Robbinsián positivism principally on three bases. They found positivism (a) in Robbins's belief that is is possible (and a scientific desideratum) to construct a positive science of economics without introducing normative considerations; (b) in Robbins's insistence on the general, abstract, and analytically independent character of economic reasoning, neither permitting nor requiring any organic integration with other social sciences; (c) in Robbins's conception of individual economic activity—a conception upon which he depends for his analytical definition of the nature and scope of economic science. In this paper we will not be concerned at all with the first of these three aspects of Robbins's work. Most of our discussion will relate to the third (with certain implications, in passing, also for the second).

ENDS, MEANS, AND ECONOMIZING

Robbins's conception of individual economic activity, and his definition of economics in terms of such individual allocation in the face of scarcity, is well-known. "Economics," Robbins declares, "is the science which studies human behaviour as a relationship between ends and scarce means which have alternative uses."[6]

The feature of human behavior called into being by this relationship is that of *choice*. "When time and the means for achieving ends are limited *and* capable of alternative application, *and* the ends are capable of being distinguished in order of importance, then behaviour necessarily assumes the form of choice. . . . It has an economic aspect."[7] Even in the "simplest case" considered by Robbins, that of "isolated man dividing his time between the production of real income and the enjoyment of leisure," there is an economic aspect to the situation. This aspect consists in the circumstance that, given the scarcity of means, their alternative applicability and his differential valuation of real income and leisure, this isolated man "has to choose. He has to economise. The disposition of his time and his resources has a relationship to his system of wants. It has an economic aspect."[8]

Economic activity, as conceived in these terms, occurs, Robbins emphasizes, also in the context of the "isolated economy" of Crusoe, and in the communist economy. But in these contexts economic analysis has little to offer. From "the point of view of isolated man, economic analysis is unnecessary."[9] By "the very *raison-d'être* of a strictly communist society" economic analysis is "debarred from any but the simplest generalizations."[10] The usefulness of economic analysis arises in the context of the exchange economy, the phenomena of which "can only be explained by . . . invoking the operation of those laws of choice which are best seen when contemplating the behaviour of the isolated individual."[11]

Here, then, we have Robbins's conception of the scope and function of economic science. Economic science has the function of explaining the phenomena of the market economy by tracing these phenomena back to the choices of the individual market participants. There can be no doubt that this conception of economics has had profound influence on the course of twentieth century economic thought. This can be seen most clearly, perhaps, by noticing how *commonplace* this view (at least insofar as microeconomics is concerned, or insofar as the need is recognized, on the part of macroeconomics, for an understanding of its "microfoundations") must seem to the modern student. Yet when Robbins wrote, his conception of economics was far from being a commonplace. Robbins found it necessary to explain, gently but firmly, that it is inaccurate and unhelpful to define economics in terms of the "causes of material welfare." This latter definition, Robbins observed, was explicit or implicit in the works of the leading neoclassical economists of the era, particularly in the works of Cannan, Marshall, Pareto and J. B. Clark.[12] Robbins was not tilting at windmills when he found it necessary to explain, a bare fifty years ago, that "it is not the *materiality* of even material means of gratification which gives them their status as economic goods; it is their relation to valuations."[13] (Indeed Robbins's own teacher, Edwin Cannan, whom Robbins had taken as his principal target, gladly took up the cudgels—in his review of Robbins's book—in defense of the material-welfare criterion.[14])

If, then, a modern economic textbook devotes an entire (brief) chapter to credit Robbins's *Nature and Significance* with the breakthrough leading up to the contemporary view that "the core of pure economic science is the general theory of choice,"[15] this is by no means an exaggeration of Robbins's influence. What is now a commonplace was, in 1932, something of a revolutionary idea; since then this idea has decisively altered the direction of mainstream economic thought. During the heyday of Keynesian influence this decisive Robbinsian influence was perhaps easier to overlook. But since the resurgence of neoclassical microeconomics this influence has become more and more apparent to the historically minded observer.

As mentioned, this influence represented the absorption of modes of economic thinking that had been developed by the Austrian School from Menger to Mises and his circle. Yet we must emphasize that anyone familiar with the work of the present day "Austrian" followers of Mises, will immediately recognize the profound differences separating the modern Austrian view of economics, from that embedded in the currently resurgent neoclassical microeconomics. We shall see that the basis for this paradox in the history of ideas lay in what Souter and Parsons identified as Robbins's "positivism." We shall argue that this "positivism" of Robbins constituted neither an accurate transmission of the subjectivist Menger–Mises tradition, nor, on the other hand, a crude distortion of it. Rather the Robbinsian statement represented an unself-conscious *simplification* of the Austrian subjectivist tradition—a simplification that certainly seems, from at least one perspective, as entirely excusable, but to which must, at the same time, be partly attributed many of the "un-Austrian" aspects of modern neoclassical microeconomics.

SUBJECTIVISM AND SUBJECTIVISM

From its very beginning, of course, the Austrian School was identified as being "subjective." Whereas the classical theory of value had sought explanations in terms of the objective conditions surrounding production, the Austrians emphasized the market processes initiated by the actions of valuing consumers. Robbins's work is certainly not inconsistent with this aspect of Austrian subjectivism (although it was apparently not relevant to the book's principal purposes to emphasize the subjectivist roots of its general perspective). A conception of economics as the science of choice, in Robbins's sense, is certainly asserting that observed phenomena become explicable only in terms of the preferences subjectively held by the independently choosing individual market participants. But explorations of subjectivism in recent years have drawn our attention to several quite different levels of subjectivism at which individual choice may be discussed. From the perspective of the more profound (or "extreme") insights into subjectivism, discussions pitched at less profound levels must indeed appear as being almost "positivistic." Robbins's characterization of economic choice does, in fact, seem to suppress the more profound insights into the subjectivism of human action. And here, we submit, is the clue to the puzzle cited earlier: Robbins's being simultaneously cited and criticized as Austrian and as being "positivistic." Let us see what all this means.

From several recent discussions of subjectivism there has emerged a sharp distinction between two distinct levels of discourse. One terminology identifies the two levels as static subjectivism and dynamic subjectivism respectively.[16] (After Professor Machlup's delightful survey of the numerous different uses made in economic terminology of the static-dynamic distinction, it is of course wholly unnecessary to spell out which of these two levels is the more profound.)[17] There are some differences between different formulations of the distinction. But a useful criterion for such a classification is supplied by the well-known contributions of G. L. S. Shackle to the analysis of human decisionmaking. In a stream of fascinating, persuasive, and by new justly famous books over the course of some two decades,[18] Shackle has been concerned to emphasize the radical *creativity* and *indeterminacy* of the human decision. Each decision is a spontaneous new beginning, not at all the inexorable outcome of some previously given configuration of preferences and obstacles. Social history is a fabric woven out of the continual emergence of such mutually interacting new beginnings. These decisions are made in the face of the need to speculate on the course of future events, when the future is shrouded in ineradicable uncertainty. Moreover the essential unpredictability of the future is itself partly the consequence of our complete certainty that the future will be shaped, in large part, by intrinsically unpredictable future human decisions. From this Shacklean perspective, a "dynamically" subjectivist view of social history sees it as being governed by forces that must be traced back to choices being made, at each and every moment, by individual market participants *whose decisions can in no manner or form be treated as flowing inexorably out of the objective circumstances* prevailing at the instant prior to these respective decisions.

This view of the subjective character of human choice is contrasted sharply with that other ("static") level of subjectivist analysis in which the creativity and inherent indeterminacy of decisionmaking is, at least tacitly, suppressed. The "statically subjectivist" view portrays the decision as indeed expressing the subjective preferences of the decisionmaker, but makes it appear as if these preferences are somehow separate from (and even, in some versions, chronologically prior to) the decision itself, and as if these preferences then "determine" the specific decision taken. The course of social history is then seen as the "inexorable" flow of events emerging from these interacting decisions (it being understood that such "inexorability" is strictly relative, of course, to the independent, "subjective" preferences of potential decisionmakers).

As Shackle and others have pointed out, the human decision envisaged in such a "statically" subjectivist view, hardly constitutes a genuine *choice* at all.[19] The very circumstance that the "chosen" course of action is seen as already inexorably implied in the given configuration of preferences and constraints, of ends and means, makes the choice "mechanical" or "automatic"—and thus not a true choice at all. True choice surely requires the realistic possibility of more than one alternative; but for the statically subjectivist view the rejected alternative is *already, before* (or at least apart from) the moment of decision, an option declared to be a sub-optimal (and thus a quite unthinkable) alternative. The circumstance that, in this statically subjectivist view, the scales of individual preference, or the relevant indifference maps, are declared to be the expression of independent subjective likes and dislikes, does not suffice to invest this "mechanical" model of decisionmaking with the characteristics of genuine choice.

Yet it is by now well-known that the sense in which modern neoclassical economics is a "science of choice" is none other than that which confines choice itself merely to the calculation of the optimal courses of action marked out by the relevant, given sets of preference rankings and constraints. For this microeconomics the phenomena of the market are, for the greater part, simply *required* to be such as to permit all such constrained optimization calculations to be simultaneously successfully carried out. There is nothing in the way in which such choices are envisaged, to suggest that it is the purposeful, alert decisions of market participants which independently *generate* the market processes which, at each moment, precipitate the market phenomena we observe. In other words it is by now well recognized that those features of neoclassical price theory to which Austrians demur, turn out to be derived precisely from these aspects of the neoclassical theory that express its unconcern with "dynamically" subjectivist considerations. It remains for us to show that, for all its Austrian credentials, the view of the economizing, allocative decision expressed in Robbins's *Nature and Significance* appears to suppress, or at least abstract from, such "dynamically" subjectivist considerations.

ROBBINSIAN CHOICE

We have referred earlier to the criticisms of Souter and Parsons directed against what they saw as Robbins's "positivism." At least part of these criticisms can be understood as expressions of dismay at Robbins's failure to recognize the "dynamic" subjectivism involved in human action. And, in the light of the careful analysis of the full subjectivism of human action more recently supplied by Mises and Shackle there can be little doubt of the validity, in this respect at least, of these early criticisms by Souter and Parsons.

The outcome of a Robbinsian act of choice, it appears, is inescapably implied in the given pattern of ends and of means the relationship between which is the prerequisite for Robbinsian choice. This outcome emerges, it seems to be asserted, in a manner almost beyond the control of the decisionmaker—it is instead "the resultant of conflicting psychological pulls acting within an environment of given material and technical possibilities."[20] To be sure the ends themselves, while given, are not fixed for all time. Ends can and do change: "sybarites become ascetics."[21] But the replacement of one set of given ends by a second set occurs *before* (or at least *outside*) Robbinsian choice itself. Whatever the process through which Robbinsian man chooses the system of ends with respect to which he must allocate his finite array of given means, this process not only lies wholly outside the scope of economic science, it lies outside the realm of economic choice itself. Economic choice, for Robbins, is circumscribed entirely by the framework of given ends and given means that makes systematic allocative behavior necessary. As Parsons points out, this unfortunate mechanical picture of choice is a consequence of the way in which Robbins treats ends as given, suppressing the futurity of the very notion of a human purpose.

There can be no objection, Parsons explains, to the treatment of means as given. "The 'conditions' of the situation in which a person acts, the means to his end are to be sure 'given' independently of his ends or desires. In this respect they are strictly analogous to the 'observations' of the scientist. But the same cannot be true of 'ends.' To be sure an 'end' may refer to a state of affairs which can be observed by the actor himself . . . *after* it has been accomplished. But at the time of inception of the action . . . such is not the case. Then it is 'subjective' to the actor."[22] An end is "the anticipation of a future state of affairs." To abstract from this essential feature of an end is to "denature" it, through the assimilation of ends to the category of "given data" for the actor.[23] The consequence of this treatment of ends as "given" to the decisionmaker must, Parsons continues, citing Souter, be to deny that action is a process of rational choice. The scale of valuation of different ends is now not itself a factor in action "but is merely a resultant, a reflection of the relative strengths"[24] of Robbins's "conflicting psychological pulls."

Human action is the expression of human purposefulness. In expressing his purposes man must choose between alternative imagined future scenarios. His imagination of these alternative futures is very much an intrinsic element of choice. At the moment of choice ends are not at all "given"; they are nailed down only through the act of choice itself. Whatever it is that accounts for the particular ends that are thus chosen to be aimed at, it cannot be the solution of a problem in constrained maximization for which these ends themselves are data.[25] A fully subjectivist treatment of choice could not, as Robbins does, avoid discussion of these matters. A fully subjectivist treatment of choice must grapple with the way the decisionmaker, with all his spontaneous creativity in the face of a radically uncertain world, *chooses* which of the infinite possible pictures of the future he adopts as the basis for the alternative scenarios among which he undertakes the path he is to pursue. Despite all its virtues, all its Austrian credentials, Robbinsian choice is portrayed in abstraction from (if not in complete denial of) the insights of truly dynamic subjectivism.

Let us sum up. We have seen that the Robbinsian contribution played a decisive and revolutionary role in diverting mainstream economics toward its modern neoclassical microeconomic form. We have seen that Robbins's contribution was made under the strong influence of the Austrian tradition. But we have seen again that the specific direction taken by modern neoclassical microeconomics is not at all that to which the Austrian tradition itself was pointing. Moreover we have seen that the source of contemporary Austrian dissatisfaction with neoclassical microeconomics consists precisely in that neoclassical failure to recognize the full subjectivism of human choice that we have now found to characterize Robbins's own formulation. Now then are we to understand Robbins's failure, in his transmission of the fundamental tenets of the Austrian tradition to the Anglo-American mainstream, to be sensitive to these subjectivist insights that, we can now see, are so crucial to the Austrian view as it has developed in this century? It might appear that only two possibilities lie before us: either the Austrian tradition as it had developed up until 1932 had itself failed to incorporate the subjectivist insights which later Austrians have learned from Mises and Shackle; or else Robbins, in bringing the Austrian message to his 1932 English readers, failed to grasp the full significance of Austrian subjectivism and was thus guilty of injecting only a garbled version of it into subsequent Anglo-American economic thought. In the remainder of this paper I shall argue that if one confines oneself to these two possibilities, then the first of them is closer to the truth, but that in fact there exists yet a third, and a more persuasive, possibility. This is that the Mengerian tradition *was* at heart fully subjectivist—so that Robbins indeed failed to transmit important aspects of that tradition; but that for many purposes these fully subjectivist aspects of the Austrian approach did not need to be invoked. What Robbins gave us in 1932 was not then a *distortion* of the Austrian view, but in fact a (possibly legitimate) *simplification* of that view. (It is for our purposes altogether unimportant whether Robbins himself was fully or even partly aware that he was giving anything other than a completely sensitive statement of the Austrian views. As Parsons indicated in 1934, any criticisms of Robbins for "positivism" must be directed not so much at what Robbins himself wrote, as at the logical implications of his formulation. The "pesitivistic" consequences implied by Robbins's work "can scarcely be said to constitute a statement of his position itself. The just criticism of him . . . is that, remaining on the surface, he fails to see and meet the very serious problems lurking underneath . . ."[26] Our position is that Robbins may, whether he so intended it or not, at least have had legitimate reason to remain on the surface.) Nonetheless, as historians of economic thought we should not fail to recognize that, whatever the justifications for and legitimacy of Robbins's simplified treatment, the extraordinary influence of that treatment has, as a result of this simplification, helped propel modern economics along a course quite different from the direction to which the Austrian tradition itself had pointed.

CHOICE AND CHOICE

It is of course true that an Austrian, explicitly and "dynamically" subjectivist, treatment of the nature of human action did not appear until Mises presented his fully developed ideas in the 1940s.[27] So that a superficially persuasive case could perhaps be made that the Austrian insights that Robbins had absorbed in the late twenties did not yet include the kinds of Mises-Shackle considerations that we have identified as unfortunately missing from *Nature and Significance*. But, on the other hand, it is not difficult to show that from the time of Menger onwards, there were frequent indications that the full subjectivist character of choice never went wholly unrecognized.[28] And it is difficult to believe that Mises of the late twenties (whose writings of the time on the epistemological character of economics came to be published as a collection of essays in 1933,[29] clearly anticipating

his more developed work of the following decade) failed to convey to Robbins his own powerful insights into the intrinsic *purposefulness* and into
the essentially *entrepreneurial* character of individual human action.[30]

The truth appears to be that while the post–World War I Austrians
were indeed steeped in a thoroughly subjectivist understanding of human
choice, it did not seem to them of crucial importance to emphasize every
single subjectivist insight for each and every analytical purpose. As Richard Ebeling has recently documented,[31] several of the Austrians cited by
Robbins had themselves offered during the twenties statements regarding economic choice that turn out to resemble Robbins's own later formulation in most important respects. What Robbins was then doing in
1932 was to follow the Austrians themselves in abstracting from certain
subjectivist aspects of choice, because, apparently, these aspects were
held to be of limited relevance to the purposes at hand.

But of course the circumstance that Robbins was merely employing
a simplification already employed by the Austrians from whom he drew,
does not, of itself, absolve either Robbins or the Austrians themselves of
the charge of "positivistic" distortion. The kind of abstraction and simplification, it may be objected, is by no means obviously possible. Either
one perceives the essentially spontaneous, undetermined, "dynamically"
subjective, character of human decisionmaking, or one does not. If the
Austrians indeed held a fully subjectivist view of choice, a critic may
surely be permitted to inquire, then how can any "simplified" version of
it, along Robbinsian lines, fail to constitute a "positivistic" distortion? The
answer to this question requires (a) that we examine more fully the relation between the Robbinsian abstraction and the fully subjectivist understanding of human choice; (b) that we recognize the state of mainstream
economics at the time Robbins offered his book to the profession.

Let us recapitulate the interrelated and overlapping features of Robbinsian economizing-allocative decisionmaking that render it a grossly
imperfect portrayal of individual choice: The Robbinsian view of decisionmaking (i) sees ends as somehow *given* prior to (or separately from)
the act of choice (failing to show how the choice of a system of ends to
replace an earlier cherished system must itself be understood in terms
of economic choice); (ii) suppresses the *futurity* surrounding the character of an end as perceived by the agent immediately prior to action; (iii)
is therefore able to abstract from the anticipation of radical *uncertainty*
that, in real life, pervades each choice act; (iv) permits it to appear as if

human choice was nothing but the mechanical resultant of conflicting psychological pulls, a conflict to which the chooser is little more than an interested observer. What we wish now to point out is that the features of human action that the Robbinsian formulation excludes (i.e. the selection of ends themselves, the futurity of ends, the uncertainty surrounding action, and the independent sovereignty of the individual over his acts of choice) represent features that, while never *wholly* absent from human action, yet influence different actions in quite different degrees. The truth surely is that for many decisions, the system of ends being consulted is (while never *entirely* beyond reexamination) taken as already well settled; that the context of action is often such that radical uncertainty is held to be of relatively tolerable proportions, and that the futurity of goals is of rather little moment; that the principal responsibility of the decision-maker is in fact sometimes not much more than to ensure the correct computation of the solution "mechanically" implicit in the given framework of required outputs and resource constraints. It is true that the act of choice must always, for Austrians, be recognized as involving more (in many cases, much, much more) than such mechanical computation. But the analyst of action may surely be excused for perceiving, within the haze of the uncertainty surrounding the inevitable futurity involved in choice, beneath the sparkle of the imaginativeness and the creativity pervading the human decision, that same stable pattern of allocative-maximizing computation that can never be absent from any decision, no matter how limited the imagined scope for uncertainty or for creativity. The very same human purposiveness that assures us that individual choice is always made with one's antennae alertly switched on to notice opportunities (that already "exist," or that may be created) worth pursuing even through the mists of an uncertain future—also assures us that each such choice at least implicitly embodies, as well, the kind of constrained maximization computation (no matter how sketchily performed) to which, in a world of complete certainty, choice would necessarily be entirely reduced. *If* it is thought useful to focus analytical attention upon this purely allocative element in human choice, it must surely be excusable to identify it in terms of a description of choice from which futurity and uncertainty have been abstracted. But, of course, this part of our discussion raises immediately the question: "*Is* it useful (or was it useful in 1932) to focus analytical attention upon the purely allocative element in human choice?"

Here we must be wary of permitting our historical hindsight such a free rein as to compel us immediately to reach an unambiguously harsh judgment concerning Robbins's procedure. We have already observed how Robbins's work can now be seen to have made decisive contributions to those unfortunate modern neoclassical developments that, from the modern Austrian perspective, have led to something of a crisis in contemporary economics.[32] It may seem difficult, therefore, to treat Robbins's formulation of the Austrian position as anything other than a deplorable aberration that has had predictably deplorable consequences.

A more sympathetic appreciation of the task faced by Robbins and the Austrians around 1930 in bringing a changed perspective to the mainstream English-language economics of the time, may perhaps soften our judgment. As Robbins himself explains, the conception of economic understanding as being constructed out of building blocks analyzing individual acts of choice was far indeed from mainstream thinking. The possibility of disentangling purely economic aspects of processes of social interaction from its attendant dense thickets of particular political, sociological, psychological phenomena, was not seen to extend beyond the Marshall-Pigou device of the measuring rod of money. Inevitably such failure to distil the purely economic processes at work beneath the masses of particular phenomena meant a clouding of the very possibility of pure theory in economics, and a tendency to succumb to the temptations of historicism. The need of the moment as it must have appeared to Austrians and to Robbins around 1930 was to reaffirm the legitimacy of economic theory, and to trace its possibility to the systematic analysis of the individual choices from which economic processes proceed. For this task, it may well have appeared, the full exposition of all the subjective subtleties of individual choice was by no means necessary. It was sufficient to emphasize the paramountcy of individual choice, to stress its relationship to the scarcity of means with respect to the ends of the moment and to point out the way in which this relationship is common to and thus transcends the myriad specific situations in which it may be concretely expressed. Robbins's presentation of the Austrian position, it may thus be argued, was a useful and legitimate simplification of the full subjectivist understanding of human choice. This simplification was legitimate, in this judgment, because, while it abstracted from the more profound subjectivist insights, it did focus on a meaningful and significant aspect of choice. This simplification was useful, because it permitted the essential Austrian message—essential for the immediate and important doctrinal purposes of the moment—to be conveyed without need to pay distracting attention to less immediately relevant features of the Austrian position.[33]

THE IRONY OF HISTORY

A half-century after the appearance of Robbins's classic work, we see it then as having been responsible for a supremely ironical historical episode. For its purposes of 1932 it presented the Austrian position in a form that (with some justice) evoked criticisms (from these deeply disturbed by the Austrian insistence upon the validity and possibility of a purely economic theory) of "positivism." These criticisms, it now seems, while in one sense entirely valid, seem less serious when viewed from the perspective of the overall Austrian purposes of the moment (with which of course the early critics themselves had little sympathy!) Nonetheless, we can now see, with the benefit of a half-century's hindsight, that the "positivism" in Robbins has indeed exercised powerful (and, to Austrians, regrettable) influence upon the course of twentieth century neoclassical microeconomics—along with its benignly successful influence toward the transformation of a science of material welfare into a science of human action.

NOTES

1. In preparing this paper the writer has had the benefit of having before him drafts of work by two authors, that relate to the theme of this paper. While certain fairly important differences separate the treatment here from that of each of these authors, I wish to acknowledge most gratefully the opportunity to learn much from each of these two works: (a) Mark Addleson, "Robbins's *Essay* after Fifty Years: The decline and Possible Rehabilitation of an 'Economics of Choice'" (1981, mimeo.); (b) Richard M. Ebeling, "The Marginalist Revolution: A Tale of Two Traditions" (a chapter in a dissertation-in-progress at University College, Cork, Ireland, entitled *Action Analysis and Economic Science, The Economic Contributions of Ludwig von Mises*).

2. Because today it is the second edition (London: MacMillan and Co. Ltd., 1935) which is widely used, all page references here are to this edition.

3. "'The Nature and Significance of Economic Science' in Recent Discussion," pp. 377–413.

4. T. Parsons, "Some Reflections on 'The Nature and Significance of Economics,'" *Quarterly Journal of Economics*, May 1934, p. 512.

5. Ibid., p. 514.

6. *Nature and Significance*, p. 16.

7. Ibid., p. 14.

8. Ibid., p. 12.

9. Ibid., p. 18.

10. Ibid., p. 19.

11. Ibid., p. 20.

12. Ibid., p. 4.

13. Ibid., p. 22.

14. E. Cannan, review of L. Robbins, *Nature and Significance, Economic Journal,* September 1932, pp. 424–27.

15. V. C. Walsh, *Introduction to Contemporary Microeconomics* (McGraw-Hill, 1970), p. 17.

16. See J. M. Buchanan, "The Domain of Subjective Economics: Between Predictive Science and Moral Philosophy," in I. M. Kirzner (ed.), *Method, Process, and Austrian Economics: Essays in Honor of Ludwig von Mises* (forthcoming, Lexington Books, 1982); G. P. O'Driscoll and M. J. Rizzo, as yet untitled book (forthcoming, Basil Blackwell, 1983), chapters 2 and 3; R. M. Ebeling, *op. cit.* See also L. M. Lachmann, "From Mises to Shackle: An Essay," *Journal of Economic Literature* 14 (March 1976), a brilliant and important paper which, however, sees the modern development of subjectivism in a manner different from that expressed in the present paper.

17. F. Machlup, "Statics and Dynamics: Kaleidoscopic Words," *Southern Economic Journal* (October 1959), reprinted in Machlup, *Essays in Economic Semantics* (Prentice-Hall, 1963).

18. Among the most important of these are G. L. S. Shackle, *Decision, Order and Time in Human Affairs* (Cambridge, 1969), and *Epistemics and Economics: A Critique of Economic Doctrines* (Cambridge, 1972).

19. See Shackle, *Epistemics and Economics, passim*; Kirzner, *Perception, Opportunity and Profit* (University of Chicago Press, 1979), chapter 13.

20. Robbins, *Nature and Significance,* p. 35.

21. Ibid., p. 26.

22. Parsons, *op. cit.* pp. 513f.

23. Ibid., p. 514.

24. Ibid., p. 516.

25. On the relationship between Robbinsian choice and the maximization of utility, see Robbins, *op. cit.,* p. 15n.

26. Parsons, *op. cit.,* p. 515.

27. L. Mises, *Nationalökonomie: Theorie des Handelns und Wirtschaftens* (Geneva: Editions Union, 1940); *Human Action* (New Haven: Yale University Press, 1949).

28. On this see R. M. Ebeling, *op. cit.*

29. L. Mises, *Grundprobleme der Nationalökonomie* (1933), also translated as *Epistemological Problems of Economics* (New York University Press, 1981).

30. L. Mises, *Human Action,* p. 253.

31. R. M. Ebeling, *op. cit.*

32. See Israel M. Kirzner, "The 'Austrian' Perspective," in D. Bell and I. Kristol (eds.), *The Crisis in Economic Theory* (New York: Basic Books, 1981).

33. The explanation suggested in the text may throw light on a circumstance that some have found difficult to understand: that several prominent Austrian economists (who were active participants in the Mises "Private Seminar" of the twenties) came to believe that by the early thirties the main insights of the Austrian tradition had become successfully absorbed into the neoclassical mainstream, so that there was therefore little further need for the distinctive Austrian tradition. While in retrospect it seems clear (as argued in the present paper) that the long-run need for a distinctive Austrian tradition became, if anything, *more* acute as a result of the absorption of Austrian influence via Robbins, we can at least understand how, from the perspective of the early thirties, it did indeed appear that the Austrians had succeeded in redirecting mainstream economics in the Mengerian direction.

RATIONALITY, ENTREPRENEURSHIP, AND ECONOMIC "IMPERIALISM"

In 1976 Gary Becker's *The Economic Approach to Human Behavior* introduced into social science a radical emphasis on the relevance of individual rationality in human behavior of all kinds, and argued that this rendered the conclusions of economic theory directly and overridingly applicable to areas of social interaction which had traditionally been treated as the "turf" of other social sciences. Brian Loasby was one economist who expressed serious reservations concerning what others have seen as "economic imperialism." Loasby was disturbed by a perspective which sees all areas of social science as being rendered subfields in a "universal" applied economics. "Becker . . . has claimed that this principle of coherent rationality not only provides a unified framework for the analysis of all human behaviour—itself a claim of astonishing ambition, if not arrogance—but that it is the only such basis—the only firm spot on which to stand" (Loasby, 1989, p. 191). Becker's position, which has been described as "hardboiled economism" (Green, 1996, p. 28), raises important issues relating to the very foundations of economic science.

In one sense, Becker's position reflects an old lesson which economists learned from Lionel Robbins in 1932,[1] viz. that economics does not deal with one specific *area* of human behavior, but rather with one specific *aspect* of *all* areas of human behavior. The self-same economizing, allocative aspect of human behavior which is salient in, say, the commercial areas of life conventionally dealt with in economic theory, is present, Robbins taught us, also in the religious or cultural fields of human endeavor. Wherever human purposefulness encounters the imperative to choose, imposed by scarcity of the necessary means needed to achieve all of one's goals, human beings will economize, allocate, and engage in constrained maximization. Similarly, Becker's position reminds us of the

From *The Driving Force of the Market: Essays in Austrian Economics* (New York and London: Routledge, 2000), 258–71. Reprinted by permission of Edward Elgar Publishing, Sheila C. Dow, and Peter E. Earl.; the original source is *Economic Organisation and Economic Knowledge: Essays in Honor of Brian J. Loasby*, ed. Sheila C. Dow and Peter E. Earl, vol. 1 (Cheltenham: Edward Elgar, 1999), 239–54.

assertion by Ludwig von Mises that economics is merely "a part, although the hitherto best elaborated part, of a more universal science, praxeology."[2] Praxeology is the general science of human action (with human action seen as deliberative choice under conditions of radical uncertainty). And human action manifests itself in all areas of endeavor:

> Choosing determines all human decisions. In making his choice man chooses not only between various material things and services. All human values are offered for option. All ends and all means, both material and ideal issues, the sublime and the base, the noble and the ignoble, are ranged in a single row and subjected to a decision which picks out one thing and sets aside another. Nothing that men aim at or want to avoid remains outside of this arrangement into a unique scale of gradation and preference."[3]

Both for Robbins and for Mises, economics is seen as the science of rational choice, and rational choice is seen as governing human action in all its departments. It might seem, then, that Becker's extension of economic analysis to govern explanation in all departments of social science is simply the consistent application of the "Austrian" (Robbins-Mises) position. The purpose of this chapter is to dispel such an impression. The Austrian tradition in economics which both Robbins and Mises were articulating, does not by itself lead to the economic imperialism of which Becker has, not without cause, been accused. There is an important difference between (a) the sense in which Becker understands the relevance of rational choice to areas outside the conventional scope of economics, and (b) the significance of Austrian insights concerning the universality of rational choice.

In fact there is something of an exquisite paradox here. On the one hand it is the universality of rational choice for Becker, which leads him almost ineluctably to see all possible explanations in social science as being reducible to applications of the standard theorems of economics. On the other hand, it will be shown that it is precisely the universality of rational choice for Mises, which entails our conclusion that the Austrian tradition which Mises represents, is unable to accept the direct applicability of the standard theorems of economics to the intellectual areas marked out by economic imperialists for annexation. All this requires careful explanation. Our explanation begins by way of an illustrative digression.[4]

A WORLD OF PERENNIAL OPTIMALITY: A DIGRESSION

What is generally known as the Coase Theorem draws attention to the possibilities which exist in free markets for spontaneous internalization of externalities through direct trading (between decision makers generating externalities, and the beneficiaries/victims of those externalities). Simple economics shows that all suboptimalities attributable to externalities correspond to unreaped potential gains from such trade. In the absence of transactions costs, it is therefore argued, it follows that all such potential gains from trade will be grasped; *all* externalities will have been spontaneously internalized. Furthermore, it came to be maintained, even in the presence of positive transactions costs, Coaseian logic argues for spontaneous market optimality despite the continued presence of externalities. After all, if transactions costs are positive, this simply means that gains from trade will be forgone due to the costs of the resources required to consummate such trade. But this merely means that such unconsummated possibilities for spontaneous internalization of externalities are, indeed, best left unconsummated: the social benefits are simply not worth the costs.

This kind of logic has been pushed to the bitter end to seriously argue that all conceivable kinds of apparent suboptimalities (e.g. those attributable to the exercise of monopoly power) must ultimately be declared (at least absent transactions costs) to be entirely consistent with social optimality, after all. As Calabresi put it:

> A misallocation exists when there is available a possible reallocation in which all those who would lose from the reallocation could be fully compensated by those who would gain, and, at the end of this compensation process, there would still be some who would be better off than before. [But this] . . . and other similar definitions of resource misallocation merely mean that there is a misallocation when a situation can be improved by bargains. If people are rational, bargains are costless, and there are no legal impediments to bargains, transactions will *ex hypothesis* occur to the point where bargains can no longer improve the situation; to the point, in short, of optimal resource allocation.[5]

And what Calabresi suggests as true for a zero-transaction-cost world, would, it is clear, *mutatis mutandis,* also be true for a world in which transactions are costly: *all* misallocations would be spontaneously traded away—since those not so traded because of transactions costs turn out not to have been net misallocations after all.

But all this leads us still further. Suppose government regulation blocks some negotiations or some trades. It might at first glance seem that if markets are not permitted to function, this surely permits misallocation to persist. But the economic logic we have cited has been applied even to this situation. Even here, the Coase-Calabresi logic *seems* to indicate, the world must be the best of all possible worlds since, after all, the regulations which block the reaping of potential gains from trade must be beneficial to some agents in society (or else it would pay those thwarted by those regulations from reaping gains-from-trade, to incur the financial and/ or political costs needed to eliminate such regulation). Clearly the benefits enjoyed by those whose protected positions are secured by regulation, are so considerable that we cannot pronounce the elimination of such regulation (even though it would ensure the reaping of potential gains from trade) to be a net social gain. The late George Stigler, pursuing this logic to its bitter end (an end many are likely to consider a *reductio ad absurdum*), argued that an economist pointing out an unwise (i.e. a misallocative) public policy, is really merely disagreeing with the valuations placed upon potential transactions by agents in the economy (or with the ethical validity of the manner in which decision-making rights are distributed among those agents). To declare a public policy to be economically "wrong" is therefore not to assert a scientific conclusion; it is merely to engage in "preaching." The world, according to its own lights, is *always* in an optimal state.[6]

But all this seems, surely, abundantly perverse. We know by casual observation that many situations in the world *are* suboptimal—not merely in "our" subjective evaluation of the alternatives, but, quite clearly and obviously, also in the evaluations of all the affected parties themselves. It is simply not the case, it is abundantly apparent, that at each and every moment the world has exhausted all relevant net-beneficial opportunities for mutually gainful negotiations. Economic logic seems to have somehow led seriously astray—even in the context of potential market activities which seem to fall squarely within the scope of conventional, non-imperialistic, economics.

THE ILLUSION OF PERENNIAL OPTIMALITY
EXPLODED: DIGRESSION CONCLUDED

The most simple and obvious explanation for where and how our economic logic has led us astray lies, it seems to us, in the assumption
concealed in that economic reasoning, to the effect that each and every
opportunity for mutually net-beneficial exchange between each and every
pair of individuals *must* be taken advantage of at the very instant when
such an opportunity emerges into existence. This assumption simply
rules out, even for the briefest span of time, the possibility of an available, as-yet unexploited opportunity for mutually net-beneficial exchange.
(This assumption thus formalizes the old, weak, joke in which an economist asserts that there are *never* any lost dollar bills to be found in Times
Square, because any such lost bills that *would* be in Times Square, will
already have been picked up.)

This obviously false assumption underlies and vitiates almost every
conclusion reached, on the basis of economic logic, in the preceding section of this chapter. It is not true that, with zero transactions costs, all
externalities must necessarily be spontaneously internalized; it is not true
that all net misallocations of resources must instantaneously have been
corrected (through the instantaneous exploitation of the entailed available potential gains from trade); it is not true that an economist pointing
out an obviously economically-flawed public policy measure is necessarily merely preaching. All these assertions are false simply because it is
entirely possible for an individual to pass up an available opportunity for
pure gain, without taking advantage of it. He may fail to take advantage
of it not because the costs of doing so (e.g. the costs of gaining the necessary information to do so) render this opportunity no longer one offering
net gain. He may fail to take advantage of such opportunity *simply because
he is not aware of its availability.* To be unaware of the availability of an
opportunity for pure gain (and thus to fail to exploit it), is not deliberately
to reject it because of the infinite cost of knowing about its existence; it is
not to be irrational; it is unwittingly to pass up an attractive opportunity
staring one in the face.

The assumption frequently encountered in economic theory that
denies any such possibility of unwittingly passing up an attractive opportunity, is based, in effect, on the assumption that the existence of available opportunities (including particularly opportunities to acquire needed

information at a worthwhile cost) is always known to all relevant parties. Austrian economics rejects this assumption, and thus insists on having us grapple with the very real possibility of unexploited opportunities for pure gain. In particular this requires us to recognize the possibility that pairs of individuals between whom exists the potential for mutually gainful trade may simply overlook such opportunities. And once we admit this very real possibility into our theoretical discussions, the idea of necessary perennial optimality immediately evaporates into thin air. There is nothing in economic reasoning which entails any such perennial optimality; the possibility of misallocated resources, of overlooked opportunities for mutually gainful exchanges, with or without transactions costs, and the possibility of genuinely economically wrong public policy, is alive and well—and fully consistent with economic analysis, properly understood.

ECONOMIC REASONING RECONSTRUCTED

Yet the theorems of economics which assume that all such opportunities have already been grasped and corrected, are certainly not without usefulness. Austrian (and, for that matter, non-Austrian) economists may not wish to see the economy as if it were, at each and every moment, in that state of affairs in which no available opportunities for gainful exchange remain. But, at the same time, they may recognize the existence of powerful tendencies which, in the absence of exogenous change, might eventually *be imagined* to culminate in such a state of affairs. There may indeed be important lessons to be learned by contrasting the world in which we live (characterized by unexploited opportunities for mutually gainful exchange) with a hypothesized world in economic equilibrium (in which no such unexploited opportunities remain). This does not reinstate equilibrium analysis as the central tool of economic understanding, but it does permit us to use equilibrium constructs as tools in helping us understand the phenomena of markets in disequilibrium. Austrian economics has indeed proceeded in this way, drawing attention (by careful analysis of such contrasting views of conceivable worlds) to the forces which are set in motion by the lure of pure entrepreneurial profit (opportunities for which exist whenever unexploited gains from trade are available for the taking).

In this perspective, understanding of market dynamics flows from the circumstance that opportunities for pure gain are created precisely when the conditions for equilibrium have not been fulfilled—so that disequilibrium conditions, by "switching on" entrepreneurial alertness to opportunities for pure profit, tend to initiate entrepreneurial actions which move toward the elimination of those disequilibrium conditions. (After all, every action taken to grasp pure entrepreneurial profit, tends to eliminate the price discrepancy of which that opportunity consists.) So that sound economic reasoning *does* show how equilibrating forces (that is, tendencies toward the disappearance of unexploited opportunities for mutually gainful exchange) are continually—despite the equally continual interference of exogenously created new opportunities—being set in motion.

DISCOVERY AND THE RELEVANCE
OF INSTITUTIONAL SETTING

It should be noticed that this entrepreneurial process of becoming alert to as-yet ungrasped opportunities for pure profit, depends crucially on the circumstance, unique to the institutional setting of the market, that earlier errors do translate into identifiable lumps of pure prospective net gain. A number of perceptive readers of (earlier drafts of) this chapter have pointed out that even in an institutional setting which does not translate errors into such identifiable lumps of pure gain, we might expect a systematic tendency for error correction. After all, if unexploited opportunities exist for mutual gain through exchange between two parties, A and B, in an institutional world in which no entrepreneurial arbitrage activity is permitted, we may nonetheless postulate eventual mutual discovery of each other, by A and B, simply as a result of the "entrepreneurial" propensity of alert human individuals to become aware of opportunities available to them—even if the gain available as a result of exchange cannot be isolated as a pure lump of gain available to any imagined "pure" entrepreneur. Our response to this thoughtful observation is that the phenomenal rapidity with which we observe markets to absorb and respond continually to new information does clearly appear to depend upon the remarkable circumstance which characterizes markets—namely that unexploited opportunities for interpersonal mutually gainful exchange, become translated into pure profit opportunities, available to pure arbitraging entrepreneurs. While there is indeed an entrepreneurial element in all human action, it is the scope offered by markets, for pure arbitraging entrepreneurship to be exercised, which is responsible for the swift adjustments of markets to exogenous changes.

It is markets, under institutional arrangements which include especially the possibility of buying at a low price in order to resell at a higher price, which are responsible for the initiation of those systematic processes of error-correction which we understand as making up the process of equilibration. While interaction between alert human beings can be expected to result in some relevant gradual mutual discovery under any institutional circumstances, the speed of such discovery processes within markets is clearly of an entirely different order of magnitude than is conceivable outside markets.

What is responsible for the initial existence of potential lumps of pure gain, under market institutions, is not any cost of transacting, of gaining knowledge, or the like, but merely sheer ignorance, utter unawareness of these opportunities (including, as we have seen, the opportunities available for deliberately acquiring relevant knowledge). The spontaneous learning required in order for misallocations (represented by unexploited exchange opportunities) to be corrected, is inspired by the circumstance that this sheer ignorance translates itself (within the institutional setting of individual rights to property and thus to market arrangements) into pure profit opportunities. Were this translation not to occur, we would be unable to rely upon any economic forces for the generation of those discoveries which had hitherto not been made. Ignorance attributable to the costs of deliberate learning may be expected to be eliminated by deliberate learning as (and if) these costs become lower. But the sheer ignorance which we have seen to occur even in the absence of costs of deliberate learning, cannot be expected systematically to disappear with any rapidity without definite cause. The lure offered by pure profit opportunities represents such a possible cause. It is only within the market setting that this cause can operate. Outside the market context we have nothing, within the realm of economic theory, upon which we can rely to generate any systematically rapid processes of mutual discovery that might tend to eliminate episodes of social suboptimality (caused by sheer ignorance).

RATIONALITY, EQUILIBRIUM, AND
THE SOURCE OF ECONOMIC IMPERIALISM

Examination of the foundations of ventures to extend the scope of economic reasoning to govern territories conventionally treated in other social sciences, reveals that the key "economic" assumptions claimed to characterize also those territories, include especially not only universal rationality, but also universally attained equilibrium. As Becker put it: "The combined assumptions of maximizing behavior, market equilibrium, and stable preferences, used relentlessly and unflinchingly, form the heart of the economic approach."[7] In Jack Hirshleifer's words:

> What gives economics its imperialist power is that our analytical categories—scarcity, cost, preferences, opportunities, etc.—are truly universal in applicability. Even more important is our structural organization of these concepts into the distinct yet intertwined processes of optimization on the individual decision level *and equilibrium on the social level of analysis*. Thus economics really does constitute the universal grammar of social science.
>
> (Hirshleifer, 1985, p. 53; emphasis added)

An examination of Becker's work in applying the economic approach to areas usually reserved to other social sciences, indeed reveals that the assumption of universally attained equilibrium is taken very seriously and quite self-consciously. Thus in his well-known analysis of marriage Becker is explicit, not only in assuming that "each person tries to find a mate who maximizes his or her well-being, with well-being measured by the consumption of household-produced commodities," but also in hypothesizing that "the 'marriage market' is assumed to be in equilibrium, in the sense that no person could change mates and become better off."[8]

Now, as we have seen, (and despite our unhappiness at the overemphasis of economists upon equilibrium analysis) there is considerable usefulness, within economics, in the ideas of equilibrium and of equilibration. The central thesis of this chapter is, however, that such usefulness cannot simply be assumed to apply also to these ideas within the territories conventionally treated by other social sciences (especially in the absence of market institutions). Equilibrium is a useful notion within the economic analysis of markets, because we understand how, within the institutional setting of the market, disequilibrium conditions tend to inspire that spontaneous process of mutual discovery of which equilibration consists. But, as pointed out in the preceding section, we have no basis whatever, in economic theory, for concluding that any similar processes of equilibration can tend systematically to exist in areas of social interaction outside the market setting.

An approach to explanation in the areas conventionally dealt with in other social sciences (that is, in areas outside the setting created by market institutions) which relies heavily on the assumption of universally attained equilibrium must therefore, in our view, be fundamentally flawed. It is one thing to postulate universal rationality in human decision-making; it is quite another thing (and, in our view quite unjustified) simply to assume as an empirical matter that all human decisions are at all times universally arranged in equilibrium patterns. (To *assume* that no married person could change mates and become better off thus appears as a totally unjustified and unrealistic assumption, thoroughly undermining the usefulness of the "economic approach" in the marriage "market.")

In the succeeding sections of this chapter we explore how and why this latter distinction is implicitly denied in the literature of "economic imperialism." This discussion will permit us to savor the paradox referred to early in this chapter. That paradox consisted, we said, in that the universality of rational choice for Becker *does* rigorously entail subordination of other social sciences to economics, while for the Austrian tradition, it is precisely the universality of rational choice (in the Mises sense) which rigorously entails our *in*ability to extend the applicability of the theorems of economics, uncritically, to other areas of social interaction.

RATIONALITY AND EQUILIBRIUM—THE MAINSTREAM VIEW

The truth is that the mainstream assumptions which, we saw in an earlier section, lead to a picture of the world as being in a perennial state of optimality, are merely the logically derived consequences entailed by the mainstream understanding of the rationality assumption itself. The very assumption of rational choice which undergirds economic theory must, if this assumption is understood as it is understood by the mainstream, necessarily mean that we are also, at the same time, assuming the equilibrium state.

For the mainstream, to assume rational choice is, as we have seen, to assume universal awareness, at each and every instant, of all the circumstances relevant to choice. (Although, ever since George Stigler's pioneering article of 1961,[9] economists have incorporated the need to search for information (in order to reduce ignorance) into microeconomic analysis, this does not in any way compromise the omniscience implied in the mainstream interpretation of the rationality assumption. The theory of search still stoutly assumes that each individual is aware, at each and every instant, of all the circumstances relevant to choice—and thus of all opportunities for worthwhile search. The only ignorance recognized as conceivable in this Stiglerian world is "optimal" ignorance, that is, ignorance which it is too costly to remove. To undertake the search necessary to remove such ignorance would be a mistake; efficiency *requires* this ignorance.) But this assumption (of universal awareness of all circumstances relevant to choice) conceals within it also the assumption that the decisions being made (besides—or rather as a result of—their all being rational) have all somehow already been modified and coordinatively arranged in a mutually sustaining (i.e. an equilibrium) pattern. No two decisions made (by two rational individuals) can be imagined as being made without these decisions having been somehow prearranged so as to be mutually sustaining—i.e. each must be such as not to frustrate the possible implementation of the other, and, further, each must not be such as to render the other decision as less than the best which its maker could possibly have made. To imagine that these two decisions are *not* mutually sustaining, is to imagine either that one decision-maker is presuming circumstances (on which he is relying) to exist which do not in fact exist, or to imagine that that decision-maker is failing to take advantage of opportunities actually available to him. In other words, to imagine that decisions are not mutually sustaining is to give up the assumption of universal rationality in decision-making—at least in the context of the mainstream interpretation of this assumption.

But it is immediately clear that if the rationality assumption implies that each pair of decisions made in the market are necessarily mutually sustaining, then the rationality assumption is also revealed to require that all decisions being made throughout the market system make up a complete system of general equilibrium. So that, for mainstream understanding of rationality, there really is no way of understanding individual behavior (for which understanding we must rely on the rationality assumption) without assuming complete market equilibrium somehow already to exist at all times. It follows, similarly, that any claim of universally rational behavior (in areas of social activity not conventionally covered in economics) must also imply the prior attainment of universal equilibrium in all areas of social interaction. If (in the preceding section) we found this universal equilibrium assumption unacceptable, and hence found the attempts to subordinate explanation in other areas of social science to the hegemony of economic theory, to be flawed, what is to blame in this regard is the assumption of universal rationality (in its mainstream interpretation). And it is here that we encounter the paradox mentioned earlier. For the "Austrian" sense in which rationality is a universal aspect of all human action, it turns out that it is precisely this universality of rationality which led us to challenge definitively the direct relevance of the equilibrium pattern in areas of social interaction outside the conventional scope of economics.

UNIVERSAL RATIONALITY IN THE MISESIAN FRAMEWORK

As was recognized already in the 1930s[10] the notion of rationality central to economics was understood by Mises to mean, essentially, purposefulness. For Mises the rationality of human action does not mean that decisions are made with full awareness of the circumstances relevant to choice. For Mises there is necessarily an element (which this writer has identified as the entrepreneurial element) in human action (a notion applicable only in a world of open-ended uncertainty) which grapples with the inherent uncertainty in which the agent is enveloped.[11] The assumption of rationality therefore means not any relevant omniscience, but simply the intent purposefulness of the human agent which inspires his alertness to opportunities (or to dangers) which he might otherwise overlook (or has in the past overlooked). It is this sense of rationality which, for Mises, characterizes human action in all its manifestations, in all areas of human interaction.

But this focus upon (what we have identified as) the entrepreneurial element in Misesian human action entails the insights developed in earlier sections of this chapter. Those insights led us to argue for a sharp difference between human action as it occurs within the institutional setting of the market, and human action as it occurs outside that setting. Within the setting of the market the entrepreneurial element in human action can be expected to set in motion a process of mutual discovery. The reasonableness of such processes of mutual discovery in markets renders the notions of equilibrium and equilibration relevant, at least, for our understanding of market phenomena. But outside the market setting, we argued, there is nothing in the character of interpersonal interaction which suggests any systematic discovery process (analogous to the discovery processes inspired, in markets, by the lure of pure entrepreneurial profit). Precisely because the notion of universal rationality, in the Misesian framework, includes the powerful possibility, at very least, of entrepreneurial error, our recognition of such universality ignites a red light warning against the uncritical transfer, to areas outside the conventional scope of economics, of the notion of equilibrium. To the degree that any extension of the applicability of economic theory requires us to invoke equilibrium notions, such extension must, for the Austrian-Misesian tradition, remain thoroughly suspect.

UNIVERSAL PRAXEOLOGY AND GAINS
FROM INTERDISCIPLINARY TRADE

It is quite true that Mises envisaged a general science of human action based on the universality of the rationality aspect of action. Certainly this common feature of human action in all its manifestations suggested for Mises that this feature can serve as the starting point for the development of theorems that cover both conventional economic interaction and other areas. We do not know (and Mises did not claim to know in any way specifically) how such theorems can in fact be developed. The universal notion of human action, Mises was convinced, could serve as an intellectual key to open up new areas of understanding. This conviction seems to have been in the nature of a prescientific hunch, which has as yet not been validated. Of one thing, however, we can be quite sure: Mises did not envisage any general science of praxeology that might be anchored in the assumption of universal, omniscience-based, equilibrium.

At the same time, while recoiling from that economic imperialism which, for Becker and Hirshleifer, derives from the assumption of universal equilibrium, we certainly need not and should not fail to recognize possible usefulness in interdisciplinary trade. No doubt many of the insights of economics (even in its mainstream version!) can be usefully incorporated into areas outside the conventional scope of economics. Much of Becker's work can no doubt be hailed in these terms. As Demsetz (1996, p. 3) put it, interaction between economics and other social sciences has, thus far, resulted in a "strong export surplus" being maintained by economics "in its trade in areas and methods with the other social sciences." Nothing in this chapter need contradict Demsetz's statement, or the spirit of interdisciplinary trade in ideas which it represents. Economics, through its insights concerning the universality of human reason and purposefulness, can, one can confidently hope, be of enormous benefit to other social sciences, *without* transforming them into colonial subdisciplines of applied economic theory.

NOTES

1. Robbins (1932, ch. 1).
2. Mises (1966, p. 3).
3. Ibid.
4. This digression is based on ideas developed earlier, out of the work of Mises and Hayek. See especially Kirzner (1973, ch. 6). The mode of exposition in the following section has benefitted from listening to a lecture by Professor Mancur Olson.
5. Calabresi (1968, p. 68).
6. See the title essay in Stigler (1982).
7. Becker (1976, p. 4).
8. Ibid., p. 232.
9. Stigler (1961).
10. See for example, Robbins (1932; 2nd edn, 1935, p. 93 and fn). *See also* Kirzner (1960, pp. 165–72).
11. See Kirzner (1973, pp. 32–37).

REFERENCES

Becker, G. (1976) *The Economic Approach to Human Behavior.* Chicago: University of Chicago Press.
Calabresi, G. (1968) "Transaction Costs, Resource Allocation, and Liability Rules: A Comment." *Journal of Law and Economics* 11 (April).
Demsetz, H. (1996) *The Primacy of Economics, An Explanation of the Comparative Success of Economics in the Social Sciences.* Jena: Max Planck Institut.
Green, David G. (1996) *Community Without Politics. A Market Approach to Welfare Reform.* London: IEA Health and Welfare Unit.
Hirshleifer, Jack (1985) "The Expanding Domain of Economics." *American Economic Review* 75(6).
Kirzner, Israel M. (1960) *The Economic Point of View.* Princeton, N.J.: Van Nostrand.
——— (1973) *Competition and Entrepreneurship.* Chicago: University of Chicago Press.
Loasby, Brian J. (1989) *The Mind and Method of the Economist. A Critical Appraisal of Major Economists in the Twentieth Century.* Aldershot and Brookfield, Conn.: Edward Elgar.
Mises, Ludwig von (1966) *Human Action. A Treatise on Economics.* Chicago: Contemporary Books.
Robbins, Lionel (1932) *The Nature and Significance of Economic Science.* London: Macmillan.
Stigler, George J. (1961) "The Economics of Information." *Journal of Political Economy* 69 (June).
——— (1982) *The Economist as Preacher and Other Essays.* Chicago: University of Chicago Press.

THE ECONOMICS OF GREED OR THE
ECONOMICS OF PURPOSE

I. INTRODUCTION

The topic I have chosen for this Keynote Address is one that has engaged critics and defenders of the market economy, as well as critics and defenders of economic science, for at least two centuries. I venture into this well-trodden territory both for personal reasons and for reasons having much to do with the theme of the Miller Upton Forum—The Wealth and Well-Being of Nations.[1] The personal angle derives from the circumstance that most of my work in economics (ever since Ludwig von Mises, back in 1955, suggested to me a topic for a paper he assigned) has, directly or indirectly, related to this theme—and resulted in my first book, published five years later. The reasons pertinent to this Miller Upton Forum have to do with the circumstance that Mises's own work, sadly neglected in modern economics, offers critically important new insights on this Forum's theme—insights that can indeed be crucial for the promotion of the Wealth and Well-Being of Nations.

I hope to show that central mainstream professional and lay criticisms of both the free market economy and economic science, melt away as soon as these Misesian insights are absorbed and appreciated. What is common to the mentioned criticism is a flawed understanding of the essence of the individual decision insofar as it is the building block of the capitalist economy, and of the structure of economic theory. These criticisms accept the myth that the success of the capitalist system is based entirely on the circumstance that market-place decisions are made by cold, calculating, selfishly materialistic, greedy individuals; and they accept the related myth that economic theory sees systematic

From *The Annual Proceedings of the Wealth and Well-Being of Nations*, vol. 3, 2010–11, pp. 17–30. Reprinted with permission from Beloit College Press.

1. I take this opportunity to express my particular pleasure at being this year's Upton Scholar. I had the personal privilege to have known President Upton. We served together for a number of years in the 'eighties as Trustees of the Foundation for Economic Education. I learned to appreciate and deeply respect Miller Upton's intellectual integrity and his commitment to the free society. It is for me a distinct honor to participate in this year's Miller Upton Forum on the Wealth and Well-Being of Nations.

chains of cause and effect as arising in market economies, only as a result of those same greedy, calculating decisions. As we shall see, it is one thing to claim that many, or most, in a given society are greedy and selfish. It is quite another thing to claim—falsely, as it turns out—that it is due to such selfish greed that free markets are able to prosper, and that economic theory can arrive at its central results. The gross fallacies in these perennial myths have, as we shall see, been unmasked again and again during the past century. What still needs to be stated in explicit terms, however, is that the truth concerning the individual decision, both in the capitalist economy and in economic theory, involves subtleties that require a substantial overhaul of central elements of mainstream economic understanding. I shall attempt to show that, by drawing attention to the entrepreneurial element in human action—an element first identified by Ludwig von Mises—we not only immediately see the emptiness of the above standard criticisms of capitalism and of economic theory, but are at the same time able to glimpse (a) a more profound understanding of economic causation, and (b) a deeper appreciation for the manner in which simple, layman-friendly economic theory can make an important contribution toward enhancing the wealth and well-being of nations.

2. ECONOMIC SCIENCE, FREE MARKETS, AND ECONOMIC MAN

It is a fact that over the past two centuries a central lesson of economics theory has taught us the spontaneously coordinative properties of free markets. This certainly does not mean that most economists have favored free markets. Much of the economic theory of the past century, at least, has in fact sought to demonstrate shortcomings in market outcomes, thus attempting to build the case for increased government regulation of free market economies, or for outright central planning. Nonetheless, it was shown over a half-century ago, familiarity with economic theory tends strongly to generate, at least, an appreciation for the spontaneously coordinative properties of markets (Stigler 1959: 52f). It is therefore no accident that writers most critical of free market arrangements, have tended to attempt to demolish the methodological foundations for mainstream economic theory. To wish to organize an economic system by central direction is to wish to refute the body of science which apparently teaches the unwisdom of such centrally planned arrangements.[2]

One route taken by these critics of free market arrangements has been to point out that the economic theory (which seems to argue for the social usefulness of such arrangements), depends crucially on the analytical construct known as *"homo oeconomicus"*—"economic man" understood to be a coldly calculating, selfishly greedy pursuer of unlimited physical pleasure (or its surrogate, unlimited pecuniary wealth). Because economic theory has indeed often seemed to assume that markets are peopled only by "economic men," it became a standard strategy to seek to demolish the central lessons of economic science by claiming that these lessons are only as true as is the truth of the *homo oeconomicus* assumption. Historicist, Institutionalist critics have again and again hammered away at the validity of this assumption; modern critics of economics have come up with novel forms of essentially the same objections to the fundamental assumptions of economic science.[3]

At the same time, critics of the capitalist system have not failed to seize on the unsavory character attributed to economic man, in order to denounce the morality of a system (the freedom of which permits free rein to such disgusting, jungle-like human traits and the success of which in fact depends upon such offensive patterns of behavior). Going back to Bernard de Mandeville's 1714 *Fable of the Bees or Private Vices, Publick Benefits,* writers have delighted in tracing capitalist success to selfish and/or wasteful economic activity.

3. HOMO OECONOMICUS AND A NEW ATTACK ON ECONOMICS

One eminent economist has, with an integrity and consistency admirable as an exercise in intellectual morality—but appalling in the *reductio ad absurdum* conclusions from which he could find no escape, was George J. Stigler. A Nobel Prize–winning star of the economics

---

2. A good deal of Ludwig von Mises's effort to focus attention on the methodological foundations of economics can be traced to his concern that the critically important teachings of economic science might otherwise be impugned by the ideologically driven enemies of capitalism.

3. For a survey of some of these new-old criticisms, see Kirzner (1990).

profession, and illustrious leader of the post–World War II Chicago School of Economics (a school of thought often seen as the fore-most intellectual spokesmen for free markets), Stigler found himself trapped into a corner from which economics must be seen as a sterile exercise without anything to teach society in regard to public policy. Stigler's astounding conclusions depend on his understanding of the individual economizing decision in markets. Stigler was too sophisti-cated to focus on greed or selfishness; he focused on the coldly calcu-lating behavior which standard microeconomics attributes to market participants. Standard equilibrium theory, the theory central to the Chicago School's understanding of the real world, assumes that ratio-nally calculating economic agents can be relied upon not to be mak-ing decisions that mistakenly anticipate other decisions that are in fact not being made, or decisions which would imply that uncaptured pockets of pure profit remain available for the taking. Pursuing the logic of such theorizing to its ultimate implications, Stigler is forced to conclude that, at each moment in time the world is, given the exist-ing legal patterns of rights assignment, the best of all possible worlds. If it seems to an economist that a change in policy (e.g., the elimina-tion of tariffs) could enhance aggregate "well-being," this turns out, in Stigler's view, to the economist's wishing to impose his scale of val-ues upon a society in which rights (including voting clout) have been assigned in a way that leads participants in the political-economic system, to decide differently. No one has made an error which the economist has discovered; it is merely that the economist would have wished that a different set of decisions could have been made. So Sti-gler finds himself, as a result of the omniscient rationality attributed by his economics to market decision makers, to conclude that eco-nomic advice offered by economists (e.g., advice to eliminate govern-ment regulation) is merely "preaching," i.e., offering to, or urging upon, voters a value system which they have, up until they hear the economic "sermon," not shared (Stigler 1982).

What we shall see in the remainder of this paper is that the fallacy in Stigler's position is (although it focuses on a different feature in the make-up of economic man) closely related to the fallacies that mar the older criticisms of economic science, and of capitalism, to which we drew attention in the preceding section of this paper.

4. TRADITIONAL RESPONSES TO
THE CRITICS OF ECONOMIC THEORY

Defenders of economic theory had traditionally responded to its critics (i.e., the critics who have challenged the realism of the model of economic man deployed in standard theory) in either of two types of response. One approach is to concede that "of course" the real world is more complicated than are the models of economic theorists, but that these models nonetheless offer useful approximations to reality, and that the conclusions drawn from these models can usefully be applied to guide public policy in the admittedly more complex world of reality.[4] The second approach, associated with a tradition including Philip Wicksteed (1910) and Lionel Robbins (1932), denies that in fact economic theory needs to invoke assumptions of selfish, materialistic greed, at all. All that is needed to generate the main theorems of economics, this defense argues, is the assumption that market participants consistently pursue their purposes (whatever these purposes may be, altruistic or selfish). (Much of formal modern theorizing, involving the assumption that market participants maximize "utility" [subject to their income constraints] have indeed attenuated the meaning of "utility" to the point where the analysis has been understood, and dismissed, as consisting of essentially empty tautologies.)

Our approach in this paper will, in broad terms, follow the second ("Robbinsian") route, with an important difference, deriving from my understanding of Ludwig von Mises's articulation of the novel concept of "human action" as constituting the analytical building block of economic science. For Robbins (1932) (and, as a result, for most of subsequent mainstream microeconomic theory) the crucial analytical unit is the individual constrained-maximization decision.[5] An economizing individual finds himself confronting a world in which he has at his disposal a given, limited, array of resources—which he seeks to transform into the utility-maximizing bundle of consumer purchases. He thus "economizes" against a given background of ends and means. The

---

4. One defense (associated primarily with eminent Chicago School economist Milton Friedman), argues that the truth of assumptions is not needed by a theory that is able, in "black-box" terms, to make valid real-world predictions.

5. Robbins, later Lord Robbins, wrote his book with ample acknowledgement of intellectual indebtedness to the Austrian School, in its 'twenties incarnation.

ends are emphatically, not confined to selfish, materialistic goals; they may include spiritual objectives and altruistic objectives—but they all call for the utilization of scarce material resources (which are given). Understanding the mathematics of constrained maximization, the economic theorist then predicts in principle the buying and selling decisions that will, from an initially given situation, (i.e., a situation in which each individual finds himself confronted by his own specific ends-means configuration) emerge from the informed decisions of all market participants, viewed simultaneously. Notice that the phrase "informed decisions" implies that market participants are aware of the decisions which other (equally "informed") decision makers are making. (After all, the given "means" available to any one economizing individual reflects, especially all the buying opportunities and all the selling opportunities, which are implicit in the decision which other similarly informed market participants are currently making.) Modern microeconomics has thus deployed the critical Robbinsian insight (that market participants are "economizing" decision makers) to reach a Walrasian analytical conclusion. In escaping from an economic man who greedily seeks materialistic selfish pleasure, modern economics has fallen into the trap of assuming that all markets are, at all times, in equilibrium. The Robbinsian economic man of microeconomics textbooks has, somehow, while no one was looking, as it were, come to be defined as an analytical entity unthinkable outside the equilibrium state. Notice that this eyebrow-raising result proceeds from the analytical presumption that the make-up of Robbinsian man permits and requires us to predict, in principle, the outcome of each individual decision—with this prediction having to be made simultaneously regarding every single participant in the market.

What has emerged then, from the Robbins-Walrasian tradition in modern microeconomics, is a body of theory that makes no attempt whatever to explain how all these individual decisions have, indeed, been brought into a state of utter mutual consistency. Instead this body of theory consists, in principle of two segments: a) one segment explaining the constrained-maximization character of each decision (whether it be a consumer decision, a potential laborer's decision, a business firm's hiring or production decision, or whatever); b) with the second segment working out the mathematical conditions which will have had to have been satisfied in order for an equilibrium state to exist. At no point does this theory, in its pure analytical form (as distinct from its less precise classroom-didactic form) seek to explain any possible equilibrating process (or, indeed, any systematic processes of market causation)!

We have stated that our approach (in abandoning the older assumptions of homo oeconomicus, the greedy, selfish seeker after what more money can buy) will, broadly, follow the Robbinsian path (rather than the path which claims that models built on the older assumptions are useful approximations to the truth). But we shall find that, following Mises's notion of "human action" (a subtle concept going beyond Robbinsian "economizing"), we will be led decisively to reject the view which sees economic theory as a theory of the equilibrium state. Instead we shall find that in reaching our understanding of the way in which human beings make decisions (i.e., in our understanding of the implications of "human action") we will have discovered the crucial element in modern Austrian economics, viz. that economic theory permits us to understand the nature of the market process (and, even more fundamentally, the nature of purely economic causation)—as this market process (and this process of economic causation) occurs under initial disequilibrium conditions.

5. MISES AND THE SCIENCE OF HUMAN ACTION

For Mises, the analytical unit for economic reasoning calls for no departure from full reality. This analytical unit is "human action," a concept grounded in the truth that human beings pursue purposes, they are *purposeful* human beings. Just as Robbins's "economizing man" pursues ends of all kinds (altruistic as well as selfish), so too Mises's *homo agens* ("acting man") pursues purposes of all kinds. So that Mises and Robbins do share their recognition that economic theory does not rest on the assumed selfish, materialistic greed of economic man. But it is in the next step that Mises goes beyond Robbins. As we have seen, for Robbins the economizing man is seen as facing a given (and known) configuration of ends and means. For Mises, however, acting man's purposefulness includes, most importantly, the entrepreneurial element of determining for himself what in fact the relevant ends-means configuration is, at each moment in his life. Whereas, in the mainstream microeconomics deriving from Robbins, there is no scope whatever for any entrepreneurship (because it is assumed that nothing remains to be discovered!); in the Misesian "science of human action," there is room for both entrepreneurial error and entrepreneurial discovery, in every single example of human action.

For Mises, in fact, the market process, the element in social interaction that generates systematic chains of economic causation, is attributed to the entrepreneurial propensity to discover pockets of available pure profit. For mainstream microeconomics there never are any available pockets of pure profit. (The mind-set of the mainstream economist has been likened to the mind-set behind the assertion that there never are any twenty-dollar bills to be picked up in Times Square—because any such bills would already have been picked up!) For Mises the market process is set into motion purely by the lure of available pure profit opportunities—with these understood to be always available as the result of (earlier) imperfect entrepreneurship.

So that, for Mises, the rebuttal of the claim that economic theory rests on the analytical myth of selfish, materialistic, greedy, economic man, is at the same time, the key to a fresh and illuminating understanding of the market process.

6. THE SAINTLY MARKET PROCESS

Thus the market process can now be understood in Misesian (and Hayekian) terms, as the mutual learning process through which, by means of entrepreneurial trial and error, grosser misunderstandings of market possibilities tend to be replaced by less erroneous beliefs (concerning opportunities available in the market). It is important to notice that this market process of mutual discovery[6] is one driven by purposefulness, not by constrained maximization; it is driven by the pursuit of pure profit.

And it is important to notice that such pursuit of pure profit has nothing essentially to do with selfish greed. It is certainly true that in our imperfect world selfish greed is, regrettably, all too prevalent. But even in a world peopled by saintly, utterly altruistic individuals, the very same market phenomena can be expected to emerge.

Imagine a society in which everyone is primarily concerned to help others. That is, imagine a society in which human beings engage in consumption (eating, wearing clothes, and the like) only in order to be able to have the strength and ability to pursue their primary philanthropic goals. Notice that these goals may be different for different people. Some individuals wish

---

6. Hayek (1978) used the phrase "Competition as a Discovery Procedure" as the title of a paper, published in his *New Studies in Philosophy, Politics, Economics, and the History of Ideas.*

to feed the hungry, others wish to care for the sick; perhaps others wish to educate and raise orphans, or to care for the elderly. All this is entirely compatible with profit-seeking entrepreneurial activity and discovery.

Business firms, in such a saintly society, would still be charging the highest possible prices, and paying the lowest possible wages. The profits won by discovering which consumers are prepared to pay the highest prices, and which workers are prepared to work at the lowest wages, would, in this saintly society, be dedicated almost entirely to lofty, philanthropic purposes. The entrepreneur whose highest altruistic goal is to eliminate the ravages of a dread disease, might, for example, manufacture furniture, squeezing the maximum legally permissible services from his workers, offering no unnecessary price-discounts to potential furniture buyers, regardless of their poverty-stricken need for moderately priced furniture. He will pursue such a strict business regimen because, by assumption, he ranks the virtue of building hospitals and promoting medical research, as higher than that of benefitting healthy, but poverty-stricken, workers and consumers. His philanthropic purposefulness leads him to be alert to all possibilities of enhancing his profits. This purposefulness, together with the similar philanthropic purposefulness of all his fellow saintly market participants, will thus generate the very same ("ruthless"?) market competition (and the same entrepreneur-driven profit-seeking market process) familiar to us from our participation in less saintly economic environments.

We have thus seen that the prosperity widely recognized as being characteristic of the capitalistic system, in no way depends on the selfish greed of the participants in that system. To be sure, the purposefulness of greedy, selfish entrepreneurs, workers, and consumers, that may fill a given society, will generate prosperity and growth in that society. But it is the pure purposefulness, the potential for entrepreneurial discovery in that society, which will be responsible for that prosperity—not the materialistic greed that may be driving that purposefulness.

And we see at the same time, that the economic analysis which has illuminated our understanding of this entrepreneurial market process, in no way depends on any necessarily unattractive features of economic man. The market process is a discovery process, driven by the alertness of entrepreneurs—and every human being is, to some extent, an entrepreneur!—to the profits generated by earlier entrepreneurial error.

7. ECONOMICS AND THE WELL-BEING OF NATIONS—I

We are now in a position to perceive the disastrous fallacy in Stigler's (tongue-in-cheek?) dismissal of all advice proffered by economic theorists. As we saw earlier, Stigler, constrained as he was by the mainstream assumption that no market participants ever lack relevant information (i.e., that they know everything which it is worthwhile for them deliberately to learn)—found himself forced to the conclusion that we live in the best of all possible worlds (i.e., "best" in terms of the existing accepted system of initial rights-assignments). Given such a perspective on the world, there is nothing that economists can offer that might, relevantly, increase societal well-being. For Stigler, we saw, all condemnation on the part of economists for existing public policy, all endorsements offered by economists by specific public policy proposals, are, at best, simply unscientific "preaching"—i.e., expressions of the economists' opinions regarding what ought to be the appropriate pattern of rights-assignment, or what ought to be the appropriate scales of value to be applied. The very circumstance that the economists are offering advice to change matters reflects the truth that the participants in the economic system (since they have not already adopted the advised policies) do *not* share these opinions. Economic advice amounts to nothing more than "preaching"—i.e., an attempt to change people's values (not to teach them how better to pursue their goals). But the perspective on economic theory which we have developed in this paper, demonstrates the utter fallacy of such attitudes toward economic advice. Everything depends on our recognition of the possibility of genuine error (Kirzner 1979).

For Stigler, genuine error is never evinced in the market. (Notice we are not denying that Stigler recognizes the possibility of genuine ignorance; but ignorance may not necessarily be an example of error. I may be ignorant of the Sanskrit language, this may not be an error on my part; I may simply, and correctly, have concluded that the cost to me of learning Sanskrit is not justified by the benefit to me of learning the language. My ignorance would then be optimal ignorance, not at all an example of error.) Stigler indeed pioneered the Economics of Information; he developed a sophisticated theory of how ignorance is deliberately minimized, subject to cost constraints. But at all points in that theory, every market participant knows as much as he wishes to know (given the [known] costs of learning). For Stigler, people always succeed in getting the best possible outcomes (given their preferences, and given the assets to which they own title). No genuine errors ever occur.

But the truth is that the market is, at all times, a showcase for the possibility of genuine error! Any market not (yet) in equilibrium demonstrates, by definition, the existence of erroneous decisions. As we have seen, the Misesian (entrepreneurial) market process is a process of mutual discovery. What is discovered in each step in this process is the fact that potentially mutually profitable transactions (now seen to be possible), up until now and for no justifiable reason (such as cost), had simply not been noticed. The competitive entrepreneurial market process is a process of error-discovery and error-correction. Because the underlying variables (consumer preferences, resource availabilities, and technological possibilities) are constantly changing, the market process never ceases—because unanticipated exogenous changes render earlier decisions erroneous. Markets never do attain equilibrium, because the tendencies toward systematic correction (read: discovery) of error, are continually disrupted by exogenous changes in tastes, in the state of technological knowledge, and in resource availabilities. Once we admit the possibility of error (more precisely, once we admit the *impossibility*, in practice, of an errorless universe), our attitude toward the potential social usefulness of economic science must surely undergo a dramatic change. Economic science can teach us, not only *that* errors are near-inevitable in any society—it can also teach society how best, and how most rapidly, to move toward the *correction* of error.

8. ECONOMICS AND THE WELL-BEING OF NATIONS—II

We have seen that the key to the discovery and the correction of error lies in the scope which a society permits its entrepreneurs. Whenever errors have been made, this manifests itself in the circumstances that pure entrepreneurial profit is available for the taking. It is the availability of pure profit opportunities which, in ways we admittedly do not fully understand, attract entrepreneurial attention. Where a method exists whereby low-cost resource services can be deployed to produce high-value consumer goods, this is evidence of earlier error. Owners of these low-value resources must have been unaware of the high-valued productive capabilities of their resources (or else they would never have permitted their resources to be available at low cost). This unawareness constitutes error—but an error that has prevented society at large from enjoying the additional value that might have been extracted from these low-value resources. These resources have, in truth, been wasted. This error and societal waste are, however, one side of a coin, the other side of which constitutes the opportunity for pure entrepreneurial profit which switches on the entrepreneurial antennae, leading them to discover (and thus also to tend to correct) where earlier errors have been made.

The winning of pure entrepreneurial profit has often been seen as a disreputable feature of the free market system. First of all, winning such pure profit seems to be taking advantage of other people's ignorance. Second, pure profit seems in no way related to effort or sweat expended, or to ownership of productive assets. Many moralists have no problem with a high wage being paid to a worker who has worked exceptionally hard; or with the fruit which spontaneously grows on a legitimately owned fruit tree, belonging to that owner. But the entrepreneur who has bought all the needed resource services at a low cost, and subsequently sells consumer goods at a much higher total value, appears to many *not* to be entitled to the gain represented by this pure profit.

This paper is not the place to address these moral concerns; I have, as it happens, written a book showing, I believe, that these moral concerns are based on an inadequate understanding of the pure economic theory of pure entrepreneurial profit (Kirzner 1989). This paper cannot address these concerns; its purpose is to point out how a more profound and subtler economic theory can explain how freedom for entrepreneurial discovery can indeed promote the well-being of nations.

The point is a simple one, but one very often overlooked. Errors deprive society of available additional goods and services. Errors are responsible for useful resources being allocated "wastefully" to uses that provide society with less than their full potential. A free market is a market into which anyone who believes he can see a better way of using resources (than is presently the case) is free to attempt to profit by his insight. Only in such a market is there the yeast which inspires discovery. Any impediments to pursuing pure profit opportunities not only block attempts that might have been socially useful—much more seriously, they switch off the current of entrepreneurial excitement and alertness which are the only source for the discovery of error. The point is that pure error may continue indefinitely. What people have not known today—in the sense that they have not known that they lack any knowledge—they may never know. It is only entrepreneurial, profit-inspired alertness to what is around the corner, as it were, that tends actively to erode error.

9. GREED, PURPOSE, PROFIT, AND THE WELL-BEING OF NATIONS

We have reached the end of our brief journey. We have seen the fallacies—yes, the errors!—in the hoary complaints that free market systems prosper purely because of human greed. What drives free markets is not necessarily greed at all, it is the purposefulness of potential entrepreneurs whose purposes, in the disposition of their pure profits, may be altruistic, selfish, or whatever. We have seen that economic science, at least in its Misesian incarnation, does not depend on the model of a materialistic, greedy *homo oeconomicus*—it depends merely on the insight that human beings do not simply choose from given menus, they act, with the entrepreneurial element in action identifying what the relevant menus should be.

And, most important of all, we have seen that all this is vitally important. Economic Science matters. A wider understanding of the fundamental, essentially simple truths of economics can help us appreciate the crucial significance for societal well-being, of the free market economy.

REFERENCES

Hayek, F. A. 1978. Competition as a Discovery Procedure. In *New Studies in Philosophy, Politics, Economics, and the History of Ideas*. Chicago: University of Chicago Press.

Kirzner, Israel. 1979. Economics and Error. In *Perception, Opportunity and Profit*. Chicago: University of Chicago Press.

———. 1989. *Discovery, Capitalism and Distributive Justice*. Oxford: Basil Blackwell.

———. 1990. Self-Interest and the New Bashing of Economics. *Critical Review* 4 (1–2), Reprinted in Kirzner, I. 1992. *The Meaning of Market Process, Essays in the Development of Modern Austrian Economics*. London: Routledge, chapter 12.

Robbins, Lionel C. 1932 [1935]. *The Nature and Significance of Economic Science*. London: MacMillan & Co., Ltd.

Stigler, George J. 1959. The Politics of Political Economists. *Quarterly Journal of Economics* 73 (4): 522–32; reprinted in Stigler, G. 1965. *Essays in the History of Economics*. Chicago: University of Chicago Press.

———. 1982. The Economist as Preacher. In *The Economist as Preacher and Other Essays*. Chicago: University of Chicago Press.

WELFARE ECONOMICS

COORDINATION AS A CRITERION
FOR ECONOMIC "GOODNESS"

INTRODUCTION[1]

From the very beginnings of economic science, economists (and the public) have been convinced that economic theories can offer impartial guidance for public policy. In other words economic science, it has always been believed, can objectively pronounce some policies to be economically "bad," and other policies to be economically "good." For the age of Adam Smith there was little ambiguity in the phrase "economically good" (or its opposite). That which increased the "wealth of nations" was clearly economically good. And for classical economists what constitutes a nation's wealth seemed reasonably clear.[2] As economics (following on the marginalist revolution) advanced through the era of neoclassicism, the precise nature of the economic criterion came to be developed far more critically and self-consciously. The emergence of the theory of welfare economics during the first half of the now concluding century consisted, to a significant degree, in attempts to grapple ingeniously with conceptual problems raised by the subjective character of utility, as distinct from objective wealth (and thus by the difficulty of aggregating a society's economic well-being). Hayek's mid-century insights concerning the dispersed character of available knowledge in society[3] further challenged the possibility of treating the economic problem facing society, as being that of achieving global efficiency in the allocation of resources. Recent critiques[4] of traditional welfare theory have radically questioned the very possibility of devising an economic criterion that might, independently of particular moral philosophical positions, be deployed in order to pronounce one economic state of affairs (or one economic policy) to be "economically better" than a second.

This chapter, building on certain earlier works,[5] sets forth a clearcut, objective criterion, *coordination*, which may satisfy the intuitive conviction

From *The Driving Force of the Market: Essays in Austrian Economics* (New York and London: Routledge, 2000), 132–48. Reprinted by permission of Springer; the original source is *Constitutional Political Economy* 9 (1998): 289–301.

of economists that their science does objectively demonstrate the economic "goodness" of some economic policies (and the economic "badness" of other policies)—without running into any of the above-mentioned difficulties which have dogged twentieth century welfare economic theory.

WHAT IT IS WE ARE LOOKING FOR

In searching for an objective criterion for service as an index of economic "goodness," we are not seeking to square the circle. Certainly "goodness" of any kind is a normative notion calling for a justification in moral-philosophical terms (which may, at least for the economist, involve subjective convictions rather than objectively established definitive conclusions). But such a criterion may nonetheless be identified in objective terms (i.e., in terms that themselves do not beg the moral-philosophical question of defining "goodness"); that criterion may then (subject to independently adopted moral-philosophical principles) serve as an objective criterion for economic goodness. An illustration from early nineteenth-century economic literature may be helpful on this point.

In 1831, Richard Whately, an Anglican cleric, delivered a course of lectures on political economy at Oxford.[6] In introducing his subject, he apparently found it necessary to defend himself against some who had questioned the propriety of a clergyman's interest in the "science of wealth." Whately's response to his critics was ingenious (and, one suspects, somewhat playful). He pointed out that research into the causes of a phenomenon (such as wealth) does not, by itself, imply any moral approbation of that phenomenon. After all, Whately argued, a medical researcher exploring the causes of a disease does not, one presumes, hope to enhance the incidence of this disease. Scientific research, Whately was arguing, is not by itself an expression of a commitment in favor of (or against) the phenomenon which is the topic of exploration.

Now certainly a policy which reduces the incidence of a disease cannot be described as "good" without additional moral-philosophical insights. But the disease itself can be defined objectively and scientifically; a policy which reduces the incidence of disease may then on the basis of independently established moral principles be pronounced as medically good policy.

What is needed for an objectively based normative economics, is a criterion which, like the criteria which identify a particular disease, can be unambiguously identified by economic science and which, again as in the case of disease, seems likely to be able to serve as a norm for goodness in the light of independently established, widely shared or otherwise assumed moral principles. For Whately, wealth offered itself as such a criterion (although, as we have seen, he was playfully coy as to whether he envisaged economic goodness to be correlated with its increase or with its decrease). But the subjectivist insights of the Marginalist Revolution rendered "aggregate wealth" unacceptable as a criterion for economic goodness.

STANDARD ATTEMPTS TO IDENTIFY THE CRITERION OF ECONOMIC GOODNESS

Economists during the early and central decades of this century labored hard in order to establish a scientifically defined criterion for economic goodness. These efforts constitute the history of twentieth-century welfare economics. From the perspective provided by an understanding of Austrian Economics at the close of the century, these efforts, ingenious and brilliant though they were, largely failed to achieve their objective. They depended either, as in Pigouvian welfare economics, on the futile idea of somehow aggregating utility across the individuals making up society, or, as in the standard interpretations of Paretian welfare economics, on the flawed notion of seeing society as a single decision making entity seeking to achieve global efficiency in its pattern of resource allocation.

From the perspective of the methodological individualism and subjectivism which nourish Austrian Economics, the idea of aggregating utility is simply meaningless (not just wrong)—since utility is seen as essentially nothing more than a degree of importance attached by a decision-making individual to an option, in his comparison of it with other options.[7] Similarly the notion of societal efficiency is viewed by Austrians as less than coherent, since not only does society in fact not make decisions, in any but a metaphorical sense, but as Hayek showed us,[8] the essence of an economic problem facing society consists precisely in the dispersed character of existing knowledge—which dispersed character renders entirely moot the notion of centralized allocative efficiency (for which centralized information must be a necessary prerequisite).

We should point out that these "Austrian" difficulties do not reflect any conceptual difficulty in deploying economic science for policy purposes.

There is no difficulty in arguing an "ought"-statement which depends, for its factual basis, on an independently established "is"-statement. These "Austrian" difficulties stem from the conceptual difficulties associated with constructing a coherent notion of what is economically good for society. The Austrian methodological tenets we have referred to seem to invalidate, as science, any global notions of economic goodness that might serve as policy yardsticks. In other words, it seems, the global notions of economic goodness needed in order to evaluate social policies must themselves remain outside science. Economic science cannot, it appears, be deployed for social-normative purposes, only because the criteria we wish to apply in our evaluations cannot be coherently defined except as pure (non-scientific) judgments of value. Positive science may not, without appealing to non-scientific judgments of value, be able to pronounce heart disease desirable or undesirable. But these judgments of value are not needed to identify heart disease (and thus to be able scientifically to identify its causes). The "economic well-being of society," on the other hand—even before one begins to consider whether it is morally worthy of being desired—is a concept which, we have argued, is simply undefined and undefinable, as long as we confine ourselves to positive categories of subjectivist and methodologically individualistic economics. Certainly such economics will, by itself, be unable to identify specific policies as able to enhance the "economic well-being of society."

But all this means that we have reached something of an impasse. Economists have always assumed that their positive findings can be of direct assistance in advising rulers. Economists have always believed that their discipline does teach us about the virtues or vices of free markets. The purism expressed in the preceding paragraphs seems to have unhelpfully propelled us rapidly toward an intellectual dead end.

In this chapter we shall argue that we can escape this impasse. The notion of "coordination" fits precisely the specifications we are seeking to apply. It refers to an objective state, which economic science is able to identify and describe and which does, in general, appear to be a matter of moral concern to many thoughtful observers of economic phenomena and economic policies. This notion is not vulnerable to the subjectivist and methodologically individualist objections which we found to challenge standard welfare economics. Economics science is thus, through the coordination notion, able, we shall maintain, to provide an objective criterion in terms of which the economic goodness and badness of economic situations or economic policies, may be judged. We certainly need moral philosophy to help judge the goodness (or badness) of greater degrees of coordinatedness; but we do not need any help from moral philosophy in order to identify the coordination concept and associate specific economic policies with either greater or lesser likelihood of generating coordination. In this way economics may, in principle, be able to provide objective measures of (what independently established moral principles declare to be) economic goodness.

COORDINATION DEFINED

A fully coordinated state of affairs, for our purposes, is one in which each action taken by each individual in a demarcated set of actions, correctly takes into account (a) the actions in fact being taken by everyone else in the set, and (b) the actions which the others might take were one's own actions to be different. An example of what we mean by a state of coordination is presented in the activities of air controllers in charge of flights into and out of a busy airport. It is generally understood that the function of the air controller is to coordinate these flights in order to ensure smooth and safe scheduling of departures and arrivals. It will be useful to consider in precisely what the air controller's coordinative responsibilities consist.

Clearly, were two airplanes to collide, we would say that the actions of their respective pilots were not mutually coordinated. Each pilot failed correctly to take into account what the other pilot was doing. Had Pilot No. 1 known that Pilot No. 2 would place his plane at the particular point and at the time at which the collision occurred, he would not have placed his own plane at that point, at that time; and similarly for Pilot No. 2. What the air controller does in coordinating flight activity is to ensure that no such failure in each pilot's taking into account the other's actions should ever occur. But of course the objective of the air controller goes beyond the avoidance of collisions. The objective is also to expedite the smooth movement of aircraft into and out of the airport, so as to minimize the time spent in unneeded waiting. A pilot held in an unnecessarily long holding pattern is, in effect, failing to have his actions coordinated with those of the other pilots—since if he were utterly sure that no other aircraft would be in his vicinity during the immediate future, there would be no reason for him not to proceed to land immediately.

We notice that the coordinative activity of the air controller is deliberately and centrally planned. It is, predominantly, "top-down" coordination. Each pilot coordinates his activity with the actions of the other pilots, in effect, by entrusting decision-making to the air controller. Having confidence in the air controller's expertise, he takes the actions of other pilots into account, not by being himself in direct communication with them, but by agreeing (at the same time as, he is given to understand, the other pilots are similarly agreeing) to obey the instructions of the controller, to whom is assigned the task of explicitly arranging the coordination of the flight patterns.

When we identify coordination as being the criterion for economic "goodness," we are asserting that, from the perspective of those whom economists aspire to serve, the function of an economic system is to coordinate the activities of its participants. For one convinced that a centrally planned economy is the economic system to be preferred, central planning (like the activity of the air controller) is the preferred instrument for the achievement of coordination. For those convinced of the virtue of Adam Smith's "invisible hand" a free market is able to achieve, spontaneously and without central direction, coordination among its primary participants, the consumers and the owners of resources. Certainly one of the tasks of economic theory is to help determine which of these two options is closer to the truth.

FURTHER REFLECTION ON THE MEANING OF COORDINATION

We were concerned, earlier in this chapter, to establish that "coordination" is a state of affairs that can (like a disease) be objectively defined and described, without the need for any value judgments or moral considerations whatever. It was only in order to identify greater degrees of coordination as being "better"—analogously to being able to describe a more effective cure for a disease as being a "better" drug—that moral judgment concerning the desirability of greater coordination—analogous to the judgment that it is morally desirable to eliminate disease—enters the picture.

This earlier emphasis of ours underscores what should by now be obvious,[9] viz. that what is meant by coordination is not the presence of a *pattern of activities* which appears pleasing to the economist, or to anyone else. People do sometimes speak of one color scheme being a better-coordinated one than a second scheme. In making those kinds of statements reference is certainly being made to the pleasing or unpleasing character of the configuration of colors. But that is not at all the way we have defined coordination for purposes of serving as a criterion of economic "goodness." An air collision is an example of imperfect coordination, in our sense of the term, not because of the tragically unfortunate character of the collision, but because of the obvious failure which the collision demonstrates, on the part of each of the two colliding pilots, to have taken adequate account of each other's actions. When we wish to take coordination as our criterion for economic "goodness," we imply, not that a coordinated state is one which reflects the beauty (in the eyes of the morally relevant public) of the particular patterns of decisions which happen to make up that state, but that we understand that morally relevant public to consider the coordinated state (because, and only because, it conforms to our definition of coordination) to be morally desirable. It is not that we define coordination by reference to what is morally beautiful. It is that we believe that moral beauty is widely perceived to inhere in the state of coordination as we have defined it i.e., as a state in which no action would be different than it is, were the agent to have known more accurately what it is that other decision-makers are doing, or what they might be prepared to do under alternative circumstances.

A COMPLICATION IN THE DEFINITION OF COORDINATION: AN IMPORTANT DIGRESSION

It should be carefully noted that the criterion we have selected as an indicator of economic goodness is, while itself entirely objective and value-free, able to be defined only against the background of some initially given pattern of property rights. Given a pattern of property rights designated, say, as A, we may meaningfully seek to judge a particular piece of legislation or an entirely different pattern of property rights, as to whether it offers greater or lesser coordinative potential than does A. That notion will be made in terms of the notion of coordination as defined from the perspective of rights system A. Without some initially given rights pattern, a notion of coordination cannot be assigned specific meaning. In particular, it will not be possible to judge "absolutely" between two property rights systems (system A and system B) in regard to their comparative coordinative potentials—without any given starting position.

To see this at the most elementary level, imagine that agent alpha prefers a marginal unit of beef over a marginal unit of chicken, while agent beta prefers the chicken over the beef. It will make all the difference in the world, in our judgment of coordination or miscoordination in regard to the distribution of beef and chicken ownership, whether we (i) begin with a situation in which alpha and beta "own" the chicken and beef respectively, or (ii) begin with a situation in which alpha, say, "owns" *both* the beef and the chicken. From the perspective of situation (i), coordination would require that alpha finish up having the beef, and beta having the chicken. But from the perspective of situation (ii), it is that initial situation (in which alpha owns both the beef and the chicken) which is the coordinated situation. From a strictly economic perspective (i.e., from a perspective which is neutral in regard to the relative morality or legality of alternative initial property rights patterns of distribution) one cannot pronounce situation (ii) as economically "bad"—even though that situation would be perceived as uncoordinated, were our initial vantage point to have been a situation in which the beef and chicken were, initially, differently distributed.

It might then seem that the notion of coordination is not entirely objective, after all. What is seen as coordination from the perspective of one particular property rights system, based presumably upon one particular adopted moral framework, may well be seen as discoordination in regard to a second property rights system, based on a different adopted moral framework. So that the coordination criterion appears, contrary to our earlier assertion, to be a morally relative notion.

But recognizing the validity of the insights presented in this section does not contradict our earlier assumptions. It is true that coordination cannot be defined except within a given, adopted moral/legal framework; nonetheless, within that framework, it offers an objective criterion. This criterion is itself admittedly unable to discriminate between the economic goodness of different moral/legal frameworks, unless one of them is taken as the relevant starting point. But this does not render the criterion itself arbitrary. The question, "How far is it to Chicago?" cannot be answered except by reference to some "arbitrarily-given" starting point. Yet the concept of distance is itself entirely objective, not at all arbitrary. As elsewhere argued,[10] the efficacy of the market process is itself not a meaningful notion unless embedded in some exogenously given moral/ legal framework. What we see in regard to the coordination norm is exactly the same case.

Moreover, we should remind the reader that the more traditional attempts, in standard welfare economics, to fashion a criterion of economic goodness, were, quite similarly, relative to the initial pattern of rights distribution. As Ezra Mishan showed many years ago,[11] a welfare optimum cannot be defined except within the framework of a given ownership pattern (since the wealth effects arising from alternative ownership patterns will affect the utility schedules or indifference maps from which welfare theory construes its patterns of optimalities). Although the specific sense in which our coordination criterion is definable only relative to a given rights framework is somewhat different from that demonstrated by Mishan in regard to the standard welfare-theoretic apparatus, the essential insight is entirely the same. And while this "relativism" should be carefully noted and respected (and while, in consequence, the scope within which "scientifically objective" welfare theory can be deployed is narrower than one might perhaps have thought), it does not destroy the objectivity of the welfare criterion, properly used. The case with the coordination criterion is entirely similar.

So that when we use the coordination criterion to assess, for example, Mises's arguments in regard to the possibility of socialist economic planning, it offers us insights which must be carefully identified. To take matters at a most simple level, it would be incorrect to assert that Mises proved that the central planners' decisions under socialism are literally uncoordinated. By definition, all the decisions of the central planners, since they are consciously arrived at within a single (attempted) "plan" must—no matter how incoherent and mistaken that plan may be shown to be—have been "coordinated" in the sense that each part of the "plan" is, at least superficially, made with awareness of each part of the "plan." What Mises showed, of course, was that at a deeper level, the central planner cannot create a true plan, since he cannot engage in "economic calculation," i.e., each part of the "plan" is necessarily made without full awareness of its true implications for other parts of the attempted plan. What this means, in terms of our notion of coordination is that the actions called for by the attempted central plan are uncoordinated in the sense that, were the various agents in the socialized economy to have the freedom to make their own decisions (with full awareness of each other's decisions and potential decisions), (i.e., were they to be assigned specific property rights), they would find it mutually beneficial not to follow the pattern of actions in fact dictated by the central plan—even if the central planner's objective was that of fulfilling the preferences of agents, to the greatest socially possible extent. The economic inadequacy of socialist planning is thus to be understood as seen from the hypothetical starting point of some (i.e., any) pattern of private property rights.[12]

COORDINATION AND COORDINATION

There is a certain ambiguity in the word "coordination" which urgently calls for our attention.[13] Sometimes we use the word coordination (as in the phrase "complete coordination") to refer to the fully coordinated state (as defined above). But at other times we use the word coordination to refer to the process in the course of which a state of discoordinatedness gradually comes to be replaced by successive states of greater and greater degrees of coordinatedness.

So that, if an economist asserts that the market "coordinates" the activities of its participants, this may mean one of two possible things. It may mean that that economist is maintaining that the market has achieved that equilibrium state in which all activities are in a state of complete mutual coordinatedness. (In that equilibrium state market exchanges are such that each participant takes into account, in effect, the plans of each other participant. So that, by confronting each market participant with the appropriate price incentives, the market may be said to be coordinating all the decisions being made, i.e., to be arranging those incentives to be operating that are able to achieve this state of complete coordinatedness.) Or that original assertion may have a quite different meaning. It may mean that the economist is maintaining that while, at any moment of time during the course of the market process of equilibration, all activities are *not* fully coordinated, nonetheless that process is tending steadily to reduce the degree of discoordinatedness that initially existed among the activities of the market participants. These two assertions are quite different assertions. Understanding what a particular assertion in fact means, and avoiding confusing that assertion with a second assertion (that may in fact not be being made at all) may be of considerable importance. An example of the importance of such understanding follows.

DYNAMIC COMPETITION AND THE
COORDINATING PROCESS

This writer has often drawn attention to the possible equilibrative properties of dynamic entrepreneurial competition.[14] From an initial state of affairs in which productive activities are not taking advantage of existing resource or technological availabilities, entrepreneurial entry, based on innovative recognition of these availabilities, may generate a dynamically competitive process during which the older inefficient producers come to be replaced by more efficient producers. It is clear that, from the consumers' point of view this process is economically "good"; it provides them with products which are cheaper and/or better, as judged by them. I would also argue that this process is "good" in that it better coordinates the preferences of consumers with the availabilities of resources (and thus with the potential actions of resource owners). It is here that critics have rebelled.

Surely, it is again and again objected, this dynamically competitive entrepreneurial entry—no matter how beneficial it may be held to be—cannot be described as coordinative.[15] After all, despite all the undenied benefits of this entry (as judged by consumers), this entry drastically disrupts ("discoordinates") the activities of those older, less efficient producers (and their employees) who are being destroyed by this new competition. Surely this kind of Schumpeterian creative destruction should be recognized as (perhaps valuably) disrupting the coordination which had previously prevailed in the industry. Up until the new innovation, production plans smoothly dovetailed with consumer decisions. As a result of the innovation those earlier plans (and all the plans, say, of potential employees who have been training in preparation for entry into the now obsolete production procedure) have been irrevocably disrupted. Surely this dynamic competition must be recognized as discoordinative! So run the objections. But our earlier discussions should have made clear why these objections are not valid; in the important sense of the term this dynamically competitive entry must be seen as coordinative, not discoordinative.

Certainly this entry disrupts the earlier-made plans of inefficient producers and their employees and suppliers. Based on their earlier, now disappointed expectations, those producers may certainly see themselves as being "hurt" by the new innovations. But those earlier plans of the inefficient producers were in fact part of the network of plans that were being made, which were poorly coordinated with other potential decisions on the part of other owners of resources. The owners of those other resources would have been ready—and, when the innovative competing entrepreneur approached them they were in fact ready—to offer resource services to the market which could have made possible the provision to consumers of better and cheaper products. The consumer who (being unaware of such possibilities) had continued to pay high prices for the inferior products of the older producers, were making decisions that were not appropriately taking into account the potential decisions of other resource owners and other potential producers. The innovative competitor who, entering the industry and pushing out the older firms, is disrupting their earlier plans, is replacing a less coordinated set of market activities, by a better coordinated set. In the "dynamic" sense of the term "coordination" (identified in the preceding section of this paper), this brash, aggressive competition is coordinative. The disruption it causes in the earlier plans of the inefficient producers is the evidence for and manifestation of the earlier state of discoordinatedness which has generated the changes (of which this disruption is a part). The apparent earlier calm which, as a result of the aggressive new competition, has been followed by sudden disruption, was in fact utterly misleading. That calm was a facade expressing the presence of as yet undiscovered (but very real) discoordinatedness; dynamic competition shattered that calm, replacing the earlier uncoordinated sets of activities by a better-coordinated set.

It is true that the disappointment of earlier-made plans of (the inefficient) producers may hit them with a sense of great pain. But, from the perspective of the coordination criterion for goodness, that pain is hardly of relevance. Notice that this assertion reflects no moral judgment of the older, inefficient producers. Their innocence need not be doubted; nor the reality or moral significance of their pain. We simply point out that the coordination criterion is not measuring goodness by any aggregate measure of well-being (because we believe that economic science cannot recognize the validity of such aggregates). In fact, well-being is not referred to in the coordination criterion at all. Moreover, the pain suffered by the older, inefficient producers has arisen only because those inefficient producers had believed (innocently, perhaps, but nonetheless erroneously, and, from the consumers' perspective, harmfully), that they could continue indefinitely to rely on the consumers' failing to take advantage of alternative available opportunities. From the perspective of the coordination criterion this "pain" thus appears to be based upon an illusion, the removal of which has definitely positive merit. What has been taken from the inefficient firms is nothing but the false expectations which their illusions had nourished, that they would be able to continue to rely on consumers' remaining ignorant of better opportunities available to them elsewhere. The coordination criterion (that is, the moral principles which pronounce this criterion to be a useful standard, among other possible standards, of "goodness") refuses to acknowledge the relevance of any pain which accompanies the realization of the falsity of such expectations. We may indeed have compassion for the pained victim of such self-delusion, but such compassion is not part of that moral dimension of social goodness which we seek to isolate by the adjective "economic," a moral dimension which the coordination criterion seems to capture very neatly.

COORDINATION AND PARETO-OPTIMALITY

It will be noticed that the coordination criterion bears a certain formal resemblance to Pareto-optimality. In this section we briefly examine this apparent resemblance, and clarify our reason for rejecting the Paretian criterion in favor of coordination.

A state of full coordinatedness is, of course, Pareto-optimal. If each participant is taking full account of actions (and potential actions) of each other participant, this clearly means that all courses of action which might be preferred by any one participant without hurting anyone else, · must already have been successfully pursued. Conversely, if a Pareto-preferred course of action *is* available, this must mean that, to some extent, participants have not taken full account of what others might be prepared to do under all relevant circumstances; Pareto-suboptimality corresponds to imperfect coordination. Yet to use Pareto-optimality as the criterion of economic goodness is not the same as using the coordination criterion; the formal congruence of the two concepts does not at all imply that the philosophical or moral meanings of these two criteria are the same. Pareto-optimality is generally understood to be a concept that ingeniously permits us to talk of the overall well-being of society without having to confront the problems of interpersonal utility comparisons. The coordination criterion does not purport to say anything whatever about aggregate well-being.

The Pareto-optimality concept (because it is generally understood as representing, in a certain limited sense, maximum possible aggregate well-being) is widely used as a criterion relevant to "social efficiency" in the allocation of society's resources (a notion seen as similar to that of individual efficiency in budgeting scarce individual resources among competing individual ends). A Pareto-suboptimal state of affairs is socially inefficient, because somehow that state of affairs reflects a failure to achieve the highest level of aggregate well-being that might have been attained. The coordination criterion implies nothing about any such notion as social efficiency. In fact it emerged as a deliberate attempt to be able to say something about the economic goodness of policies or situations *without* becoming embroiled in the well-known analytical and conceptual difficulties which render the notion of social efficiency unacceptable to Austrian economists.[16]

Because the Pareto-criterion is understood to be concerned with aggregate well-being, its serviceability as a yardstick of economic goodness depends on our willingness to accept aggregate well-being—defined in terms of satisfaction of individual preferences—as a relevant moral norm. Notice that this does not mean that in making judgments based on Pareto-optimality considerations, standard welfare economics has committed itself morally to this norm.[17] It merely means that, in using Pareto-optimality as the criterion for goodness, it is presuming that those to whom welfare economics provides technical advice do share this moral commitment. Nonetheless use of the Paretian-criterion does, somewhere along the line, presume a moral acceptance of the satisfaction of individual preferences as an important element of "goodness." Use of the coordination criterion involves no such moral commitment at all, on anybody's part. Use of the coordination-criterion presumes that those advised by the economist are morally concerned that members of society undertake their actions in a way that does not inevitably spell disappointment and/ or regret (such as must ultimately ensue from patterns of action which incorrectly anticipate and depend upon the actions of others in the system). This moral concern is clearly a different one from that generally understood as implicit in the deployment of the Pareto-criterion.

CONCLUSION

There is no doubt that when the layperson is led to believe that a particular piece of legislation is good economic policy, he understands that to mean that this legislation overwhelmingly tends sooner or later to improve chances for the greater overall prosperity of society, with "prosperity" itself being understood by the layperson to be measurable in fairly definite terms. Economists have struggled mightily to render this vague notion of global economic "goodness" precise and objectively definable. One criterion after another has been proposed, only to have it be rejected on theoretical-consistency grounds. For economists concerned to preserve the sense of economic meaningfulness strictly on methodologically individualistic grounds, and aware of the challenge posed for economic meaningfulness by the circumstance of dispersed knowledge, the difficulty of devising an acceptable criterion for economic goodness has been particularly daunting. In this chapter I have outlined the case for taking "coordination" (particularly in the process sense of this word) as the criterion for which economists have been searching.[18]

NOTES

1. Helpful comments on an earlier draft were gratefully received from members of the Austrian Economics Colloquium at New York University. The author is especially indebted for stimulating and insightful criticisms and suggestions contributed by David Harper and Sanford Ikeda.

2. There were, of course, differences among classical economists concerning the precise definition of wealth. On this see Kirzner (1960, pp. 29–32).

3. See Hayek (1949, 1945).

4. See e.g. Hausman and McPherson (1993).

5. See Kirzner (1963, pp. 33–44, 297–309); (1973, ch. 6); O'Driscoll (1977); Cordato (1992).

6. See Whately (1855, p. 25).

7. For a classic statement of these problems in welfare economics, see Robbins (1935, chs III and VI). Readers of Robbins's book will be aware of the extensive influence of Robbins's ideas upon this chapter.

8. Hayek (1944, 1945).

9. The assertion in the text is contrary to the (surprisingly) opposite interpretation of this writer's position suggested by Daniel Klein (1997, p. 331).

10. See Kirzner (1994).

11. Mishan (1976). I am indebted to Mario J. Rizzo for reference; see also Rizzo (1980).

12. This exposition of Mises's economic calculation demonstration of the impossibility of socialist central planning may, concededly, seem forced. Certainly Mises himself intended to show that, from the perspective of the central planners themselves, their "plan" must necessarily fail to be a true plan, since the planners *cannot* be aware of the full consequences of each part of their plan for each other part. We do not at all question the validity of this assertion, and it is of course the basis of our discussion in the text. However, in order unambiguously to rank the economic "goodness" of the market economy and the centrally planned economy respectively, this assertion may not be sufficient. Conceivably, "unplanned" socialism (i.e., socialism with its fatally flawed central "plan") might in some sense be judged economically superior to the literally unplanned outcomes of the competitive market. The coordination criterion enables us to translate Mises's own demonstration (of the impossibility of a true central plan) into a coordination-based assessment of the relative economic superiority

of the market economy and the centrally planned economy respectively. For such a translation, we have argued in the text, some initial private-property pattern of rights assignment must be assumed, in order for a coordination-based comparison to be able to be rigorously attempted.

13. On this see Kirzner (1992, pp. 190–92).

14. See e.g. Kirzner (1973, p. 81).

15. See e.g. Klein (1997, p. 331 and fn 7).

16. For literature directly or indirectly critical of the notion of social efficiency, see Littlechild (1978, pp. 77–93); Rizzo (1979b) and Rothbard (1979); Egger (1979, pp. 118–22).

17. On this point we must disagree with the position taken by Hausman and McPherson (1993).

18. We must readily grant that even if the arguments in this chapter are accepted, we have not yet firmly established the usefulness of the coordination concept as the criterion for economic goodness. The serviceability of the coordination criterion, as a device with which to rank a series of alternative policies, has yet to be concretely demonstrated. Nevertheless, casual consideration of such welfare issues as the socialist calculation debate, suggests that the coordination criterion can fairly easily be used for at least some evaluative purposes. In addition, the *formal* congruence of this criterion with the Paretian criterion, noticed earlier in the text, suggests further scope for the serviceability of the coordination criterion, along lines traditionally pursued within the standard Paretian welfare economics.

REFERENCES

Cordato, R. E. (1992) *Welfare Economics and Externalities in an Open-ended Universe,* Boston, Dordrecht, London: Kluwer.

Egger, J. B. (1979) "Comment: Efficiency is Not a Substitute for Ethics," in M. J. Rizzo (ed.) *Time, Uncertainty, and Disequilibrium,* Lexington, Mass.: Lexington Books.

Hausman, D. M. and McPherson, M. S. (1993) "Taking Ethics Seriously: Economics and Contemporary Moral Philosophy," *Journal of Economic Literature* 91, pp. 671–731.

Hayek, F. A. (1945) "The Use of Knowledge in Society," *American Economic Review* 35. Reprinted in Hayek (1949).

—— (1949) *Individualism and Economic Order,* London: Kegan Paul.

Kirzner, I. M. (1960) *The Economic Point of View,* Princeton, NJ: Van Nostrand.

—— (1963) *Market Theory and the Price System,* Princeton, NJ: Van Nostrand.

—— (1973) *Competition and Entrepreneurship,* Chicago: University of Chicago Press.

—— (1992) *The Meaning of Market Process, Essays in the Development of Modern Austrian Economics,* London: Routledge.

—— (1994) "The Limits of the Market: the Real and the Imagined," in Möschel *et al.* (1994), republished as chapter 4 in the present volume.

Klein, D. (1997) "Convention, Social Order, and the two Coordinations," *Constitutional Political Economy* 8, p. 331.

Littlechild, S. C. (1978) "The Problem of Social Cost," in *Spadaro* (1978).

Mishan, E. J. (1976) *Cost-Benefit Analysis*, rev. edn, New York: Praeger.

Möschel, W., Streit, M. E., and Witt, U. (eds) (1994) *Marktwirtschaft und Rechtsordnung*, Baden-Baden: Nomos.

O'Driscoll, G. P., Jr. (1977) *Economics as a Coordination Problem: The Contributions of Friedrich A. Hayek*, Kansas City: Sheed, Andrews and McMeel.

Rizzo, M. J. (ed.) (1979a) *Time, Uncertainty, and Disequilibrium*. Lexington, Mass.: Lexington Books.

────── (1979b) "Uncertainty, Subjectivity, and the Economic Analysis of Law," in Rizzo (1979a).

────── (1980) "The Mirage of Efficiency," *Hofstra Law Review* 8, pp. 648ff.

Robbins, L. C. (1935) *The Nature and Significance of Economic Science*, 2nd edn, London: Macmillan.

Rothbard, M. N. "Comment: The Myth of Efficiency," in Rizzo (1979a).

Spadaro, L. M. (ed.) (1978) *New Directions in Austrian Economics*, Kansas City: Sheed, Andrews and McMeel.

Whately, R. (1855) *Introductory Lectures on Political Economy, Delivered at Oxford in Easter Term, 1831*, 4th edn, London: John W. Parker.

WELFARE ECONOMICS: A MODERN
AUSTRIAN PERSPECTIVE

Among the most notable of Murray Rothbard's many contributions to
the literature of modern Austrian economics is surely the major paper
on utility and welfare theory that he wrote for the 1956 Mises Festschrift
(Rothbard 1956). This writer can personally attest to the excitement
engendered by the lucid manner in which this paper deployed Austrian
insights to illuminate fundamental theoretical issues (concerning which
contemporary economics was floundering) and by the characteristic eru-
dition which Rothbard poured into that single essay. Whether or not one
fully accepted Rothbard's conclusions, it was impossible not to glimpse
the power of consistent Misesian thinking which that paper so excel-
lently exemplified. The present chapter, written thirty years later, seeks
to reexamine a small part of the terrain covered by Rothbard's essay. In
offering a modern Austrian perspective on welfare economics we shall
be emphasizing some of the same basic Austrian tenets that Rothbard
so rightly insisted on thirty years ago. While our perspective may not
entirely dovetail with some of Rothbard's conclusions, we venture to
hope that our observations concerning welfare economics be judged to
be in the same subjectivist, methodologically individualistic tradition that
Rothbard's work has so valuably carried forward for so many years.

SOME OBSERVATIONS CONCERNING WELFARE ECONOMICS

Welfare economics, in its numerous incarnations, has sought to offer criteria by which it might be possible scientifically to evaluate the economic
merits of specific institutions, pieces of legislation or events. Such evaluation would have to transcend the narrow economic concerns of specific
individuals whose interests might be involved, and to express, somehow, a
perspective flowing from the economic interests of all individuals in society.

From *The Meaning of Market Process: Essays in the Development of Modern Austrian
Economics* (New York and London: Routledge, 1992). 180–92. Reprinted by permission of the Mises Institute; the original source is *Man, Economy and Liberty: Essays in
Honor of Murray N. Rothbard*, ed. W. Block and L. Rockwell (Ludwig von Mises Institute, 1988).

As we shall see, Austrian economists have been particularly sensitive to the difficulties that must beset such an undertaking. Indeed, many of the difficulties have been recognized again and again by the economic profession at large, and it is for these reasons, of course, that welfare economics has undergone so many attempted reconstructions "from the ground up."

We shall briefly survey the more important of these attempts from a perspective that seeks consistently to apply the following (related) Austrian concerns.

1. Methodological individualism: we shall refuse to recognize meaning in statements concerning the "welfare of society" that cannot, in principle, be unambiguously translated into statements concerning the individuals in society (in a manner which does not do violence to their individuality).

2. Subjectivism: we shall not be satisfied with statements that perceive the economic well-being of society as expressible in terms (such as physical output) that are unrelated to the valuations and choices made by individuals.

3. An emphasis on process: we shall be interested in the economic well-being of society not merely in terms of its level of economic well-being (however defined) but also in regard to the ability of its institutions to stimulate and support those economic processes upon which the attainment of economic well-being depends.

WELFARE ECONOMICS—SOME HIGHLIGHTS OF ITS PAST

1. During the period of classical economics it was, of course, taken for granted that a society was economically successful strictly in so far as it succeeded in achieving increased wealth. Adam Smith's *Inquiry into the Nature and Causes of the Wealth of Nations* expressed this approach to the economics of welfare simply and typically. It was taken for granted that a given percentage increase in a nation's physical wealth (with wealth often seen as being able to be seen as consisting of bushels of "corn") meant a similar percentage increase in the nation's well-being. From this perspective a physical measure of a nation's wealth provides an index of that nation's economic success, regardless of its distribution. A bushel of wheat is a bushel of wheat. Clearly this notion of welfare offends the principles of methodological individualism and subjectivism; it was swept away by the marginalist (subjectivist) revolution of the late nineteenth century.

2. Marshall and Pigou sought to preserve certain central elements of the classical approach, while avoiding the trap which sees well-being as identified with (or directly proportional to) physical wealth itself. They focused attention not on goods themselves, but on the *utility* of those goods. In principle a nation's physical wealth, given its pattern of distribution, corresponded to a given level of aggregate utility. Moreover they believed this aggregate to be measurable, in principle, by the "measuring rod of money." They sensed no problem in conceiving of "aggregate utility"; they thought of utility as something that could be compared and aggregated across individuals. They certainly did not see utility as associated uniquely with an individual act of choice; rather, they saw it as a kind of psychological shadow that closely followed physical wealth. (Its central advantage over wealth, as an index of well-being, was that it incorporated the refinement of diminishing marginal utility. It was no longer acceptable to consider a bushel of wheat to be identical, welfare-wise, with every bushel of wheat: the margin of consumption by the individual must be considered. But it was still considered valid to treat one dollar's worth of utility as entirely equivalent to a second dollar's worth of utility.)

This approach to welfare economics is clearly unacceptable to economists who have absorbed the Misesian (and Rothbardian) lessons concerning the true meaning of utility in economic analysis. Utility, for Austrians, is not a quantity of psychological experience; it is merely an index of preferability as expressed in acts of choice. To attempt to aggregate utility is not merely to violate the tenets of methodological individualism and subjectivism (by treating the sensations of different individuals as being able to be added up), it is to engage in an entirely meaningless exercise: economic analysis has nothing to say about sensations; it deals strictly with choices and their interpersonal implications.

3. The approach to welfare economics that has, of course, been central to economics for the past half-century is that which revolves round the notion of Pareto optimality. A change is seen as enhancing the economic well-being of society if it renders some of its members better off (in their estimation) without rendering any others worse off. This approach certainly avoids the problems of interpersonal comparisons of utility, and would thus seem to be consistent both with the methodological individualism and with the subjectivism that Austrians insist upon. Several points, however, need to be noticed.

While the notion of Pareto optimality is indeed concerned with the individual members of society it none the less reflects a supra-individual conception of society and its well-being. After all, a Pareto-optimal move is considered to advance the well-being *of society*—considered as a whole. Otherwise it is not at all clear what is added (to the bald observation that the change is preferred by some and objected to by none) by the judgement that the move is "good for society." Indeed the Pareto criterion turned out to become an integral element in the development of the idea that society faces an "economic problem"—that of allocating its resources among its competing goals in the most efficient manner. Societal inefficiency in resource allocation came to be identified with suboptimality according to the Pareto criterion.

Now this notion of society facing its economic problem in the resource allocation sense arose, as is well known, as an extension of the concept of individual economizing behaviour that was articulated so definitively by Lionel Robbins in 1932. But, as has before now been recognized, this extension is in fact an illegitimate extension, not at all faithful to the spirit of Robbins's formulation. Robbins was concerned to identify the economic problem facing the *individual*. It is the individual who has goals and who deliberately deploys his perceived resources in order to achieve his goals most efficiently, so far as is possible. To transfer this important concept of individual allocative choice to society as a whole is, at best, to engage in metaphor. Society, as such, neither possesses goals of its own nor deliberately engages in allocative choice. In so far as the idea of Pareto optimality came to reinforce the faulty and misleading notion of society's "economic problem," it was part of an approach to the analysis of economic welfare that fell grievously short of consistent adherence to the principles of methodological individualism.

HAYEK AND THE CRITIQUE OF WELFARE ECONOMICS

It was against this mainstream notion of society and its purported allocative problem that Hayek's famous 1945 paper (Hayek 1949b) was directed. Hayek's attack might, it is true, be seen as not being *primarily* against the welfare notion that was embedded in the idea of society's economic problem. Hayek focused on the circumstances of dispersed knowledge. The relevant information that "society" would have to possess in order to solve its economic problem is widely dispersed. Society is thus simply not in a position to address its supposed economic problem (even if, for the sake of discussion, this societal allocative task could be held to be meaningful). Hayek's critique might thus be seen as emphasizing the problems obstructing the practical solution of a nation's economic problem, rather than as a critique of the standard conception of that problem itself. But Hayek's paper constituted, none the less, a profound—if indirect—critique of the very meaningfulness of societal efficiency as developed, for example, in the Paretian context.

For once it is recognized that the relevant information *is* inevitably and definitely dispersed among many minds, it is impossible to avoid the conclusion that the notion of social efficiency is correspondingly devoid of meaning. Social efficiency must refer to the extent to which the allocation of social resources corresponds to the priorities implied in the relative urgencies of social goals. But in order for the notion of "social resources" to be meaningful, and in order for the notion of "relative urgencies of social goals" to be meaningful, it must, at least in principle, be possible to imagine a single mind to which the relevant arrays of social resources and social objectives are simultaneously given. Hayek's insight concerning dispersed knowledge was, in effect, to deny such a possibility. Thus dispersed knowledge turns out to be not merely a phenomenon that constitutes a practical difficulty with which would-be planners must grapple, but a phenomenon (not necessarily the only one) that robs the very concept of social efficiency of its meaningfulness, even in principle. To choose *presupposes* an integrated framework of ends and means; without such a presumed framework allocative choice is hardly a coherent notion at all (Buchanan 1964). Hayek's insight into the subjectivism of knowledge and information has thus decisively dislodged the foundations of Paretian welfare economics, at least in so far as those foundations have been held to support the concept of social choice and social efficiency. (More recent extensions by Hayek and others of this subjectivism of information to encompass also Polanyi's idea of "tacit knowledge"—knowledge incapable of being deliberately communicated to others—have rendered these damaging implications for standard welfare economics even more destructive (Hayek 1979: 190).

CO-ORDINATION AS A HAYEKIAN
WELFARE CRITERION

Several writers, pursuing the implications of these Hayekian insights, have seen the concept of "co-ordination" as offering a normative yardstick consistent with these subjectivist and methodologically individualistic insights (Kirzner 1973: ch. 6; O'Driscoll 1977). As discussed, the notion of social choice (and thus of the efficiency of such choice) has been fatally undermined (except at the level of metaphor). If Jones (who prefers Smith's food to his own enjoyment of a day's leisure) fails to trade with Smith (who prefers the labour of Jones over his own food), we may not be able to say that society has failed efficiently to allocate the food and labour time between Jones and Smith, but we could surely still say that Jones and Smith have failed to co-ordinate their activities and their decisions. It seems plausible and intuitively appealing to perceive co-ordination— permitting each agent to achieve his goals through the simultaneous satisfaction of the goals of the other agent—as constituting a desideratum transcending the individual goals of the respective agents. Failure to achieve co-ordination might thus be seen as a failure of the social apparatus to achieve a supra-individual result—but such a judgement relies not at all on any notions inconsistent with subjectivism or with methodological individualism.

It is of course true that the fulfilment of the co-ordination norm appears to be formally equivalent to the fulfilment of the Paretian welfare criterion. Any suboptimal situation (in the Paretian sense) clearly corresponds to the failure of a pair of market participants to trade with one another on feasible, mutually attractive terms—in other words, it corresponds to a failure to achieve co-ordination. But, unlike the Paretian norm, the co-ordination norm escapes interpretation as a yardstick for social efficiency in social allocative choice. Co-ordination does not refer to the well-being achieved through its successful attainment; it refers only to the dovetailing character of the activities that make it up.

Thus Hayek's emphasis on the dispersed character of knowledge appears to provide not merely the definitive critique of standard Paretian welfare economics, but also the basis for an alternative normative yardstick, one thoroughly consistent with the tenet of methodological individualism. Scope for this new normative yardstick is provided precisely by the circumstance of dispersed knowledge. Fragmented knowledge is responsible for activities that are *not* mutually co-ordinated. The "social" problem faced by Hayek's economic society is precisely that of overcoming the discoordination to be expected to flow out of such fragmentation.

There is a deeper issue here. If one abstracts from the fragmented character of information, if one treats all existing information as if it were known to all market participants, one is, of course, abstracting from the possibility of discoordinated activities. With the Hayekian "economic problem" assumed to be out of the way in this fashion, it might seem that the standard (Paretian) economic problem comes back into its own, invulnerable to Hayekian strictures. The problem facing society, on such assumptions, would appear to reduce to that of achieving Paretian optimality in respect of the relevant social objectives, in the face of its limited resources. But, surely, if we assume away the dispersed character of information, the standard economic problem facing society presents no challenge at all. If we can assume that what is known to one is known to all, then (averting our gaze from the remaining quibbles which the methodological individualist might have against the concept of social efficiency) it seems difficult to imagine the possibility of any social allocation of resources that might be pronounced socially *inefficient*. Given perfect mutual knowledge it appears obvious that all possible Pareto-optimal moves *must have already been implemented.* To imagine otherwise would be to imagine that agents deliberately refrain from taking advantage of available opportunities known by them to exist. Knowledge of all such opportunities, and knowledge of all relevant transaction costs, must appear inevitably to lead to Pareto optimality (given these transaction costs)—achieved either through market activity or through centralized organization (with the latter choice itself determined by comparison of the respective transaction costs).

So Hayek's insights concerning fragmented knowledge might appear to provide not merely a critique of standard welfare criteria, and also a substitute yardstick (in terms of the co-ordination norm)—they might appear at the same time to salvage welfare economics from the extinction to which it would be doomed by the inevitability of perpetual optimality. But the situation is not quite so simple.

HAYEK IN THE PANGLOSSIAN WORLD

The truth is that many of the observations made in the preceding sections might seem to be vulnerable to serious challenge. Such challenges, it would seem, can be launched at several distinct levels, with the challenges stemming precisely from the paralysis arising from the inevitability of perpetual optimality. On the one hand it might appear that the circumstance of fragmented knowledge does *not* salvage welfare economics from the extinction spelled by perpetual optimality. Further it might be argued that Hayek's insights in fact deepen the perplexities created by such Panglossian concerns. We shall in the present section develop these challenges. In subsequent sections we shall rebut these challenges, showing how the observations made in the preceding sections with regard to Hayekian welfare economics *can* be defended (despite the challenges developed in the present section). Moreover we shall use our discussion to point out a novel sense in which "co-ordination" offers a normative criterion that escapes Panglossian paralysis. (It will be in the context of the latter discussion that we shall deploy the third Austrian tenet referred to at the outset of this chapter, that of maintaining a concern with *processes* rather than exclusively states of affairs.) We turn now to develop the apparent challenges to Hayekian welfare economics referred to at the outset of this section.

The difficulties that we must face up to, in considering the Hayekian thesis of dispersed knowledge and information, consist in the fact that, from a mainstream perspective, the Hayekian "knowledge problem" might appear not to be a problem at all, in the relevant sense (see chapter 9). To point out that knowledge is scattered in society is, it might be argued (contrary to our earlier assertions), not necessarily to note that standard welfare analysis is inapplicable—it is merely to point out that such standard welfare analysis is to be carried on in the context of a hitherto unsuspected cost, the cost of ascertaining and of communicating information. Dispersal of knowledge and information indeed introduces new costs for the acquisition of the knowledge necessary for economic choice. But surely the presence of a novel class of costs does not, in principle, render inapplicable the standard criteria for the evaluation of social efficiency.

Moreover, once it is recognized that the fragmentation of information complicates standard welfare analysis without vitiating it, it seems appropriate to point out that the Panglossian paralysis referred to earlier offers threats as serious for a "co-ordination"-based approach to welfare analysis as for the mainstream approach. After all, any discussion of Jones and Smith "co-ordinating" their activities must refer to a potential for co-ordination in the context of the relevant resource constraints confronting the respective parties. Surely, then, the availability and costliness of information acquisition must be counted as part of these "relevant resource constraints." If engineer Jones, Sr, and farmer Smith can exchange engineering services for food, with mutual gain, it may seem that only a co-ordination failure could prevent such exchange from taking place. But it will not constitute a co-ordination failure if Jones, Jr, schoolboy, refrains from enrolling in an engineering programme on his graduation from high school if the costs of the training programme are too high. Similarly, it might appear, all co-ordination "failures" attributable to Hayekian knowledge fragmentation turn out not to be failures at all once one properly considers the cost of searching for the information needed to bridge the dispersed knowledge gaps. If Jones, Sr, and Smith fail to engage in mutually gainful exchange as a result of knowledge dispersal, they are not, it might be contended, acting suboptimally from a social point of view; they are fully taking advantage of each other's availability in the context of their limited knowledge of each other's situation. To pronounce this state of affairs to be socially inefficient or "uncoordinated" might seem to be succumbing to a temptation warned against in elementary economics, namely that of pronouncing welfare judgements without regard to resource scarcities. Participants in an economy can be counted upon to engage in mutually gainful exchange transactions in so far as their knowledge permits. Moreover, in so far as participants are aware of worthwhile possibilities for learning useful information that may reveal as yet unexploited opportunities for mutual gain, they can surely be counted upon to engage in such useful learning. It does seem, then, that, in a world of dispersed information as in a world of omniscience, suboptimality or states of discoordinatedness cannot be postulated to exist (if one properly includes the costs of information acquisition).

Indeed it might be contended that it is precisely Hayek's dispersed information insights that are capable of focusing needed attention on the costs of learning and of knowledge communication. Once the paralysing assumption of perfect knowledge has been dropped it becomes impossible to avoid grappling with the economics of learning and communication. Our contention thus far is that, once such economics of learning and communication has been taken into account, Panglossian perpetual optimality paralysis sets in once again. At all times agents will be engaging in the optimal mix of decisions (including decisions to learn and to communicate). No pair of decisions can be pronounced uncoordinated, given the costs of learning.

DISPERSED KNOWLEDGE, OPTIMAL
IGNORANCE AND GENUINE ERROR

We shall discover, however, that these contentions are invalid. The Panglossian paralysis we have found to afflict mainstream welfare economics is *not* a threat to the Hayekian co-ordination approach. It is *not* the case, we shall see, that Hayek's fragmentation of information does nothing more than complicate matters through the introduction of a new cost. Rather, the dispersal of knowledge creates scope for a genuinely fresh approach to normative analysis. This is so because such dispersal of knowledge necessarily involves not merely new costs (of learning and communication) but also the very real possibility of what we may call *"genuine error."*

This writer has elsewhere argued (Kirzner 1979a: ch. 8; 1985a) that genuine error, so often exorcised from economic analysis, in fact deserves a central place in that analysis. Genuine error occurs *where a decision maker's ignorance is not attributable to the costs of search, or of learning or of communication.* In such cases the decision maker's ignorance is *utter* ignorance, i.e. it is a result of his ignorance of available, costworthy, avenues to needed information (which includes, of course, the possibility of his being altogether ignorant of the very existence of valuable information). At the level of the individual decision maker we may describe his activity as having been suboptimal when he subsequently discovers himself to have inexplicably overlooked available opportunities that were in fact worthwhile. He cannot "condone" his faulty decision making on the grounds of the cost of acquiring information, since the information was in fact costlessly available to him. He can account for his failure only by acknowledging his utter ignorance of the true circumstances (i.e. his ignorance of the availability of relevant information at worthwhile low cost). Such utter ignorance cannot be explained in cost–benefit terms; it is simply a given.

Two implications of the phenomenon of utter ignorance, of genuine error, may be noticed. First, the injection into economic reasoning of the possibility of genuine error introduces a degree of "looseness" into our understanding of economic processes that is of great importance. It is no longer true that the configuration of exogenous variables, tastes, resource availabilities and technological possibilities, unambiguously marks out the course of individual activities. This is because, while these data do mark out the optimal opportunities, we cannot be confident that such optimal opportunities will be known to the relevant decision makers— even if we make provision for deliberate processes of search and learning. We cannot be sure that available processes of search and learning are known to those who might benefit therefrom. The second implication (flowing from recognition of the phenomenon of genuine error) is that we must now recognize the possibility of corrective actions within an economy that are not to be traced to shifting cost patterns. Corrective action may be set off by the sudden ("entrepreneurial") discovery by a market participant of a hitherto unperceived opportunity for pure profit. Let us now return to examine Hayek's dispersed information.

We objected that the introduction of the need for costly search, learning and communication (forced upon us by Hayek's insight) does not really threaten the mainstream economizing view. The fragmentation of knowledge, we pointed out, merely introduced an additional cost dimension— that of mobilizing and centralizing scattered bits of information. We now see that the fragmentation of knowledge is likely to affect matters far more seriously and fundamentally. *The fragmentation of knowledge injects into the picture scope for genuine error, resulting from utter ignorance.* Pursuing once again the line of reasoning introduced earlier (and subsequently challenged in the preceding section) the circumstance of dispersed and fragmented knowledge compels us not merely to recognize a practical difficulty to be encountered in seeking to address society's allocative efficiency problem—this circumstance undermines the very meaningfulness of such a social "economic problem." Given the scope for genuine error we now see to be implicit in the circumstance of dispersed information, we see that this circumstance indeed erodes the meaningfulness of the concept of social allocative efficiency. Before we can even begin to contemplate what we may mean by social allocative efficiency we must somehow confront the problem of overcoming that utter ignorance which obstructs the relevancy of the efficiency concept for social policy. It is here that the norm of "co-ordination" is to be perceived in a fresh light, rather different from that co-ordination norm discussed earlier.

CO-ORDINATION AND CO-ORDINATION

We must distinguish carefully between (a) a possible norm of co-ordination in the sense of a co-ordinated state of affairs and (b) a possible norm of co-ordination in the sense of the ability to detect and to move toward correcting situations in which activities have until now been discoordinated (see also chapter 8). The distinction between these two possibilities corresponds to the two different meanings of the word "co-ordination": it may refer to the activities being carried out when these activities are indeed dovetailing with one another; alternatively it may refer to the process through which initially clashing, discoordinated activities are somehow being hammered out in a manner such as to approach a more smoothly dovetailing pattern of activities. The discussion earlier in this paper implicitly referred to co-ordination only in the first of these two senses. (It is for this reason that we were able to note formal equivalency between the co-ordination norm and the norm of Pareto efficiency.) We wish now to draw attention to the possible relevance of the second co-ordination norm for a modern Austrian approach to welfare economics.

Once we have identified genuine error as a culprit responsible for a failure of a society's economic system to fulfil its functions successfully, we have placed ourselves in a position to appreciate the meaning of this second co-ordination norm. Without the phenomenon of utter ignorance, we have seen, our *first* co-ordination concept (like its Paretian counterpart) turned out to be of little normative interest. After all, we noted, given the absence of utter ignorance, all activities must be carried on in optimal fashion. Even if some activities are being carried out "erroneously," because of incomplete information, we saw, we could hardly describe these activities as being suboptimal or "wrong"—after all, they took advantage of every scrap of information it was judged worthwhile to lay their hands on. In this sense the world at all times is at a Pareto optimum, in a state of full co-ordination—the best of all possible worlds, given the costs of change. But injection of the possibility of genuine error arising out of simple utter ignorance introduces us to the possibility of *genuine* discoordination—and to the possibility of evaluating the institutional environment in terms of its potential to inspire genuine discovery (of opportunities previously overlooked as a result of utter ignorance). Thus a norm of co-ordination looms into centre stage in the sense of permitting us to ask what potential a society's economy possesses to inspire such pure discovery of its earlier genuine errors. Such an approach to welfare economics is made possible by our escape from the Panglossian world; that escape was, in turn, made possible by our emphasis on genuine error (arising out of utter ignorance); we have seen in this chapter that scope for genuine error is widened most considerably by the circumstance of dispersed and fragmented information identified by Hayek. It is for this reason that we see Hayek's criticisms of standard approaches to welfare analysis as opening the door, at the same time, for the possible reconstruction of normative economics along truly Austrian lines, i.e. in a manner fully consistent with (a) subjectivism, (b) methodological individualism and (c) an emphasis on dynamic processes.

REFERENCES

Hayek, F. A. (1949b) "The use of knowledge in society," in *Individualism and Economic Order*, London: Routledge & Kegan Paul (originally published in *American Economic Review* 35 (4) (1945): 519–30).

Hayek, F. A. (1979) *Law, Legislation and Liberty*, Vol. 3, *The Political Order of a Free People*, Chicago, IL: University of Chicago Press.

Kirzner, I. M. (1973) *Competition and Entrepreneurship*, Chicago, IL: University of Chicago Press.

Kirzner, I. M. (1979a) *Perception, Opportunity and Profit*, Chicago, IL: University of Chicago Press.

Kirzner, I. M. (1985a) *Discovery and the Capitalist Process*, Chicago, IL: University of Chicago Press.

O'Driscoll, G. P., Jr (1977) *Economics as a Coordination Problem, The Contributions of Friedrich A. Hayek*, Kansas City, KS: Sheed, Andrews & McMeel.

Pareto, V. (1927) *Manual d'économie politique*, 2nd edn, Paris.

Rothbard, M. N. (1956) "Toward a reconstruction of utility and welfare economics," in M. Sennholz (ed.) *On Freedom and Free Enterprise*, Princeton, NJ: Van Nostrand, pp. 224–62.

AUSTRIAN ECONOMICS, THE COORDINATION CRITERION, AND CLASSICAL LIBERALISM

I. INTRODUCTION

Classical liberalism consists of a set of political ideals reflecting, for perhaps most of its adherents, both (a) "absolute" moral convictions, and (b) purely "instrumental" utilitarian considerations. These latter considerations are usually identified with the conclusions of economic science. Economics, and in particular Austrian Economics, is generally held to teach that economic efficiency, prosperity and success can be expected to result from free market arrangements. In this way, Austrian Economics is seen as an important intellectual foundation for classical liberalism. This paper explores the interface thus held to exist between science and political conviction.

2. WERTFREIHEIT AND ALL THAT

This topic is, of course, an old one.[1] Max Weber famously criticized members of the German Historical School for illegitimately injecting their personal judgments of value into their scientific work, thus rendering their conclusions (Weber argued) invalid as science. Austrian economists (and especially Ludwig von Mises) generally accepted Weber's exhortation to keep science *wertfrei*.[2] When Gunnar Myrdal wrote his *The Political Element in the Development of Economic Theory* (first Swedish edition, 1929), he gave the Austrian School high marks for refraining from permitting their political aims to shape their science.[3]

A first version of this article had been presented at the XXth Session of Université d'Eté de la Nouvelle Economie, University of Aix en Provence, September 3, 1997. From *Le Journal des Economistes et des Etudes Humaines* 8, 2/3 (June/September 1998): 187–200. Reprinted by permission of De Gruyter.

1. The author offers no apologies for being old-fashioned enough to take for granted throughout this paper that "ought" statements differ categorically from "is" statements; and in particular, that science is able to deal with the truth-content of the latter statements with an objectivity not possible in regard to the former.

2. On the "*wertfreiheit*" doctrine, see also Kirzner 1994.

3. See Myrdal 1954, p. 128.

Yet this did not prevent Austrian economists (like all economists) from permitting their scientific conclusions to lend crucial support for specific policy positions they saw as being logically implied by those conclusions. In this they were following the path pioneered in 1831 by Richard Whately who, when criticized (as a clergyman) for engaging in research in the morally questionable science of wealth, pointed out that a scientist exploring the science of wealth does not necessarily have to aim at increasing wealth; after all, a medical researcher doing research on a disease, does not necessarily have to aim at promoting that disease![4] Similarly, the scientific autonomy of a research project is not affected or contaminated by its being subsequently employed by those with an interest either in promoting or eliminating the phenomenon being researched. Economics as a *wertfrei* science is not contaminated, nor need its conclusions be rendered in any way suspect, by its ability to serve a particular set of political objectives.

Having recognized all this (and we shall in a later section of this paper return to examine critically a line of recent work generally challenging the possibility of any economics being independent of moral entanglements) however, one hastens also to recognize, at the same time, the danger to scientific integrity and reputability posed by the deployment of positive scientific conclusions in order to further particular political or ideological objectives. Not only is there the danger that the economist may, wittingly or unwittingly, illegitimately tailor his conclusions to fit such extra-scientific objectives. There is the perhaps even more serious danger that, even if (or precisely when) the economist arrives at his conclusions on purely objective and scientific grounds, these conclusions may be decisively dismissed in the world of public opinion—because this objectivity is simply not trusted. "Everyone knows," it will be asserted with casual cynicism, "that anyone wishing for financial reasons to promote a particular policy, can easily stimulate the appearance of a professionally-crafted research study 'proving' that policy to be the very best for society. . . ."

It was for this reason that Mises, the passionate ideologue on behalf of classical liberalism, insisted—in fact he *passionately* insisted—on the

---

4. Whately 1855, p. 25. Compare also the statement made by Mises a century later: "The objectivity of bacteriology . . . is not in the least vitiated by the fact that the researchers in this field regard their task as a struggle against the viruses responsible for conditions harmful to the human organism." Mises 1960, p. 36.

wertfreiheit of the economist. Precisely because he believed that economic science *can* offer powerful support for classical liberalism, he saw it as crucially important that the reputability and objectivity of that science be maintained beyond suspicion. Economics demonstrates truths which society can ignore, Mises held, only with the direst consequences. The economist has a *duty* to teach society those truths—for the sake of the very survival of civilized society. But the economist's teachings can have the desired effect, Mises realized, only if the economist *qua scientist* maintains an austere detachment from the political-ideological debates to which his science may be able to make crucial contributions.[5]

3. THE POSSIBILITY OF A SCIENCE
OF WELFARE ECONOMICS

In the history of economics a significant role was played by attempts to fashion an objective science of economic welfare. If it could be shown scientifically that Policy A conduces to greater economic well-being for society than that produced by Policy B, then economic science supports Policy A. To be sure economic well-being is but one component of a more comprehensive concept of society's overall well-being. So that although Policy A might be *economically* superior to Policy B, Policy B might be militarily, or medically, or morally superior to Policy A. But at least economics would, through an economics of welfare, in principle be able to contribute a clear-cut piece of advice—admittedly merely *economic* advice—to those charged with the responsibility of determining which policy is best, overall, for society. Even after the simplistic view of the old classical economists (to the effect that aggregate physical wealth produced provides a simple, valid yardstick for measuring economic success) was given up, as a result of the marginalist revolution, it was still hoped that more sophisticated economic theorizing would be able to identify a concept of economic welfare that could be used for the clearcut crystallization of policy recommendations, at least from the strictly economic point of view.

Notice what successful fulfilment of this hope would have meant. It would have meant the achievement of a body of scientific normative economics. That is, we would have achieved, in principle, the ability to deploy objective, impartial economic analysis in order to demonstrate

5. See Kirzner 1978.

unambiguously that one policy is economically better for society as a whole, than a second policy. To disagree with such a conclusion (unless, indeed, on the basis of *non*-economic considerations) would be to express a disagreement not on the basis of a legitimate difference of opinion, but simply as a consequence of ignorance (or dulness in the comprehension of) objectively established scientific propositions.

Economists during the early and central decades of this century indeed labored hard in order to establish the framework for such a scientific normative economics. These efforts constitute the history of twentieth century welfare economics. From the perspective provided by an understanding of Austrian Economics at the close of the century (and quite distinctly from a modern line of criticism directed against welfare economics which we shall take up later in this paper), these efforts, ingenious and even brilliant though they were, largely failed to achieve their objective. These efforts depended either, as in Pigouvian welfare economics, on the futile idea of somehow aggregating utility across the individuals making up society, or, as in the standard interpretations of Paretian welfare economics, on the flawed notion of seeing society as a single decision-making entity seeking to achieve global efficiency in its pattern of resource allocation.

From the perspective of the methodological individualism and subjectivism which nourish Austrian Economics, the idea of aggregating utility is simply meaningless (not simply wrong)—since utility is seen as essentially nothing more than the degree of importance attached by a decision-making individual to an option (in *his* comparison of it with other options).[6] Similarly the notion of societal efficiency is viewed by Austrians as less than coherent, since (not only does society in fact not make decisions, but) as Hayek showed us,[7] the essence of an economic problem facing society consists precisely in the dispersed character of existing knowledge—which dispersed character renders entirely moot the notion of centralized allocative efficiency (for which centralized information must be a necessary prerequisite).

6. For a classic statement of these problems in welfare economics, see Robbins 1935, chapters III and VI. Most of what is presented in the present paper is consistent with (if it does not actually duplicate) many of the positions elaborated in Robbins's book.

7. Hayek [1945/1948].

We should point out that (in contrast to certain modern criticisms of welfare economics that we consider later in this paper), these "Austrian" difficulties do not reflect any conceptual difficulty in deploying economic science for policy purposes. (There is no difficulty in arguing an "ought" statement on the basis of an independently established "is" statement.) These "Austrian" difficulties stem from the conceptual difficulties associated with constructing a coherent notion of what is economically good for society. The Austrian methodological tenets we have referred to seem to invalidate, as science, any global notion of economic goodness that might serve as policy yardsticks. In other words, the global notions of economic goodness needed in order to evaluate alternative social policies must themselves remain outside science. Economic science cannot be deployed for social-normative purposes, only because the criteria we wish to apply in our evaluations cannot be coherently defined except as pure (non-scientific) judgments of value. Positive science may not, without appealing to non-scientific judgments of value, be able to pronounce heart disease desirable or undesirable. But those judgments of value are not needed in order to identify heart disease (and thus to be able scientifically to identify its causes). The "economic well-being of society," on the other hand,—even before one begins to consider whether it is morally worthy of being desired—is a concept which is undefined and undefinable, as long as we confine ourselves to positive categories of subjectivist and methodologically individualist economics. Certainly such economics will, by itself, be unable to identify specific policies as able to enhance the "economic well-being of society."

But all this means that we have reached something of an impasse. Economists have always assumed that their positive findings *can* be of direct assistance in advising rulers. Economists have always believed that their discipline teaches us about the virtues or vices of free markets. The purism expressed in the preceding paragraphs seems to have unhelpfully propelled us rapidly toward an intellectual dead end.

It is at this point that modern Austrian economics suggests a way out of this dilemma, a way, as it were, to eat one's cake and yet have it, too. The *coordination* criterion[8] permits us to retain our methodological individualism and yet, at the same time, to be able to make scientific

8. For background on the emergence of the coordination concept in modern Austrian Economics, see Kirzner 1973, chapter 6; O'Driscoll 1977; Cordato 1992, pp. 45–54.

pronouncements with direct implications for the rankings which evaluating policy makers must assign to alternative social policies and arrangements.

4. THE COORDINATION CRITERION

The coordination criterion does not seek to rank alternative social arrangements by comparing outcomes, nor by applying any yardstick of global efficiency. It considers only the extent to which these alternative arrangements promote patterns of individual action *which take appropriate mutual account of one another.* A set of arrangements which stimulates actions which tend systematically to be mutually inconsistent, is clearly, in an altogether objective sense, different from a set which promotes mutual consistency. The former set tends to encourage decisions which must be frustrated (because they presume actions of others which are in fact not being taken). Or it tends to encourage decisions which must be regretted (because, even though they are successfully carried out as planned, they turn out to fail to have anticipated the actions of others which are in fact creating profitable opportunities which are now not being grasped). Here we have a scientifically meaningful, objective criterion, to which judgments of value may now be arbitrarily (that is, non-scientifically) attached. It is a scientifically definable criterion which does not do violence to our methodological individualism or subjectivism. It is a criterion in regard to which personal or political judgments of desirability can be considered. If we (in our capacities as citizens or rulers) *prefer* a less coordinated state of affairs, economic theory may show us scientifically which institutional arrangements are most likely to generate the frustration and regret we cherish. If, on the other hand, we deplore frustration and regret, valuing coordination over discoordination, then economic theory may be able to show us scientifically how to set up institutional arrangements that promote the harmonious dovetailing of activities. While our familiarity with our fellow human beings may convince us that very few are likely systematically to cherish a state of social chaos, as scientists we need not take explicit note of this circumstance. The coordination concept permits, in principle, the economist to make clearcut positive statements which can easily be used (in conjunction with independently held non-scientific judgments of value) logically to arrive at definite policy recommendations.

Because some ambiguities concerning the meaning of the coordination criterion have surfaced in recent debates, it may be useful to devote a short discussion to the meaning of the coordination criterion.

5. THE MEANING OF THE COORDINATION CRITERION

We define a coordinated state to exist when each action being taken—within a system of activities with which we have chosen to be concerned—correctly and adequately takes account of all other actions (within that same system). For an agent engaged in action A to be "taking account" of another action B, means that the choice of action A is not the consequence of the decision-maker's ignorance of the reality of action B. Notice that we do not require that the decision-maker actually know that action B is being taken, merely that his choice is the same as if he did know. (A vendor who brings newspapers to sell may not know specifically who will wish to buy his newspapers, but he has correctly acted as if he did.) We may distinguish between a narrower sense of the coordinated state, in which the above definition refers only to positive acts, and a broader sense of the coordinated state in which (a) the notion of "an action taken" includes also decisions *to refrain* from engaging in positive acts, and (b) in which the state of coordination involves taking into account not only the actual actions taken by others, but also their willingness to take actions under a variety of hypothetical situations. An example of what we have called coordination in the narrower sense is where I leave my home to buy a newspaper correctly assuming that the newspaper vendor will be there with a paper which he wishes to sell to me at a price I am willing to pay. An example of what we have called coordination in the broader sense would be where I make an offer to pay an unusually high price for an item which I wish to buy, correctly judging that, even though this item has *not* as yet been offered for sale in the market, my offer will inspire some owners of this item to agree to sell.

It will be observed that these notions of coordination all refer to systems of human action. They do not refer to arrangements of inanimate objects which constitute, for some observer, a pleasing pattern. One may of course refer to the trees, plants and flowers in a garden as being coordinated (or not). But that use of the term coordination is *not* the one we have in mind.

Although our definition of coordination may seem to have referred to systems of independently acting agents, it was in fact couched in terms broad enough to include systems of actions guided (or even controlled, to some extent) by a central decision-maker. Thus we think of an air controller coordinating flights into and out of a busy airport. The directions he provides to individual pilots (which directions will guide their actions in the cockpit) are, if he successfully coordinates these flights, such as correctly to take into account the actions which the other pilots in the area (actions which are *also* being guided by the air controller's instructions to *them*) are taking. (The notion of coordination in this context may be one that is "narrow," in the sense described above (that is, successful coordination may consist in avoiding collisions). Or it may be "broad" (as where successful coordination embraces also the goal of achieving the highest possible number of safe landings and take-offs in a given time period). A system of traffic lights may similarly be seen as coordinating traffic flows, either in a narrow or a broad sense of the coordination notion.

What constitutes coordination, in these air controller or traffic light examples, is not (at least for the purposes of *our* definition) defined by the distaste which the air controller, or the traffic engineer may have for collisions or for wasted time (caused by unnecessary waiting). Coordination, in these cases, (and as in the usual economic contexts), consists in the achievement by each aircraft pilot (or driver of a vehicle) of a set of actions which (from *his* perpective) correctly takes account of the actions of the other pilots (or drivers). The circumstance that a driver simply obeys a traffic *light* signal (without actually knowing or even thinking about what other drivers are about to do) is nonetheless consistent with our description of his "taking account" of the actions of other drivers. An efficient traffic signal system directs traffic in a manner such that each driver *is*, in effect, taking appropriate effect of the actions of other drivers.

The coordination notion we have identified is identified in methodologically individualistic terms (that is, in terms of the preferences of the agents themselves, not of any "social" preferences, nor even, as we have seen, of the preferences of any traffic controller or similar centralized decision-maker). But it is, at the same time, a "social" concept, a supra-individual concept. To describe a situation as constituting an uncoordinated state of affairs is to describe, not an individual's state of well-being (or the separate states of well-being of a number of individuals), but a quality of a social institution, one created by the relationship existing between individual actions being taken. Because this particular quality is one concerning which individual participants in the social situation are likely to hold (separate, but probably mutually consistent) preferences, it is a quality suitable for service as a criterion for social policy-making. Of course such service is itself outside the scope of value-free science, involving as it must, personal preferences of policy-makers. But the social quality we have described as consisting in the notion of coordination is one about which pure economic science may be able to have much to say, that does not depend on the preferences of any would-be policy-maker. In fact it is a notion which goes to the heart of what constitutes economic science. But before showing this to be the case, it is necessary to digress in order to take note (as promised several times earlier in this paper) of a line of recent criticism of normative economics to which we believe the coordination criterion is *not* vulnerable.

6. VALUE-FREEDOM, MORAL PHILOSOPHY, AND NORMATIVE ECONOMICS: A DIGRESSION

A line of recent work has argued that there is virtually no statement in economics which can be made without, at least implicitly, relying upon the conclusiveness of some specific moral considerations. Much of this work has been summarized in a masterly survey paper by Hausman and McPherson.[9] For our purposes the relevant parts of Hausman and McPherson's discussions are those criticizing the very notion of a welfare economics that should be able to avoid becoming entangled in moral philosophy debates.[10] Thus economists often like to think of themselves as technicians discussing "efficiency" in complete abstraction from distributive considerations. But a concern with efficiency already, these authors argue, presupposes a specific moral basis; and to believe it possible to make a sharp distinction between efficiency and equity issues (so as to be able to discuss the former in abstraction from the latter) presupposes further moral (and other) considerations. In general, Hausman and McPherson claim, "[d]istinguishing better from worse economic policies

9. Daniel Hausman/McPherson 1993, pp. 671–731. See Hausman/McPherson 1996.

10. A good deal of what they have to say in this regard overlaps the discussion in Paul Streeten's "Appendix" to Gunnar Myrdal, *The Political Element in the Development of Economic Theory, op. cit.*, pp. 208–17, to which the authors make grateful reference in their paper (p. 675, footnote 6).

and outcomes . . . inescapably relies on moral judgments."[11] Traditionally economists came to "look to levels of utility or of preference-satisfaction as the fundamental measure of human well-being for evaluative purposes. . . ."[12] But "for some purposes central to moral reasoning, preferences may not form a suitable basis [for evaluation of individual and hence of social well-being]."[13] Preferences may be based on faulty information, or they may be "idiosyncratic or based on highly contestable beliefs."

Earlier critics of welfare economics used these (or similar) criticisms to argue that economists, qua scientists, should refrain from making recommendations. Hausman and McPherson use these arguments to urge economists to make their moral presuppositions explicit, and to make sure they are adequately grounded in moral philosophy. From the point of view of the *wertfreiheit* ideal outlined earlier, it would follow from the foregoing that (if Hausman and McPherson's arguments are valid) the earlier economists were right: economists have no business making recommendations at all. A scientific welfare economics is a contradiction in terms. Without endorsing either the title or the substance of welfare economics (which we have roundly criticized on entirely different, viz. Austrian, grounds) we must point out certain evident weaknesses in the line of reasoning represented by Hausman and McPherson. Specifically we shall argue (a) that Hausman and McPherson's critique of the possibility of an "amoral" welfare economics is open to challenge, and (b) that (even if we accept their critique of the possibility of an "amoral" welfare economics) the coordination criterion outlined in this paper (and offered as an "amoral," technical basis for purposes of policy advice), seems invulnerable to the Hausman-McPherson line of criticism.

(a) Hausman and McPherson, we have seen, point out that when economists express a concern for efficiency, they can do so only on some moral basis; that when economists evaluate policies or outcomes on the basis of the extent to which individual preferences are satisfied, they can do so only on some moral basis. But, as Paul Streeten put it many years ago,[14] "[a]lthough economists cannot say which of two situations is better, they can throw light on certain features, and thus help others to make

---

11. *Op. cit.*, p. 689.
12. *Ibid.*
13. *Op. cit.*, p. 690. See also the references there to the work of Amartya Sen.
14. *Op. cit.*, p. 214.

their decision." And although Streeten himself rejects this view (at least in the context of the distributional implications of alternative policies), this view seems correctly and validly to reflect what welfare economists have believed themselves to be doing. The welfare economist does *not* himself have to endorse the moral judgment that individual preferences are to count in evaluating alternative social outcomes. But, if he believes himself to be advising those who do share that moral judgment (and this belief on the part of the economist involves *no* moral judgment itself), then this procedure seems a perfectly consistent and valid one, *without* his having embroiled *himself* in any moral debate whatsoever.

Having said this in defense of classical welfare economics, we must immediately concede that many expositions of welfare economics proceed in a way which *is* vulnerable to the Hausman-McPherson critique. Many expositions, as we saw earlier, do make it appear that the removal of an "inefficiency," say, unambiguously improves the economic well-being of society (instead of saying that such a removal enhances the extent to which individual preferences are likely to be satisfied). And our own "Austrian" critique of welfare economics earlier in this paper, on grounds independent of Hausman and McPherson, was couched in terms referring to such expositions. Our point here is merely that traditional welfare economics is not essentially committed to such expositions, and thus not necessarily vulnerable to the Hausman-McPherson critique (while still being vulnerable to the Austrian critique offered earlier in this paper).

(b) But quite apart from the above, it seems important to emphasize that the "coordination criterion," as a basis for offering technical, "amoral," advice to policy-makers, is certainly *not* vulnerable to the Hausman-McPherson line of criticism. An uncoordinated set of actions is less coordinated than a fully coordinated set. This is an "is" statement not relying upon any moral considerations whatsoever. Economists may be able to rank policies according to the degree to which they promote or obstruct coordination. Nothing is being implied, in the making of such rankings, concerning the moral significance of the purposes of those engaged in the relevant actions, nor in the moral significance of a coordinated set of such actions (as compared with an uncoordinated set). To be sure, consideration of one aspect of alternative policies (such as their respective coordinative properties) may obscure possibly morally more significant aspects of these policies (such as their income-distributive effects, in the opinion of many moral judges). But scientific attention to one aspect of a multi-dimensional phenomenon does not *by itself* depend on the moral judgment that this one aspect is morally more significant than others. To repeat the medical analogy used earlier in this paper, research attention to cancer-causing aspects of a particular diet does not itself constitute a declaration that other aspects of that diet (say, its effect upon heart disease) are morally less significant. In fact, as seen earlier, such research does not itself depend on the moral judgment that cancer is a disease to be fought, rather than a boon to be promoted. Certainly those to whom this medical research is hoped to provide practical advice (on how to fight or to promote cancer) have *their* moral agenda. And, to be sure, a cancer research project which is engaged in by a researcher hired by a group with such a moral agenda, is ultimately selected by that moral agenda. But the research itself can, at least in principle, remain detached from the moral convictions which inspired it.

The truth of course is that each and every human action, including antiseptically scientific research, is *inspired* by some morally relevant judgment of value, be this inspiration the pursuit of abstract truth, the pursuit of fame and wealth, or the elimination or promotion of a disease. But the *wertfreiheit* position outlined at the outset of this paper maintains the possibility, in principle, of engaging in an activity which in and of itself does not logically presuppose any *specific* moral conviction, in a manner which is not distorted by that specific moral conviction which may in fact have ultimately inspired this particular activity. The researcher engaged in science in order to earn a living can, perhaps precisely because he wishes to make a good living as a researcher, detach his research from any personal financial considerations.

It follows that, while the economist might not have selected the coordination criterion for attention unless there were those who seek his advice (on morally relevant grounds) in regard to that particular criterion, his technical analysis of the consequences of alternative policies for their coordinative or discoordinative impact, may be carried on *without* becoming embroiled in moral debates.

But we claim that coordination has an even more fundamental claim on the economist's attention qua objective scientist. The phenomenon of spontaneous coordination has, ever since the beginning of modern economics two centuries ago, been at the heart of what captured the economist's purely scientific interest.

7. ECONOMIC SCIENCE AND THE COORDINATION NOTION

From the very beginnings of modern economics in the eighteenth century, economists have continually glimpsed, at least, the remarkable circumstance that markets are somehow, without centralized direction, able to achieve socially desirable outcomes. As argued earlier in this paper, the history of economic thought reveals that economists did not, in general, succeed in pinning down satisfactorily in what precise scientific sense we are entitled to describe market outcomes as socially desirable. Nonetheless the ability of markets to stimulate mutually gainful exchanges among market participants was never far from economists' attention. Early neoclassical economists may have seen this as an ability of markets spontaneously to achieve maximum aggregate utility; later welfare theorists may have seen this as an ability to allocate social resources efficiently. Our discussion thus far in this paper permits us to see the ability to stimulate mutually gainful exchange as the ability spontaneously to coordinate the independently taken actions of a large number of individuals. The work of Friedrich Hayek on the role of markets in communicating knowledge sharpens our understanding of the coordinative properties of markets.

As Hayek taught us, the basic requirement for market equilibrium to exist is that all agents be correctly aware of all actions of other agents (including the actions they *might* take under different sets of hypothetical circumstances). Market disequilibrium consists in situations where such complete mutual awareness has not been attained, even in effect. When economists claim that markets "work," they are simply claiming that disequilibrium situations (in which complete mutual awareness is absent) tends to generate spontaneous processes of mutual discovery. In other words, using the terminology employed in the preceding pages, markets tend to coordinate. If we can declare this proposition (that markets tend to coordinate) to be arguably the central insight of economics, then we will have established the coordination notion (which we have seen as able to serve as an appropriate criterion for economic policy-making) as indeed at the heart of economic understanding.

Our reference to Hayek's insights concerning the knowledge-discovery properties of markets alerts us, we should note, to a certain ambiguity in the term "coordination." Our definition of coordination, in the preceding section of this paper, was couched in terms of the "coordinated state" (in which actions were taken with full awareness, in effect, of all other actions). Hayek's insights into the market process as a process of mutual discovery, permit us to see that the word "coordination" may be used (*besides* its use as a noun describing a completed state of affairs in which actions *are already* fully coordinated) *also*, but differently, as a verbal noun referring to a *coordinating process*. That is, "coordination" may refer to a process in the course of which a less coordinated set of actions (less coordinated as a result of inadequate mutual awareness among market participants), gradually gives way (as an aspect of the equilibrating process of market competition) and comes gradually to be replaced by a more fully coordinated set of actions. One may, in seeking within economics for a criterion to serve would-be policy-makers, wish to take note of these two distinct (but related) potential criteria: (a) the criterion of coordin*atedness* (referring to the success with which the fully coordinated state has been or is likely to be achieved), or (b) the criterion of coordin*ating* (referring to the rapidity, smoothness and sensitivity, with which states of *dis*coordinatedness may tend to stimulate the mutual discovery process through which greater degrees of coordinatedness may be hoped for).

8. COORDINATION, ECONOMIC SCIENCE, AND CLASSICAL LIBERALISM

We are now in a position to return to our original theme, the exploration of the interface between economic science and the political/ideological ideal of classical liberalism. We have now within our grasp a criterion for choice among competing political ideologies, through which economic science can be brought to bear upon the non-scientific preference-ranking we seek to make. As argued in an earlier section, the coordination concept permits us, in principle, to make scientific pronouncements concerning alternative social-institutional arrangements that will permit the policy-maker to make informed choices among them.

In particular, we immediately see, the basis in economic science for favoring classical liberalism is within our grasp. Economics does teach us the spontaneously coordinative properties of free markets. So that if (on admittedly *non*-scientific grounds) we prefer greater coordinatedness to less, the "advantages" of the free market have been established "scientifically."

This conclusion is certainly an important one; but we must not exaggerate its significance. We may be satisfied that the coordination criterion is sufficient to point to classical liberalism as a program worthy of enthusiastic support, but others may disagree. They may grant that economics teaches that markets tend to coordinate, but may claim (a) that this tendency is never (in the face of continual external shocks) able to achieve a sufficiently adequate degree of coordinatedness, to warrant strong support for classical liberalism, or (b) they may argue (again, admittedly on non-scientific grounds) that coordination should not necessarily be seen as an overridingly significant criterion for social policy; they may point to other possible economic criteria (for example, income equality, environmental quality, etc.) as providing what they maintain to be morally significant ideals. The choice between these competing possible criteria must certainly be a non-scientific one. Can we still claim that economic science teaches the advantages of a free market society?

The answer, of course, is that "we," in our capacity of citizens (not scientists), must determine the criteria we wish to employ in policy-making. Economics alone cannot help us definitively in this regard (although it can assist us in recognizing, perhaps, that certain criteria we hold dear may be mutually inconsistent, and so on). Economics draws out attention to the extraordinary, counter-intuitive property of free markets, that they do tend to coordinate the independently made decisions of millions of individuals.

Those of us who are ideologically predisposed to classical liberalism are entitled to draw upon these scientific conclusions in support of this ideological position. But we must respect the need for the economist himself, in his capacity of economist, to proceed more austerely and in a morally detached manner. The economist, qua scientist, must maintain his impartiality between alternative ideological visions. He must be open-minded in his scrutiny of scientific work the conclusions of which seem to threaten ideological positions which he might, in his capacity of citizen, hold dear. Even though his own moral attitudes, as citizen, lead him to embrace the conclusions of economics in regard to the coordinative tendencies of free markets, he should understand that other citizens who hold dear other rankings of moral values (e.g., those who value egalitarianism) may possibly, and validly, use conclusions of economics to demonstrate the *un*desirability of classical liberalism.

What the classical liberal can be confident in is that, based on his own ranking of degrees of moral significance, the central results of economic theory point unequivocally to the conclusion that the institutional arrangements which classical liberalism upholds, not only conform *directly* to his own moral convictions, but also have the extraordinarily remarkable property of tending to guide countless individual private property owners to undertake activities which harmoniously but uncannily tap the productive potential inherent in the initial pattern of resource ownership—without disappointment and without regret.

REFERENCES

Cordato, R. E. (1992) *Welfare Economics and Externalities in an Open-Ended Universe: A Modern Austrian Perspective*, Boston, Dordrecht, London: Kluwer.

Hausman, D. M. & McPherson, M. S. (1993) "Taking Ethics Seriously: Economics and Contemporary Moral Philosophy," *Journal of Economic Literature*, Vol. XXXI, June, pp. 671–731.

Hausman, D. M. & McPherson, M. S. (1996) *Economic Analysis and Moral Philosophy*, New York and Melbourne: Cambridge University Press.

Hayek, F. A. [1945/1948] "The Use of Knowledge in Society," *American Economic Review*, no. 35, pp. 519–30; reprinted in Hayek, F. A.: *Individualism and Economic Order*, Chicago, University of Chicago Press.

Kirzner, I. M. (1973) *Competition and Entrepreneurship*, Chicago: University of Chicago Press.

Kirzner, I. M. (1978) "Foreword," to Ludwig von Mises, *The Ultimate Foundation of Economic Science: An Essay on Method*, Kansas City: Sheed, Andrews and McMeel, Inc.

Kirzner, I. M. (1994) "Value-freedom," in Boettke, P. J. editor, *The Elgar Companion to Austrian Economics*, Aldershot, Hants and Brookfield, Vermont: Edward Elgar.

Mises, L. von (1960) *Grundprobleme der Nationalökonomie*, translated as *Epistemological Problems of Economics*, Princeton, New Jersey: Van Nostrand.

Myrdal, G. (1954) *The Political Element in the Development of Economic Theory*, Cambridge: Harvard University Press, first Swedish edition 1929.

O'Driscoll, G. P. (1977) *Economics as a Coordination Problem: The Contributions of Friedrich A. Hayek*, Kansas City: Sheed Andrews and McMeel.

Robbins, L. C. (1935) *The Nature and Significance of Economic Science*, 2nd edition, London: Macmillan, chapters III and VI.

Streeten, P. (1954) "Appendix" in Myrdal, G.: *The Political Element in the Development of Economic Theory*.

Whately, R. (1855) *Introductory Lectures on Political Economy, Delivered at Oxford in Easter Term, 1831*, 4th edition, London: John W. Parker.

ETHICS AND MORALITY

ALTRUISM, SOCIAL RESPONSIBILITY, AND THE MARKET ECONOMY

In a paper largely dedicated to goodnatured (but deadly serious) criticism of the ethical underpinnings of laissez-faire capitalism, Professor Paul Samuelson of M.I.T. has, tongue in cheek, drawn a picture of the ideal world as envisaged by the individualist. "Physicists have a model of a dilute gas. The air in this hypothetical balloon I hold in my hand is supposed to consist of a number of hard little atoms in continuous motion. So small is each atom as to make the distances between them very large indeed. It is a lonely life, and the encounters between atoms are very few and far between—which is indeed fortunate since the encounters are envisaged by the physicist as involving collisions with elastic rebounds. Something like this is pictured by the extreme individualist. Daniel Boone, who moved farther west when he could begin to hear the bark of his neighbor's dog, would regard this model of a dilute gas as very heaven."[1]

This vision of the laissez-faire economy strives to caricature, not so much the selfishness, as the coldness and the impersonality which critics of the market claim it to promote. But the picture presents quite closely the view of capitalism as a society of wholly selfish individuals entirely callous to the goals, the strivings, and the sufferings of others. And this view of capitalism has been used again and again by its critics to assail the moral foundations of the system. The analysis by economists of the workings of the price system has to some extent reinforced this moral condemnation. A model of the world relying upon profit-maximizing businessmen and utility-maximizing consumers has inspired critics of the market to identify both the market itself and its economic analysis, as the works of the devil. Whether it is a nineteenth-century John Ruskin inveighing against the "selfish" Political Economy of a John Stuart Mill,[2] or twentieth century socialist critics insisting on the continued relevance and dominance of Marx's avaricious capitalists[3] or condemning the "impersonal nexus of the capitalist market" for making "profit and

From *The Hillsdale Report*, vol. 11, no. 4 (1972): 1–6. © Hillsdale College 1972. Reprinted with permission from Hillsdale College Department of External Affairs.

loss the ultimate and pervasive evaluative criteria of human worth"[4]—the market economy is identified as the social manifestation of man's egoistic impulses. Profit maximization is perceived as unbridled greed, competition as harsh and ruthless, and privacy of property as inhospitable and uncharitable. A symposium [at Hillsdale College in November 1972, at which this paper was delivered] devoted to an examination of the extent of man's responsibility to be his brother's keeper can hardly avoid coming to grips with this now ancient denunciation of capitalism as entailing the systematic abandonment of such responsibility. Certain recent developments in the perceived function of the market make it desirable to go over afresh ground that economists have frequently traversed in grappling with this denunciation.

We will not follow those who, execrating altruism as the "morality of self-immolation," as the "creed of self-sacrifice—the primordial weapon used to penalize man's success on earth, to undercut his self-confidence, to cripple his independence, to poison his enjoyment of life, to emasculate his pride, to stunt his self-esteem and paralyze his mind"[5]—glory in capitalism precisely because of its being considered liberated from such a curse. Nor, on the other hand, will we walk with Oscar Wilde in disparaging capitalism for almost exactly the opposite reason, viz. that it makes possible and necessary the practise of altruism, seen as degrading and demoralising to both giver and receiver.[6] Instead we will simply take it as a datum that a widely shared ethical view is that which perceives profound moral worth in taking account of the goals and needs of others, and man's adjusting his own actions so as to help in some way in the achievement of these goals and in the alleviation of these needs. We will examine the nature of a market system in order to assess its compatibility with this widely shared ethic. Briefly our conclusion will be that (as is the case with respect to other ethical values), the market is neutral toward the pursuit of altruistic impulses. A market system in a society of would-be altruists will tend to permit them as individuals to practise mercy and kindness as efficiently as it would minister to the egoistic greed of a world of avaricious and selfishly materialistic individuals. The market does not depend, for the source of its motive power, upon the selfishness of its participants; neither does it, in its operation, penalize the unselfish. In particular, and contrary to much current opinion, there is in general no need for the altruistic impulses of socially responsible market participants, to impose upon the business firms they control a systematic policy of deliberately avoiding the maximization of profits.

ON THE MAXIMIZATION OF PROFIT

That the maximization-of-profit assumption is not identical with the assumption of selfishness has been made abundantly clear by numerous writers. The profit-maximization assumption occupies so central a place in economic theory (and current debates concerning the validity of the assumption have so deeply touched the question of how capitalism operates) that no discussion of altruism in the market can avoid the task of pointing out once again that an imperative to be one's brother's keeper does not require (more accurately, is powerless to accomplish) a failure to seek maximum profits, properly understood. If the term "maximization of profits" means anything at all, famed economist Ludwig van Mises explains, it is merely an expression of the very category of action, the insight that in all market transactions man aims at increasing to the utmost the advantage derived. And "economics refers to every kind of action, no matter whether motivated by the urge of a man to eat or to make other people eat."[7]

The theorist distinguishes between actions directed at goals which are desired for their own sakes (acts of consumption) and actions toward goals which are desired only because they are prerequisites for still more ultimate goals (acts of "production"). The categorization of an act as either selfish or unselfish can avoid ambiguity only when applied directly to acts of consumption, or (if applied to acts of "production") by reference to the consumption goals which the acts of production are intended to make possible. The acquisition of food is not an act of consumption; it is an act of "production." Whether the purchase of food represents an altruistic act or not depends upon whether the food is designed to be placed at the disposal of the hungry poor or not. The determined drive to obtain the means needed to achieve unselfish purposes cannot be denied the moral approbation accorded to altruistic actions. But no judgement concerning a drive to obtain means can be made without reference to the ends for which the means are intended.

Now, in a market system based on specialization and division of labor, the majority of acts of "consumption," selfish and unselfish, depend upon prior money purchases in the market. Accordingly the resolute pursuit of consumption goals, selfish or unselfish, necessitates a similarly determined drive for money income. To the observer, however, this drive for money income is visible only *separately* from the acts of consumption toward which this drive is directed. The possibility that the drive for money income, or maximum pecuniary profits, may be for the sake of completely unselfish ultimate purposes, is thus lost sight of. (Nor is avoidance of this oversight made any easier, of course, by the empirical circumstance that so many income earners do, in fact, use so much of their money incomes in other than altruistic fashion.)

Error in this respect is made even easier by the fact that the context in which acts of "production" are carried out, frequently permits elements of "consumption" to become intimately entangled in the actions taken. The businessman's ultimate values, selfish and unselfish, help determine his decisions even in the sphere of his commercial activities. He may furnish his office more luxuriously than is strictly required by his business needs; he may, on the basis of personal friendship, or out of sentiments of pity, pay an employee more than austere attention to money profits would justify. So that where a businessman deliberately *excludes* altruistic motives (of the latter type) from entering into the area of his commercial activities, this easily comes to be interpreted as inherently selfish (in spite of the possibility that this businessman's profits may be intended for even more worthwhile, altruistic purposes than those now being ignored.) Again the ease with which the theorist analyzes the commercial actions of businessmen into a "pure" monetary-profit-maximizing component separate from other (possibly altruistic) "consumption" components, and the frequent tendency for price theory to operate with models of business decision making confined to the first component, have helped bring about the popular characterization of commercial activity as essentially selfish—and have thus fueled current demands that business decisions be made with awareness of "social responsibilities" other than the maximization of profits.

All this was seen with unsurpassed clarity by Philip Wicksteed over sixty years ago. He explained, with characteristic patience and persuasive charm, that the mark of the economic relation between two parties to an exchange, is not any selfishness that might motivate the traders (since their purpose in trading may in fact be to achieve some quite altruistic goals)—but rather the circumstance that *each of the parties enters into the exchange for the sake of some one other than the second party to the exchange.* This Wicksteed labels *non-tuism,* as distinct both from egoism and from altruism. The economic relationship is a non-tuistic one, Wicksteed makes clear, in that one engages in economic transactions with other market participants not in order to further *their* purposes.[8] Trusteeship provides Wicksteed with a helpful illustration. Trustees who have no personal interest whatever in the administration of the estates to which they give time and thought will often drive harder bargains—that is to say, will more rigidly exclude all thought or consideration of the advantage of the person with whom they are dealing—in their capacity as trustees than they would do in their private capacity. Thus we see that the very reason why a man feels absolutely precluded from in any way considering the interests of the person with whom he is transacting business may be precisely the fact that his motive in doing business at all is absolutely and entirely unselfish. . . . The transaction . . . becomes more rigidly "economic," just because my motive in entering upon it is altruistic."[9] We shall find that this trusteeship example will be especially useful to us when we come to consider the corporate business firm.

ON GIFTS, GRABS, AND EXCHANGES

The above discussion throws light on one aspect of the profound transformation from a pre-market society to a market society that was initiated by the Industrial Revolution. This transition can be viewed as consisting of a drastic expansion in the range and importance of "non-tuistic" interpersonal relationships, to which both egoism and altruism are irrelevant, and a corresponding relative shrinking in the scope of those interpersonal relationships in which the egoism or altruism of motives directly matters. The analytical distinction between "production" (to which questions of altruism are not of direct relevance) and "consumption" (to which such questions are of unquestioned relevance) has, in the development of market societies corresponded roughly to an institutional separation between "business" activities and "household" (or consumer) activities. One need not be happy that this historical development has widened the scope of activities in which non-tuism is the distinguishing feature; one may legitimately regret the "coldness" of the resulting market place; but one must not confuse this development as requiring or depending upon, a suppression of any altruistic motives that human beings might otherwise permit themselves. Even if the institutional separation between business and consumption were as complete as is the analytical separation between them, it would no more be correct to accuse a business system of necessary selfishness than it would be to describe it as engaged in endless fasting (punctuated only by business luncheons), simply because business activities do not of themselves involve dining.

Indeed, the institutional separation between the earning of income in business activities, and the spending of it in consumption activities, and the enormous growth in the scope of the former, have combined to produce results which can only be welcomed by those who value altruistic impulses and fear selfish ones. Quite apart from the enormous productivity of the resulting expansion of division of labor and exchange, which has brought about rising living standards for all, the emergence of the market society based on private property has (a) sharply narrowed the field in which greed and selfishness can inflict damage upon others, and (b) substituted the exchange relationship (in which each participant wins a *right* to what he receives) for the relationship in which there is danger that charity may corrupt both giver and receiver by making "the former self-righteous and the latter submissive and cringing."[10] To the extent that the widening of the market replaces mutually profitable exchange for giving and receiving, it has removed the need for altruism (substituting the dignity of right in place of the possible humiliation of receiving a gift) without inhibiting the fullest exercise of altruistic motives where still needed. Mises has pointed out most penetratingly, in this regard, that those who demand that the needy be given help as a matter of right rather than suffer the indignity and humiliation of receiving charity from compassionate donors, cannot at the same time consistently complain of the coldness and impersonality of the market. The market relationships that replaced feudal structures, were those that substituted rights based on contract for benefits received as a result of grace, or of fidelity.[11] The coldness and impersonality of the exchange relationship derives precisely from the substitution of contractual rights in place of the gifts of benevolence. At the same time the market system, based as it is on the privacy of property rights (and barring the criminal invasion of rights), limits the possibility that one man's greed and selfishness can harm others. Selfishness and greed can harm others only in situations where rights are not private, such as within the family, or in the context of community-owned property. Where property is not private it indeed requires specific regard for the needs of others to prevent one from exploiting the commonly available source at the expense of others. The rearrangements of ownership patterns which result from market activity, even where made strictly out of selfish motives, are never (at least as viewed prospectively by the participants in these voluntary transactions themselves) harmful. Harmful effects of selfishness and greed may be searched for possibly in the legal system whereby rights are assigned in the first place, or in those activities of society which are not channelled through the market—but can never be found in the levels of well-being of those participants in market exchange whose needs have been selfishly ignored by their trading partners.

Thus market exchanges, because they are non-tuistic, are, while "cold and impersonal," for that very reason exempt from the possibility of any degrading aspects of altruism. And again, to the extent that market exchanges are conducted within the given framework of private rights, they provide no room within which egoistic market participants might inflict harm on others. We turn now to consider currently fashionable doctrines which insist, in effect, upon the abandonment of the non-tuistic character of business activity, especially as carried on by corporate enterprises.

THE SOCIAL RESPONSIBILITY OF BUSINESS DOCTRINE

For several decades now there has developed the doctrine which declares it to be the social responsibility of business firms, especially of large corporate firms, to act in a manner other than that which promises to maximize the firms' profits (as usually defined). The rationale for this doctrine is somewhat complex. On the one hand businessmen are often exhorted to be "socially responsible," because this is the right, moral thing to do; on the other hand they are advised (or even warned) that social responsibility is in their own genuine longrun profit interest, properly understood. We will not attempt here to examine the social-responsibility-of-business doctrine in detail. We wish merely to assess briefly the relevance of the doctrine to our own theme, the place for altruism and of being one's brother's keeper in the market society. Let us note some of the confusions in this regard.

It need not be questioned that some aspects of social responsibility may indeed be consistent with the properly understood profit-maximizing interests of business firms. Goodwill may be achieved by business support for worthy causes; educational institutions serving as valuable sources of skilled manpower may warrant judicious corporate support. Such support should, from the point of view of business firms,

and of the economist, be correctly labelled. Such support is not the generous, profit-sacrificing contribution of deeply altruistic businessmen, but
rather the deliberate investment of farsighted non-tuistic management.
Moreover, it would seem to be nobody's business but that of the firm
itself (and its stockholders) when that firm should or should not make
such investment. At any rate to the extent that social responsibility fits
this pattern it does not, of course, constitute any problem for the position
we have taken in this paper. We are fully aware that much private philanthropy is consistent not only (of course) with utility maximization, but
even with selfishness. There is certainly no reason, therefore, why corporate philanthropy should be inconsistent with non-tuism.[12]

We know, however, that while appeals for social responsibility may be
couched in terms consistent with corporate "enlightened" profit maximization, they do in fact frequently require managers to consult the goals,
needs and interest of groups other than their stockholders, and even when
these are in direct conflict with stockholder interests. There appear to be
two bases for such appeals and demands. First, there seems to be a belief
that corporations ought to behave like gentlemen, so that the crudities
of relentless profit-seeking ought to be softened by courtliness, compas-
sion, and cooperation. Society is simply no longer prepared to tolerate the
breaches of good manners of which profit-maximizing corporate activities are considered guilty.[13] Second, these demands frequently rest on the
belief that strictly profit-oriented behavior by corporations will, through
market failure, generate undesirable social results; that the avoidance
of such results requires that somehow corporate behavior be modified,
and that this can be achieved by impressing upon corporate management
the view that their stewardship over corporate assets represents responsibilities not merely to their stockholders, but even more importantly, to
society at large. Indeed, if corporations fail to respond to these demands,
they are warned that society will not stand idly by: ". . . if business does
not accept a fair measure of responsibility for social improvement, the
interests of the corporation may actually be jeopardized. Insensitivity
to changing demands of society sooner or later results in public pressures for governmental intervention and regulation to require business
to do what it was reluctant or unable to do voluntarily. . . . Experience
with governmental and social constraints indicates that the corporation's self-interest is best served by a sensitivity to social concerns and a
willingness, within competitive limits, to take needed action ahead of a

confrontation . . . Moreover, indiscriminate opposition to social change not only jeopardizes the interest of the single corporation, but also affects adversely the interest all corporations have in maintaining a climate conducive to the effective functioning of the entire business system."[14] Both of these grounds for demanding limitations on the maximization of corporate profits are vulnerable to severe criticism.

To argue that corporations should act as compassionate gentlemen is to insist on treating as a human being an institution which is a "person" only in the eyes of the law, and which is in fact ideally suited for the non-tuistic role appropriate for purely commercial relationships. To be sure, the image which consumers, rightly or wrongly, have of the corporation, may importantly affect its sales revenues, and we have already noticed that, to the extent that this is the case, some sacrifice of immediate profits for the sake of a less obnoxious corporate image may be wisely undertaken in order to achieve longer-run profits. But to humor the consumer in this way does not, surely, require that we deliberately endorse the myth of the corporation as a quasi-natural person capable of outraging us by its (his? her?) coldly non-tuistic behavior.

We have seen earlier that a businessman's ultimate values, selfish and unselfish, inevitably come to be entangled in his business activities as an individual, and help determine his decisions in the sphere of commerce as they do in his private consumption choices. But to the extent that his relationship to a corporation insulates a stockholder from direct contact with corporate decisions, we would expect his values to play less of a role in influencing those decisions. Of course corporate managers have their own cherished values, selfish or unselfish, and they may be tempted to permit these values to influence their decisions concerning the disposition of corporate assets. But to the extent that the indulgence of managers' cherished values is a matter of indifference to stockholders, any such influence upon corporate disposition of assets constitutes an unwarranted intrusion of managers' "consumption" goals into their activities as "trustees" over corporate assets.[15] We have seen earlier how Wicksteed's trustees steeled themselves against permitting their own possibly altruistic impulses to interfere with their non-tuistic stewardship of their trust. (It may well be the case that the personal sacrifice to the corporate managers (or to Wicksteed's trustees) of reining in their altruistic impulses may be so significant that competition for the services of competent executives or trustees forces stockholders to explicitly or implicitly grant to them a degree of discretion within which it is the managers' rec-ognized privilege to indulge his own charitable tastes. But this is a matter strictly between stockholders and management, and is entirely similar to the competitive pressures which lead stockholders to authorize con-sumer comforts of all kinds for their executives.)

Earlier in this paper mention was made of the institutional separation between the earning of income in business activities, and the spending of it in consumption activities. The truth is that the emergence of the cor-porate form of business activity has been one of the powerful ingredients which have contributed to such a separation in contemporary capitalism. Those who make the daily decisions for corporate business are indeed trustees hired to act non-tuistically in order to fulfil stockholders' hopes for profits from their investments. The gentlemanly virtues of compas-sion and altruism are thus supremely irrelevant for corporate decision making. Final goals and values are simply irrelevant to corporate profit making,[16] which is strictly instrumental—a neutral means toward the purposes, gentlemanly or otherwise, of those to whom the profits will accrue. To insist on "humanizing" the corporation by charging it to live up to a compassionate code of ethics is to misunderstand the ethical neu-trality of purely business activity and to overlook the ideal opportunity for such purely business activity for which the corporate form of business makes such superb institutional provision. To be sure, stockholders in a free society should have the privilege of creating corporations charged with carrying out philanthropic functions. If they choose to channel such activities through business corporations there need be no objection. (The question of the legitimacy or desirability of stockholder majority rule on such matters, is, however, quite another problem.) But the fact that some stockholders may wish to integrate their altruistic impulses with the activities of the business enterprises which they control, should not con-ceal the complete propriety of corporate enterprises whose stockholders choose to channel their altruistic impulses separately from the business activities of their corporation.

The second basis for demanding that corporations be run on other than profit-maximizing lines (viz. the belief that without some voluntary or involuntary restraints on corporate maximization of profit, market fail-ure will lead to undesirable social consequences) has been criticized even more severely. In effect corporate managers are being told that they are civil servants whose responsibility is not solely to their employers, but also to society at large, inasmuch as their activities affect many others besides stockholders. Both Milton Friedman and Friedrich von Hayek have pointed out the grave dangers to the market economy inherent in such a view, Friedman, in fact, pronouncing it a "fundamentally subversive doctrine." "If businessmen are civil servants rather than the employees of their stockholders then in a democracy they will, sooner or later, be chosen by the public techniques of election and appointment."[17] Already, indeed, we hear proposals for the appointment of public interest representatives on the boards of large corporations. Dr. Arthur Shenfield has accurately commented on these proposals that they involve a change in "the whole corporate system and hence the essential nature of the American economy." [See *The Hillsdale Report*, Vol. ii, No. 1] Concerning such appointments Dr. Shenfield asks: "Who would appoint the public interest representatives? To whom would they be responsible? What knowledge would they have to control the malfeasances of their board colleagues? . . . Either, and fortunately this is the more likely, the system would become a sham. Or it would become a centrally planned economy . . ."[18] Stockholders should (again without conceding the relevance of majority rule) be free to charge their employees with pursuing any socially worthwhile responsibility they choose, (just as any individual should be free to renounce profits for the sake of fulfilling what he believes to be in the social interest). But to demand that stockholders turn over control over their corporate employees to representatives of the public, in order to correct alleged market failures, is to naively believe that those who deny any validity at all to the beneficent operation of Adam Smith's invisible hand, might endorse the proposal that economic activity be continued as private enterprise so long as each individual be exhorted to act not for the sake of his own welfare, but for that of all society.

CONCLUSION

Two and a half centuries ago Mandeville shocked his contemporaries by arguing slyly that the private vices of avarice and luxury result in benefits to society at large. The moralists of his time refused to accept a thesis that private immorality can generate socially beneficial results. Erroneously identifying commercial activity with immoral egoism, critics of the market have, ever since Adam Smith, similarly attributed to the pursuit of profits not only private vice but also undesirable social consequences. The unhampered market requires correction, and in particular, governmental correction, in this view, not only to redress allocative inefficiencies which the critics ascribe to the market process, but also because the unhampered market depends upon and encourages a pattern of selfish behavior which, the critics believe, must leave the weak and the unfortunate uncared for.

It seems unlikely that the curious morality of compulsory or vicarious "altruism" (with A forcing B to be C's keeper)—of which so large a portion of our governmental budgets consist—would have gone for so long without serious challenge, were it not generally believed that the market is somehow not only incapable of deploying voluntary altruism efficiently, but indeed is instrumental in extinguishing altruistic impulses altogether. That the market system has been phenomenally successful in reducing the urgency of the need for charity, through the steady increase of mass standards of living, is well recognized. This paper has emphasized the complete ability of the market to serve effectively the wishes of those of its participants who wish to further the goals and alleviate the suffering of their fellows. To the extent that this aspect of the market is generally overlooked, we can unfortunately continue to expect a widening of the effort to substitute tax collecting in place of voluntary acts of unselfishness, and of the effort to impose upon business executives under the rubric of social responsibility, burdens which they are incapable of bearing.

NOTES

1. P. A. Samuelson, "Modern Economic Realities and Individualism," *The Texas Quarterly*, Summer, 1963. (Reprinted in *Collected Scientific Papers*, Vol. 2, p. 1407.)

2. J. Ruskin, "*Unto This Last*" (Oxford University Press, 1934), p. 109.

3. P. A. Baran and P. M. Sweezy, *Monopoly Capital* (Monthly Review Press, 1966), pp. 42–44.

4. E. K. Hunt, *Property and Prophets* (Harper and Row, 1972), p. 174.

5. Ayn Rand, *Capitalism: The Unknown Ideal* (Signet Books, 1967), p. 312.

6. Oscar Wilde, "The Soul of Man Under Socialism" in D. Mermelstein (Editor), *Economics: Mainstream Readings and Radical Critiques* (Random House, 1970), p. 608.

7. L. Mises, *Human Action* (Yale, 1949), p. 243.

8. P. H. Wicksteed, *The Common Sense of Political Economy* (London, Routledge & Kegan Paul, 1949), Vol. 1, p. 174. For further discussion of Wicksteed's non-tuism see I. M. Kirzner, *The Economic Point of View* (Van Nostrand, 1960), pp. 64–67.

9. Wicksteed, *op. cit.* p. 175.

10. L. Mises, *Human Action* (Yale, 1949), p. 834.

11. Mises, *ibid.* See also K. Boulding, *Economics as a Science* (McGraw-Hill, 1970) pp. 127, 130. Sir Henry Maine made famous the description of the movement of "progressive societies" as one from status to contract. (*Ancient Law,* London, 1861, p. 151, cited in F. A. Hayek, *Constitution of Liberty,* Chicago, 1960, p. 154.)

12. For a recent interesting example of an economist's analysis of corporate philanthropy see C. M. Douty, "Disasters and Charity: Some Aspects of Cooperative Economic Behavior," *American Economic Review* (September, 1972).

13. R. A. Anthony, "The Trouble with Profit Maximization," *Harvard Business Review* (Nov./Dec., 1960) reprinted in D. S. Watson (Editor), *Price Theory in Action, A Book of Readings* (Houghton Mifflin Company, Boston, 1969) Second Edition, p. 79.

14. Committee for Economic Development, *Social Responsibilities of Business Corporation* (New York, 1971), pp. 28–29.

15. F. A. Hayek, "The Corporation in a Democratic Society: In Whose Interest Ought It To and Will It Be Run?" in *Studies in Philosophy, Politics and Economics* (Chicago, 1967), p. 305.

16. An interesting problem in this regard is set by the need to specify time preferences for optimal corporate investment decisions. See J. Hirshleifer, "On the Theory of Optimal Investment Decision," *Journal of Political Economy* (August, 1958).

17. M. Friedman, *Capitalism and Freedom* (Chicago, 1962), pp. 133–34.

18. A. Shenfield, "Consumerism," *The Hillsdale Report,* Vol. 11, No. 1, p. 3.

THE UGLY MARKET: WHY CAPITALISM IS
HATED, FEARED, AND DESPISED

One of the most intriguing paradoxes surrounding modern capitalism is the hate, the fear, and the contempt with which it is commonly regarded. Every ill in contemporary society is invariably blamed on business, on the pursuit of private profit, on the institution of private ownership. Those who have pierced the shrouds of hate and ignorance with which the critics of the market have enveloped it, inevitably come to ask themselves why so valuable a social institution is held in such universal contempt and dislike. The question is one which has a scientific fascination of its own. But the question has significance extending far beyond mere scientific curiosity. As Mises pointed out, "A social system, however beneficial, cannot work if it is not supported by public opinion."[1]

Those who are convinced that the market system is uniquely capable of mobilizing and developing the resources available to a society in a manner able most faithfully to reflect the wishes of its members, while it protects and nourishes their political and economic liberties, have for a long time been aware of the unfortunate validity of this statement. The ability of the market to serve society has been and is continually being undermined by the attacks levelled by its ideological opponents and by the powerlessness of the public to withstand these attacks. Public opinion has come to be moulded in a direction overwhelmingly antithetical to a market orientation. The "anticapitalist mentality" has come to pervade the thinking of the masses who are the market's chief beneficiaries, of the intellectuals and social scientists who might have been expected to be its principal interpreters and exponents, as well as of the entrepreneurs and business leaders who constitute its pivotal instruments. It is surely a tribute to the extraordinary vitality and power of the market system that in the face of such deep mistrust, and in the teeth of massive and well-nigh crippling state interventions (deriving largely from this anticapitalist

From *The Freeman / Ideas on Liberty*: http://www.thefreemanonline.org. © 2008 *The Freeman / Ideas on Liberty*. All rights reserved. Reprinted by permission of the Foundation for Economic Education. Originally appeared in print in *The Freeman* 24, 12 (1974): 20–32.

mentality), the system still continues to support an enormously complex division of labor and to generate an unprecedentedly high flow of goods and services. How long this can be continued in the face of widespread lack of confidence in the efficiency and morality of the system, must seriously trouble those concerned for the very survival of the system.

An understanding of the nature and sources of this anti-capitalist mentality is, therefore, crucially important. If this mentality is to be dispelled, its principal features must be clearly pointed out, and its sources identified. A number of scholars have addressed themselves to this task. A series of papers by various writers was published under the editorship of Hayek two decades ago,[2] drawing attention to the anti-capitalist bias of historians, and relating this to the hostility toward the early emergence of capitalism in the eighteenth and nineteenth centuries evinced at the time by the aristocracy and the intellectuals. Almost four decades ago Hutt[3] brilliantly analyzed the causes, not so much of the existence of the anti-capitalist mentality itself, as of the surprising inability of the economists to influence public opinion toward an appreciation of the beneficent operation of the competitive market process. More recently both Mises[4] and Stigler[5] have sought to explain the emergence of the strong antipathies shown toward the market system by so many, including the intellectuals who might have been expected to be its most enthusiastic supporters. Historians of economic thought have, and no doubt will, chart the vagaries in the attitudes of economists themselves toward the social usefulness of a decentralized system of decision-making based on private property.

The following discussion of the anti-capitalist mentality will attempt to identify three distinct levels at which this mentality demands analysis: *First,* we will notice the objections explicitly raised by the critics of capitalism. It is through these charges, criticisms and denunciations that the anti-capitalist mentality finds overt expression. *Second,* we will identify the analytical premises which inform (or misinform) the stated criticisms expressive of the anti-capitalist mentality. Any attempt to respond to the criticism raised at the first level must sooner or later search out the weaknesses of the analytical bases—at the second level—for these criticisms. *Third,* we will take note of the deeper attitudes which have inspired the various forms of anticapitalist mentality. Whatever the stated, specific denunciations of capitalism, whatever the errors in economic analysis which are implicit in these denunciations, a thorough understanding of the anti-capitalist mentality cannot avoid ultimately coming to grips with the deep-seated prejudices and engrained habits of thought which are, both consciously and unconsciously, responsible for the antipathy shown to the market system. We will now take up in turn the three levels which we have identified.

THE STATED CRITICISMS

The list of denunciations of the market system is both well-known and long. They range from those which condemn the system on moral grounds to those which attack it on more narrowly economic grounds. We will make no attempt to do more than merely recite this list. It is not our main purpose here to grapple with these criticisms. Rather we list them to indicate the range of expression of the anti-capitalist mentality, and more importantly, to distinguish these stated criticisms sharply from their theoretical underpinnings, and from the unstated attitudes to which they are, in large measure, to be ascribed.

The market system is indicted as feeding and responsible for the *materialistic aspects* of modern society. It is blamed as promoting and permitting the expression of *selfishness* and *greed*. It is charged with *encouraging fraudulent behavior*. It is denounced as *debasing the tastes of the public* through advertising, fraudulent or otherwise, leading them to demand products and services which are in fact harmful and degenerating. The system is held accountable for the destruction of the environment. It is denounced for destroying the self-esteem of its workers, for generating profound alienation, despondency and despair within society, as well as for widespread insecurity and anxieties. The inequality in incomes which characterizes capitalist countries is denounced as evil in itself and socially deleterious in its consequences. This inequality is condemned as exemplifying the fundamental injustice of the market system; it is perceived as expressive of economic oppression and exploitation. The market system is made to shoulder responsibility for *racism*, for *sexism*, for *imperialism*. The market is given failing grades in its strictly economic functions. It is seen as producing shoddy, dangerous products, for the *profit of the businessman rather than for the use of the consumer*. It is seen as generating cataclysmic spasms of *overproduction, unemployment and monetary crisis*. It is seen as *subverting the operation of political democracy*. It is blamed for the corruption of government and for the *concentrations of dangerous centers of economic power in big business*.

No doubt this list is an incomplete one. But it does present the range of anti-capitalist clichés with which we are all familiar. Sooner or later the anti-capitalist mentality expresses itself in one or several of these charges, denunciations and criticisms.

Before reviewing the *theoretical bases* for these criticisms, it is important that one observation be made. This is that while in most cases these denunciations can be sustained only in the context of particular theoretical views (so that the revelation of fallacies in these views renders these objections harmless) the objections themselves are usually raised without benefit of any *explicit* theoretical framework. An undesirable aspect of capitalist reality is observed, whether it is the prevalence of fraud or unemployment, or racism, or greed. This aspect is then uncritically attributed to capitalism itself. The circumstance that, in the nature of things, undesirable features of capitalist reality—or, for that matter of any reality—abound, must in some measure account for the continual reappearance of old denunciations of capitalism in new guises despite their earlier refutations.

ANTI-CAPITALIST THEORY—THE STIGLER-ZWEIG THESIS

We now turn then, to examine the theoretical bases which nourish the overt denunciations of the market system listed in the preceding section. In this we confine ourselves to those (often merely implicit) views of anti-capitalists which seem most clearly vulnerable to critical scrutiny. It is not, to repeat, our purpose here substantively to deal with the objections listed in the preceding section. Nor, in fact, do we necessarily maintain that each and every one of these objections is entirely without force. But in examining the analytical "vision" expressed by the anti-capitalist mentality, we find it expedient to draw attention only to those aspects of it which, we believe, dispassionate consideration reveals to be flawed. In fact our purpose in setting forth the theoretical underpinnings of anti-capitalism is to illustrate what may be termed the Stigler-Zweig thesis.

This thesis is that the traditional training of the professional economist predisposes him toward a free enterprise view on economic affairs. This thesis has support from more than one quarter within the ideological spectrum. In a well-known paper a dozen years ago, Stigler advanced this thesis: "the professional study of economics makes one politically conservative," (with a "conservative" defined as one "who wishes most economic activity to be conducted by private enterprise, and who believes that abuses of private power will usually be checked, and incitements to efficiency and progress usually provided, by the forces of competition.")[6] More recently Michael Zweig has expressed, on behalf of the New Left, the similar view long held by socialist critics of orthodox economics: that marginalist analysis (with which orthodox economics is held to be completely identified) is not only "irrelevant," but that it can be "pernicious," so that "marginalism is fundamentally counter-revolutionary."[7] In an essay introducing a volume of readings which includes many contributions from both the New and Old Left, Lekachman, too, has registered his opinion that marginalism is "a highly conservative notion."[8]

Our survey of the theoretical groundwork of the anti-capitalist mentality will confirm this thesis. We will discover, that is, that this theoretical vision is inconsistent (to say the least) with that which underlies economic analysis. So that *this* level of discussion of the anti-capitalist mentality must perceive it, as Mises has insisted again and again, as the *denial of economic science*.

It is to be observed that the Stigler-Zweig thesis, or a variant of it, is relevant not only to the theoretical bases for these anticapitalist objections which are strictly economic in character, but also to those which underlie the denunciations concerned with the morality of the market system. The habits of thought engendered by economic analysis enable one to avoid ethical judgments which are mutually inconsistent or which otherwise rest on logically invalid foundations.

If the preceding section consisted of a list of well-worn denunciations of capitalism, the following pages will turn out to offer a catalogue of those fallacies which teachers of introductory economic theory find themselves again and again forced to unmask.

(a) One man's gain must be another's loss: Innocence of economics is often most dearly manifested by the refusal to recognize that free exchange must have been viewed as (at least prospectively) beneficial by both sides to the deal. The error of insisting that gain in the market must be at someone else's expense is responsible for a wide range of denunciations of the market. These include charges of exploitation of sellers by buyers (as in the case of labor), and of exploitation of buyers by sellers (as in the case of landlord relations). This error is responsible for the perennial willingness of critics of capitalism to prohibit exchanges in which they perceive one of the parties to be receiving inordinate benefit. The error is, further, one of the foundations for the condemnation of profits

in general, and thus of the entire market system insofar as it is the social manifestation of the profit motive.

(b) Blaming the waiter for obesity: Failure to perceive the degree to which the notion of consumer sovereignty manifests itself in the market is responsible for what Stigler has called blaming the waiter for obesity. In the most naive forms of this fallacy, the market system is condemned for the efficiency and abundance with which it ministers to consumer tastes which the critic does not share. To a large degree the condemnation of capitalism for "materialism" reflects this aberration. (One recalls that not only the market has been condemned for its materialism, but economists have been denounced for their interest in such a debased topic as the material side of human existence.) To some degree the condemnation of business for producing shoddy or dangerous products reflects a failure to understand that consumers are simply unwilling to sacrifice as much as would be necessary to enjoy a higher level of quality and safety. There can be no doubt that current denunciations of capitalism for its effect upon the environment must, to some extent, be seen as reflecting a value placed upon the quality of the environment which is higher than that placed by consumers in general.

To a certain extent, the charges of racism and sexism leveled against capitalism are expressive of the same blindness toward the direction in which causes and effects are related in the market process. At somewhat less naive levels of discussion, the "blaming the waiter for obesity" fallacy resurfaces as an attack on advertising and selling effort in general. If it is not the waiter himself who is to be the culprit, it is the neon sign outside the restaurant, or the tempting aroma of good food escaping there from, which are perceived as the villains. It is perhaps because elementary economics in fact generally fails to make clear the role of selling effort in the entrepreneurial process of seeking to serve the market, that this particular form of the obesity fallacy is advanced so triumphantly by economists who ought to know better.

(c) Petulance at Costs (or the denial of scarcity): To a surprising extent the criticisms of anticapitalists turn out to reflect merely an impatience at the costs inevitably associated with the achievement of desired goals. Again and again undesirable features of the economic landscape are cited as evidence of the failure of the market. (Incidentally, the same fallacy is, to be sure, often committed in the course of pro-capitalist criticisms of socialist economies.) Here it is not so much that the critic ignores or

disagrees with the values of consumers, as that he simply refuses to recognize that efficiency in achieving more highly valued goals may necessitate the deliberate renunciation of otherwise important goals which happen to be less urgently valued. Long working hours, poor working conditions, loss of pristine environmental beauty may, elementary economics teaches us, be evidence not of the failure of the economic system (whether capitalist or socialist) to achieve its goals, but of the very efficiency with which it channels resources away from less crucial goals toward those more highly valued. Some aspects of what the critics deplore as worker alienation, or of the anxiety and insecurity felt by market participants, would surely be appraised rather differently were they recognized as the inevitable costs of division of labor or of a social system in which freedom of entry for competitors is the prime motive force. At a somewhat more subtle level, the often deplored garishness and pervasiveness of modern advertising take on a different aspect when perceived as a social cost made necessary by the sheer multitude of products from which the consumer in successful capitalism must choose. The very affluence of capitalism, it turns out, reveals a new guise in which scarcity manifests itself—the scarcity of information on what to consume out of the available riches. Anti-capitalist critics—it turns out—are ill-equipped to perceive these insights of elementary economics.

(d) The fear of anarchy: As Hayek has repeatedly pointed out, one of the clichés of our age sees a blemish in anything that "is not consciously directed as a whole," that this is a "proof of its irrationality and of the need completely to replace it by a deliberately designed mechanism."[9] In particular, this fallacy is related to "the inability, caused by the lack of a compositive theory of social phenomena, to grasp how the independent action of many men can produce coherent wholes, persistent structures of relationships which serve important human purposes without having been designed for that end."[10]

There can be no doubt that this "lack of compositive theory of social phenomena" is the view underlying an enormous volume of anti-capitalist criticism. The anti-capitalist mentality, it is clear, is to a great extent coextensive with ignorance of, or a refusal to acknowledge, the insights into the market *system* which economics theory reveals. Once it is taken for granted that a society unplanned from the top must generate incessant chaos, it becomes easy enough to seize on targets that may be held to exemplify that chaos. Even where critics of capitalism recognize the determinateness of market forces, they see them as nonetheless chaotic in the sense that these forces are believed to lead in socially undesirable directions.

(e) Fear of the consequences of greed: Closely related to the preceding analytical prejudice is that which tends to attribute undesirable consequences to the market simply because the market permits greedy or selfish individuals to act out their impulses. Because freedom to trade means freedom to act greedily or selfishly, it is believed the consequences of laissez-faire must inevitably tend to be nasty, brutish and jungle-like. What is being implicitly denied in this respect is the ability of the market process to harness the greed of its participants so as to serve the wishes of the other participants. Refusal to perceive the constraints upon individual actions imposed by the market permits anti-capitalists to interpret those aspects of the economics landscape which they deplore as the only-to-be-expected, sinister consequences of a social system based on selfishness and greed.

(f) Blaming the market for the results of intervention: As is well known, the market system is frequently criticized for features of contemporary economic society which are, in fact, to be attributed to state *interference* with the market. Of course, to the extent that it is *contemporary* capitalism which is being attacked, there can be no objection to this. However, such criticisms of capitalism, it all too frequently turns out, are in fact deployed to attack not the statist interference with the market process, but the market system itself. We have here a simple analytical failure to recognize, within the complex tangle of modern capitalism, the consequences of its market elements, from those of non-market admixtures. This analytical failure manifests itself in many of those objections to capitalism which relate to absence of competition generated by government-imposed barriers to entry (or from limitations on international trade), or to maladjustments arising from government price controls of various kinds or to cyclical maladjustments (including large-scale unemployment) generated by massive government monetary expansion. In all such criticisms, what is at issue is the theory maintained (perhaps implicitly) by the critics that the undesirable features being exposed are to be attributed, not to departures from the market, but to the untrammeled workings of the market process itself.

(g) The "Nirvana Fallacy": As the final entry in our (doubtless incomplete) list of analytical fallacies, we present what Professor Demsetz has

labeled the "Nirvana Approach."[11] (In fact we will present it in a somewhat broader context than that identified by Demsetz.) Demsetz explains that "those who adopt the Nirvana viewpoint seek to discover discrepancies between the ideal and the real and if discrepancies are found, they deduce that the real is inefficient."[12] There can be no doubt that many critics of capitalism are judging its efficiency and/or morality by comparison with some ideal norm that can have little relevance for real problems. In so doing they overlook the fact that improving an imperfect world must take place against the background of that imperfect world; that it is usually simply impossible to remake whole systems in their entirety; that even where this is possible, the costs of doing so may make imperfection relatively attractive and efficient.

The nirvana attitude of many anti-capitalists manifests itself in various ways. Thus the market is frequently blamed for the distribution of incomes to which it gives rise without regard to the circumstance that the market presupposes some initial distribution of resource ownership (especially in regard to the resources embodied in human beings themselves). Or, where marginal analysis is indicted for accepting without challenge the institutional structure (including the existing property rights system) within which marginal adjustments are contemplated to be made, there is no awareness on the part of the critics, of the *costs* (transaction and policing) of remaking the social system from the very foundations. Or, again, as Demsetz has shown, critics who have pointed to externalities or other circumstances spelling inefficiency, have frequently ignored, in their calculations, the cost of resources that would be required to correct these inefficiencies.

THE SOURCES OF THE ANTI-CAPITALIST MENTALITY

Our survey of anti-capitalist criticisms of the market, and our identification of the analytical confusions which have frequently supported these criticisms make it of special interest to review now the underlying psychological attitudes and prejudices which might fuel this mentality. The very recognition of the confusions which abound in the theoretical underpinnings for so much anticapitalist criticism, make it clear that such criticism must be nourished by deeply held values and prejudices. The literature cited earlier in this paper, together with several additional sources, yield the following inventory of attitudes from which anti-capitalism might easily be expected to spring.

(a) Mises has dwelt at length on the *resentments* which can arise from *frustrated ambitions,* of the *envy* on the part of the intellectuals and the white collar workers of the good fortunes enjoyed by successful entrepreneurs.

(b) Similar in important respects must be judged the widespread views that economic inequalities are somehow immoral and seriously undesirable per se. Here the often vicarious envy of the wealthy and sympathy for the poor must be judged as predisposing observers of capitalist inequalities toward "sinister" interpretations of the sources of these inequalities.

(c) Deep-seated contempt for greed and for self-centered activities is clearly responsible for a readiness to believe the worst about capitalism.[13]

(d) An almost similarly deep-seated contempt for the low tastes of the masses and thus for the businessmen who cater to these low tastes is responsible for treating the *market* as vulgar and crass. It becomes, in fact, all the easier to blame the vulgarity of mass tastes upon the businessmen who minister to them.

(e) Closely related to high-brow disdain of mass tastes, must be listed man's love for the natural over the artificial, his preference for more spaciousness and simplicity over urban congestion and complexity. Since the spectacular success of industrial capitalism was accompanied by the loss of the simple, natural life for which so many of us yearn, capitalism itself has come to be the villain.[14]

(f) And again, the yearning for simplicity abuts on the deep-rooted unwillingness of men to be forced to be efficient. Modern capitalism is despised and feared because it successfully mobilizes available resources to serve socially needed purposes.

(g) Widespread *fear of economic power* must be considered one of the attitudes responsible for anti-capitalism. While what Professor Petro has recently called the "economic power syndrome"[15] is often accompanied by an explicit theoretical position which denies the role of consumer sovereignty, it seems clear that in many instances the syndrome in fact *precedes* the theoretical position needed to support it. Thus the very success of capitalism in organizing production in efficient, large scale productive units is responsible in fact for the suspicions which have led to its being so bitterly attacked.

(h) Professor Hutt has pointed out that opponents of economics are often the victims of what he calls "custom-thought"[16]—intellectual inertness. To be sure custom-thought may work in more than one direction.

But the long list in the preceding section of this paper of economic falla-cies subscribed to by anti-capitalists suggests that intellectual inertness might indeed play a not insignificant role in the anti-capitalist mentality.

(i) Finally we notice, as an explanation for the persistence of so many elementary fallacies, the role of the "corruption of opinion by interest." Professor Hutt[17] has provided a full review of the role of "power thought" in this regard. Here again, of course, opinion can be corrupted by inter-est in more than one direction. But when one thinks of the businessmen who stand to gain from governmental protection against domestic or for-eign competition and of the many who, rightly or wrongly, believe that a different order of things would redound to their benefit, it cannot be denied that this must be counted an important source of anti-capitalism.

WRESTLING WITH THE ANTI-CAPITALIST MENTALITY

Traditionally apologists for capitalism have addressed themselves to the specific stated objections and accusations advanced by the detractors of the market. In attempting to do this they have, of course, found it nec-essary to search out the logical fallacies which support these objections. At the same time awareness of the more deeply rooted prejudices which seem to be responsible for the continued vitality of the anticapitalist men-tality, raise doubts as to the efficacy of this strategy for the ideological defense of the market. Recognition of the three-level character of the anti-capitalist mentality emphasized in this paper can be of help in identi-fying what must be faced. At the level of stated objections, there is an enormous variety of possible manifestations of the mentality. Refutation of one particular objection in one form does not prevent its reappearance in some other form. Clearly, for this reason, theory has a crucial role to play in refuting the analytical fallacies responsible for entire groups of possible objections and denunciations of the market. On the other hand, the very generality of theoretical discussion makes it possible for critics of capitalism to fail to see how the theories relate to *particular* features of the market which seem to invite criticism. The proper *application* of theory is, of course, in many ways more difficult than theorizing itself.

Moreover, economic theory is for various reasons not well-adapted for the task of combating anti-capitalism. Theorists are scientists whose attempts at maintaining *value-freedom* in their work seem to render them unprepared to serve as apologists for a particular system of social organi-zation. Again, the *sophistication* of modern theory is hardly conducive to the correction of popular misconceptions. (We recall that Edwin Cannan, for this reason, appealed for *simple* economics.) There are grounds for believing that the character of much contemporary theory, especially in its emphasis on equilibrium conditions, is not well suited for the explication of the social function of the market.[18] At the ideological level defense against the anticapitalist mentality seems to require continual new applications of fundamental theory to new situations.

But on the other hand, our awareness of the role of theoretical fallacy and of the impact of the multitude of specific denunciations of the market, must make us cautious in imagining that the anti-capitalist mentality can be dispelled by any device that fails to come to grips with each of these levels of its manifestation. No matter how successfully one or more of the underlying anti-capitalist prejudices may be neutralized, the possibility of logical error yet remains and the availability of apparently undesirable features of capitalism ready to be used in its denunciation has not yet been eliminated. Moreover, the formidable list of anti-capitalist prejudices must raise doubts concerning the likelihood that they can be successfully neutralized by any simple means. To be sure, any advance is desirable if its costs are acceptable. But the degree of advance needed to make a visible dent in the anti-capitalist mentality must require the most careful examination of the costs involved in any proposal.

Many students of capitalism have pointed out that, despite its advantages, there may well be grounds for predicting its replacement by other systems. One thinks of Schumpeter's thesis in this regard. One possible reason for arguing that capitalism is unstable, is that it is a social system which generates a negative public opinion so powerful as to spell its ultimate death. This paper has attempted to identify the sources of this tendency. Only by recognizing the nature and the power of these forces can we hope, through patient teaching and discussion, to dispel the hate and the ignorance which surround the free market.

NOTES

1. L. Mises, *Human Action* (Yale, 1949), p. 862.

2. F. A. Hayek (Ed.), *Capitalism and the Historians* (Chicago, 1954).

3. W. H. Hutt, *Economists and the Public, A Study of Competition and Opinion* (London, 1936).

4. L. Mises, *The Anti-Capitalistic Mentality* (Van Nostrand, 1965).

5. G. J. Stigler, "The Intellectual and the Market Place," *National Review* (Dec. 1963).

6. G. J. Stigler, "The Politics of Political Economists," *Quarterly Journal of Economics* (November 1959); reprinted in *Essays in the History of Economics* (Chicago, 1965), pp. 52–53.

7. M. Zweig, "A New Left Critique of Economics," in D. Mermelstein, (Ed.) *Economics: Mainstream Readings and Radical Critiques* (New York, 1970), p. 25.

8. R. Lekachman, "Special Introduction" in Mermelstein, *op. cit.,* p. xi.

9. F. A. Hayek, *The Counter-Revolution of Science* (Free Press, 1955), p. 87.

10. *Op. cit.,* p. 80 (italics supplied). *See also* F. A. Hayek, *Individualism and Economic Order* (London, 1949), pp. 7 ff.

11. H. Demsetz, "Information and Efficiency: Another Viewpoint," *Journal of Law and Economics* (April 1969).

12. *Op. cit.,* p. 1.

13. One thinks here in particular of Ruskin.

14. See the above cited *Capitalism and the Historians.*

15. See S. Petro, "The Economic-Power Syndrome," in *Toward Liberty* (Mises Festschrift) Vol. II, p. 274.

16. *Economists and the Public,* p. 50.

17. *Op. cit.,* chapters 3 and 4.

18. One thinks here in particular of Professor Buchanan's plea that economics be understood as a sophisticated catallactics, the theory of exchanges and of markets, see his "What Should Economists Do?," *Southern Economic Journal* (January 1964).

The title of this chapter is, of course, the same as that of the celebrated paper which Frank Knight published over seventy years ago, in which he set forth what is probably the most powerful and profound ethical critique of the market economy ever written.[1] Certain central elements in that critique have succeeded in establishing themselves as part of this century's conventional wisdom concerning capitalism: they have come to be routinely restated in and absorbed from today's principal textbooks in economics.[2] The circumstance that a number of Knight's most eminent students have, in the latter half of this century, come to be identified as the most prominent defenders of capitalism has not, in the mainstream perspective, suggested serious questioning of the validity of Knight's criticisms. Rather this perspective seems to conclude that convincing defenses of capitalism can be achieved only by confining analysis within a narrow economic frame of reference (permitting one to ignore, at least, Knight's ethical worries), or by remembering that Knight himself was careful not to imply that his critique requires us to deny significant merit to capitalism nor to suggest that his critique in and of itself established the ethical inferiority of capitalism to other possible systems of economic organization.

The thesis of this chapter will, contrary to mainstream acceptance of Knight's criticisms, be that Knight's ethical objections to the market economy are in fact in large part (though certainly not completely) based on a flawed understanding of how that economy works and what it achieves. It follows that a good deal of conventional textbook wisdom on these matters is similarly flawed. Our concern here is not primarily with Knight's own views as they matured over his extraordinarily distinguished career; this is certainly not the place to examine the

Many of the ideas expressed in this chapter were first put forward in earlier versions. See in particular Kirzner (1973, ch. 6; 1985, chs 2, 4, 6; 1989).

From *The Driving Force of the Market: Essays in Austrian Economics* (New York and London: Routledge, 2000), 88–102. Reprinted by permission; the original source is *The Ethical Foundations of the Market Economy*, ed. H. Sieber (J. C. B. Mohr, 1994). © Mohr Siebeck Tübingen.

evolution of Knight's thinking concerning the ethics of capitalism during the half century following the publication of his 1923 paper. We take Knight's 1923 paper as a point of departure only because of the originality and trenchancy of its critique, because of its seminal influence on mainstream twentieth-century thinking about capitalism, and because it exemplifies the source of what we see as the central fallacy in that mainstream thinking—viz. a flawed conception of the nature and function of competition in the market economy.

Although we shall, on these grounds, seek to refute many of Knight's ethical criticisms of capitalism, we certainly do not wish to claim that such refutation unequivocally establishes the invulnerability of that system to all ethical criticisms. For example, a number of Knight's profound observations raising possibly disturbing questions about the less immediate consequences of the system's operation will be seen to be entirely unaffected by our claims in this chapter. "While men are 'playing the game' of business, they are also moulding their own and other personalities, and creating a civilization whose worthiness to endure cannot be a matter of indifference" (Knight, 1935, p. 47). Our claim here is simply that what we claim to be the invalidities in Knight's critique can also not be matters of ethical indifference.

It will be noted that our disagreements with the mainstream ethical criticisms of the market economy do not derive from disagreements concerning ethics itself. (Knight himself, by the way, is careful to avoid resting his criticisms on any specific ethical foundations; instead he is mainly content to point to aspects of capitalism which would appear to raise as-yet-unresolved ethical questions.) Our disagreements will be seen to derive from divergent ways of understanding the functions and the operation of the market economy. Central to these disagreements are the ambiguities surrounding the nature and role of competition in the capitalist system.

THE MEANING OF COMPETITION

For Knight (and for mainstream economic thought throughout the century) competition means the state of affairs spelled out in the model of perfect competition (Knight 1923, p. 47 fn. and p. 50). The ethics of competition, for Knight, boils down to an ethical analysis of the ethics of the perfectly competitive world, and of the extent to which real world markets approximate that model. It was, after all, Knight himself who had in his

Risk, Uncertainty and Profit (Knight, 1921, pp. 76–86) definitively articulated the conditions necessary for such a state of affairs. As his eminent student George Stigler has made clear (Stigler, 1957), it was this articulation by Knight which finally crystallized what modern economists have understood by the term "competition." And it was to be Knight who led the Chicago School's insistence[3] that the model of perfect competition was able to serve economists adequately in their search for theoretical understanding of real world varieties of market competition.

From this Knightian perspective the real world market system can be understood by reference to the model of perfect competition. Although, to be sure, the real world does not fulfill all the conditions required by the model, nonetheless it is that model which enables us to understand whatever systematic market forces real world capitalism reveals. Although a part of Knight's ethical critique of capitalism relates to the divergences between real world capitalism and the "ideal" model of perfect competition, the bulk of his critique refers to the (ethically) less-than-ideal outcomes to be expected from a hypothetically perfectly competitive world itself. It is this perspective which modern textbooks have adopted. And it is to this perspective that we shall, in this chapter, attribute the flawed understanding of the market which we blame for the errors in the Knightian (and contemporary mainstream) ethical critique of the market economy.

We shall—on well established "Austrian" lines—claim that real world competition is to be understood, not by reference to an "ideal" model of perfect competition; but strictly in terms of dynamic ("entrepreneurial") forces—precisely the forces which are explicitly banished from the perfectly competitive model. At issue here is not whether the perfectly competitive model affords us a realistic picture of market economy (few mainstream economists claim that it does), but whether it captures the essence of how the competitive market economy works. Mainstream ("Knightian") theory maintains that the competitive market economy displays systematic regularities only to the extent that it can be reasonably fitted into the perfectly competitive mold. Subsequent generations of Chicago theorists would maintain that as a matter of fact the real world competitive market economy can so be fitted.

Austrian critics of mainstream theory maintain on the other hand, that the systematic regularities displayed by the market economy can be explained only by recognizing that the economy is, at any given point in time, significantly subject to active entrepreneurial forces for which the model of perfect competition can, by definition, find no place. The active competition which is so obvious a feature of real world capitalism is, in this Austrian view, to be understood as exemplifying these dynamic, entrepreneurial forces (rather than an approximation of the conditions established in the model of perfect competition).

THE OPEN-ENDEDNESS OF THE MARKET ECONOMY

Perhaps the most important implication of this disagreement concerning the nature and role of real world competition is that the Austrian view of competition portrays the market economy as "open-ended" (in a sense very shortly to be explained), while the mainstream view sees it as "closed-ended." In the mainstream view the "data" (i.e. tastes, resource endowments, technological possibilities) are, because they are data, seen as "given." They mark out the possibilities for improved allocation in the short run, and for growth in the long run. Optimal available courses of action are implicit in the data. These courses of action set out the boundaries for economic improvement. The economic process is judged in terms of its ability successfully to exhaust these possibilities—but it is out of the question for these possibilities to be transcended. Except as a possibly accidental change in the data, there is no room here for surprise or for discovery—only for efficient or inefficient performance in regard to the system's functions. In this sense the system is a closed one, strictly circumscribed by its data. In the mainstream view the data are given not only in the simple sense of the term, but also in the sense that they are, in principle, known. While many relevant items of information may not in fact be known, at least it is assumed that the costs required to obtain relevant knowledge *are* known. What renders the world closed-ended is, in the final analysis, the assumed completeness of knowledge which this mainstream view expresses. To seek to understand the market economy in terms of the perfectly competitive model is to portray that closed-ended economy as fulfilling its functions by confronting each of its participants with a similarly closed-ended choice situation. Prices and opportunities are arranged to permit (and ensure) those interlocking decisions which constitute the details of the system's fulfillment of its functions. Each situation confronting the individual, and rigorously entailing the relevant optimizing decision, is a closed-ended situation: it consists of a fully specified (i.e. fully known) choice context providing scope for only one ("single-exit") solution.

By contrast, the Austrian view of the world sees it as open-ended, not merely in the sense that realities necessarily diverge from the conditions of the abstract model of the economic theorist, but, more fundamentally, in the sense that what makes the system work is precisely its open-endedness—an open-endedness created by sheer ignorance of relevant possibilities. For the Austrian view competition consists of series of discovery steps,[4] revealing possibilities which were no part of any set of "data." These steps of entrepreneurial discovery are seen as inspired by the pure profit possibilities inherent in the sheer ignorance which pervades the open-ended economy. The function of competition, in this open-ended world of sheer ignorance, is to achieve those discoveries which change the position of the frontiers separating knowledge from ignorance. It is dynamic competition which expands the domain of what is known, continually shifting the location of profitable opportunities and thus continually inspiring yet further discoveries expanding the domain of what is known. These discoveries include not only discoveries of new goods to be produced, new methods of production to be utilized, and new sources of available natural resources, but also discoveries of new needs and desires deemed worthy of fulfillment. The economic process and the essence of its social function is not primarily one of achieving efficiency, but one of revealing knowledge the very availability of which has up until now not been suspected. Let us examine this proposition somewhat more carefully.

THE FUNCTION OF THE MARKET

For the mainstream view (underlying the Knightian ethical critique of the market economy) the function of the market is to efficiently allocate social resources among the multiple competing relevant social goals. Successful fulfillment of this function would occur where "every productive resource [has been placed] in that position in the productive system where it can make the greatest possible addition to the total social dividend as measured in price terms," and rewards have been assigned to "every participant in production by giving it the increase in the social dividend which its co-operation makes possible" (Knight, 1923, p. 48). Knight's critique proceeds to argue that successful fulfillment of this function does not constitute the fulfillment "of a sound ethical social ideal, the specification for a utopia" (ibid.). Much of what we shall have to say in the following pages stems from an entirely different view of what constitutes the social function of the market economy. Our disagreement with Knight's ethical critique of capitalism rests primarily on a refusal to accept successful fulfillment of the mainstream allocative-efficiency function, as the relevant yardstick with which to measure the ethical achievement of the market system.

For us the function of the market system is to inspire those acts of discovery through which potentially discoverable possibilities can be identified and brought into view. In particular, this function has been described as a "coordinative" function, in that the sheer ignorance which pervades the market economy at a given instant, is likely to be generating sets of decisions which are failing to exploit all available opportunities for mutually gainful exchange among market participants. These decisions are thus "uncoordinated"; a well-functioning market would tend most effectively to stimulate those mutual discoveries which will bring decisions into coordination, permitting fullest exploitation of the potential for mutually gainful exchanges.

It should be clear that this difference in the perceived function of the market economy can make all the difference in the world in one's assessment of the ethical significance of a "successfully functioning" market economy. Much of our quarrel with Knight, depends upon his taking it for granted that the most one can expect from the market system is an efficient allocation of social resources.

SHEER IGNORANCE AND KNIGHTIAN UNCERTAINTY

At first glance it may seem puzzling that we have attributed to Knight a view of the market and of its function which assumes, in principle, the completeness of knowledge concerning relevant information (such as the costs of obtaining needed knowledge). Surely it was Knight who had in his celebrated *Risk, Uncertainty and Profit* emphasized that what separated the real world from the economist's model of perfect competition is precisely that the real world is characterized by uninsurable uncertainty (as contrasted with risk). Surely the essence of Knightian uncertainty is the inescapable open-endedness of real world ignorance which the notion of uncertainty seeks to capture. How then can we charge Knight with the error of assuming complete knowledge?

This is not the place to attempt a full elucidation of this paradox. We certainly do not wish to deny the paradoxical quality of our criticism of Knight; but we must emphatically point out that this paradox is not one of our own making. The insistence on the part of the Chicago School on the centrality of the perfectly competitive model in explaining real world capitalism is of course well known; this insistence has in fact ample basis in Knight's own teaching. The key to solving the puzzle (concerning Knight's attitude to uncertainty) appears to lie in Knight's view[5] that uncertainty cannot be overcome or escaped, that there is nothing in the market process that can systematically narrow the range of uncertainty introduced by the brute fact of the unknowable future. The Knightian entrepreneur is subject to uncertainty, but possesses no capacity to overcome that uncertainty. It follows that for Knight what occurs systematically in real world markets cannot be explained in terms of any systematic market elimination of uncertainty. There *is* no way, with or without a market, to grapple with uncertainty. (Knight was in fact convinced that, on balance, entrepreneurial losses are likely to outweigh entrepreneurial profit (Knight, 1921, p. 347).) What occurs systematically in real world markets can, therefore, be accounted for only by postulating that, for all the uncertainty which characterizes the real world, it is the model of perfect competition which nonetheless successfully captures the systematic elements in the real world. To understand the real world as a *system,* it is necessary to view it as somehow more or less precisely portrayed in the perfectly competitive model from which all uncertainty has been carefully removed. Uncertainty introduces an inescapable fuzziness into the picture; but the picture itself is that marked out by the perfectly competitive model.

It appears, then, that to treat uncertainty as utterly inescapable can lead to precisely similar ways of understanding the real world economy as are sustained by the assumption that the economy is characterized by the complete absence of uncertainty. What permits the Austrian view of the competitive world to understand it as an open-ended system within which a systematic "discovery procedure" is able to occur, is not so much recognition of sheer ignorance, as the recognition of the vincibility of that ignorance. For the Austrian view, the market process is systematic only insofar as that view understands how ignorance generates market opportunities which inspire discovery. A refusal to recognize any such discovery procedure compels a choice between two alternatives: either to abandon any notions of systematic market processes, or to perceive such systematic market processes as arising in spite of inescapable ignorance and uncertainty. The latter alternative is equivalent to the assertion that ignorance and uncertainty can—for the purposes of the relevant explanatory theory—be imagined simply not to exist.

Let us return to our main theme: the claim that an Austrian view of the market as a process of competitive discovery can undermine much of the mainstream ethical case against the market economy. It will be useful to review Knight's classic criticisms. The criticisms that we are concerned with fall into two groups: (a) contentions that real world divergences from the conditions of the perfectly competitive model mean that the market economy must fall short of the efficiency standard which that model represents; (b) contentions that the efficiency attained under the conditions of perfect competition can itself be challenged from the ethical perspective.

THE REAL WORLD AND THE PERFECTLY COMPETITIVE MODEL

Mainstream writers, following Knight, routinely point out that, however useful the model of perfectly competitive equilibrium may be as an explanatory framework for the real world, the latter world in fact displays many features that are utterly inconsistent with the model. So that real world capitalism must, to a greater or lesser extent, invariably fail to achieve the allocative efficiency associated with that model. Under this heading Knight (1923, pp. 50–52) lists: imperfect divisibility and mobility of goods and services; imperfect market knowledge and costly communication between traders (leaving "wide margins for 'bargaining power'" [ibid., p. 50]); imperfect knowledge by potential buyers of the precise usefulness of what they may buy; monopolistic combinations that may arise in "free" markets. Each of these features of the real world violates one or more of the conditions for the perfectly competitive model. Outcomes must, therefore, be expected to diverge from those benign results predicted by the model.

Our reaction to these valid positive observations is that they represent valid normative criticisms of free markets only to the extent that one has accepted the perfectly competitive model as the relevant normative ideal. If one sees the function of the market as that of achieving an efficient allocation of social resources (i.e. that allocation achieved in the perfectly competitive model) then it is reasonable to see these features of the real world (that Knight has identified) as inevitable sources of inadequate market performance of its assigned function. We have seen that for Knight (and for the subsequent twentieth century mainstream) efficient resource allocation is indeed seen as the market's function. For Chicago School economists, indeed, the virtues of the market consist precisely in the market's assumed approximation to the outcomes of the perfectly competitive model. So that imperfect divisibility, imperfect knowledge, and so forth do seem to cast serious shadow on claims for market success.

But, as explained, we wish to escape such a view of the market's function. Recognition of the uncertainty inherent in an open-ended world, recognition of the human propensity for entrepreneurial discovery and innovation, permit us to recognize a social function played by the market economy for which there is no counterpart in the perfectly competitive model. This social function, we have seen, is to stimulate and inspire those discoveries—of the abilities and plans of others, of the availability of resources, of one's own potential needs and desires, and of hitherto unsuspected technological possibilities—which can enhance mutual coordination among the plans made by market participants and the exploitation of unnoticed production possibilities inherent in existing economic circumstances. While the model of perfect competition is, for this perspective on markets, a highly interesting construction, it does not and cannot serve as the relevant normative ideal for the economic problems of the real world. These problems are, as Hayek pointed out in his celebrated 1945 paper (Hayek, 1945), not those of securing optimum social efficiency in resource allocation, but those of mobilizing scattered information—and, we may add, those of inspiring the discovery of entirely new bits of information—in order to enhance the usefulness of decisions made.

From this perspective, it is clear, many of the mainstream criticisms of the market economy (adumbrated by Knight in the above cited passages) melt away as wholly beside the point. Not only does it turn out that these perceived "imperfections" of the market have been so identified only by setting up an inappropriate criterion as the ideal, in fact it can be shown that the alleged imperfections are likely to be positive advantages to the market in its fulfillment of (what we maintain to be) its true social function. As has often been pointed out by Austrians as diverse in their views as Schumpeter and Mises, the dynamic market process is one which is able to proceed only because the conditions for perfectly competitive equilibrium are absent. Imperfect divisibility, imperfect knowledge, and sizes of firms rendering industries oligopolistic rather than perfectly competitive, are important prerequisites for the creation of those entrepreneurial acts of discovery which enable the market to fulfill its true function. It is not, of course, that imperfect divisibility, imperfect knowledge, and the like are to be seen as in themselves evidence or expressions of market success. Imperfect knowledge is not a goal of Austrian economics! Instead it is simply to be noted that to wish away these features of the real world is, given the relevant economic problems we face, to wish away the very "frictions" which are indispensable prerequisites for taking steps toward the solution of these problems.

It may be worth noting that our perspective on the mainstream (Knightian) criticisms of the market are not quite the same as the valuable critique of those criticisms which Demsetz offered many years ago by characterizing those criticisms as representing a "nirvana approach." In Demsetz's words, "The view which now pervades much public policy economics implicitly presents the relevant choice as between an ideal norm and an existing 'imperfect' institutional arrangement" (Demsetz, 1969, p. 1). Demsetz cogently points out that such an imagined choice imagines away the possibly high cost of making the transition between a given "imperfect" arrangement and an ideal one. When such transition costs are taken into account, the "imperfect" arrangement may turn out to be the best attainable one, after all.

The critique offered by Demsetz is able to accept the mainstream identification of the perfectly competitive model as the societal ideal. It is thus able to agree with the mainstream identification of features of the real world as being, in principle, "imperfections" (as compared with the ideal). It simply (and most valuably) points out, however, that recognizing the costs of transition from an actual to an "ideal," may render that "ideal" no longer so ideal after all. Certainly Demsetz's perceptive critique is (within the scope of the mainstream perspective) entirely and importantly valid. But our own disagreement with the mainstream criticisms is more radical in our rejection of the perfectly competitive model either as the relevant normative ideal or as a useful positive explanatory tool.[6]

**THE ETHICS OF COMPETITION
AND THE ETHICS OF DISTRIBUTION**

The second group of Knightian criticisms of the ethics of competition arise mainly out of his dissatisfaction with the distributional outcomes of the perfectly competitive model itself. Knight argues the ethical inadequacy of this distributional outcome on a number of grounds, including the following: (a) the ethical character of this outcome can be no stronger than the principle "that productive contribution is an ethical measure of desert" (Knight, 1923, p. 54)—a principle which Knight rejects; (b) "productive contribution" is measured in terms of price which "does not correspond closely with ethical value or human significance" (ibid., p. 55), (c) market distribution is based on resource ownership, with the ethical justification for such ownership being, in Knight's view, highly questionable (ibid., p. 56). (Knight's criticisms of the distributive outcome of the market also reflect ethical convictions which, while perhaps questionable in themselves, do not depend on the centrality of the perfectly competitive model. For example Knight seems to dismiss outright any possibility of inheritance providing an ethically valid basis for ownership. In general Knight recognizes only "effort" as providing an ethically valid claim to ownership rights. He seems not to be prepared to recognize that inferior competence should be a barrier against being able to demand, on ethical grounds, an income that might have been earned with greater competence (since, after all, society does recognize an ethical obligation to support the entirely helpless). For the purposes of this chapter we are not concerned with this aspect of Knight's dissatisfaction with capitalist distribution.)

Our quarrel with the above Knightian criticisms of capitalist distribution (criticisms echoed in many subsequent mainstream textbooks) arises entirely from the extent to which these criticisms fail to recognize any discovery dimensions in the competitive market process. Knight's criticisms apply, in principle, to a perfectly competitive world in which incomes are distributed strictly in terms of J. B. Clark's theory of marginal productivity. It is in the context of such a world that it may be in order to question, on ethical grounds, the appropriateness of reward according to the market value of productive contribution derived from initially assumed patterns of resource ownership. Our claim is that distribution in the real world market economy characterized by dynamic, entrepreneurial competition, introduces a dimension of possible ethical worthiness which has nothing to do with "productive contribution" (however valued) and in no way depends upon (ethically valid or invalid) resource ownership rights.

This newly introduced dimension of possible ethical worthiness concerns just title to what one has discovered. It is not possible to provide here a full-length analysis of what discovery means and how it may introduce distinctive ethical considerations into discussions of distributive justice.[7] A few brief observations are however in order.

We distinguish sharply between acts of production (including the production of knowledge in acts of deliberate search) and acts of discovery. The former are the subject matter of mainstream micro-economics; they are deliberate transformations of resource services into outputs. The resources services, being sufficient to generate the outputs, are, in a certain sense, already, that output. To possess the inputs is potentially already to possess—or at any rate, to have within one's grasp—the outputs. If ownership rights in inputs are recognized as valid, this recognition itself implies the validity of the ownership of the corresponding outputs. Conversely, in order to establish ethically valid ownership of output, it is necessary to show that (somewhere along the line of legitimate transfers of ownership rights which have led up to the present) output ownership grew directly out of input ownership. Challenges to the legitimacy of output ownership may fairly be grounded in challenges to the legitimacy of input ownership. Acts of discovery are quite different.

Acts of discovery are non-deliberate. They involve alert individuals becoming aware of resources, or possibilities of deploying resources, to which no one else has established any claim. So to discover a resource, or a new way of using a resource is in effect to create that resource, or its new use. Such creation is in no way to be seen as the planned conversion of input into output. It is to be seen as the creation of something entirely new, *ex nihilo*. Legitimacy of ownership in regard to what has been discovered cannot derive from ownership of any inputs, since the discovery is not attributed to any inputs. A discovery occurs *ex nihilo*. One may wish to argue that a discovery is to be attributed to the human-capital quality of alertness possessed by the discoverer. However, as argued elsewhere (Kirzner, 1979, pp. 186–89), following Schumpeter, such alertness cannot be treated as an economic input. An input is a resource (of which its owner is already aware) deliberately deployed in a planful act. Alertness may indeed be deserving of credit for a discovery; but alertness is not deliberately deployed in discovery. As noted in passing earlier, deliberate search (in which alertness may certainly be deployed) is an act of production of knowledge, not one of discovery.

It may at first glance appear that, if acts of discovery are not the outcome of deliberate plans, then the fortunate consequences of discovery must be ascribed to sheer good luck—sharply eroding, in the eyes of many, the ethical claim of the discoverer to what has been discovered. We must insist that this is not the case. To declare an outcome not to have emerged as a result of a planned act, is not necessarily to pronounce that outcome to be ascribable only to sheer luck. There is a category of gain which is neither the planned consequence of an act of production, nor the wholly fortuitous outcome of a blind stroke of luck. This category refers to gains which have been noticed. To notice something worth acquiring is (while we can certainly recognize the element of luck in the circumstance that something was there "waiting" to be noticed) to bring something into existence that was hitherto, for all intents and purposes, non-existent. While the act of noticing (unlike the outcome of a successful search) was not deliberately undertaken, yet the discovered gain is not something which random good luck has thrust into the hands of a sleeping beneficiary. To notice an opportunity worth grasping is to have created something. Only she (or he) who has noticed the opportunity and has grasped it, and no one else, is responsible for and is to be credited with the discovery.

Such discovery is not to be credited to effort, but is nonetheless to be credited to a quality of the discoverer. To say that, because the discovery was not the result of the deployment by the discoverer, of *his* inputs, it therefore belongs to society in general, is to deny that the discovery was made by him (or her) and no one else. Elsewhere this writer has argued that our insights concerning discovered gain appear to coincide with those rather widely shared moral intuitions which are sometimes expressed in the principle of "finders, keepers."

Our point in this paper is not to insist on the moral right of the discoverer. Rather we wish to simply draw definitive attention to an aspect of real world capitalism which appears to bring into one's moral field of vision dimensions of possible ethical significance which are, and must be, entirely absent from the world of perfect competition at which Knight's ethical misgivings were addressed (and to which subsequent mainstream ethical comment has been directed). In the real capitalist economy incomes of all kinds are embedded in an open-ended world of uncertainty in which discoveries are continually being made. The standard theoretical categories of income, such as wages, rents, and interest, are categories taken from the Clarkian perfectly competitive world (in which marginal productivity is the sole operative determinant of income) but are not to be found, in their pure form, in the real world. In this real world incomes invariably partake, to a greater or lesser degree, of the character of pure entrepreneurial profit. To the extent that the Knightian ethical misgivings concerning capitalist distribution derive from exclusive concentration on the marginal-productivity slicing up of the pie produced under perfectly competitive conditions, they must be pronounced irrelevant for a capitalism in which entrepreneurial discovery plays a significant role in income distribution.

CONCLUDING REMARKS

Our thesis has not been to promote any particular ethical perspective upon capitalism. Instead we have merely asked that ethical evaluation of capitalism should proceed from an adequate and full understanding of its operation. An evaluation undertaken from an Austrian perspective recognizing the dynamic entrepreneurial dimension to real world competition will, we believe, show the fallacies in or irrelevance of many of the ethical criticisms of capitalism that have become central to the twentieth century conventional wisdom.

NOTES

1. Knight (1923), all reference here will be to the republished version of that paper in Knight (1935, ch. 2).

2. For a typical and careful example, see Baumol and Blinder (1991, ch. 29).

3. On this see Chamberlin (1957, ch. 15). See also Stigler (1952) and Friedman (1953, p. 38).

4. On this point see particularly Hayek (1978).

5. On this point see Knight (1921), and the discussion in Kirzner (1973, pp. 82 ff.).

6. For discussion of some overlap between Demsetz's position and my own, see Kirzner (1973, pp. 231 ff.).

7. For such a more detailed analysis see Kirzner (1989).

REFERENCES

Baumol, W. J., and Blinder, A. S. (1991) *Economics, Principles and Policy,* San Diego: Harcourt Brace Jovanovich.

Chamberlin, E. (1957) *Toward a More General Theory of Value,* London: Oxford University Press.

Demsetz, H. (1969) "Information and Efficiency: Another Viewpoint," *Journal of Law and Economics* 12, pp. 1–22.

Friedman, M. (1953) *Essays in Positive Economics,* Chicago: University of Chicago Press.

Hayek, F. A. (1945) "The Use of Knowledge in Society," *American Economic Review* 35, pp. 519–30.

———— (1978) "Competition as a Discovery Procedure," in F. A. Hayek (ed.) *New Studies in Philosophy, Politics, Economics and the History of Ideas*, Chicago: University of Chicago Press, pp. 179–90.

Kirzner, I. M. (1973) *Competition and Entrepreneurship*, Chicago: University of Chicago Press.

———— (1979) *Perception, Opportunity and Profit*, Chicago: University of Chicago Press.

———— (1985) *Discovery and the Capitalist Process*, Chicago: University of Chicago Press.

———— (1989) *Discovery, Capitalism and Distributive Justice*, Oxford: Basil Blackwell.

Knight, Frank H. (1921) *Risk, Uncertainty and Profit*, Boston, MA: Houghton Mifflin.

———— (1923) "The Ethics of Competition," *Quarterly Journal of Economics* 37, pp. 579–624.

———— (1935) *The Ethics of Competition and Other Essays*, New York: Harper.

Stigler, G. J. (1952) *Five Lectures on Economic Problems*, lecture 2, London: Macmillan, pp. 12–24.

———— (1957) "Perfect Competition, Historically Contemplated," *Journal of Political Economy* 65, pp. 1–17. Reprinted in G. J. Stigler (1965) *Essays in the History of Economics*, Chicago: University of Chicago Press, ch. 8.

THE MORALITY OF CAPITALIST SUCCESS

It is an honor for me to present this C. A. Moorman Memorial Lecture. Over the years I have been greatly impressed by this distinguished lecture series. I am grateful to President Brown and to the Directors of the Moorman Foundation for the privilege of addressing you this afternoon. My talk today will be devoted to only one small aspect of a much larger subject, surrounding which there exists a very substantial (and still growing) literature. This larger subject is the ethics and morality of the capitalist system of economic organization. During recent years many writers have sought for features or consequences of capitalism upon which overall moral judgements of it might somehow rest. This lecture does not attempt to grapple with this kind of comprehensive task. Rather we focus on one small aspect of that task—one on which an economist may have something specific to say. This aspect of the larger task is the analysis of whether and how the *efficiency* of capitalism has any contribution to make toward winning moral approbation for capitalism.

Let me explain. Disagreements concerning the morality of capitalism between its defenders and its detractors have revolved around such issues as the justice or injustice of capitalist income distribution, or the role of selfishness and greed in capitalism, or the extent to which capitalism promotes the qualities of prudence, diligence and thrift. Such moral debates have concerned the ethical defensibility of capturing pure profits, or the extent to which capitalism coincides with or is a necessary condition for a society of free individuals.

In these wider debates the economist does indeed have *some* role to play. In order to reform an opinion concerning, for example, the justice or injustice of capitalism (or even, recognizing Hayek, concerning whether notions of justice have any internal coherence at all when applied to capitalism), a thorough understanding of the workings of the capitalist system is an important prerequisite. And the same is true for most of the dimensions of morality along which capitalism may be sought to be measured. But the economist's role, in these questions, is a limited one.

From the C. A. Moorman Memorial Lecture Series, Culver-Stockton College, November 13, 1980. Reprinted by permission.

The economist is, after all, not professionally competent to illuminate the nature of specific moral values, such as justice, or freedom; he can merely clarify the extent to which the capitalist system promotes or subverts these values.

Our concern in this paper, on the other hand, is with a criterion or norm the *very meaning of which* depends on rather thorough understanding of subtle economic issues. Our concern is with the economic success or "efficiency" of capitalism, and its meaning for the moral qualities of that system of economic organization. "Efficiency" is very much a specifically economic criterion. And it is for this reason that this economist, fully aware though he is of his limited competence to make pronouncements on ethical issues best left to professional philosophers, dares to offer some observations on the ethics of capitalist efficiency.

The issue happens to be one of considerable importance for capitalism. On the one hand more and more perceptive observers of the modern world are coming to the conclusion that the free market system—the core of capitalism—is the pattern of societal arrangement able to promote maximum production and efficiency. On the other hand more and more of these thoughtful observers are searching critically for the moral foundations of capitalism. Productivity and efficiency by themselves, it is held, treated as strictly technical matters unrelated to ethical norms, are simply not sufficient to capture hearts and stir enthusiasms. If capitalism is to survive, it can only be because the public recognizes the cogency of its moral claims. And yet, it is frequently pointed out, the economic success of capitalism,—its capacity to address the problems of hunger and want, its ability to provide the material basis for the satisfaction of man's aspirations—can hardly be totally irrelevant for a judgement on its overall moral worth. It is this last issue that we shall examine today. To what extent may a moral justification of the capitalist system rest upon its generally acknowledged economic efficiency? Our concern, then, is not with the dignity of individualism, the value of freedom, the ethics of competition, or the justice of property—but with the morality of economic success.

THE MEANING OF ECONOMIC SUCCESS

A word of clarification may be in order. Economic success is not to be measured by the number of cars, or the number of telephones, or the number of calories, enjoyed per capita. Economic success is not, except in the very crudest of senses, to be measured by the dollar figure attained by Gross National Product, or other aggregate magnitude. Economic success, we have understood since Lord Robbins explained it for us a half-century ago, refers not to the sheer volume of output itself, but to the efficiency with which available resources have been deployed in achieving that output. Capitalism is a successful economic system not because it provides more cars but because it avoids waste; its success is reflected not in the quantity of production so much as in the extent to which this quantity approaches the maximum ideally possible with available resources. Two economies may be enjoying roughly the same standard of living, yet differ sharply in their economic successfulness, as we wish to define it. The one economy may be achieving its standard of living by having effectively deployed its skimpy resources so as to minimize waste, incompetence and mismanagement, and to encourage growth, innovation, and efficiency. The second economy, while initially enjoying a vastly larger volume of resources, may have been reduced to its standard of consumption (similar to that of the first economy), as a result of faulty patterns of resource allocation, inappropriate incentives, and sheer waste. To be sure economic success, defined in efficiency terms, tends to assure higher standards of living (with any given volume of available resources) than would be delivered by inefficient economic performance,—clearly this *is* the important practical point about the desirability of efficiency. But this does not mean that in discussing the economic successfulness of capitalism we are referring directly to the level of consumption which it makes possible. In what follows we are therefore *not* considering the morality of high standards of living. Rather we will be concerned with the moral aspects of those societal arrangements which permit that society to achieve efficiency.

Certain features of this economic efficiency should be particularly emphasized for the purposes of our discussion. We should remember that the concept of efficiency does not prejudge the desirability of particular goals. The term "level of consumption" is often taken to refer to consumption in terms of a well-defined group of consumer satisfactions. So that if one individual skimped, say, on food expenditures in order to make a donation to a hospital drive, it will be said that he lowered his level of consumption in order to engage in philanthropy. But the notion of efficiency, unlike "standard of living," is certainly not confined in such a way as to exclude attention to the efficiency with which philanthropic goals are pursued. Efficiency is a concept relating to the effectiveness with which available means are deployed in the pursuit of given purposes—no matter what the character of these purposes may be. In earlier times economics was thought of as having to do with certain kinds of things or certain kinds of satisfactions (such as money, or material goods, and the like). As economic science came to be refined, however, it was recognized that what is common to economic phenomena is not their material or pecuniary character, but rather their relating to the manner in which human beings systematically pursue purposes—no matter what the character of these purposes. It was this which moved the great Austrian economist Ludwig von Mises to describe economics as a *science of human action*. Let us take note of some of the implications of this breadth in the notion of efficiency.

THE ETHICS OF INDIVIDUAL EFFICIENCY

Our discussion of the efficiency concept has made it clear that the concept is one that is applicable to the pursuit of purposes—whether these purposes are morally attractive or not. An evil man intent on achieving the most revolting of ends will, in pursuing these hellish purposes, certainly seek to be as efficient as possible. He will surely seek to avoid fulfilling goals of lesser importance to him if these preclude the satisfaction of more important desires—whether or not these latter desires are less morally revolting than the former. In other words the search for efficiency cannot, by itself, be hailed as a simple virtue. Presumably efficiency in the pursuit of evil partakes of the very same moral reprehensibility as applies to the evil goals themselves. Again, efficiency in the pursuit of goals judged to hold high moral worth, would enjoy the same moral approbation as is accorded to these goals themselves. It is not so much that efficiency is morally *neutral*; rather it is that the moral evaluation of efficiency cannot be undertaken except in terms of the particular goals in the service of which it is being achieved. Efficiency is strictly a matter of maintaining consistency with a given ranking of goals; the morality of its pursuit hinges entirely on and must be derived from the morality of the goals toward which it is being directed.

To be sure there were attempts in the earlier literature to elevate efficiency into a distinct human value. The avoidance of waste does, for example, appear to have significantly wide applicability in art, music and literature. Nonetheless it seems difficult to see how the pursuit of efficiency in the fulfillment of wicked ends can itself avoid being damned. So that any moral approval of efficient pursuit of worthy ends must surely be attributed to the worthiness of those ends, rather than to any aesthetic qualities inherent in efficiency per se. These observations concerning the ethical dimensions of individual efficiency are introduced here only to facilitate our subsequent discussion of parallel issues as they relate to social efficiency under capitalism. Let us turn, then, to consider the moral dimensions of the efficiency notion as it applies to the free market economy as a whole, rather than to its individual participants.

SOCIAL EFFICIENCY AND ETHICAL NEUTRALITY

It should be pointed out that, at one important level, social efficiency partakes of the same derivative character we have emphasized with respect to the individual. The social efficiency achieved by the market must, at this level of discussion, derive any moral worth it may have from the worthiness of the individual purposes whose fulfillment it facilitates. An outstanding British economist of an earlier era elegantly expressed the basic idea seventy years ago:

> The network of interchanges created and sustained by the economic forces is, morally, socially, and aesthetically, absolutely indifferent. It serves to enable every man to pursue his purposes, such as they are, beyond the range of the direct applicability of his own faculties and resources to them. It enables the saint who has the will but not the power to do some great deed to enlist the cooperation of the sinner who has the power but not the will to do it. But in order to make the sinner help him to the accomplishment of his purposes he has been obliged himself to help the sinner to the accomplishment of his. . . . And so, under the all-covering cloak of money payments for services and commodities, and sales of instruments and supports of life for money payments, all purposes and impulses, of love and of lust, of narrow greed and of broad beneficence, of enlightened and productive insight, of blind, tangled and self-confuting gropings, all destructive and reckless passions, all wasteful and desolating vices, all noble ambitions, all vulgar or refined enjoyments, all fruitful enterprises, and all foolish or wicked schemes of industrial waste, enter the open market and draw to themselves the efforts and services of men in proportion not to their worthiness or fruitfulness, but to the means they

command of furthering the purposes of others; for they secure the co-operation of all sorts and conditions of men, not in the measure in which such men sympathise with them, but in the measure in which by serving them they will forward their own purposes. (P. Wicksteed, *The Common Sense of Political Economy* [1910]. London: Routledge and Kegan Paul, 1933, pp. 395f).

Precisely because the market serves both saints and sinners, it seems important to avoid the danger of praising the efficiency of the market, the economic success of capitalism, for moral virtues it does not possess. The market *may* efficiently minister to saintly purposes; but, on the other hand, it may minister to other purposes. The moral value of the efficiency of the market, just as that of the efficiency of the individual, depends, at least to this extent, entirely on the saintliness of its participants. The market indeed possesses enormous *potential* for good, for the furtherance of inspired purposes and lofty goals. But this seems, at this point in our discussion, to exhaust the ethical merit which attaches to the efficiency of the market, considered in abstraction from particular historical context. This does bear emphasis. The understandable urge, on the part of defenders of capitalism, to see its economic success, too, as somehow an ingredient in the *moral* case for capitalism, may involve misunderstanding and hence serve to discredit the otherwise valid claims of capitalism for ethical approbation.

Defenders of capitalism are justifiably quick to reject criticisms of it which denounce the many kinds of consumption goods produced by capitalism that fall short of the ideals of high quality and noble purpose. The market system is not to be blamed, it is properly pointed out, for the crassness of tastes demonstrated by consumers. To blame the market for faithfully catering to these preferences, would be equivalent, to use George Stigler's delightful metaphor, to blaming the waiter for obesity. The efficiency of the market is *supposed* to minister, and without grumbling, to the crudest as to the most elevated of consumer desires. But while this defense of the market properly rejects the groundless assertions which ascribe the shoddy, sorry products of some industries to capitalism itself (rather than to the tastes of consumers), this defense can hardly succeed in ascribing independent moral worth to the effectiveness with which decadent tastes may be served.

Of course, to recognize the moral neutrality of market efficiency, in the abstract, is in no way to deny that the by-products of market efficiency may be highly desirable from numerous perspectives. A number of writers (including Mises, Rothbard, and Hazlitt) have pointed out that market exchange transactions are, historically, probably responsible for such amiable social characteristics as sympathy and friendship. It is unlikely, these writers argue, that these characteristics would have emerged in the absence of the advantages to be derived from social cooperation via exchange (as opposed to conflict). Certainly any overall moral evaluation of capitalism should take such factors into account (along with other morally relevant aspects of the free market). But we are here concerned not with the moral evaluation of the *by-products* of economic success under capitalism; our concern here is with economic efficiency itself. So far, it seems, efficiency appears to hold no clear independent claims to our moral enthusiasms. And yet, we shall maintain, the economic success of capitalism *does* possess attributes which, if properly understood, may well command our moral admiration. Let us see how this is the case.

THE EFFICIENCY OF SOCIETY

Thus far in our discussion of the notion of efficiency, we have proceeded as if the concept applies to society in as simple a fashion as it applies to the individual. But this is by no means the case. In fact as soon as we seek to extend the notion of efficiency to a society certain serious difficulties immediately present themselves. For the individual member of society—or for that matter for Robinson Crusoe—the notion of efficiency is clearcut. At a given moment in time the individual has a variety of goals which he would like to pursue. The means available to him are, however, insufficient to permit fulfillment of all of these goals. Some must remain, at least to some extent, unfulfilled. The notion of efficiency refers then to the individual's concern to ensure that of all the purposes which must perforce remain unfulfilled, none is more important to him than any of those that are fulfilled. The simplicity and coherence of this notion arises out of the circumstance that at a given moment in time an individual does indeed perceive himself to be in command of given scarce resources, and does indeed possess the ability to arrange his goals in an unambiguous ranking of priorities. But when one wishes to discuss efficiency as a *social* notion, both these features of the individual decision setting are immediately seen to be absent. Society simply does not "choose" in the way an individual chooses. The resources available to a society of any size are never known simultaneously to any single choosing mind. Nor does society itself (in any but a metaphorical sense) possess goals of its own that might be ranked in order of social importance. Rather each of the individuals that make up society possesses his or her own private goals. How, from the countless private decision-settings involving individual members of society, can we construct a notion of *social* efficiency—of society concerned that no goal of superior social importance be wastefully displaced by the fulfilment of some other goal of lesser social significance?

Today's lecture is not the occasion for a full scale exploration of this difficult analytical issue. But it is necessary to state briefly the position on this question which underlies the subsequent discussion. This position is as follows: First, the problem cannot be avoided by simply refusing to recognize, at the social level, *any* counterpart to the notion of efficiency (that we understand in straightforward fashion at the individual level). There surely does exist a sense in which we understand that an economy may be organized along institutional lines that prevent it from achieving those levels of individual well-being that might have been achieved within a differently structured institutional setting. There must be some way of rendering conceptually precise the sense in which this economy is not as efficient as it might have been—even though each of its individual members successfully achieves the highest levels of satisfaction attainable within the given opportunity framework. Second, a notion of social efficiency cannot—at any but a very crude metaphorical level—be salvaged by treating society *as if* it *does* possess a single ranking of goals with respect to which the given volume of available resources (treated as if they were known to a single mind) are to be allocated. The simplifying assumptions needed to render such a notion of social efficiency coherent are either entirely too fantastic or are of a character as to beg the very questions sought to be grappled with. As Hayek taught us long ago, to imagine that the given volume of resources is somehow fully known to a single mind, is to imagine away the central circumstance underlying the need for arrangements conducive to social efficiency. Third, we may describe one economic system as more economically successful, as a system, than a second, if the first is better able to induce the *coordination among individual actions* that is necessary if individuals are to achieve high levels of goal-fulfillment. Imagine a group of individuals whose preferences and current endowments are such as to afford numerous opportunities for mutually profitable exchanges. In order for these exchange opportunities to be consummated, individual decisions need to become mutually coordinated: individuals must correctly anticipate the willingness of each other to engage in exchange. A society may then be described as economically unsuccessful if it performs poorly in terms of promoting this kind of coordination. Each of the individuals may, given the barriers of mutual ignorance, be making decisions of greatest possible effectiveness—yet, because of some "supra-individual" failure, each of them remains unable to attain goals which superior coordination among them might have brought within reach. This kind of social economic failure may be considered to represent social inefficiency—the individuals in society are not achieving what they *might* have achieved; the resources available to society are not, therefore, being used to greatest advantage. This social efficiency concept does not entail any social ranking of priorities, nor does it presume initial knowledge on the part of a single mind of all available resources and opportunities (in fact it is entirely consistent with the possibility that some available resources and opportunities are, initially, known to no one at all).

It is in this sense that we consider free market capitalism to be a remarkably successful and efficient economic system. The high standards of living achieved under the free enterprise system are to be credited to the ability of the market continually to reveal where profitable opportunities exist and to bring these to the attention of market participants, with amazing swiftness and effectiveness. And it is in the light of this "coordination" view of social efficiency that we shall argue a case for recognizing a possibly significant moral element to the economic success of capitalism.

SOME ECONOMICS OF SOCIAL EFFICIENCY

We have explained that the social efficiency achieved by capitalism must be understood in terms of the *coordination of individual actions.* How does the free enterprise system in fact succeed in coordinating myriads of individual decisions without central direction? A complete answer to this question would comprise a very large fraction of the entire science of economics. Indeed, as economists explore the frontiers of their discipline they are continually discovering new subtleties beneath the surface of this question, and new insights into its solution. I must content myself here with the briefest statement of this solution; in so doing I shall emphasize the critical role played by *discovery* in the social coordinating process of the market.

Absence of coordination occurs when market participants undertake actions which, if they had been better informed, they would have avoided. Some actions *should* have been avoided because (although these actions can be successfully carried out) they ought to have been replaced by other feasible actions able to offer superior results. Other actions should have been avoided because they are simply not feasible; their successful completion depends upon actions of other market participants which will in fact not occur. Now both these kinds of mistaken actions are mistaken as a result of faulty anticipation of the actions of others. Either one pessimistically fails to anticipate the actions of others and hence fails to grasp superior available opportunities; or one overoptimistically anticipates actions of others that will not, in fact, occur, so that one fruitlessly chases after non-existent opportunities. Both kinds of mistake, it is clear, consist in an absence of coordination among the actions of market participants. Absence of coordination represents the state of imperfect knowledge concerning one another's attitudes and abilities. If the free market system is indeed successful in replacing such a state of mutual ignorance by one of improved knowledge, this must, then, depend on a *discovery process*. This is what the famed Austrian economist Friedrich Hayek has in mind when he refers to the competitive market process as a "discovery procedure."

The market generates mutual discovery through its central, defining activity—the competitive quest for pure entrepreneurial profit. Absence of coordination implies available opportunities overlooked, non-existent opportunities futilely pursued. Such profit opportunities missed, and such loss situations grasped, tend to ignite discovery. The lure of pure profit tends to uncover opportunities hitherto missed, the sting of losses teaches its own salutary lesson. The gradual discovery of true possibilities and their limitations constitutes the coordinating process of the market. It is this process that tends to direct resources into products for which consumers are prepared to pay more, rather than into those for which consumers are prepared to pay less. It is this process that tends to teach producers to employ resources less urgently needed elsewhere in the market rather than resources more urgently in demand. It is this process that tends to assure owners of resources that the value to society of the marginal output of their resources might render it worthwhile for them to place these resources at the service of others rather than to enjoy them in the form of leisure or direct consumption use. In other words, the economic success of capitalist society (and thus the cornucopia of good things which it makes possible for its members to earn) consists in the rapidity with which errors are discovered and exploited. This, then, is the meaning of the social efficiency of capitalism; it differs in important respects from individual efficiency. These differences may be significant for our own present inquiry.

INDIVIDUAL EFFICIENCY AND SOCIAL EFFICIENCY

Efficiency by an individual in the pursuit of his goals adds nothing to our understanding that he pursues these goals. To pursue goals *means* to refrain from actions inconsistent with those announced goals. To be inefficient, as Benedetto Croce recognized at the turn of the century, is somehow to be impossibly in contradiction to oneself. Or, as a modern economist has put it, to maximize utility (i.e. to seek efficiency in consumption) is nothing but telling the truth. If one fails to achieve achievable goals because of laziness, one is not being inefficient at all, in this line of argument; one is simply confessing that those unachieved goals in fact rank lower than that of enjoying slothful slumber. It was due to this circumstance that we found it difficult to summon up moral enthusiasm for individual efficiency abstracted from the particular goals being sought.

But *social* efficiency is of a quite different character. As noted earlier societies do not choose; societies do not pursue goals (in any but a metaphorical sense). If social efficiency is achieved, this represents a phenomenon *not at all* implicit in the datum that its individual members pursue purposes. In fact social efficiency represents a circumstance so remarkable as to require, as mentioned earlier, virtually an entire science for its explication.

This point may be emphasized somewhat further by noting that there *does* exist, at the level of the individual, an aspect of action that bears an analogy to the role of discovery at the societal level. But at the individual level discovery remains *outside* the efficiency framework, as usually conceived. Efficiency for the individual occurs within the given framework of perceived ends and means. The discovery of new goals worthy of pursuit, or of available resources hitherto not known, permits the individual to transcend these given frameworks. Whatever the moral significance (if any) that one may wish to perceive in the individual discoveries by which he is able to escape the constraints of one efficiency framework and immerse himself into one less restrictive—it must at least be recognized that discovery is not already *implicit* in the pursuit of the originally perceived goals. Similarly the social discovery process through which the market achieves coordination, is a phenomenon not contained in the initial datum (consisting in the goals pursued by its members). The fact that it is this discovery process in which we have seen social efficiency to consist, thus decisively destroys the completeness of the analogy between individual and social efficiency. Let us now observe the implications of this for the moral evaluation of capitalist success.

THE VALUE OF SOCIAL EFFICIENCY

What we have learned from our brief foray into the economics of the market process, deserves recapitulation. We have seen that this process is not one which "automatically" assures the allocation of social resources in a pattern faithfully reflecting the relative importance of social goals. Individual efficiency, we saw earlier, is nothing more than the consistent implication of goal pursuit. It is automatic in the sense that its absence is, given the ranking of goals and availability of means, unthinkable. Social efficiency, emerging out of processes of inter-individual discovery, is by no means automatic. It is not difficult at all to imagine circumstances, or institutional arrangements which perversely affect the learning process. When we refer to the "miracle of the market" we may indeed be falling into cliché—but something of a miracle the market certainly is. It is on this ground that one may submit that the coordinating process of the market does after all possess positive moral significance. When we observe an individual efficiently pursuing worthy purposes, his efficiency is indeed worthy, but only in the sense that he is pursuing worthy purposes. It is for this reason that efficiency in pursuit of unworthy purposes can hardly escape the verdict of unworthiness. At the social level, however, efficiency consists in the achievement of something quite distinct from the specific goals cherished by individual market participants—it consists in the attainment by market participants of a steady improvement in mutual knowledge. Such mutual knowledge of each other's preferences and abilities is not at all "automatically" forthcoming. Its achievement does appear to hold moral significance, since such knowledge is so crucial for successful social cooperation. And social cooperation for mutual benefit does surely hold moral significance, quite apart from the character of these benefits. If your situation and mine are such as to render exchange between us mutually profitable, then it is in some sense a genuine "pity" if such exchange fails to occur, because of our ignorance of each other's willingness to trade. The exploitation of the opportunity for such exchange, made possible by the discovery process of the market, avoids the "tragedy" of such failure. To be sure the objects or services that we might wish to exchange may not pass the moralist's scrutiny—but this merely recognizes that a miraculous gift may possibly come to be deployed for less than laudable purposes.

The social efficiency achieved under capitalism is not, therefore, a matter of moral indifference. If individual members of society are to be able to fulfill worthy goals to the utmost feasible extent, this calls for social cooperation. Social cooperation depends on mutual knowledge. In providing the vehicle for steadily improving mutual knowledge the market is creating something of social value; it seems difficult to deny that participants in this social process of improving mutual knowledge are engaged—knowingly or not—in a noble enterprise.

THE MORALITY OF CAPITALIST SUCCESS

Advanced capitalist societies have succeeded in providing their citizens with standards of consumption unprecedented in history. We do not claim that the provision of high levels of consumption is itself a noble undertaking, simply because such consumption is the goal of individual aspirations. Nor do we claim that mere consistency in the pursuit of goals commands our moral wonder—apart from the moral status of these goals themselves. What we do say is that underlying the extraordinary flows of consumer goods and services which capitalism makes possible, is a delicate and wholly remarkable process of social coordination. This process of social coordination consists of a systematic—but spontaneous and undirected—series of mutual discoveries. This process holds such potential for the benefit of individual members of society that, unplanned and undesigned as it is, it seems difficult to deny its moral significance. That this seems in any way surprising is surely to be ascribed to the twin dangers that confront virtually any piece of economic reasoning: either the danger that it be dismissed as trivial, or the danger that it be denied as false. For those to whom the market process does not exist at all, it can certainly hold no ethical relevance. Again, for those who take the market process for granted, the achievement of social efficiency can be no more exciting than the "automatic" efficiency invariably attained by individual agents. Only those with full awareness of the extraordinarily complicated process of learning made possible by the market, are in a position to recognize its moral significance.

Of course, to recognize the moral significance of the economic success of the market economy, is not, by itself, to endorse the overall morality of capitalism. Such overall recognition must depend, in addition, upon judgments concerning many other critical and controversial aspects of the system. But our purpose today has been, as announced at the outset, a limited one, to explore the morality of capitalist *success*. We have found that capitalist success depends upon a social discovery process able to transform chaos into fruitful cooperation. It is in this discovery process, holding so much potential for good, that the morality of capitalist success is to be seen.

ECONOMIC SCIENCE AND THE MORALITY
OF CAPITALISM

INTRODUCTION

In this paper we explore the old theme that economic science (more precisely, a flawed but widespread understanding of economic science) is at least partly responsible for the tragically mistaken view that a successful free market society must be an immoral society. That this view has enjoyed widespread currency will hardly be denied by anyone; and in some intellectual quarters it will not be doubted that this widespread currency was responsible in the twentieth century for disastrous public policies. The thesis under discussion here is that this mistaken view can be traced, at least partly, to an unfortunate understanding of economic science. A more careful understanding of the foundations of economics can make a contribution to a more accurate (and more favourable) moral image for capitalism.

The ethical misinterpretation of economic science
Throughout its history, economic science has explained the achievements of free markets in enhancing national wealth, in promoting socially gainful exchange and division of labour, in attaining efficiency in the social allocation of resources, in promoting economic coordination among members of society. Indeed, these teachings of standard economic science have led to its being recognised, by friend and foe of capitalism alike, as the intellectual foundation for any case for capitalism. Foes of capitalism have for over a century and a half recognised standard economic theory as the enemy which must be destroyed if capitalism is to be discredited in the market for ideas. Friends of capitalism have recognised the positive role of sound economics in generating understanding of and appreciation for the public benefits conferred by economic liberty.

Too often, however, economic science has been presented in a manner that sees these benefits as arising strictly from patterns of individual

From *Economy and Virtue: Essays on the Theme of Markets and Morality*, ed. Dennis O'Keeffe (London: Institute of Economic Affairs, 2004), 88–100. First published by the Institute of Economic Affairs, London, 1980. Reprinted by permission.

behaviour which most ethical observers denounce as immoral. The problem is, of course, an old one, and one well recognised. It goes back at least to Mandeville, who argued that "what we call evil in this world . . . is the grand principle that makes us sociable creatures, the solid basis, the life and support of all trades and employments . . ." It led to early denunciations of economics by moralists such as Ruskin (who pronounced the classical economists, and those who could read their work with acceptance, as having entered into an "entirely damned state of soul"). Economics seems to explain the success of a free market society by its reliance upon the untrammelled interplay of the decisions made by selfish, materialistic individuals. Economics has not, in public perception, been able to shake itself free from its dependency (in terms of arguing the efficiency and affluence of a market society) upon *Homo economicus,* defined in a way that portrays him, in Frank Knight's characterisation, as "the selfish, ruthless object of moral condemnation."

To be sure, modern economists of virtually all schools have, certainly since Robbins's 1932 *Nature and Significance of Economic Science,* recognised that economic theory does not require selfish and materialistic agents, only agents who are "rational," i.e. consistently self-interested (with altruistic motives being included as possible "interests" of the individual). Yet the educated layperson might be excused for believing otherwise. Despite lip-service to the idea that the criterion for economic behaviour is no more restrictive than that it be concerned with optimal allocation of scarce resources for the attainment of objectives of all kinds, economists seem continually to be referring to a much narrower set of concerns. Despite Frank Knight's insistence some three-quarters of a century ago that the "idea of a distinction between economic wants and other wants must be abandoned," economists (including some of his own most eminent disciples) continually measure economic success as if the notion of a specifically "economic" objective for society is indeed well defined—as the maximisation of aggregate "wealth" or "value," measured in money.

PEOPLE THINK WE HAVE TO TOLERATE IMMORALITY
IN ORDER TO ENJOY THE ADVANTAGES OF CAPITALISM

Consequently, close to three hundred years after Mandeville, public perception concerning the teachings of economics on capitalism is still mired in paradox. It is widely believed that capitalist prosperity derives from the freedom that the system offers to the greedy, the grasping and the gouging, to cheat and to exploit. Even if public opinion has, during the past decade, swung round toward a more favourable view concerning free markets, this has not meant that any more benign perception of capitalist morality has emerged. Rather what has happened is that a widely shared cynical attitude has crystallised, to the effect that the immorality of unbridled economic freedom is seen as a price worth paying for the enjoyment of the luxuries of Western capitalism. That such an attitude is a highly brittle one should be obvious: the enemies of the market have only to wait for any faltering in the growth of prosperity, for any reason whatever, in order to exploit the apparently obvious lesson. That lesson is that economic immorality does not, after all, pay. The paradox of Western economics, that economic immorality promises economic prosperity, will have been triumphantly exploded.

It is not true that the invisible hand
depends on the acts of immoral people
If only for this reason alone, therefore, it is worthwhile to insist upon exorcising from economics those tendencies to see market achievements as the paradoxically benign outcomes of unethical behaviour. We must insist that it is one thing to claim that individuals acting strictly in regard to their own objectives are led, as if by an invisible hand, to coordinate their decisions with those being made by others. It is quite another thing (and quite fallacious) to insinuate that this invisible hand derives its cunning strictly from the moral failures of market participants. We must insist that the coordinative properties of free markets would be as fully relevant for societies of saintly altruistic market participants as for ruthlessly selfish and materialistic participants.

Hypothetical sainthood and the free market
It is perhaps worthwhile, in order to drive home this insight, to outline very briefly how a free market would operate in an imaginary society of saintly individuals in which each consumer is primarily concerned to help others, and engage in what we would ordinarily call consumption (such as eating, buying new clothing, and the like) only in order to be able to carry out his primary, philanthropic objectives. Sometimes it is thought, even by economists who should know better, that if everyone is selflessly concerned to help others, then the price system must collapse.

Even if it is understood that utility maximisation by consumers can be held to apply even to such a selfless society (simply by recognising that a desire to help others must be incorporated into utility theory), yet it is thought that the price system must break down because of the absence of the profit motive. In a society of selfless saints there seems at first glance no way to incorporate a profit-maximising motive that might drive the price system in the way envisaged in microeconomic theory. Surely individuals for whom the well-being of others takes precedence over their own material consumption will not conduct their business affairs by charging their customers the highest prices they can obtain and paying their workers the lowest wages they can get away with. And if the compass of profit maximisation has, in such a society of saints, been abandoned, it would appear that the conclusions of price theory can no longer be supported. All the elegant marginal equalities demonstrated, as a result of the assumption of profit-maximising behaviour, in the theory of the firm must be given up. In this society of pure altruists none of the efficiency properties ascribed to a well-functioning price system would seem to hold. So might run the argument.

This argument is clearly quite mistaken. Identifying the fallacy that this argument expresses will be instructive in clarifying the nature and function of the business firm in the real world of capitalism-without-saints.

Capitalism-without-saints
The truth is that profit-maximising business firms, charging the highest possible prices, and paying the lowest possible wages, would emerge in the purely saintly society in exactly the same way as in ours. The profits won in business activity would, in the saintly world, no doubt be dedicated to lofty, saintly, philanthropic purposes, instead of being devoted to grossly selfish, materialistic enjoyments on the part of the successful entrepreneurs. But that is all. In conducting his business, an entrepreneur who has no interests other than to eliminate the ravages to humanity of dread diseases would act strictly on profit-maximising principles. By hypothesis his highest (in fact his only true) goal is to combat disease. All else (including enhancing the well-being of his workers, or of his business customers, not to speak of his own material well-being) must and will be subordinated to the overall objective of winning the greatest volume of profit in order to fight disease. The results demonstrated by the theory of the firm hold without modification.

The point is, of course, that to maximise profits is merely an instrumental goal. Saint and sinner alike may seek to maximise profits; they differ only in the uses to which attained profits will subsequently be dedicated. (In exactly the same way saint and sinner alike may drive on a highway from city A to city B, using the same road map and following the same driving principles; they differ only in the ways in which they will respectively enjoy city B's varied endowments.) The profit motive and thus the price system depend for their driving force not upon the ubiquity of selfish or materialistic goals, but upon the ubiquity of *human purposefulness*. In a society based on division of labour and freedom of entrepreneurial entry, those intent on attaining resources with which to fight disease, or other saintly objectives, have every incentive to engage in business ventures to maximise pecuniary profit.

Our purpose in emphasising this simple point is to throw light on the nature and role of the entrepreneurial firm in capitalist society. It is, after all, upon the objective of unadorned profit maximisation that most critics have poured their most mordant scorn. It is the profit-maximising entrepreneur who is seen as unfeeling, ruthless and selfish, as cunningly exploitative and chronically dishonest. It is because his activity is understood to be central to the workings of the free market that the market society is believed to rely upon systematically unethical behaviour for its driving force. But the truth is that profits are not ultimate objectives; only consumption objectives are. Profits are instrumental goals to be deployed for the attainment of immediate (consumption) objectives. The morality or immorality of pursuing profits depends entirely on the morality or immorality of pursuing those consumption objectives.

Moreover, it follows that the profit maximisation objective of business activity relies, as Philip Wicksteed pointed out 85 years ago, *not* upon selfishness but upon what he called "non-altruism." That is, to maximise profits implies not that the businessman is unable to recognise any higher purpose than his own enjoyments, but that he has some purposes that rank higher, at the moment, than the purpose of enhancing the welfare of those with whom he is now trading, to which he intends to dedicate the profits he wins. We might emphasise, perhaps in modification of Wicksteed's position, that we do not posit that purely profit-maximising entrepreneurs have no regard for the welfare of their workers and customers, merely that such regard ranks lower, on the entrepreneur's utility scale, than those other objectives for which profits are being pursued. It should be further observed that, while for theoretical purposes it is convenient to deal with the purely profit-maximising entrepreneur, economists have always been well aware that real-world entrepreneurs are free to modify the purely instrumental objective of maximising profit by introducing "consumption" objectives (such as those of caring directly for the well-being of one's workers and one's customers) into one's "business" activities. While the price system certainly does rest upon the concept of pure profit maximisation, the socially benign properties of the price system in the real world do not depend upon the existence in that world of only those analytically pure agents which people the theoretical system. There is no difficulty in applying price theory to a world in which businessmen integrate some of their consumption objectives directly into their profit-making activities; social coordination can be achieved through the free market also in a world in which businessmen do urgently and genuinely care for the well-being of their workers and customers.

IN AT LEAST ONE SENSE CAPITALISM
IS ETHICALLY NEUTRAL

It should hardly be necessary to expand on the obvious truth that to deny that capitalism depends for its success upon unethical behaviour is not at all to maintain that unethical behaviour is somehow excluded from or by the capitalist rules of the game. To point out that the economics of a free market society of saints need not be essentially different from the economics of real-world capitalism is not to anoint capitalists as saintly. The important truth surely is that, at least in one most significant sense, capitalism is an ethically neutral system, that is, it efficiently promotes the fulfilment of goals of all ethical stripes. Certainly the capitalist economies encountered in modern economic history have not always been peopled by businessmen of overwhelmingly selfless, saintly or otherwise particularly ethical character. And there may indeed be sociological or psychological theories linking the morality of man's behaviour to the economic system (capitalist, socialist, or whatever) in which they participate (there is of course a considerable literature of conflicting theories in this regard). Our thesis is merely that the economics of capitalist prosperity— clearly the most arresting feature of the system—is independent of the particular ethical principles subscribed to by the participants in a capitalist society.

Property rights protect welfare even
when entrepreneurs are morally corrupt

There is, however, one sense in which it may be important to relate capitalist success to an implication of capitalist rules of the game in regard to unethical individual behaviour. While capitalism is certainly consistent with grossly selfish or otherwise unethical behaviour, the property rights framework of capitalism is such as to eliminate the social harm one might be inclined to attribute to such repugnant behaviour. A consistently enforced and protected set of property rights must mean that however deplorable a person's behaviour may be, such behaviour is quite powerless to harm others in any literal sense. Without property rights, the selfish greed of one agent in the economy must rob the others of the potential use of the scarce social resources devoured by the greedy one. With property rights securely in place, greed may breed covetousness, it may be responsible for uncharitable behaviour; but in terms of any danger of this actually reducing the well-being of others, we must pronounce it to be quite harmless. Where the capitalist rules of the game are respected and upheld, A's unethical behaviour is simply unable to violate B's property rights. Not only, as emphasised earlier in this chapter, does the free market not depend upon unethical behaviour for its driving force, but in fact the free market system insulates its participants from any direct harm that might be perpetuated by unethical behaviour, however defined.

WHY IT IS WRONG TO LINK FREE
MARKETS WITH GREED: A SUMMARY

We are now in a position to sum up our reaction to the widely held cynical attitude that capitalist prosperity arises only because the free market encourages repugnantly selfish behaviour and the pursuit of contemptibly materialistic objectives. We may summarise our reaction in the form of the following assertions:

1. It is not the case that free market success in satisfying wants and coordinating purposeful plans, depends on any necessarily unethical (or even materialistic) set of consumption objectives being pursued by market participants.
2. It is not the case that such free market success depends on unethical behaviour by business entrepreneurs.

3. While the free market system is certainly (neutrally) consistent with all kinds of unethical behaviour by its participants, the rules of the system protect each participant from direct harm being perpetrated against him/her through the unethical behaviour of others.

Despite our apparent rejection of the central Mandeville thesis, that public benefits arise from private vices, we should not lose sight of a fundamental feature of the market system. This is that the wonderfully productive social arrangement based on division of labour, specialisation and entrepreneurial discovery and social coordination through the price system works by harnessing the productive powers of individual participants to further, mutually, the consumption purposes of other participants. This means that the standard of living a person enjoys in the market economy is also advanced by the participation in that economy of individuals acting unethically, immorally or repulsively (and that one's own participation furthers the purposes of those immoral and repulsive others). When we draw the seductive picture of "economic harmony" in which everyone is "helping" someone else and making himself useful to him, we insensibly allow the idea of "help" to smuggle in with it ethical or sentimental associations that are strictly contraband. We forget that the help may be impartially extended to "destructive and pernicious or to constructive and beneficent ends . . ." So that private vices may, certainly, generate public benefits. The moral neutrality that we have claimed for the market economy does not guarantee that the benefits which market participants derive from their participation may not have been indirectly generated by the ethically deplorable behaviour of others. Moral neutrality merely means that ethically deplorable behaviour is not necessary for the success of the market economy.

We can be serious in our concerns with ethics and morality and at the same time we may support and participate in the capitalist economy without compromising our ethical commitments. To do so will indeed not exempt us from the responsibility to condemn and reject the deplorable behaviour, the greed, corruption and deception that we continually encounter in free market (as in other) societies. But we may extend such support and justify such participation secure in the conviction that we are not thereby automatically endorsing such greed, corruption, degeneracy or deception. Greed, corruption, degeneracy and deception are not prerequisites for a functioning and prosperous market economy.

Economists can help discourage misunderstandings concerning the role of unethical behaviour in markets by distinguishing carefully between the form of the market economy in theory, and the substance that makes up the market economies of the real world. At the formal level there should be no scope for misunderstanding. At this level there is no need to measure a society's success in the misleading terms of aggregate material wealth, or income in purely money terms. At this level, the obtrusive reality of a world made up of the imperfect human beings we are need not delude us into concluding that the driving force for market coordination is fuelled by our moral imperfections.

With a clear understanding of the secret of capitalist success as consisting strictly of the human purposefulness of its participants (and the capacity of this purposefulness to stimulate entrepreneurial alertness leading to mutual discovery and coordination), we may, if we wish to do so as moralists, attempt to improve capitalist reality without jeopardising its blessings. We may pursue whatever courses of action that ethical (and didactic) wisdom can identify in order to uplift ourselves and our fellow human beings—without interfering with that delicate and marvellous spontaneous social process through which "men who have never seen or heard of each other, and who scarcely realise each other's existence or desires even in imagination, nevertheless support each other at every turn, and enlarge the realisation each of the other's purposes."

My plea is that economists should seek to present our science to the world in a manner which, precisely by emphasising the abstractions of pure theory, discourages that disastrously erroneous perception of the ethical implications of the free market process, which muddy thinking about complex reality all too frequently tends to project.

SOME ETHICAL IMPLICATIONS FOR CAPITALISM
OF THE SOCIALIST CALCULATION DEBATE

The debate that raged in the interwar period between the Austrian economists (who argued the thesis that under socialism it would not be possible to engage in rational economic calculation) and socialist economists
(who rejected that thesis) was, narrowly conceived, a debate in positive
economics. What was being discussed was certainly not the morality of
capitalism or of socialism. Nor, strictly speaking, was the debate even
about society's economic well-being under socialism; it concerned the
ability of central planners to make decisions that take appropriate account
of relevant resource scarcities, in the light of consumer preference rankings. To be sure, the extraordinary interest which surrounded the debate
and the passions that lurked barely below its surface testified to the powerful *implications* of the debate for crucial issues in welfare economics.
The Austrians were not merely exploring the economies of socialism;
they were in effect demonstrating that, as an economic system attempting to serve the needs of its citizens, socialism must inevitably fail. But,
even if the debate is interpreted in its broadest terms, as a debate in welfare economics, it represented a sharp break with traditional polemics
relating to the socialism-capitalism issue. Traditionally the arguments
for or against capitalism had, until 1920, been deeply involved in ethical
questions. Mises's 1920 challenge to socialism, in contrast, was explicit
in making no attempt to address any claims concerning the alleged
moral superiority of socialism. He simply argued that, as an economic
system, socialism was inherently incapable of fulfilling the objectives of
its proponents; central planners are unable to plan centrally. For Mises
this issue seemed paramount. "Everything brought forward in favour of
Socialism during the last hundred years, in thousands of writings and
speeches, all the blood which has been spilt by the supporters of Socialism, cannot make Socialism workable."[1] This challenge lifted the debate

From *Social Philosophy and Policy* 6, 1 (1988): 165–82. Reprinted by permission of
Cambridge University Press.

1. L. Mises, *Socialism, An Economic and Sociological Analysis,* trans. J. Kahane from
2nd German edition [1932], (London: Jonathan Cape, 1936), p. 135.

from being an emotional one concerning the alleged injustices arising out of a system that allows selfish capitalists to indulge their greed, to a scientific level that could, at least in principle, permit dispassionate analysis of the economics of socialism. Whatever one's ethical preferences as between socialism and capitalism might be, Mises was asserting, it must be pointed out that socialism necessarily fails to satisfy the criteria for a rational economic system.

In this paper it will be argued that, properly understood, the Austrian position in the socialist calculation debate did—in spite of everything in the preceding paragraph—hold important implications for the ethical appraisal of capitalism. Neither Mises nor Hayek appears to have been aware of these ethical implications (although we cannot rule out the possibility that, perhaps subconsciously, these implications played a role in undergirding their defense of capitalism as an economic system). My argument thus maintains that the debate not only broke new ground in the scientific analysis of socialism; it was at the same time capable of enriching the moral appraisal of capitalism. This potential for enriching moral discourse was a potential that depended strictly on the scientific content of the debate. What the Austrian side of the debate contained, we shall see, was the possibility of a new way of understanding, not merely socialism, but also the operation of the capitalist system. In arguing the inability of central planners to achieve what the decentralized market is able to achieve, Mises and Hayek were, in effect, teaching us revolutionary lessons in positive economics about the capitalist system. These lessons do not depend on, and may be studied independently of, any ethical judgments concerning capitalism. But my contention will be that once these lessons have been adequately learned, once we understand capitalism as Mises and Hayek came to understand it, it is difficult to avoid recognizing the possible implications these lessons hold for an ethical assessment of capitalism. Paradoxically, therefore, it turns out that Mises's attempt to lift discussion concerning capitalism and socialism to the level of dispassionate science carried with it implications for a "feedback" capable, in turn, of enriching the nonscientific moral judgment of capitalism. I should perhaps add that this kind of ethical byproduct of science is not at all atypical of economics. Most moral judgments concerning economic systems are rooted, explicitly or implicitly, in some specific understanding of how these systems respectively operate. It is entirely to be expected, therefore, that a revolutionary lesson in the way capitalism works should carry with it correspondingly revolutionary implications for the moral appraisal of it.

I. THE SOCIALIST CALCULATION
DEBATE: AN ABRIDGED HISTORY

The history of the debate I provide in this section is deliberately abridged. The abridgement is motivated not merely by the obvious objective of remaining within reasonable space constraints,[2] but also, quite frankly, in order to highlight those features of the history that illustrate my thesis. The justification for this selective history is the judgment that what are important, both for the general history of economic ideas and for the history of the debate itself, are indeed those segments of the debate to which I will be drawing attention.

Before 1920 the questions of how and whether socialism could work as an economic system were rarely taken up. Where these questions were raised (as by Gossen, Pareto, and Pierson[3]) the discussion failed to be taken account of either by economists in general or by socialist theoreticians. In 1920 Mises threw out his challenge to socialists by asserting flatly that "in the socialist community economic calculation would be impossible."[4] Mises's reasoning focused on the role played in the market economy by the prices of factors of production. It is these prices which "furnish a basis for reckoning. Where there is no market there is no price system, and where there is no price system there can be no economic calculation."[5] Because socialism is, by definition, the system in which all factors of production are owned by the state ("Society"), it follows that there can be no market for factors. "Exchange relations in productive goods can only be established on the basis of private property in the means of production. If the Coal Syndicate delivers coal to the Iron

---

2. Two excellent book length histories (both sympathetic to the Austrian side of the debate) are: T. J. B. Hoff, *Economic Calculation in the Socialist Society*, trans. from Norwegian edition (1938), (London: W. Hodge, 1949); D. Lavoie, *Rivalry and Central Planning, The Socialist Calculation Debate Reconsidered* (Cambridge: Cambridge University Press, 1985).

3. For detailed references, see Hoff, *Economic Calculation*, p. 1; L. Mises, *Socialism*, p. 135.

4. Mises, *Socialism*, p. 131.

5. Ibid.

Syndicate a price can be fixed only if both syndicates own the means of production in the industry. But that would not be Socialism."[6]

Mises's article was reproduced virtually verbatim in his 1922 *Die Gemeinwirtschaft*. Although that book was a full-length treatment of socialism (its English translation is described in its subtitle as "An Economic and Sociological Analysis," and runs to more than five hundred pages), Mises himself describes "the doctrine of the impossibility of economic calculation in a socialist community" as constituting the "gist" of the book. The book's publication was followed by a large volume of socialist responses. As Mises noted in the second edition of the book, "socialists of all kinds have poured out attempts to refute my arguments and to invent a system of economic calculation for Socialism."[7] During the 1920s these writings attempting to refute Mises's thesis were mainly German and Italian.[8] But the literature of the 1930s most heavily involved English language writers. This latter literature had its beginning, perhaps, in Fred M. Taylor's presidential address to the American Economic Association in December 1928, "The Guidance of Production in a Socialist State."[9] Taylor envisaged a central authority fixing (nonmarket) prices for productive factors and altering these prices through a system of trial and error. Taylor's suggestion for solving the socialist calculation problem was taken up in considerably greater detail by Oskar Lange in a 1936 article which came to be recognized as the definitive socialist position (at least at the theoretical level) in response to Mises. At about the same time A. P. Lerner was writing along similar lines.[10] It was also about this time that F. A. Hayek edited a collection of classic papers addressing the calculation problem (including not only a translation of Mises's original

6. Ibid., p. 132.

7. Ibid., p. 135.

8. See Hoff, *Economic Calculation*, p. 131 footnote, and entire chapter 11.

9. F. M. Taylor, *American Economic Review*, vol. 19, no. 1 (March 1929), reprinted in B. J. Lippincott, ed., *On the Economic Theory of Socialism* (University of Minnesota Press, 1938; reprinted by McGraw-Hill, 1964).

10. O. Lange, "On the Economic Theory of Socialism," *Review of Economic Studies*, vol. iv, numbers 1,2 (October 1936 and February 1937), reprinted in Lippincott, *Economic Theory*, (subsequent page references will be to the Lippincott edition). A. P. Lerner, "Economic Theory and Socialist Economy," *Review of Economic Studies*, vol. ii (1934); and "A Note on Socialist Economics," *Review of Economic Studies*, vol. iv (1936); see also, A. P. Lerner, *The Economics of Control* (New York: MacMillan, 1944).

1920 paper, but also several papers that preceded Mises). Hayek introduced the collection with an essay on "The Nature and History of the Problem," and concluded the volume with an essay on "The Present State of the Debate."[11] In these two papers Hayek lucidly restated the Misesian argument and presented the major socialist response to that argument, together with his own critical assessment of them. Although Hayek was not able to deal fully with Lange's argument (which had not yet appeared in print),[12] nonetheless his papers constituted an influential and powerful updating of the Mises position. Mises's side of the debate came to be known as the Mises-Hayek position.

It seems, therefore, historically valid to perceive the debate as crystallizing into a confrontation between the Mises-Hayek position on the one hand, and the Lange-Lerner suggested solution on the other hand. In the postwar literature on comparative economic systems it was this confrontation that was highlighted, and (as already noted) it was the Lange-Lerner position that came to be cited in that literature as providing the satisfactory socialist response to the Mises-Hayek arguments. For this literature the Taylor-Lange-Lerner trial and error approach using non-market prices constituted the decisive refutation of Mises's original assertion denying the economic workability of central planning.[13] Mises and Hayek, it should be emphasized, never conceded that Lange's argument addressed their concerns.[14]

Looking back on this confrontation from the perspective of a half century of subsequent development in economic thought, it appears illuminating to interpret the confrontation as one involving two quite inconsistent alternative paradigms. Professor Lavoie has provided the definitive interpretation of the debate along those lines.[15] The Lange-Lerner approach proceeded strictly along the lines of neoclassical equilibrium theory; the

11. Both papers were reprinted in F. A. Hayek, *Individualism and Economic Order* (London: Routledge and Kegan Paul, 1949).

12. Hayek did address Lange's solution (together with those of several others) in "Socialist Calculation III: The Competitive 'Solution,'" in *Individualism and Economic Order*, chapter six (original paper first published in *Economica*, vol. vii, no. 26, May 1940).

13. See Lavoie, *Rivalry*, p. 13, for a list of postwar writers who took this position.

14. See Hayek, "Socialist Calculation III"; see also L. Mises, *Human Action* (New Haven: Yale University Press, 1949), pp. 700–706.

15. See D. Lavoie, *Rivalry*.

Mises–Hayek position sees it as an entrepreneurial-competitive discovery process. A good deal of the complete (and somewhat mystifying) failure of the two sides of the debate to reach any sort of mutual understanding seems to stem from the circumstance that they were unwittingly working within entirely different theoretical frameworks. It is this that explains how, for the Austrians, the suggestions of Lange and Lerner failed even to begin to address the calculation problem which they had identified as existing in the centrally planned economy. It is this that explains how, nonetheless, Lange and Lerner (and a host of postwar writers) genuinely believed that the trial-and-error proposal had decisively refuted the Austrian claims regarding the unworkability of central planning.

This writer has elsewhere[16] developed an interpretation of the calculation debate that sees the Austrians as having been forced, during the course of the debate, toward a far greater degree of self-awareness than they had possessed at the outset of the debate. Much of the confusion in the debate appears, as I have noted, to stem from the circumstance that the Austrians were initially unaware of any fundamental difference that separated their understanding of the theory of the market from that of other schools of economic thought.

In 1931, before Lange and Lerner, Mises could write the following: "Within modern subjectivist economics it has become customary to distinguish several schools. We usually speak of the Austrian and the Anglo-American Schools and the School of Lausanne. . . . [The fact is] that these three schools of thought differ only in their mode of expressing the same fundamental idea and that they are divided more by their terminology and by peculiarities of presentation than by the substance of their teaching."[17]

It was the confrontation with the response of critics such as Taylor and Lange which taught the Austrians how profoundly their theory of the market differed from that of the neoclassical orthodoxy. Only ten years after writing about the insignificance of the differences between the Austrian School and the other schools of economic theory, at the end of a

---

16. See I. M. Kirzner, "The Economic Calculation Debate: Lessons for Austrians," *The Review of Austrian Economics*, vol. 2 (1987).

17. L. Mises, *Epistemological Problems of Economics*, trans. G. Reisman, (New York: Van Nostrand, 1960), p. 214. The passage appears in a paper whose original German version was published in 1931.

decade in which the Lange-Lerner position was articulated, Mises was writing very emphatically about the fundamental character of these differences. "What distinguishes the Austrian School . . . is precisely the fact that it created a theory of economic action and not of economic equilibrium or nonaction. . . . The Austrian School endeavors to explain prices that are really paid in the market, and not just prices that would be paid under certain, never realizable conditions. It rejects the mathematical method . . . because it does not emphasize a detailed description of a state of hypothetical static equilibrium."[18] In subsequent sections of this paper I will briefly outline the lessons in self-awareness which the Austrians learned, and take note of the characteristic understanding of the market economy which the Austrian position came explicitly to embody. But I must first set out the Lange-Lerner position in some detail.

II. THE LANGE-LERNER APPROACH

Oskar Lange proposes that the centrally planned economy should operate on a trial and error procedure essentially similar to the procedure he believes to characterize the competitive market economy. In developing this proposal (which he considers as no more than an elaboration of the Fred M. Taylor plan) Lange reveals with great clarity exactly how he understands the operation of a competitive market economy. Central to this understanding is the assumption that each decision by consumers, producers, and resource owners is made "only on the basis of a *given* set of prices. . . . The prices are regarded by the individuals as constants independent of their behavior."[19] This assumption is central, in particular, to the trial and error procedure which Lange attributes to the market. "The solution by trial and error is based on what may be called the *parametric function of prices,* i.e., on the fact that, although prices are a resultant of the behavior of all individuals on the market, each individual separately regards the actual market prices as given data to which he has to adjust himself."[20] At the outset a set of random prices is assumed given to each market participant; each participant makes his buying and selling decisions on the basis of these given

18. L. von Mises, *Notes and Recollections* (South Holland, IL: Libertarian Press, 1978), p. 36. See Foreword (by Margit von Mises) pp. viii–ix, for the information that the book was completed in 1942.

19. Lange, "Theory of Socialism."

20. Ibid., p. 70; italics in original.

prices. If the demand for a commodity exceeds its supply, competition of buyers will cause its price to rise; if the opposite is the case, competition of sellers will cause it to fall. Thus a new set of given prices is generated, and the process is repeated. "And so the process goes on until the objective equilibrium condition is satisfied (i.e. that demand for each commodity is equal to its supply) and equilibrium finally reached."[21]

It is this picture of the market that underlies Lange's views concerning the workability of socialism. Careful consideration of this picture reveals its key features. It is a picture thoroughly characteristic of standard neoclassical textbook price theory. As already noted, Lange's picture concentrates, of course, on market equilibrium, but this is so to a degree perhaps not immediately apparent. As Hayek showed many years ago,[22] to assume the perfectly competitive conditions (that underlie Lange's "parametric" treatment of prices) is already to assume a degree of knowledge on the part of market participants which it is the function of real market processes to generate. In particular, the parametric treatment of price really requires us to renounce any ambition to understand, say, *how* competition by buyers causes price to rise when demand exceeds supply (since we have been told to assume that at each instant each buyer believes that price is not subject to his own actions).[23] In Hayek's phrase the standard neoclassical treatment of competitive price "*assumes* the situation to exist which a true explanation ought to account for as the effect of the competitive process."[24]

I shall argue in the following sections that it is here that the nub of the disagreement exists. For the Austrians, Mises and Hayek, the essence of the market is perceived precisely in that "true explanation" which is absent from Lange's narrowly neoclassical understanding of the market. This essential element in the market process, it turns out, is simply not able to be duplicated under socialism. Indeed, nothing in Lange's proposal offers any suggestion or assertion as to how it might be so duplicated, since Lange utterly failed to recognize this element at all. Given

21. Ibid., p. 71.

22. F. A. Hayek, "The Meaning of Competition," in *Individualism and Economic Order,* chapter v.

23. On this see I. M. Kirzner, *Competition and Entrepreneurship* (Chicago: University of Chicago Press, 1973), pp. 42, 91ff.

24. F. A. Hayek, *Individualism and Economic Order,* p. 94.

an Austrian understanding of market processes, Lange's proposal must appear well-nigh incomprehensible. It purported to show how socialism could simulate the competitive market, but failed entirely to address the problem of simulating the market's most essential element. But my goal in this paper is not to explicate the misunderstandings in the debate. It is to draw out the ethical implications of the Austrian position. My procedure will be to show how this Austrian position was itself crystallized through the course of the debate. Thereafter I will attempt to demonstrate the ethical implications of this position.

III. THE CRYSTALLIZATION OF THE AUSTRIAN POSITION

We may distinguish several elements in the developing self-awareness on the part of the Austrians. These are: (a) the role assigned to market prices; (b) welfare aspects of the market process; and (c) the interpretation of the competitive market process. I take these up briefly in order.

(a) A superficial student of Mises's original statements (of 1920 and 1922) on the calculation problem might be excused for concluding that Mises's understanding of the role of market prices in achieving social efficiency did not differ substantially from Lange's emphasis on the parametric character of prices. For Mises in 1920 and 1922, market prices provide an adequate basis for calculation because they confront each market participant with social valuations which *already* reflect the activities and preferences of all other market participants.[25] But after the debate had run its course we find Mises altogether explicit in setting forth a quite different understanding of the nature and role of market prices. In particular he emphasized that prices are not in any sense *given* to entrepreneurs but are the results of their own activity *as individual agents.* "The entrepreneurs, eager to earn profits, appear as bidders at an auction, as it were. . . . Their offers are limited on the one hand by their anticipation of future prices of the products and on the other hand by the necessity to snatch the factors of production away from the hands of other entrepreneurs competing with them. . . . The essential fact is that it is the competition of profit-seeking entrepreneurs that does not tolerate the preservation of *false* prices of the factors of production."[26] We thus see that it was during the period of the calculation debate that Mises came to articulate with

---

25. Mises, *Socialism*, p. 115.
26. Mises, *Human Action*, pp. 332–35; italics in original.

clarity his treatment of prices as expressing the outcome of entrepreneurial actions, rather than as parameters to which entrepreneurs adjust. We
shall see that this treatment has significant implications.

(b) For neoclassical economics, the normative criterion that came to
be applied to a society in assessing the effectiveness of its economic system was that of the efficient allocation of society's resources among the
competing available uses for them. It is now well recognized that this criterion was an *extension* of Lionel Robbins's concept of the activity of individual economizing. In other words, neoclassical normative economics
treats the entire economy exactly as the economizing individual treats his
own little economic world, viz., as if all relevant data for decision making are, in principle, already known or readily ascertainable. As we shall
see, this approach to judging the effectiveness of an economic system is
thoroughly alien to the Austrian view. Yet the Austrians themselves had
not always understood this. As late as 1935 Hayek defined "the economic
problem" as being the "distribution of available resources between different uses," and he declared that this is "no less a problem of society than
for the individual."[27] Hayek was clearly entirely satisfied to extend Robbins's notion of economizing to the level of society-wide "choices." He
was apparently quite unaware of the extraordinary assumptions concerning the availability of information that would have to be made in order to
sustain this extension. Yet, only two years later, we find Hayek asserting
that the "central question of all social sciences [is]: How can the combination of fragments of knowledge existing in different minds bring
about results which, if they were to be brought about deliberately, would
require a knowledge on the part of the directing mind which no single
person can possess?"[28] And by 1940 we find Hayek applying this very
insight to criticize the socialist position in the calculation debate. The
"main merit of real competition [is] that through it use is made of knowledge divided between many persons which, if it were to be used in a centrally directed economy, would all have to enter the single plan."[29] And,
ten years after his extension of the Robbinsian notion of economizing to
society as a whole, we find Hayek, in effect, completely repudiating his
earlier statement of the economic problem facing society. "The economic

27. Hayek, *Individualism and Economic Order*, p. 121.
28. Ibid., p. 54.
29. Ibid., p. 202.

problem of society is thus not merely a problem of how to allocate 'given' resources—if 'given' is taken to mean given to a single mind which deliberately solves the problem set by these 'data.' It is rather a problem of how to secure the best use of resources known to any of the members of society, for ends whose relative importance only these individuals know. Or, to put it briefly, it is a problem of the utilization of knowledge which is not given to anyone in its totality."[30]

It seems inescapable that it was Hayek's experience during the latter 1930s (during which he was confronted by the Lange-Lerner suggestion for economic calculation under socialism) that sensitized him to the dubious meaning that can be attached to the idea of the efficient allocation of social resources. It was out of this debate, it seems evident, that there emerged Hayek's now celebrated insights concerning the dispersed knowledge that challenges societal "efficiency." And it was in following up these calculation-debate-generated insights that modern Austrians have explored the possibility of developing a new approach to normative economics based on the concept of *coordination*.[31]

(c) Perhaps the best known element in the modern Austrian understanding of markets is that which sees the market as a "discovery procedure,"[32] an on-going process of spontaneous and induced change. It was Mises who in his 1940 *Nationalökonomie* (revised and translated as *Human Action* in 1949) emphasized with unsurpassed clarity how important it is to see the market as an entrepreneurial process rather than as a state of equilibrium affairs. And by 1940 Hayek was pointing out that some of the socialists following the Lange-Lerner proposal were guilty of "excessive preoccupation with problems of the pure theory of stationary equilibrium" and failed to understand how real-world markets are likely to have the advantage in regard to the rapidity of "adjustment to the daily changing conditions in different places and different industries."[33] Yet it

30. Ibid., pp. 77f.

31. See Gerald P. O'Driscoll, Jr., *Economics as a Coordination Problem: The Contribution of Friedrich A. Hayek* (Kansas City: Sheed, Andrews and McMeel, 1977; I. M. Kirzner, *Competition and Entrepreneurship*, chapter 6 ("Competition, Welfare, and Coordination").

32. See F. A. Hayek, "Competition as a Discovery Procedure" (first delivered as a lecture in 1968), in *New Studies in Philosophy, Politics, Economics and the History of Ideas* (Chicago: University of Chicago Press, 1978).

33. Hayek, *Individualism and Economic Order*, p. 188.

must be acknowledged that in his earliest statements on the socialist calculation issues, Mises reads as if the central feature in his appreciation
for markets is their continual ability to generate near-equilibrium prices
and near-equilibrium patterns of resource allocation. Under "the economic system of private ownership of the means of production," Mises
claimed, "all goods of a higher order receive a position in the scale of calculations in accordance with the immediate state of social conditions of
production and of social need."[34] Once again, we must conclude, it was
the experience of the socialist calculation debate that sharpened Austrian
self-awareness. At the outset Austrians genuinely believed that the overlap between their own theory of markets and that of the other schools of
economic thought was so overwhelming as to subordinate the differences
between them. It was the calculation debate that demonstrated that, quite
the contrary, these differences ran so deep as to generate radically divergent understandings of how markets work.[35]

IV. THE AUSTRIAN PERSPECTIVE
ON THE CALCULATION DEBATE

It will be useful to sum up what we have learned. The Austrian position
in the debate depends, we now appreciate, on a very special theoretical
understanding of market. Markets work, on the Austrian view, because
they are characterized by continual processes of entrepreneurial discovery. These processes are set in motion by the maladjustments that are, at
each moment, caused by imperfect information, itself simply the manifestation of Hayek's dispersed knowledge. What drives the market process is the entrepreneur's eagerness to discover pockets of pure profit.

34. L. Mises, "Economic Calculation in the Socialist Commonwealth," trans. S.
Adler from the 1920 German article, F. A. Hayek, ed. *Collectivist Economic Planning:
Critical Studies on the Possibilities of Socialism* (London: Routledge and Sons, 1935),
p. 107.

35. We interpret these changes in the Austrian articulation of their position as increasing self-awareness of the implications of the Mengerian paradigm, rather than as
any substantive modification in Austrian theory, for reasons that need not detain us
here. For discussion of these issues, see D. Lavoie, *Rivalry and Central Planning*, p. 26;
and I. M. Kirzner, "The Economic Calculation Debate: Lessons for Austrians"; see also
I. M. Kirzner, "Ludwig von Mises and Friedrich von Hayek: The Modern Extension of
Austrian Subjectivism," N. Leser, ed., *Die Wiener Schule der Nationalökonomie* (Vienna:
Böhlau, 1986).

In seeking to grasp these profits, entrepreneurs are not merely discovering opportunities for gain for themselves; they are at the same time discovering the nuggets of information possession of which can eliminate the above-mentioned maladjustments. The crucial role in the creation of these profit opportunities (and their discovery) is played by market prices. These prices, themselves the expression of entrepreneurial bids and offers, reflect on the one hand the degree of discovery already achieved by the market process, and on the other hand the extent to which full coordination has not yet been achieved. Price movements are simply expressions of entrepreneurial discovery, of steps being taken in the coordinating process of the market.

From this perspective on the market it is clear how centrally planned economies are, by definition, precluded from simulating any of the essential functions of the market process. The basic driving element in the market process, entrepreneurial eagerness for pure profit, is *necessarily* excluded from the socialist economy. There is nothing that can quite replace it. Lange's opinion that the socialist economy can simulate the achievement of market equilibrium overlooks the critical assumption needed to make equilibrium theory relevant at all—the assumption that entrepreneurial discovery processes can be relied upon to proceed swiftly and "noiselessly." The net effect of taking this assumption entirely for granted is to assume away that imperfection of knowledge, that dispersal of information, which is the very root of the economic problem.

We are now in a position to assess the ethical implications which I believe to be entailed by this Austrian view of the market process, a view which, as we have seen, emerged from the socialist calculation debate.

V. THE DISCOVERY VIEW VERSUS THE ALLOCATION VIEW

Throughout the history of socialism it is the question of distributive justice that has at all times been the most central issue. It is this issue that has fired enthusiasms, lifted hearts, inspired revolutions. Whatever Marx's own views on this issue may have been,[36] it cannot be doubted that socialists the world over have been and still remain convinced that the capitalist market economy represents an immoral system of exploitation

36. On this see A. Wood, "The Marxian Critique of Justice," *Philosophy & Public Affairs*, vol. 2 (Spring 1972), and W. Baumol, "Marx and the Iron Law of Wages," *American Economic Review*, vol. 73, no. 2 (May 1983), p. 306.

and economic injustice. I shall argue that the Austrian side of the calculation debate implied a response to these ethical criticisms of capitalism—
a response that has not yet been explicitly articulated. This implied
response differs sharply, I shall claim, from the standard neoclassical
responses.

Neoclassical-type defenses of market justice have depended heavily on
two (often only implicit) premises: (a) the premise that *initial* resource
endowments can be taken as justly held in the first place, and (b) the
premise that market-generated incomes can be taken as approximating
their equilibrium levels. It is upon these implicit premises, for example,
that J. B. Clark's celebrated defense of the economic justice of capitalism
was constructed.[37] Clark argued, on the basis of the marginal productivity
theory of resource price, that each resource owner tends, in the capitalist economy, to receive the value of the productive contribution he has
permitted to be made with his resources. Since the laborer receives the
full value of the productive contribution that his sweat and effort have
generated, the capitalist cannot be accused of robbing him of any slice
of the final product. What the capitalist himself receives is no more than
the value contributed by the capital resources which *he* has committed to
production. Since the validity of the capitalist's ownership of his capital
resources is being taken for granted in this defense, it follows that all
incomes are justly received. But it is clear that this convenient conclusion for capitalism rests, in effect, on faith that in the capitalist economy
incomes reflect substantially perfect mutual information on the part of
all market participants. And, indeed, Clark makes no attempt to justify
the grasping of pure entrepreneurial profit (other than to treat it as somehow less significant because it is a strictly temporary share that is being
rapidly eroded, at each instant, by the forces of competition). Once again,
it seems, the possibility of incomes resulting from the existence of serious market error is virtually ignored.

It should be noted that this equilibrium view of the market that underlies neoclassical defenses of capitalist justice itself implied a very definite
view of the distribution problem. Not only does equilibrium imply perfect mutual awareness on the part of market participants, it carries with

---

37. See J. B. Clark, *The Distribution of Wealth: A Theory of Wages, Interest and Profits*
(New York, 1908), esp. chapter 1; see also M. Friedman, *Capitalism and Freedom* (Chicago: University of Chicago Press, 1962), chapter x.

it a perspective on the aggregate economy that permits it to be treated analogously to the economic situation confronting the individual. Since, in principle, all information existing in the economy is able to be centralized (since we assume *everyone* to know how to command every piece of information existing anywhere), it is quite natural to treat the economic problem facing society as essentially a problem of the efficient allocation of known resources among competing known uses. (I have noted earlier in this paper how it was the calculation debate that moved Hayek to renounce this view of the economic problem and to focus on the problems raised by genuinely dispersed information—i.e., information so dispersed as to defy centralization, even in principle.) But this way of perceiving society's economic problem as an allocation problem implies, in turn, that the problem of distribution is *a problem of sharing out a given pie.* This given pie was not, it is true, seen by the neoclassicals as given societal *output*; but it was seen in the form of given arrays of "society's" resources which are to be shared out—with full awareness that the sharing out of resource services implies the sharing out of the corresponding pie-to-be-produced.

It is this view of distribution, as a case of sharing out a given pie, that is emphatically ruled out by the Austrian side of the calculation debate. Let us remember that it was precisely the equilibrium view of the market (which we have seen to underlie the neoclassical defense of the capitalist ethic) which informed the socialist side of the calculation debate as represented by Lange.

From the developed Austrian perspective on the debate, the fundamental brute fact of dispersed knowledge transforms not only our understanding of markets, how they work, and how they address society's economic problem. Awareness of the fact of dispersed knowledge transforms, in addition, our perception of the problem of distribution. What is distributed in markets is not a known, given pie—neither a pie of produced national output, nor a pie of given societal resources. What is to be distributed is *an aggregate which must be discovered* in the course of the very market processes through which it is "distributed." In fact, the circumstance that aggregate output (and aggregate available resources, too) must be discovered in the course of the market process renders the entire notion of "distribution" highly dubious. Not only must the aggregate volume of societal resources, and certainly the aggregate volume of societal output, be discovered; in fact, from the Austrian perspective, each and every income receipt is, to a degree, a discovered income. This is perhaps most easily seen in the case of the winning of pure profit, but it is also the case to a greater or lesser degree for each unit of resource income received. Let us consider the nature of pure profit.

Pure profit is the surplus remaining in the hands of a vendor of a good after he has deducted *all* the costs assumed in order to be able to make the good available to the buyer. In the case of simple arbitrage, where an entrepreneur is able to buy an item in a market where price is low, and, without incurring any cost of transportation, to sell the same item simultaneously in a second market where the price is high, pure profit is the difference between these two prices. In the case of entrepreneurial production, pure profit is what is left out of total revenue to the entrepreneur-producer after deducting *all* the costs of production (including all interest charges, transportation and delivery costs, and the like) needed to achieve delivery of the product to its buyer.

In the equilibrium world of standard neoclassical economics, with full knowledge assumed on the part of all participants, analysis proceeds as if pure profits never do occur. The possibility of more than one price existing at a given time for an item is not considered. The profits that are discussed in the theory of the producing firm are not pure profits at all, but rather quasi-rents earned on the firm's fixed capital assets. (Thus a producer may be using his factory, built in the past and thus calling for no new current cost sacrifices, using two million dollars worth of current inputs to produce three million dollars worth of product. But the million dollars of "profit" so won is not true profit; since the productive capacity of the factory is known to everyone, the producer could have leased his factory to other producers for up to a million dollars, which they would be prepared to pay, since the factory enables them to generate this net revenue. So our producer, in calculating his total costs of production, would have to include this sacrifice of a million dollars of lease-revenue foregone, leaving no pure profit at all.)

But for the Austrian view pure profit is not only possible, it is central to the understanding of market processes. Pure profit emerges, in this view, because genuinely dispersed information is a fact of life. An entrepreneur may indeed be able to buy an item for two dollars and sell it for three. A producer may indeed be able to produce an item for two million (*including* the cost of foregone lease-revenue at current market prices for the lease of his factory) and sell for three million. All this is possible because of genuinely dispersed information, i.e., information so dispersed that market participants are unaware of the nature and the very existence of the information which they lack. It is only this circumstance which makes possible the existence of two prices—and thus a pure profit opportunity—in the same market for essentially the same item. (The bundle of resources which are capable of producing a given product is treated, in this context, as essentially the same item as that product.) Absent genuinely dispersed information, no pure profit opportunities can be imagined to exist. Any apparent price differentials cannot qualify as profit opportunities since, absent genuinely dispersed information, such differentials must be treated as necessary to cover the cost of obtaining needed (and known-to-be-needed) information (or of otherwise transferring the purchased item to its point of high-priced sale). Without genuinely dispersed information no "unexplained," "unnecessary" price differentials can be imagined. True pure profit opportunities, evidenced by genuine price differentials, are not *necessary*, in the sense of being *needed* to permit the item purchased at the low price to be sold at the higher price. True profit opportunities are the result of sheer ignorance. Their exploitation is a matter of the *discovery that replaces sheer ignorance by full awareness*. It is to be emphasized that discovery is quite distinct from deliberate search. Deliberate search is engaged in when one has already known that there is something worth being searched for. If one has already known that there is something worthy to be searched for, the reason for its not having already been found must lie in the perceived cost of the search. Pure discovery occurs when one notices the existence of something that could, in principle, have been costlessly grasped earlier. The reason for its not having already been grasped lies, therefore, not in any cost of finding it, but in earlier sheer ignorance concerning its existence. To grasp pure profit is to notice the presence of two market prices *for the same* item. Pure profit is won through discovery.

Once we have grasped the nature and origin of pure discovery, we can perceive how discovery may occur not only in the context of pure profit opportunities, but also in regard to all market transactions. Pure profit occurs only in the absence of equilibrium, and it is not difficult to see how each market transaction in disequilibrium shares significant elements in common with the grasping of pure profit. We must distinguish sharply between (i) the transactions undertaken in a world of perfect relevant information (such as under equilibrium conditions) and (ii) those undertaken in the real world of open-ended possibilities for ignorance (and thus for discovery). The first are undertaken by simply exercising one's preferences between given, fully known entities (even if these entities are "fully known" only in the sense that one knows the precise statistical odds governing the payoffs to be expected from them). There is no room for surprise in these transactions. The second kind of transactions, on the other hand, are undertaken in contexts in which the ever-present possibility of surprise is of the essence. If the first kind of transaction results in an improvement in one's situation, this improvement must be described as having been deliberately grasped. This improvement was clearly visible to all; grasping it did not involve any creative leap, any entrepreneurial daring. But if the second kind of transaction, that taken under disequilibrium conditions, results in an improvement in one's situation, one sees this improvement as having been *discovered.* Through the fog of conflicting possibilities and potential surprises, one has "seen" the prospect for gain. This gain has been "discovered" in a sense very similar to that in which we have seen pure profit to be the result of pure discovery.

Not only are the individual transactions (including especially the market transactions which yield income receipts) characterized by discovery. The aggregate outcome of these countless acts of discovery under disequilibrium conditions must also be seen as a discovered outcome. The market process, carried on by definition under disequilibrium conditions, is a process of discovery. The incomes generated by this disequilibrium process are discovered incomes. We must now contemplate the possible ethical significance of this important insight.

VI. OBSERVATIONS ON THE FINDERS-KEEPERS ETHIC

A person is hiking on a mountain trail, on land owned by no one; he notices a beautiful mountain flower, picks it, and brings it home with him. There are probably few who would question the hiker's right to have done this. Moreover, if another person grabs the flower from the hiker's lapel on his way home, there are probably few who would not agree that that person is robbing the rightful owner of his flower. Let us examine the ethical premises that underlie these views concerning the property rights of our mountain hiker in this beautiful flower. What is it that confers upon him the ownership rights in this flower? Granted that the flower was ownerless when he noticed it, what transformed it into becoming his private property? I will submit that the ethical grounds for the view that the hiker is the owner of the flower are those usually described as the finders-keepers principle. I wish to maintain that this finders-keepers principle is of considerable ethical significance. In seeking to persuade the reader of this importance I do not need to persuade him of its definitive validity. My purpose is thus not to advance this principle itself; it is to draw attention to its profound relevance for an understanding of widespread attitudes toward the ethics of private property. I wish, that is, to point out what appears to be the underlying moral intuition that nourishes the fairly widespread view that this beautiful flower (and all other objects similarly discovered in an ownerless state) properly belongs to its discoverer.

This finders-keepers ethic confers ownership of the flower upon its discoverer not because his claim antedates any other possible subsequent claims,[38] but because finding and taking the flower is seen as giving him a unique moral claim over it that possesses greater weight, on the scales of justice, than any other possible claim can possess. This unique moral claim appears to arise from the circumstance that the undiscovered flower, blooming unseen was, in a certain sense, a nonexistent flower. It existed for no human mind, so that, regardless of philosophical profundities, its physical existence was economically and socially irrelevant. The discoverer of the flower, appreciating its beauty and worth, is in effect *creating* this flower, as it were *ex nihilo*; it is his perception of the flower that brings it within the scope of human interest. Its subsequent existence as a valued object, the pleasure it is able to give to human beings, is to be attributed to the discoverer's perceptive alertness. He originated the flower; he created it; the finders-keepers principle declares that the flower is therefore his own. This *seems* to be the moral intuition that underlies the finders-keepers ethic.

VII. THE FINDERS-KEEPERS ETHIC
AND THE DISCOVERY VIEW

If the widespread (implicit) acceptance of this finders-keepers principle is acknowledged, it seems difficult to avoid recognizing the profound ethical implications of the Austrian side of the calculation debate which I

---

38. See Robert Sugden, *The Economics of Rights, Cooperation and Welfare* (Oxford: Basil Blackwell, 1986), p. 88, for a view of the finders-keepers rule that appears to differ from that developed here.

have identified in this paper. That side of the debate sees the market pro-cess, we saw, as a process of discovery in the context of open-ended scope for ignorance. Each unit of income received, we saw, was, at least in some degree, discovered income. In particular, the important species of capital-ist income, pure profit, was won only as a result of pure entrepreneur-ial discovery. Aggregate national output comes into existence through countless mini-processes of productive discovery. Implied in these mini-processes of discovery are in turn the countless elements of resource incomes which are discovered wages; the employer discovered a way of putting the laborer's hands to worthwhile productive use; the laborer discovered an employer capable of putting his (the laborer's) hands to worthwhile productive use. To the extent that a resource owner (such as a laborer) is acting—in a world pervaded by ignorance—to secure the highest-paid use for his resource, his discovery of the employer does mean that he, the resource owner, has in a sense acted "entrepreneurially"; in a sense, he has *created* the opportunity to secure that high income. Had he not seen, "created," this opportunity, he would be putting his resource to work at a less rewarding task; the higher-valued contribution to produc-tion of which this particular unit of resource is capable might never have been noticed. In a world of disequilibrium, all market participants are to a certain extent intent on noticing better opportunities for themselves; to the extent that this generates discoveries that might otherwise have been missed, this transforms their incomes from being mere quid-pro-quo payments in exchange for productive services into being genuine creations. What I grasp when I discover an income opportunity in the market place is an opportunity that others have not yet perceived. It is, therefore, exactly as if I have grasped a discovered mountain flower that has been ownerless (because no one had perceived it up until now). The same finders-keepers ethic that declares the mountain flower to belong rightfully to its discoverer, surely declares these discovered incomes won by resource owners in the market to be rightfully theirs.

These ethical implications of the Austrian side of the calculation debate have both a positive and a negative side. The negative class of implications are those that challenge the standard perspectives on the ethics of distribution. Those perspectives start, we have already noticed, from the notion of a given pie to be distributed. It is not easily appreci-ated how heavily standard views on distributional ethics depend on this premise of a given entity that must somehow be shared out among an array of claimants. As soon as we perceive how unrealistic such a starting point is, we are instantly liberated from the ethical baggage which that starting point entails.

The positive class of implications of the Austrian side of the calculation debates are those which I have associated with the finders-keepers ethic. As soon as we appreciate the nature of the market as an ongoing process of mutual discovery, we are in a position to recognize the possible applicability of this ethic to a wide range of seemingly surprising cases.

Mises and Hayek never did realize these ethical implications that follow from their position in the calculation debate. But, again, Mises and Hayek were themselves less than completely appreciative of the fundamentally different understanding of the market which their position reflected. Just as one byproduct of the calculation debate was the more careful articulation of this fundamentally different understanding, it is possible that yet another byproduct—one still to be carefully articulated—is the crystallization of a novel approach to capitalist morality. It is toward such a crystallization that this paper wishes to point.

THE MORALITY OF PURE PROFIT: THE LOGIC
AND ILLOGIC OF A POPULAR PHOBIA

Discussions concerning the justice of capitalism have multiplied in recent decades, and a good deal of the debate has, directly or indirectly, concerned the morality of pure entrepreneurial profit. Certainly no aspect of capitalist income distribution has seemed to clash more sharply with commonly accepted notions of justice and fairness, than has the phenomenon of pure entrepreneurial profit.

The wages of labor have been explained and largely accepted as the market-determined, productivity-based, value of labor contributed. Arduous effort has been justly rewarded; the laborer has earned his wage by the sweat of his brow. Rent on land and interest on capital have likewise been rationalized as the market-valued counterparts to the marginal productivity of owned assets.[1] To the extent that observers are prepared to recognize the legitimacy of individual ownership in land resources and capital goods, these income categories are reconciled with commonly held criteria for justice in income receipts. He who justly owns the tree, is justly entitled to the fruit of the tree. All this is closely similar to what Milton Friedman has referred to as the "capitalist ethic": "To each according to what he and the instruments he owns produces."[2]

But the winning of pure entrepreneurial profit cannot easily be justified under the rubric of the capitalist ethic. By definition pure entrepreneurial profit is won through sale of a product (or any good) at a price in excess of its *full* cost of production (or of the price at which it had been acquired). Once the term "full cost of production" is interpreted exhaustively, it becomes clear that pure profit cannot be rationalized as the counterpart to any productive contribution (of an owned asset or personal service). The entrepreneur has not earned his pure profit by the expenditure of effort, because the full value of all productive effort he may have

From *Le Journal des Economistes et des Etudes Humaines* 4 (1993): 315–28. Reprinted by permission of De Gruyter.

1. The present writer does not, in fact, accept this particular rationalization of interest income—but this is not the point here.

2. Friedman 1962, pp. 161–62.

contributed has already been subtracted (from gross revenue) in arriving at the pure profit concept. Nor can the entrepreneur lay claim to his pure profit as being the spontaneously grown fruit of any owned "tree," since pure profit is not being attributed to any owned asset whatsoever. Inevitably, perhaps, pure entrepreneurial profit has come to be viewed as hardly obtainable without unjust exploitation and/or deceit.

Despite all this, the position we take in this paper is *not* that the justice of pure entrepreneurial profit requires an innovative defense in the face of a strong prima facie case against it. Quite the contrary, we shall endeavor to explain why the case for the justice of such pure profit—a case which we believe to be simple and compelling—has come to be implicitly rejected in common discourse. The puzzle we shall seek to solve is thus not that of justifying pure profit, because we believe the solution to that puzzle to be simple and straightforward. Rather, precisely because that solution appears to us to be so simple and convincing, the puzzle which we shall address here is the corresponding problem: why is this solution ignored or rejected?

Now, we do not wish to appear naive. There are no doubt ample plausible grounds, in the psychology of envy, in the phenomenon of perennially invincible economic ignorance, for the continued widespread suspicion of pure entrepreneurial profit. Nonetheless we wish to explore the situation more carefully. Perhaps what we have termed the simple and straightforward solution to the dilemma of the justice of pure profit is not as simple or as straightforward (or as true) as we have claimed. If we believe that widespread acceptance of the moral legitimacy of pure profit is a necessary condition for a society's ability to enjoy the fruits of untrammelled capitalist growth, then these questions are not idle ones. They may be profoundly important for the long term welfare of modern economics.[3]

In the following two sections we review briefly what we have termed the simple and straightforward case for the justice of pure entrepreneurial profits. In subsequent sections we will then seek to account for the apparent failure of this approach to convince the public at large. In the concluding section we briefly trace out some implications of our explorations, for the role of economic education.

---

3. For an earlier discussion of some of these issues, see Mises 1956.

I. THE NATURE OF PURE PROFIT: A PRELUDE
TO AN INQUIRY ON THE JUSTICE OF PROFIT

We have pointed out the apparent problems, for the ethics of justice, presented by the phenomenon of pure profit. These problems reflect and
express, in turn, the elusive nature of the entrepreneurial role. If pure
profit is that which remains (out of gross revenue) after *all* factor costs
(both explicit and implicit) have been deducted, then it would appear as if
this residual share is received by someone who (or, at any rate, by an analytical abstraction that) contributes absolutely nothing to the production
process. Not only does this, at first glance, fly in the face of conventional
notions of just desert, it also raises conundrums in positive economics,
and especially concerning the nature of the entrepreneurial role.

The entrepreneur is clearly the most visible player on the business
stage. A theory of the capitalist economy must certainly be able to identify
with clarity and precision exactly in what his functional contribution to
the market process consists. Yet the very definition of pure entrepreneurial profit appears to require us to see the entrepreneur as having done
nothing at all that can be considered a contribution to production. There
is not only a glaring ethical question casting the shadow of undeservedness over the profits which the entrepreneur has won. There is also the
obvious positive-economics problem: why have the buyers of output paid
more for that output than is needed to cover the costs of *all* necessary
productive contributions? Or again, why have sellers of input services
accepted an aggregate of payments which fall short of the price which
ultimate buyers of output are in fact paying for that output? It will not
do to portray the entrepreneur as being in command of scarce valuable
information (for which buyers are prepared to pay, because the full array
of necessary input services is insufficient, absent this scarce information,
to yield the final output). This will not do because, of course, if specific
"information" is needed to convert inputs into output, then that information, too, is an input. We must deduct, from the entrepreneur's gross
receipts, the full market value of that information in order to arrive at the
pure profit figure.

It appears as if the entrepreneurial role evaporates as soon as we focus
analytical attention upon it. As soon as we attempt to grasp hold of it, it
appears to disintegrate into nothingness. What we have termed the simple and straightforward solution to the ethical dilemma which shrouds

pure profit, emerges, in fact, from a clear understanding of the elusive entrepreneurial role.

The entrepreneurial role (and thus the nature of pure profit) was extensively explored during the three decades beginning about 1890. Although we will find inadequacies in these early discussions, we must recognize certain valuable insights which they contain. In the course of expounding his marginal productivity theory of capitalist justice, John Bates Clark explained that pure profit emerges only as a result of dynamic change: it has no place in the state of static equilibrium. When an exogenous shock (such as a new invention) impinges upon an equilibrium situation, "economic friction" may temporarily delay the achievement of the relevant new equilibrium conditions. Gaps may occur separating input values from output revenues; pure profits or pure losses may emerge. Where an innovation has been beneficial it is the entrepreneur who has initiated it; what has attracted him to do so has been the prospect of "friction"—generated (temporary) profits made possible by the innovation.

Clark has perhaps not satisfactorily solved the ethical problems surrounding pure profit (because he has not been able—as his own theory of justice seems to require—to identify profit with any marginal productivity-based revenue). But he has successfully achieved a solution to the puzzle of what *causes* pure profit. Pure profit is caused by dynamic change initiated by the entrepreneur; it is a disequilibrium phenomenon which has been temporarily kept in existence by economic frictions.[4]

The American economist Frederick B. Hawley saw the contribution of the entrepreneur not in his innovative capacity, but in his willingness to assume the risks attendant on production. Profits are the reward for this entrepreneurially provided service. Such a reward is necessary because there is an "irksomeness of uncertainty" which would prevent "industrial risks [being] assumed without the expectation of a compensation in excess of the actuarial value of the risk."[5] Although Hawley seems not to have been concerned to defend the ethics of profit, such a defence could no doubt be constructed on the basis of his approach. The entrepreneur provides a specific, irksome, necessary service; he may be considered to deserve the reward which provides the inducement to provide this service. If one is willing to define pure profit in a manner which will not

4. Clark 1899, pp. 410f.
5. Hawley 1893, p. 460.

require such rewards to be treated as a cost of production, then Hawley has apparently solved both the positive and the normative problems surrounding pure profit.

It was Frank Knight who put his finger, however, on the central weakness of Hawley's theory. Hawley has been assuming that the entrepreneur knows the true actuarial value of the risk being taken. But, as Knight emphasized, there is an important difference between risk and uncertainty. It is only uncertainty, uninsurable, indeterminate and inherently immeasurable, which can be responsible for pure profit. "A little consideration will show that there can be no considerable 'irksomeness' attached to exposure to an insurable risk, for if there is it will be insured; hence there can be no peculiar income arising out of this alleged indisposition."[6]

Frank Knight's own theory of profit drew on elements he found in Clark and Hawley. Clarkian dynamic change is, by itself, not able to generate profit *in the absence of uncertainty* (since such change can be anticipated). Profits must be "offered" to overcome the irksomeness, not of risk-bearing, but of uncertainty bearing. Such profits are created in the course of the dynamic changes which render the world radically uncertain. Whether such uncertainty results in profits or in losses depends upon the pure luck with which entrepreneurial judgment is intertwined.

Knight's theory explains profit in a way which satisfactorily accounts for it without seeing it as a market value offered in exchange for the fulfilment by the entrepreneur of a needed social function. But he has done so without addressing the ethical legitimacy of profit. If pure profit is deemed "undeserved," because it does not arise out of any provided service, or as the "fruit" of any owned asset, Knight's explanation of it as caused by uncertainty has not removed the taint of undeservedness. In fact this taint of undeservedness may be deemed to be deepened by Knight's attribution of pure profit to pure luck. (Knight himself apparently felt that the entrepreneur's rendering himself vulnerable to pure loss, somehow justifies his retaining any pure profits which good luck might confer upon him.)

In order to proceed beyond the valuable, but yet limited, insights provided by Clark, Hawley, and Knight, we will find it necessary to draw on certain observations concerning the entrepreneurial role, and concerning

6. Knight 1921, p. 46.

the pure profit share, which were made by the Austrian economist, Ludwig von Mises.

The Misesian theory of profit may appropriately be termed the "arbitrage theory" of profit. In this view profit emerges as the price discrepancy between two markets, today's market (in which, say, productive resource services are bought and sold) and tomorrow's market (in which the output of these productive services will be sold). Such discrepancies arise when today's market prices are (after making allowance for interest) out of line with the true, higher values which will become apparent in the market of tomorrow. In Mises's words: "What makes profit emerge is the fact that the entrepreneur who judges the future prices of the products more correctly than other people do buys some or all of the factors of production at prices which, seen from the point of view of the future state of the market, are too low."[7]

Mises's view of profit as a disequilibrium phenomenon is fully in line with the insights of Clark, Hawley and Knight. But Mises has identified the entrepreneurial role in a simple but revolutionary way. The essence of that role is not any innovative potential contributed by the entrepreneur. Nor does it consist in the provision of uncertainty bearing (although, to be sure, Mises's entrepreneur may well be innovative and certainly does expose himself to Knight's open-ended uncertainty). Rather the essence of the entrepreneurial role consists in the entrepreneur's judgment concerning the true values (that will be revealed in tomorrow's market) as compared with the (possibly mistaken) values expressed in today's market price. Profits are won through superior vision exercised by the entrepreneur. It is because this writer finds this Misesian insight into the nature of pure profit (and of the entrepreneurial role) to be inherently plausible and satisfying, that we take it as an appropriate basis for an assessment of the ethical character of pure profit.

2. THE JUSTICE OF PURE ENTREPRENEURIAL PROFIT

We have identified entrepreneurial profit as won through superior vision, through the entrepreneur's more correct anticipation of future conditions. The gap between the present market value of resources and the (discounted) market value of output (as it will in fact turn out to be in the future) is caused by the erroneous judgements currently being made (by others) in

---

7. Mises 1962, p. 190.

the market. The entrepreneur sees a prospective increment of value which others have somehow failed to see. We shall now argue that the profits so won satisfy a criterion for economic justice which makes it irrelevant and unnecessary to ask whether these profits have been "deserved" (in the sense of corresponding to effort expended, to productive contribution achieved), or have somehow "grown" (like fruit) from any owned assets (like trees).

Our basis for declaring such questions to be irrelevant is the insight, now within our grasp, that profits represent not a *produced* gain, not a *windfall* gain, but a *discovered* gain. In the world of standard economics it is assumed that economic gains must be classified as either the deliberately achieved goals of human effort, or as windfalls attributable to sheer luck (or as the outcomes of effort and luck intertwined). We argue that the Misesian insight we have described, permits us to recognize the possibility of a *third* source for gain, neither deliberate production nor stroke of good fortune, but sheer *discovery*.

A discovery is not a deliberate act of production, because, prior to the moment of discovery, there was no plan to achieve such discovery. But, it is also true, a discovery is far more than a stroke of good luck. A discovery is made when a human being notices something significant for him. There may, certainly, be an element of good fortune in the *availability* of this gain, its presence in the place and at the time when it can be noticed by the discoverer. But the act of discovery itself is neither a fortunate chance nor a deliberately productive act (such as, for example, would be a deliberate search undertaking for gain the existence of which is already known in advance). The act of discovery is a spontaneous, creative act on the part of the discoverer, in which his alertness and judgment combine to make him aware of the significance of what is within his grasp. Because this act is a spontaneous one, it cannot be compressed within the model of the deliberately planned productive project, in which (one might perhaps have been tempted to say) the discoverer has deliberately deployed his alertness and his judgement to achieve a discovery. Once the discoverer has become aware of his having a potential discovery within his grasp, he has *already* made the relevant discovery (and any subsequent acts of deliberate search will indeed *not* be discoveries at all).

But the very circumstances which have permitted us to see that an act of discovery is neither a deliberately productive act nor a mere stroke of good fortune, should permit us to recognise the relevance of an ethical principle entirely distinct from the ethical principles which we conventionally apply to productive acts and to strokes of good luck, respectively. This new ethical principle is that often presented as "finders, keepers."

A "finders, keepers" ethic declares that the finder of a hitherto unowned object becomes its rightful owner not because he has expended effort or used up resources in its production, not because he (more than others) is entitled to that which good luck has showered upon him, but because he, and no one else, *has brought the found object into economic existence.* Before it was found, that object did not exist in any relevant sense; it figured in nobody's plans, it affected nobody's decisions. Its discoverer has brought it into relevant existence. The finders, keepers ethic declares him, and no one else, to be its rightful owner.

The entrepreneur who buys resources below their "true" values (as revealed in subsequent market prices for outputs) and wins profits by selling the outputs at higher prices, has recognized increments of value which others overlooked. He has "found" these increments of value; he has brought them into relevant existence. Were he not to have "seen" (and grasped) these increments of value, they would not have come into existence. He has created them; he is, by the finders, keepers principle, entitled to them.

So that the entrepreneur is entitled to his pure profits *not* because he has contributed resource services to a productive process, *not* because such profits are to be seen as the fruit of any assets the entrepreneur owns—but simply because he, the entrepreneur, and no one else, discovered the availability of these profits.[8]

Once we have identified the true nature of pure profit as a wholly discovered gain, its legitimacy and the justice of its receipt follows immediately from the finders, keepers principle. Of course, nothing we have written here concerning pure profit has validated the finders, keepers principle itself. Certainly a rejection of that principle would demolish our defence of the justice of pure profit. But if, as we in fact believe, the finders, keepers principle is widely supported, then our defence of the justice of pure profit stands. In fact, we maintain, it stands in such a simple and straightforward fashion, that an explanation is called for, for the widespread scepticism concerning capitalist justice, especially as it concerns the phenomenon of pure profit. In the following sections of this paper we take up in turn several possible explanations for this persistent scepticism concerning the justice of pure entrepreneurial profit.

8. For more detailed discussion of this view see Kirzner 1989.

3. THE ROLE OF IGNORANCE

An obvious candidate for fulfilling such an explanatory role is the phenomenon of *economic ignorance*. The fact that an economic insight is simple, even obvious, once it has been grasped, is in no way inconsistent with the phenomenon that that insight remains widely unknown and ungrasped. It may seem obvious that a world of radical uncertainty must provide innumerable opportunities for pure gain attributable to superior entrepreneurial vision. But habitual patterns of thought may, nonetheless, obscure perception of this obvious truth. This must seem only all the more plausible when we remember that mainstream economics has, so to speak, painted itself into an analytical corner where such truths are wholly invisible. By adopting the assumption of complete (relevant) information, mainstream economics has made it very easy indeed to overlook the very possibility of what we have termed discovery. The world of mainstream economic theory is one from which open-ended uncertainty has been wholly excluded; it has found room for imperfect knowledge only in the context of in-principle-knowable frequency-probabilities held to govern events.

It is true, of course, that most laymen do *not* view themselves as living in the model economy depicted in the textbooks of mainstream economic theory. Most laymen certainly do not see themselves as living in a world bereft of genuine surprise and of opportunities for genuine creativity. Economic ignorance cannot, after all, be wholly blamed upon mainstream economic theory. So that persistent ignorance concerning the role of discovery, and concerning the possible relevance of a finders, keepers ethic, may certainly be attributed to failure to grasp—no matter whose the blame for this may be held to be—the true nature of the competitive market process as one of the continual perception, by entrepreneurs, of pre-existing mutual ignorance among market participants. That this kind of ignorance may be responsible for widely held ethical condemnation of pure profit is at the same time both depressing and, perhaps, encouraging. It is depressing to the extent that evidence of widespread ignorance concerning obvious matters, must always be depressing. But this very circumstance may, at the same time, offer an ounce of encouragement in that it suggests, after all, a potential for improvement (through economic education). We shall return to this latter point in the concluding section of this paper.

4. RESENTMENT AT DISCOVERED GAIN

A second candidate (for the explanation of persistent scepticism concerning discovered gain) does not invoke the notion of economic ignorance at all. It is possible for one to accept a finders, keepers ethic, to grasp the discovered nature of entrepreneurial gain, and yet to challenge its justice. This may be done by denouncing, on ethical grounds, the very idea of "profiting as a result of the ignorance of others." While recognizing that the entrepreneur has gained only through the discovery of information available, in principle, to everyone, a critic may argue that a gain achieved only through deliberately failing to make others aware of that which they themselves "ought" to have known, has been achieved unethically. There is only a fine line, such a critic might maintain, separating gain so won from gain achieved through deliberately *deceiving* another. To cheat another, this argument could run, may occur not only through deliberately misleading this other, but also through knowingly permitting (for one's own gain) this other to refrain from taking advantage of that which is, unbeknownst to this other, in fact within his grasp. Not to let him know what he is overlooking is (when one might have costlessly so let him know) in this view to act reprehensibly. To benefit oneself by so acting is, in this view, close to gaining by sheer deception.[9]

Of course it may be pointed out that the very notion of finders, keepers does, to some extent, appear inconsistent with such a line of ethical criticism. Every "finder," it can be pointed out, might have drawn the attention of others to his find. His appropriation of his find represents, after all, the achievement of gain as a result of the ignorance of others. But the critic may nonetheless insist on his line of criticism without necessarily abandoning the finders, keepers principle. He could argue that while the finder-keeper has indeed gained through the ignorance of others, such ignorance was not concerning something "within the grasp" of others. These others were not in the position where they "ought to have known" about something readily available to them. This contrasts, the critic might continue, with a profit-making entrepreneur who has discovered a gap in prices, and who is grabbing gain which those from whom he bought and those to whom he sold "should" have known about. To appropriate this gain, it may be held, is hardly distinguishable from cheating these others.

9. For further discussion on this point see Kirzner 1989, chapter 7.

Our comment on this candidate for an explanation, must be a classificatory one. This ethical argument criticizing pure entrepreneurial profit *can* after all, be classified as an ethical objection to the finders, keepers principle—if not in all its manifestations, then at least in those manifestations of it which are most relevant for pure entrepreneurial profit.

5. THE EQUILIBRIUM PERSPECTIVE

Yet another candidate (for the explanation of persistent scepticism concerning the justice of pure entrepreneurial profit) may be suggested in what we may term "the equilibrium perspective." Here we refer not so much to the preoccupation, on the part of the theoretical mainstream in economics, with the equilibrium state, as to a widespread attitude among non-economists. This attitude is one which sub-consciously but tenaciously insists on perceiving important features of reality as being in equilibrium, or, at least, in demanding, perhaps childishly, that they *should* be in equilibrium (regardless of excuses based on ignorance). Such an attitude is not prepared to accept these features of reality as being "out-of-sync" with the underlying facts. It is not prepared to see these features as being necessarily and properly in transit (because of inconsistency with the underlying facts). From such a perspective it is easy to assume that all relevant knowledge has *already* been absorbed (or, ethically equivalently, that it "should" so become absorbed). This attitude surely operates to reinforce the ethical condemnation (noted in the preceding section) of "gaining as a result of the ignorance of others." It differs from the view noted in the preceding section, in the following respect.

The view noted in the preceding section proceeds from the (tacit) assumption that knowledge which is within my grasp is knowledge to the fruits of which I am ethically entitled. No one has the moral right to snatch those fruits away (simply due to that person's having in fact *already* discovered that which I could and should have discovered, and which I presumably would in fact very soon have discovered). The attitude being noted in the present section goes further. It argues, at least implicitly, that knowledge that is, in principle, available at zero cost, *belongs to all mankind*. There is no excuse for the economy *not* being in equilibrium, and there is no justification for gain won by exploiting the "aberration" (consisting in de facto disequilibrium, profit-generating situations).

While this explanation, for persistent scepticism concerning the justice of pure profit, might be classified (as was that noted in the preceding section) as simply a form of rejection of the finders, keepers ethic, there seem grounds to see this explanation as reaching to additional considerations. The attitude being now noted appears implicitly to assume that sheer ignorance is not only able to be costlessly eliminated (as it is by definition) but that its early elimination *is so assured* that to take advantage of its very temporary existence is unethical. This ethical judgement is thus grounded in a factual assumption (not necessarily shared by those whose rejection of the finders, keepers principle we noted in the preceding section). The circumstance that this factual assumption (which we are here attributing to non-economists) is similar to that built into the equilibrium models of mainstream economic theorists, is certainly of more than passing interest, but must not detain us further in this paper.

6. CONSIDERATIONS OF ENVY

We have already noted that envy is, of course, a most plausible explanation for an attitude of disgust at pure entrepreneurial profit. What we wish to point to in the present section, however, is a somewhat more subtle sense in which envy may emerge (and thus lead to the condemnation of pure profit). This has to do with the psychological tendency noted in recent literature, for people to treat the existing situation as being the *normal* one. This tendency is no doubt to be linked with that noted in the preceding section (a tendency we dubbed "the equilibrium perspective"), but the tendency being here noted operates not by treating available knowledge as somehow belonging to all, as by seeing gains won by innovation as unjust exploitative gains achieved by shattering that which is "normal." In the words of a contemporary writer: "The entrepreneur . . . arouses suspicion among conformists. He (or she) breaks from the pack . . . The majority in the community regard the would-be entrepreneur as flippant, brash, disloyal to time-honored institutions, opportunistic and worse. We respond to his failures with vindictive indignation: 'I told you so!' . . . Success of the entrepreneur, on the other hand, throws the masses into confusion. The masses who work as diligently as ever according to conventions cannot understand why the demand for their products are disappearing, making them poorer, while the entrepreneur is swarmed by customers, making him rich . . . At this point, people in the community will feel . . . unjustly dealt with by the shady character, and they will demand restitution."[10]

No doubt one may classify this kind of envy as rooted in total ignorance of the discovery role of the entrepreneur (and such ignorance was noted earlier as a "candidate"). But this kind of ignorance-generated envy seems to call for attention in its own right in that it expresses itself as the implicit refusal to recognize scope for innovative improvement. The critics, in the present case, are not ignorant concerning the nature of discovery due to an implicitly faulty "social science" (as was the case in the earlier section in which "ignorance" was canvassed as a "candidate"); rather they are ignorant because they are imbued with an attitude instinctively hostile to change per se. Even where they are forced to concede that change is in some sense progressive and beneficial, they are strongly inclined to view it as unfairly and unethically disrupting the lives of honest and deserving citizens displaced by the change. In no way are they prepared to recognize the possibility that these deserving citizens are overlooking obvious (or less obvious) ways of improving methods of production.

In other words the envy which we now see as an explanation for a hostility to pure profit maintained on ethical grounds, takes its form *precisely* from the *correct* economic science view of profit (*i.e.* as resisting completely all attempts to treat it as a kind of factor income that can be rendered consistent with equilibrium conditions).

7. THE EX POST PERSPECTIVE

Yet a further consideration may be introduced as adding an element of explanation (for the persistently widespread scepticism concerning the justice of pure profit). Although perhaps not itself an independent "explanation," this new consideration offers a fresh element for understanding the "blind-spot" widely encountered concerning the nature of discovery. We are referring here to the circumstance that profit is observed (by others) only ex post. Hind-sight is seldom sensitive to the completeness with which successful discoveries were hidden from view prior to their having been so discovered by daring, visionary innovators. Such hindsight does not see the profitable gap in price (separating input from output) as attributable to earlier faulty vision (on the part of market participants who

10. Choi 1993, chapter 7.

had undervalued inputs)—because hindsight cannot fully reconstruct the completeness of earlier ignorance. From this ex post perspective, the explanation for profit must inevitably be sought in exploitative behavior or in deceptive (or virtually deceptive) practices.

8. A ROLE FOR ECONOMIC EDUCATION

If we are correct in the preceding discussions, several conclusions seem to emerge. First and foremost is the conviction that sound economic insight concerning the nature of the market process is an essentially necessary prerequisite for a consistent and coherent ethical evaluation of pure profit and, indeed, of capitalism in general. So long as the observer thinks of the market as being at all times in a state of (relevant) normalcy, it becomes inevitably difficult for him to recognize the relevance to the winning of pure profit, of any finders, keepers principle. Second, our discussion has revealed the probable set of attitudes which appear to reinforce that ignorance of the economics of the market process to which we have been referring. Awareness of these attitudes must surely be useful for any educational effort directed at enhancing wider economic understanding of the market process.

These conclusions point to a certain complication surrounding the goal of economic education. Traditionally, economic educators have usually preferred to see their objective as that of transmitting scientific truth. Certainly critics of economics have, no doubt with some justification, continually questioned the accuracy (and perhaps the sincerity) of this view.[11] But even where economic education has, openly or otherwise, had an ideological or policy-oriented objective, it has proceeded by pointing out the implications of (what it has maintained, at least, to be) the scientifically true understanding of economic processes. The economics teacher may have taught students to favor different economic policies, but has not deliberately sought, qua economics teacher, to change students' moral judgements. If, however, economic education is to have the objectives suggested in the preceding paragraph, it will be embarking on a campaign designed to alter the *moral* evaluation by the public, of certain aspects of capitalism. It is true that this campaign will not seek *directly* to alter the values held precious by those being educated. It will not seek to impart ethical insights or moral sensitivity per se. It will merely permit

---

11. A well-known example of such criticism is Myrdal 1954.

those being educated to recognize the relevance of *given* moral principles (*e.g.* the finders, keepers ethic) to economic phenomena (*e.g.* pure entrepreneurial profit) to which such principles had been (incorrectly) thought not to apply. Nonetheless such an approach may leave some economic educators troubled.

I find nothing, in such an educational objective, inconsistent with scientific objectivity. A medical researcher whose studies have convinced him that smoking enhances cancer risks for non-smokers, may legitimately permit his research to be used in a campaign designed to alter peoples' views on the ethics of smoking. To be sure, use of science to alter moral evaluations of specified acts may be beset by temptations which threaten to corrupt scientific integrity. Those seeking to alter moral evaluations may proceed by obfuscation, through invoking unscientific arguments and irrelevant data, all in the interest of some specific, prejudged moral outcome. But the plausibility of the danger that such temptations might arise, does not in the slightest affect the possibility of a wertfrei scientist legitimately putting his results at the service of those with an axe to grind (with due safeguards against the possible misuse of his results by others).

All science, as Bishop Whately noted over a century and a half ago, may be undertaken in order to achieve extra-scientific objectives. The cancer researcher may be inspired by the lofty (but extra-scientific) objective of battling disease. Such extra-scientific objectives need not, logically, entail corruption of the scientist's own wertfreiheit-constrained scientific methodology. If inappropriate moral judgments are being made as a result of faulty or incomplete economic understanding, no apologies need be made for the deliberate deployment of more complete economic understanding in order to straighten out people's confused moral thinking. The danger that economic education may be corrupted into propaganda for fixed moral pre-judgments certainly exists. But, as a matter of logic, the existence of such danger does not, by itself, render such an undertaking (*i.e.* the deployment of sound economics to straighten out confused moral thinking) in any way corrupt. On the contrary, the importance of securing moral judgments not based upon confused thinking, may well render such deliberate deployment of scientifically established conclusions fully consistent with the loftiest objectives of scientific work.

REFERENCES

Choi, Y. B. (1993), *Paradigms and Conventions: Uncertainty, Decision Making and Entrepreneurship*, Ann Arbor: University of Michigan Press.

Clark, J. B. (1899), *The Distribution of Wealth*, New York and London: Macmillan.

Friedman, M. (1962), *Capitalism and Freedom*, Chicago: University of Chicago Press.

Hawley, F. B. (1893), "The Risk Theory of Profit," *Quarterly Journal of Economics*, volume 7, July.

Kirzner, I. (1989), *Discovery, Capitalism and Distributive Justice*, Oxford: Basil Blackwell.

Knight, F. H. (1921), *Risk, Uncertainty and Profit*, Boston and New York: Houghton Mifflin.

Mises, L. (1956), *The Anti-Capitalist Mentality*, Princeton: Van Nostrand.

Mises, L. (1962), *Planning for Freedom and Other Essays and Addresses*, second edition, South Holland: Libertarian Press.

Myrdal, G. (1954), *The Political Element in the Development of Economic Theory*, Cambridge: Harvard University Press.

THE NATURE OF PROFITS: SOME ECONOMIC
INSIGHTS AND THEIR ETHICAL IMPLICATIONS

In everyday business terminology, the term "profit" has a fairly well-understood meaning (constructed, in the main, out of accounting categories). In considering the ethical acceptability of business profits, however, it is necessary for the economist first to disentangle the various analytically separate elements that together comprise such business profits. As is well understood in elementary economic theory, most of these separate elements turn out to be identical, in their economic significance, to nonprofit elements. The owner of a business may work long hours; at least part of his business profits must be seen as the equivalent of the wages he could have earned by working for another firm. The owner of a business may have his own funds invested in his firm; part of his business profits must be seen as the equivalent of the market interest income he could have obtained by investing at the market rate of return in, say, corporate bonds. It is plausible, therefore, to assume that ethical acceptability of such nonprofit elements of accounting profit raises no new questions beyond those generally relevant to nonprofit incomes in capitalist society. The sense in which business profits pose a special challenge for an ethical appraisal of capitalist distribution, therefore, arises strictly from the residual "pure economic profit" element contained in business profits. After filtering out, from accounting profit, all elements that can be construed as market return on capital owned, or implicit wages of management, there remains the possibility of a residual category that cannot be imputed to any factor owner; it appears to be related to the role of the entrepreneur in a way that does not permit it to be treated as his wage, or as market return on his investment. In the last analysis, the ethical evaluation of business profits thus revolves around the nature of "pure economic profit"—both in regard to its economic function and its economic causes. As we shall see, understanding the economic nature of pure entrepreneurial profit may well open up fresh insights concerning

From Robin A. Cowan and Mario J. Rizzo, eds., *Profits and Morality* (Chicago: University of Chicago Press, 1995), 22–47. © 1995 by The University of Chicago. Reprinted by permission of The University of Chicago.

the ethical acceptability of business profits as broadly understood in everyday discourse.

ETHICS AND ECONOMICS INTERTWINED

Much of what we shall argue here depends on recognizing the ethical implications of economic insights. We shall not, that is, attempt to offer any innovations in ethical theory. We shall not attempt to persuade the reader to modify any ethical principles to which he subscribes. Instead, we shall proceed to suggest to the reader that the *application* of these ethical principles to the evaluation of pure profit demands, as a prerequisite, an appreciation for the true *economic* nature of entrepreneurial profit, along lines that may appear novel and even strange. Once the economic insights necessary for this appreciation have been accepted, we believe, the appropriate ethical evaluation—different though this may turn out to be from that reached conventionally—follows entirely without strain.

It is because of this that the "nature of profit" becomes so central to the task of its ethical evaluation. As we shall see, it is only as a result of careful attention to the economic nature of pure profit that we find ourselves forced to reject standard defenses of the ethics of pure profit. And it will turn out to be the case that from still more careful attention to the economic nature of pure profit there will emerge an understanding of it which opens up fresh dimensions of ethical relevance. It is toward this latter understanding, and a perception of these fresh dimensions of economic relevance, that this chapter sets its aim.

The beginning of wisdom in regard to pure profit is a full appreciation of how difficult it is to understand profit—or, at least, to understand profit in the way we are accustomed to understand the economics and the ethics of other kinds of incomes under capitalism.

THE ECONOMIC AND ETHICAL
PROBLEMS OF PURE PROFIT

Let us begin with two commonplace observations. The first observation is that many of us regard as justly earned those receipts which can be attributed to the efforts of the recipient. To the extent that a person's sweat is solely responsible for a particular output, we tend to regard it as unjust for that particular output to be appropriated by anyone else. The second commonplace observation is that many of us regard the fruit of a tree justly to belong to the legitimate owner of that tree. If a justly owned asset spontaneously yields a return, without the effort of any human being, we tend to regard it as entirely acceptable for that return to accrue to the owner of that asset. We do not need, for present purposes, to delve into the philosophical underpinnings supporting these two widespread convictions.[1] They are together sufficient to highlight the problem—at once ethical and economic—raised by pure profit. The *economic* problem raised by pure profit is that it seems to be *uncaused*. We can neither trace it to anyone's effort, nor to the spontaneous fruitfulness of any productive source. This is so, as we shall emphasize, simply as a matter of sheer definition. To the extent that a receipt *can* be attributed to the effort of the recipient, it qualifies immediately as a wage (implicit or explicit). To the extent that the receipt can be seen as attributable to the pure spontaneous fruitfulness of an owned asset, it qualifies immediately as a property-income component of accounting profit. It is only after all such elements have been filtered out, as we have seen, that we arrive at pure profit. This pure profit then appears to present an economic puzzle: if it was not created by any human effort, nor emerged as the fruit of any kind of "tree," how could it possibly have come about?

But at the same time this very difficulty presents a strictly ethical aspect. Whoever grasps this pure profit can lay claim to it on the basis of neither of the two intuitive convictions referred to earlier. He has not expended effort in its creation or acquisition, nor is he the owner of any asset from which it spontaneously emerged. The economic dilemma thus turns out to be matched by a mirror-image ethical difficulty.[2] If this pure

---

1. We take these widespread ethical intuitions for granted, not because we believe they are self-evidently true and correct but because our goal is to understand pure profits in terms of widely held ethical convictions. (This will hold, in particular, also for our use of the finders-keepers ethic later in this chapter.) It follows, of course, that our arguments will properly be held at least partly irrelevant by those who, in fact, refuse to accept those widely held ethical institutions.

2. Throughout this chapter we will be referring to the ethical "difficulty" or "problem" associated with pure profit. Of course, no difficulty or problem will exist for one who, indeed, believes that the phenomenon of pure profit is ethically undefendable. Although we will be using the terms "difficulty" and "problem," it is not our intention, in so doing, implicitly to beg the ethical question involved. From the perspective reached by the end of this chapter, suggesting a possible line of ethical justification for pure profit, it seems useful to introduce discussion by focusing on what will eventually be seen, we shall argue, to have been only apparent difficulties and problems.

profit, economically uncaused as it appears at first glance, must be attributed to pure chance, or to the exploitation of buyer ignorance, this very circumstance appears to render its grasping by an individual seriously vulnerable to ethical challenge. Exploitation of consumer ignorance, of course, raises issues of fraud. And even the beneficiary of pure good fortune does not at all enjoy that intuitive ethical approval of his fortunate situation which, for many of us, attaches to the recipient of that produced by the sweat of his brow, or to the owner of the fruit-bearing tree. We can no longer appeal to a widely shared notion of simple justice to support his grasping of profit. Let us return to ponder on the apparently "uncaused" character of pure economic profit.

If we begin with an institutional framework which recognizes private self-ownership rights and the possibility of acquiring ownership rights in productive resources, we have no difficulty in accounting for the emergence of factor incomes. The worker is able to command a wage for his labor because that labor produces an item for which a consumer (and hence an entrepreneur intending to sell to the consumer) is prepared to pay. Because labor services are scarce, market competition ensures a positive wage to productive labor. The owner of a fruit tree is able to command a price for the fruit of his tree because, given his ownership of the scarce fruit, consumers are, in competition with one another, prepared to pay positive prices to acquire that fruit. Given widespread preference for earlier rather than later receipts, the market for loanable funds yields interest income to lenders, because the borrowers find it worthwhile to offer interest, and scarcity of loanable funds makes it necessary for them to do so. But there seems, on the face of it, to be no earthly reason why, when a consumer buys an item, he should pay a price for it which is *more* than sufficiently high to cover *all* costs of resource services (including the borrowing of necessary capital funds) needed to deliver that item to his doorstep at the time he wishes to buy it. The portion of this purchase price which accrues as pure profit is paid, it appears, for nothing at all. It does not pay for the performance of any productive service rendered. It does not pay for the use of capital funds. It cannot be rationalized as being paid in return for the provision by the seller of necessary information— because, to the extent that this *is* the reason why this payment is being made, it follows that it is payment for a service rendered and thus not pure profit after all. It seems that the pure profit portion of the purchase price can emerge only as the result of a fluke, an aberration, and/or of virtual fraud on the part of the seller (who somehow, as the result of consumer ignorance, extracts a price higher than that strictly necessary to provide the consumer that which he is buying). And it is here that the ethical side of the problem of profit comes clearly into focus. It follows from the very circumstance that there appears no economic justification (in the sense of "valid explanation") for the payment of pure profit, that the grasping of such profits must necessarily fail to meet both of the two commonly held criteria for deservedness mentioned earlier. A payment is economically justified if the relevant conditions of supply and demand mark out a positive market clearing price. The circumstance that such justification is absent in the case of pure profit leaves pure profit in an ethical limbo. One is simply unable to point to any quid pro quo (such as effort, or the fruit of an owned tree) corresponding to the grasped profit. The ethical problem of profit emerges directly from the economic nature of pure profit.

PURE PROFIT AND THE ENTREPRENEURIAL ROLE

The problematic nature of pure profit is mirrored, of course, in the problematic nature of the entrepreneurial function itself. From the perspective of conventional economic theory this function is a notoriously elusive one. The entrepreneur assembles all the productive services needed to produce a product. He assumes the cost represented by the market values of all these services and receives the market value of the produced output. He retains whatever surplus remains, as pure entrepreneurial profit (or, if the residual is negative, he suffers entrepreneurial loss). But in stipulating that he assumes the costs embodied in the market value of *all* productive services needed for the product, we of course mean to include also all those services provided by the entrepreneur himself which could, in principle, have been hired in the marketplace. His labor services and the services of the assets he owns could have been provided from the outside. In identifying the peculiarly entrepreneurial character of his role, we must certainly not obscure this role by failing to distinguish it analytically from the provision of these nonentrepreneurial services with which the entrepreneurial role is often in real life packaged together. The computation of residual pure profit, as we saw previously, requires that we net out, from the gross revenue obtained from the sale of output, not only out-of-pocket expenditures made by the entrepreneur to command the productive services he buys in the market, but also the market values of the nonentrepreneurial services the entrepreneur himself provides. The pure profit residual accrues to the pure entrepreneurial role played by the entrepreneur. But of what does this role consist? What does the entrepreneur, qua entrepreneur, contribute to the emergence of the product? After all, the productive services he assembles (including his own nonentrepreneurially contributed services) are, by stipulation, together *fully* sufficient for the production of the product and its delivery to the purchaser. The list of assembled services *must* be a complete one. Inputs produce output; the entrepreneur assembles *all* the inputs needed for the output. With *all* the needed inputs in hand, what else could possibly be needed? It appears, at first glance, as if the purely entrepreneurial function disintegrates into nothingness as soon as we attempt to grasp hold of it.

Pure profit accrues to the entrepreneur. But we cannot seem to perceive what it is that the entrepreneur *does*. And, as seen previously, we seem to be unable to understand why the prices paid by purchasers are high enough to leave a residual pure profit. We don't know what the function of the entrepreneur is, and we don't understand how and why he is ever able to retain his residual pure profit. The ethical problem we found to surround pure profit thus parallels our mystification concerning the function and role of the entrepreneur. Much of what follows here is concerned with the explication of the entrepreneurial function.

SOME LEADING THEORIES OF ENTREPRENEURIAL PROFIT

It will be useful, both for its own sake and as preliminary to our own theory of profit, to provide a brief review of the principal economic theories of entrepreneurial profit developed during the heyday of entrepreneurial theorizing (1890–1920).[3] The several major approaches we shall identify attest to the intense interest displayed by the early neoclassical economists in the pure profit concept and in the entrepreneurial role.

3. This section draws substantially upon the material in my *Discovery, Capitalism and Distributive Justice* (Oxford: Basil Blackwell, 1989), chap. 3. The history of theories of profit and entrepreneurship is a rich one. See in particular R. F. Hebert and A. N. Link, *The Entrepreneur: Mainstream Views and Radical Critiques*, 2d ed. (New York: Praeger, 1988). My brief review makes no attempt at completeness in coverage; instead, it identifies several key approaches, an understanding of which (and of the shortcomings of which) can, I believe, conduce to an appreciation of the Misesian theory discussed here.

This contrasts sharply with the virtual silence on these matters which characterized the subsequent half-century of economic thought. We shall identify what we believe to be weaknesses in these approaches but also point out the valuable insights contained in them. Wherever possible, we shall take note of the possible implications which these theories hold for the ethical evaluation of pure profit.

J. B. Clark

Clark's observations on profit occur peripherally to his exhaustive analysis of distribution under conditions of static equilibrium.[4] Under static conditions there is no profit. All incomes are marginal productivity incomes. "Profit has no place in such static conditions. The two incomes that are permanent and independent of dynamic changes are the products, respectively, of labor and of capital. Each of them is directly determined by the final productivity law . . . ."[5] Profit emerges only as a result of dynamic change. Suppose a new invention improves the methods of production. This may result in permanently higher wages. "Wages now tend to equal what labor can now produce, and this is more than it could formerly produce."[6] However, as a result of "economic friction," wages may be temporarily lower than their new, higher, static level, leaving a profit margin between output value and production costs, which the entrepreneur is able to grasp. "The interval between actual wages and the static standard is the result of friction; for, if competition works without let or hindrance, pure business profit would be annihilated as fast as it could be created—entrepreneurs, as such, could never get and keep any income . . . Dynamic theory has to account for the whole of that friction on which *entrepreneurs'* shares depend; while static law determines what wages will be, when the friction shall have been completely overcome, and what they would be at this instant, if friction were immediately to vanish."[7] Clark is apparently satisfied with the justice of such entrepreneurially grasped profit—despite the circumstance that it does not fit into his own marginal productivity ethic (which declares wages, for example, to be justly earned only because they correspond to what labor has

---

4. J. B. Clark, *The Distribution of Wealth* (New York: Macmillan, 1989).
5. Ibid., p. 201.
6. Ibid., p. 405.
7. Ibid., pp. 410–11.

contributed to the total output). Clark notes that were it not for the friction which permits a temporary profit to entrepreneurs, the latter "would have no incentive in self-interest to make any improvements, and it is clear that additions which are difficult and costly would be in danger of not being made. Profit is the lure that insures improvement . . . To secure progress, this lure must be sufficient to make men overcome obstructions and take risks."[8] Yet it is not clear how this renders the grasping of these profits ethically acceptable for Clark. Clark does not appear to recognize any productive service to have been rendered by the entrepreneur, even when he has introduced improvements in productive methods. After all, all that is produced through the new methods is produced by the input services being used. So we do not quite understand how Clark's productivity criteria for distributive justice have been met by the entrepreneur, permitting him to enjoy (the admittedly temporary) profits made possible by economic friction.

On the other hand, Clark *has* provided a solution to the problem of what causes profit to exist at all. Profits are not uncaused; they are caused by economic frictions which prevent the immediate disappearance (through competitive activity) of the profits initially generated by dynamic change. Clark has, importantly, identified pure profit as a disequilibrium phenomenon, and has at least given a name to the source responsible for the temporary persistence of disequilibrium: "economic frictions."

F. B. Hawley

Hawley was an important (but now almost forgotten) U.S. profit theorist at the turn of the century. He is prominently cited by Frank Knight in his survey of profit theories, and Hawley's theory, while sharply criticized by Knight, is recognized by him to contain a valuable element of what Knight believes to be a correct theory.[9] Hawley's work had a profound influence on subsequent U.S. textbook treatments of profit, an influence continuing well after World War II.[10]

8. Ibid., p. 411.

9. Frank H. Knight, *Risk, Uncertainty and Profit* (Boston: Houghton Mifflin, 1921), pp. 41–48.

10. On this see Martin Bronfenbrenner, "A Reformulation of Naive Profit Theory," *Southern Economic Journal* (April 1960): 300–309.

Hawley identifies the "distinguishing function of the *entrepreneur*" as the "assumption of risk," and saw pure profit as "the economic reward for services rendered by the assumption of industrial risk."[11] Were no one to be prepared to assume this industrial risk, it would not be possible for production to occur. Profit provides a reward for this entrepreneurially provided service, and thus also an inducement persuading the entrepreneur to provide this service. It is important, Hawley contends, not to confuse this reward and inducement with the amount an unwilling risk bearer pays in order to insure himself against the risk of loss. This latter payment, "a sum sufficient to cover the actuarial or average losses incidental to the various risks of all kinds necessarily assumed by the entrepreneur and his insurers," is already included among the costs of production.[12] Hawley maintains that production will not occur unless the entrepreneur can be induced to assume risk, through the prospect of a surplus over and above *all* costs, including the cost of insurance. This is so, Hawley argues, because there is an "irksomeness of uncertainty" attached to each *particular* business project, even where the businessman has confidence in the validity of his actuarial judgment over the long run (during which time losses and gains will tend to offset each other).[13] It is because of this that Hawley asserts that "industrial risks will not be assumed without the expectation of a compensation in excess of the actuarial value of the risk."[14]

It will be observed that Hawley's theory of profit does, within its own framework, adequately address the economic (and, by implication, also the ethical) problem surrounding profit and the entrepreneurial role. The entrepreneur does provide a service, a service that is both essential for the emergence of output and not able to be purchased on the market. Profit is not uncaused, it is caused by the need, if product is to be forthcoming, for the (inescapable) risk of business to be assumed. The consumers are forced to pay prices high enough to permit profits, or else they would not

11. F. B. Hawley, "Enterprise and Profit," *Quarterly Journal of Economics* 15 (November 1900): 75.

12. F. B. Hawley, "Reply to Final Objection to the Risk Theory of Profit," *Quarterly Journal of Economics* 15 (August 1901): 610.

13. Ibid., p. 604.

14. F. B. Hawley, "The Risk Theory of Profit," *Quarterly Journal of Economics* 7 (July 1893): 460.

find the products they wish to buy. Hawley does not appear to have much concerned himself with the ethics of profit. He wished to teach economists how correctly to characterize the phenomenon of profit. Yet we can see for ourselves how an ethical defense might be constructed on the basis of Hawley's theory. The entrepreneur provides a special service, one irksome for him to provide; he may be deemed entitled to the reward the market provides as an inducement to him for so providing this needed service.

Yet the framework that Hawley has offered seems unredeemably flawed. Knight put his finger on its central weakness. Hawley assumes "that the 'actuarial value' of the risks taken is known to the entrepreneur."[15] Knight was himself to emphasize, however, that there is a fundamental difference between risk and uncertainty. For Knight "uncertainty" is a term reserved for that which is, as a consequence of the utter unpredictability of future events, inherently indeterminate and immeasurable. So long as Hawley provides no room, in his analytical scheme, for such open-ended, uninsurable uncertainty, he has not rendered plausible the nature of the peculiarly entrepreneurial function. As Knight pointed out, "[A] little consideration will show that there can be no considerable 'irksomeness' attached to exposure to an insurable risk, for if there is it will be insured; hence there can be no peculiarity income arising out of this alleged indisposition."[16]

Frank H. Knight

Knight constructed his own uncertainty theory of profit out of elements he found in Clark and Hawley. Clark was right in associating profit with dynamic change; Hawley was right in associating the entrepreneurial function with the residual bearing of uncertainty. But it was left for Knight to forge out of these ideas what he believed to be the correct theory of profit and of the entrepreneurial role. Clarkian dynamic change is, by itself, not enough to generate profit, because it is possible for change to be anticipated.[17] If an increase in the productivity of labor can be generally anticipated, competition among prospective employers will immediately force wages up to the new, higher level. It is only to the extent that change is responsible for ignorance of the future that it can be associated with the

15. Knight (1921), p. 43.
16. Ibid., p. 46.
17. Ibid., pp. 35–37.

phenomenon of profit. And this insight leads Knight to locate the source of profit not in dynamic change itself but in the open-ended uncertainty of the future for which such change is responsible. For Knight it is this inescapable difference between what has been anticipated and what actually occurs, which is responsible for entrepreneurial profit (and loss). So that profits are not forthcoming because an inducement must be offered to overcome some irksomeness of uncertainty bearing; profits and losses are forthcoming because the uncertainty of life continually generates unexpected gains or unexpected losses. The entrepreneur has (certainly as a result of the inducement offered by the prospect of possible profit) placed himself in the position of residual claimant. Knight goes into considerable detail concerning the qualities required for the entrepreneurial function, involving, as it thus does, both *responsibility* for and *control* of an enterprise in an uncertain world.[18] But for an understanding of Knight's view of the nature of entrepreneurial profit it is sufficient to focus on the extent to which entrepreneurial *judgment* (which for Knight appears to refer to the judgment required for the successful carrying out of routine managerial tasks in an uncertain world) and *pure luck* are inevitably intertwined in the generation of residual profit.[19] Because the entrepreneur exposes himself to residual uncertainty the element of luck plays a decisive part in determining whether the residual left, after paying all contractual income, will be positive or negative.

So that, for Knight, pure profit is not exactly uncaused. It is an implication of the need to operate in a world of uncertainty. In such a world somebody, or everybody, must be left exposed to the vagaries of pure luck. Entrepreneurs choose to occupy such exposed positions; their luck may be good or bad—profits may be positive or negative. Consumers do not deliberately pay a price higher than necessary to cover all costs of production; if they pay such higher prices this is because the course of events happens to have been such as to force the current output price up higher than had been anticipated when the contractual income payments for factor services were agreed upon. Profit emerges because a world of uncertainty is necessarily one in which "a condition of perfect equilibrium is no longer possible."[20] A world of continuous disequilibrium is one in

18. Ibid., p. 271.
19. Ibid., pp. 277–83.
20. Ibid., p. 272.

which residual incomes are continually being subjected to unanticipated shocks and readjustments. It is not correct to characterize profits as "having to be paid" in order to induce entrepreneurs to enter (although the *possibility* of such profits may indeed provide such inducement); in fact, Knight believed rather strongly that, on balance, losses outweigh profits. Profits (or losses) emerge simply because, in an uncertain world, matters never do turn out to be exactly what the best judgment anticipated as being likely to happen.

What Knight has given us, then, is a theory of profit which sees it as caused by uncertainty-bred conditions of market disequilibrium. It should be noted that while this certainly does explain how the phenomenon of profit arises, it does so in a way which does *not* see profit as the market value offered in exchange for the fulfillment by the entrepreneur of any valuable social function. To be sure, profit and loss are inseparably associated with the entrepreneurial role, and, to be sure, Knight sees a *most* important place for this role in the capitalist process of production.[21] But the nature of these associations is such that even where profits, rather than losses, have been achieved, these can hardly be seen as payment for the entrepreneurial services rendered. We would rather have to say, according to Knight, that the provision of entrepreneurial services is inseparable from consequent exposure to the possibility of loss and the possibility of profit. Since, on balance, there never may be net profits won by the entrepreneurs in the economy, these net profits cannot, even if they occur, be seen as market generated payments made for, and necessary to induce the provision of, the services of entrepreneurs.

In other words, Knight has, in his own way, solved the purely economic problem of pure profit without being concerned with, and without offering any clues to the solution of, the ethical problems we identified earlier. Where an entrepreneur has won profits there still seems no way of subsuming these profits under the category of justly received incomes (according to the everyday consensus mentioned earlier as providing rough criteria for ethical acceptability). Although by focusing upon uninsurable uncertainty (rather than upon insurable risk) Knight has no doubt restored legitimacy to Hawley's "irksomeness of uncertainty,"

---

21. In fact, Knight (1921) argued that it is the entrepreneur (who, while himself owning no inputs, assembles them to generate output) who must be considered the real "producer" of capitalist output (p. 271).

nonetheless Knight's perspective does not, as we have seen, permit profit to be seen as paid for (and thus ethically justified by) the provision of this service of irksome-bearing. While we now understand what Knight wishes us to see the entrepreneur as doing, we are, therefore, still unable to see how this renders the winning of profit legitimate. In fact, it would seem eminently plausible for a critic to argue that the entrepreneur has no inherent right to the lucky profits that came his way. (Knight himself may well have felt that the entrepreneur's vulnerability to the losses generated by bad luck, somehow makes it not unfair for him to be permitted to keep the proceeds of good luck.[22] But this surely depends on the validity of Knight's conviction that, in general, losses more than cancel out profits.)

J. A. Schumpeter

We list Schumpeter's well-known theory of profit not because his theory offered a fundamental insight not already covered in our brief review of the literature but because of the centrality and prominence of his theory, and because of certain important fresh nuances to be noticed in that theory. For Schumpeter profits are created by entrepreneurial innovations. He sees the entrepreneurial function as consisting in the "carrying out of new combinations," which change the methods of production and/or the products produced.[23] The energy and leadership qualities of the entrepreneur provide him with the initiative and the will needed to break away from the routine activities of everyday business. It is not so much a matter of originality and ingenuity of invention as of power and determination "in getting things done,"[24] of introducing into practice the inventions that others can see as well as he can.[25] These entrepreneurial innovations

---

22. See Knight's statement: "Both in abstract ethics and from the standpoint of social interest in adequate motivation, a proposal to reduce high profits raises the question of using the proceeds to reduce losses" ("Profit," in *Encyclopedia of the Social Sciences* 12, reprinted in *Readings in the Theory of Income Distribution*, ed. W. Fellner and B. F. Haley (Philadelphia: Blakiston, 1949), p. 546.

23. See Joseph Schumpeter, *The Theory of Economic Development* (Cambridge, Mass.: Harvard University Press, 1934), pp. 74ff.

24. J. A. Schumpeter, *Capitalism, Socialism and Democracy*, 3d ed. (New York: Harper and Row, 1950), p. 132.

25. Schumpeter, *Theory of Economic Development* (1934), pp. 88–89.

together make up the "perennial gale of creative destruction" which, for Schumpeter, is an unmistakable characteristic of capitalism.[26]

The profits won by the Schumpeterian entrepreneur are not windfall profits; they have been deliberately created. By innovating a new technique or a new product the entrepreneur creates a profit-surplus of revenues over costs, for as long as it takes the nonentrepreneurial "imitators" to compete away that difference. For Schumpeter risk and uncertainty have nothing to do with profit (although he would not deny that entrepreneurial activity is inseparable from exposure to uncertainty). Schumpeter believed that the risk associated with an entrepreneurial venture is borne by the capitalist, not the entrepreneur. The profits of innovation are not a reward paid by the market but a gain created by jolting the economy out of its routine pattern.

The similarity between Schumpeter's understanding of the nature of pure profit and that perceived by J. B. Clark is obvious. For Clark, too, as seen earlier in this section, profits emerge as the result of the dynamic change associated with industrial progress. Schumpeter was to recognize this similarity. In surveying neoclassical contributions to the theory of enterprise (in his monumental *History of Economic Analysis*), Schumpeter described Clark's contribution as being "the most significant of all: he was the first to strike a novel note by connecting entrepreneurial profits, considered as a surplus over interest (and rent), with the successful introduction into the economic process of technological, commercial, or organizational improvements."[27]

What distinguishes the Schumpeterian view of pure profit from that of Clark seems to be entirely a matter of nuance. Clark does not seem to emphasize as Schumpeter does the *deliberate* character of profit creation; he does emphasize, more than Schumpeter appears to do, the *temporary* nature of profit, noting (as we have seen) that it is only "economic friction" which somehow prevents its instantaneous disappearance. The lure of profit stimulates the entrepreneur to introduce technological innovations, with the impression somehow being conveyed that the market is already clearly *offering* these fleeting profit opportunities in

---

26. Schumpeter, *Capitalism, Socialism and Democracy* (1950), p. 87.

27. J. A. Schumpeter, *History of Economic Analysis* (Oxford: Oxford University Press, 1954), p. 894. See also Schumpeter, *Theory of Economic Development* (1934), pp. 128–29, where Clark's theory is described as the closest to Schumpeter's own.

exchange for innovation (rather than their being deliberately engineered by the Schumpeterian entrepreneur's leadership and determination). As we saw earlier, Clark's theory solves the problem of what causes profits: profits are caused by economic frictions which prevent the immediate disappearance (through competitive activity) of the profits initially generated by dynamic change. For Schumpeter, it would seem more accurate to describe his theory as solving the causal problem in profits slightly differently: profits are caused by entrepreneurial innovations; they tend to be ground down to zero by the competition of imitators. As we have seen, Clark's theory of profit was not more than a footnote, as it were, to his comprehensive marginal productivity theory of income distribution under static equilibrium conditions. Schumpeter's theory of entrepreneurial innovation, on the other hand, was the central element in his understanding of the capitalist process.

SOME LESSONS LEARNED FROM THE LEADING THEORIES

Consideration of the theories briefly sketched in the preceding section can significantly advance understanding of the phenomenon of pure profit. These theories point unerringly to the *disequilibrium* character of profit. It turns out that the problem which we encountered, at the outset of this chapter in explaining the economic causes of profit, was a problem only because we were, at least implicitly, seeking for causes that could operate steadily under settled circumstances. We were looking for a service provided steadily by the entrepreneur that could be understood as commanding a settled market price. Inevitably, we found ourselves forced to acknowledge that, to the extent such a steady service and such a settled market price could be identified, we were no longer dealing with the purely entrepreneurial role and with pure profit. The work of Schumpeter and Knight (in whose ideas, as we have seen, we can find echoes of insights present in the work of Clark and Hawley) incisively identifies profit as a gain that has no place at all in the settled scheme of the equilibrium state. Profits appeared to be without cause, because in the settled scheme of things that was the background of our quest, there can in fact be no profit. Real world profits do exist; they have their cause in the circumstances responsible for and which accompany the real world state of disequilibrium. For Schumpeter profits are created through the leadership with which the entrepreneur propels the economy away from its earlier somnolent state of equilibrium. For Knight profits are caused by the inevitable failure of market participants, in the disequilibrium world of uncertainty, to correctly anticipate subsequent conditions.

Yet these solutions to the *economic* problem of pure profits have not provided any help in decisively establishing ethical justification for profit. The ethical challenge, we saw, arose out of the circumstance that profit is neither a property income (comparable to the fruit that grows on a tree that is legitimately owned), nor an income paid as compensation for a productive service rendered. It was this that seemed to place pure profit under an ethical cloud. Consideration of the Schumpeterian and Knightian disequilibrium theories of profit appears, at first glance, to suggest that, indeed, even after as economists we understand how profits arise, one might yet conclude that they lack ethical justification. For both Schumpeter and Knight it is still the case that profits cannot be defended as the fruits of any owned tree, nor as the market value of any provided service. It is true that a consistent defender of private property rights could claim that, since no violation of property rights occurs either in the Schumpeterian or the Knightian scheme of things, the resulting ownership patterns cannot be pronounced unjust. (This is, indeed, the central thesis of Nozick's entitlement theory of justice.)[28] But in regard to pure profit it seems safe to say that many people are, at the intuitive level, simply not satisfied by the entitlement theory. (Perhaps their intuitive misgivings about profits are such as to lead them to question the very property system, consistent application of which appears to legitimize these apparently undeserved gains.)

In the Knightian theory of profit, with its emphasis on the consequence of sheer luck, the undeserved nature of profit appears particularly bothersome. It seems, to critics of capitalist distribution, entirely arbitrary to declare one individual to be the just owner of that which came his way only as a result of a chance occurrence in no way attributable to his efforts.[29] (As noted earlier, it is likely that Knight found himself able to defend profits on the grounds that those who stand to win profits are exposed to losses which, on balance, more than offset the profits.)

28. Robert Nozick, *Anarchy, State and Utopia* (New York: Basic Books, 1974), chap. 7.

29. Critics of capitalism have, indeed, even challenged the notion of self-ownership on precisely these grounds; see for example J. Roemer, *Free to Lose: An Introduction to Marxist Economic Philosophy* (Cambridge, Mass.: Harvard University Press, 1988), p. 154.

Schumpeterian profits are certainly not primarily a matter of luck; they are deliberately created by determined entrepreneurs. As such they might seem to be ethically defendable as the outcome achieved by deliberate effort. Yet such a defense presents something of a puzzle. Once the "imitators" will have absorbed and duplicated the innovations pioneered by the entrepreneur, equilibrium will once again have been attained; no portion of output revenue will then revert to the entrepreneur. It must appear puzzling that the contribution made by the entrepreneur is somehow held to cease as imitators copy his trade secrets. If it is eventually obvious that the nonentrepreneurial factor services are by themselves entirely sufficient to generate the new product or the new production technique (so that the full value of the output becomes justly imputed to them alone), this might be held to be equally valid and relevant immediately after introduction of the entrepreneurial innovation. If, on the other hand, it is held that, absent the pioneering effort of the entrepreneur, the new technique might never have come to pass at all, and that this entitles him to a share of the output revenue, then it is not clear why this does not entitle him to a similar share for as long as the revenue stream endures. In a nutshell, the Schumpeterian concept of profit does not facilitate its being easily fitted into a productivity-return ethical category. Let us turn to yet another theory of profit, similar in spirit, to a degree, to both the Schumpeterian and Knightian theories, but yet providing a unique twist that can perhaps help us in solving not only the economic problem of profit but also the ethical problem as well.

THE ARBITRAGE THEORY OF PURE PROFIT

This theory of profit is that of the Austrian economist Ludwig von Mises. It seems appropriate to call it the *arbitrage* theory of profit[30] because it focuses on the sense in which profit is simply the price discrepancy between two markets, today's market (in which, say, productive resource services are bought and sold) and tomorrow's market (in which the output of these productive services will be sold). Arbitrage opportunities arise when today's market prices are (after taking interest expense into account) out of line with the true, higher values that will be revealed in tomorrow's market. As Mises said, "What makes profit emerge is the fact that the entrepreneur who judges the future prices of the products more

---

30. On this see further Israel M. Kirzner, *Competition and Entrepreneurship* (Chicago: University of Chicago Press, 1973), pp. 85–86; Hebert and Link (1988), p. 152.

correctly than other people do buys some or all of the factors of production at prices which, seen from the point of view of the future state of the market, are too low. Thus the total costs of production—including interest on the capital invested—lag behind the prices which the entrepreneur receives for the product. This difference is entrepreneurial profit."[31]

The Misesian theory shares with Schumpeter's theory and with Knight's theory the insight that profit is a disequilibrium phenomenon. (Arbitrage profits are possible only because arbitrage activity has not yet squeezed them out of existence.) But the emphasis in the Misesian discussion is on the ability of the superior entrepreneur to identify, more correctly than others are able to do, where today's market undervalues future output. "An entrepreneur can make a profit only if he anticipates future conditions more correctly than other entrepreneurs. Then he buys the complementary factors of production at prices the sum of which, including allowance for the time difference, is smaller than the price at which he sells the product."[32]

Schumpeter's emphasis was on the leadership and determination expressed by the entrepreneur in creating new procedures of production. Mises's emphasis is on the superior perception on the part of the entrepreneur as to where resources services are currently undervalued.

Knight's emphasis was on the extent to which luck can benefit the agent who exposes himself to residual uncertainty. Mises's emphasis is on the vision exercised by the superior entrepreneur. Mises does not, of course, underestimate the role of uncertainty in creating opportunities for profit.[33] "The ultimate source from which entrepreneurial profit and loss are derived is the uncertainty of the future constellation of demand and supply. If all entrepreneurs were to anticipate correctly the future state of the market,

31. Ludwig von Mises, *Planning for Freedom and Other Essays and Addresses*, 2d ed. (South Holland, Ill.: Libertarian Press, 1962), p. 190.

32. Ludwig von Mises, *Human Action* (New Haven: Yale University Press, 1949), p. 291.

33. Murray N. Rothbard ("Professor Hebert on Entrepreneurship," *Journal of Libertarian Studies* 3, no. 2 (Fall 1985): pp. 281–86) has argued that this recognition and emphasis by Mises on the role of uncertainty in the generation of pure profit is inconsistent with the interpretation which the present writer has given Mises's theory. For Rothbard, an "alertness" theory of profit must do away with uncertainty. Although I have not been able to follow Rothbard's reasoning on this matter, the reader may wish to explore this issue further. See also Herbert and Link (1988), pp. 132f.

there would be neither profits nor losses."[34] But for Knight profit appears to arise, *after* the entrepreneur has taken up his exposed position, by a fortunate change which everyone (including, very possibly, this entrepreneur) has failed to foresee. For Mises, on the other hand, the profit-making entrepreneur is he who (while everyone else has failed to see the course of future events) sees the opportunity created by the errors of the other market participants. For Knight luck is a decisive factor generating profit; for Mises superior vision is the decisive factor in the grasping of profits.

We emphasize these nuances of difference between Mises, on the one hand, and Schumpeter and Knight, on the other, because, as we shall try to show, it is these differences which hold important implications for the ethical evaluation of pure profit.

PURE PROFIT AND THE ETHICS
OF DISCOVERY: AN OVERVIEW

Once we identify profit as the result of the circumstance that the entrepreneur "anticipates future conditions more correctly than other entrepreneurs,"[35] we have within our grasp the solution to the ethical problem of profit identified earlier in this chapter. The entrepreneur "sees" the future more accurately than others do. Because others see the future inaccurately, there is generated a gap between the present market value of resources and the (discounted) market value of output (as it will, in fact, turn out to be in the future). The entrepreneur, in seeing the future more accurately, in effect sees this gap. (Indeed, it is the very prospect and incentive of gaining from such perceived gaps which concentrate and focus the entrepreneurial vision to more accurately glimpse the future.) What the entrepreneur sees is a prospective increment of value which others, although in no way handicapped as compared with our entrepreneur, have somehow failed to see. (In fact, the increment of value is nothing but the market expression of this failure on their part correctly to see the future.) We argue that profits grasped by the entrepreneur are in the nature of an unowned, unperceived object first discovered by an alert pioneer, who, in the view of many, becomes the legitimate private owner of that which he has discovered, on the basis of the "finders-keepers" ethic.

34. Mises, *Human Action* (1942), p. 291.
35. Ibid.

Up until now our discussion concerning ethics referred to only two criteria on the basis of which general opinion seems prepared to endorse ethical acceptability of gain. These were (a) compensation for productive service rendered, and (b) gain directly derived ("fruit from an owned tree") from private property legitimately possessed. We now wish to recognize a third criterion, a criterion that (although apparently widely accepted in everyday discourse) appears alien to the world scheme of economics but is, we believe, crucially important to the evaluation of outcomes in an uncertain world. It is on the basis of this "finders-keepers" criterion that we shall argue the ethical defensibility of pure entrepreneurial profit. In the following pages we shall develop somewhat more fully (a) the nature of discovery, and (b) the discovered character of pure entrepreneurial profit.

THE MEANING OF DISCOVERY[36]

In the world of standard economics there is a widely employed scheme of classification the assumed exhaustiveness of which we wish to challenge very vigorously. In this scheme it is assumed that economic gains can be understood either as the deliberately achieved goals of human effort, or as windfalls attributable to sheer luck. (In addition, of course, this scheme recognizes the possibility of sequences of events in which luck and effort intertwine.) No other category of cause besides planned result of deliberate activity, and fortunate outcome of sheer good fortune, is recognized. If an outcome was not deliberately aimed at, it must be seen as purely lucky. We wish to insist that a third possible source for economic gain, a source entailing ethical implications of an entirely different character, must be recognized. This source is deliberate human discovery, not to be attributed to unaided luck but (at least in part) to the alert attitude on the part of the discoverer. It is the alertness of human beings that enables them to notice and profit by what they find.

Standard economics understands the meaning of search activity. One decides to search for an object, or for an item of information, in exactly the same way as one decides to engage in every other kind of deliberate productive activity. Such a decision is seen as rigidly determined by the value of the prospective find to the searcher, in conjunction with

36. This section draws substantially upon chap. 2 of my *Discovery, Capitalism and Distributive Justice* (1989).

the relevant costs of search. The determination is, in the economics of search, seen as being made in the context of assumed probabilities governing the techniques of deliberate search.

Deliberate search, however, is not at all the same as spontaneous, alert discovery (although, certainly, the two may occur together). Someone looking up a telephone number in a telephone directory is engaged in deliberate search. Someone who, walking along a city boulevard, notices a public telephone and realizes that this will permit him to make an important telephone call, has made a discovery. (Someone who notices the availability of a telephone directory and is thereby spurred to undertake a search for an important telephone number presents an example of how discovery and deliberate search may be intertwined.)

The special ethical relevance of spontaneous discovery arises precisely from the circumstance that it can be classified neither as a deliberate activity nor as an occurrence strictly attributable to blind chance. If I deliberately produce output using only legitimately acquired productive resource services, commonplace ethical intuition is inclined to recognize my just title to what I and my resources have produced. If I am lucky in the sense that a fortune has fallen from heaven directly in my lap, commonplace ethical intuition is not at all clear on the legitimacy of my claim to sole ownership of this fortune; after all I did not lift a finger in achieving this windfall. Critics are often inclined to argue that such windfalls somehow belong to "all mankind." It is not a simple matter to rebut such a position on the basis of commonplace intuition. What I claim here is that he who alertly grasps an opportunity for gain—an opportunity in principle available to others but which has remained ungrasped because as yet not noticed—occupies a distinct ethical box, neither that labeled "producer of output with legitimately owned resources," nor that labeled "lucky beneficiary of windfall gain." The ethical box occupied by the alert discoverer of an available opportunity might well be labeled "finders-keepers."

The finder (i.e., the discoverer) of this opportunity might lay claim to what he has discovered, not because he deliberately produced it but because he alertly noticed it. He might reject the criticisms of those who denounce private appropriation of lucky windfalls on the grounds that these criticisms are not relevant to his situation. Criticism of ownership based on pure luck cannot apply to the gains won by alert discovery. The lucky winner in a *purely* chance situation has done *nothing* to generate this outcome, which is unrelated to his efforts, his actions, his thoughts, and his purposes. The opportunity noticed by the discoverer is the direct creation of that discoverer's alertness, vision, and self-confidence. He was not deterred by the opinions of others; he saw what he saw and grasped it. He did not produce it deliberately; his unique vision brought it into economic existence. In a very real sense, he created what he discovered.

The creative aspect of alert discovery deserves to be emphasized. It seems plausible to attribute the finders-keepers ethic to the insight that the discovered object owes its very existence, as it were, to the discoverer. Had he not discovered it, that object would, for all *human* intents and purposes, be nonexistent; it would not figure in anyone's plans, purposes, or evaluations. An object produced out of the producer's owned resources is considered the just property of the producer because it *is* those resources, simply in different form; the pie *is* the sum of the ingredients out of which it has been baked. But a discovered object has been created, as it were, ex nihilo; its discoverer is considered its owner, not because he owned the inputs from which it has been produced but precisely because it has *not* been produced out of inputs. The discovered object has been brought into existence from nonexistence, simply through its having been discovered. Its discoverer is, in an ethically relevant sense, its creator.

The person into whose lap falls a valuable object has *not* created that object (assuming that others notice its fall just as soon as that person himself does). He is simply the location where sheer, blind luck has placed that object. The person who, owning resources, has deliberately employed them to produce output has not created that object out of nothing; he has deliberately fashioned it out of owned inputs. The discoverer of an object, available to but unnoticed by everyone else, has, in the relevant sense, created that object out of nothing, simply by virtue of the alertness of his personality. That alertness links the discovered object indissolubly with his personality; commonplace ethics finds this link sufficiently convincing to place the discovery in an ethical box entirely distinct from that labeled "windfall gain."

THE DISCOVERY CHARACTER OF PURE PROFIT

The arbitrage theory of profit, which we identified earlier with Ludwig von Mises, permits us to see entrepreneurial profit as a wholly discovered gain. Both the economic problem of profit and the ethical problem of profit dissolve once one recognizes the discovered character of pure profit. Profits, we found, cannot conceivably arise in equilibrium conditions; this is because equilibrium is, by construction, a state in which nothing (that is relevant to the analysis) remains to be discovered. Profit arises strictly in disequilibrium precisely because disequilibrium conditions are the directly implied consequences of as yet ungrasped opportunities "waiting," as it were, to be discovered. The appearance of an arbitrage opportunity between two markets is simply the manifestation of the failure of those selling in the low-priced market to be aware of buyers in the other market who are prepared to pay more; of the failure of those buying in the high-priced market to be aware of sellers in the other market who are prepared to sell for less. These failures in mutual awareness constitute an as yet undiscovered opportunity for pure profit. The entrepreneur who notices the price gap is making the relevant discovery. In grasping the profit constituted by this price gap he is, by his superior alertness, bringing into existence and into reality something of which no one was aware. It seems intuitively appealing to see the entrepreneur as the just owner of what he has discovered, not because he has provided a productive service, not because he claims the benefit conferred by pure luck, but because he is the finder, the creator of what he has discovered, and is thus entitled to be its keeper.

Our assertion that discovery-generated profit is not to be understood as the market value of a productive service provided by the entrepreneur perhaps may be challenged as an unnecessary complication. It perhaps may be argued that, even if one grants the crucial role of discovery in generating profit, this need not prevent us from seeing profit as a factor income. So that all that is required in order to understand pure profit within the traditional, Clarkian scheme is to recognize its emergence as due to deployment of a newly identified factor, the entrepreneurial propensity to discover. There is no need, it may be held, to justify pure profit in terms of a finders-keepers (i.e., a creators-keepers) ethic. Pure profit may be justified, surely, as being simply the additional value we can attribute to a factor service furnished by a particular class of factor owners, that is, to the service of discovery provided by entrepreneurs. We believe this argument to be faulty; it is *not* possible, we maintain, to treat entrepreneurial discovery as a productive factor.[37]

37. For further discussion of this point see Israel M. Kirzner, *Perception, Opportunity, and Profit* (Chicago: University of Chicago Press, 1985), pp. 187–88; and my *Discovery and the Capitalist Process* (Chicago: University of Chicago Press, 1985), pp. 27–28.

The key point is that, by its very nature (following from the sharp distinction drawn above between pure discovery and deliberate search), the pure propensity to make discoveries—or alertness—*is not capable of being deliberately deployed*. If one focuses on any such deployable propensity, in fact one must not be thinking of pure discovery at all but of a kind of deliberate search. In the market context pure entrepreneurship is not for hire—because if "entrepreneurial" services are, in fact, the object of sellers' offer to sell and buyers' offer to buy, then clearly the true entrepreneurs *are those doing the buying*—the services they are buying are not the relevant entrepreneurial services at all. It is these buyers' alert discovery (of the worthwhileness of deploying the services they are buying) which constitutes the element of pure discovery in the situation. To put the matter somewhat differently, an entrepreneur never perceives his alertness, his discovery potential, *as a valuable, available factor able to command incremental value*. Either he already perceives the available incremental value or he does not. (If he perceives the existence of this incremental value but must now search to ascertain the precise route to its realization, what we have is the *already* perceived opportunity of *producing* valuable knowledge through search, not a potential pure discovery at all.) If he does not yet perceive the availability of any incremental value, there is nothing, in the range of deliberate actions available to him, which promises any such gain at all. An engineer asked to identify the productive agents "needed for" the production of a product may certainly list, as one of these agents, an intangible such as "knowledge." But he will not list "initiative," or "awareness of the opportunity to produce the product," because the very notion of what is needed in order to produce a product presupposes the *prospect* (based, obviously, on an *already* existing initiative, on an *already* possessed awareness of the productive possibilities) of producing (if the listed necessary productive ingredients are forthcoming).

It is for these reasons that the pure profit perceived and grasped by the successful entrepreneur cannot be justified as simply the market value of a special kind of productive service he was able to provide. The notion of a market value (which presupposes sellers knowing they can provide the service they propose to sell and buyers knowing the service is available for purchase) is simply not applicable to pure discovery (to which we have seen the pure profit must be traced).

FURTHER REFLECTIONS ON THE
DISCOVERED NATURE OF PURE PROFIT

This insight into the discovered nature of pure profit is closer to the Schumpeterian than to the Knightian view of profit, but it permits us to see something not so easily seen in the Schumpeterian view. The difference between the Misesian view and that of Knight is a decisive one. Although for both profit is a disequilibrium phenomenon associated strictly with the open-ended uncertainty of an unexpectedly changing world, it emerges quite differently for each of them. For Knight it emerges because the world has changed in a way that was expected by nobody, including the profit-winning entrepreneur; his profit *is* in the nature of a windfall. For Mises, on the other hand, profit is won through the superior vision of the entrepreneur, through his power to *transcend* the uncertainty which has misled other market participants to undervalue present resources.[38] The relation between Misesian profit and Schumpeterian profit is a more subtle one. For Schumpeter profit is deliberately created as the pioneering, innovating entrepreneur disturbs the somnolent calm of the existing routine. This disequilibrating activity consists in acts of creativity, or at any rate, in introducing into practice the creative novelties thought up by others. (Schumpeter labeled the entrepreneurial process the "perennial gale of creative destruction.")[39] So that one might be tempted to apply a creation ethic to Schumpeterian profits, too. We must not, however, forget that Schumpeter insisted that it is no part of the function of entrepreneurial leadership "to 'find' or to 'create' new possibilities. They are always present, abundantly accumulated by all sorts of people. Often they are also generally known and being discussed by scientific and

38. I have sometimes been (justifiably) criticized for making it seem as if the Misesian entrepreneur can win profits but never suffer losses. The superior vision of the entrepreneur sees profit opportunities; this explains profits but does not account for losses. The truth is, of course, that losses arise in exactly the same context as do profits, namely, when entrepreneurs, acting in an uncertain world, act to grasp what they think they see. Those who correctly see what others have not seen make profits. Those who "see" what, in fact, is not there to be seen (so that they buy resources at prices not justified by subsequent output values) suffer entrepreneurial losses. It is because we recognize that entrepreneurs are *interested* in making profits rather than losses that we are unable to treat losses and profits, as Knight does, as being wholly symmetrical.

39. Schumpeter, *Capitalism, Socialism and Democracy* (1950), p. 87.

literary writers. In other cases there is nothing to discover about them because they are quite obvious."[40] Clearly, it would be difficult to apply a finders-keepers ethic to this kind of picture of the entrepreneurial function. On the other hand, the arbitrage view of profit is not inconsistent with the notion of innovative production possibilities. Earlier discussion of this view of profit by the present writer have sometimes been misunderstood in this regard. The emphasis placed on the superior vision of the entrepreneur has been interpreted as denying him genuine creativity, since that which can be seen presumably exists, in *some* sense, before it has been noticed. For similar reasons, critics often wish to emphasize the inherent unknowability of the future; the future, they insist, is *not* to be considered as a rolled-up tapestry to be gradually unrolled as time passes but as something that is being continually created out of nothing in the course of the events and decisions which make up the flowing sequence of human history. They are thus unhappy with the arbitrage view on the grounds that it appears to deny this inherent unknowability and inescapable uncertainty of the future. How can we ascribe to the entrepreneur the capacity of seeing into the future when the future is not yet "there" to be seen? If we insist on viewing the entrepreneur as arbitrageur, are we not thereby suppressing the entrepreneur's role as innovator and creator of new products, new techniques, and new ideas?

Our view is that while entrepreneurship may very well (and in the real world certainly very frequently does) manifest itself in acts of innovative and technical creativity, the economic significance of such acts is yet to be seen in the strictly arbitrage aspect of such activity. The innovator is entrepreneurial in that he believes he has discovered a new way of deploying inputs—a way that will reveal the present market as undervaluing these inputs. The creativity we have emphasized in regard to entrepreneurial profit grasping consists not in the concrete innovative creations through which profit opportunities are identified and grasped but in the circumstance through which these innovative creations compel us to recognize how the market has (in regard to these innovative possibilities) undervalued the relevant inputs. It is the discovery of a price gap which others have failed to see which makes up, for the pure theory of entrepreneurial profit, the relevant creative aspect. So long as one is confined (as one is within the Schumpeterian framework) to recognizing entrepreneurial

40. Schumpeter, *The Theory of Economic Development* (1934), p. 88.

creativity only insofar as it is manifested in changed techniques of production, one's attention is deflected from the pure discovery element contained in every successful entrepreneurial venture.

It is true that the future is not a rolled-up piece of tapestry. Rather it
is a tapestry that is being continually woven by the actions of individuals who are able to choose freely. Yet it should be clear that the successful entrepreneur, who located a new store in an area he believes will
shortly become rather heavily populated, is in fact "seeing" the future.
Although that future must be created by the further choices of many
freely choosing persons, the entrepreneur has "seen" it—more correctly
than others have. His purchase of the land on which to build his store
has taken advantage of the market's failure to value that land at its full
value—in terms of the services it can and will provide to this larger future
population.

In talking of "more correct" or "less correct" entrepreneurial vision,
in referring to noticing opportunities others have failed to notice, we are
not, of course, attributing any kind of *moral culpability* to those who have
failed to see the future correctly. If we use the term "error" to describe the
failure of others to see what the successful entrepreneur sees, this term
is used strictly as a metaphor. No one can be "blamed" for not foreseeing
the future course of events correctly. But, on the other hand, we must not
deny "credit" to the entrepreneur who *does* correctly see the future. He is
not simply the lucky beneficiary of a chance turn of events. He really did
guess the future correctly, not perhaps with certainty but with sufficient
conviction to inspire him to undertake his venture. When that venture
turns out to have been a profitable one, we are entitled to describe the
successful entrepreneur as having made a discovery; he should, for many
of us, be entitled to keep that which he found.

TOWARD A BROADER THEORY OF DISTRIBUTIVE JUSTICE[41]

Although this chapter has focused narrowly on the ethical acceptability of
pure profit, its central insights point to a broader issue, that of distributive justice in general. We conclude this chapter by briefly drawing attention to this broader context. The truth is that the traditional approach to

41. For an elaboration of the broader agenda appealed for in the text see, in general,
my book *Discovery, Capitalism and Distributive Justice* (1989); see especially chap. 7 for
certain qualifications to the ideas set forth perhaps too unequivocally in this chapter.

distributive justice has suffered, we maintain, by failing to incorporate considerations relating to the ethical status of discovered gains. Once we recognize the nature of discovery, we appreciate that the total "pie" which is being "distributed" is, in fact, a pie the very size of which is being discovered, in fact created, during and through the very process of distribution. By this we do not mean simply that (as is, of course, well recognized in the literature of distributive justice) the size of the total social output, being a function of the incentive system, is itself determined, to some extent, by the distributive pattern adopted. Instead, we are referring to the circumstance that a significant proportion of production activity is inseparably intertwined with the pure discovery engaged in by market participants in their entrepreneurial roles. Real world production is, almost inevitably, partly a matter of entrepreneurial vision in identifying where resources can be obtained, what products are worthwhile producing, what techniques will be most successful and most economical, and so forth. The size of total output and, in particular, the size of the total complex of available resources is something that cannot, even in principle, be thought of in isolation from the system of rewards assigned to entrepreneurial discovery.

There never is a "given pie," or even a given complex of resources (from which to "bake the pie") available to society. So that the notion of "distribution" (and hence "distributive justice"), a notion presuming something "there" to be distributed, is a highly problematic one.[42] The notion of a given pie or given available resources rules out any possible query as to whether, perhaps, any of the output attributable to the resources ought to accrue to him who *created* the resources ex nihilo, as it were. After all, the resources are seen as somehow "given," before the issue of distributive justice makes its entry.

It is our position, indeed, that in confining attention to the issue of how given output, or given resources, are to be justly distributed, theorists of economic justice have illegitimately blocked from consideration a most important series of possibilities. These possibilities arise out of the circumstance that, in our real world of open-ended uncertainty, an enormous contribution to the total size of output is made by those whose alertness has brought to society's attention the availability of resources,

---

42. For an earlier criticism of the notion of distribution, based on considerations not emphasized here, see Mises, *Human Action* (1949), p. 255.

the availability of techniques, and the desirability to consumers of specific kinds of output. Appropriate rewards (and incentives) for this kind of contribution requires that we step outside the framework of a given available set of goodies that must be shared out. We require a perspective which recognizes that, quite apart from the attribution of these goodies to relevant inputs, there is also the primordial issue of how it came to be discovered at all, that these inputs and worthwhile output possibilities were, in fact, available. The theory of pure profit outlined in this chapter finds its place in such a broader-gauged approach to economic justice.

INSTITUTIONS

THE PRIMACY OF ENTREPRENEURIAL DISCOVERY

INTRODUCTION

An economically successful society is one whose members pursue the "right" set of coordinated actions. The "ideal" economic organization for a society consists, therefore, of the pattern of institutions and incentives that will promote the pursuit of the "correct" set of actions by its members. Economic theory has, in general terms, been able to enunciate the conditions to be fulfilled if a set of actions is to be "correct." These optimality conditions are, not surprisingly, governed basically by the available resources and technological possibilities, on the one hand, and, on the other, by the pattern of consumers' tastes. The "economic problem" faced by society is then often viewed as being somehow to ensure that the various economic agents in society indeed undertake those actions that will, all together, satisfy the conditions for optimality. While this formulation is 'in some respects not quite satisfactory, it will serve reasonably well in introducing my discussion of the role of entrepreneurial discovery.

PATTERNS OF ECONOMIC ORGANIZATION

In theory there exist a variety of possible patterns of economic organization for society, ranging from completely centralized decision making at one extreme, through an array of "mixed" systems, to pure laissez-faire. Several related observations may be made.

First, *all* these possible systems of economic organization involve making *decisions*—with greater or lesser degree of decentralization.

Second, these decisions will necessarily involve an *entrepreneurial element*—regardless of the degree of decentralization sought.

Third, one dimension along which the effectiveness of each of the alternative patterns of societal economic organization will need to be

From *Discovery and the Capitalist Process* (Chicago and London: The University of Chicago Press, 1985), 15–39. Reprinted by permission; the original source is *Prime Mover of Progress: The Entrepreneur in Capitalism and Socialism,* ed. A. Seldon (Institute of Economic Affairs, 1980). First published by the Institute of Economic Affairs, London, 1980.

assessed will therefore be that of measuring the *success with which entre-preneurial activity can be evoked in that pattern of organization.*

These observations call for some elaboration.

The Entrepreneurial Element in Decisions

I have asserted that decisions necessarily involve an entrepreneurial element. What do I mean by the "entrepreneurial element" in decision?

The *non*entrepreneurial element in decisions is easy to pin down. In most textbooks of microeconomics, this nonentrepreneurial element is often made to appear the *only* element in decision making. The non-entrepreneurial element in decision making consists of the task of cal-culation. A decision maker is, in this context, seen as seeking to achieve an array of goals (or to "maximize" some goal or utility function) with the scarce resources available. In seeking to arrive at the optimal decision, the decision maker must therefore calculate the solution to what, in the jargon of economics, is called a "constrained maximization problem."[1] Correct decision making, in this nonentrepreneurial sense, means cor-rect calculation; faulty decision making is equivalent to mistakes in arithmetic.

This nonentrepreneurial aspect does not have to assume initial omni-science; it is entirely possible for the incompletely informed decision maker to calculate (i.e., to decide) how much knowledge to acquire.[2] But this nonentrepreneurial aspect does presume, at least, that the decision maker has a clear perception of the scope of his ignorance and of how this ignorance can be reduced; in a sense he knows precisely what it is that he does not know. And it is here that we can recognize the scope for the other element in decision making, the entrepreneurial element.

For the truth is that the calculative aspect is far from being the most obvious and most important element in decisions. When a wrong deci-sion has been made, the error is unlikely to have been a mistake in calcu-lation. It is far more likely to have resulted from an erroneous assessment of the situation—in being overoptimistic about the availability of means or about the outcomes to be expected of given actions; in pessimistically underestimating the means at one's disposal or the results to be expected from specific courses of action. Making the "right" decision, therefore, calls for far more than the correct mathematical calculation; it calls for a shrewd and wise assessment of the realities (both present and future) within the context of which the decision must be taken. It is with this aspect of decision that we will be dealing in analyzing the entrepreneurial element in subsequent discussion.

No matter how centralized or decentralized a decision-making system may be, its decision makers will regret their decisions if the entrepreneurship embodied in these decisions is of poor quality. Whatever the institutional context, a correct decision calls for reading the situation correctly; it calls for recognizing the true possibilities and for refusing to be deluded into seeing possibilities where none exist; it requires that true possibilities should not be overlooked, but that true limitations not be overlooked either. It is therefore my contention that alternative systems of economic organization have to be appraised, in part, with an eye to the respective success with which they can evoke entrepreneurship of high quality.

Entrepreneurship in Received Economic Theory

It is by now fairly well recognized that standard economic theory has developed along lines that virtually exclude the entrepreneurial role. This has largely been a result of the tendencies, long dominant in neoclassical economics, to exclude all elements of unexpected change, to focus attention almost exclusively on equilibrium states of affairs, and to treat individual decisions as immune from the hazards of error.[3]

As Frank Knight of Chicago explained many years ago, in a world from which the troublesome demon of unexpected change has been exorcized, it is not difficult to imagine away any need for entrepreneurship.[4] In such a world we can reasonably expect decision makers, given sufficient time, to have come somehow to perceive the world correctly. To decide, in such a world, involves nothing more than to perform those calculations we have described as constituting the nonentrepreneurial element in decision making.

In a world of unchanging certainty, where the future unfolding of events is anticipated with assurance and accuracy, selecting the optimal course of action is not a task that challenges the entrepreneurial qualities of vision, daring, and determination. Indeed, it is difficult to imagine how such a world could ever fail to be in anything but a state of optimality. To be sure, such a world must be envisaged as bounded by resource scarcities. But it is difficult to imagine how anyone in such a world—given these resource limitations, and given the accepted structure of ownership—can ascribe any perceived shortcomings to faulty decision making. Such an imaginary world is not paradise, but it can hardly fail to be the closest to paradise imaginable within the given limitations of supply and the given institutional framework.

When this theoretical framework is uncritically adopted, it becomes easy to fall into the error of tackling economic problems with nonentrepreneurial analytical tools. It becomes natural to assume that the correct decisions are being made, from the viewpoint of the relevant decision makers; that the problems encountered are to be attributed to inadequate resources or to a faulty institutional structure. What is overlooked, in such treatments, is the possibility that a great deal of want and misery are the result of nothing less mundane than *sheer error* on the part of decision makers, that is, of decisions made that, from the decision maker's own point of view, are suboptimal. That such errors may and do occur requires us to recognize scope for entrepreneurial error, for decisions made with faulty assessments of the facts of the world, future as well as present, upon which the decision is to impinge.

Certainly, in a perspective which simply assumes that decision makers, in all circumstances, regardless of institutional environment, inevitably and unerringly find their way to the correct decisions there is little point in inquiring into the circumstances that are most conducive to alert, entrepreneurially successful decision making. It is a fundamental insight—upon which, I believe, the proceedings of today's colloquium are being conducted—that simply to assume correct decision making is to beg far too large a fraction of the essential question confronting us. We begin, in other words, with a healthy awareness that the world is very far from being the best of all possible worlds—even from being the best of those worlds possible with available resources and within existing institutional environments.

It is from this beginning that we are led to appreciate the primordial importance of our question: What institutional circumstances or arrangements, which system of economic and political institutions, can be expected most successfully to evoke those qualities of entrepreneurial alertness upon which the quest for optimality in decision making necessarily depends?

Entrepreneurship as a Scarce Resource

It might perhaps be argued that, important as the quality of entrepreneurship undoubtedly is, it does not involve any really new considerations beyond those usually taken into account in studying the conditions for optimality. All that has been established in the preceding pages, it may be held, is merely that we must bear in mind the need for a special resource, entrepreneurship, which has often been incorrectly taken for granted. Instead of viewing entrepreneurship as exercised flawlessly, tirelessly, and universally, we must begin to recognize that it is a scarce, valuable resource of which our economic models had better begin to take careful account. But all this, it may perhaps be maintained, does not justify our demand that we transcend the standard maximizing model of decision making. All that has to be done, it may be contended, is to incorporate into our list of required resources the flow of required entrepreneurial services and to ensure that available stocks of such service flows be used optimally. Social optimality, it may be contended, will now be judged within a broader framework in which there is recognition of both the demand for, and availability of, the service of entrepreneurial vision.

More particularly, in respect of the question I have described as primordial, it may be objected that it is fundamentally inappropriate to inquire into the comparative effectiveness of alternative institutional frameworks, for the evocation of entrepreneurship. It will be objected that, since entrepreneurship is a resource no different, for pure theory, from other resources, any comparison among alternative social economic systems must begin with the assumption of some *given*, initial stock of that resource. It will not do to begin a comparison between different economic systems by suggesting that the very pattern of institutional arrangement may have important implications for the initial size of a particular stock of resource. Different economic systems may certainly differ in the efficiency with which they deploy and allocate given resource supplies; but, it may be argued, if we postulate some given supply of a particular resource in one economic system, there can be no objection in principle to supposing any other system to begin with exactly the same supply of that resource.

My response to this line of argument (and thus my defense of the validity of the central question to be addressed here) rests on the insight that entrepreneurship cannot usefully be treated simply as a resource, similar in principle to the other resources available to an economic system.

THE PRIMACY OF ENTREPRENEURSHIP

What is important is to insist that entrepreneurial alertness differs in fundamental respects from the resources ordinarily discussed in decision making. These differences will justify my contention that there may be important differences between different economic systems in respect to their success in harnessing entrepreneurial alertness for making error-free decisions.

A cardinal quality of a potential resource, in the economists' analysis of decisions, is that the decision maker can deploy it, if he so chooses, in specific processes geared toward the achievement of specified goals. What the decision maker has to decide is whether to deploy a particular resource, and how and in what quantity to deploy it. He must decide whether to use it at all, and whether to use it for one purpose or for another. The quality of entrepreneurial alertness cannot be discussed in these terms.

Entrepreneurial Alertness Is Not a Conventional Economic Resource. If an entrepreneur's discovery of a lucrative arbitrage opportunity galvanizes him into immediate action to capture the perceived gain, it will not do to describe the situation as one in which the entrepreneur has "decided" to use his alertness to capture this gain. He has not "deployed" his hunch for a specific purpose; *rather, his hunch has propelled him to make his entrepreneurial purchase and sale.* The entrepreneur never sees his hunches as potential inputs about which he must decide whether they are to be used. To decide *not* to use a hunch means—if it means anything at all—that a businessman realizes that he has no hunch (or that his hunch is that it will be best to be inactive for the time being). If one has become sufficiently alerted to the existence of an opportunity—that is, one has become sufficiently convinced regarding the facts of a situation—it becomes virtually impossible to imagine *not* taking advantage of the opportunity so discovered.

Entrepreneurship is thus not something to be deliberately introduced into a potential production process: it is, instead, something primordial to the very idea of a potential production process awaiting possible implementation. Entrepreneurial alertness is not an ingredient *to be deployed* in decision making; it is rather something in which *the decision itself is embedded* and without which *it* would be unthinkable.

It is true that *knowledge* (e.g., in the sense of technical expertise) may be deployed. A person may certainly decide that it does not pay to use his knowledge in a specific manner. Or he may decide that it does pay to use it. Here knowledge is a resource at the disposal of the entrepreneur. He is conscious of his knowledge as something to be used or not. But this refers only to knowledge of how to achieve specific goals, not knowledge of whether it is worthwhile to attempt to achieve a goal at all. A distinguishing feature of entrepreneurial insight consists precisely in the absence of awareness by its possessor that he does possess it. A would-be entrepreneur may agonize over whether to embark on a particular venture. His trauma arises not from deciding whether to use his entrepreneurial vision; it stems from his unsureness of what he "sees."

Entrepreneurial Opportunity May Be Blocked by Lack of a Resource but Not of Insight. Again, it is integral to a necessary resource (in the usual sense) that a decision maker may feel its lack. A decision maker may say, "I have all the ingredients necessary to produce ice cream, except sugar." The opportunity to achieve a particular goal is blocked only by lack of some necessary resource. But it is absurd to imagine a decision maker saying (on a commercial venture about the profitability of which he is profoundly skeptical) that he sees a profitable opportunity the exploitation of which is blocked only by lack of entrepreneurial insight. It would be absurd because this entrepreneur is (correctly or otherwise) convinced that he does *not* see any profitable opportunity in this venture at all.

To repeat what was stated earlier, all this does not apply to *technical* knowledge which an entrepreneur may know exists and which he knows he lacks. It is certainly possible for a decision maker to say, "I have all the ingredients for ice cream, but I lack the relevant recipe." He may know that a recipe exists, and that it is a good one, without knowing what it is. But for a man to refrain from a particular productive venture because he is not convinced that it is sound—even if it turns out that he was wrong—is not to refrain from it because he has been unable to lay hands on the appropriate vision; it is to refrain because he is convinced (rightly or wrongly) that, with respect to this venture, the *best entrepreneurial alertness finds nothing to be seen.*

Entrepreneurial Alertness Is Not a Potential Stock Available to Society. It is because of this inherent *primacy* of entrepreneurial alertness and vision (as contrasted with deployable resources)[5] that we cannot avoid the question to be addressed in this paper—the varying degrees of success with which alternative economic systems can inspire entrepreneurial alertness. We do not view the *potential* stock of entrepreneurial alertness in a society as some quantity "available to be used by society." (Were this the case one could proceed to inquire how different systems variously succeed in most effectively using this uniformly *given* stock.) Instead we recognize the quality of entrepreneurial alertness as something which *somehow emerges into view at the precise moment when decisions have to be made.* As we shall see, this opens up the important possibility that the institutional framework within which decisions are made may itself vitally affect the alertness out of which those decisions emerge.

THE COST OF ENTREPRENEURSHIP

This line of argument points to a further related insight: *entrepreneurship is costless.* In using any quantity of a scarce resource (in the usual sense of that term) the decision maker is always viewed as choosing between alternative goals to which the scarce resource might be applied. The goal forgone is the cost of using the resource for its present purpose. In the case of entrepreneurial alertness, however, a decision maker never considers whether to apply some given potential alertness to the discovery of opportunity A or opportunity B. As already argued, the opportunities (or any one of them) are either perceived or not perceived; alertness is not something about which a decision can be made *not* to deploy it. (In this we distinguish sharply between pure alertness, on the one hand, and "deployable" scarce inputs that may be useful in decision making, for example, time, technical knowledge, managerial expertise, on the other.) To recognize that opportunity A exists need not preclude simultaneously recognizing that opportunity B exists.

Conversely, to fail to recognize that opportunity A exists cannot be explained in terms of the high cost of so recognizing it; if opportunity A has not been recognized, the failure represents some shortcoming in entrepreneurial alertness, not the outcome of a decision to deploy it for the discovery of other opportunities.

Faulty Entrepreneurship Means Alertness Remains Untapped. That in the real world we encounter innumerable instances of faulty and inadequate entrepreneurship must be interpreted, therefore, not as evidence of the absolute scarcity of entrepreneurial alertness (with the existing stock of it having been applied elsewhere), but as evidence that the alertness costlessly available has somehow remained latent and untapped. The central question then looms even more significantly than ever: What institutional frameworks are best suited to tap the reservoir of entrepreneurial alertness which is certainly present—in potentially inexhaustible supply—among the members of society?

THE QUALITIES OF ENTREPRENEURSHIP—
THE UNCHARTED FRONTIER

Although, as Ludwig von Mises pointed out long ago,[6] *all* individual action is entrepreneurial, and although I have described entrepreneurial alertness as in principle inexhaustible, I have also been careful to notice that potential alertness may be (and so often is) untapped and inert. We know, certainly, that individuals display vastly different degrees of entrepreneurial alertness. Some are quick to spot as yet unnoticed opportunities, others notice only the opportunities revealed by the discoveries of others. In some societies, in some climates, among some groups, it appears that entrepreneurial alertness is keener than in others. Studies of economic development have come to recognize that the qualities called for in successful entrepreneurship are not uniformly distributed and certainly do not appear to be in infinite supply.

It would certainly be desirable to be able to identify with precision those human qualities, personal and psychological, which are to be credited with successful entrepreneurial alertness, drive, and initiative. It would be most valuable to be able to study the short-run and long-run impact upon the development of these "entrepreneurial" qualities of alternative social, economic, and institutional frameworks. It would be important to know, for example, if a comfortable sense of security discourages noticing new opportunities. If "independence" or "economic freedom" encourages entrepreneurial drive and initiative, this would be significant information. Likewise, does "competition" encourage alertness to new opportunities?

Research on Psychological Aspects Is Desirable. Up to the present, little systematic work appears to have been done on these questions. Observations made are likely to be based on "common sense" or on anecdotal foundations. It is certainly necessary to go beyond this elementary stage. Indeed, an important frontier of knowledge, largely unexplored, appears to consist of those aspects of psychology, such as temperament, thirst for adventure, ambition, and imagination, that are likely to throw light on the development of the qualities of entrepreneurship and on the ways alternative institutional arrangements may affect such development. It is to be expected and very much to be desired that research should proceed on this frontier during the years ahead.

Applied entrepreneurial theorists should look to this research with considerable interest; it is to be hoped that their own needs and interests will help to define the directions along which this research proceeds and to formulate the questions it seeks to answer.

My tentative observations here will suggest that a number of important general statements can be made even before we enjoy the systematic knowledge I anticipate will emerge from research into the psychology of entrepreneurship.

THE INCENTIVE FOR ENTREPRENEURIAL DISCOVERY

Were entrepreneurship a scarce resource in the usual sense, economists would have no difficulty in spelling out, at least in general terms, the kinds of incentives capable of coaxing out the desired quantity of entrepreneurial discovery. Potential entrepreneurs would have to be offered rewards that more than offset the costs of exercising entrepreneurship. This, after all, is how economists understand the role of incentives; this is how the price system is perceived to offer, via the resource market, the incentives required to stimulate resource supply and to allocate it among alternative uses. But the special aspects of entrepreneurship render this kind of incentive system inappropriate to entrepreneurial alertness and discovery.

Since entrepreneurship is costless (no incentive at all is needed, in principle, to activate entrepreneurial vision), and since on the other hand entrepreneurial vision is not uniformly and continuously "switched on" to take advantage of all opportunities, we are very much concerned to identify what it is that *does* "switch on" entrepreneurial vision and discovery.

With scarce resources in the usual sense, it is meaningful to talk of the kind of incentive that needs to be "offered" to owners to stimulate supply. We can imagine, that is, that some entrepreneur already has a fairly clear picture of the results to be obtained from deploying the relevant resource in some particular line of production. We can then talk of whether it is worthwhile for him to offer the resource price required to overcome the cost of supplying the resource. The point is that the notion of a needed incentive, in this usual sense, presupposes the clear perception, even before the deployment of the service, of its usefulness in production.

As has already been emphasized, such a perception is ruled out by definition in the case of entrepreneurial alertness. No one "hires" or "offers incentives" to the entrepreneur. To hire an "entrepreneur" *is to be an entrepreneur*—simply shifting the problem back to the incentives that might galvanize *this* latter entrepreneur into action. It cannot be sufficiently emphasized that (*a*) until an opportunity *has* been discovered, no one knows how much to offer as an incentive for its discovery; and (*b*) once the opportunity has been discovered, it is no longer relevant to inquire into the springs of entrepreneurship—since it will already have been exercised.

The Promise of Pure Gain Is Entrepreneurial Incentive. There seems one statement, however, that can be made about the incentives required to excite entrepreneurial alertness. It is a statement which sees such incentives as having little in common with the character of and role for incentives in the usual sense. It can be stated with considerable confidence *that human beings tend to notice that which it is in their interest to notice.* Human beings notice "opportunities" rather than "situations." They notice, that is, concatenations of events, realized or prospective, which offer *pure gain.* It is not the abstract *concatenation* of these events which evokes notice; it is the circumstance that these events offer the promise of pure *gain*—broadly understood to include fame, power, prestige, even the opportunity to serve a cause or to help other individuals.

Two individuals walk through the same city block teeming with hundreds of people in a variety of garbs, with shops of different kinds, advertising signs for many goods, buildings of different architectural styles. Each of these individuals will notice a different set of items out of these countless impressions impinging on his senses. What is noticed by the one is not what is noticed by the other. The difference will not merely be one of chance. It is a difference that can be ascribed, in part, to the *interests* of the two individuals. Each tends to notice what is of interest *to him.*

A difference between the price of apples traded in one part of the market and the price of apples traded in another part may pass unnoticed. It is less likely to pass unnoticed if it constitutes a phenomenon of interest to its potential discoverer. A concatenation of possible events (in this case the possible purchase of apples at a lower price, to be followed by their sale at a higher price) may not be noticed at all unless the potential discoverer stands to gain from the price differential. *In order to "switch on" the alertness of a potential discoverer to socially significant opportunities, they must offer gain to the potential discoverer himself.*

This kind of incentive—the incentive that somehow converts a socially desirable opportunity into a personally gainful one—is not needed to ensure pursuit of that opportunity *after* its discovery. Once the socially desirable opportunity has been perceived, individuals may be persuaded (or threatened) to act on that opportunity simply by suitable choice of reward (or punishment). The kind of incentive here under discussion is that required to reveal opportunities that have *until now been perceived by no one at all.*

PERFORMANCE OF ALTERNATIVE ECONOMIC SYSTEMS UNDER ENTREPRENEURIAL INCENTIVE

How do alternative socioeconomic systems appear likely to perform in terms of this kind of incentive? We will consider a free market economy, a centralized (socialist) economic system, and a regulated market economy. Our concern is solely with the comparative scope they hold for entrepreneurial incentives.

Entrepreneurship in the Free Market

The free market is characterized most distinctively, for our purpose, *by freedom of entrepreneurial entry.* Given some accepted system of property rights, individual participants are free to enter into mutually beneficial trades with each other. Production decisions involve judgments about buying inputs on factor markets in order to sell output in product markets. Market prices therefore guide the decisions which determine the allocation of society's resources among alternative lines of output. Were the market to have attained full equilibrium, it may, under specific assumptions, be described as having attained an optimal allocation of resources.[7] But (especially in view of ambiguities surrounding the interpretation of "social optimum" and of the possibility that not all the specific assumptions will be fulfilled in practice) this is *not* the interesting proposition—even were it reasonable to view the free market economy as in continuous equilibrium.

What is important about the market economy is that unexploited opportunities for reallocating resources from one (low market valued) use to another of higher value offer the opportunity for pure entrepreneurial gain. A misallocation of resources occurs because, so far, market participants have not noticed the price discrepancy involved. This price discrepancy presents itself as an opportunity to be exploited by its discoverer. *The most impressive aspect of the market system is the tendency for such opportunities to be discovered.*

The Discovery Process of the Market. It is in a sense similar to this that Hayek has referred to the competitive market process as a "discovery procedure."[8] The essence is not that market prices offer spontaneously developed "signals" able faultlessly to coordinate millions of independently made decisions. (This would occur only in equilibrium; in disequilibrium the prices which prevail would *not* so perfectly coordinate decisions.) It is rather that the disequilibrium situation—in which prices do not offer the correct signals—is one which offers entrepreneurs the incentives required for the discrepancies to be noticed and corrected. In the course of this entrepreneurial process, new products may be introduced, new qualities of existing products may be developed, new methods of production may be ventured, new forms of industrial organization, financing, marketing, or tackling risk may be developed. All the ceaseless churning and agitation of the market is to be understood as the consequence of the never-ending discovery process of which the market consists.

Entrepreneurship in the Socialized Economy

Little work has been done on the analysis of entrepreneurship in fully socialized societies. The great debate on economic calculation under socialism carried on between the two world wars in many respects revolved around precisely this issue but was couched in terms which unfortunately permitted its central importance to be overlooked. The attempts by Oskar Lange (of Poland) and others to show how a socialist system could be set up that would permit decentralized decisions by managers of socialist enterprises on the basis of centrally promulgated "prices," along the same lines as the price system under the free market, unfortunately completely overlooked the entrepreneurial character of the price system.

Lange relied on the "parametric function" of prices, that is, on that aspect of prices which permits each decision maker to treat them as equilibrium prices to which he must passively adjust himself.[9] But in this view of the market (and hence of the possibility of a socialist "price" system), Lange failed to recognize that the distinctive aspect of the market is the manner in which prices *change*, that is, that market prices are in fact treated nonparametrically. It is one thing to imagine that socialist managers can be motivated to obey rules on the basis of centrally promulgated "prices"; it is quite another to take it for granted that the *non*parametric function of price (in which, that is, price is *not* being treated as a datum but is subject to change by individual market participants), a function which depends entirely on entrepreneurial discovery of *new* opportunities for pure profit, can be simulated in a system from which the private entrepreneurial function is completely absent.

Alertness by "Price" Planners and Plant Managers. Under a Lange-type system, alertness would be called for at a number of levels. Officials deciding on the "price" structure must do so by what they know about the performance of the economy under earlier "price" structures and by what they anticipate to be the pattern of consumer demand and of resource supply in the period ahead. In promulgating a list of "prices" it is necessary to determine, first of all, the list of commodities and of resource services for which "prices" are to be set. The construction of this list requires an enormous volume of entrepreneurial alertness on the part of these officials. After all, some products should not be produced at all; others very definitely ought to be produced, but officials may be quite ignorant of them or of their urgency. This is of course more particularly likely to be true of new and innovative products and product qualities. But it could occur with any product whatever.

Again, the Lange system would call for alertness by socialist plant managers. They would have to identify sources of resource supply; they would have to notice technological possibilities that may not hitherto have been known, or that, given the old price structure, may not have been economic. They would have to notice the need for and possibility of any number of changes (innovative or otherwise) which changed patterns of tastes, for example, might make worthwhile. There is certainly nothing in Lange's own description of his system to suggest how this might be ensured.

Will Available Options Be Noticed? How? The question the entrepreneurial theorist must ask is not whether, given available known options, the relevant socialist official is operating under an incentive system that will make it personally gainful for him to select the optimal course of action for society. Our question is rather whether there is any assurance that relevant options will in practice be noticed as being available. What might motivate an official to notice an opportunity not yet adopted (but which it might be highly valuable to pursue)? It will not do to suggest that some higher official arrange matters so that when the (lower) official does notice the opportunity he can personally benefit by its adoption. This merely passes our question up the line: What might motivate this higher official to notice the opportunity?—and even to notice its worthwhileness *after* it has been brought to his attention?

We will, for the present, ignore the question of how a newly discovered valuable social opportunity is revealed, even after the event, as having been such. Our question will confine itself to asking how it might be ensured that such social opportunities constitute at the same time privately gainful opportunities for their potential discoverers. It is doubtful in the extreme if ideals such as benevolence or patriotism can be relied upon, in general, to enable a potential discoverer to identify his own personal interest with that of the discovery of an opportunity for a reallocation of resources desirable for society.

We might imagine, of course, a system in which there is not merely decentralization of decision making, in the Lange sense, but also freedom for socialist managers to buy and sell on behalf of the state (when discrepancies among socialist "prices" might have been discovered) and to retain for themselves some fraction of the price differential. If such trading is restricted to those who are already socialist managers, we will have to examine the mechanism of selection of managers to see whether it indeed ensures that those with entrepreneurial skills tend to become socialist managers (since the socialist state would not be permitting others to "prove" their entrepreneurial skills in this way). On the other hand, if entrepreneurial trading is to be open for all (raising, let me of course note, the obvious question of access to society's capital to be risked in such ventures), then clearly we have moved closer and closer toward a "mixed" capitalist system in which private entrepreneurs might be free to seek profits within a system of state-controlled prices (a regulated system which will be briefly considered below).

Individual Decision Makers Cannot Profit under "Market" Socialist Schemes. We may talk of various schemes for "market" socialism along Lange's lines, in which some decisions are left to lower-ranking officials to be made on the basis of centrally designed systems of "prices." No matter how extensive the degree of decentralization thus achieved, however, a critical condition for the socialist quality of the system appears to be that neither at the level of the central design of "prices," nor of individual managers' decisions made on the basis of these "prices" may decisions be made primarily in order that the decision maker can profit personally from errors discovered. Those responsible for designing the system of socialist "prices" are clearly not participants in any entrepreneurial market; their function is to impose "prices" upon the socialist "market."

To imagine that in this socialist "market" freedom of entry for private profit-making entrepreneurial activity is to be permitted is surely to compromise fatally the definition of a socialist economic system. But without such freedom of entrepreneurial entry, market socialism has a fatal flaw: it has not succeeded in identifying any way by which errors, whether of omission or commission, can be systematically avoided by decision makers. It has not identified any way the discovery and avoidance of error redounds directly to the personal benefit of the discoverer. It has not identified how the unsuspectedly inefficient socialist venture might so reveal itself to a socialist decision maker in advance as a threat to his own well-being; it has not identified how the currently undreamed of venture, of critical benefit to society, might reveal itself to a socialist planner as one offering him personal gain.

Incentives to Socialist Managers Deny the Essential Role of Entrepreneurial Discovery. I do not deny the possibility of arranging incentives to socialist managers to produce more, or to produce with a smaller labor force or lower energy consumption. Nor do I even deny the possibility of offering incentives that will reward innovation. Incentives can certainly be structured to reward inventors and innovators of new products and new production techniques. Recent extensive study of innovation in the Soviet Union has, for example, confirmed the significant vitality of the innovative process there (although the process lags more or less behind that in capitalist economies).[10] But to reward managers for meeting or exceeding target output quantities presupposes that *it is already known* that more of these outputs is urgently required by society; to reward managers for introducing a new product is to presume that *it is already known* that this particular new product—or else *any* new product—is socially more important (taking into account the resources required for its production) than the product it replaces; to reward managers for introducing innovative methods of production is to presume that *it is already known* that the additional inputs called for by the new technique are less costly to society than those the technique avoids—or else that *any* change in production technique must be an improvement over those currently employed.

That these matters may already be known is in many instances entirely plausible. But if they *are* assumed already known, we are simply assuming away the need for entrepreneurial discovery. The task is to ensure the discovery—by someone, somewhere, who possesses power to set things into motion—of which products (existing or new) should be produced (and in what quantities), the urgency of which the current conventional wisdom has *failed* to recognize. The problem is to identify techniques of production whose usefulness has up until now *not* been perceived. Not all innovation is socially desirable; not all expansion of lines of output is socially desirable. What is required is an incentive system to convince decision makers that when they discover opportunities others will deny to exist, they (the discoverers) will be the gainers.

Thus, far, in all the discussion of varieties of socialism, of incentive systems and planning theories, I have not seen *this* problem addressed. Nor is it at all apparent how, without fundamentally compromising the essential defining criteria for socialism, it can be solved.

Entrepreneurship in the Regulated Market Economy[11]

Most societies in the modern world have allowed their economic systems to follow neither the pattern of pure socialism nor that of pure capitalism. They consist of market economies that have been circumscribed by more or less extensive systems of state intervention. Convinced that the unhampered market will generate undesirable price structures or undesirable arrays of output qualities, working conditions, or other undesirables, the state intervened, replacing the laissez-faire market by the regulated market. Price ceilings and price and wage floors, transfer of income, imposed safety standards, child labor laws, zoning laws, prohibited industrial integration, prohibited competition, imposed health warnings, compulsory old-age pensions, and prohibited drugs are among the countless controls that possibly well-meaning public officials impose. What is the role of entrepreneurial discovery in the regulated market?

Genuine—but Inhibited—Entrepreneurial Incentive. Despite the controls, regulations, and interventions, there exist in such systems genuine markets for both resource services and consumer products. Although the prices which emerge in regulated markets may have been more or less drastically distorted in the regulatory process, they are (except for directly controlled prices) nonetheless market prices. To the extent that entrepreneurial entry remains free, discrepancies in these prices provide the incentives for entrepreneurs to capture pure profit, leading to a process of entrepreneurial competition acting at all times to modify the existing price structure.

Nevertheless, it is not difficult to perceive the many ways entrepreneurial discovery may come to be inhibited or redirected under regulatory constraints. And regulation raises new and important questions concerning the way the agents of the state (whether legislators or officials in other stages of regulation and its enforcement) come to notice where opportunities for supposedly beneficial regulation may exist. Let us take up these latter questions first.

Knowledge and Discovery Are Absent in Price Setting and Resource Allocation. Government regulation takes the general form of imposed price floors, price ceilings, mandated quality specifications, and similar measures. We will assume that the hope surrounding such government impositions is that they will confine market activities to desired channels and at desired levels. But it is by no means clear how officials will know what prices to set, or if their earlier decisions have been in error. It is not clear how officials will *discover* those opportunities for improving the allocation of resources (which, after all, we can hardly assume to be automatically known at the outset of a regulatory endeavor). The regulator's estimates of the prices consumers are prepared to pay, or of the prices resource owners are prepared to accept, are not *profit-motivated* estimates. But estimates of market demand conditions, or of market supply conditions, that are not profit motivated cannot reflect the powerful, discovery-inspiring incentives of the entrepreneurial quest for profit.

It is, further, not clear how it can be ensured that government officials who perceive market conditions more accurately than others will tend systematically to replace less competent regulators. It is not clear what proxy for entrepreneurial profit and loss there might be that could inspire officials to see personal gain for themselves in successful discovery. What regulators know (or believe they know) at a given moment is presumably only partly correct. No systematic process seems available through which regulators might come to discover what they have not known, especially since they have not known that they enjoy less than complete awareness of relevant situations. *If they do not know what they do not know, how will they know what remains to be discovered?*

Quite apart from the question of the entrepreneurship required to engage in regulation believed to be desirable, we must, in the context of the regulated market economy, also consider the impact of regulation upon the pattern and direction of entrepreneurial discovery in the marketplace. There is a serious likelihood that regulatory constraints may bar the discovery of pure profit opportunities (and thus of possibilities for socially beneficial resource reallocation).

Damaging Effects of Regulatory Controls and Price Ceilings. A good deal of regulation consists in creating *barriers to entry*. Tariffs, licensing requirements, labor legislation, airline regulation, and bank regulation, for example, do not merely limit numbers in particular markets. These kinds of regulatory activity tend to bar entry to entrepreneurs who believe they have discovered profit opportunities in barred areas of the market. Such barriers may, by removing the personal gain which entrepreneurs might have reaped by their discoveries, bring it about that *some opportunities may simply not be discovered by anyone.* An entrepreneur who knows that he will not be able to enter the banking business may simply not notice opportunities in the banking field that might otherwise have seemed obvious to him; those who are already in banking, and who have failed to see these opportunities, may continue to overlook them. Protection from entrepreneurial competition does not provide any spur to entrepreneurial discovery.

Imposed price ceilings may, similarly, not merely generate discoordination in the markets for existing goods and services (as is of course well recognized in the theory of price controls); they may inhibit the discovery of wholly new opportunities. A price ceiling does not merely block the upper reaches of a given supply curve—further increases in supply to meet demand. It may also inhibit the discovery of as yet unsuspected sources of supply (which in the absence of the ceiling might have shifted the entire supply curve to the right—made supplies marketable at lower prices—as these sources came to be discovered) or of wholly unknown new products.

The imposition of price ceilings, which has switched off the lure of pure profits in this way, is not accompanied, as far as can be seen, by any device that might, in some alternative manner, lead a potential discoverer to associate a discovery with his own personal gain.

CONCLUSION

This discussion has focused attention on a neglected aspect of economic decision making, the urgency for incentives for the "entrepreneurial" discovery of what opportunities exist for economic action. Pursuing this point further, I have pointed to the need for critical assessment, within any economic system of organization, of the way the system permits the potential discoverers to identify their own personal interest with the successful discovery of socially desirable opportunities for change. In the briefest possible framework, I have considered aspects of the socialist system and of the regulated market economy, in contrast to the laissez-faire market system.

A great deal of work is waiting to be done in the economics of entrepreneurship. It has been my purpose to emphasize the enormous stake society—under whatever economic system it may operate—holds in the successful pursuit of such research.

NOTES

1. That is, the problem of achieving maximum desirable results without overstepping the constraints imposed by the limited resources available. This emphasis on maximization is to be traced to the influence of Lionel H. Robbins, *The Nature and Significance of Economic Science* (London: Macmillan, 1932).

2. The literature on the economics of search proceeds on this basis. The classic article is G. J. Stigler, "The Economics of Information," *Journal of Political Economy* 69 (June 1961): 213–25.

3. An elaboration of this theme is in my *Competition and Entrepreneurship* (Chicago: University of Chicago Press, 1973), chaps. 1–3.

4. F. H. Knight, *Risk, Uncertainty and Profit* (Boston: Houghton Mifflin, 1921).

5. A fuller discussion of this insight is in my *Perception, Opportunity, and Profit* (Chicago: University of Chicago Press, 1979), chaps. 9, 10.

6. In Ludwig von Mises, *Human Action* (New Haven: Yale University Press, 1949), p. 253.

7. A complete discussion of this central theorem of welfare economics is in W. J. Baumol, *Economic Theory and Operations Analysis,* 4th ed. (Englewood Cliffs, N.J.: Prentice-Hall, 1977), chap. 21.

8. F. A. Hayek, "Competition as a Discovery Procedure," in *New Studies in Philosophy, Politics, Economics and the History of Ideas* (Chicago: University of Chicago Press, 1978).

9. Oskar Lange, "On the Economic Theory of Socialism," in Oskar Lange and Fred M. Taylor, *The Economic Theory of Socialism,* ed. Benjamin E. Lippincott (New York: McGraw-Hill, 1964), p. 70. The initial statement by Mises demonstrating the problems in socialist economic calculation was "Die Wirtschaftsrechnung im sozialistischen Gemeinwesen," *Archiv für Sozialwissenschaften und Sozialpolitik* 47 (April 1920): 86–121, reprinted in *Collectivist Economic Planning,* trans. and ed. Friedrich A. Hayek (London: Routledge and Kegan Paul, 1935). Hayek's own response to Lange is contained in his *Individualism and Economic Order* (London: Routledge and Kegan Paul, 1949).

10. Joseph S. Berliner, *The Innovation Decision in Soviet Industry* (Cambridge: MIT Press, 1976).

11. Further discussion of this theme is in my "The Perils of Regulation: A Market-Process Approach," Occasional Paper of the Law and Economics Center, University of Miami, 1978, reprinted in this volume, chap. 6.

THE LIMITS OF THE MARKET
THE REAL AND THE IMAGINED

Conventional wisdom asserts the existence of important limits to the operation of markets. Even economists who generally champion the efficiency properties of the market readily concede that significant and widespread cases of market failure provide a valid rationale for government policies suspending or modifying the operation of the market. Our thesis in this chapter, building on insights developed in modern Austrian economics, is that if the nature and functions of the market are properly understood, it must be acknowledged that the market never fails to fulfill those functions. In this sense, the asserted "limits of the market" do not in fact exist. We shall, for reasons which will become obvious, refer to these limits (which we are denying) as, "inner limits." We hasten to add that, as we shall see, this denial of the existence of any "inner" limits to the market does not, by itself destroy the possibility of economically justified active governmental policies. But acceptance of our thesis will, nonetheless, alert us to the searching and challenging questions which must be asked before such policies can in fact be justified on strictly economic grounds.

While this chapter will thus sharply criticize what is generally understood by the term "limits of the market," we will at the same time emphasize a different, valid, and indeed insufficiently appreciated sense of the term. In this different sense, the term "limits of the market" do not refer at all to any kind of market failure. Instead the notion refers to the institutional pre-requisites for the very existence of the market. We shall refer to such limits as the "outer" limits of the market. We wish to emphasize the insight that, for its very emergence and existence, the market must rely on the presence of extramarket institutions, without which the idea of a market process must be a mere dream. These genuine limits to the market, because they do not refer to market failure, cannot provide

From Israel M. Kirzner, *The Driving Force of the Market: Essays in Austrian Economics* (New York and London: Routledge, 2000), 77–87. The original source is W. Möschel, M. E. Streit, and U. Witt, eds. *Marktwirtschaft und Rechtsordnung* (Baden-Baden: Nomos, 1994).

any rationale for governmental suspension of markets. But they certainly do point our thinking concerning markets toward the extramarket ethics or legal principles which may, practically speaking, be the necessary basis for those institutions upon which the market itself must rest. Our quarrel with economists concerning this latter point relates to a certain tendency within modern economics to understand the establishment of private property—that bedrock institution required for the very idea of markets—as somehow historically and conceptually independent of ethics. Such "economic" theories of property rights, explaining these rights in terms of blind, amoral, economic forces acting in the prehistory of market societies, in effect deny the existence, or at least the relevance, of "outer" limits to the market.

To sum up our argument in this chapter, then, we will be concerned (a) to deny those "inner limits" to the market which economists affirm in the doctrine of market failure; and (b) to insist upon the importance of those "outer limits" to the market which economists in effect deny in the economic theories of property rights. Proper appreciation for the true ("outer") limits to the market, and recognition for the utter absence of "inner limits" to the operation of the market are both important for understanding the appropriate economic role for government in the market society, and the appropriate limitations for that role. But we shall argue further that it is our very appreciation for the reality of the market's "outer limits" which conduces to our understanding of how imaginary are those alleged "inner limits" implied by the theory of market failure.

Section I of this chapter will present our definition of the market and what we consider to be its central function. Section II will apply these insights to the elucidation of the impossibility of market failure, once the true function of the market is properly understood. Section III will elaborate our thesis concerning the very real outer limits of the market, in terms of its institutional prerequisites, and will apply the thesis to refer critically to the economic theory of property rights. Finally, section IV will develop our assertion that the mistaken notion of "inner limits" to the market may, at least in part, be attributed to insufficient appreciation for the reality of the market's outer limits.

I

A market economy is a societal arrangement in which the ultimate decisions concerning the disposition of individually held rights to goods and services are exercised by the relevant individuals themselves. In such a pure market economy all the economic outcomes, exchanges, allocation of resources, prices of productive factor services and of consumer goods and services, outputs, methods of production and modes of organization and the structure of production, are all determined by the interplay of voluntary decisions of property owners.

In neoclassical economics the textbook statements concerning the function of the market refer routinely to the achievement of an efficient allocation of society's resources. (It is with reference to this criterion of efficient societal resource allocation that market failure theorists find the market wanting.) Following upon Hayek's 1945 critique of the very notion of societal efficiency in a world of dispersed information (and mindful of the traditional Austrian rejection of notions of global welfare), modern Austrian economics has dismissed the idea that the function of the market is to allocate resources efficiently. Since information is in fact scattered, it is hardly relevant to apply as a yardstick a notion of global efficiency which could have meaning only for an omniscient mind possessing global control over all economic activity. Instead, the function of the market has been seen as one of *coordinating* the plans of independently acting market participants.[1] In particular, this function has been interpreted as that of promoting the mutual discovery by market participants of the availability of and needs for exchangeable goods and services (Hayek, 1978; Kirzner, 1985, chs. 1, 2 and 3; Kirzner, 1989, ch. 4).

It should be noticed that while this view of the functions of the market rejects—on methodologically individualist grounds—holistic treatment of society as faced by the Robbinsian challenge of efficiency in resource allocation,[2] it certainly does recognize a supra-individual function for the market. Successful achievement by the market of this "social" function requires that it spur those discoveries that will promote those sets of individual decisions which will best enable individuals severally to fulfill their respective objectives, in light of their own endowments and in conjunction with the opportunities implicit in the endowments and objectives of others.[3] What it is important to emphasize is that this coordination function, promoting the exploitation by individuals of the potential for mutually gainful exchanges amongst them, can be defined only against the background of given individual rights to endowments. *If* individual A possesses money and is hungry, while individual B possesses a surplus of food but lacks money, *then* we can appraise social mechanisms in regard to their effectiveness in promoting the coordinating mutual discovery by A and by B of the gains to be achieved by exchange. It would have been idle to speculate concerning "coordination" (in regard to the distribution of food and money between A and B) in the absence of some initial given position (reflecting the given initial endowments). If it were possible to talk sensibly of the total utility to A and B (corresponding to alternative distribution of food and money between them) then, of course, (as in neoclassical welfare theory in its many variants), one might imagine being able to assess outcomes in terms of a global optimality criterion. Then, as in mainstream economic discourse, the market might be seen as having the function of computing the solution to that set of simultaneous equations marking out the relevant optimal pattern of allocation. The market might be assessed in terms of its success in regard to this function. But the Hayekian point is that such assessments must, given the impossibility of centralized access to all available, dispersed bits of information, remain entirely imaginary. Instead, the modern Austrian approach argues, we can recognize that markets encourage the identification and exploitation by individuals of hitherto unnoticed opportunities for mutually gainful exchange or cooperation. It is this tendency toward supra-individual coordination which constitutes the discovery function of the market. This function is to alert market participants to possibilities for gain that may, without being yet known to anyone, be inherent in the current pattern of ownership and of preference. This function is, to use modern Austrian terminology, to overcome the "knowledge problem."

II

Market failure theorists focus attention on situations where (as, for example, in the presence of externalities), individual self-interested decision-making produces a globally suboptimal outcome. Individual self-interested decisions pay attention only to private gains and private costs. Where, however, externalities exist, an activity may, for example, generate costs to others, such that what appears to the individual as an optimal choice, affording him significant net gain, may in fact be causing damage to others which outweighs, in some social sense, the gain to himself. Such cases are held to be examples of "market failure."[4] While the economic literature following on Ronald Coase's seminal paper (1960) valuably drew attention to the market's own potential for the private internalization of externalities,[5] this literature yet left ample scope for what appeared to be market failure. Where transaction costs render private internalization unfeasible, markets generate suboptimal outcomes. Cases such as "prisoner-dilemma" situations, situations involving so-called "public goods" (in which "free-riding" is feasible and tempting), provide models of market failure. and thus call for governmental suspension of the market. By limiting the freedom of individuals to act without regard to the social consequences of their actions, governments may hope to improve the allocation of resources (over what would have occurred as a result of market failure).[6]

What we wish to argue in this section is that none of these situations (in which self-interested individual decisions generate what are held to be socially suboptimal outcomes) constitutes valid examples of what could properly be called market failure—in the context of the understanding of the function of the market as developed in the preceding section. In none of these situations has the market failed to tend to coordinate individual decisions in the light of the relevant property right endowments.

Standard theory pronounces these situations to be cases of market failure because that theory, blandly assuming a perspective of imagined omniscience (and skillfully side-stepping the problems of interpersonal comparisons of utility) believes it possible to identify the resulting market outcomes as socially inferior to patterns of resource allocation attainable through government intervention. From this perspective the market must, in such situations, fail to achieve that which is its assigned function to achieve, viz. a socially optimal pattern of resource allocation. But, from the perspective outlined in the preceding section, matters appear quite differently.

From this latter ("Austrian") perspective, the function of the market is to overcome the knowledge problem, i.e. to promote the coordination among individual decisions so as to enable market participants to take advantage of available opportunities for mutually gainful exchange. But, as noted, such coordination can be defined only in the context of a given pattern of individual rights. Within such a context it is the function of the market to promote mutual discovery and, thus, coordination. In situations characterized in mainstream theory as cases of market failure, the pattern of rights is such as to create unsustainably high costs of internalizing troubling externalities. In the light of such costs the resulting market outcomes—no matter how "suboptimal" they may appear from the perspective of omniscience—do tend to promote discovery of relevant information, encouraging fullest exploitation of all available opportunities for mutually gainful exchange. We must, after all, remember that the concept "all available opportunities for mutually gainful exchange" can be spelled out only after taking due account of (a) initial endowments, and (b) of relevant transaction costs. So that, given the high costs of internalizing externalities, the *de facto* distribution of rights (allowing, say, a manufacturer to pollute a river without having to pay for so doing) constrains the discovery procedure of the market faithfully to tend to reflect the given rights framework (by tending to disseminate information concerning the relevant realities to all market participants).

To say that the market process works successfully in the context of externalities is certainly not to pronounce the market outcome socially optimal (if only because we have questioned the meaning of social optimality in a world of dispersed information). Nor is it, in and of itself, to declare governmental attempts compulsorily to internalize externalities, to be a definite error (since, after all, governmental policy may seek to reflect citizens' preferences as these are understood in moral or political terms, rather than in the narrow, austerely "scientific" terms within which economic science is confined). But to recognize that the market process of mutual discovery works in the presence of externalities no less effectively than it does in their absence, should alert us to one serious potential for harm in such governmental policies. To the extent that such policies suspend or inhibit the market process, they are obstructing a process of discovery without offering any substitute for it. Let us not forget that the market process has the function of alerting market participants to opportunities which nobody has expected. To initiate governmental policies to grapple with externalities is, in effect, to pretend knowledge which no one can, in principle, honestly claim to possess.

Where cooperation is of real or imagined mutual benefit to a group of individuals, the market will of course provide scope for such cooperation. The market does, as has often been recognized,[7] make it possible for groups within it to organize themselves in communes or other organizations on strictly socialist principles, if they choose. (This, let us not forget, is how capitalist firms come into existence.) But the market will do more than simply *permit* cooperation. It will offer the incentives for members of such groups *to discover* the fact that cooperation would be mutually gainful. Where the structure of property rights is such as to make it economically feasible for private internalization of external effects to occur, the market will generate the incentives sufficient *to alert* market participants to the benefits so to be gained. The market process has no "inner limits" (in the sense that it fails to encourage necessary cooperation among individuals to form firms or organizations of a size best able to participate in the open-ended competitive process of the market). It is true that the market will not inspire cooperation where the transactions costs of so doing are prohibitive (even though such cooperation may appear highly desirable from a perspective which sees these transactions costs as in principle avoidable—say, through government compulsion). But this does not exemplify market failure or the existence of limits to the effectiveness of the market in alerting participants to opportunities inherent in the given set of rights—with all the benefits and costs that such a set of rights implies. Let us turn now to take note of the real limits to the market—limits which many economists have tended to ignore.

III

These limits on the market are imposed by its institutional prerequisites. Without these institutional prerequisites—primarily, private property rights and freedom and enforceability of contract—the market cannot operate. It follows that those institutions cannot be created by the market itself. The institutions upon which the market must depend must have been created or have evolved through processes different from those spontaneous coordinative processes which we have seen to constitute the essence of the market's operation. It can in fact be shown[8] not only that, of course, we cannot, without a market, rely on spontaneous market processes of coordination to establish the institutions needed for the market to operate, but also that we cannot rely upon *any* spontaneous social forces to foster those institutions. So that these institutional requirements for the market constitute what we have termed the "outer limits" to the market. They mark out the boundaries beyond which any coordinative processes (such as those generating the sets of mutually reinforcing expectations which constitute the system of property rights) must necessarily be of a non-market character.

Emphasis on the nature of these outer limits is important in that it can assist in winning proper recognition for the role of shared ethical principles in the emergence of societal institutions. Surely the principal historical basis for the institution of private property rights or for the institution of enforceability of contract has been man's moral convictions concerning the simple justice of owning what one has produced with one's own effort, or has discovered through one's own alertness, and the injustice of appropriating (through violence or dishonesty) what another has produced, discovered, or otherwise justly acquired. Such shared moral convictions may certainly have evolved over time, and have been partly shaped by economic conditions. But we cannot fail to acknowledge the sharp difference which separates what occurs as a result of spontaneous economic processes *within* market societies, from the complex webs of historical experience which come to be crystallized in the shared moral intuitions which support the institutions which frame market societies. The former processes are themselves intrinsically amoral, they tend to express, faithfully and neutrally, the preferences and values of market participants. The latter crystallization of shared moral intuitions consists, at each moment in history, of sets of explicit or tacit ethical convictions nourishing people's evaluation of and expectations concerning the acts of others. No understanding of the market can afford to ignore the fundamental insight that its institutional foundations are to be sought directly, not in economic considerations but in ethical ones.[9]

The thrust of these observations of ours concerning the outer limits of the market must be to question the perspective insisted upon in the literature seeking to develop the "economic analysis of rights."[10] That literature tends to dissolve the sharp difference we have asserted separating the character of market processes from the character of the processes leading up to the crystallization of the institutions upon which markets must rest for their very existence. That literature would, if carried to the extreme, entirely deny the relevance of outer limits to the market. It would, in this extreme form, recognize both inside and outside the market, only the impersonal, amoral force of costs and benefits. This "economic" force would be seen as operating uniformly within the relevant constraints, whether these be those of secure property rights (as within the market society), or of brute force and fear (as in the Hobbesian jungle). A consequence (of this denial of the relevance of the outer limits to the market) must surely be to weaken the perceived moral basis for the assignment of rights. As a critic of the economic analysis of rights has pointed out, that analysis "offers plenty of good reasons for those assignments of rights which seem intuitively clear to us, but the reasons have nothing to do with the inherent 'rightness' . . . or the 'wickedness' [of the positions of victims of civil wrongs and of those of the wrongdoers]"

(Fried, 1978, p. 98). Our purpose in this section is not only to deplore this "sundering of ethical decisions from decisions about rights" (Fried, 1978, p. 96), but to insist (albeit without working out here the proof[11]) that we cannot, in order to arrive at the market institutions of a free and civilized society, in fact rely upon impersonal economic forces to transform a Hobbesian jungle into a stable and ordered system of law. There are outer limits to the market, and to the benignly coordinative properties of the spontaneous economic forces which operate within it. These forces can only be relied upon provided a widely shared ethic already exists which firmly recognizes the "rightness" of the property rights system and the corresponding "wrongness" of theft and fraud.

IV

We have argued in this chapter against the existence of the inner limits to the market asserted by market failure theorists, and in affirmation of the existence of the outer limits to the market (in effect denied by the economic analysis of rights). Our denial of inner limits to the market should alert us to the potential dangers in government suspension of or interference with markets. Our affirmation of outer limits to markets should drive home the need for society-wide acceptance of shared ethical perspectives (and, most likely, for governmental, extra-market enforcement of the rights system implied in such shared ethical perspectives). But it seems important also to emphasize the existence of the market's outer limits in order to appreciate the impossibility of inner limits to its effectiveness.

As noted in sections I and II, the function of the market process can be defined only with respect to some given initial set of endowments. Only after we can assume some such given initial set, can one define the task of achieving coordination among market participants (so that the opportunities for mutually gainful exchange implicit in the endowment set, together with the preferences of the participants, can be discovered and exploited). It was this insight which led us to recognize that such phenomena as externalities do not generate market failure (at least in the framework of the market's essential function as we explained it to be).

What we wish to point out is that this recognition rests upon an understanding of the importance of the rights framework of the market. For economists who fail to appreciate this importance, welfare conclusions are sought which refer hardly at all to the initial pattern of ownership. For them welfare conclusions are sought relevant to the resources available to society as a whole (as well, of course, as the preferences of individual members of society). For us, on the other hand, who see the function of the market as consisting in the coordination of decisions among holders of rights, the pattern of initial distribution of such rights looms into a position of pivotal importance. If market outcomes, resulting from externalities, are deemed somehow unfortunate, this is seen immediately as attributable, not to the failure of the market to coordinate with respect to the given rights system, but to the pattern of rights which the system has, rightly or wrongly, taken as its initial framework. As we have noted there is significant merit in being able to distinguish sharply between a possibly faulty functioning of the market (a possibility we have denied) and a possibly erroneous initial distribution of rights (a possibility we must certainly recognize[12]).

Toward the attainment of such a more insightful understanding of markets and their function, we suggest that our emphasis on the nature and importance of the outer limits to the market can make a useful contribution. The uniquely valuable character of the spontaneous forces of the market process rests entirely on nonmarket-generated institutions which frame the market. Seeing the outer limits of the market with clarity can help economists avoid the analytical fog which has led so many to see inner limits to the effectiveness of the market where no such limits in fact exist.

NOTES

1. On this see Kirzner (1973, ch. 6), O'Driscoll (1977), Cordato (1992).

2. Robbins (1935, ch. 1).

3. On this point see Buchanan (1964).

4. Bator (1958). See also Schotter (1990, ch. 4).

5. An example of this literature is Buchanan and Stubblebine (1962).

6. Of course, public choice theory has pointed out the fallacy of ignoring the very real possibilities for "government failure"—but that is not our topic in this chapter.

7. See Nozick (1974, pp. 250f.). See also Coase (1937).

8. For such a demonstration, see Kirzner (1992, ch. 10).

9. For a vigorous presentation of this point see North (1992).

10. A classic in this literature was Demsetz (1967). Note that the criticism in the text does not contradict the substance of Demsetz's most interesting analysis—only the suggestion it conveys that rights have evolved historically in a moral vacuum.

11. On this, see above, note 8.

12. For a detailed discussion of the relationship between the problems of externalities and possible flaws in the legal system establishing and protecting property rights, see von Mises (1966, pp. 654–61).

REFERENCES

Bator, Francis (1958) "The Anatomy of Market Failure," *Quarterly Journal of Economics* (August).

Buchanan, James M. (1964) "What Should Economists Do?," *Southern Economic Journal* 30 (January).

Buchanan, James M. and Stubblebine, William Craig (1962) "Externality," *Economica* xxxi, pp. 371–84.

Coase, Ronald H. (1937) "The Nature of the Firm," *Economica* n.s. 4, pp. 386–405.

—— (1960) "The Problem of Social Cost," *Journal of Law and Economics* 3, pp. 1–40.

Cordato, Roy E. (1992) *Welfare Economics and Externalities in an Open Ended Universe: A Modern Austrian Perspective*, Boston, MA: Kluwer Academic Publishers.

Demsetz, Harold (1967) "Toward a Theory of Property Rights," *American Economic Review* LVII (May), pp. 347–59.

Fried, Charles (1978) *Right and Wrong*, Cambridge, MA: Harvard University Press.

Hayek, Friedrich A. (1945) "The Use of Knowledge in Society," *American Economic Review* 35, pp. 519–30; reprinted in *Individualism and Economic Order*, Chicago: University of Chicago Press, 1948.

—— (1978) "Competition as a Discovery Procedure," in *New Studies in Philosophy, Politics, Economics and the History of Ideas*, Chicago: University of Chicago Press.

Kirzner, Israel M. (1973) *Competition and Entrepreneurship*, Chicago: University of Chicago Press.

—— (1985) *Discovery and the Capitalist Process*, Chicago: University of Chicago Press.

—— (1989) *Discovery, Capitalism and Distributive Justice*, Oxford: Basil Blackwell.

—— (1992) *The Meaning of Market Process: Essays in the Development of Modern Austrian Economics*, London: Routledge.

Mises, Ludwig von (1966) *Human Action, A Treatise on Economics*, 3rd edn, Chicago: Henry Regnery.

North, Gary (1992) *The Coase Theorem, A Study in Economic Epistemology*, Tyler, TX: Institute for Christian Economics.

Nozick, Robert (1974) *Anarchy, State and Utopia*, New York: Basic Books.

O'Driscoll, Gerald P., Jr. (1977) *Economics as a Coordination Problem: The Contributions of Friedrich A. Hayek*, Kansas City: Sheed, Andrews and McMeel.

Robbins, Lionel (1935) *An Essay on the Nature and Significance of Economic Science*, 2nd edn, London: Macmillan.

Schotter, Andrew (1990) *Free Market Economics: A Critical Appraisal*, 2nd edn, Oxford: Basil Blackwell.

POLICY

TAXES AND DISCOVERY:
AN ENTREPRENEURIAL PERSPECTIVE

The central theme of this paper will take the form of a rather basic criticism of an unstated premise of the accepted theory dealing with the economic effects of taxation. If this criticism is accepted as sound, it will raise serious questions concerning the completeness (if not the very validity) of the conclusions arrived at through application of the standard theory. In order to reformulate the theory of taxation to take adequate account of our basic criticism, a significant array of new theoretical challenges will have to be grappled with. Thus this paper implies not only a broad attack on orthodox taxation theory, but also an extensive positive agenda for its reconstruction. But it by no means attempts to undertake these formidable tasks. (In fact it must be freely confessed that it is not clear that economics yet possesses the conceptual and analytical tools necessary for these tasks.) It confines itself to the far more modest (and, I hope, achievable) objective of articulating the basic insight underlying my criticism and of identifying some of the theoretical issues that are raised by awareness of this basic insight.

THE PREMISE OF ORTHODOX THEORY

Underlying the standard theory that assesses the economic consequences of taxation is the premise *that taxes are introduced into a world in which available opportunities for gainful actions are given and known* (in the sense to be defined below) to relevant decision makers. Acceptance of this premise has meant that the economic impact of a tax is explored only insofar as it may affect the relative preferability for the decision maker of already-perceived alternative courses of action (the fully known benefits of which may be affected unequally by the tax). No consideration is given to the possibility that the tax may have, perhaps, significant impact upon the very perception by the prospective taxpayer of what array of

From *Discovery and the Capitalist Process* (Chicago and London: University of Chicago Press, 1985), 93–118. Reprinted by permission of the Pacific Institute; the original source is *Taxation and Capital Markets,* ed. Dwight Lee (Cambridge, Mass.: Ballinger Publishing Co., for the Pacific Institute for Public Policy Research, 1985).

opportunities are available for his choice, or of what their pretax benefits for him may in fact be. In other words, no consideration is given to the possibility that taxation may affect what it is that decision makers *discover* to be the situation in which they act. The effect of taxation upon incentives has been explored on the premise that the degree to which the taxpayer can successfully discover the true state of affairs surrounding him is left unaffected by all taxation patterns (and it is often assumed, in fact, that the taxpayer is able to discover this state of affairs with *complete* success in all circumstances). I shall argue that this basic premise is likely to be, in general, unfounded. Once the possibility is recognized of there being a linkage between what a person is to be taxed and what opportunities that person discovers to be available for his taking, we must recognize further the need to modify substantially the conclusions reached by standard theory (on the basis of this challenged premise) concerning the effect of specific taxes upon what prospective taxpayers decide to do. Let me elaborate briefly on two quite different senses in which the notion of *incentives* may be relevant to the economic analysis of taxation.

INCENTIVES AND INCENTIVES

Ordinarily economists treat the concept of an incentive as referring to the provision of an encouragement for a decision maker to select a particular one out of an array of *already perceived alternatives*. What is already perceived about these alternatives is taken to be not only the possible courses of action themselves, but also key elements, at the very least, concerning the respective consequences that can reasonably be expected to follow from pursuing these courses of action. To provide an incentive to encourage the decision maker to select course of action *A*, rather than courses of action *B*, *C*, . . . , means to seek to modify the consequence of these various courses of action in such a manner as to render the perceived consequences of *A* more desirable than those of *B*, *C*, ... Typically this is likely to take the form of arranging an enhancement of the value to the decision maker of the perceived consequence of *A* itself. In other words, the way to induce the decision maker to adopt course of action *A* is, to use the economists' opportunity-cost phraseology, to overcome the cost of sacrificing *B*, *C*, ... Whereas, absent this inducement, course of action *B* might have been judged to promise greater rewards than action *A*, the provided incentive (enhancing the total value of *A*'s consequences) renders *A* more desirable than *B*. The high cost of rejecting *B* has been met by increasing the payoff on action A. It is easy to understand how taxes (and subsidies) may be deployed in this way to provide the incentives designed to encourage taxpayers to pursue courses of action which the taxing authorities would like them to pursue.

To encourage work rather than leisure it may be deemed necessary to increase after-tax labor income (without affecting the desirability of relevant forgone leisure); to encourage saving rather than the immediate consumption of income it may be deemed necessary to offer tax exemptions on that portion of income directed toward saving (while leaving unchanged the severity of the tax bite on other income). These tax measures provide tax-based incentives to encourage work, or saving, through modifying the rewards of working, or saving, in such a way as to outweigh the perceived costs of working, or saving. Let us call this kind of incentive an *incentive of the first kind*. I wish to draw attention to an altogether different notion of an incentive that will be of critical importance for the theme of this paper.

This second, entirely different, incentive concept does not operate by overcoming the cost, to the decision maker, associated with his adoption of the to-be-encouraged option A; it does not operate by enhancing the value of A's consequences so as to make these consequences appear more valuable, all in all, than those of B, C, ... Rather, this second kind of incentive operates to encourage the adoption of A by making A more likely to be *noticed* by the decision maker. In other words, it may be the case that even *without* any new incentives, course of action A may *already* have in fact involved consequences more desirable than those of B, C, . . . —but that his preferred action A, would, in the absence of new incentives, *not* have been adopted *simply because it would have failed to have been noticed as a possibility by the decision maker.* Here the incentive takes the form not of altering the *relative* attractiveness of the payoffs to A, B, C, . . . but of somehow enhancing the potential of course of action A to *attract attention.* There is no need to offer incentives in order to overcome the opportunity cost of rejecting course of action B. A is *already* offering greater rewards than B. Thus, if the authorities, in this situation, wish to structure taxes in order to provide taxpayers with incentives to pursue course of action A, any tax policy generated sweetening, for the taxpayer, of the anticipated value of the consequences of undertaking A does not affect action through the enhancement of the relative desirability of A. Rather, the incentive to undertake A operates, under the specified assumptions, *through its inducement to discover* the possibility and/or the attractiveness of A. I will refer to this kind of incentive as an *incentive of the second kind*.

It should perhaps be pointed out that an inducement to discover A is not at all the same as an inducement *deliberately to undertake the search effort* (involving possibly significant search costs) that might reveal the existence and value of A. A decision maker might indeed be convinced that, by the expenditure of a specified degree of search effort, he could locate a superior course of action—but that the cost of the necessary search effort was so high as to make the whole search not worthwhile. And tax authorities might indeed then be able, perhaps, to provide sufficient enhancement of the value of the to-be-searched-for course of action so as to make the expensive search appear worthwhile after all. But *this* kind of inducement to search is evidently no different from any of the incentives of the first kind discussed earlier. This kind of inducement is designed to overcome the costs of undertaking an already perceived course of action, namely, that of deliberately searching for a superior course of action (to be undertaken subsequent to the search). This kind of inducement operates (as do all incentives of the first kind) by enhancing the relative desirability of an already perceived (and already correctly evaluated) course of action (the act of searching). The sense in which incentives of the second kind can be said to serve as inducements for discovery is quite different.

Discovery may be induced by incentives of the second kind, not by rendering an already perceived possibility of costly search worthwhile, but by sparking interest in a possible but hitherto *unnoticed* course of action (or at least a course of action whose net desirability had not been noticed). One cannot deliberately search for an opportunity if one is totally unaware of the very possibility of its existence. (One of the avenues through which incentives of the second kind may spark interest in hitherto unnoticed possibilities may of course take the form of sparking interest in the possible worthwhileness of deliberate search itself. But then the reason the search would, absent these new inducements, not have been undertaken deliberately had nothing to do with the costliness of the search effort. The to-be-expected results of a search would, in such cases, be such as to render such cost well worth while; the search would have failed to be undertaken because the very possibility of such a search, or of its likely and valuable successful outcome, was somehow—in the absence of the new incentives—not perceived.)

The theme of this paper can now be concisely stated in terms of the two kinds of incentives described above. This theme is that the standard theory of the economic effects of taxation proceeds exclusively through the analysis of the incentive (or disincentive) effects of taxation in the context of the first kind of incentive concept; what needs to be introduced is an analysis of taxation that takes into account the role of incentives (and disincentives) of the second kind.

THE INCENTIVE OF PURE PROFIT

The foregoing suggests rather clearly that the reconstruction of the economic theory of taxation that I am calling for must proceed through a reconsideration of the theory of the economic effects of the taxation of pure entrepreneurial profit. That this is so emerges immediately from the insight that the incentive role of pure profit is entirely that of the *second* kind of incentive discussed in the preceding section. Although the disincentive effects of taxation upon profit have been frequently referred to in the tax literature, it appears that these references have had only the *first* kind of incentive effect in mind. I shall argue in this section that this latter understanding of the incentive effect of profit (and hence of the disincentive effect of profit taxes) is valid only to the extent that accounting profit (upon which taxes may be levied) includes elements other than pure entrepreneurial profit. With respect to the *pure* profit component, I shall maintain, the *only* relevant incentive category is that which I have labeled the second kind.

Pure profit is captured by the entrepreneur when he succeeds in selling an item (a good or a service) at a price that exceeds the price for which he purchased that item (or the total of the outlays incurred in producing that item and making it ready for sale). Pursuing this definition, we observe that all payments necessary to command the services of relevant productive factors have already been included in the outlay total to be subtracted from the sales proceeds in arriving at the pure profit that has been won. By definition, therefore, pure profit is a sum that cannot be described as necessary for the production of the item sold (or for its availability for sale at the relevant selling price). Pure profit contains no element needed to ensure the availability of the item to be sold. All necessary costs of production, including all outlays (such as selling costs, delivery costs, and the like) needed to ensure that the item to be sold will be forthcoming at the appropriate time and place are included in the total deducted from sales revenues in arriving at the profit amount. Pure profits are not needed to provide the economic incentives necessary to evoke relevant productive effort. Notice that this means, of course, that even without the presence of pure profits, sales revenues are, by being sufficient to cover all the necessary factor service outlays, sufficient to overcome the pull exercised by the bids of entrepreneurs in other industries, competing to secure the services of these factors for other productive uses. Any incentive role that may be ascribed to pure profit can therefore not take the form of the first kind of incentive role identified earlier (in which an income receipt provides the incentive to the decision maker to undertake a given course of action by rendering the consequences of that course of action preferable to those of alternate courses of action). Here the course of production action (undertaken in the profitable line of production) would, we have seen, have been worth adopting even if the pure profit amount was not forthcoming from the sales revenues. The possibility that pure profit fulfills an incentive role can therefore exist only in the *second* of the senses I identified earlier (in which an income receipt provides the incentive for a course of action to be undertaken by enhancing the potential of that course of action, and of its worthwhileness, to attract entrepreneurial attention).

That this indeed may be an incentive role provided by pure entrepreneurial profit follows from the very concept of entrepreneurship and from the theory of pure entrepreneurial profit. The very possibility of the emergence of pure entrepreneurial profit rests, after all, on the circumstance that worthwhile opportunities may simply not be noticed. Were all worthwhile opportunities to be noticed at all times (i.e., were all opportunities for producing items whose prospective sales revenues fully covered necessary costs of production to be immediately noticed), then we could hardly expect that sales revenues would ever exceed costs of production. No buyer would pay for an item a sum larger than the perceived minimum outlay sufficient to obtain the availability of that item. The possibility of sales revenue's exceeding cost of production arises solely out of the possibility that desirable courses of action may not be noticed (or that their desirability may not be noticed).

Thus the incentive role of pure entrepreneurial profit fits naturally into the theory accounting for its very existence. Profit is generated by earlier failure of market participants to notice worthwhile possibilities. The profit thus generated sparks interest in these overlooked possibilities.

The incentive of profit thus works not to affect the relative attractiveness of already perceived opportunities, but to attract notice to the most desirable (but possibly not yet perceived) of the existing opportunities. The concept of entrepreneurship is closely linked to that of alertly noticing hitherto unnoticed opportunities. As we shall see, there is every reason to recognize the possibility of pure profit as providing the incentive that inspires entrepreneurial discovery of such hitherto unnoticed opportunities. These insights certainly hold considerable relevance for understanding the impact of profit taxation.

I note, in concluding this section, that accounting profit may, of course, not conform at all closely to the pure entrepreneurial profit I have been discussing here. As is well known, accounting profit figures may contain very significant components of a variety of different analytical categories, especially interest and wages of management. To the extent that interest must be paid in order to compete for capital with other branches of production or to dissuade potential investors from succumbing to the lure of more immediate consumption possibilities, or to the extent that wages of management must be paid in order to attract talent away from other pursuits, accounting profits may well be needed to secure the availability of the resource services for this branch of production as against competing branches. To this extent accounting profits may certainly be held to perform the first kind of incentive role identified earlier. The effects of the taxation of accounting profit must certainly deal, as standard theory does, with the *first* kind of disincentive effect of such taxation. (My contention is that such analysis covers only part of the full effects of such taxation.) The discussion in this section has referred *only* to the pure profit element.

At the same time we must not forget that, just as accounting profit is likely to embrace elements other than pure entrepreneurial profit, so also may other accounting categories such as wages, or interest, include elements of pure profit. Let me elaborate briefly on this theme.

THE UBIQUITY OF PURE PROFIT

I have argued that the reconstruction of the theory of taxation called for in this paper must proceed by way of a reconsideration of the economic effects of the taxation of pure entrepreneurial profit. This does not mean, however, that such reconstruction would leave unaffected the theory dealing with the effects of the taxation of income categories other than accounting profit. The truth of that pure entrepreneurial profit is a ubiquitous economic phenomenon, present in a variety of economic circumstances and captured by a variety of economic agents. As Ludwig von Mises wrote, "In any real and living economy every actor is always an entrepreneur."[1]

What this means is that every action in the market economy reflects the actor's alertness to aspects of his situation that might otherwise have escaped attention. In a changing, open-ended world, acting man is never exempt from the self-generated pressure to ensure that his decisions not overlook available opportunities. Action never does consist merely in selecting the highest valued of a given array of opportunities; it always embraces the simultaneous *identification* of what the relevant opportunities (and their values) really are at the moment of action. While we usually think of pure entrepreneurial profit as generated by the independent businessman through acts of purchase and sale, the truth surely is that an element of profit is captured whenever, say, a worker moves out of an industry where his marginal productivity and therefore his wages are low and obtains a job in another industry or location where compensation for similar skills is higher. This wage differential is the incentive that attracts the worker to change jobs; it can hardly be described as an incentive of the first kind—only a small fraction of it may be needed to render the new job more attractive than the old. Clearly the wage differential acts as an incentive for workers to become alert to the most desirable employment opportunities, in exactly the same way as price differentials attract potential entrepreneurs to buy at low prices and sell at higher prices. The role of incentives of the *second* kind (as I have called them in this paper) is a ubiquitous one. Thus the reconsideration of the economic theory of taxation that I call for in this paper is by no means confined to taxes explicitly levied on profit receipts. The reconstruction and the reconsideration I call for have implications that extend to most kinds of taxes, to greater or lesser degree.

Nonetheless, having recognized the entrepreneurial element in all human action, and having asserted the possibility that incentives of the second kind play roles in almost every kind of economic receipt, we must acknowledge that the adviser on tax policy can hardly be the purist the present section might appear to demand. Assertions concerning the impact of taxation upon analytical categories must, for the purposes of tax policy, be translated into assertions that relate, broadly if not precisely, to empirically identifiable classes of receipts. It is for this reason that most of the subsequent discussion is directed toward the impact of taxation upon accounting profit, insofar as a significant element in it is likely to be pure entrepreneurial profit in the more obvious sense. By "pure profit in the more obvious sense" I mean the difference between the amounts paid and received by an entrepreneur in paired buying and selling transactions (including in the buying transaction the purchase of all factor services needed to make possible a subsequent selling transaction of a produced item).

PURE PROFIT THAT PROVIDES
NO INCENTIVES FOR DISCOVERY?

I have discussed some of the pitfalls surrounding attempts to identify empirical expressions of the analytical category of pure entrepreneurial profit. The discussion was conducted on the basis of insight into the special character of the incentive provided by pure entrepreneurial profit, namely, that this represents the *second* kind of incentive that I distinguished earlier. It was this insight into the special character of the pure profit incentive that suggested that the impact upon entrepreneurial discovery exercised by the taxation of profit urgently needs to be taken into account. We must now consider the possibility that the winning of pure entrepreneurial profit—in the form of a surplus of sales revenues over total relevant purchase outlays—may be accompanied by *no* incentive effects whatever.

This possibility was raised, in a somewhat different context, by Professor Shackle[2] many years ago. Shackle distinguished between two possible sources of pure profit: "imagination and knowledge" and "luck." In Shackle's view a goal for tax policy should be to avoid discouraging the exercise of imagination and knowledge; but he believed that the taxation of lucky gains involved no such disincentives. The problem remaining for Shackle was the practical one: "How are we to determine when a high rate of profit is due to luck and when to instructed imaginative enterprise?"[3] Only if such a determination can be made is it possible to hope to answer positively the central questions Shackle poses for tax policy in regard to profit: "Is it possible to devise a form of tax by which the majority of actual ventures will be caused to yield some revenue, but which will leave the incentive to enterprise, that is, the *ex ante* attractiveness of every venture, entirely unaffected? Can such a tax be so fashioned that actual gains realized *ex post* are taxed at lower rates when they accrue to those who have been able rather than merely lucky?"[4]

Shackle's understanding of the incentive role that pure profit plays in evoking "instructed imaginative enterprise" on the part of the "able" is perhaps not quite the same as my interpretation of pure profit as providing incentives "of the second kind." But the questions he has posed are of direct relevance for our inquiry as well. May it not, after all, perhaps be the case that a realized difference between sales revenue and purchase outlay corresponded to nothing that provided any incentive (of the second kind) for discovery but was instead merely the outcome of a lucky break? To point out that the emergence of pure profit is evidence of hitherto overlooked opportunities is by itself not sufficient to establish that the entrepreneur who captures such pure profit was inspired to his discovery ex ante by the incentive effect of that prospective profit. May it not, in any particular situation, perhaps be the case that in fact the entrepreneur was the fortunate beneficiary of good luck with nothing at all attributable to his own entrepreneurial alertness? And in addition may it not perhaps be that the nature of the changes that generated the profit margin were so drastic as to have been clearly beyond the scope of possible human anticipation, making it idle to speculate on the incentive power that the prospect of profitability might have had on the entrepreneur's decisions?

If indeed a significant fraction of realized pure profits is to be ascribed to sheer luck and therefore held to have played no incentive role whatever, then much of my concern in this paper would appear to be beside the point. Theorists claiming to account for the consequences of the taxation of profit may well be thought to be responsible to consider the special kind of incentive role (the "second" kind) that pure profit may fulfill in inspiring discovery. But they may be held to be justified in ignoring the second kind of incentive if it turns out that that category of income receipt held to exemplify this second kind of incentive is in fact largely a matter of sheer luck and in no way responsive to, or a result of, "instructed imaginative enterprise." Were we to believe that pure entrepreneurial profit is indeed mainly a matter of sheer good luck, were we to believe that the successful entrepreneur, looking back on his wise decisions, can honestly state that the prospect of the profit eventually grasped played no incentive role in inspiring those decisions—then we would seem to have great difficulty in claiming that the taxation of pure profit operates to discourage alert decision making. And our critique of orthodox taxation theory might seem safe to ignore.

Professor Shackle's own suggestion for distinguishing between lucky profits and profits won through shrewd entrepreneurial judgment, depends heavily on his own ("focus-value") theory of decision making under uncertainty. His suggestion involves the identification of "that one rate of profit which [the entrepreneur] had most vividly in mind when he decided that the venture was sufficiently attractive to warrant his embarking on it."[5] It should be observed that this way of putting the matter makes it clear that the emergence of a profit rate other than the one most "vividly in mind" would be (in Shackle's terminology) the emergence not of an "unexpected" course of events, but of a "counter-expected" course of events.[6] The profit that might emerge would, that is, even if far above that "most vividly in mind," represent an outcome that had at least been considered. Moreover, the framework of Shackle's discussion is one in which "the venture" was one clearly defined, at the moment of decision, quite apart from the rate of profit to be associated with it. The sense in which the vividly anticipated rate of profit served as an incentive to undertake the venture is thus quite different from that I have identified as "incentive of the second kind." Perhaps our appreciation of this difference between Professor Shackle's frame of reference and that developed in this paper may permit us to see the nature of what Professor Shackle considers to be profit due to luck through somewhat different spectacles.

THE COUNTER-EXPECTED AND THE UNEXPECTED

As we have seen, Shackle identifies a portion of realized pure profit as merely the result of luck, by showing it to have been "counter-expected." Viewing matters from this perspective, it is difficult not to agree with Shackle that the taxation of this portion of profit can have no disincentive effect on entrepreneurial action. But it must be submitted that this understanding of the scope for "imaginative enterprise" seems far too narrow. It may be suggested that a broader view of the entrepreneurial role would permit us to see that what is important is not so much the distinction between the expected (in Shackle's sense of the prospect "most vividly in mind") and the counter-expected, but rather the distinction between what has been considered as a possible contingency and what has somehow not been considered at all. (The latter is what Shackle, p. 73, calls the "unexpected event," i.e., the "contingency which has entirely escaped attention"). This distinction will permit us to recognize the possible incentive character of profit resulting from sheer luck, at several distinct levels.

For me, to choose entrepreneurially calls for more than merely to identify, out of an array of conceivable outcomes perceived as available, what appears most vivid. To choose entrepreneurially must include also the step of "discovering" those courses of action, and those arrays of potential outcomes, that one believes to be relevantly conceivable. Now we know very little about how "incentives of the second kind" operate; we know little about how the attractiveness of an outcome (or an array of possible outcomes) of a course of action stimulates the discovery of the possibility of this course of action. But we do know, if only in a very general way, that potentially attractive outcomes somehow do tend to stimulate attention.[7] We do seem likely to notice what we are personally interested in, more than we are likely to notice what holds no interest for us. From the perspective of our analysis of "incentives of the second kind," we recall that the profit incentive is not called for to stimulate *adoption* of perceived courses of action. Were we to be concerned with what stimulates the entrepreneur to *undertake* a risky, already perceived course of action, we would have to agree that considered but counter-expected outcomes can have played no role in stimulating the relevant assumption of risk by the entrepreneur.[8] Our concern, however, in the context of incentives of the second kind, is with the discovery of possibilities *worthy of consideration*. If, say, very attractive potential outcomes help attract attention to a relevant course of action that may be available, then even if after consideration of this possible course of action it turns out that *those* outcomes are indeed, in the end, counter-expected—but the course of action is adopted nonetheless because of other more vivid (if not quite as attractive) outcomes—surely we must concede that those very attractive outcomes have played their incentive role in the discovery of the adopted course of action. These insights are already sufficient for us to recognize that at least some portion of apparently "lucky" profits (that portion which entrepreneurial foresight had rendered "counter-expected" but not "unexpected") may have played an incentive role in stimulating adoption of the profitable course of action (by rendering that course of action sufficiently noticeable to have been discovered). But we can go even further.

The insights contained in the preceding paragraphs do not, after all, affect our understanding of profits that were in fact not merely counter-expected but indeed totally unexpected. Outcomes of an adopted course of action that were so far from the decision maker's field of vision as to have escaped his notice altogether must surely, even according to these insights, appear to have totally lacked any incentive role in the fortunate adoption of that course of action. Yet I shall argue that the distinction between the counter-expected and the unexpected permits, in the light of my identification of incentives of the second kind, a different view even of this kind of lucky profit. My argument depends on appreciating the *open-ended* character of the entrepreneurial decision-making context.

INCENTIVES IN AN OPEN-ENDED WORLD

Although I have made frequent reference to what I have called "incentives of the second kind" (those that encourage *discovery* of courses of action, or their desirable outcomes, that might otherwise escape attention), I have not yet given attention to the paradox inherent in the very notion of this second kind of incentive. How, one must surely ask, can an enhancement of the desirability of a particular course of action which by the very definition of this kind of incentive *has not yet been noticed* inspire its discovery? How can an *unnoticed* potential outcome, no matter how attractive, affect behavior? How can the attractiveness of an unknown opportunity that awaits one around the corner possibly inspire one to peer around that corner?

It would be presumptuous and misleading to suggest that I know how to answer these questions. We do not know (and this appears to hold true not only for economists but for psychologists as well) precisely how human beings are inspired by the attractiveness of unknown opportunities. But there can be no doubt that such inspiration has been of enormous importance throughout recorded human history. The sources of the entrepreneurial energy and alertness are still urgently in need of very basic research. Yet we know that the driving force behind this energy and this alertness is firmly rooted in the nature of the unknown—precisely the opposite of the economic motivations that govern nonentrepreneurial endeavor. Ordinary, nonentrepreneurial economic motivation operates within a given (real or assumed), closed set of circumstances. In such circumstances the drive to succeed is motivated by the visible outcomes promised by success, in relation to the perceived necessary sacrifices required by the given, closed framework. The drive that spurs entrepreneurial energy and alertness, on the other hand, appears to have its source in the very open-enededness of the entrepreneurial context.

What switches on the entrepreneurial antennae appears to be the potential entrepreneur's awareness that the situation holds unknown possibilities unconstrained by known constraints. It is the entrepreneur's awareness of the *open-enedness* of the decision context that appears to stimulate the qualities of self-reliance, initiative, and discovery.[9] It is here that we encounter once again, in a different context, the distinction between what Professor Shackle called the "counter-expected" and what he called the "unexpected."

What is counter-expected relates to the given, closed decision context. The decision maker knows enough, or at least thinks he knows enough, to be convinced that a considered outcome or event is not to be expected. Even if the counter-expected character of this outcome or event derives from an assessment of the probability of its occurrence (including in the notion of probability any relevant notion of "subjective probability" or of Shackleian potential surprise that one may wish to invoke), the conviction not to expect it resides, in these circumstances, in the set of given constraints viewed as governing the relevant probabilities. To stimulate entrepreneurial alertness, on the other hand, what is needed is the awareness of the *open* character of the situation one is confronting.

From this perspective, the truly unexpected character of an outcome or an event emerges—paradoxically, perhaps—as an aspect of it that is related, possibly in an essential manner, to that which inspires successful entrepreneurial decision making. Entrepreneurial talent consists in peering into an unknown future and arriving at an assessment of relevant features of that future. The circumstance that this assessment occurs against the background of the realization that this future that one is assessing is, after all, an unknown future is at the heart of what stimulates shrewd entrepreneurial assessments. In peering into the future one is aware that *nothing* is known with certainty about it, not the parameters of any probability functions, or potential surprise functions or anything else.

From this perspective a profit component that emerges from a "lucky" entrepreneurial decision—in the sense that it would be wholly unreasonable to believe the decision maker seriously entertained any expectation that this particular profit component might emerge—is not at all to be dismissed as having played no incentive role. While this particular result was certainly wholly "unexpected" (in Shackle's sense, particularly), it is precisely the entrepreneur's awareness of the potential that the situation held for the wholly unexpected that may have stimulated action and discovery.

To announce in advance to potential entrepreneurs that "lucky" profits will be taxed away is to convert open-ended situations into situations more and more approximating those of a given, closed character. The complete taxing away of pure entrepreneurial profit can, it is clear, succeed only in removing from potential entrepreneurs all incentive for paying attention to anything but the already known (with the "already known" to be interpreted as including what is known concerning the possibilities for costly, deliberate search in the context of a given stochastic environment).

THE TAXATION OF ENTREPRENEURIAL
DISCOVERY: REMARKS ON MORAL ASPECTS

The taxation of pure profits, we saw earlier, involves none of the disincentives ("of the first kind") usually discussed in the economic theory of taxation. Without the insights argued in this paper concerning the "second kind" of disincentive that may be associated with the taxation of pure profit, therefore, there appears to be no purely economic reason whatever not to tax away pure profit. (It should be remembered that pure profit is calculated, for our purposes, after deducting from gross revenues an amount sufficient, prospectively, to counterbalance the related risk of economic loss.) Now this conclusion, that the taxation of pure profit entails no undesirable allocative consequences—a conclusion this paper wishes to deny—turns out to reinforce a widely held view of the morality of profit. In this section I take note of this circumstance. I will, further, show that the insights of this paper (pointing out the economic disincentives involved in the taxation of pure profit) permit us to draw attention to moral aspects of pure profits that are not widely appreciated. Thus the questions raised in this paper about the economic desirability of the taxation of profit weaken, at the same time, the moral grounds for considering such taxation wholly justified.

Economic profit has, in the popular judgment, frequently been held to be morally inferior to wage remuneration. This moral inferiority attached to profit appears to be derived from its *surplus* character: profit is a receipt over and above the portion of output needed to ensure the maintenance of existing productive potential. From this perspective many critics of the capitalist system (and perhaps some of its defenders as well) have seen the theories advanced by economists to account for economic profit as somehow seeking to redeem the moral questionableness of profit. The late Joan Robinson put this point of view most bluntly by asserting that the "unconscious preoccupation behind the neo-classical system was chiefly to raise profits to the same level of moral respectability as wages. The labourer is worthy of his hire. What is the capitalist worthy of?"[10]

Now whatever the moral justification economic theory may provide for the share of profit received by the *capitalist,* it should be noticed that such justification does not yet extend to the category of pure entrepreneurial profit. By definition such profit consists of the surplus after the returns to *all* necessary factors of production, including interest on invested capital, have been set aside. No penny of pure entrepreneurial profit can be justified as *needed* to ensure the availability of any necessary productive service. Nor, by the same token, can any penny of pure profit be justified as being the *reward* of any necessary productive effort.

It may be observed that this apparent lack of moral justification for pure profit parallels with precision my discussion of how the category of pure profit possesses no incentive character (of the "first kind") whatever. Everything that is being done in the course of the profitable productive activity would be done even without one penny of profit. The circumstance that removes any incentive character (of the first kind) from pure profit is the same circumstance that, in the popular view, seems to render it morally unjustified. Thus economic reasoning arguing for the economic innocuity of profit taxation is closely related to the reasoning that upholds the moral justification of such taxation.

The reasoning in this paper concerning the disincentive effects of profit taxation impinges on these considerations with obvious significance. On the one hand, my reasoning supports, of course, the insight that pure profit fulfills no incentive role of the first kind. But more important, we have seen that an altogether different incentive role (that of the second kind) is fulfilled by pure profit. Understanding this incentive role for entrepreneurial discovery that is fulfilled by pure profits does not of itself invalidate the reasoning I have cited questioning the moral justifiability of pure profit. After all, it still remains the case that no penny of pure profit was *necessary* to be paid to make it worthwhile for the owner of a productive service to put that service to work for this profitable undertaking; no penny of profit represents the *reward* for productive effort.

Nonetheless our emphasis upon the second kind of incentive role played by pure profit does have several possible moral implications. (1) Pure profit is indeed not necessary, in the narrow meaning of the word, to ensure availability of relevant productive services, *given widespread awareness of the worthwhileness of this productive undertaking.* But it may yet be, as we have seen, that the incentive role of pure profit was a crucial factor in attracting the attention of the successful entrepreneur. It could well be that without such pure profit this productive undertaking would *not,* after all, have been undertaken. (2) Pure profit is indeed not received *in exchange for* any necessary productive service rendered. It is captured by entrepreneurs who were inspired to undertake courses of action whose profitability was "unexpected" by the market at large. This circumstance permits us to recognize profits as having been "created" or, at least, "found" by the insightful entrepreneur. In this way it may be possible to defend the moral justifiability of pure profit by what has been called the "finders-keepers" ethic.[11]

Thus the questions this paper asks concerning the economic desirability of the taxation of pure profit do tend to dovetail, in a clearly specified sense, with the related questions concerning the moral justifiability of such taxation.

THE ECONOMICS OF TAXATION:
THE SCOPE FOR RESEARCH

In this paper I have critically questioned the unstated premise of the standard theory of taxation. My criticism has rested on our insights into what I have described as incentives of the second kind. But to offer these questions and state these insights is not yet to formulate an economic theory of taxation (or even of the taxation of pure profit); far less is it to develop theoretically sound and administratively practical tax policy. A number of difficult theoretical and practical problems block the way to these goals, at least for the time being. My listing of some of these problems may be organized under two main headings: (*a*) problems arising out of our ignorance concerning the precise disincentive impacts of different patterns of profit taxation; (*b*) problems arising out of the practical and empirical difficulties of identifying the pure profit components that are part of more conventional accounting categories, and hence the difficulties in identifying which taxes may in fact involve disincentive effects (of the second kind).

Unsettled Issues Related to the Disincentive
Impact of Profit Taxation

I have pursued the insight that the pure profit inherent in economic opportunities may play an incentive role in inspiring the entrepreneurial discovery of those opportunities. This suggested strongly that the taxation of pure profits involves a disincentive not discussed in the standard literature on the economics of taxation. I linked this kind of disincentive to the circumstance that taxing away pure profit tends to convert an "open-ended" situation (which inspires entrepreneurial alertness) into the closed situation in which the alert, wide-awake, resourceful entrepreneur reverts to being the merely routinely consistent, optimizing decision maker within the given, perceived constraints. What is left unclear after these insights are acknowledged is the extent to which the *partial* taxation of profits affects the incentives for discovery. On the one hand it might appear that if profits provide incentive, then *any* reduction in the profit received must be presumed to weaken the incentives for discovery. On the other hand, however, it might be argued that a given percentage tax on prospective pure profit does not significantly erode the *open-endedness* of the situation. It is not, it may be held, the *absolute* levels of pure profit that confer the *open-ended* character upon the entrepreneurial situation. Thus at least moderate taxation of profit may perhaps only slightly affect its incentive power.

Research into the extent of disincentive exercised by this kind of partial taxation of profit might consider the example of the entrepreneurial *partnership*. In such a partnership, too, each entrepreneurial partner can expect only a portion of the pure profits that the partnership may win through his own alertness. To what extent, one wonders, is the individual entrepreneur likely to be better motivated, more likely to perceive opportunities for pure gain, than the entrepreneur who is aware that whatever his own entrepreneurial insight perceives must be shared with a partner, or with the government?

Again, although I have emphasized the importance of pure profits as providing incentives of the second kind, we possess little knowledge of the different degrees in which these incentives might operate in different contexts. The circumstance of "open-endedness" may perhaps operate quite differently in different concrete situations. It appears that such differences in context can be distinguished along several dimensions.

It is well known that entrepreneurial endeavor (and thus pure entre-preneurial profit) may find scope at three distinct levels:[12] (*a*) the level of pure arbitrage, where paired buying and selling transactions are simul-taneous (so that what the successful arbitrageur must "see" is entirely in the virtual present); (*b*) the level of pure speculation, where simultaneity is absent, so that entrepreneurial alertness must assess the future (but where what is to be sold is physically identical with what was bought); (*c*) the level of productive *creativity*, where not only is simultaneity absent, but the entrepreneur must also, so to speak, "be alert to" the possibil-ity of combining given inputs into novel forms of product or of obtain-ing given forms of product from novel combinations of input. At each of these levels the incentive for the entrepreneur to "see" correctly is to be attributed to the open-endedness of the environment. But to see a *pres-ent* price differential may call for human qualities different from those that make for shrewd speculation regarding the future. And the qualities of mind and character that stimulate "alert" creativity in production may be altogether different from those that inspire shrewd speculative vision into the future. Research into the sources of entrepreneurial alertness, and into the incentive effects of pure profit, must presumably treat each of these different kinds of entrepreneurial visions separately.

Or again, in modern capitalism a good deal of entrepreneurial vision is exercised *within* complex organizations. In the large modern corporation, for example, there may be many levels at which alert corporate execu-tives may enjoy sufficient discretionary scope, and be stimulated by suf-ficiently significant opportunities for pure gain for themselves, to require us to recognize these possibilities as representing important examples of entrepreneurial activity. There is every reason, however, to believe that the personal qualities undergirding successful entrepreneurship *within* the modern corporation may fail to overlap entirely with those qualities making for successful entrepreneurship in more conventional contexts. The effect of the taxation of the "pure profit" component in corporate executive rewards may turn out to be significantly different from the effect of taxation on other kinds of entrepreneurial profit. (One possibility for relevant research is suggested by the insights contained in Professor Henry Manne's thesis that legal prohibitions on "insider trading" operate to block the incentives to entrepreneurial discovery on the part of corpo-rate executives).[13]

The Identification of Pure Profit

The second main heading under which I organize my listing of urgent research needs in the area of entrepreneurial incentives is the empirical identification of pure profits. For policy purposes, any propositions concerning the disincentive effects of the taxation of pure profits must be translated into corresponding statements referring to measurable accounting categories. But we have already seen that accounting profits are both wider and narrower than the category of pure entrepreneurial profit to which my discussions concerning the "second kind" of incentives have pertained. Accounting profits are wider than the category of pure profits, since the former may include implicit interest on invested capital and other nonentrepreneurial categories. Accounting profits are narrower than the category of pure profits insofar as the latter may include elements of entrepreneurial receipts won by the owners of resources, including labor. All this means that the empirical identification of the profit base with respect to which policy pronouncements are to be made calls for careful and insightful research. Professor Shackle was concerned, we saw, with the practical problem of measuring the portion of pure profit attributable to entrepreneurial imagination (as distinct from that attributable to sheer luck). For me, as I noted earlier, Shackle's problem need not perhaps appear to hold significant relevance for practical tax policy. But as we see, measurement difficulties are likely to be severe even if no attempt is made to separate out elements (within the overall category of pure profit) attributable to sheer luck.

But the measurement problem touches on deeper theoretical issues as well as policy issues. The category of pure profit is, after all, one that is linked essentially to *decisions*. Accounting categories, on the other hand, are linked specifically to *periods of time*. Where a long-run decision has been a profitable one (for example, a shrewd decision to build a plant capable of producing what later turns out to be a product in high demand), the entrepreneur may reap immediate accounting profit (as where he sells the plant to eager manufacturers when the strong demand has become apparent to all). But the entrepreneur's profitable decision may not be translated into accounting profits until later periods (as when the entrepreneur operates the plant himself, in a market for which the profitability of this line of production has not yet become widely apparent). Within any given accounting period, therefore, the bare amount of accounting profit recorded reveals little definitive concerning the timing and the nature of the entrepreneurial decisions inspired by these profits.

The problems listed in this section certainly do not exhaust the research agenda that my position seems to call for, if meaningful tax policy is to take account of these concerns. Nor, again, does my position in this paper itself hold promise of any straightforward solutions to these problems. Nonetheless the questions raised, with respect to orthodox tax theory, do appear to demand the attention of theorists and policy analysts. It is for this reason that, inconclusive as my explorations have been, it seems necessary to offer them for consideration.

NOTES

1. Ludwig von Mises, *Human Action* (New Haven: Yale University Press, 1949), p. 253.

2. My critical discussion here of Professor Shackle's position pertains only to the one paper cited (first published in 1949). I certainly do not wish to suggest that that paper adequately represents the comprehensive view on pure profit developed by Professor Shackle in the course of a number of later works.

3. G. L. S. Shackle, *Expectations in Economics* (Cambridge: Cambridge University Press, 1952), p. 96.

4. Ibid., pp. 95–96.

5. Ibid., p. 99.

6. See Shackle, *Expectations in Economics*, pp. 73n, 96.

7. On this see the doctoral dissertation, B. Gilad, "An Interdisciplinary Approach to Entrepreneurship: Locus of Control and Alertness" (New York University, 1981).

8. It should be noted in this respect that, since *other* courses of action do not involve this riskiness, the incentive needed to render this risky course of action preferred must be of "the first kind."

9. See the dissertation cited in note 7.

10. Joan Robinson, *Economic Philosophy* (Harmondsworth, Middlesex: Penguin Books, 1962), p. 57.

11. For more discussion of the "finders-keepers ethic" and its relevance for entrepreneurial profit, see Israel M. Kirzner, *Perception, Opportunity, and Profit* (Chicago: University of Chicago Press, 1973), chaps. 11 and 12.

12. I am indebted to Professor L. M. Lachmann for drawing my attention to this classification.

13. See Henry G. Manne, *Insider Trading and the Stock Market* (New York: Free Press, 1966).

THE PERILS OF REGULATION:
A MARKET-PROCESS APPROACH

INTRODUCTION

Economists have for at least two centuries debated the merits of government regulation of the market economy. In recent decades, however, this debate appeared to die down, and for a number of years it seemed that economists, with very few exceptions, subscribed to (and indeed helped propagate) a strongly approving view of extensive government intervention in the marketplace. Only recently has the pendulum of professional opinion begun to swing away from a definitely interventionist position, permitting a renewal of the classic debate about government regulation of the economy.

The position in favor of extensive government regulation of the market, of course, must be sharply distinguished from the views of radical critics of capitalism. The interventionist position, unlike that of radical critics, in general thoroughly appreciates the role of the market system in the efficient allocation of resources. The interventionist position fully accepts the central theorem of welfare economics concerning the Pareto optimality achieved, on appropriate assumptions, by the competitive market in general equilibrium. Intervention, however, is said to be required by the real-world impossibility of fulfilling the assumptions needed to hold for a perfectly competitive equilibrium to prevail. Because of chronic "market failure" attributable to the violation of these assumptions, the interventionist position deems it essential that government actively modify the operation of the free market by extensive, even massive, doses of intervention and regulation. The interventionist position holds that the market economy, suitably modified by a judicious combination of government controls on prices, quality of outputs, and the organization of industry, can achieve reasonably satisfactory results. This position came

From *Discovery and the Capitalist Process* (Chicago and London: The University of Chicago Press, 1985), 119–49. Reprinted by permission of the Law & Economics Center, George Mason University; originally published as *The Perils of Regulation: A Market-Process Approach* (Coral Gables, Fla.: Law and Economics Center, University of Miami School of Law, 1979).

418

to be so entrenched in professional opinion that, supported (as it always has been) by the layman's intuition, interventionism became a virtually unchallenged orthodoxy.

Only recently has this orthodoxy begun to crumble. Both the layman and the economist have come to suspect that government interventions, especially those limiting competition and controlling prices, are consistently responsible for undesirable consequences. Confidence in the ability of government officials to construct a useful program of controls that would correct "market failure" without generating new problems attributable to government action itself has been rather thoroughly shaken. For many members of the public, and even for many economists, the crumbling of orthodoxy has come as a sharp surprise, if not a jarring shock. Economists now must rethink the theory of the market. They have begun to see that the assumption that the market can approximate a competitive equilibrium is more robust than hitherto believed. They have argued that government regulation produces its own undesirable distortions in market outcomes. Finally, economists have begun to understand that the political economy of regulation tends to ensure that market interventions are far more likely to be undertaken to further the well-being of special interests (not excepting those of the regulators themselves) than of the public at large.

This essay, too, draws attention to problems that appear to be the inescapable results of government regulation of the market. However, the approach taken here differs substantially from those just mentioned in that it does not postulate instantaneous or even rapid achievement of a general equilibrium in the free market; nor does it emphasize the undesirable distortions in equilibrium conditions introduced by government regulation. And to simplify matters, the discussion will relate to controls assumed to be deliberately introduced and enforced by legislators and officials intent on nothing but the welfare of the consuming public. The position developed here argues that intervention tends to interfere harmfully in the *entrepreneurial process* upon which the most basic of the market's virtues (conceded in principle by its interventionist critics) must surely depend.

To avoid misunderstanding, it should be emphasized that I do not wish to minimize the impact of those implications of regulation upon which my own argument does *not* rest. There can be little doubt that much regulation has been inspired, consciously or not, by considerations other than the goal of contributing to the public weal.[1] And the propensity of government interventions to generate tendencies toward suboptimal equilibrium configurations has certainly been amply demonstrated by economists from Bastiat to Friedman.[2] I merely contend that, valid though these approaches to a critique of interventionism undoubtedly are, they do not exhaust the phenomena to be explained. To sharpen the presentation of the approach taken here, regulations are assumed to be introduced and enforced with only the public welfare in mind. Many of regulation's undesirable consequences undoubtedly can be attributed to the tendency for regulation to serve the interests of regulators. I maintain that, quite apart from such difficulties, regulation generates economic confusion and inefficiency. This confusion and inefficiency are perceived more clearly by assuming, for the sake of argument, that those *other* difficulties (arising out of the regulators' self-interest) are absent.

INTERVENTIONISM AND SOCIALISM: A PARALLEL

The surprise and dismay experienced today by so many economists and others at the manifest failure of well-meaning interventionist measures to create anything but inefficiencies of their very own is reminiscent in many ways of the surprise and disquiet experienced some sixty years ago when Mises first demonstrated on theoretical grounds, the inability of a socialized economy to perform the economic calculation needed for social efficiency. It is instructive to pursue this parallel further, for properly understood, Mises's theoretical argument regarding the socialist (that is, nonmarket) economy suggests useful insights into the problems of the hampered (that is, regulated) market economy. It was the earlier failure (by Mises's readers) to understand the operation and function of the market economy that led them to assume uncritically that a socialist society, in principle, need encounter no difficulty in the attainment of social efficiency. The realization that this assumption was far from obviously justified occasioned the surprise and disquiet following Mises's famous article. The now crumbling orthodoxy upon which the interventionist approach until very recently has rested reflects misunderstandings concerning the operation and function of markets. And those misunderstandings bear a remarkable likeness to those pointed out by Mises, and later by Hayek. These deep-rooted misunderstandings, in turn, appear responsible for the surprise and dismay occasioned by the realization that government regulation may itself be the problem rather than the solution it had so obviously seemed to be.

The hampered, regulated market, of course, is not at all the same thing as the fully socialized economy which Mises and Hayek studied. In the socialized economy there is no market at all, free or otherwise, for the services of material factors. In the socialized economy, therefore, there can be no market prices for such factor services. This absence of market prices is crucial to the Mises-Hayek critique of socialism. The regulated market economy, on the other hand, no matter how hampered it may be, *is* unquestionably a market economy, in which prices emerge through the interplay of profit-seeking market transactions. The Mises-Hayek critique of socialism, therefore, is certainly not applicable, as it stands, to the regulated market.

A brief review of the Mises-Hayek critique of socialism nonetheless proves helpful for a critical appraisal of regulation. For the Mises-Hayek discussion offers an appreciation for the operation of the market process by revealing the enormous difficulties confronting socialist planners trying to emulate the market economy's achievements without a market. This discussion also reveals the hazards besetting the path of regulators seeking to improve on the market's performance. Just as the attempt to seek social efficiency through central planning rather than through the spontaneous market process, in the Mises-Hayek view, must necessarily fail, so too, for essentially similar reasons, must attempts to control the outcomes of the spontaneous market by deliberate, extra-market, regulatory action necessarily tend to generate unexpected and wholly undesired consequences.

I turn, therefore, to a brief review of the debate on socialist economic calculation, drawing particular attention to a widespread failure to appreciate fully certain important elements in the Mises-Hayek critique. It is these important elements, indeed, that will be found to be the basis for this essay's critical analysis of government regulation of the market economy. These elements underlie our perception of the parallel between a critique of the regulated market on the one hand and of socialism, without any market at all, on the other.

Mises and Hayek on Socialism

Mises's demonstration of the economic calculation problem facing the socialist planning authorities was first presented in 1920.[3] The demonstration was subsequently repeated in more or less similar terms (with critical attention paid to the attempts of socialist writers to respond to his challenge) in several of Mises's later works.[4] Hayek first addressed the problem in two essays, which respectively introduced and summed up the debate concerning socialist calculation (in the volume of essays on the subject that he edited in 1935).[5] An important third essay, published in 1940, contains Hayek's most complete appraisal of the issues.[6] Many writers on the Continent, in England, and in the United States attempted to meet Mises's arguments, the best-known socialist contribution being that of Oskar Lange.[7] A thorough survey of the state of literature at the onset of World War II, provided by a Norwegian economist, was made available in English in 1949.[8]

For Mises, the defining element in socialism lies in its collective ownership of the means of production, in particular land and capital. It follows, therefore, that under socialism there exists no market for these factors of production or for their services; without private ownership, there can be no market exchanges between individual owners; and without market exchanges, of course, there can be no ratios of exchange—that is, there can be no market prices. Mises finds in the absence of factor prices the essence of the difficulty. Without prices, socialist decision makers (the central planners and their subordinates, the managers of socialized enterprises) do not have available relevant indicators (prices) of the relative economic importance of the various factor services in their various alternative uses. Socialist planners cannot know whether the allocation of a unit of a particular resource to a specific line of production is more or less desirable than its replacement by some quantity of another resource which is technologically capable of substituting for the first. Planners cannot know in advance where efficiency is likely to be attained, nor do they have any way of assessing ex post whether or to what extent such efficiency may have been achieved.

Professor Armentano illustrates Mises's point by imagining a socialist director choosing between the construction of a power plant that uses fossil fuel and one that uses nuclear fuel. Since the state owns all of the resources, no objective money prices exist for any of the alternative projects' required resources. The socialist planner has no way of knowing which project is cheaper, which promises the greater return on investment, which, in sum, offers the most efficient way to produce electricity. "If and when the power plant is built at a particular point with particular resources, it will represent an 'arbitrary' and not an economic decision."[9]

Hayek's most complete discussion of the problem of socialist calculation appeared in 1940 as a review article analyzing particularly the contributions of two socialist economists, Oskar Lange and H. D. Dickinson.[10] Both Lange and Dickinson conceded that economic calculation is unthinkable without factor prices.[11] They pointed out, however, that a price need not mean merely an exchange ratio established in a market; the notion of price, they maintained, can be understood more broadly as "the terms on which alternatives are offered." Using price in this broader sense, they argued, there is every possibility for setting up a socialist economy in which "prices" are announced by the planning authorities and are used as guides in the decisions of socialist managers (who are instructed to obey specified rules in which these "prices" appear). These writers believed the authorities could handle the adjustment of prices on the basis of trial and error, with the relation between perceived supply and demand indicating to the authorities where adjustments should be made. In this fashion, the socialist writers held, a socialist economy could achieve an efficient allocation of resources without markets in the material factors of production, and without profit-maximizing entrepreneurial decisions.

Hayek's critique of the Lange-Dickinson proposals was long and detailed. He considered their approach to be a vast improvement as compared with the earlier socialist reactions to Mises, in which the nature of the problem was hardly perceived at all. Yet he continued to find the Lange-Dickinson proposals seriously deficient both in their perception of the problem to be solved and of the practical difficulties confronting the suggested solution. The difference, Hayek wrote, between the "system of regimented prices" proposed by the socialist economists "and a system of prices determined by the market seems to be about the same as that between an attacking army in which every unit and every man could move only by special command and by the exact distance ordered by headquarters and an army in which every unit and every man can take advantage of every opportunity offered to them."[12]

Some Thoughts on the Socialist Calculation Literature
Despite Hayek's powerful critique of the Lange-Dickinson proposals, the postwar textbook literature, curiously, came to present the results of the

interwar debate as if Mises's original claim (to have demonstrated the impossibility of economic calculation under socialism) had been decisively refuted by Lange, Dickinson, and Lerner.[13] Several writers have noted that this view conveyed by the literature is seriously mistaken.[14] A careful review of the debate surely reveals that the Lange-Dickinson-Lerner solution hardly comes to grips with the difficulties that Mises and Hayek explained. The textbook literature did not so much ignore the arguments of Mises and Hayek *as it failed to understand the view of the market process, which underlies their critique of socialist calculation.* Indeed, the authors of the socialist proposals themselves offered their solution from a perspective on the nature and function of the market economy that differed sharply from the "Austrian" perspective shared by Mises and Hayek. My purpose in drawing attention to this defective view of the market reflected in the Lange-Dickinson literature is not merely to throw light on the socialist calculation debate (an issue only tangentially relevant to our own theme of efficiency in the regulated market economy); for the insights into the market process expressed in the Mises-Hayek view and overlooked in the Lange-Dickinson proposal become crucial to a critique of the economics of regulation.

Lange's response to Mises placed much emphasis on the *"parametric function of prices,* i.e., on the fact that . . . each individual separately regards the actual market prices as given data to which he has to adjust himself."[15] For Lange, each person in the market treats prices as if they were equilibrium prices to which he must adjust himself passively. If the market prices happen *not* to be equilibrium prices, then these market prices must somehow change "by a series of successive trials"—prices rising where demand exceeds supply, and so on.[16] Lange does not address the question of *how* market prices actually change if each person at all times considers prices as given data to which he must silently adjust himself.

For Lange, indeed, the function that prices play in the efficiency of markets is simply the function that the equilibrium set of prices would fill. Prices, that is, provide the parameters to guide market participants in engaging in the set of activities that are consistent with equilibrium conditions. Lange understandably held that this function of prices could be simulated in a socialist economy. Socialist managers can be given lists of "prices" to which they can react according to well-defined rules (analogous to, but of course not identical with, the "rule" that capitalist decision makers are assumed to follow: that is, to maximize profits), Lange believed the task of ensuring that the lists of "prices" would be those required to ensure overall efficiency in the socialist economy could be fulfilled by again simulating (what he thought to be) the market trial and error procedure.

But here lies Lange's cardinal misunderstanding: he assumed that there exists in the market a procedure (involving "a series of successive trials") whereby prices are somehow adjusted toward equilibrium *without essentially altering the "parametric" character and function of prices* (that is, without departing from the supposition that each person separately regards market prices as given data, which he is unable to change). The market process through which prices are adjusted toward equilibrium, however, is a process in which prices are *not* treated as given parameters but are themselves hammered out in the course of vigorous and rivalrous bidding.

In emphasizing exclusively the "parametric" function of market prices. Lange misunderstood the central role of the market. The primary function of the market is *not* to offer an arena within which market participants can have their decentralized decisions smoothly coordinated through attention to the appropriate list of given prices. The market's essential function, rather, is to offer an arena in which market participants, by entrepreneurial exploitation of the profit opportunities offered by disequilibrium prices, can nudge prices in the direction of equilibrium. In this entrepreneurial process prices are *not* treated as parameters. Nor, in this process, are prices changed impersonally in response to excess demand or supply. It is one thing for Lange to assume that socialist managers can be motivated to follow rules with respect to centrally promulgated given "prices" (in the way capitalist decision makers can be imagined to treat given equilibrium market prices).[17] It is quite another to assume that the *non*-parametric function of price in the market system, the function dependent on entrepreneurial alertness to opportunities for pure profit, can be simulated in a system from which the entrepreneurial function has been wholly excised.

That Lange did not understand this nonparametric function of prices must certainly be attributed to a perception of the market system's operation primarily in terms of perfectly competitive equilibrium. (Indeed, it is this textbook approach to price theory that Lange explicitly presents as his model for socialist pricing.[18]) Within this paradigm, as is now well recognized, the role of the entrepreneurial quest for pure profit, as the key element in bringing about price adjustment, is completely ignored. It is not difficult to see how Lange could conclude that such a (nonentrepreneurial) system might be simulated under socialism.

Mises and Hayek, by contrast, saw the price system under capitalism from a totally different—an Austrian—perspective. For these writers, the essence of the market process lies not in the "parametric" function of price, and not in the perfectly competitive state of equilibrium, but in the rivalrous activity of entrepreneurs taking advantage of disequilibrium conditions. The debate between Lange-Dickinson on the one hand and Mises-Hayek on the other can best be understood as a clash between two conflicting views of the price system. Mises's views on the market as a process have been expounded extensively in a number of his works.[19] The idea of the market as a *dynamic process* is at the very heart of his system. Hayek's perception of the price system was articulated (during the same period in which his critical essays on socialist calculation were written) in a remarkable series of papers on the role of knowledge and discovery in market processes.[20]

That the postwar textbooks incorrectly presented the debate on socialist calculation as having been decisively won by Lange must be attributed not to ideological bias (although this may not have been entirely absent) but to an utter failure to understand the flaws in Lange's discussion (flaws that Hayek indeed had identified). Not recognizing the Austrian background of Hayek's critique, Anglo-American economists saw in Lange a cogent application of standard price theory; Hayek's critique simply was not understood.

The Market Process: An Austrian View[21]

Before returning to the theme of efficiency in the regulated economy, it is useful to review some Austrian lessons to be drawn from the socialist calculation debate. The Austrian understanding of the market as a dynamic process of discovery generated by the entrepreneurial-competitive scramble for pure profit may be spelled out in terms of a brief discussion of several key concepts. A sensitive appreciation of these ideas will alert us to problems raised by government regulation of the market that might otherwise easily be overlooked. It is partly because the terms convenient for the exposition of these concepts also are used in non-Austrian contexts, with rather different meanings, that the ideas developed here are so often misunderstood and therefore require brief elaboration.

Competition. What keeps the market process in motion is competition—*not* competition in the sense of "perfect competition," in which perfect knowledge is combined with very large numbers of buyers and sellers to generate a state of perennial equilibrium—but competition as the rivalrous activities of market participants trying to win profits by offering the market better opportunities than are currently available. The existence of rivalrous competition requires *not* large numbers of buyers and sellers but simply *freedom of entry.* Competition places pressure on market participants to discover where and how better opportunities, as yet unnoticed, *might* be offered to the market. The competitive market process occurs because equilibrium has not yet been attained. This process is thwarted whenever nonmarket barriers are imposed blocking entry to potential competitors.

Knowledge and Discovery. As Hayek has emphasized, the competitive market process is a discovery procedure.[22] If all that needed to be known were already known, then the market would already have attained full equilibrium, the state in which all decisions correctly anticipate all other decisions being made within the market. An institutional device for social organization that mobilizes existing knowledge and brings it to bear upon decision makers is necessary because realistically people never do have command even over all the information that is already known somewhere.[23] Market equilibrium is thinkable only if we can presuppose the full mobilization of existing knowledge; so also centralized economic control would be thinkable (whether by Lange-Dickinson-Lerner proposals or other devices) if we could assume existing knowledge already to be fully mobilized. It is just because, without a market, such prior mobilization is so difficult to assume that a market is seen to be a prerequisite for economic calculation.

The competitive market process is needed not only to mobilize existing knowledge, but also to generate awareness of opportunities whose very existence until now has been known to no one at all.[24] The entrepreneurial process, moreover, disseminates existing information through the market. The process itself is a continual one of the discovery of opportunities. The discoverer of these opportunities himself, at least, has had no inkling whatever of their very existence. The market, in other words, is not merely a process of search for information of the need for which men had previously been aware; it is a discovery procedure that tends to correct ignorance where the discoverers themselves were totally unaware that they indeed were ignorant. A realization that the market yields knowledge—the sort of knowledge that people do not at present even know they need—should engender among would-be social engineers who seek to replace or to modify the results of the free market a very definite sense of humility. To announce that one can improve on the performance of the market, one must also claim to know in advance what the market will reveal. This knowledge is clearly impossible in all circumstances. Indeed, where the market process has been thwarted, in general it will not be possible to point with certainty to what *might* have been discovered that has now been lost.

Profit and Incentives. In standard treatments of price theory, decision makers are assumed to maximize utility or "profit." The profit for which entrepreneurs are so eager (and which for Austrians drives the market process) is *not* that "profit" maximized by the firm in the standard theory of the firm. The standard theory assumes that the firm confronts definitely known and given cost and revenue possibilities. For the theory of the firm, therefore, to maximize profits does not mean to *discover* an opportunity for pure gain; it means merely to perform the mathematical calculations required to exhaust the *already fully perceived* opportunity for gain that the given revenue and cost curves might present. The urge of would-be entrepreneurs to grasp profit, by contrast, is the force which *itself reveals* the existence of gaps between costs and revenues. This distinction is of considerable importance.

It is elementary to the theory of the market that the market performs its functions by virtue of the *incentives* it offers to those who make "correct" decisions. For example, the incentive of the higher wages offered by industries in which the marginal productivity of labor is greatest attracts labor to more important uses. Such incentives tend to ensure that once a superior use for a given factor (or group of factors) is discovered, it becomes worthwhile for factor owners to forgo alternative ways of putting their factors to work. This is well understood. What is not always understood is that the market also offers incentives for the *discovery* of new opportunities (for the most useful employment of factors), that is, for the exploitation of opportunities that until now have remained unexploited. These opportunities have remained unexploited *not* because of high costs, and not even because of the high cost of searching for them.

They have remained unexploited simply because of sheer oversight, possibly including oversight of the opportunity to find them through deliberate search. Pure entrepreneurial profit is the market form in which *this* kind of incentive presents itself. The availability of pure entrepreneurial profit has the function not of outweighing the costs associated with withdrawing inputs from alternative uses, but of alerting decision makers to the present error of committing factors to uses less valuable to the markets than others waiting and able to be served.

Market Prices. Market prices in the Austrian view are not primarily approximations to the set of equilibrium prices. Instead, they are (disequilibrium) exchange ratios worked out between entrepreneurial market participants. On the one hand, these exchange ratios with all their imperfections reflect the discoveries made up until this moment by profit-seeking entrepreneurs. On the other hand, these ratios express entrepreneurial errors currently being made. Market prices, therefore, offer opportunities for pure profit. And we can rely on these opportunities to create a tendency for market prices to be changed through the rivalrous bidding of alert entrepreneurs. The course of market prices, in other words, is closely bound up, in *two* distinct ways, with the incentive system of pure entrepreneurial profit. First, the configuration of market prices at any given moment must be attributed to the pure profit incentives that have until now determined bids and offers. Second, this present configuration of market prices, together with existing and future conditions of supply and demand, is responsible for the opportunities for pure profit. The discovery and exploitation of these opportunities will constitute the course of the market process in the immediate future. From this perspective on market prices it is not difficult to perceive how small must be the resemblance to them of any centrally promulgated set of socialist "prices." The entrepreneurial drive for pure profit plays no role at all in the determination of socialist "prices."

REGULATED MARKET ECONOMY

I shall assume, as noted at the outset of this essay, that government regulation of the market economy is generated by dissatisfaction with market outcomes. Legislators or other government officials (perhaps in response to public outcry, or in anticipation thereof) are disturbed either by the high price that certain would-be purchasers are asked to pay in the market or by the low price (for example, farm prices or the wages of labor) received by certain sellers in the market; or they are disturbed by the quality of goods or services being offered for sale (for example, because of the absence of safety devices) or by the unavailability in the market of goods or services that they believe to be important. They are disturbed by the conditions under which workers are expected to work, or they are disturbed by the pattern of income distribution generated by the market, by unemployment, or by "profiteering," or by the side effects (such as environmental pollution, or spread of disease, or exposure of the young to pornography) generated by uncontrolled market activity.

Hoping to correct what are perceived to be unsatisfactory conditions, the government intervenes in the market. It seeks to replace the outcomes expected to result from unchecked market transactions by a preferred configuration of prices and outputs, to be achieved not, as under socialism, by replacing the market by central ownership of factors, but by imposing appropriate regulations and controls. The laissez-faire market is replaced by the regulated market. Price ceilings and price and wage floors, transfers of incomes, imposed safety standards, child labor laws, zoning laws, prohibited industrial integration, tariff protection, prohibited competition, imposed health warnings, compulsory old age pensions, and prohibited drugs are all examples of the countless controls that well-meaning public officials impose.

In the face of these controls, regulations, and interventions there remains, nonetheless, a genuine market both for factor services and for consumer products. Government controls constrain and constrict; they rearrange and repattern the structure of incentives; they redistribute incomes and wealth and sharply modify both the processes of production and the composition of consumption. Yet within the limits that such controls impose, buying and selling continue, and the constant effort to capture pure entrepreneurial gain keeps the market in perpetual motion. Government regulations drastically alter and disturb opportunities for entrepreneurial gain, but they do not eliminate them. These controls thoroughly influence the prices that emerge from the interplay of entrepreneurial competition. But unless directly mandated prices are involved, exchange ratios still reflect the outcome to date of the entrepreneurial process.

Traditionally, criticism of government intervention involves one or more of several general lines of argument.[25] First, critics may argue that

the admitted failure of market outcomes to meet successfully the aspirations of regulators is a result not of market failure to achieve peak efficiency, but of inescapable scarcity. If costs are fully taken into account,
efforts to improve outcomes must be found to be doomed to failure or
to lead to even less preferable outcomes. Second, critics may agree that
from the viewpoint of the value system adopted by the would-be regulators market outcomes might be improved upon. But, these critics maintain that the market faithfully reflects consumers' values. Regulation in
such circumstances therefore must violate consumer sovereignty, if not
consumer freedom.

Third, critics may argue that the unwished-for market outcomes are
to be attributed not to the free market, but to earlier government interventions in the market which have hindered the corrective forces of the
market from doing their work. Additional regulation, it is then pointed
out, either may be unnecessary (since the earlier interventions can simply be eliminated) or may compound the problems. Fourth, critics may
argue that whether or not the undesirable outcomes of the market are (in
the sense appropriate to economic science and not necessarily from the
viewpoint of the regulators' values) to be regretted, government regulation is simply incapable of achieving improvement. The technology of
regulation is such that its full costs outweigh by far any benefits that may
be achieved.

The Austrian lessons drawn from the preceding survey of the debate
about socialist economic calculation suggest that another set of considerations, until now not sufficiently emphasized in the literature, deserve to
be included in the list of causes to which one might attribute the failures
of regulation. These considerations constitute a separate line of criticism
of government intervention, to be added to the other lines of criticism
(where one or more of these may be relevant).[26]

Government Regulation and the Market Discovery Process

The perils associated with government regulation of the economy
addressed here arise out of the *impact that regulation can be expected to
have on the discovery process, which the unregulated market tends to generate.*
Even if current market outcomes in some sense are judged unsatisfactory, intervention, and even intervention that can successfully achieve its
immediate objectives, cannot be considered the obviously correct solution. After all, the very problems apparent in the market might generate

processes of discovery and correction superior to those undertaken deliberately by government regulation; deliberate intervention by the state not only might serve as an imperfect substitute for the spontaneous market process of discovery; but also might impede desirable processes of discovery the need for which has *not* been perceived by the government. Again, government regulation itself may generate new (unintended and undesired) processes of market adjustments that produce a final outcome even less preferred than what might have emerged in the free market.

Here I discuss critically the impact of government regulation on the discovery process of the unregulated market at four distinct levels. First, I consider the likelihood that would-be regulators may not correctly assess the course the market might itself take in the absence of regulation. Second, I consider the likelihood that, because of the presumed absence of entrepreneurial incentives operating on government decision makers, government regulatory decisions will fail to exploit opportunities for social betterment waiting to be discovered. Third, I consider the likelihood that government regulation may stifle or inhibit desirable discovery processes which the market might have generated. Finally, I consider the likelihood that government regulation may influence the market by creating opportunities for new, and not necessarily desirable, market discovery processes which would not be relevant in an unregulated market.

The Undiscovered Discovery Process

We assumed earlier that regulation is demanded because of undesirable conditions that emerge in the market in the absence of regulation. But the urge to regulate, to control, to alter these outcomes must presume not only that these undesirable conditions are attributable to the absence of regulation, but also that the speedy removal of such conditions cannot be expected from the future course of unregulated market events. To attribute undesirable conditions to absence of regulation, moreover, also may require the denial of the proposition that were a better state of affairs indeed feasible, the market probably would have already discovered how to achieve it.

More specifically, many demands for government intervention into the market rest on one or both of two possible misunderstandings concerning the market discovery process. Demand for government intervention, on the one hand, might grow out of a failure to realize that the market already may have discovered virtually everything worth discovering (so that what appears to be obvious inefficiency might be able to be explained altogether satisfactorily if government officials had all the information the market has long since discovered and taken advantage of). Demand for regulation, on the other hand, may stem from the belief that unsatisfactory conditions will never be corrected unless by deliberate intervention. Such demands for regulation might be muted, that is, were it understood that genuine inefficiencies can be relied upon in the *future* to generate market processes for their own correction. (This second misunderstanding itself may rest on either of two bases. First, the tendency of markets to discover and eliminate inefficiency simply is not recognized. Second, by contrast, it is assumed, far too sanguinely, that market processes are *so* rapid that our awareness of an unmistakably unsatisfactory condition proves that some kind of market "failure" has occurred and that one cannot rely on future corrective processes.)

These misunderstandings, so often the foundation for demands for intervention, surely derive from an unawareness of several basic principles of the theory of market process. These principles show that, first, were knowledge perfect, it would be inconceivable that unexploited opportunities could yet remain for rearranging the pattern of input utilization or output consumption in such a way as to improve the well-being of all market participants; second, the existence of such unexploited opportunities, reflecting imperfect knowledge throughout the market, expresses itself in the unregulated market in the form of opportunities for pure entrepreneurial profit; and third, the tendency for such pure profit opportunities to be discovered and exploited tends more or less rapidly to eliminate unexploited opportunities for improving the allocation of resources.[27] These principles of the theory of market process suggest that if genuine inefficiency exists, then (perhaps because of a recent sudden change in conditions of resource supply, of technology, or of consumer tastes) the market has not yet discovered *all that it will surely soon tend to discover.*

These principles may be denied either by expressing a lack of confidence in the systematic tendency for imperfect knowledge to be spontaneously improved or by attributing to the market the ability to attain equilibrium instantaneously (that is, by assuming that ignorance is not merely a disequilibrium phenomenon, but that ignorance disappears the very instant it emerges). Both denials may lead to demands for government intervention. The denial based on a lack of confidence about improving knowledge leads to the belief that current inefficiencies will not tend to be corrected spontaneously (and also to the propensity to see inefficiency where the market *already* has made necessary corrections). The denial based on the belief in instantaneous correction of disequilibrium conditions leads to the view that existing inefficiencies somehow are consistent with market equilibrium and that therefore extramarket steps are called for to achieve correction.

The Unsimulated Discovery Process

Government regulation takes the general form of imposed price ceilings and floors, of mandated quality specifications, and of other restraints or requirements imposed in interpersonal market transactions. The hope surrounding such government impositions, I continue to assume, is that they will constrain market activities to desired channels and at desired levels. But what is the likelihood that government officials, with the best of intentions, will *know* what imposed prices, say, might evoke the "correct," desired actions by market participants? This question parallels that raised by Mises and Hayek with respect to "market" socialism.[28] Government officials in the regulated economy do enjoy the advantage (*not* shared by socialist planning officials) of making their decisions within the framework of genuine market prices. But the question remains: How do government officials know what prices to set (or qualities to require, and so forth)? Or to press the point further: How will government officials know if their earlier decisions were in error and in what direction to make corrections? In other words, how will government officials *discover* those opportunities for improving the allocation of resources, which one cannot assume to be automatically known to them at the outset of a regulatory endeavor?

The compelling insight underlying these questions rests heavily on the circumstance that officials institutionally are precluded from capturing *pecuniary* profits in the market, in the course of their activities (even though they are as eager as anyone else for entrepreneurial "profit" in the broadest sense of the term). The regulators' estimates of the prices consumers are prepared to pay, or of the prices resource owners are prepared to accept, for example, *are not profit-motivated estimates*. The estimates are not profit motivated at the time of an initial government regulatory action, and they are not profit motivated at each subsequent date when modification of a regulation might be considered. But estimates of market demand conditions or market supply conditions that are not profit motivated cannot reflect the powerful, discovery-inspiring incentives of the entrepreneurial quest for profit.

Nothing in the course of the regulatory process suggests a tendency for as yet unperceived opportunities of resource allocation improvement to be discovered. Nothing ensures that government officials who might perceive market conditions more accurately than others will tend systematically to replace less competent regulators. There is no entrepreneurial process at work, and there is no proxy for entrepreneurial profit or loss that easily might indicate where errors have been made and how they should be corrected. What regulators know (or believe they know) at a given moment presumably remains only partly correct. No systematic process seems at work through which regulators might come to discover what they have not known, *especially since they have not known that they enjoy less than complete awareness of a particular situation.*

The problem raised here is not quite the same as the one identified in other literature critical of government intervention. It is often noted, for example, that government officials are not motivated to minimize costs, since they will not personally benefit from the resulting economies.[29] The problem raised here differs importantly from such questions of incentives for adopting known efficiencies. For even if one could imagine an official so dedicated to the citizenry that he would ensure the adoption of all known possible measures for cutting costs, one cannot yet imagine him somehow divining *as yet undiscovered* techniques for cutting costs. What the official knows, he knows, and what he knows that he does *not* know, one may imagine him diligently undertaking to find out, through appropriate cost-benefit-calculated search. But one can hardly imagine him discovering, except by the sheerest accident, those opportunities for increasing efficiency of which he is completely unaware. The official is not subject to the entrepreneurial profit incentive, which somehow appears continually and successfully to inspire discovery of hitherto undreamed of possibilities for eliminating unnecessary expenditures. Nothing within the regulatory process seems able to simulate even remotely well the discovery process that is so integral to the unregulated market.

The Stifled Discovery Process

The most serious effect of government regulation on the market discovery process well might be the likelihood that regulation, in a variety of ways, may discourage, hamper, and even completely stifle the discovery process of the unregulated market. Indeed, that much regulation is introduced as a result of unawareness of the market's discovery process already has been noted.

Government regulation plainly might bar exploitation of opportunities for pure entrepreneurial profit. A price ceiling, a price floor, an impeded merger, or an imposed safety requirement might block possibly profitable entrepreneurial actions. Such restraints and requirements may be designed to block *particular* activities. If so, the likelihood is that since the possibility of such activities is so clearly seen and feared, the blocked activity may provide standard rates of return, but *not* particularly profitable ones in the entrepreneurial sense. Regulated restraints and requirements, though, are also likely to block activities that have *not* yet been foreseen by anyone, including the regulatory authorities. Regulatory constraints, that is, are likely *to bar the discovery* of pure profit opportunities.

That government regulation diminishes competition is common knowledge. Tariffs, licensing requirements, labor legislation, airline regulation, and bank regulation reduce the number of potential participants in particular markets. Government regulation, therefore, is responsible for imposing monopolylike inefficiencies ("deadweight" welfare losses) upon the economy. But such losses by no means constitute the full impact of the countercompetitive measures often embodied in regulatory constraints.

The beneficent aspect of competition in the sense of a rivalrous process, as noted earlier, arises out of *freedom of entry*. What government regulations so often erect are *regulatory barriers to entry*. Freedom of "entry," for the Austrian approach, refers to the freedom of potential competitors to discover and to move to exploit existing opportunities for pure profit. If entry is blocked, such opportunities simply may never be discovered, either by existing firms in the industry, or by regulatory authorities, or for that matter by outside entrepreneurs who *might* have discovered such opportunities were they allowed to be exploited when found.

From *this* perspective on regulation's anticompetitive impact, it follows that much regulation introduced explicitly to *create* or *maintain* competition is no less hazardous to the competitive-entrepreneurial process than are other forms of regulation that restrict competition. Entry of competitors, in the dynamic sense, need not mean entry of firms of about equal size. For example, entry might imply the *replacement,* by merger or other means, of a number of relatively high-cost producers by a *single* low-cost producer. Antitrust activity designed ostensibly to protect competition might *block* this kind of entry. Such regulatory activity thus blocks the capture of pure profit, obtainable in this case by the discovery and implementation of the possibility of lowering the price to consumers by taking advantage of hitherto unexploited, and perhaps unsuspected, economies of scale.

The literature critical of government regulation often draws attention to the undesirable effects of imposed prices. A price ceiling for a particular product or service (rent control, for example) tends to generate artificial shortages (of housing). A price floor for a particular product or service (minimum wages, for example) tends to generate an artificial surplus (teenage unemployment). These important, well-recognized consequences of imposed prices flow from the efforts of the regulators to legislate prices at other than equilibrium levels.

Quite apart from the discoordination generated by such imposed prices in the markets for *existing* goods and services, price (and also quality) restraints also may well inhibit the discovery of wholly new opportunities. A price ceiling does not merely block the upper reaches of a given supply curve. Such a ceiling also may inhibit the discovery of as yet unsuspected sources of supply (which in the absence of the ceiling would have tended to shift the entire supply curve to the right) or of as yet wholly unknown new products (tending to create supply curves for wholly new graphs).[30] The lure of pure profit tends to uncover such as yet unknown opportunities.

Price and quality restraints and requirements and restrictions on organizational forms operate (in a generally understood but not precisely predictable way) to inhibit entrepreneurial discovery. Price ceilings, for example, not only restrict supply from known sources of natural gas (or from known prospects for search), but also inhibit the discovery of wholly unknown sources. Drug testing regulations, as another example, not only reduce the flow of new pharmaceutical drugs where successful research might have been more or less predictable, but also discourage the entrepreneurial discovery of wholly unknown research procedures. Against whatever benefits might be derived from government regulation and intervention, one is forced to weigh, as one of regulation's intrinsically immeasurable costs, the stifling of the market discovery process.

The Wholly Superfluous Discovery Process

There is yet one more aspect of government regulation's complex impact on the discovery process. Whether intended by the regulatory authorities or not and whether suspected by them or not, the imposition of regulatory restraints and requirements tends to create entirely new, and not necessarily desirable opportunities for entrepreneurial discovery.

That such opportunities may be created follows from the extreme unlikelihood that government-imposed price, quality, or quantity constraints introduce anything approaching an equilibrium configuration. These constraints, on the contrary, introduce pure profit opportunities that would otherwise have been absent, as they simultaneously reduce or possibly eliminate other opportunities for pure profit that might otherwise have existed. This rearrangement of opportunities for pure profits, of course, is unlikely to be the explicit aim of regulation; nor even, indeed, is such rearrangement ever likely to be fully *known* to the authorities. Market ignorance is a fact of economic life. It follows that the replacement of one set of (unregulated) prices by another set of (partly regulated) prices, simply means that regulation has generated a possibly major alteration in the pattern of the discovery process. The now regulated market will tend to pursue the altered discovery process.

This regulation-induced alteration in the pattern of market discovery is closely related to the often noticed circumstance that regulation may result in a different set of *equilibrium* market consequences. Such consequences, moreover, may not have been correctly foretold by the authorities and, indeed, may be wholly undesired by them. Regulation often imposes costs not immediately recognized.[31] Unless, quite fantastically, the regulatory authorities (somehow all acting in completely coordinated fashion) are perfectly informed on all relevant data about the market, they will *not* generally be able to perceive what new profit opportunities they create by their own regulatory actions. Inevitably, therefore, the imposition of a set of regulatory constraints on a market must set in motion a series of entrepreneurial actions that have *not* been anticipated and, therefore, that may well lead to wholly unexpected and even undesired final outcomes.[32]

The one kind of new "profit" opportunity created by regulation that is by now well anticipated, though hardly desired of course, involves bribery and corruption of the regulators. There is widespread understanding of the unwholesome channels into which the entrepreneurial quest for pure profit inevitably tends to be attracted if arbitrary restraints on otherwise profitable activities are imposed.[33]

The basic insight underlying these conclusions, in sum, is a simple one. The competitive-entrepreneurial process, being a process of discovery of the as yet unknown, can hardly be predicted in any but the broadest terms. The imposition of regulatory constraints necessarily results, therefore, in a pattern of consequences different from and, most plausibly, distinctly less desirable than what would have occurred in the unregulated market. One might therefore refer to this unplanned, undesired pattern of consequences of regulation as the wholly superfluous discovery process.

DISCOVERY, EVIDENCE, AND ILLUSTRATION

The preceding discussion is theoretical and general, providing no hints of possible verification of its conclusions. While this discussion relies on highly plausible insights into the character of human action, a reader may believe himself justified in demanding evidence that might support the discussion's rather strong conclusions. Yet such evidence can hardly be furnished, and it may be instructive to spell out the reasons.

Evidence about Discovery

Econometricians have endeavored to measure the consequences of particular economic policies. Much of their ingenuity and sophistication has been called forth to grapple with the formidable problem of describing *what might have occurred* in the absence of particular policies. The problem of describing concretely what might have happened but did not, it should be noted, exists even in situations in which all the alternatives before relevant decision makers are clearly defined, so that one at least knows the list of options from among which choices would have been forthcoming. The problem derives from the circumstance that it is not possible, without more or less sophisticated conjecture, to be confident as to which of an array of options a particular decision maker *might* have selected in hypothetical circumstances.

This problem becomes infinitely more formidable if one wishes to describe, in specified hypothetical circumstances, *what might have been spontaneously discovered*. Here the problem is not merely that a particular decision maker's preferences are unknown. The problem is that one cannot imagine what specific, now unknown opportunities might have been discovered in the relevant hypothetical circumstances.

One should not be surprised, therefore, that the losses from the regulatory stifling of market discovery processes are difficult to single out. Indeed, one should not be surprised that analysis, too, has tended to overlook such losses. Therefore one can only hope to draw brief attention to studies that perhaps can provide some illustrative flavor of the kinds of losses attributable to regulatory constraints, to which I have sought to direct attention. For purposes of such illustration, I draw on work focusing on the discovery process initiated by the lure of entrepreneurial profit in technological innovation and in corporate entrepreneurial endeavor.

Discoverers: Innovators

Much recent work by economists is devoted to gaining insight into the process of technological innovation. A small part of that work has considered the impact of government regulation on innovative activity at the technological frontiers. Although the authors of these studies are not primarily concerned with the impact of regulation upon entrepreneurial incentives, it is difficult to read their work without noticing its direct relevance to this essay's concerns.

A 1971 Brookings Institution volume, for example, was devoted to a symposium examining technological change in regulated industries (in particular electric power, telecommunications, and air and surface transportation).[34] In the analytical framework within which this examination was conducted, brief attention is paid to the thesis (attributed, perhaps too hastily, to Schumpeter) that it is "the incentive to earn very large profits" which "spurs entrepreneurs to introduce new techniques," so that the limits on possible profits imposed by regulatory commissions may inhibit such innovation.[35]

A similar possible link between regulatory constraints and the possible slowing down of the processes of technological discovery is noted particularly in the context of drug research in the pharmaceutical industry. The classic paper by Professor Peltzman, examining the impact of the 1962 drug amendments upon drug research, together with the work of others, has led to widespread discussion of the possibility that drug research in the United States lags seriously behind that of other countries.[36] Peltzman's results do not prove that regulation inhibits entrepreneurial discovery, which means the discovery of hitherto unknown opportunities, unknown even in the sense that it had not been known that they were there to be discovered. That is, Peltzman's findings would fit in equally well with a theory of search based on the assumption of awareness of discoverable opportunities waiting to be researched if the cost were not too high. Nonetheless, once attention is focused on entrepreneurial discovery, it is difficult to avoid linking Peltzman's results with the postulation of an entrepreneurial discovery process hampered by regulatory constraints.

Discoverers: Insiders

Another important area in which the role of entrepreneurial discovery has been explicitly explored is that of decision making by corporate managers. In his definitive study of the issue, Henry Manne discusses the impact upon the exercise of entrepreneurship in the corporate firm of regulatory restrictions on insider trading.[37] Manne's study thoroughly examines the entrepreneurial role and its expression in a world of corporations. The study identifies the incentives of entrepreneurial profit needed to evoke the entrepreneurial role and the part that insider trading, in the absence of regulatory prohibition, might play to provide profit opportunities to reward entrepreneurial success. Restrictions on insider trading, Manne shows, no matter how plausible the motives underlying the regulatory restrictions may appear, tend to inhibit the exercise of entrepreneurship in corporate firms.[38]

CONCLUSION

This essay draws attention to some less obvious drawbacks of government regulation of the market. These drawbacks are rooted in the way regulatory restrictions, restraints, and controls interfere with the spontaneous discovery process that the unregulated market tends to generate. These drawbacks are also to be clearly distinguished from other disadvantages that flow from government intervention.

The peculiar character of the perils of regulation identified here closely parallels certain economic problems associated with the operation of the socialist economy. The review of the Mises-Hayek criticisms of the possibility of economic calculation under socialism provides a classic source for an Austrian perspective on the market process, and simultaneously the review provides important lessons for an understanding of the dangers inherent in regulation.

Recognition of these dangers can be most helpful in explaining the inefficiencies and the stagnation that appear so consistently to beset modern interventionist economies. It is in the nature of the subject, however, that the recognition of these perils does not lead easily to the provision of clear-cut examples of such regulatory damage. Nonetheless, in a modest way it is possible to illustrate these perils from contemporary discussions of palpable problems.

An emphasis on the perils of regulation that arises out of concern for the market process does not, in and of itself, justify the absolute condemnation of government regulation of the market process. Such condemnation would require full consideration, in addition, not only of other perils than those discussed here, but also of the hoped-for benefits sought through regulation of the market. Ultimately, public policy must depend on the value judgments of the policymakers or of those they wish to serve. But, no policy decisions with respect to government regulation can be properly arrived at without a full understanding of all the dangers inherent in such regulation. And such a full understanding arises particularly out of studying the market process of entrepreneurial discovery.

NOTES

1. For the literature on private incentives for public regulation, see George J. Stigler, "The Theory of Economic Regulation," *Bell Journal of Economics and Management Science* 2 (Spring 1971): 3–21; reprinted in Stigler, *The Citizen and the State* (Chicago: University of Chicago Press, 1975); Richard A. Posner, "Theories of Economic Regulation," *Bell Journal of Economics and Management Science* 5 (Autumn 1974): 335–58; Sam Peltzman, "Toward a More General Theory of Regulation," *Journal of Law and Economics* 19 (August 1976): 211–40.

2. The most trenchant recent criticisms of government regulation from this perspective include Ludwig von Mises, *Human Action* (New Haven: Yale University Press, 1949), part 6; Milton Friedman, *Capitalism and Freedom* (Chicago: University of Chicago Press, 1962); Friedman, *An Economist's Protest* (Glen Ridge, N.J.: Thomas Horton and Daughters, 1972).

3. Ludwig von Mises, "Die Wirtschaftsrechnung im sozialistischen Gemeinwesen," *Archiv für Sozialwissenschaften und Sozialpolitik* 47 (April 1920): 86–121; reprinted in *Collectivist Economic Planning*, trans. and ed. Friedrich A. Hayek (London: Routledge and Kegan Paul, 1935).

4. Ludwig von Mises, *Socialism: An Economic and Sociological Analysis*, trans. J. Kahane (New Haven: Yale University Press, 1951), part 2, sect. 1; this edition is translated from the second German edition (published 1932) of Mises's *Die Gemeinwirtschaft* (originally published in 1922); see also Mises, *Human Action*, part 5.

5. Hayek, *Collectivist Economic Planning*.

6. Friedrich A. Hayek, "Socialist Calculation: The Competitive 'Solution,'" *Economica* 7 (May 1940): 125–49; reprinted as "Socialist Calculation III: The Competitive

'Solution,'" in Hayek, *Individualism and Economic Order* (London: Routledge and Kegan Paul, 1949).

7. Oskar Lange, "On the Economic Theory of Socialism," in Oskar Lange and Fred M. Taylor, *On the Economic Theory of Socialism*, ed. Benjamin E. Lippincot (New York: McGraw-Hill, 1964).

8. Trygve J. B. Hoff, *Economic Calculation in the Socialist Society*, trans. M. A. Michael (London and Edinburgh: Hodge, 1949).

9. Dominic T. Armentano, "Resource Allocation Problems under Socialism," in *Theory of Economic Systems: Capitalism, Socialism, Corporatism*, ed. William P. Snavely (Columbus, Ohio: Merrill, 1969), pp. 133–34.

10. Hayek, "Socialist Calculation III." Reviewed particularly were Lange, "On the Economic Theory of Socialism," and Henry D. Dickinson, *Economics of Socialism* (London: Oxford University Press, 1939).

11. Thus they agreed with Mises and Hayek that efficiency is impossible without indicators of value and that any hope of solving the problem by direct mathematical methods (for example, by solving the Walrasian equation system) is illusory.

12. Hayek, *Individualism and Economic Order*, p. 187.

13. Abba P. Lerner, *The Economics of Control* (New York: Macmillan, 1944).

14. See most recently Murray N. Rothbard, "Ludwig von Mises and Economic Calculation under Socialism," in *Economics of Ludwig von Mises*, ed. Laurence S. Moss (Kansas City: Sheed and Ward, 1976).

15. Lange, "On the Economic Theory of Socialism," p. 70.

16. Ibid., pp. 70–71.

17. This assumption, of course, is vulnerable to serious question. See James M. Buchanan, *Cost and Choice* (Chicago: Markham, 1969), chap. 6; G. Warren Nutter, "Markets without Property: A Grand Illusion," in *Money, the Market, and the State: Essays in Honor of James Muir Waller*, ed. Nicholas A. Beadles and L. Aubrey Drewry, Jr. (Athens: University of Georgia Press, 1968). It is important to note that the argument stated in the text does *not* depend on any doubt concerning managers' ability and motivation to obey rules. Were socialist managers to be given price lists, then we may assume for the purposes of the present discussion that they *could* make decisions *as if* they were intent on maximizing "profits." (Of course, the profits maximized in equilibrium contexts are not pure entrepreneurial profits. This distinction is discussed later in this essay.)

18. Lange, "On the Economic Theory of Socialism," pp. 65–72.

19. Particularly in Mises, *Human Action*, chap. 15.

20. Hayek, "Economics and Knowledge," "The Use of Knowledge in Society," and "The Meaning of Competition," all reprinted in *Individualism and Economic Order*. In this respect the work of Austrian-born Joseph A. Schumpeter is of considerable relevance for the Austrian view of the market; see particularly Schumpeter, *The Theory of Economic Development*, trans. Redvers Opie (New York: Oxford University Press, 1961); this work first appeared in German in 1912 and was first translated by Opie in 1934.

See also Schumpeter, *Capitalism, Socialism and Democracy* (New York: Harper and Row, 1950), chap. 7.

21. This section draws freely from my *Competition and Entrepreneurship* (Chicago: University of Chicago Press, 1973), and *Perception, Opportunity, and Profit* (Chicago: University of Chicago Press, 1979).

22. Friedrich A. Hayek, ed., "Competition as a Discovery Procedure," in *New Studies in Philosophy, Politics, Economics and the History of Ideas* (Chicago: University of Chicago Press, 1978).

23. See Hayek, "Economics and Knowledge," "The Use of Knowledge in Society," and "The Meaning of Competition."

24. See Kirzner, *Perception, Opportunity, and Profit,* chaps. 2, 8, 9.

25. Once again, we assume away criticisms based on the view that regulation may be motivated not by the wish to benefit consumers, but by the wish to benefit the regulators and those they regulate.

26. While these considerations support a stance critical of regulation, in and of themselves they do not necessarily declare regulation to be wrong, or even inefficient. Given sufficiently strong value judgments on the part of would-be regulators—whether in favor of environmental purity, of an egalitarian distribution of wealth, of freedom from pornography or disease, of national prestige, of the enrichment of the arts, or of whatever—criticism of intervention, from the perspective of these value judgments, may (properly) carry little weight. The economist's task, however, is to spell out as fully as possible the consequences of alternative policies, so that policy decisions at least will not be taken on the basis of erroneous assessments of their likely consequences. The discussion in the following pages does not offer an airtight case against intervention but draws attention to possibly grave perils of intervention, perils that seem to have been taken fully and explicitly into account neither by the literature critical of interventionist policies nor, a fortiori, by the uncritical proponents and supporters of government regulation.

27. Here an improvement in the allocation of resources (given the initial pattern of resource distribution) is defined as a change in the pattern of input utilization and/or input consumption that improves the well-being of each member of the economy. Although this definition is close to the norm of Paretian welfare economics, it does *not* invoke the notion of aggregate welfare.

28. "The Austrian finds no detailed explanation in welfare economics of how government is supposed to obtain the information necessary to carry out its assigned tasks. The knowledge required . . . is not to be found collected in one place, but rather dispersed throughout the many members of the economy." Stephen C. Littlechild, *The Fallacy of the Mixed Economy: An "Austrian" Critique of Economic Thinking and Policy* (London: Institute of Economic Affairs, 1978), p. 40. See also Gordon Tullock, *The Politics of Bureaucracy* (Washington, D.C.: Public Affairs Press, 1965), p. 124: "Administrative problems . . . could . . . be of such complexity that the centralization of information necessary to make decisions effectively in a bureaucracy might not be possible."

29. It is even most cogently pointed out that the very notion of cost, seen from the perspective of the regulator, is unlikely to coincide with any notion of cost that one might wish to consider relevant to the quest for efficiency. See Buchanan, *Cost and Choice*, chaps. 5 and 6.

30. Professor Machlup valuably refers to the "fertility of freedom" in generating discovery of new possibilities. Fritz Machlup, "Liberalism and the Choice of Freedoms," in *Roads to Freedom: Essays in Honour of Friedrich A. von Hayek*, ed. Erich Streissler (London: Routledge and Kegan Paul, 1969), p. 130.

31. Murray L. Weidenbaum, "The Impact of Government Regulation" (study prepared for the Joint Economic Committee, Subcommittee on Economic Growth and Stabilization, United States Congress, July 1978). See also Ernest C. Pasour, "Hide and Seek: Hidden Costs of Government Regulation," *World Research INK* 2 (December 1978): 5.

32. "There is ample evidence that imagination and innovation are not stilled by restrictive legislation—only diverted to figuring out ways around it." Friedman, *Economist's Protest*, p. 149.

33. See, for example, Nicholas Sanchez and Alan R. Waters, "Controlling Corruption in Africa and Latin America," in *The Economics of Property Rights*, ed. Eirik Furubotn and Svetozar Pejovich (Cambridge, Mass.: Ballinger, 1974); Edward C. Banfield, "Corruption as a Feature of Governmental Organization," *Journal of Law and Economics* 18 (December 1975): 587–605; and Simon Rottenberg, "Comment," *Journal of Law and Economics* 18 (December 1975): 611–15.

34. William M. Capron et al., eds., *Technological Change in Regulated Industries* (Washington, D.C.: Brookings Institution, 1971).

35. Ibid., p. 8. See also chap. 2.

36. Sam Peltzman, "An Evaluation of Consumer Protection Legislation: The 1962 Drug Amendments," *Journal of Political Economy* 81 (September–October 1973): 1049–91. See also David Schwartzman, *Innovation in the Pharmaceutical Industry* (Baltimore: Johns Hopkins Press, 1976).

37. Henry G. Manne, *Insider Trading and the Stock Market* (New York: Free Press, 1966).

38. Although there are many other studies illustrating the hidden distortions generated by regulation, I do not cite them here, since they do not obviously call our attention to the market discovery process and its modification as a result of the regulatory constraints.

REJOINDER [THE CASE FOR FREE MARKETS]

Professor Alec Nove's passionate case on behalf of benevolent government activism in the market economy raises many familiar criticisms of the claim that markets work best for society when left completely alone. I would certainly not wish to identify myself with all those whom Nove criticises; nor would I assert that every one of Nove's points is without merit. But one general presupposition of Nove's deserves to be sharply rebutted.

This is that a case for *laissez-faire* must necessarily rest on the assumption that markets are "perfect," that "there are innumerable competitors who are price takers, products are homogeneous, entrepreneurs operate with quasi-perfect knowledge" and there is a "timeless world quasi-instantaneous adjustment. . . ." Perhaps some proponents of free markets fit this caricature. For others Nove's use of this kind of straw man suggests that he has failed grievously to understand the economic case for free markets.

That case (which Nove might perhaps best study through the works of modern exponents of Austrian economics—for example, S. C. Littlechild's *The Fallacy of the Mixed Economy*, HP80, IEA, 1978) rests upon totally different foundations. It rests primarily on the insight that, where allocative errors are being made, the incentives best likely to reveal errors, and to inspire the corrective action of alert decision makers, are those that promise alert discoverers the prospect of pure gain in an environment permitting full freedom of entry. The focus is thus upon the role of prices that are *not* market-clearing, upon incentives for entrepreneurial discovery in a world in which pure profits are certainly *not* zero, and in which knowledge is *never* assumed to be widespread.

The case for free markets rests *not* upon the imaginary state of affairs under unattainable and largely irrelevant conditions for equilibrium. It

From *Economic Affairs* (January–March 1985): 49. Copyright of *Economic Affairs* is the property of Blackwell Publishing Limited. Reprinted by permission of John Wiley and Sons, publisher.

rests only upon the ability of dynamic, "imperfect" markets to generate a continuing, spontaneous process of *error-discovery*, one that has the tendency continually to nudge decisions away from those errors that must otherwise inevitably and incessantly emerge as a result of continually changing conditions.

THE ANATOMY OF ECONOMIC ADVICE, PART I

As is the case with virtually all branches of human knowledge, economic knowledge and understanding are valued not only (or even primarily) for their own sake, but for their *usefulness* in practical terms. The enormous sums expended each year on economic research and economic education certainly would not be forthcoming if it were not expected that such research and education could help promote wise policies leading to prosperity and economic well-being.

Indeed, there can be no doubt that those advocating free-market policies (in *The Freeman* or elsewhere) do so firmly convinced that such advocacy grows naturally out of economic understanding. I certainly share this conviction. Yet the path leading from valid economic understanding to sound economic policy advice is not straightforward. To proceed from an "is" statement to an "ought" statement is, in all contexts, fraught notoriously with philosophical hazards. In the context of economics these dangers are compounded further by the subtleties that complicate the sources of economic understanding itself.

Our attempt to clarify the basis in economic science for valid and useful economic advice will proceed as follows. In the present article we elaborate on the apparent paradox involved in offering "scientific" advice (that is, advice supported or even entailed by science) in the economic arena. In the second article we shall examine the philosophical foundations of economic science itself (with a special interest in its potential in regard to economic policymaking). In the concluding article we will try to draw together our various insights and to formulate our conclusions in regard to the scientific validity of economic advice.

THE "SCIENCE" AND THE "ART" OF POLITICAL ECONOMY: A NINETEENTH-CENTURY DILEMMA

The founding fathers of economics, including, most prominently, Adam Smith, generally saw their discipline as constituting what came to be called an "art"—that is, a body of advice on how to achieve a well-defined objective—the enhancement of national *wealth*. Although the title of Adam Smith's classic was *An Inquiry into the Nature and Causes of the Wealth of Nations* (suggesting it to be a disinterested scientific inquiry, concerned neither to promote increased national wealth nor to prevent it), Smith himself has usually been seen to have conceived his subject as an art (setting forth ways to increase national wealth).[1] But thoughtful economists of that period had serious misgivings about such an approach.

Some of the classical economists following Smith indeed wrestled with the relation between a science of political economy and an art of political economy. One such economist was Richard Whately, who was not only an economist of note but also an Anglican archbishop. He felt the need to defend himself in regard to his interest in the science of wealth (an interest his critics apparently thought of as unbecoming a clergyman). Whately pointed out (in an 1831 lecture at Oxford) that the conclusions of political economy can be deployed in policies designed to *reduce wealth* (if wealth be seen as morally suspect)—just as they can be used to formulate policies for *increasing* wealth!

At one stage in his academic career Nassau Senior, one of the most prominent early nineteenth-century political economists, flatly denied the very possibility of such an art.[2] Although Senior later retreated from this categorical position, he was never completely reconciled to the idea of political economy as an art. In his 1860 presidential address to The Section of Economic Science and Statistics (of the British Association), almost a quarter century after his denial of the possibility of an art of political economy, Senior insisted that the political economist is concerned only with the production or distribution of wealth—regardless of whether "wealth be a good or an evil." He clearly believed that, *qua* economist, the economist has no business offering advice. "Whenever he gives a *precept*, whenever he advises his reader to do anything, or to abstain from doing anything, he wanders from science into art. . . ."[3]

As the nineteenth century wore on, Senior's qualms came to be ignored. Particularly on the Continent, economists paid scant heed to Senior's admonitions. The German Historical School (which dominated continental economics during the closing decades of the century) made no attempt whatever to separate their substantive economics from advocacy on behalf of specific social programs. For them it was precisely this advocacy that gave economics its importance as a branch of knowledge. Joseph Schumpeter cited the testimony of a student in a class taught by a prominent leader of the School, to the effect that the mood in the classroom resembled that of an election rally.

It was the great sociologist Max Weber who recognized the danger to the reputation of economics as an objective science that was posed by such a politicized attitude. He maintained that the scientific character of any social science *requires* that it be meticulously impartial as between different judgments of value. This ran counter to the dominant perspective in German economics. At a meeting of German-language social scientists held in 1907, Weber's position was the subject of bitter disagreement. Weber insisted that scientists who disagree sharply on moral priorities should, despite this, be able, at least in principle, to agree on the positive propositions of their discipline. We shall return very soon to comment further on this Weberian doctrine of *wertfreiheit* (freedom from value judgments).[4]

THE TWENTIETH CENTURY: THE ECONOMICS OF WELFARE

By the end of the nineteenth century, mainstream economic theorists no longer saw their discipline as concerned with material wealth. Instead they focused on the subjective sense of well-being that human beings hope to derive from their wealth and from their economic activities. This led them (particularly in England) to see economics as primarily concerned with "welfare." Very soon they were speaking of the "economics of welfare" (the new title of A. C. Pigou's 1920 book, itself the second edition of a 1912 book titled *Wealth and Welfare*). To think of economics as the science able to *promote* economic welfare seemed an innocuous small step. Thus for much of the first half of the twentieth century it was taken almost for granted that the economist is the expert who formulates policies to be implemented in order to promote aggregate economic welfare. It seemed to be obvious that economists had the professional duty of advocating policies they believed would, scientifically, enhance social well-being. And even economists squeamish about the philosophical coherency of any notion of aggregate well-being were able to devise more carefully formulated versions of welfare economics by reference to "Pareto optimality" or similar sophisticated constructions.

It was during this period that economists began to find ample employment opportunities in government. As the tide of public opinion turned (during the second quarter of the century) decisively in favor of massive government intervention in the market economy, economists increasingly saw their discipline as capable of generating very definite policies for enlightened governments to follow. Economists were placing their science (particularly the branch that made up "welfare economics") at the service of political parties. Inevitably this tended to raise those same gnawing questions concerning the objectivity and impartiality of that science which had so troubled Max Weber. More and more, it seemed, *any* political program, *any* proposal for economic legislation, could find economists prepared to present a "scientific" case in its support.

MISES AND WERTFREIHEIT

Ludwig von Mises, the towering Austrian School economist of the twentieth century, was an ardent champion of Weber's *wertfreiheit* principle for all social sciences, and particularly for economics.[5] He believed that the objectivity of the science requires nothing less than its complete detachment from the personal preferences and value judgments of its practitioners. Implicit in Weber's *wertfreiheit* principle is the conviction that it is, at least in principle, *possible* for the economist to pursue his science in detachment from his own personal judgments of value. In fact, however, some twentieth-century philosophers have challenged (and do still challenge) this, maintaining that it is an illusion to believe that one can suppress one's value judgments while engaging in one's science. Inevitably, they argue, one's science reflects one's moral presuppositions. Mises may have agreed that to maintain such detachment may be difficult—but he would have emphatically rejected claims that it is impossible. It is the scientist's obligation to the reputation and integrity of his science, Mises would have insisted, that he insulate his scientific work from any hint of "contamination" arising from personal predilections. The medical researcher exploring the links between cigarette smoking and cancer must pursue his laboratory testing and his statistical analysis without that research being affected in any way by his own preference for smoking or his own fears concerning the disease. So too must the economist's analysis of markets, of regulation, and their consequences be utterly independent of his own moral opinions concerning liberty, the inequality of incomes, or whatever.

Mises's position offers a fascinating illustration of the ambiguities and complexities involved in the *wertfreiheit* principle. Gunnar Myrdal was a prominent twentieth-century Swedish social scientist. (His positions on economic policy were so utterly at odds with those of Mises, that when, in 1974, Myrdal and F. A. Hayek were joint recipients of the Nobel Prize in economics, it was widely understood that these choices represented a kind of ideological balancing act, with Hayek's approving views on free markets being counterbalanced by Myrdal's advocacy of comprehensive government control of the economy.) In 1930 Myrdal published a German-language book that examined the history of economics and concluded that most of the leading economists during that history had injected political presuppositions and ideals into what they presented as scientific investigations. This book was translated into English in 1955. Fritz Machlup (himself an eminent Austrian-trained twentieth-century economist who had been a pupil of Ludwig von Mises and who treated Mises at a personal level with exemplary loyalty) wrote a review of this published translation. Machlup drew attention to Myrdal's declaration that (unlike the other schools of economic thought) the Austrian School of economics was *not* guilty of injecting political ideals into their scientific work. Machlup found this approving judgment surprising. "How did the anti-interventionist writings of the Austrian von Mises escape Myrdal's attention?" he asked. Apparently Machlup was not able to reconcile Mises's stated insistence on *wertfreiheit* and detachment from ideological precommitments with Mises's eloquent writings in favor of laissez faire and the free-market economy.

In fact a reader of Mises's work cannot fail to sense a paradox surrounding the *passion* with which Mises wrote his economics. By the time we reach the third part of this series, we shall hopefully have resolved this paradox. Here we shall merely identify it and relate it to the broader challenge of extracting useful *advice* from *wertfrei* economic science.

LUDWIG VON MISES AND THE IMPORTANCE OF ECONOMICS

Mises was, as we have seen, convinced that economics must be pursued dispassionately—as a *wertfrei* discipline—but he wrote with white-hot passion about the dangers that face mankind should it ignore the truths which academic science reveals. He concluded his magnum opus, *Human Action,* with the following searing sentences: "The body of economic knowledge is an essential element in the structure of human civilization; it is the foundation upon which modern industrialism and all the moral, intellectual and therapeutic achievements of the last centuries have been built. It rests with men whether they will make proper use of the rich treasure with which this knowledge provides them or whether they will leave it unused. But if they fail to take the best advantage of it and disregard its teachings and warnings, they will not annul economics; they will stamp out society and the human race."[6]

It is this passionate conviction on the utter importance of the teachings of economic science that accounts for the attention which Mises paid to the philosophical status of those teachings. Mises believed that the enemies of the free society can maintain their advocacy of central planning and massive government intervention in (or replacement of) the market economy only by ignoring or denigrating economic science. He saw all the attempts to question the validity of the foundational propositions of economics as driven by the ulterior motive of discrediting laissez-faire economic policy. Because Mises believed that only laissez-faire policies can sustain modern civilization, he felt driven to clarify and defend the philosophical foundations of what he called "modern economics." (For Mises, modern economics was the body of economic teachings rooted in the classical economics of Adam Smith and his followers, as refined and reformulated by the so-called neoclassical economists, including especially the founder of the Austrian School, Carl Menger and his followers, among whom was Mises's own teacher, the eminent Eugen von Böhm-Bawerk.)

Mises's clarifications of the foundations of neoclassical economic theory included, in particular, his defense of economics from the Marxist charge that conventional economists are merely the lackeys of Wall Street, advocating free markets only in order to serve their capitalist paymasters. Mises saw clearly that, unless economists purged their science of any taint of personal bias (that is, as expressing personal judgments of value), their teachings would be vulnerable to such dismissal. Precisely because he saw free markets as the essential prerequisite for civilized, prosperous society, and because he believed that disinterested economic analysis definitively supported this view, Mises was terrified by the possibility that economic science was to be dismissed as nothing but capitalist propaganda. Fritz Machlup saw Mises's advocacy of laissez faire (his "anti-interventionist" writings) as an example of precisely that departure from impartiality in the pursuit of economic science, for which Myrdal had indicted so many economists (but for which had declared the Austrian School, in general, as having been *not* guilty). We shall return, in the third essay in this mini-series, to examine the validity of Machlup's charge.

Most economists of the postwar period did not pay much attention to these concerns. It is true that Milton Friedman, one of the leading scholars of the eminent Chicago School, advocated (in an influential 1953 essay) what he called "positive economics" (in which economic propositions could be established that might command the assent of scholars regardless of their personal predilections). But this came to be viewed primarily as an exercise in methodology, presenting the case for treating economics as a strictly empirical (as opposed to a *logical*) discipline (rather than as a case for *wertfreiheit*).

From time to time more serious attention was devoted to the *wertfreiheit* issue. Thus a leading historian of thought, Terence W. Hutchison (who was, as it happens, a scholar in the methodology of economics who had bitterly criticized Mises's own methodological writings), wrote a book on the subject. But few other economists gave much thought to the dangers to their impartiality (or to their perceived impartiality) that may lurk in their policy pronouncements. And some economists otherwise deeply influenced by the Austrian School, and Mises in particular, expressed strong reservations against the *wertfreiheit* doctrine. Thus Murray Rothbard, a leading disciple of Mises, argued for the explicit articulation of the ethical principles on the part of the economic scientist offering policy advice.

Recently a noted exponent of free-market economic policymaking, Daniel B. Klein, called on economists to deploy their science to modify the political-economic choices of the public.[7] Klein contended that economists who themselves value the free society have a moral *obligation* to help mold public opinion toward an appreciation for liberty. Economists are in a unique position to do this because they enjoy a respected professional reputation. Instead of spending their time talking to each other in the language of abstract mathematical models, economists ought to be engaging in "public discourse," talking to Everyman about issues of practical public policy. Klein surveys a swath of literature in which economists, both advanced scholars and frustrated graduate students, bemoan the irrelevance of the academic work being done by the economics profession. He finds the profession locked into a mindset in which it is in the rational professional interest of the individual economist to *avoid* addressing Everyman on realistic issues, focusing instead on the abstract models upon which professional repute and rewards (perversely) depend. In urging the economist to tell Everyman what is good for him, Klein is clearly urging the economist to see his professional responsibility as extending beyond the strictly positive. The economist must not only—or even primarily—concern himself with the understanding and prediction of chains of economic cause and effect; he must also deploy that understanding to advise (and even to exhort) the man in the street as to what are his best (and worst!) courses of action.

CASTIGATED ECONOMISTS

In urging the economist to tell the public what economic science sees as good for them, Klein was explicitly rebelling against the position taken by George J. Stigler, the Nobel-laureate Chicago School economist. In 1982 Stigler published a book in which he castigated economists (from Adam Smith to Stigler's own time) for doing precisely what Klein wished them to do (that is, to tell the public what is good for them). Stigler strongly protested against economists being "preachers" (treating the public as mistaken, perverse children whose behavior can be improved if they are properly instructed through appropriate moral suasion).

For Stigler the economist should refrain from "preaching" not because of any concerns that such preaching violates their scientific objectivity and moral neutrality. Rather Stigler denounced such preaching because to preach economic policy is to believe—quite mistakenly, in Stigler's opinion—that the economist knows what is economically good for the public better than the public itself knows. Stigler carries the assumption of perfect knowledge (which has notoriously characterized many of the models constructed by economic theorists in order to account for real-world facts) to a consistent, but extreme, degree. He assumes, in effect, that all that economics might be able to teach is *already known* to the public and to its political agents. The economist may think the outcome to be expected from a given policy to be undesirable, but if the public adopts that policy this proves that the public in fact *desires* that very outcome. The economist who denounces that policy as "wrong" is simply revealing that he has a set of objectives different from those that are in fact being pursued by the public.

Certainly the history of economics reveals little unanimity among economists concerning the possibility and the usefulness of the *wertfreiheit* principle. The prestige associated with the teachings of economic science, and the importance that educated public opinion attaches to them, have waxed and waned during that history. The views of economists themselves as to whether or not they have an obligation to enlighten the public on economic policy have varied widely. It is against this rather confusing background that we shall try to clarify the legitimacy of ("scientific") *advice* to the public by economists.

FROM "IS" TO "OUGHT"

In the second of this series we shall review the foundations of the strictly positive lessons taught by economic science. That is, we shall briefly set forth the nature of the economic reasoning that establishes the existence of chains of cause and effect in the economic sphere. In this regard we shall follow the Austrian tradition in economic reasoning, particularly as developed in the relevant writings of the twentieth-century leaders of that tradition, Mises and F. A. Hayek. What will emerge from this examination is insight into the powerful market tendency to systematically translate consumers' rankings of needs, and physical resource constraints, into corresponding patterns of resource allocation. This systematic translation, we shall see, follows from the purposefulness of human action, the entrepreneurial propensity of human beings to discover what is of interest to them, and from the information-communicating capabilities of the market price system. This will lead us directly to the third and final part of this series.

In that third article we shall examine what implications this Austrian perspective holds for the possibility of offering impartial advice on public-policy issues, such that the advice does *not* reflect any personal or ideological preferences of the economist offering it. Only if this possibility exists can the doctrine of *wertfreiheit* be upheld consistently by the policy adviser; only if this possibility exists can the objectivity and impartiality of the advising economists be preserved; only if this possibility exists can we hope to uphold the scientific repute of economics. Our conclusions in regard to these questions will enable us to clarify some of the paradoxes we have encountered in the present article. They will provide us, in particular, with an understanding of how the teachings of free-market economists need not compromise their objectivity and impartiality, and may, nonetheless, be presented with passionate conviction and dedicated advocacy.

NOTES

1. See for example J. N. Keynes, *The Scope and Method of Political Economy* (1st ed., 1891) 4th ed. (London, 1930), p. 39n.

2. On this see Marian Bowley, *Nassau Senior and Classical Economics* (London: George Allen and Unwin, 1937), p. 54.

3. See the text of this presidential address in R. L. Smyth, ed., *Essays in Economic Method* (London: Duckworth, 1962), p. 21.

4. For a more detailed discussion of the *wertfreiheit* principle, see Israel M. Kirzner, "Value Freedom," in Peter J. Boettke, ed., *The Elgar Companion to Austrian Economics* (Aldershot: Edward Elgar, 1994), pp. 313–19.

5. See Ludwig von Mises, *Human Action*, 3d ed. (Chicago: Contemporary Books, 1966), pp. 881–85.

6. Ibid., p. 885.

7. Daniel B. Klein, *A Plea to Economists Who Favour Liberty: Assist the Everyman* (London: Institute of Economic Affairs, 2001).

THE ANATOMY OF ECONOMIC ADVICE, PART II

How can positive science (consisting entirely of "is" statements) be translated into "ought" statements within the framework of economic understanding? In the first part of this series we drew attention to some of the paradoxes surrounding economic advice. In particular we drew puzzled attention to the *passionate* advocacy by Ludwig von Mises of free-market arrangements—the same Ludwig von Mises who insisted on an attitude of purest, disinterested *wertfreiheit* ("value-freedom") on the part of all social scientists. In the present article, as a step toward clarifying these paradoxes and puzzles, we discuss the nature of the strictly positive central propositions of economics. We shall find that a careful appreciation for the manner in which economic science accounts for the existence of chains of economic cause and effect can help us see how knowledge of these chains can sustain very definite ways of providing advice and guidance to economic policymakers. Statements describing chains of cause and effect are "is" statements. But, as we shall see, these statements *can,* in a carefully defined sense, generate the "ought" statements of which economic advice consists.

CAUSE AND EFFECT IN ECONOMIC AFFAIRS

Economic science was established as a branch of knowledge in the eighteenth century, when the classical economists recognized that there exist systematic chains of cause and effect in economic phenomena (just as they exist in regard to physical phenomena). Although subsequent progress in economic theorizing radically altered the way in which economics understands economic cause and effect, it was the classical economists who, by establishing the idea of systematic chains of cause and effect, established the scientific discipline of economics.

The very perception of a scientific discipline of economics (or "political economy," as it was called by the classical economists of the late eighteenth and early nineteenth centuries) carries revolutionary implications for public policy. As Mises emphasized again and again, the discovery of regularities in economic phenomena means that statesmen concerned with public policy can no longer treat the economy as putty that they are free to mold into whatever shape they believe best for society. Every political act, every legislative constraint over economic activity, and every public subsidy must now be recognized as entailing specific consequences. Before instituting any tariff, before granting any right of monopoly, before printing any money, before imposing any kind of price control, those responsible for state policy must ask themselves whether they have fully taken into account *all* the consequences that are likely to follow from these actions. There *are*, the classical economists had shown, "laws" of economics that must be respected and taken into account if economic disaster is to be avoided.

But how can such "laws" possibly exist? Surely an intuitive *impossibility* blocks any conceivable "laws" from existing. It is one thing to observe and understand regularities and causal or functional relationships in physical phenomena. But to expect such regularities and relationships in economic phenomena (which represent the outcome of the independently made decisions and actions of millions of freely choosing individual agents) seems to be glaringly counterintuitive. There seems to be no way of ensuring that freely choosing agents "obey" the regularities that a science might declare to be determinative.

This intuitive difficulty is the fundamental reason why both economic theorists and philosophers have, during the past two centuries, puzzled and argued over the very possibility of an economic science, and over its epistemological character. The present series of papers (and this one in particular) are informed by the insights and philosophical framework identified with the Austrian School of Economics, and especially with the thought of its leading twentieth-century representatives, Mises and F. A. Hayek.

In this framework the focus of attention is on the *purposefulness* of human beings, and on the way in which the expectations and knowledge of these human beings are *systematically* modified by economic experience. Changing economic experience alters the terms on which individual agents in fact find themselves able to choose; that experience also teaches agents where they had over-optimistically or over-pessimistically misjudged the terms on which others were prepared to trade with them; that experience also alerts individual agents to opportunities for the future that had hitherto not existed or that have until now not been noticed. Economic theory is able, in this analytical framework, to provide understanding of how exogenous changes in resource availabilities, technical knowledge, and consumer preferences may systematically change market phenomena, and thus determine the course of production and the patterns of resource allocation. To illustrate this approach to economic reasoning, let us take perhaps the most basic of the "regularities" in the market economy, the "law" of supply and demand.

THE "LAW" OF SUPPLY AND DEMAND

This basic understanding of the behavior of market prices identifies the nature and the direction of the forces operating in the market for each product and for each resource. This understanding sees the market for any given item, be it a product for human consumption (such as milk or the services of an opera singer), or a resource (such as farmland for growing crops or the services of an engineering instructor for the training of engineers), as being continually modified by market experience in systematic fashion. At any given time "too much" or "too little" of the given item may be offered for sale (or sought to be bought). ("Too much" being offered for sale means that, *at current prices,* more of an item is being offered for sale than is being bought. "Too little" being offered for sale means that, at current prices, more of the item is being sought to be bought than sellers wish to sell.) *The "law" of supply and demand focuses attention on the existence of spontaneous market forces tending to "correct" these imbalances.*

Where "too much" has been offered for sale, falling prices (for the relevant item) tend to encourage some ("marginal") sellers to cut back on its production and to encourage potential buyers to seek additional quantities for purchase. Where "too little" has been offered for sale, rising prices for the relevant item tend to encourage potential sellers to increase production (and thus the quantities they will offer for sale) and to discourage some ("marginal") buyers from continuing to buy. Were this process of adjustment in a given market to be permitted to continue indefinitely (that is, were the costs and techniques of production for the relevant item, on the one hand, and the preferences of the consumers, on the other, to remain indefinitely unchanged while market adjustments continued), the market for that item might be imagined to attain "equilibrium." Market equilibrium corresponds to the imaginary state of affairs in which neither "too much" *nor* "too little" of an item is being offered for sale. In such an imagined state of equilibrium there would be no scope for market forces to be set into motion. Prices and quantities offered for sale and sought to be bought are, in such an imagined state of equilibrium, such that no tendencies are set in motion for any of them to change.

Contrary to what many students of economics have been taught to believe, the "law" of supply and demand does *not* (when it is properly understood) declare that each market is at or near equilibrium at each moment. Nor does it declare (the less-objectionable form of the above) that markets tend rapidly to achieve equilibrium. Rather the "law" declares that, to the extent that a market, at any given moment, is *not* at equilibrium, this will itself set into motion forces predominantly pushing the market *in the direction* of equilibrium.

However, it should be understood and emphasized, the continual changes in the relevant exogenous variables (for example, the costs of production, the availability of resources, and the patterns of consumer preferences) will almost inevitably ensure that the equilibrium position for a market at any given moment is different from what that position was at any earlier moment. So the market forces unleashed by the disequilibrium conditions at one moment will almost certainly *not* ensure the attainment of equilibrium at any subsequent moment.

Nonetheless, it is reasonable to point out, the more gross imbalances present in the market at any given moment will, according to the "law" of supply and demand, tend to be corrected. An "oversupply" places pressure on prices to fall, discouraging marginal sellers from some production and encouraging additional purchases, and thus tending to eliminate the imbalance. A "shortage" operates in the reverse, but equally benign, direction. Let us examine why the elimination of these "imbalances" can legitimately be described as "benign." In the final article of this series, this will help us to understand the sense in which economic theory can, in scientifically objective fashion, promote sound economic-policy advice.

MARKET IMBALANCE—WHY IS IT REGRETTABLE?

Let us consider the case of "overproduction" in a particular market (a market seen as isolated and insulated from other markets). Due to miscalculation or other error, the decisions of producers in this market have overestimated the eagerness of buyers to buy. The amounts offered for sale, and the prices expected and asked by potential sellers, are not matched by the decisions of potential buyers (and thus by the prices at which potential buyers expect to be able to buy, and at which they are willing to buy). This imbalance corresponds to decisions that have turned out to have been *disappointing*, and to decisions that turn out to have been *regrettable*. Some potential sellers (who might otherwise have offered to sell for lower prices, but who mistakenly held out for higher prices) are *disappointed* in that their plans to sell at higher prices cannot be successfully carried out. Those sellers may also *regret* their refusal to offer to sell at lower prices, or they may regret their decisions to produce in the first place. The failure of the decisions of some of the potential sellers to dovetail with corresponding decisions of potential buyers reveals the "error" of all of those decisions and is the source of both disappointment and regret.

A different, more accurate pattern of decisions, by *both* potential buyers and potential sellers, might have permitted them to achieve more successful fulfillment of plans than has in fact occurred. When a pair of market participants *might* have engaged in voluntary exchange to *mutual advantage* (for example, at a lower price), their *failure* to have done so (due to "error") seems, at least at first glance, to have been unambiguously unfortunate—for everybody. *Nobody*, it seems at first glance, has gained anything by the fact that potential steps to mutual advantage were not taken.

So, if we are correct in this judgment, the market process, which according to our "law" of supply and demand initiates continual market tendencies toward the correction of such imbalances, would appear to be benign. It tends to discover and to correct "erroneous" market decisions—that is, decisions which operate to frustrate the exploitation of potentially mutually gainful exchanges.

Although we have been careful to express this approving judgment (for the outcome of the "law" of supply and demand) strictly in tentative terms, we shall find that it in fact holds more robustly than we have suggested. As we shall see in the final article of this series, it tends to hold even when we drop the special assumptions made in this section. There is a definite sense in which the "positive" theory of supply and demand leads ineluctably to an understanding of its socially benign character (that is, of its "normative" implications). We have in fact glimpsed here the basis for scientifically based economic *advice*. But the present article has not yet completed its exposition of the "positive" operation of the "law" of supply and demand. Before proceeding further we must explore more carefully exactly *how* this "law" achieves its magic—its tendency to correct market imbalance. We shall find that the "normative" discussion of this section can help us understand the "positive" operation of the competitive market process.

HOW THE MARKET WORKS*

As we have seen, market imbalance reflects and expresses decisions that have been made in error. Market participants have been disappointingly left with unsold goods. Had they known this previously, they might have produced fewer units of these goods; they might even have gone into entirely different lines of production; or they might have been happy to have sold for lower prices (the only reason for their having failed to do so being their erroneous conviction that they could obtain higher prices).

Notice that this understanding of market imbalance refers, in effect, to *two* distinct kinds of error. One kind of error made by participants in the market we have considered is that mutually gainful exchange opportunities have simply not been taken advantage of. (Thus when market prices have been "too high," generating offers to sell that have been rejected, this is likely to mean that mutually gainful sales *could*, in principle, have occurred at lower prices.) A second kind of error has meant that some market participants have been led to *believe* (quite erroneously) that (*nonexistent*) opportunities for mutually gainful exchange really did exist. The first of these two kinds of error is thus *to fail to recognize existing opportunities*. The second kind of error is *to "see" opportunities which in fact do not exist*. One might describe the first kind of error as one of undue pessimism (failure to see opportunities really staring one in the face); the second kind of error might be described as one of undue and unjustified over-optimism. This insight can help us understand the process of market adjustment, the operation of the "law" of supply and demand.

Let us consider the errors of over-optimism. Whenever such an error occurs, it is discovered (and thus presumably corrected) almost *inevitably*.

---

* Much of the material in this article, and especially the material in this section, is covered in greater detail in my monograph *How Markets Work: Disequilibrium, Entrepreneurship and Discovery* (London: Institute of Economic Affairs, 1997).

One's market experience *reveals* where one has been over-optimistic; the opportunities that one had over-optimistically expected to encounter simply do not happen. Such chastening experience tends, almost inevitably, to rein in over-optimistic market anticipations. Such experience "teaches" where and how more realistic expectations are in order. Where over-optimistic would-be sellers had, for example, refused to sell for lower prices (confidently, but erroneously, expecting to sell at higher prices), their disappointing experience in the market tends to teach them to lower their asking prices.

But the *other* kind of error (that expressing undue pessimism) does not seem capable of "automatic" correction in any similar way. An opportunity (for mutually beneficial exchange) that was not seen today by the relevant parties (and therefore not taken advantage of) may not be seen tomorrow either (even if it still exists tomorrow). Let us take an example. If different prices for "the same" item have been prevailing in different parts of "the same" market, this is a scenario in which potentially mutually advantageous trading opportunities *have* existed, but have been missed. After all, in any market in which buyers have been buying at higher prices while some sellers have been selling at lower prices, we have a situation where these buyers and these sellers could obviously have benefited by trading *with each other* at some price lower than those higher prices at which the buyers have been buying, but higher than those lower prices at which the sellers have been selling. Clearly these market participants were simply unaware of what was going on elsewhere in this same market. But there seems no obvious manner in which such unawareness might be spontaneously replaced by superior market information. There seems no obvious way through which the market might tend to replace widely divergent market prices with less divergent prices.

It is here that the spontaneous market process depends on *entrepreneurial alertness* for one of the most fundamental (and widely recognized) tendencies in free, competitive markets: that prices for the same item do move toward a single price throughout the market.

ENTREPRENEURIAL ALERTNESS

One of the less obvious, but nonetheless most powerful elements acting in markets is entrepreneurial alertness—the propensity of human beings to notice that which it is in their interest to notice. Sooner or later buyers paying unnecessarily high prices do tend to discover where they can obtain comparable goods at significantly lower prices. Sellers selling for unnecessarily low prices do tend to discover where they can find buyers willing to pay higher prices. Moreover, sooner or later entrepreneurs will discover that they can grasp pure profit simply by buying at the lower prices and selling at the higher prices. We do feel convinced that widely diverging prices in the same market for a given product or resource will give way in this fashion to competitive forces tending to push these diverging prices toward each other. Errors of undue pessimism do tend to be corrected in this way—as a result of entrepreneurial alertness.

So the "law" of supply and demand explains chains of economic causation along each of two distinct dimensions. First, as we have seen earlier, it operates toward the correction of market imbalances for given items. Second, it operates to correct such imbalances at the same time as it corrects the phenomenon of divergent prices for each such item. The forces of supply and demand operate to correct "wrong" decisions that are unduly optimistic, at the same time as it operates to correct "wrong" decisions that are over-pessimistic.

THE BROAD SCOPE OF OUR ANALYSIS

Our discussion thus far has been extremely simple both in its assumptions and its substance. We have talked of the market for a "given item" while assuming this market to be isolated and insulated from all other markets. When one broadens one's analytical perspective to include the markets for innumerable products and resources that may be bought and sold, and to include not only simple buying and selling decisions but also decisions on what to produce and how to produce, it might appear that we are now in a world of mind-boggling complexity, for which our simple analysis has little relevance. But this is *not* the case. The insights of the previous sections do have immediate relevance even for the most complicated of interlocking markets.

Consider, for example, a market in which a particular item C is produced by combining input A with input B, in accordance with some production recipe. Imagine that such production is highly profitable. The combined costs of inputs A and B are, at a given level of output, significantly lower than the revenue obtainable from selling C in the consumer-goods market. This scenario may seem fairly complicated (in comparison with the scenarios discussed earlier). But we should notice that this scenario is one in which buyers are paying higher prices than necessary, and sellers are selling at lower prices than necessary—exactly as in the single-item market discussed in the preceding section. Thus those selling A and B at prices summing to less than the price being paid for C *could,* in principle, have produced C and sold it for the higher price (since *only* A and B are needed to produce C). The profitability of this line of production results from a (disguised) divergence of prices "for the same item" in the same market (that is, it results from the circumstances that *everything* needed to produce C can be bought for less than the market price for C). Thus this profitability can be expected (unless we postulate monopolistic control of access to resources A and B) to tend to attract competitive entrepreneurial attention. This will tend to eliminate the profitability of this line of production (by pushing the price of C and the sum of the prices of A and B closer together).

Although this is not the place to do so, similar analysis can demonstrate the broad relevance of our earlier discussion of the "law" of supply and demand to key aspects, at the very least, of complex market scenarios.

CAUSE AND EFFECT IN ECONOMIC AFFAIRS

Our discussion has illustrated the way in which simple economic theory accounts for the existence of definite and systematic chains of cause and effect in economic affairs. There do exist definite ways in which economic decisions made in any one period tend to take systematic account of the other decisions being made in the same markets. In this way decisions do mold each other in systematic fashion. And we have seen how the manner in which such "molding" tends to occur appears, at least at first glance, to deserve being called "benign." This simple analysis will help us understand, in principle, how economic theory can lead toward making judgments on the "goodness" of specific policy initiatives through an understanding of the likely consequences of such initiatives.

We are now ready to tackle, in the final article in this series, the question posed at the beginning of the first article: Can positive economic understanding be translated into scientifically objective and valid *economic advice?*

THE ANATOMY OF ECONOMIC ADVICE, PART III

In the first article of this trilogy we explored some of the ambiguities and difficulties that surround the very idea of "economic advice" based on economic science. In the second article we set forth some of the basic foundations of economic science (with special reference to what the science can teach us about what we called the "benign" character of the spontaneous market process). We are now ready to draw together the various strands of our discussions and to set forth the scientific legitimacy of economic advice based on an accurate understanding of the nature and significance of the free-market process.

As was developed in the preceding article, economic science has explicated the nature of the forces that govern the market process. What we saw was that the market process is made up of powerful tendencies set into motion by "erroneous" market decisions. Such "erroneous" (that is, uncoordinated) market decisions are responsible for "imbalances," in which over-optimistic expectations are frustrated and disappointed, while overpessimistic expectations are translated into overlooked opportunities for mutually beneficial exchanges. The market process consists partly of forces that tend to modify over-optimism, replacing erroneously hopeful decisions by more realistic market bids and offers (and more realistic production plans); and it consists, in addition, of "entrepreneurial" tendencies toward the discovery of hitherto overlooked opportunities. At any given time these coordinative tendencies are operating to eliminate the earlier errors—at the same time as "exogenous" changes in consumer preferences, resource availabilities, and technological possibilities are altering the very framework against which "error" is to be defined.

To the extent that production decisions are geared, not to the satisfaction of current consumer needs, but to the satisfaction of future needs, our above capsule description of the market process must be deepened. We must recognize that a production decision may be "over-optimistic" not only in overestimating the urgency of consumer demand for today's fresh milk, but also in overestimating the future demand for a particular style of automobile. Such a production decision may be "over-pessimistic" not only in failing to realize that today's market will express an unsatisfied demand for cheese products (which might have been even more profitable than the production of fresh milk), but also in failing to realize that (perhaps as a result of advances in medical research), in five years' time the demand for fresh fish (and thus the profitability of now producing fishing trawlers) may increase substantially.

To recognize all this does not require us to change our basic understanding of the nature of the forces that make up the market process. It merely requires us to recognize that these forces operate along channels that permit us to apply our elementary understanding of the "law" of supply and demand to levels of intertemporal complexity not noticed previously. Ultimately, however, the intertemporal coordinating forces unleashed by the "law" of supply and demand operate in ways fundamentally similar to the operation of this "law" in the simplest of markets. Market decisions are continually modified to take more realistic account of future possibilities; entrepreneurs are continually alert to the possibilities of discovering hitherto unnoticed gainful opportunities (whether these opportunities are short-run or long-run in their nature).

IS THE MARKET PROCESS REALLY BENIGN?

Our discussion in the preceding section (and in parts of the preceding article) may suggest that each step of the market process is, at least in its tendency, socially beneficial. After all, this process tends to correct the erroneous expectations that individuals may have. It tends to discourage individuals whose over-optimism might otherwise inspire them to undertake projects doomed to failure. And it tends to inspire individuals to discover hitherto overlooked ways in which they can be useful to each other. To the extent that we would hope that such opportunities would be discovered, the market process, it would seem, is "benign" in its tendency. But what about the possibility that the successful achievement of mutually beneficial exchange between parties A and B is seen by party C as an undesirable development? (Economists term such situations "externalities.") We may consider several different scenarios.

a) Suppose, as a result of newly discovered trade possibilities between A and B, C (who had previously enjoyed B's spending as a customer in his store) now finds his income reduced. Of course he is dismayed by the newly discovered mutually gainful exchange opportunity between A and B. (C would be similarly dismayed if, as one who used to buy from A at a low price, he now finds himself forced to match the higher price that B is now paying A in their newly discovered mutually gainful exchange.) While C certainly feels himself to have been "hurt" by the discovery, does this compromise our earlier judgment that the latter discovery is socially beneficial? The basis for our earlier judgment was the implicit assumption that the trade between A and B benefits them both (which is certainly the case) without affecting anyone else negatively (which is not the case in our present scenario).

Without entering into any deep philosophical issues revolving around comparisons between the "harm" suffered by C and the gains enjoyed by A and B, let us carefully notice that C has not really been harmed at all. What has happened is merely that C, who had enjoyed income received by selling to B as a result of B's earlier ignorance, is now no longer able to do so. (Or, in our alternative case, C, who had enjoyed being able to buy cheaply from A, as a result of A's earlier ignorance, is now no longer able to do so.) C has not been harmed in the sense of having lost any of his physical assets. Nor, as we shall see, has he been harmed in the sense of having lost some of the established true value of his assets; his "harm" consists strictly in his having now to live with a more realistic assessment (by himself and others) of what his physical assets are worth, and have really been worth, to others. Up until now he has, as is presently apparent, been extracting an unrealistically and unjustifiedly higher value from others, in exchange for what was really a lower-value asset.

But what if the exchange between A and B does indeed physically harm C; suppose that what A sells to B is his service as a musician and that this music played by A is so loud and so repulsive to C that the latter feels as if physically assailed. Let us consider this as scenario b).[1]

b) A sells live music to B; C's life is totally disrupted by what he considers atrocious noise. Surely we cannot describe the discovery by A and B of this opportunity for mutually gainful exchange as constituting an unambiguously socially benign development. Surely the gain to A and to B has to be offset, at least in part, by the harm caused to C. Let us distinguish two cases: (i) one in which the law recognizes C's right not to be disturbed by other people's music and (ii) one in which the law does not restrain individuals from disturbing others with their noise. In case (i), C's right not to be disturbed will certainly have to be taken into account by A and B. They will, if they wish to trade with each other, have to pay C to persuade him to permit them to do so. If C accepts such a payment, we would have a three-way trading arrangement in which everyone (at least in his own estimation) has been made better off. B gets to hear music at a total cost that he apparently believes to be worthwhile; A plays his music for a net price (after paying C) that he finds worth his while; C, while he must now sacrifice his peace and quiet (to which he is legally entitled), finds that the payment he receives from A and/or B is more than sufficient to make it worthwhile to do so. Everyone (to whom the trade between A and B is of relevant interest) has gained from trade.

In case (ii), in which the law does not recognize any right not to be disturbed by the noise of next-door music-lovers, C's pain will be legitimately ignored by A and B (unless of course they choose to act altruistically to consider C's suffering). But C has a way of making sure that his pain is taken into account by A and by B; he can offer them money to sign a contract undertaking not to play music during agreed-on periods. If they accept his money, C will consider himself to have gained (since he has purchased peace and quiet, to which he had not previously been legally entitled). If they do not agree to such a contract, C will indeed suffer from the music; but it is the legal system that is the source of this pain. The market process merely translates the legally recognized rights of A and B into corresponding realities. In both case (i) and case (ii) the market process benignly tends to reveal all relevant opportunities for mutually beneficial gain—within the given framework of legally recognized (and enforced) individual rights. We may approve or disapprove the morality of the legal system of rights, but given that system, whatever it may be, the market process benignly tends to inspire mutual discovery; it tends to bring about coordination among the decisions of all those who are considered relevant by society's adopted system of law.

HAS ECONOMICS PROVEN THE MARKET PROCESS TO BE MORALLY GOOD?

We have seen that elementary economic reasoning shows that the market process tends to promote the discovery of hitherto overlooked possibilities for mutually beneficial exchanges. We have therefore described the process as "benign" in its tendency. Does this mean that the market process is morally "good"? Have we shown that, since the market process is economically good, we have scientifically demonstrated that public policies which promote the market process are morally good policies, while those which hinder the process are morally bad? Have we used science-based "is" statements to generate morally compelling "ought" statements? Careful examination of our reasoning will show that we have not demonstrated any necessary moral goodness in the market process—but that we have nonetheless succeeded in securing a valid basis for economic policy, properly understood.

What we have called the "benign" results that tend to flow from the spontaneous market process are benign in a very special, limited, sense. It seems a pity that Jones, who prefers a (which he does not have) to b (which he does), is somehow (let us say as a result of unnecessary ignorance—unnecessary in the sense that it could be eliminated with virtually zero cost) held back from trading with Smith, who prefers b (which he does not have) to a (which he does). A market process that tends to reveal to both Jones and Smith a way in which they can mutually benefit each other (without harming anyone else) seems to be an obviously "socially" beneficial process. But the beneficial character of this process is strictly relative to Jones's and Smith's given preferences. If these preferences are, in a moral sense, praiseworthy, the process that promotes their fulfillment can be seen as morally praiseworthy too. But suppose that the a which Jones prefers is a cholesterol-laden dessert that is likely to trigger a heart attack; suppose further that the b which Smith prefers is a hectic ride on a wildly unsafe motorcycle on a busy highway. Surely many observers would think the world a morally better place without the implied exchange. But—and this is the important point—the economist who applauds the market process is doing so not as a moralist; he is doing so strictly within the "instrumentalist" framework of his profession. He is pointing out that, from a purely economic point of view (that is, in terms of given preferences and given resources), free exchange is "beneficial" in its tendency, for all relevant parties.[2]

An educational psychologist who has been consulted on the best color that might be chosen for the walls of a classroom may recommend a bright color that will stimulate alertness and learning. But before pronouncing this color to be morally superior to other possible classroom-wall colors, we would want to be sure that the classroom is to be used for morally good teaching purposes. If the classroom is to be the arena in which students are indoctrinated into hateful ideologies, we would probably consider a color which slows down the learning process to be morally superior to the alertness-inducing color. "Goodness" is strictly relative to the professional focus of the expert. For the educational psychologist this focus is the promotion of alertness to new information—regardless of the moral status of that information. For the economist the professional focus is the fulfillment of mutually beneficial opportunities for exchange, based on given preferences and resources—regardless of the moral status of those preferences.

But if this is properly understood, it does not appear to be wrong to label a coordinative economic policy to be "good economic policy," since it does promote mutual discovery among the Smiths and the Joneses. The economist who argues that one economic policy is economically better than another policy is doing so strictly within his professional framework.

WHAT WE HAVE NOT CLAIMED

There are other claims that are not implied by our claim on behalf of the economic goodness of the market process. To show this does not, however, call for philosophical or moral insight; it simply requires rigorous economic reasoning.

For example, take the idea that free markets maximize national wealth. Now the great economists who were the founding fathers of the discipline—the "classical economists"—did indeed define their science as the "science of wealth." It is well known that the (short) title of Adam Smith's classic work is *The Wealth of Nations*. As we noted in the first article, Smith, followed by the other classical economists, took it for granted that the objective of good economic policy is to increase national wealth. Yet the very meaning of the term "aggregate national wealth" (especially if confined as it was in classical economics to material wealth) begins to crumble away, as a scientifically useful term, as soon as it is subjected to analysis.

Two bushels of wheat may certainly appear as more wealth than one bushel. But are they also more wealth than, say, a package of one bushel of wheat and one sack of potatoes? And even when we consider only wheat, are we sure that two bushels owned by a single wealthy person constitute more wealth than one bushel that has been somehow distributed among several desperately poor large families? Simply drawing attention to the valuation problems of adding up apples and oranges, or to the complications introduced by the insights of subjectivist (and especially, Austrian) economics, explains why economists at the end of the nineteenth century sought to replace the criterion of aggregate national wealth by less-physical concepts. One such concept, which came to be associated particularly with the work of British economist A. C. Pigou, was that of the aggregate national "economic welfare." What good economic policy seeks to maximize, according to this approach, is the aggregate economic well-being of the members of society.

But the idea of treating individual economic welfare as something that might in principle be added together with someone else's individual economic welfare is one which could hardly be sustained. In particular Austrian economics, which had pioneered the subjectivist understanding of consumer utility, could never accept any such aggregate notion. Moreover, attempts to replace direct notions of aggregate welfare by less-direct formulations (that is, those implied in the notions of aggregate efficiency in the allocation by society of its economic resources) are easily seen to be doomed to failure.

Thus, it turns out, economic policy advice cannot meaningfully claim to be based on the idea that a particular policy should be described as economically "good" because it tends to promote aggregate wealth, or aggregate economic welfare, or a more efficient allocation of a society's economic resources.[3] We seem to be forced back to the more modest (but yet enormously important!) claims examined earlier—that certain economic policies may be shown to promote mutual discovery by potential market participants (and may therefore be considered to be "economically good" policies). Sometimes, as we have indicated, this is expressed by pointing out that such policies promote "coordination" among the decisions made in a society. They tend to alert relevant market participants about the possibilities available to them, tending thus to ensure that potentially beneficial opportunities for innovative production, and mutually gainful exchange, do not go unnoticed and unexploited. Implicit in the work of Ludwig von Mises, however, are insights into several additional criteria for judging economic policies to be good or bad.

LUDWIG VON MISES AND THE GOODNESS (OR BADNESS) OF ECONOMIC POLICIES

Mises never did fully explain the basis on which he felt able to pronounce an economic policy to be good or bad. He never (as far as I am aware) explicitly discussed the "coordination" criterion for good economic policy to which we have repeatedly referred. But there are grounds for believing our position in this article to be consistent with Mises's philosophical and economic perspectives. In his explicit discussions Mises seems to have grounded his judgments (on the goodness or badness of economic policies) on one or more of three separate foundations:

Self-Frustrating Economic Policies: A policy that can be shown by economic science to bring about results that are emphatically not desired by the policymakers themselves is bad policy. A classic Misesian example of this was the policy of urban residential rent control. Whatever the merits might be of the results hoped for from a policy of rent control, it must be pronounced a bad policy. Economic analysis shows that it tends to generate housing shortages—which were not (one hopes!) the objective of the legislators.

Unsustainable Policies: A policy that can be shown to be inherently impossible to be successfully carried out is an obviously flawed policy. For Mises a policy of monetary inflation (to fuel a boom in the initiation of long-term capital-using ventures) is a bad policy because economics shows how extremely unlikely it is that any such sustainable boom will result. Such a boom can be sustained only through long-run consumer sacrifices, which the consumers are not in fact prepared to make. Such policies amount to attempts to run simultaneously in two opposite directions. Economics can show that a particular policy cannot expect to be successfully completed. Such a policy may be described as bad policy.

Violations of Consumer Sovereignty: Mises (like most economists) apparently supposed that most people believe it to be a "good thing" for members of society to fulfill their preferences. He therefore shared the conviction of most economists that a policy which structures a society's allocation of resources in patterns clearly at odds with the dynamics of consumer preferences is an economically "bad" policy. A policy that creates a pattern of excise taxes tending to nudge consumer purchases away from goods and services the consumers prefer, toward goods and services legislators believe to be "better" for consumers—is a policy that Mises believed to be "bad," because it violates consumer sovereignty.[4]

SCIENCE AND PASSION

We noted in the first article in this series that writers have been puzzled by the passion with which Mises denounced what he believed to be bad economic policies. Fritz Machlup, an eminent economist and devoted student of Mises, was one of these writers. Mises's passion seems, at first glance, difficult to reconcile with his own insistence on the absolute necessity for scientific *wertfreiheit*—detached objectivity—in social science. When Mises denounced socialism as a disastrous economic system—one that tends to impoverish society, to bring misery on its members, and to threaten the very survival of Western civilization—he waxed passionate. He was firmly convinced that economic science shows all this to be true. (In particular he was convinced that economics demonstrates how the most benevolent of would-be national planners would not be able to plan [that is, to coordinate individual activities] at all! Thus a policy of socialism—that is, a system in which an integrated, single, national plan is sought to replace the "anarchy" of innumerable individual plans in a free-market society—is one that is simply impossible to carry out [just as would be a policy aiming to run in two opposite directions at the same time].)

But by now it should be clear that there is no inconsistency in Mises's positions. Because Mises believed—on objective, scientific grounds—that socialism is a sure recipe for misery and worse, he believed it to be his moral duty to communicate his belief to society with whatever passion might be able to command attention and inspire political relief. Machlup may have seen this as a violation of *wertfreiheit*. Mises would have vehemently disagreed. His passion was—like the passion of someone earnestly preaching the health dangers of tobacco smoking—based on cold, objective science.

As we saw in the first article, the eminent economist George Stigler believed that any "preaching" by any economist for any particular economic policy is, on grounds of consumer sovereignty, out of order. Stigler believed that the public already knows full well what the likely results of any economic policy are likely to be. If the economist is preaching against a policy voluntarily adopted by the public through its political channels, he is simply attempting to promote what he believes to be better for society over what society believes to be better.

But economic science surely has, again and again, revealed how particular policies result in outcomes not foreseen by policymakers, or by those who elected or appointed them. Economics shows how imperfect knowledge may be responsible for enormously valuable (and completely overlooked) opportunities remaining unexploited. It is no violation of consumer sovereignty to demonstrate where such ignorance has been (or is likely to be) responsible for disastrous results. In fact, to demonstrate this is to promote consumer sovereignty. As long as the philosophical and moral detachment of economic science is well understood, this science can be used, in a *wertfrei* manner, to inform the public of what it does not yet know. Where the results of such ignorance are likely to be serious, the economist (in his capacity now of a citizen fully alive to society's suffering) may consider it his moral obligation to bring the results of his objective scientific researches to the attention of the public. Such moral obligation may indeed be expressed with Misesian white-hot passion— but this is, in principle, in no way inconsistent with the cold objectivity with which those researches were conducted.

NOTES

1. This scenario has been extensively explored in a literature pioneered by Nobel laureate Ronald H. Coase; see his celebrated paper, "The Problem of Social Cost," *Journal of Law and Economics*, Vol. III (October 1960).

2. For the classic statement of these insights, see Lionel C. Robbins, *An Essay on the Nature and Significance of Economic Science*, 2d edition (London: Macmillan, 1935), especially Ch. VI.

3. See further my paper, "Welfare Economics: A Modern Austrian Perspective," published as chapter 11 in Israel M. Kirzner, *The Meaning of Market Process, Essays in the Development of Modern Austrian Economics* (London: Routledge, 1992).

4. For a pioneering discussion of coordination, as introduced into normative economics by eminent Austrian economist Friedrich A. Hayek, see Gerald P. O'Driscoll, *Economics as a Coordination Problem, The Contributions of Friedrich A. Hayek*. See also my "Coordination as a Criterion for Economic 'Goodness,'" published as chapter 7 in Israel M. Kirzner, *The Driving Force of the Market, Essays in Austrian Economics* (London: Routledge, 2000). See also Israel M. Kirzner, *Ludwig von Mises: The Man and His Economics* (Wilmington, Del.: ISI Books, 2001), pp. 163–71.

TOWARD AN AUSTRIAN CRITIQUE OF GOVERNMENTAL ECONOMIC POLICY

In preceding articles we outlined the way in which Austrian economists understand the entrepreneurial competitive market process that is responsible for the law of supply and demand. In the present article we pursue this understanding further, to permit us to see why government interventions in spontaneous market processes tend to frustrate and obstruct the coordinative tendencies that the market process generates. The most extreme sense in which such obstruction may occur is in the pure socialist economy (in which all productive activities are governed wholly by a central planning authority). Here the obstruction is total; market tendencies toward spontaneous coordination are completely paralyzed. But less extreme (less "total") forms of government intervention, particularly so-called "mixed" systems, incorporating significant central regulation of market activity, will be seen to suffer from the same kind of difficulty—the frustration of market tendencies toward spontaneous coordination.

MISES ON SOCIALISM

It was in 1920 that renowned Austrian economist Ludwig von Mises enunciated his thesis that centralized socialist planning was, in a definite sense, simply *impossible*. What he meant by this provocative assertion has often been misinterpreted. Mises did not claim that a socialist system cannot exist; nor did he predict unequivocally that such a system cannot survive for many years. What Mises meant was that, with the best will in the world, with the most dedicated and incorruptible central planners in the world, it is simply impossible *to plan centrally* for an entire economy. The decisions made by the central authorities in an economy without a market for productive resources cannot possibly take into account all the alternatives that would, in principle, need to be taken into account in order for decisions to be able to be described as socially efficient. Without

From *The Freeman / Ideas on Liberty:* http://www.thefreemanonline.org. © 2008 *The Freeman / Ideas on Liberty.* All rights reserved. Reprinted by permission of the Foundation for Economic Education. Originally appeared in print in *The Freeman* 50, no. 4 (2000): 16–18.

a market for productive resources (and thus without market *prices* reflecting the urgency with which consumers in *other* industries are demanding the services of these resources), central planners have no way of ensuring that resources flow to satisfy the more urgent, rather than the less urgent, demands among consumer preferences.

In a market economy the price of a resource expresses the priority with which consumers wish entrepreneurs to direct that resource for the satisfaction of their preferences; a high resource price means that entrepreneurs, somewhere, are aware of a productive employment for this resource that consumers value highly. For an entrepreneur to allocate this resource to any particular industry, he must, in the market competition for the resource, outbid other entrepreneurs; that is, he must be convinced that he has identified a use for it which consumers value more highly than consumers value alternative uses for that resource. Without themselves necessarily being aware of the nature and value of these alternative uses, the entrepreneurs are led, yes, as if by an invisible hand, to allocate resources in a way that takes account, in effect, of these alternative uses.

But for the central planners, operating as they must without market prices for resources (since there can, by definition, be no resource markets in the socialist economy), a decision made as to whether to allocate steel to the construction of a bridge or to the construction of an apartment building cannot be made on the basis of any measures of alternate urgencies of need; there simply are no such measures. The central authorities may decide to build the bridge, but their decision is not "rational" (in the sense of expressing a rational selection among alternatives). Central planning, in the ordinary sense of the term "to plan" (which expresses the idea of taking into account the need to balance conflicting objectives), is, as Mises showed, impossible.

THE MYTH OF SO-CALLED "NONMARKET" PRICES

In the interwar debate that ensued as a result of Mises's provocative assertion, one attempted socialist response stood out among the others. This was the suggestion, offered separately in the 1930s by two competent socialist economists, Oskar Lange and Abba P. Lerner, that socialist planning might be possible, provided decisions, to be made by socialist employees, could be guided by nonmarket "prices" for resources—that is, by prices promulgated by a central authority, *without* any resource market, but as based on regular reports to the authority of shortages or surpluses of each particular resource during the preceding production period. Space limitations do not permit us here to spell out the details of this suggestion. As we shall see, its central, damning weakness is the notion that resource "prices" can be promulgated without the spontaneous interplay of the bids and offers of profit-hungry competing entrepreneurs.

Remarkably, but in a sense disastrously, mainstream economics for some four decades ignored this weakness and pronounced the Lange-Lerner suggestion a valid and definitive solution to the problem identified by Mises. Only during the past two decades have economists finally conceded the power of Mises's argument. In an outstanding 1985 revisionist work devoted to the socialist economic calculation debate—a work rooted in the Austrian understanding of the market process—Donald Lavoie effectively dissected the fallacies that underlay the mainstream illusion that Lange and Lerner had solved the Misesian dilemma.* The source of the illusion is the mainstream preoccupation with states of equilibrium, to the exclusion of any appreciation for the way in which the dynamically competitive ventures initiated by profit-seeking entrepreneurs are responsible for the calculative usefulness of real-world market prices. To imagine that a central planning bureaucracy might generate numbers in a manner that might remotely resemble the way in which prices are generated in the course of market competition is fundamentally to misunderstand the way markets work.

To put this in somewhat different terms: the mainstream's willingness to accept the Lange-Lerner notion of nonmarket "prices" parallels precisely that mainstream's enunciation of the "law of supply and demand" in strictly equilibrium, nonentrepreneurial terms. Mises's (and also F. A. Hayek's) refusal to acknowledge meaningfulness in such nonmarket "prices" parallels precisely the Austrian insistence on understanding the law of supply and demand as the manifestation of an entrepreneurial process.

THE ECONOMICS OF GOVERNMENT INTERVENTION

Our articulation of the Austrian version of the law of supply and demand, and our corresponding understanding of the Austrian refusal to accept the Lange-Lerner solution (in terms of centrally promulgated nonmarket prices) to the socialist economic calculation problem first identified

---

* Donald Lavoie, *Rivalry and Central Planning: The Socialist Calculation Debate Reconsidered* (New York: Cambridge University Press, 1985).

by Mises permits us to push the logic a little further. It seems reasonable to interpret Mises's well-known *general* rejection of government intervention (not only for the socialist model, but more particularly for the "mixed" economy) as a consistent application of his insights into the impossibility of rational central planning in a socialist economy. Each and every act of government regulation constitutes, no matter what noble intentions for social betterment such regulation may reflect, an act of interference with the spontaneous market process generated by entrepreneurial competition.

No one claims that the results of this spontaneous market process are, at any given moment, those that would express perfect social efficiency as seen from a vantage point of imagined omniscience. What Austrians claim for the spontaneous market process is that it is the *only* procedure available to less-than-omniscient humans to move systematically in the direction of social efficiency, properly defined and understood. For government regulators to believe themselves able systematically and deliberately to improve on the results of the free-market competitive process is not only arrogantly to assume themselves able to approximate the omniscience needed to do so; it is also to fail to realize how their activities are inevitably destined to distort and/or paralyze that market process through which society grapples creatively and constructively with its lack of omniscience. It was Ludwig von Mises who, in his critique of the possibility of socialist planning, drew indirect attention to the central planner's crippling lack of the knowledge necessary to plan centrally. It was Mises's subtle understanding of the dynamics of the competitive market process that made him, more than all other twentieth-century economists, the complete skeptic regarding the social usefulness of government intervention in otherwise market economies.

We commenced this four-part series with an Austrian critique of the textbook version of the law of supply and demand. Consideration of the Austrian understanding of that law in terms of a competitive-entrepreneurial process of mutual discovery and coordination led us to a thoroughly negative perspective concerning well-meaning attempts to "maintain competition" through so-called antitrust policies. We have now concluded with brief attention to the manner in which the Austrian view leads, not only to a critique of the pure socialist economy, but also toward the critique of interventionism in *all* its forms.

Well-meaning efforts at improving the economic performance of society have all too often tended to focus on the provision of incentives to spur the "right" set of activities by individual members of the economy. The attitude underlying this widespread tendency assumes, that in the absence of such carefully structured incentives, individuals are likely to be motivated to undertake sets of actions which will either prove to be mutually inconsistent and uncoordinated (resulting in their partial frustration), or fail to permit society to exploit all the services of the factors of production available to it resulting in unemployment or under-employment of resources. Only deliberate centrally governed arrangements concerning the appropriate incentives, relating specifically to taxation patterns, subsidies, and the regulation of business, it is believed, can succeed in steering an economy to full and efficient use of its available means of production. Recently developed "Austrian" insights into the nature of the dynamic competitive process and of entrepreneurial discovery, suggest strongly that a totally different attitude toward economic incentives may be in order.

These insights (developed particularly in the work of Mises, Hayek, and their followers in the "Austrian revival" among economists in the USA, UK and elsewhere) focus on the role of *pure discovery* and on the subtle (and as yet only imperfectly understood) factors that stimulate it. The conventional notion of an incentive refers to the prospective reward that must be dangled before a decision-maker in order to make it worthwhile for him or, of course, her to put a particular unit of resource (over which he has command) to a more socially desirable use rather than to some other use (including, particularly, its direct employment in the form of unproductive leisure). This conventional idea of an incentive is of unquestionable importance, although it by no means follows that a market is unable spontaneously to provide the optimal array of such incentives. But the scope for this kind of incentive is limited strictly to

From *Economic Affairs* 4, 2 (1984): 4. Copyright of *Economic Affairs* is the property of Blackwell Publishing Limited. Reprinted by permission of John Wiley and Sons, publisher.

contexts in which the relevant alternatives *are already obvious* to the relevant decision-makers. The newer work of the "new" Austrians has drawn our attention to the circumstance that in general what has to be done is—even when it would be lucrative for the decision makers to do it—*not known at all* to them (nor, not incidentally, to anyone else). So what is required is a type of incentive that might stimulate the *discovery* of such lucrative, but completely unknown, opportunities.

Notice that the situation is rather different from the context in which a gifted teacher can stimulate his students to the discovery of undreamed-of knowledge. There the teacher himself, at least, knows the riches that await the students' discovery. In the economic context the problem is that *no one* knows in advance what is most urgently "waiting" to be discovered. Now, there is no doubt that we have here an important, and very largely uncharted, field for new research into the shape of the economic environment most conducive to the stimulation of useful discoveries. However, although much remains to be researched in this subject, there is every reason to believe that we do already understand the general contours of such an environment. What is important is that these general contours are *sharply inconsistent* with the position envisaged by many policy makers whose thinking runs in terms of the more conventional notion of incentives.

So, far from pointing in the direction of deliberate structuring of such conventional incentives, the Austrian work suggests that, to stimulate discovery of socially valuable opportunities for change, what is required is primarily an environment in which *freedom of entry* into newly discovered opportunities is not obstructed, either by concern to protect those with vested interests in older ways of doing things or by a social attitude toward pure entrepreneurial gain that condemns it as somehow unjustly exploited from honest toilers or defenceless consumers.

COMPETITION, REGULATION, AND THE MARKET PROCESS: AN "AUSTRIAN" PERSPECTIVE

MARKET RESULTS

The benign-results critique of government regulation stems from the belief that markets can at all times be reasonably assumed to be at or close to competitive equilibrium. The market system is taken to be so efficient as to ensure that at all times prices are approximately at the levels necessary to clear their respective markets. Far from being chaotic, the market is seen as a powerful coordinating institution that matches up would-be buyers with would-be sellers, ensuring that all feasible, mutually beneficial exchange opportunities are successfully consummated. Shortcomings alleged to be visible in the market allocation of resources are, in this view, seen as shortcomings only by those who disagree with consumer preferences, or who fail to understand the inescapable constraints imposed by scarcity. Even if we are prepared to attribute the most disinterested and selfless of motives to the regulators, to tamper with the benign results attributed to the market must be to divert the course of production, of the allocation of resources, from the channels marked out by the preferences of market participants themselves (in the light of given resource endowments) to other arbitrarily imposed—"less benign"—channels. In this view, the precise sequence of market events through which equilibrium within and between markets might be achieved is of less significance than the circumstance that such balance may at all times be considered to have already been approximately achieved.

In order to conclude that the results of the market are indeed benign, this view relies heavily on the assumption of perfectly competitive markets. The equilibrium held to be approximately attained in and between markets is the perfectly competitive market equilibrium—and it is the favorable evaluation of competitive equilibrium by welfare economics that informs the anti-regulation conclusions of this view. It is not surprising that economists supporting government regulatory policies have, without need to reject the equilibrium view of markets, nor the welfare

From *Cato Policy Analysis* No. 18, September 30, 1982. Cato Institute. Reprinted by permission.

theorems to which the policies are linked, simply been able to point to the highly specific assumptions needed before a favorable verdict on the unregulated market can be pronounced. And perhaps the most important of these assumptions has indeed been that of perfect competition—that the market consists of so many small buyers and sellers that for each of them the market price may be taken as a datum, not affected by the pricing, output, or purchase decisions of any one of them. This specific assumption fails to fit the facts of modern markets. This is so obviously true that many economists, precisely because they have, on market equilibrium grounds, generally looked with disfavor upon government regulation, have nonetheless frequently considered it desirable that the government intervene to guarantee a reasonable approximation of perfectly competitive conditions.

It is not necessary to dwell on the pointed questions that proponents of regulation can raise, and have raised, against this view (with respect both to the relevance of the assumptions necessary for this view to be tenable and to the validity of the thesis that markets successfully equilibrate). So we turn now to the Austrian critique of regulation.

THE MARKET AS PROCESS

In this second view it is not claimed that at any given time the market has attained even an approximation of the equilibrium state. It is merely argued that wherever equilibrium conditions have not yet been fulfilled, this very circumstance creates incentives for systematic changes that tend to eliminate the existing imbalances. The case against the regulation of the market (even by well-meaning and conscientious public servants), rests upon insights into this corrective process and into its socially benign character. Long before this corrective process can possibly lead to even approximate coordination, changes in the basic data of the market (individual preferences, the endowments of resources, and available technology) will have rendered the hypothesized state of full equilibrium (defined with respect to the initial state of the data) utterly irrelevant. But the discrepancies continually stimulate, in turn, changes in these existing patterns of resource allocation.

Emphasizing the properties of the process market transactions make up, rather than the allocative pattern achieved by the process, underscores the complete irrelevance of utopian notions of perfect coordination. In this view of the market economy, to judge a real-world economic system against the yardstick of perfect coordination is not merely to treat far too seriously the possibility of perfect coordination (and thus of markets in full equilibrium) it is grossly to misunderstand the essential economic problem faced by complex societies. The truth is that, as Hayek explained four decades ago, the economic problem faced by society consists of the need to ensure that, as far as possible, the available bits of scattered knowledge of separate individuals be somehow mobilized to contribute to relevant decisions that affect the societal pattern of resource allocation. To try to measure the success with which a society addresses its economic problem, with a yardstick reflecting a pattern appropriate to hypothesized centralized omniscience, is akin to an attempt to assess the efficiency of an allocation pattern for scarce resources by comparing its results with those that might be imagined for a world in which scarcity is absent: The whole problem is how best to cope with scarcity. Similarly the socio-economic problem is how best to cope with the inescapable decentralization of knowledge.

Given the irrelevance of using the omniscience yardstick and the complications that compound the economic problem facing society when the consequences of kaleidic change in the basic data are taken into account, it becomes clear that a normative criterion other than perfect coordination must be found. The "process" view suggests that the appropriate criterion should be sought in the capacity attributed to the market process, of serving as a "discovery procedure" (the phrase is Hayek's). What occurs during the market process of interacting individual decisions, Hayek argues, is that participants tend to discover relevant aspects of each other's abilities and desires. Here, then, we have a relevant conceptual yardstick by which to assess both the operation of a market economy and policy recommendations made to modify its operation. Our question need never be: Are the results of the market process such that there is nothing remaining yet to be discovered, or even reasonably close to such a state? Rather, we must ask: Can the institutional structure (or proposed modifications to it) stimulate a reasonably steady and significant flow of (correct) mutual discoveries? To the extent that positive answers to this question can be provided, we have identified a socially "benign" process. To the extent that a proposed modification enhances the propensity of the system to stimulate (correct) discoveries, it represents a "benign" proposal; on the other hand, if the proposal is likely to hamper or distort the discovery procedure, it is "harmful."

Of course, the adoption of the process approach does not mean that we are entirely uninterested in results. After all, the effectiveness with which the process stimulates discoveries may be able to be gauged, in part, by observing results. But even where this is the case, results are referred to not because of the absolute desirability of the pattern of allocation that they display, but because of the extent of the already made discoveries that they reveal. Let us see how, from the process perspective, the market economy successfully coordinates the activities of its participants.

THE MARKET AS DISCOVERY PROCEDURE

In a market economy decisions are made independently by many market participants in their capacities as consumers, owners of resources, or as entrepreneur-producers. These decisions are made on the basis of what individuals think are the best options available to them. Since the available options will themselves be the results of the individual decisions of others, individual decisions are being made on the basis of assessments of the anticipated individual decisions of others. These assessments are clearly likely to be in greater or lesser error. Buyers may offer high prices because they erroneously believe that no one is able or prepared to sell for less. Sellers offer to sell at low prices because they think no one is prepared to buy for more. Producers refrain from producing an item because they mistakenly believe that the resources needed to produce it can only be obtained at a cost that would place the product out of the reach of potential consumers. Or they produce a second item at a high cost because they think potential buyers are more eager to buy it. And so on.

Each of these mistaken decisions will systematically tend to bring about rather specific kinds of consequences. Overestimating a prod-uct's appeal to consumers will result in market losses. When a producer overestimates production costs or underestimates a product's appeal to consumers, he overlooks opportunities to make a profit that will tend to attract more perceptive entrepreneurs. As a result of these elementary and well-known kinds of profit or loss experiences, market participants learn to assess more accurately the limits of possible, mutually beneficial transactions with their fellow participants.

Note that we do not say that these disappointments and profit discoveries eliminate all the errors that have been made. We say merely that market activity based on error generates the incentives and the experiences that tend to identify where the errors have been made, and to stimulate less erroneous activity. A seller who is disappointed in his expectation of securing a high price will learn that he can expect, at best, only a lower price. A seller who has accepted a price lower than the price being paid by buyers elsewhere in the market helps create a situation in which the same item is being traded at two different prices—thus offering the opportunity to alert entrepreneurs to buy at the lower price and resell at the higher price. Such clearcut opportunities for pure profit tend to attract attention, to become exploited and thus eliminated—in the course of which the initial error itself is likely to be corrected. The sequence has an almost poetic quality: 1) errors manifest themselves in the creation of profit opportunities or of experienced disappointments; 2) profit opportunities tend to be discovered and exploited; disappointments tend to give overly optimistic market participants more realistic information; these tendencies combine toward 3) the elimination of the initial errors (and of the profit opportunities and the disappointments which they generated). The impetus toward mutual discovery is provided by the market consequences of the initial discovery-failures.

PROFIT, ENTREPRENEURSHIP, AND THE DISCOVERY PROCESS

It is important to notice the role played in this process of market discovery by pure entrepreneurial profit. Pure profit opportunities emerge continually as errors are made by market participants in a changing world. The inevitably fleeting character of these opportunities arises from the powerful market tendency for entrepreneurs to notice, exploit, and then eliminate these pure price differentials. The paradox of pure profit opportunities is precisely that they are at the same time both continually emerging and yet continually disappearing. It is this incessant process of the creation and the destruction of opportunities for pure profit that makes up the discovery procedure of the market. It is this process that keeps entrepreneurs reasonably abreast of changes in consumer preferences, in available technologies, and in resource availabilities.

As we have noticed, profit opportunities reflect price discrepancies. And, indeed, such price discrepancies reflect past error. But the profit opportunity so created exerts a powerful, attractive force upon entrepreneurial alertness. While, in general, error by itself may appear likely to stimulate its own correction, the error that generates pure profit opportunities makes entrepreneurs more aware of these opportunities, thus stimulating its own elimination.

Our conviction that opportunities for pure profit will tend to be pounced upon by alert entrepreneurs should not, of course, be distorted to suggest that pure profit opportunities will, at all times, have already been pounced upon before they have even emerged. Entrepreneurial error is continually with us. On the other hand, neither should the perennial existence of error suggest that no systematic market forces are present tending to its elimination. The driving force behind the market process of continual discovery of continually emerging error is entrepreneurial alertness. The truth is that we (whether economists, or psychologists, or businessmen) know very little about the sources and the nature of entrepreneurial alertness. But we know enough to understand that the market depends upon it for its remarkable ability to serve as a social discovery procedure. If, as we wish to claim in this article, the free market must depend only on this entrepreneurial discovery process for its socially benign character, it behooves us as policymakers to understand thoroughly the subtle aspects of this process and to take every step possible to avoid hampering or distorting its course.

Entrepreneurial alertness is not confined to noticing already existing price differentials. Entrepreneurial alertness goes far beyond the exploitation of perceived opportunities for instantaneous arbitrage in today's markets. The speculative entrepreneur who, anticipating a rise in price of a particular item, buys now at the low price in order to reap pure profit by selling tomorrow, or in twenty years' time, is acting upon the stimulus of his "alertness" to an absence of coordination between what is available today and what will be needed tomorrow, or in twenty years' time. If this speculative entrepreneur turns out to have been correct, this absence of coordination will be seen retrospectively as arising out of the errors of those others who failed to anticipate correctly the future market trends. It was their error that created the intertemporal price discrepancy that attracted the notice and interest of the successful speculator-entrepreneur.

And we may take the matter even further. Not only may the intertemporal profit opportunity be noticed by the speculator, he may in fact create it. The imaginative, innovative entrepreneur who buys today's resources cheaply in order to market tomorrow, or in twenty years' time, a totally new idea, has acted to bring the allocation of society's resources into greater coordination with the true possibilities that his own creative genius reveals already to exist. From a historical perspective, what would be revealed as the "errors" of those earlier generations who had not yet dreamed of the potential discoveries "waiting" to be made are "corrected" through the creative process of entrepreneurial innovation. No matter whether entrepreneurial alertness manifests itself in the perception of arbitrage opportunities, or of purely speculative opportunities, or of opportunities for technological or marketing innovation, it is this alertness that drives the corrective discovery process of the market.

COMPETITION AND ENTREPRENEURSHIP

We should notice, in addition, that the entrepreneurial discovery process constitutes an essentially competitive process. This crucially significant insight deserves brief elaboration.

As we have seen, the dynamic of the market process comes from the implementation of entrepreneurial discoveries. For such implementation it is necessary, of course, that entrepreneurs be free to act upon their discoveries—no matter how this may redound to the disadvantage of those who have not themselves made these discoveries. Such freedom to act requires that no entrepreneur be blocked from entry into any line of market endeavor. Freedom of entry is the legal and institutional prerequisite for the discovery procedure of the market.

It is easy to see how freedom of entry for alert entrepreneurs who think they have discovered opportunities for pure profit must be a source of fear to those whose "errors" have kept consumers less well-served than they might have been. For those selling at high prices (when the same item is available at lower prices), the competition of arbitrageurs spells a rapid end to their high prices. (For those buying at the lower prices this competition from arbitrageurs spells a similar threat.) For those using scarce resources to produce a product less urgently needed by consumers than a second product (producible with the same resources) not now being produced, the competition of the innovative entrepreneur who comes to bid for these scarce resources in order to produce the second product must indeed seem a most serious competitive threat. For each of those threatened, it would seem eminently desirable that these brash, innovative, iconoclastic, and disrespectful entrepreneurs be prevented from entering—and disrupting—these existing markets. Clearly the dynamic of entrepreneurial discovery operates by continual disruption of the quiet life that would, in its absence, be enjoyed by those pursuing established (and partially "erroneous") patterns of market behavior.

In the sense in which businessmen understand the meaning of competition, the entrepreneurial discovery-process of the market is essentially competitive: It operates only insofar as no one in the market is protected against the entry of newcomers. The freedom to enter not only makes potential entrants more alert to "gaps"—areas of potential profit; the awareness of such freedom will also make incumbents more alert to threats of potential entry. The incumbents will then seek to forestall entry by appropriate, "entrepreneurial" modification of their own activities.

To stimulate the alertness of entrepreneurs in this way—that is, to guarantee the competitive character of the market process—we do not need to postulate that the market for any particular item already includes a large number of buyers and sellers. We certainly do not need to postulate—as the more traditional terminology of technical economics has assumed is necessary for the existence of perfectly competitive conditions—that each market participant views himself as powerless to choose his price bids or offers. All we need to postulate is that there exist no extra-market barriers to the entry of potential competitors to any particular line of endeavor. In arguing that the benign properties we have attributed to the market process depend upon its competitive character, we do not mean that these properties rest upon the outcome of a competitive process, during which so many market participants have entered as to render each of them atomistically impotent. What we are saying is that the conditions which stimulate the competitive process—i.e., the complete absence of institutional restrictions upon entry—tend to guarantee the mutual discovery process.

GOVERNMENT REGULATION—
OBSTACLE TO THE DISCOVERY PROCESS

We are now in a better position to see how the Austrian view of the market outlined in this article may lead to a critical stance toward government regulation, and how the basis for such a critical stance differs from that of the more orthodox, neoclassical defense of the free market. We may put the matter quite succinctly: For reasonably successful coordination within a decentralized decision-making system, the discovery process constituted by competitive-entrepreneurial alertness to profit opportunities is crucial. Attempts at improvement by direct regulation are likely to be based on erroneous information (because the regulators cannot utilize the discovery process of profit pursuit) and are likely to block or distort the market's own delicate discovery process.

Let us suppose that the need to regulate is asserted on the basis of some perceived "undesirable" phenomenon arising from the unregulated market. For example, the prices of certain goods are held to be "too high" (milk to consumers?), or "too low" (wheat prices received by farmers?). Or the quantity available of a certain product is held to be "too low" (medical care?) or "too high" (unsafe toys?). And so on. Let us imagine (perhaps fancifully) that government decisionmakers are motivated solely by the urge to induce a pattern of phenomena that faithfully reflects consumer preferences (which they believe to have been somehow frustrated by the uncoordinated free market). Our discussion should have made clear that these selfless, public-minded officials lack the means to be able to respond to the innumerable rankings of preference (by consumers and owners of resources) of which they may initially not be directly aware. There is no way they can know the "correct" price or the "correct" quantity for any particular product or resource. There is nothing (corresponding to the entrepreneurial motive to discover pure profit opportunities) that could lead them systematically to discover where failures of coordination in fact exist.

More serious is the fact that direct controls by government on prices, quantities, or qualities of output production or input employment may unintentionally block activities which have, as yet, not been specifically envisaged by anyone. Where these blocked activities turn out to be entrepreneurially profitable activities (perhaps as a result of unforeseen changes in data), the likelihood of their being discovered is then sharply diminished. Without necessarily intending it, the spontaneous discovery process of the free market has thus been, to some extent, stifled or distorted.

We saw earlier how important for the competitive-entrepreneurial discovery process is the potential for unfettered entry by profit-seeking entrepreneurs into existing markets. Inevitably, government regulatory restrictions block such entry. In the relevant sense, such restrictions are anti-competitive. They tend to frustrate the discoveries that the competitive process is likely to generate. Even where government regulation (perhaps inspired by a mistaken ideal of "competition" in which any significant size is suspect per se) is designed to "maintain competition" (e.g. by blocking mergers), this too must be set down as anti-competitive. For example, this may block the entrepreneurial process by which the optimum scale for the producing firm might be discovered.

It is easy for competent government officials to imagine that they know what is good for the economy. But this is likely to mean that in the incredibly complex economies of our time, it is easy for well-meaning individuals not to realize their ignorance in specific instances. For private entrepreneurs, the device for the communication of such unsuspected missing information is provided by the attractiveness of the opportunities for pure profit which such missing information generates. Not only are regulators unable to benefit by such profit-inspired discoveries; their direct intervention in the marketplace can hardly fail to frustrate, stifle, and distort the socially benign discovery process that depends on freedom of entry into branches of activity for which the social desirability has not yet been established.

It follows that the harmful effects of regulation (as judged from the perspective of consumer preferences, not from that of arbitrarily adopted canons of social importance) are not necessarily found in palpable failure (as expressed, for example, in shortages, or gluts, or other "obvious" absences of coordination). The harmful effects of regulation also may manifest themselves in cases where there is an absence of coordination of which no one is aware. The point is that regulation may be responsible for such absences of coordination not being discovered. The marvel of the competitive-entrepreneurial market is its ability to inspire coordinative activities the very need for which would, in the absence of the market, never be revealed.

Indeed, the "invisible hand" of the free market is invisible also in the sense that the very problems of coordination it tends to solve are invisible even to the most dedicated of scientists—or government regulators.

SELECTED BIBLIOGRAPHY

Hayek, Friedrich A., ed. "Competition as a Discovery Procedure." In *New Studies in Philosophy, Politics, Economics and the History of Ideas.* Chicago: University of Chicago Press, 1978.

———. "Economics and Knowledge." *Economica* 4 (February 1937): 33–54. Reprinted in F. A. Hayek, *Individualism and Economic Order.* London: Routledge and Kegan Paul, 1948.

———. "The Use of Knowledge in Society." *American Economic Review* 35 (September 1945): 519–30. Reprinted in *Individualism and Economic Order.*

Kirzner, Israel M. *Competition and Entrepreneurship.* Chicago: University of Chicago Press, 1973.

———. *Perception, Opportunity, and Profit.* Chicago: University of Chicago Press, 1979.

———. *The Perils of Regulation: A Market-Process Approach.* Coral Gables, Fla.: University of Miami School of Law. 1978.

Lavoie, Donald C. "Rivalry and Central Planning: A Re-examination of the Debate over Economic Calculation under Socialism." Unpublished doctoral dissertation, New York University.

Littlechild, Stephen C. *The Fallacy of the Mixed Economy: An "Austrian" Critique of Economic Thinking and Policy.* Washington: Cato Institute, 1979.

Mises, Ludwig von. *Human Action: A Treatise on Economics.* New Haven: Yale University Press, 1949.

Sowell, Thomas. *Knowledge and Decisions.* New York: Basic Books, 1980.

THE GOALS OF ANTITRUST: A CRITIQUE

A significant portion of public policy discussion in Western economics during the twentieth century has concerned the perceived need to "protect" or to "foster" competition. Policy initiatives stemming from these discussions have come to constitute so-called "antitrust" or "competition" policy. An enormous literature concerning antitrust came, during the first three-quarters of the century, to make up the area in economics known as "industrial organization." In this literature, "competition" was defined in such a way as to suggest that it is unable to survive the rigors of the capitalist process, unless vigorously protected or fostered by government. The dominant, orthodox, view of economists in this area was, until relatively recently, accordingly strongly in favor of aggressive antitrust legislation and enforcement. This antitrust policy is designed to outlaw "anti-competitive" acts and business practices. More recently a definite reaction to this earlier orthodoxy has emerged in the economics profession. The central insight that has informed this reaction has been that many of the business activities, earlier held to be "anti-competitive," and therefore condemned by orthodox antitrust doctrine, can in fact be seen to be activities that we would *expect* from benignly vigorous competitors.[1] In the view of the scholars leading this reaction, it is necessary to take a broader ("multidimensional") perspective on the role of competition in modern economic society. Such a perspective, it is held, can reduce the danger that a well-meaning public policy effort at proscribing anti-competitive behavior along one particular dimension, may *itself* be *erecting barriers* against competition along other dimensions.[2]

A feature common both to the earlier orthodoxy (strongly supportive of vigorous antitrust policy) and the more recent reservations concerning antitrust policy, is thus the conviction that, in the absence of governmental action, it is possible (and indeed likely) that business firms may undertake actions which, at least along one dimension, *are* anti-competitive. So that even those who articulate reservations concerning the overall wisdom

Unpublished paper reprinted by permission of Israel M. Kirzner. Originally published in Spanish under the title "Los Objetivos de la Política Antitrust: Una Critica" in *Información Comercial Española Revista de Economía*, 1998, no. 775, pp. 67–77.

of antitrust, recognize that unhampered market behavior is likely, in some respects at least, to run counter to the ideal of competitive enterprise. In this paper we will challenge this shared conviction, as reflecting a fundamentally limited understanding of the nature of market competition. When a more insightful view of the meaning and role of competition is adopted, the unfortunate consequences of conventional antitrust policy, we shall argue, become unmistakably clear. Our conclusion will thus certainly reinforce the more recent literature expressing strong reservations concerning traditional antitrust doctrines—but we shall do so from a distinctly more radical point of departure.[3] In what follows we will thus strongly argue against antitrust policy in the light of an articulated theoretical perspective which sees such policy as *inherently* and *necessarily* *anti*-competitive, in the most consistent and meaningful use of the adjective "competitive." Our position will be that in free markets "competition" is *not* a frail flower calling for protection; it is a vigorous plant that can be eliminated, under normal conditions, only by deliberate *governmental* policy (including well-meaning antitrust policies!). We will deploy our perspective to criticize both the goals and the tools of traditional antitrust theory; and we will argue that the "global" trends in modern international economics render our critique even more relevant to today's public policy discussions.

THE MEANING OF COMPETITION

Obviously our dissatisfaction with both of the above points of view in the existing, dominant antitrust literature is, in part, a semantic one. But our position on the relevant meaning to be assigned to the adjective "competitive," stems ultimately from a substantive disagreement with the dominant literature concerning the character of the real world competitive market process. For the literature we are criticizing, real world competition is an imperfect approximation to an abstract ideal, the ideal of so-called "perfect" competition. The real world market process is seen as a rough and crude version of an ideal situation. The economic virtues of this real market process are measured by the degree of its (necessarily imperfect) approximation to that ideal. Our position, on the other hand, is that real world competition, the competition which flesh-and-blood business people engage in (and are subject to), itself ensures *in full* all the virtues which economic theory can possibly ascribe to competitive market processes. From this perspective the so-called "ideal" of perfect competition is not only, as we shall see, not competitive at all (an admittedly semantic issue); in addition that "ideal" model emerges as almost entirely irrelevant to the manner in which markets do, can, or should operate. All this requires some brief elaboration.

For the dominant literature, "competition" refers to the state of affairs in which the number of competitors is so great, and mutual information so complete, that each of the competitors is utterly *unable to exercise any market power*. (This focus on absence of market power stems from the perception that *monopoly* [seen as the polar opposite of competition] is characterized precisely by the presence of significant power to determine price.) In the ideal state of "perfect competition" no single market participant is able to affect price (by withholding supply, or by refraining from manifesting demand) even in the slightest. Each participant in a perfectly competitive market is a "price-taker." Clearly, under such conditions no potential seller can compete for customers by cutting price, no potential seller can ensure the availability to him of goods, by competitively offering prices higher than others are paying. Indeed, in the most complete model of perfect competition, market participants lack the power to engage in *any* of the business practices (e.g. improvement of the quality of the goods produced, or of services provided along with the product) which real world practice considers to be *essentially* competitive practices. We have here, then, surely the semantic confusion that real world competition is, in this dominant academic terminology, seen as competitive only to the extent that its outcomes approximate an "ideal" in which *no* competitive activity (as such activity is understood in everyday business usage) is possible at all! (The dynamic steps of business activity taken in the real world to outstrip one's competitors, are, in accordance with this semantic confusion, seen as being in themselves expressions, not of competitive activity, but of "monopolistic" power!) It is from this semantic and doctrinal point of departure that the dominant antitrust literature is (despite the disagreements we saw regarding the usefulness of antitrust policies) at least unanimous in recognizing many business practices as being, to some extent, anti-competitive. Any activity (e.g. a merger between hitherto competing firms, reducing the number of firms in an industry) which nudges the market *away* from the ideal of "perfect competition," is in this way seen as anti-competitive. Even those who (as in the recent reaction against anti-trust policy which we have noticed above) argue that some prohibitions against anti-competitive activities may be unwittingly erecting barriers against competition, do not disagree with the dominant mode of discussion. They merely point out that a policy which moves the market situation toward the perfectly competitive ideal along one dimension, may be at the same time, and perhaps more significantly, moving that situation *away* from that ideal along another dimension. Our position is entirely different.

Our perspective on competition focuses not on absence of market power as the crucial criterion, but *on the constraining effect* (upon the behavior of incumbent and prospective business firms) of *competitive entry,* (or of the threat of competitive entry). In this view of the matter, unfettered, complete competition refers not to the model of complete absence of market power [i.e. to the model of "perfect competition"], but to a world into which there is complete freedom for competitive entry, i.e. a world in which no incumbent firms possess privileged positions assuring them of protection against potential entrants. In this view of things the competitive process consists in those business activities, inspired by the lure of pure entrepreneurial profit, engaged in competitively by new entrants into the market or, (of equal significance) by incumbent firms innovating in ways designed to *forestall* the competitive activity of new entrants. A competitive act, in this view and in this terminology, is an act taken with full awareness that others are free to enter and to attempt to offer market participants the most attractive opportunities they can imagine. To cut price competitively is not (as it would be seen in the dominant view and terminology) to act non- (or, anti-) competitively, with some measure of market power, but to engage in that dynamic, entrepreneurial, competition inspired by freedom of entry. To innovate a new line of product, or a new productive technique is not (as it would be seen in the dominant view) to engage non- (or anti-) competitively in an activity inconsistent with complete absence of market power, but to engage actively and competitively in the dynamic, entrepreneurial process made possible by freedom of entry.

From this perspective of ours, antitrust policy must be seen as *essentially* and inherently *anti*-competitive. In proscribing activities (inspired by the lure of pure entrepreneurial profit) which represent the exercise of market power, such antitrust policy is *interfering* with those powerful and benign competitive market forces set in motion by freedom for entrepreneurial entry. The truth surely is that our reliance on the capacity of markets to coordinate impersonally and without central direction multitudes of independently made individual decisions, depends on the freedom of entrepreneurs to enter the market with more attractive offers to the market wherever these entrepreneurs perceive the possibility of so grasping available pure entrepreneurial profit. Anything which hampers such entrepreneurial entry is—even if it is held to bring the configuration of market outcomes closer to the perfectly competitive model—anticompetitive, to the extent that competition consists, as we have argued, in entrepreneurial entry and the threat of its entry. The reasonableness of our focus upon freedom of entry as the criterion for competitiveness, (not only insofar as concerns the semantic issue, but more importantly, insofar as we are concerned with the coordinative effectiveness of the market process), can perhaps best be tested by examining the traditional goals of antitrust policy.

THE GOALS OF ANTITRUST

Professor Jacquemin has usefully identified the traditional goals of antitrust policy as including one or more of the following three objectives: (a) the "diffusion of private economic power," (b) the protection "of the economic freedom of market competitors," (c) the achievement of "allocative and productive efficiency."[4]

(a) The Diffusion of Private Economic Power: This objective, which is rooted not in economic thought but in relatively crude public opinion concerning the dangers of "big business," has certainly been the political force behind many antitrust policy initiatives in Western countries during the past century and longer. Although at first glance it might seem that the state of "perfect competition," with *complete lack of power* on the part of individuals to affect (i.e. to "control") prices, would be the ideal goal in regard to this popular objective, second glances are likely to lead to a different conclusion. What is presumably feared by the public in its "gut" fear of "big business monopolies," is not so much the ability to affect price per se, but the ability to control price *without fear or concern for the reaction of others*. Freedom of entry, and the awareness, on the part of "big players" that such freedom implies the very real threat of entry, is enough effectively to blunt the danger of concentrated economic power. It is by now well recognized that historical examples of concentrated economic power were almost invariably created by governmental grants of immunity against entry.

(b) The Protection of the Economic Freedom of Market Competitors: Here the concern is to prevent "powerful firms" from endangering "the existence of weaker firms."[5] European concern for this goal may be motivated somewhat differently from the traditional U.S. concern; (in that the latter has been motivated perhaps more strongly by a belief that *consumer* welfare may depend on the survival of the weaker competitors). Nonetheless, regardless of the precise source of interest in this particular objective of antitrust policy, it seems difficult to argue that its successful achievement depends on attainment of the perfectly competitive state of affairs—with its infinite number (or, at any rate, *very* large number) of firms.

(c) Allocative Efficiency: It is surely this objective of antitrust, an objective that emerged during the second quarter of this century, (as a result of the expanded influence and development of neoclassical welfare economics), which has been the primary concern of professional economists. And it is here that the state of perfect competition—which welfare economists long held to be necessary and sufficient for allocative social efficiency—came to be seen as an implicit (if ideal) criterion for public policy. Under the influence of these conclusions of neoclassical welfare economics, economists came to see antitrust policy as a tool for achieving greater social efficiency in the allocation of its resources. It is therefore this objective of antitrust policy which renders the state of perfect competition the relevant yardstick, in the eyes of the antitrust literature which we are criticizing. We must therefore deal specifically with the claim that each governmental action taken to nudge the market unambiguously closer to the perfectly competitive ideal, in fact enhances the attained degree of "social efficiency" in the allocation of resources.[6] What is at issue is the very meaning of "societal efficiency."

For the literature we are criticizing, the notion of societal efficiency is clearcut, and presumes an unproblematic possibility of seeing society (as a whole) as a single decision-maker with a single, integrated ranking of societal preferences (sought to be satisfied by efficient deployment of "society's" scarce physical resources). The perspective for which we have argued here, however, maintains, following Hayek,[7] that the inevitable fact of life created by the *dispersed* character of private information renders the very idea of efficiency in societal resource allocation almost incoherent. Not only is there no single mind in fact making the decisions which determine the pattern of resource use in the market economy;

more importantly: even if there were such a single mind, it would *not* have before it all the items of information (currently existing and known to—or potentially discoverable by—individuals in the economy) with reference to which any kind of efficiency would have to be judged. The function of a market economy, in this view, is precisely that of *eliciting* these items of information and of ensuring that they will tend to be brought to bear upon production decisions. The process through which the market fulfils this function is the process of entrepreneurial competition, in which earlier errors (i.e. failures to exploit potentially discoverable items of information) come to be corrected *through the grasping (by entrepreneurial entrants) of the pure profits created precisely by the pre-existing errors.* Enhanced societal economic performance, in this view, does *not* consist of a pattern of activities somehow closer to an imagined—but essentially irrelevant—ideal state of perfect information (which is *presupposed* in the model of perfect competition). Rather, it consists in the error-correcting activities inspired by the lure of entrepreneurial profit, a lure which inspires *competitive entry*.

In a world of dispersed information and ineradicable uncertainty, improved economic performance can only be achieved through a process of dynamically competitive entrepreneurial entry. Any interference with such a process, even when motivated with the best of intentions, can be seen only as obstructing the process of economic error-discovery. It is the competition we have associated with entrepreneurial entry, rather than the "competition" which the mainstream literature has associated with the model of perfect mutual information, upon which society depends in its goal of enhancing economic performance.

POWER, RESOURCE OWNERSHIP, AND ENTREPRENEURIAL ENTRY

It is of course true that ownership of productive resources (or of the capital funds permitting such ownership) confers a measure of economic power. To the extent that the distribution of such ownership is unequal (as indeed it must almost inevitably be under a system of free enterprise), economic power over the pattern of resource allocation (and over the gains to be reaped by efficiently serving consumers) is unequally shared by market participants. But, unless one proposes antitrust policy (or, as it is often called in Europe, competition policy) as a redistributive tool for the achievement of economic equality among citizens, it is surely odd to demand such policy on the mere grounds of size—so long as the size of a firm (and the size of its capital assets) does not obstruct the efficiency-enhancing properties of freedom of competitive entry (and of the threat of such entry). And here we must spell out certain often-overlooked aspects of competitive entry.

What is necessary for competitive entry, it must be emphasized, is not the prior possession of productive resources—but merely freedom for potential entrepreneurs to perceive and to grasp opportunities for pure entrepreneurial profit. Pure entrepreneurial profit is not a gain which somehow grows out of productive resources initially owned by the entrepreneur. Pure entrepreneurial profit requires, in fact, *no* prior ownership *of anything at all* (so that inequality in resource ownership, and in the power which such ownership confers, is irrelevant to the competition constituted by freedom for entrepreneurial entry). What is required for the grasping of pure entrepreneurial profit is simply the freedom to "enter" (meaning the freedom to buy resources at prices the sum of which [including relevant interest amounts] is lower than the price at which one expects to be able to sell the product produced with these resources). *No* prior ownership of anything is, in principle, required in order to be able to take advantage of such opportunities. Nor does ownership of resources confer superior command over such opportunities. It is superior entrepreneurial perceptiveness and prescience alone which are necessary and sufficient for the grasping of pure profit opportunities. Some further clarification on this point is in order.

Antitrust policies do nothing and can do nothing to enhance the pace of entrepreneurial discovery. To the extent that one accepts our thesis (in the preceding section) that superior societal economic performance depends upon the entrepreneurial correction of earlier errors (arising out of the dispersed character of knowledge), it should be clear that antitrust policy can only *obstruct* economic progress (by obstructing that entrepreneurial entry upon which true competitiveness depends).

Economic and business history demonstrate amply that the size of firms is utterly insufficient ultimately to control the direction of production, or obstruct economic improvement—so long as entrepreneurial entry remains unobstructed.

It is certainly true that an entrepreneur can grasp pure profits through innovative production only by acquiring the necessary productive resources. But he can, *in principle,* acquire such resources (once he has become convinced of the profitability of a projected plan of production), by borrowing in the capital market.[8] But our assertion (that the grasping of entrepreneurial profit does not depend on already owned resources) carries with it a crucially important corollary: no matter how large a volume of resources a firm may possess, its ability to grasp pure profits depends, not upon the size of that volume of resources, but upon the firm's entrepreneurial vision regarding ways of deploying those resources innovatively and profitably. Unless such vision is present, those resources will remain in conventional standard lines of production (unless indeed they are bid away by more enterprising producers); *with* such vision present, innovation expresses, not ownership of resources, but simply the entrepreneurial grasp of how to obtain command over resources in order to deploy them in fresh, profitable ways.

To proceed entrepreneurially to gain command over (hitherto undervalued) resources *means*, therefore, to proceed competitively to enter markets precisely by placing oneself in a relatively powerful position (as compared with other firms which have failed to do so). For public policy to obstruct such entrepreneurial-competitive acquisition of economic power is therefore essentially to obstruct the entrepreneurial-competitive process. To *define* competition as that state in which *no* participants possess economic power (as does the mainstream "perfect competition" literature) is thus, as we have seen, to employ a terminology which assigns the adjective "competitive" to describe the state of affairs in which scope for entrepreneurial-competitive entry is completely absent.

THE TOOLS OF ANTITRUST

The principles we have stated in developing our understanding of the competitive process, and its general implication for an evaluation of antitrust, must now be briefly illustrated by reference to selected tools of antitrust. This is not the place for any comprehensive and detailed survey of the classic measures employed to implement antitrust policy. Our purpose in the space available here is simply to illustrate, in barest outline, the force of our reasoning in regard to several typical antitrust tools.

i) Obstacles against Mergers

Anti-merger measures are typical of antitrust policy activity, and of the economic theory which the antitrust literature expresses. It stands to reason that, if the perfectly competitive model is taken as the ideal, mergers represent reductions in the degree of competitiveness within the respective markets. Fewer, larger, firms constitute an industry further away from the perfectly competitive ideal than one with more numerous, smaller firms. The larger size of the newly merged firm confers greater market power than that possessed by smaller firms. Obstacles against mergers thus appear as important weapons in the pro-competitive antitrust arsenal. Our position, as we have developed it in this paper, clearly sees things in a diametrically opposite way.

From our perspective, an agreement of two firms (in an industry made up, say, of relatively small firms) to merge, represents entrepreneurial activity aimed at achieving entry (into the particular field of production) on a quantitative scale which has hitherto not been attempted. Plausibly, this attempt is based on the *entrepreneurial* vision of lowering costs (whether fabrication costs, managerial costs, marketing costs, or whatever). Because such entry is possible, not only to these merging firms, but also to other firms (including firms entirely new to this industry), it is an essentially competitive move (in our terminology). Not only is it competitive in the sense of competing in a fresh way with existing firms; it is competitive also in the sense that this move can be matched at any time by similar (or even better) moves on the part of other firms. Even if the merger is undertaken in the hope of dominating a particular industry and its market, it remains a competitive step (since it cannot, absent governmental obstruction against entry, prevent the entry of others). Even an attempt to become the sole producer in an industry into which entry is open to all (an attempt often described as a bid to become the industry monopolist), is necessarily a competitive step (a) in that others were free to make such attempts, so that this step was taken in competition with others; (b) in that, since others are still free to enter the "monopolized" industry, the "monopolist," even if he *is* (at least for the moment) the sole seller in the industry, *is* competing with potential entrants. To obstruct such mergers is to obstruct the competitive-entrepreneurial process.

ii) Outlawing Price-Agreements
Collusion among (otherwise competing) firms in regard to prices is a typical "anti-competitive" practice targeted by antitrust. Such collusion, (often compared to the cartellization of an industry) is seen as in effect imposing monopoly-price dominance over the market. Our perspective permits

us to recognize that, whatever the motivation of the agreement, such an agreement does *not* affect the dynamic competitiveness of its market—so long as entry is free and unobstructed. The collusive attempt of a group of powerful firms to keep prices high may indeed be an attempt to use economic muscle to extract more from consumers, by eliminating inter-firm price competition. This may indeed therefore appear to be the case in which economic power coincides with anti-competitive behavior. Pro-hibition of such collusive behavior may therefore appear, as antitrust the-ory maintains, to constitute a distinctly pro-competitive measure.

From the perspective we have articulated in this paper, however, mat-ters appear differently. So long as entry is unobstructed, any attempt to use economic muscle to resist competition is essentially self-defeating. This does not mean that such attempts cannot be made—nor even that they may not temporarily be effective. *It means that even attempts to resist competition are themselves competitive steps.* This is so because any attempt to resist competition is made *subject* to competition. We must remem-ber that to compete does not, in our terminology, mean to act in a way necessarily consistent with the (so-called) perfectly competitive state. It means to act to grasp what are perceived to be prospective profits in the face of the knowledge that others are equally free to pursue these prof-its. It is no secret that a single firm may seek to grasp profit by charg-ing a "high" price—and then discover that it has made entrepreneurial *losses* by having *thereby* invited new competitors into the industry. A group of colluding firms may be acting in entirely similar fashion. We must always remember that no one knows, in advance, what the "cor-rect," competitive-equilibrium, price is. It is the process of dynamic com-petition itself which reveals which price is "too high," and which "too low."[9] A collusive agreement to maintain a "high" price may, whatever its motive, turn out to have been an entrepreneurial step through which an industry has discovered the minimum price for a product at which production of it can be successfully sustained. An attempt to cartelize an industry through a collusive price-fixing agreement turns out, so long as entry into that industry has not been blocked (as we saw in the case of an attempt to "monopolize" an industry through merger), to be a com-petitive step taken in the dynamic entrepreneurial process. Any obstruc-tion to this process of dynamic competition, *including* prohibition against price collusion, constitutes an obstruction to the discovery process of market competition.

iii) Prohibitions against "Predatory" Price Cuts

Predatory pricing is a term used to describe a policy of a large firm in an industry which seeks (a) initially to eliminate its smaller rivals by forcing them out of business through price cuts so steep that these rivals cannot match them; and (b) subsequently monopolistically to raise its prices with impunity (once the rivals have been driven out of business). Antitrust measures to prohibit such price-cutting are then seen as measures taken to preserve active competition in an industry. Our position is that, unless entry into this industry is blocked by government, there is no reason to believe that such "predatory" attempts can be successful in freezing entrepreneurial competition in this industry. Indeed, even if a *single* firm now "controls" the entire industry (but does not enjoy, and has not enjoyed, governmental protection against the entry of other firms), we must recognize that its position has been gained, in the plainest sense of the verb "to compete," through competition. And it can continue to be successful only to the extent that it competes successfully against the potential competition of other firms who may be tempted to enter the industry. At every step, this now apparently dominant firm has been forced, through fear and anticipation of the actions of others, to serve the consumers in terms dictated by competition.

It is now well-known[10] that the pattern of behavior envisaged in the theory of predatory pricing is unlikely to be effective (and has not, apparently, occurred historically in the manner once popularly thought to have been the case). But, important though this insight certainly is, our position does not depend on the effectiveness, or rather, the lack of effectiveness of predatory pricing. Our position is based on the insight that in the case of free entry, "monopoly" positions, even where acquired through attempted predatory pricing are, in truth, positions acquired and able to be maintained only in the face of competition, and therefore only by competitive behavior on the part of the "predator." No one can know when a price cut that eliminates a competitor is intended to establish a "monopoly" (rather than to compete effectively with that competitor); more to the point, even an attempt to establish a "monopoly," taken in the face of freedom of entry, is itself a competitive step. (And it is because a "monopoly" position can be preserved, in the face of potential competition, only by competitive behavior, that we have been compelled, in the preceding sentences, to place the term "monopoly" in inverted commas.)

iv) Prohibitions against Price Discrimination

The source of the rationale for such prohibitions is the economic truth that price discrimination cannot occur under perfect competition. "With homogeneous products and perfectly elastic demand functions in the factor and product markets, prices . . . would be identical."[11] The ability to charge different prices for the "same" product to different buyers is therefore seen as evidence of monopoly power. In the U.S. several of the basic antitrust laws (the Clayton Act of 1914, and the Robinson-Patman Act of 1936) saw price discrimination as a way of eliminating competition, and of exploiting a monopoly position once it has been acquired. The appreciation for the competitive process which has informed this paper, points to an entirely different perception of the matter.

In this paper we have seen the competitive process as being made up of discrete entrepreneurial moves each seeking to grasp pure profit opportunities (created by the existing discrepancies between real world conditions on the one hand, and a pattern of perfectly competitive equilibrium on the other). What is required in order to set this process in motion, we have seen, is simply the freedom to grasp the profit opportunities one perceives (or believes oneself to have perceived). The economist does not need (even though he might be able) to defend the morality of the practice of price discrimination, in order at least to recognize that (so long as it is engaged in without protection against the competition of others) such practice is simply part of the competitive process. It is such not only because it occurs under free and open competition; it is part of the competitive process also because it is part of the "discovery procedure" through which the market can arrive at the "true" price (i.e. the "equilibrium" price). When a seller (or a buyer) tests different buyers (sellers) by asking (offering) different prices, he is in this way contributing to and participating in that process of exploration and discovery, which makes up the market process. To prohibit price discrimination is to block this avenue of market exploration.

The key to understanding our position, as against that of the antitrust literature (not only in regard to price discrimination but also in regard to other tools of antitrust) is to recognize that no one knows, and no one can possibly know, in advance, what "the" market price "ought to be." If one *could* know that price, then clearly the price discriminator who charges some buyers higher prices, could be seen as gouging additional profit by virtue of his monopoly position (which gives him the power to do so). But once it is recognized that no one does or can know the "correct" price, it becomes apparent that a price discriminator is simply "feeling" his way, by grasping (or, rather, by attempting to grasp) profit opportunities he believes to be available to him. Because we understand that the grasping of profit opportunities is the manner in which market participants nudge the market toward greater internal coordination, we must reject governmental prohibitions against price discrimination as being distinctly (and typically) *anti*-competitive measures taken by the antitrust authorities.

THE GLOBAL ECONOMY AND
ANTITRUST: A FINAL OBSERVATION

As we stand at the threshold of the twenty-first century, we have become abundantly aware of the "globalization" of economic activity. The older models of international trade, in which essentially independent economies traded with each other, are becoming replaced by a vision of a single world economy. In this context those who have argued for strong antitrust policy within national economies, have, in a world of multinational giant firms, understandably become increasingly concerned about the threats to world competitiveness posed by the sheer size and power of such mega-firms. There is a growing demand for international governmental cooperation to grapple with such threats. Our position in this paper clearly indicates that the real threat to the world economy is constituted, not by large international firms, but by the growth of government and, in particular, by the trend to supra-national governmental structures. (Of course, the supreme threat, in this regard, would be a "world-government," i.e. a supra-national structure covering the entire globe, which possesses the ultimate governmental power to compel obedience.)

The truth is that as international trade expands, the growth in firm size (and the consequent growth in global concentration) offers the world not less, but more competition. As Professor McCloskey has pointed out in regard to the growth of inter-regional trade within the U.S. during the past century: "Those very improvements in transport and communication that made large enterprises possible also made possible national and international competition. The number of firms grew smaller, but at the same time their region of marketing grew larger."[12] What was relevant to the U.S. during the past century, is entirely relevant to the world economy at the beginning of the next century.

What we have here is the simple insight which has inspired this paper. Once we recognize that the *process* of competition depends entirely and solely upon freedom of entry, we see immediately that circumstances (such as "globalization") which open up given regions of the world market to new entry (as from outside those regions), constitute not threats to competition, but in fact new sources of dynamic competitiveness. The goal of public policy must surely not be to stifle such new sources of competition. The proper role for government is surely not (as in antitrust legislation) to block entrepreneurial activity but rather (as, for example, in the cancellation of such legislation) to open up markets to unfettered entrepreneurial entry.

NOTES

1. One of the most perceptive works expressing this insight is Brozen (1982).

2. On this see, for example, Demsetz (1994).

3. Our position is based primarily on the insights of Ludwig von Mises (1966, pp. 273–79). For a work which thoroughly and critically explores traditional antitrust policies from a perspective substantially similar to my own, see Armentano (1982).

4. See Jacquemin (1994, pp. 29–30).

5. Jacquemin (1994, p. 29).

6. Our discussion avoids attention to certain criticisms (e.g. those based on "second-best theorems") which have been raised *within* the mainstream literature concerning use of the perfect competition model in this way.

7. Hayek (1945).

8. We have italicized the phrase "in principle" in order to recognize that an entrepreneur's ability to borrow may, in practice, itself depend on such resources as his personal ability to convince potential capitalists of the reliability of his undertakings. Nonetheless, the principle asserted remains valid. In principle, *any* resource (including the personal charisma needed to attract lenders) can be hired.

9. See Hayek (1968).

10. This now well-known aspect of so-called "predatory pricing" was first explored and established in McGee (1958); see also Koller (1971).

11. Armentano (1982, p. 168).

12. See McCloskey (1977), cited in Brozen (1982, p. 39).

REFERENCES

Armentano, Dominick T. *Antitrust and Monopoly; Anatomy of a Policy Failure* (New York: Wiley, 1982).

Brozen, Yale. *Concentration, Mergers, and Public Policy* (New York: Macmillan, 1982).

Demsetz, Harold. "Antitrust: Concepts, Reasoning, and the U.S. Experience," in Demsetz and Jacquemin, *Anti-Trust Economics—New Challenges for Competition*

Policy (Lund, Sweden: Institute of Economic Research, Lund University Press, 1994).

Hayek, Friedrich A. "The Use of Knowledge in Society," *American Economic Review,* 35: pp. 519–30.

———. "Competition as a Discovery Procedure" (1968), published in Hayek, *New Studies in Philosophy, Politics, Economics and the History of Ideas* (Chicago: University of Chicago Press, 1978).

Jacquemin, Alexis. "Goals and Means of European Anti-trust Policy after 1992," in Demsetz and Jacquemin, *Anti-trust Economics—New Challenges for Competition Policy* (Lund, Sweden: Institute of Economic Research, Lund University Press, 1994).

Koller, II, Roland H. "The Myths of Predatory Pricing," *Antitrust Law and Economics Review,* Vol. 4 (Summer, 1971): pp. 105–23.

McCloskey, D. "Hunting the Unicorn: Some Doubts on the Rise of the Corporate Economy, Managerial Capitalism, Monopoly Capital, and the Like 2" (presented at Economic History Conference, Harvard University, September 1977).

McGee, John S. "Predatory Price Cutting: The Standard Oil (N.J.) Case," *Journal of Law and Economics,* Vol. 1 (October 1958): pp. 137–69.

von Mises, Ludwig. *Human Action: A Treatise on Economics,* 3rd Revised Edition (Chicago: Contemporary Books, 1966).

ENTREPRENEURSHIP AND AMERICAN
COMPETITIVENESS

ABSTRACT

Israel Kirzner explains that entrepreneurship is characterized by alertness to economic opportunities. Government cannot be expected to identify opportunities that others do not see, he notes, nor is it clear how entrepreneurial alertness can be taught. Competition is the key to fostering entrepreneurship.

Commentators:
Carol Steinbach
Katsuro Sakoh

"The way to wake up America is not to spend costly resources on expensive alarm boxes. It is to open the shutters and permit the sunlight of opportunity to perform its own stimulation. Opening up the economy, eliminating restrictive regulation would stimulate alertness and compel existing firms to stay on their toes to forestall aggressive competition by others."—Israel Kirzner

"What distinguishes Europe's movement, born of economic decimation and the realization that the coal mines, steel mills, textile factories and auto assembly lines will never again support the work force they once did, was the Europeans' awareness that the jobless and the disadvantaged—those with low income, poor or outmoded skills and little prospects for employment—should be warmly included in this new drive toward entrepreneurialism. Indeed, many Europeans believe they should be a major focus of it."—Carol Steinbach

"A common but mistaken impression in the United States is that the Japanese economy is controlled by giant corporations. But almost 80 percent of today's total employed workers, and 99 percent of the total business establishments, are in the small business sector."—Katsuro Sakoh

From Stuart M. Butler and William J. Dennis, Jr., eds., *Entrepreneurship: The Key to Economic Growth* (Heritage Foundation and National Federation of Independent Business, 1986), 15–29.

DR. ISRAEL KIRZNER: I was strap hanging last week in the New York subways, and I noticed an ad that was trying to stimulate interest in the New York State lottery. It was a series of little panels—steps you have to take to become a millionaire. The first panel showed two strap hangers, one of them with his eyes closed and one of them with his eyes open. And the caption said, "Step number one is, wake up." And then it proceeded to say, "As you are reading this ad already, you are ahead of the game." That intrigued me. In fact it suggested to me that the subtitle of my talk might be: How to Wake America Up.

Entrepreneurship was involved in that ad—a sort of high-level entrepreneurship. It was trying to attract my attention to a particular message to alert me to an opportunity I might be interested in. The ad writer was already alert to his opportunity to wake me up to notice that particular opportunity that might interest me.

In some sense the current ferment about entrepreneurship and the need to stimulate it is a recognition that this country is not fully awake, that it is overlooking opportunities staring it in the face and that something needs to be done about it. It is often said that this country seems to have fallen behind in the competitive race with other countries who are its rivals in commerce and industry. And it is suggested that if entrepreneurship within this country somehow can be stimulated it would enhance the U.S. competitive position in the world.

Proponents of this view often go on to suggest that entrepreneurship must be stimulated by operating on two fronts. The supply of entrepreneurial talent needs to be increased, and it is thought that perhaps this can be done by teaching and encouraging young people to become entrepreneurs. The second front consists of lowering costs of engaging in entrepreneurial endeavors, such as lowering the cost of raising capital or dealing with labor.

These are well-meaning views, held by thoughtful and well-meaning persons. Yet at least in part these views are seriously in error. Not that I am against lowering the cost of doing business; not that I am against encouraging young people to be entrepreneurs. But there is a rather subtle intermingling of truth and error in these views that I would like to disentangle.

Let us go back and ask what entrepreneurship is and why it is important. To do this, it might be useful to emphasize two quite different aspects of economic activity. One important aspect, of course, is that of acting efficiently. Efficient economic action is a key aspect of economic endeavor. A second and quite different aspect of economic endeavor is the discovery of opportunities.

First, what does it mean to be efficient or inefficient? To be inefficient in a given activity is to engage in that activity in a wasteful manner. It is to use up an unnecessarily large volume of resources in achieving a given goal—or alternatively to fail to achieve the maximum output available from a given volume of resources. To act efficiently, on the other hand, is to pursue goals in a consistent manner that accurately reflects their relative importance. Someone once put it this way, "To be efficient is to tell the truth." To be efficient, in other words, is to act in a manner that faithfully reflects the announced hierarchy of importance with respect to various goals that have been set. To be inefficient is to announce interest in a certain goal and then in fact to pursue a different goal—or to refer back to the subway, it is to set out to go uptown and in fact take the downtown train. Observe that acting efficiently cannot occur without a clearly identified framework of given goals, with respect to which truthfulness can be identified.

Let us turn to the second aspect of economic activity, namely the activity of noticing opportunities. To notice opportunities means to notice new goals worthy of pursuit. It is to notice the availability of resources that had perhaps hitherto been overlooked, or that had hitherto not been available at all. Or it is to discover an earlier error in judgment in ranking the various goals. To act efficiently is one matter. To notice opportunities is a quite different matter. Both are important. Both are intertwined in actual economic activity. Once opportunities have been identified, they must of course be pursued efficiently. In the process of pursuing objectives efficiently, the tendency is certainly to remain alert to the possibility of new opportunities that hitherto had not existed or hitherto had been overlooked.

Producers must operate on these two fronts. They engage in the cost-conscious production of goods that they believe consumers will be prepared to buy. In this way they tend, of course, to faithfully execute consumers' relative evaluations of alternative products. The "truth" that efficient producers tell is the truth with respect to consumer evaluations. But at the same time producers must be alert to the possibilities of producing new goods or perhaps producing the same goods with new, less costly methods of production. This aspect of business activity is, of course, the entrepreneurial aspect. And it is this alertness that constitutes the heart of entrepreneurship.

There is a key relationship between this notion of entrepreneurship alertness—and competition. We all know that competition among producers, though painful to those producers, is highly beneficial to the consuming public. It is competition that keeps producers on their toes. But keeping producers on their toes requires more than that they and their competitive producers simply be efficient. It requires also that they and their competitors be entrepreneurially alert. What keeps producers on their toes is their awareness that others are being alert. If competitive pressure means the pressure exercised upon producers by their being aware that others may be discovering better opportunities of serving the public, then clearly competition and entrepreneurship are merely two sides of the same coin.

This notion of competition is very different from the textbook case of perfect competition identified as a state of affairs where innumerable small market participants exist. That is not what I have referred to here as competition, and it is certainly not what businesses mean by competition. And it is not the form of competition that keeps producers on their toes. That competition arises from the pressure exercised upon producers by their awareness that others are intent and alert on discovering new ways of serving the public.

Entrepreneurship is the key to change. Change *per se,* of course, need not be for the better. A new product is not necessarily a better product, or a new system of organization, necessarily a better system of organization. To the extent that change is desirable, however, entrepreneurship is required to discover it, not merely to discover the possibility of change but to discover the desirability of change and to weed out those possibilities for change that are not in the interest of the consuming public.

In this sense, entrepreneurship initiates desirable change by the mechanism of identifying pure profit possibilities, that is, profit possibilities that have not hitherto been discovered.

While entrepreneurship is thus a key factor in initiating change, it also has a primary and crucially important role in anticipating, noticing, and responding to changes that already have occurred or are about to occur in the market itself. So entrepreneurship does not merely initiate, it also responds to changed conditions, new preferences, new patterns of population location, and newly discovered technological possibilities that create opportunities for entrepreneurial endeavor.

Let me emphasize that entrepreneurial alertness is not the same thing as deliberate search. Search is important, but to search deliberately may consist of simple, efficient activity. If we know that someone has planted a $50 bill somewhere in this room, we can then engage in systematic search. That would not be entrepreneurial. To be entrepreneurially alert would be to realize that it was a $50 bill worth looking for. The discovery or realization that there are opportunities here that might usefully be searched for is entrepreneurial. The realization that there are cost-effective search possibilities is entrepreneurial. Search by itself need not be *per se* entrepreneurial.

All of this can perhaps be expressed in terms of the much maligned free lunch. In the view of many economists, free lunches simply do not exist. All lunches, they say, are to some extent costly. The least costly lunch can be efficiently pursued perhaps, but not a free lunch because there are none to be pursued. But this view is profoundly wrong. The truth is that free lunches are everywhere, available to be picked up for nothing. There are unseen opportunities that are available to be grasped. Those are the free lunches. And it is the awareness that free lunches are abundant that switches on entrepreneurial alertness, that gets those entrepreneurial juices moving.

What makes these free lunches available is the perception of something that the competition has not yet perceived. It is those two straphangers standing there, one asleep and one awake. The one awake sees an opportunity that the other has overlooked. Such opportunities would not exist if all others were fully alert. Awareness of opportunities is a part of the competitive process whereby one competitor inches ahead of the others.

If alertness to opportunities is desirable, how can we, as a society, encourage such entrepreneurial endeavor? How do we as a society encourage activity considered to be desirable? Ordinarily we do so by diverting resources from less desirable activities toward rewarding those who engage in more desirable activities. There are goals that we as a society perhaps may consider worthwhile, but less worthwhile than others that we wish to encourage and subsidize. Therefore we tax the first and subsidize the second. That is how to encourage activity. The lunch that is stimulated in this way is not a free lunch because the resources that reward the subsidized activity are taxed away in some sense from the activities that are being given up in order to encourage the activities that we wish to stimulate.

But what if the activity that we wish to stimulate is that of noticing truly free lunches, that of entrepreneurially identifying opportunities for pure net gain. This does not mean encouraging opportunities that society has already noticed or encouraging the pursuit of search possibilities identified as worthwhile. This asks a very different question. "How can we stimulate people to be alert to opportunities that neither we nor they have specifically recognized, but which we are sure are available to be identified if we could only wake up?"

This means we cannot identify specific activities for subsidy. We cannot know which new lines of business call for stimulation, since if they were known, we would not be proposing the encouragement of entrepreneurial activity. Nor surely will we succeed in stimulating entrepreneurship by lowering the cost of doing business in general, or by lowering the cost of doing business for small firms or for new firms, because we do not know where in fact the opportunities exist. There may very well be opportunities that small businesses can exploit and can discover. But we do not know what they are. We would surely wish to stimulate a discovery at all levels wherever discovery is possible. But we as a society cannot know in advance where those opportunities specifically exist because, if we did, we would already be the entrepreneurs.

How do we encourage genuine discovery? We can easily subsidize innovation and change. I understand that in the Soviet Union there is a substantial program of incentives for innovation. But that reminds me of the kinds of innovation that deans of colleges very often demand of their faculty, new courses, new programs. Sure enough they get them. But there is no guarantee whatsoever that such innovations are in the interest of the consuming public. Innovations for the sake of innovation may be worthless or worse. So subsidizing innovation and change is not at all the issue. It is the innovations that are in the public interest.

How about teaching entrepreneurship? Here I must agree with a distinguished colleague of mine who has pointed out that, if you can teach it, it ain't entrepreneurship. What is taught may be very worthwhile. But teaching how to start up and run a new business is not necessarily teaching people how to be entrepreneurial. It is possible to teach useful skills for entrepreneurs; they may be worth support and encouragement and may very well be socially worthwhile. But it should not be thought that that constitutes teaching entrepreneurship, as the techniques of pure discovery simply cannot be taught.

So back to square one. How can we stimulate entrepreneurship? Perhaps the earlier observations concerning the linkage between competition on the one hand and entrepreneurship on the other may be of some help. I would suggest that the way to keep potential entrepreneurs awake and on their toes is to make sure that decision makers are subject to, and that they are aware that they are subject to, the keen stimulating winds of competition.

This may sound like a circular line of thinking, since competition is necessarily entrepreneurial. It sounds as if I am suggesting that the way to stimulate entrepreneurial alertness is to stimulate entrepreneurial alertness. Certainly the way to stimulate entrepreneurial alertness is to create an atmosphere in which competitors are free to be alert and each one is aware of that. There is nothing that concentrates the mind so wonderfully as the awareness that others are concentrating their minds to discover better ways of serving the customers' needs.

The way to stimulate entrepreneurship then is to ensure that free entry into each and every potentially profitable entrepreneurial activity is guaranteed. It is to withhold protective privileges from all incumbent producers. So we have almost come full circle. There is a widespread perception that the international competitiveness of American products somehow requires a revival of the entrepreneurial spirit. The point has been reached where it appears that the way to revive the entrepreneurial spirit is to foster the competitive spirit within the American economy, to refrain from discouraging entry and entrepreneurial discovery. Any blockage against entry is a signpost that says "Don't bother to be alert. You might as well be asleep here."

The way to wake up the U.S. is not to spend costly resources on expensive alarm clocks. It is to open the shutters and permit the sunlight of opportunity to perform its own stimulation. Opening up the economy and eliminating restrictive regulations would stimulate alertness and compel existing firms to stay on their toes to forestall aggressive competition by others. Strengthening international competitiveness implies encouraging a sense of openness—the sense that there is a wide open world out there full of $50 bills, full of free lunches, waiting to be discovered, and the awareness that, if you do not discover them, the fellow next door will. That, I believe, should successfully wake up the U.S.

MS. CAROL STEINBACH: As a journalist who has covered entrepreneur-ship since the 1970s, I find two elements of the phenomenon particularly exciting. First is its dynamism and the many highly creative people who are at the forefront of developing new entrepreneurial policies. This has made it an extremely rewarding subject to cover. Second, I find entre-preneurship an appealing and hopeful approach to making real inroads against poverty and creating new avenues for economic growth and job creation.

Last October, I traveled with eleven U.S. economic development prac-titioners to Great Britain and France to observe firsthand their emerg-ing enterprise development movement. Europeans are trying desperately hard to become entrepreneurial. They see our net job creation perfor-mance over the last decade and they salivate. And a growing number of Europeans are convinced that economic revitalization depends to a large extent on becoming more flexible, loosening the rigidities that beset their economic system. Many believe that the keys to diversification and growth rest with small firms and new enterprises.

But transforming Europe into a hotbed of entrepreneurialism will not be easy. It involves no less than changing a traditional mindset that deval-ues commerce into one where people see starting their own business as a viable option. To succeed, it must confront a class system that is still rigid; a political system beset by ideology and centralism; an educational system that is simply not adapted to entrepreneurial training; a lack of broad entrepreneurial support in the economy and the society, particu-larly from the private sector; and governments that, no matter how sup-portive, are really neophytes in this arena.

Nonetheless, what distinguishes Europe's movement, born of eco-nomic decimation and the realization that the coal mines, steel mills, tex-tile factories, and auto assembly lines will never again support the work force they once did, was the Europeans' awareness that the jobless and the disadvantaged—those with low income, poor or outmoded skills, and little prospect for employment—should be warmly included in this new drive toward entrepreneurialism. Indeed, many Europeans believe they should be a major focus of it.

In the U.S., when we talk about entrepreneurs, the image is of a white male engineer going to a venture capitalist to get money to develop his bril-liant high-tech idea into a product that will make them both rich—and quick. But, by contrast, in Great Britain, the movement toward entrepreneurialism comes from the poorer, distressed areas. It gets lip service from the central government and the private sector, but very few resources. In France, the central government has created a cabinet level department to promote what they called the *Economie Sociale,* and that is their big effort at entrepreneurialism. But again, it is really a very bottom-to-top movement, based on distressed areas and unemployed people left out of the mainstream. And that is understandable. Structural unemployment has hit so hard there that they are hoping that, if they can create a mindset that values entrepreneurialism in such conditions, it will spread to the rest of society. The private sector, moreover, is hardly involved in any of this in Europe.

We did not visit a city where we were not told by envious Europeans how much more entrepreneurial is the American psyche than the European. And of course in the large context this is correct. But in another sense, we found the Europeans were a bit ahead of us. In the United States, there has been no widespread systematic effort to encourage self-employment among those whom the economy has left behind. And in the isolated examples where the attempt has been made, only rarely are these efforts accompanied by the necessary support systems and by the nurturing faith that these entrepreneurs, too, really can succeed.

Here are some of the most interesting lessons we found in the European programs:

Lesson One. European income support systems are being transferred into more than just a safety net against poverty. By redirecting their focus and resources toward enterprise development and self-employment, the Europeans are trying to create a ladder for motivated recipients to climb out of poverty.

As in the U.S., European countries confront high welfare costs, a shortage of jobs, and disincentives and barriers to work built into their transfer system. Their response has been to launch a broad-scale socioeconomic experiment. The British and French programs are being run by a conservative and a socialist government, respectively. What they do is to permit their unemployed citizens to use welfare and jobless benefits to start their own enterprises. In the U.K., the "entrepreneurs" receive a weekly government allowance for one year while their fledgling businesses are getting off the ground. The French approach is to offer laid-off workers the option of taking their benefits in a six-month lump sum to use as seed capital for business. Similar programs exist in other European countries.

As of last August, the more than 43,000 Britons in the scheme were operating a variety of enterprises. Most popular were building trades, domestic services, toy manufacturing, computer services, and—not surprisingly—consultants. So far, the results have been impressive. More than 70 percent of the British firms were still in business 18 months after start up. An early survey suggests that each new enterprise is creating an average of one and a half jobs.

As of March 1984, 135,000 French had opted for the scheme. Enterprises there span the range of high technology manufacturing to janitorial services. The bulk are in the service industries, and a government evaluation suggests that between 60 and 80 percent of the enterprises started under the French scheme have survived for three years.

I would say that, in the U.S., programs of this type should be undertaken mainly by state and local governments. The federal government's best role is to remove some of the prohibitions that bar demonstration programs. Indeed, some initiatives of this kind are already in preliminary stages. Federal legislation in October 1984 expanded the states' authority in experimenting with Aid to Families with Dependent Children. Although the federal legislation did not specify the encouragement of the entrepreneurship alternative, it appears that all the states would need to implement such schemes would be a waiver from the Department of Health and Human Services. They would not need any new federal legislation to try this. So the State of Minnesota is preparing to apply for waivers to adopt the British style program for some of the Aid to Families with Dependent Children recipients. The intent is to pay them a weekly or biweekly allowance—the format is not set—and then help them in starting the new enterprise.

Lesson Two. Large, private firms can help rebuild the economy in communities where they must close plants or fire workers. Enterprise and job-creating strategies, as a centerpiece of such efforts, can have a positive impact on even the hardest hit areas.

We heard the term redundancy frequently during our visit to Europe. It is a catchall phrase to describe the factories and the workers whose products and skills can no longer be justified on economic grounds. We were all familiar with the scenario but we found some significant differences in the ways this nation and its employers respond. The best U.S. firms tend to offer severance pay, relocation assistance, retraining, and job counseling for the workers they have to dislocate. In Europe, on the other hand, we found an exciting lesson in the emerging attempts by European corporations to go beyond these traditional types of assistance and stimulate job creation and new business growth in the wake of plant closings.

The program begun nine years ago by British Steel is Europe's showcase example. In the later 1970s, the corporation embarked on a massive industrial restructuring plan which, by 1983, was to slash 150,000 employees from its work force and to write off billions of dollars of outmoded plant and equipment. To cushion the blow, British Steel in 1975 spun off a wholly owned subsidiary, BSC Industry, Ltd. This subsidiary had a single mandate: create jobs in steel closure areas.

At first BSC Industry focused principally on providing cash incentives to recruit other large firms to the distressed steel areas, but this approach proved to be expensive and not very fruitful. So the company decided to undertake a more comprehensive effort to provide a broad range of assistance to small firms and would-be entrepreneurs. During the past three years, BSC Industry's program has been expanded to eighteen steel closure areas in England, Scotland, and Wales. The subsidiary became independent of British Steel in 1984.

BSC Industry directs its efforts in four ways. First, it markets heavily a new image for distressed steel communities. It refers to them as "opportunity areas," not distressed areas. And it tries to provide the psychological climate for indigenous development and, where possible, to attract employers from elsewhere.

Second, it provides comprehensive business assistance, including loans and seed financing, to foster the development of new businesses and to help assure that the existing firms survive and grow. It also has spurred the formation of independent public/private partnerships to bring together a wide variety of resources in a united effort to regenerate distressed steel communities.

Finally, and most interesting, BSC is converting many of its redundant facilities into incubators for entrepreneurs. Its nine entrepreneurial workshops now house about 400 businesses that employ around 1,500. Through the seed financing program, it has made about 800 loans to collateral-poor entrepreneurs. Ninety percent have been for less than 25,000 pounds. Overall, as of March 1984, the company had assisted 1,500 firms in creating about 20,000 jobs to replace the 150,000 that had to end. It estimates that the total will reach about 36,000 new jobs as of next year.

Lesson Three. Small seed finance programs are a necessary component of successful entrepreneurship and enterprise development initiatives. Studies of new enterprise formation in the U.S. consistently have found that the lion's share of new businesses, perhaps as high as 90 percent, is started with capital drawn from the owner's personal savings and the famous "FFA Network"—friends, family, and associates. For high-tech startups with good growth potential, the burgeoning venture capital industry can be a source of financing. These informal networks work just fine for entrepreneurs in well-off communities, but they are not much help to the less privileged. The U.S. suffers from real seed capital gaps, especially in poorer communities.

To compensate for a lack of seed capital, the British and the French have launched a hodge-podge of innovative, small seed-financing schemes. Some are run by the government; some are run by the private sector. Similar kinds of programs in the U.S. could help expand access to startup business capital for U.S. entrepreneurs. One of the most intriguing models we found was the informal investment clubs that are dotted throughout France. One club, called Feminotre, has copied a model from Africa known as the Tontine. Thirteen women pooled their savings, and then they spun off one of their members to start a business.

The Europeans probably do more for seed capital than Americans do. The U.S. fares better at expansion capital and some of the second round financing. France has created some government programs that provide money from the tax base to small businesses that create jobs. There also are efforts underway there to encourage private banks to provide some of these small seed capital infusions. These banks are very different from U.S. banks. They are centralized, and there are almost no local banks. Great Britain is trying tax incentives. They have a program where private investors who make equity investments in small firms can write off the investment pound-for-pound against their income.

Lesson Four. Entrepreneurial training programs are successful. In their quest to be more entrepreneurial, Great Britain and France are relying heavily on a variety of new initiatives to train their citizens to make their own jobs. We were struck by the sheer magnitude of programs. Achieving the lofty goals set forth for these programs will be a formidable task, particularly in the communities hardest hit by industrial decline, where generations of children followed their fathers and mothers into the mills, mines, and assembly lines. It may be that the old adage is true: that entrepreneurs are born, not made, and that Europe's high hopes for entrepreneurial training will come up short.

We found elements in these programs that could be especially useful in the U.S. It was not so much the type of training or curricula—what we offer does not differ greatly in kind. The lessons stemmed from the magnitude and variety of enterprise training efforts, particularly the willingness to experiment with financial mechanisms and policy support by government, and from the attempts to integrate training with other economic development programs. Finally, and most important, we could learn from European efforts to target entrepreneurial training to the unemployed and to distressed areas.

Lesson Five. Small enterprise workshops are a useful tool. The U.S. is no stranger to business incubators. In recent years, a number have sprouted up in urban, suburban, and rural communities. Briefly, these are the workshops that rent individualized space to entrepreneurs to run their businesses within a complex where many other small businesses are also operating. They share common facilities and services, and they generally have on-site managers and other professionals who can offer either free or low-cost business assistance and psychological support.

The extensive experience with workshops in Europe—particularly in Great Britain where the concept is highly refined—could be transferable to the U.S. Europe not only has more workshops, but the Europeans have developed some sophisticated models. They are also experimenting with many new concepts.

Several features of the European workshops were especially impressive. First was the establishment of workshops in redundant industrial communities, distressed areas, and public housing projects. The second was the desire to use existing buildings and facilities for workshop complexes. The third, and most interesting, feature was the willingness to allow work spaces to be used for pre-business product development. Some workshops now include spaces for freelancers, for people who want to work on a project-by-project basis, and even for people who are trying to develop their hobby into a profit-making enterprise. Finally, there is clearly a belief in Europe that work spaces can be more than simply attractive supportive places to work. In what is a relatively new development in the workshop concept, some communities are trying to create complexes that offer a broad range of amenities—both for tenants and to attract community residents and tourists. Some, for instance, have space for retail outlets, restaurants, common exhibition areas, a library, a park, and a museum. This is all in the workshop/work space.

Lesson Six. Some of the European efforts to regenerate closing businesses have been successful. Not all businesses fail because the marketplace no longer demands their goods or services. Poor management, temporary capital shortage, retirement, or voluntary closure by the owner all account for a significant percentage of the companies that annually cease operations. A variety of efforts is under way in Europe to regenerate still solvent business of all sizes. France, for instance, has developed programs to regenerate closing businesses by converting them to co-ops. One program dispatches a "relay manager" to an ailing industry, and the mission is to turn the firm into a co-op within six months and then leave behind a team of workers to manage it. A second program seeks to make co-ops from healthy enterprises where the owner is retiring or dies without an heir to take over. This is a particularly important problem in Europe. France, Great Britain, and the other nations experienced a rash of business startups immediately following World War II, and now France estimates that as many as 60 percent of the companies, small and mid-size businesses, will confront the owner retirement question in the next five years.

These then were some of the most intriguing programs we saw. We came to believe that many would be transferable to the U.S. and could help to stimulate enterprise development within our own entrepreneurial culture. Some may be especially helpful in extending the benefits of entrepreneurialism to those who traditionally have been left out of the U.S. economic mainstream or who were left behind by economic and demographic shifts.

DR. KATSURO SAKOH: Japan is not very popular these days, especially in the U.S. Congress. Once viewed as a nation of purposeful, innovative, hardworking people, Japan is now seen as something of an economic pariah. The main reason for this change in attitude, it seems, is that Japan has been too successful economically and too competitive in the world market. It is important to remember, however, why Japan's economy and its industries are successful and competitive today. It is in large part because of the actions of the U.S. government following World War II.

Under the U.S. occupation, Japan's traditional feudal society collapsed, the old leaders were purged, and old economic orders, such as Zaibatsu cartels, were dissolved. In short, the Japanese gained unprecedented individual freedom. And for the first time, practically any Japanese citizen, regardless of age, class, or family background, could venture into business and succeed. Not only did established businesses prosper under fresher and younger management within this freer environment, but thousands of new enterprises, such as Honda, Yamaha, Sony, and Suzuki were born.

Even though thousands of new companies were born in this new environment, many of them did not survive. A few survived and today are huge, internationally known corporations.

A common but widely held misconception about Japan is that its economy is controlled by giant corporations. But, in fact, almost 75 percent of all employees work in small companies that make up 99.5 percent of Japan's total business establishment. Small businesses are defined as those with fewer than 300 workers in the case of manufacturing, fewer than 150 in the case of wholesale trade, and fewer than 50 employees in services and retail. These numbers indicate that Japan is very much a small business–oriented country and that these small businesses are the main source of jobs and economic vitality.

In the last ten years, roughly seven million new workers entered Japan's labor force, and nearly 90 percent of them are employed by small businesses. Moreover, most of today's large and successful companies in Japan were started through garage entrepreneurship. Those entrepreneurs, or innovative young managers, made the Japanese economy extremely dynamic and competitive after World War II. Whether or not Japan will be able to maintain high growth depends on whether or not small and new companies will be able to play an important role in its economic future.

Through deregulation, privatization, and incentive policy, the Japanese government is trying to create an economic environment favorable to the establishment of small businesses. After all, it was the growth of small businesses after World War II that set the stage for Japan's rapid economic development.

MENGER, CLASSICAL LIBERALISM, AND
THE AUSTRIAN SCHOOL OF ECONOMICS

A series of valuable recent papers has reflected increasing current interest in the political and ideological stance of the founding economists of the Austrian School. What is particularly intriguing about this literature is that it offers what appears, at least superficially, to be a set of sharply differing readings and assessments of this politico-ideological stance. Especially in regard to Carl Menger, we are offered apparently contradictory assessments. He was a champion of laissez faire; he favored substantial state economic intervention; he had no clearly defined and articulated political position at all—each of these views of Menger and the early Austrians is to be found expressed somewhere in the literature. Each of these views is supported by citations from the early Austrians. The purpose of the present paper is to reconcile the apparent inconsistencies presented in these earlier papers.

Our conclusions will be: (1) that the early Austrians, especially Menger, occupied a position which recognized both the efficacy of markets and scope for useful governmental economic intervention; (2) that this half-full, half-empty position was not articulated in any deliberate, integrated fashion, so that individual remarks can be cited that might suggest more extreme positions than the one in fact occupied; (3) that this half-full, half-empty position nonetheless expressed an understanding of markets which, *taken by itself,* strongly suggested a more radical appreciation for free markets than the early Austrians themselves in fact displayed. It is this latter circumstance, we surmise, which explains how, when later Austrians arrived at even more consistently laissez-faire positions, they were seen by historians of thought as somehow simply pursuing an Austrian tradition that can be traced back to the founders.

As must be apparent, the development of this thesis, while at first glance in conflict with the various contributions to the current literature on this topic, in fact differs from them only in matters of emphasis. Indeed the present paper contains very little that is new: it draws most

From *History of Political Economy,* Volume 22, No. 5, pp. 93–106. © 1990 Duke University Press. All rights reserved. Republished by permission of the copyright holder, Duke University Press. www.dukeupress.edu.

of its ideas from the existing literature, merely weaving these ideas into what makes up, we wish to maintain, a more acceptable, integrated story. Writers have pointed out that the cup was not full; writers have pointed out that the cup was not empty; writers have even pointed out that the cup was half-full, and half-empty. We will not merely confirm the half-full, half-empty reading but help explain, perhaps, why the cup could seem quite full to some observers while appearing quite empty to others.

MENGER, THE AUSTRIANS, AND
LAISSEZ FAIRE: SOME PARADOXES

Stephan Boehm has drawn our attention to one strand of the conventional wisdom in regard to the Austrian School from the time of Menger onwards, namely the identification of the Austrians as "rigorous defenders of laissez-faire and outspoken apologists of the capitalist system."[1] Against this traditional view of the Austrians Boehm marshals powerful evidence from Menger's own writings: "Menger presents a list of five legitimate tasks ascribed to the state, respectively 'improvement of the situation of the working class, just distribution of income, encouragement of individual ability, thrift and entrepreneurial initiative.'"[2] If this (ambitious!) list of governmental responsibilities were not sufficiently impressive, Boehm cites both Menger and Böhm-Bawerk as emphatically, even vehemently, rejecting charges that they followed a laissez-faire, "Manchester" approach to social policy. Menger, Boehm cites, maintained explicitly that "nothing could be more opposed to his school than to vindicate the capitalist system. In fact, the only thing that he appreciated in Schmoller was his passionate concern for the poor and weak."[3]

1. Stephan Boehm, "The political economy of the Austrian School," in *Gli economisti e la politica economica*, ed. Piero Roggi (Naples: Edizioni Scientifiche Italiane, 1985), 249.

2. Boehm, "Political economy," 250, citing Carl Menger, "Die Social-Theorien der classischen National-Oekonomie und die moderne Wirtschaftspolitik" (1891), reprinted in Menger's *Gesammelte Werke*, 3:245.

3. Boehm, "Political economy," 251, citing Carl Menger, *Die Irrthümer des Historismus in der deutschen Nationalökonomie* (1884), reprinted in *Gesammelte Werke*, 3:93. Boehm could also have emphasized the interventionist flavor of Friedrich von Wieser's later work; see especially his *Social economics*, translated from the German edition of 1914 by A. F. Hinrichs (New York: Adelphi, 1927), 408–16. See also Professor Streissler's remark that "Wieser was by instinct at least an unabashed paternalistic

Yet the view that the Austrian economists were indeed uncompromising advocates of laissez faire—and certainly the view that they were *perceived* as such—cannot be summarily dismissed. Erich Streissler has, particularly in his recent work, drawn our attention to newly available material supporting this view of Menger. As is well known, Menger spent several years as tutor to Crown Prince Rudolph of Austria. Rudolph was required to prepare essays setting forth the lectures he had heard from Menger. These lecture notes, with corrections by Menger, have recently been rediscovered by Brigitte Hamann, who provided typewritten copies to Streissler. From these essays Streissler has concluded that Menger taught Rudolph "a liberalism possibly even more rigorous than that of Adam Smith. In 'normal' cases economic action of the state is always harmful: it is only to be allowed in 'abnormal' cases."[4]

Perhaps even more persuasive, in regard to the perception of the Austrian School as champions of noninterventionism, are the personal reminiscences of Ludwig Mises. Mises studied at the University of Vienna in the very early years of this century, and he became one of Böhm-Bawerk's best-known disciples. His name is invariably cited as a prominent participant in Böhm-Bawerk's famous seminar at the university. There can be little doubt that Mises was thoroughly familiar with the political stance of the members of the Austrian School. Although he did not study under Menger, he could not but have been aware of what Menger's political views were understood to be. For Mises there seems to have been not a shadow of doubt that the Austrians saw themselves (and were seen by their contemporaries) as vindicating not merely an abstract science of economics (against historicist challenges), but also at the same time the effectiveness of the market economy (against its socialist and statist detractors).

In a chapter entitled "The political aspects of the *Methodenstreit*" Mises describes the alliance between Schmoller and his Historical School, and the Bismarckian policies in Prussia which "began to inaugurate its Sozialpolitik, the system of interventionist measures such as labor legislation, social security, pro-union attitudes, progressive taxation, protective

---

interventionist, if not to say finally a fascist" ("The intellectual and political impact of the Austrian school of economics," *History of European Ideas* 9.2 [1988]: 200). Recently Carl G. Uhr has referred to Menger as a "moderate social-minded liberal" who was "no uncritical defender of laissez faire" (in a book review, *HOPE* 21.1 [Spring 1989]: 152).

4. Streissler, "Intellectual and political impact," 201; see also his n. 2 for further details on the Menger-Rudolph lecture-essays.

tariffs, cartels, and dumping."[5] It is true that Mises recognized that when "Menger, Böhm-Bawerk and Wieser began their scientific careers, they were not concerned with the problems of economic policies and with the rejection of interventionism by Classical economics. They considered it as their vocation to put economic theory on a sound basis and they were ready to dedicate themselves entirely to this cause."[6] But this passage is followed by the flat assertion that "Menger heartily disapproved of the interventionist policies that the Austrian Government . . . had adopted."[7] A skeptic might be tempted to wonder if Mises (writing in 1969) was not perhaps independently reading into his teachers' attitudes the laissez-faire stance which he himself came to adopt in his own career. But a fair-minded reader of Mises's many references to the political implications of the *Methodenstreit* will find it difficult to avoid concluding that Mises is simply expressing the generally held perception of the Austrians as being strongly opposed to the statist intervention espoused by the Historical School.

And yet, as cited by Boehm,[8] we find Gunnar Myrdal describing the Austrians as being the rare nineteenth-century economists who did not inject political motives into their economics: "In Austria, economics has never had direct political aims."[9] Apparently Myrdal's reading of Austrian economics found it neither tendentiously interventionist nor seeking to promote laissez faire.

To round out our sketch of perceptions of the Austrian School's political stance (or lack of such) we must refer to a most explicit statement by Nikolai Bukharin, the eminent Marxist theorist and economic scholar, who spent time as a participant in Böhm-Bawerk's seminar and wrote a book-length, trenchantly Marxist critique of Austrian economic theory. In his preface to the Russian edition of this book Bukharin refers to his having chosen to attack the Austrian School (rather than other schools of modern economics): "Our selection of an opponent for our criticism probably does not require discussion, for it is well known that the most

5. Ludwig von Mises, *The historical setting of the Austrian school of economics* (New Rochelle, N.Y.: Arlington House, 1969), 30.

6. Mises, *Historical setting*, 18.

7. Ibid.

8. Boehm, "Political economy," 248.

9. Gunnar Myrdal, *The political element in the development of economic theory* (Cambridge: Harvard University Press, 1953), 128.

powerful opponent of Marxism is the Austrian School."[10] Of course, to be a powerful opponent of Marxism is not yet to be a champion of laissez faire. Yet it seems clear that the Austrians were seen as providing a strong intellectual defense of capitalism.[11] Nothing in their writings, it appears, could suggest any principled reasons for doubting the effectiveness of capitalist institutions in promoting human economic welfare.

This, then, is the situation in which we find ourselves. Evidence apparently exists to support the view that the Austrians were proponents of laissez faire, the view that they were sympathetic to interventionism, and the view that they were unconcerned with the political implications of their doctrines. Let us consider independently, quite apart from any of the cited evidence, what one might *expect* to conclude, in terms of political implications, from the economic theory of the Austrian School, especially in its initial, Mengerian incarnation.

MENGER AND THE MARGINAL UTILITY REVOLUTION

A certain ambiguity has come to surround the question of the degree to which Menger's *Grundsätze* represented a revolutionary, pioneering contribution to the economics of his time. The traditional view among historians of thought has seen Menger's work as one of the three basic contributions to the "marginal utility revolution" (besides being a manifesto upholding the theoretical method in economics, in opposition to the historical method that had become entrenched in German economics). From this traditional reading of Menger, his book was a frontal, pioneering, revolutionary attack on classical orthodoxy. Yet at the same

---

10. Nikolai Bukharin, *Economic theory of the leisure class*, reprint of first (1927) U.S. edition (New York and London: Monthly Review Press, 1972), 9.

11. This Marxist perception of the Austrians as spearheading the bourgeois counter-revolutionary intellectual campaign has persisted, sometimes in bizarre fashion, into our own time. Thus Maurice Dobb has misread Schumpeter's reference to Böhm-Bawerk as "the bourgeois Marx" (*History of economic analysis* [Oxford: Oxford University Press, 1954], 846) to mean that Schumpeter saw Böhm-Bawerk primarily as leader of the "conscious *apologists* of the existing system" (Dobb, *Theories of value and distribution since Adam Smith* [Cambridge: Cambridge University Press, 1973], 193). Schumpeter, of course, meant nothing of the kind by this way of describing Böhm-Bawerk. Rather he wished to draw attention to Bawerk's comprehensive, system-embracing theoretical perspective on capitalism—one which matched Marx's own view in grandeur of scope. Nonetheless Dobb's remark confirms the point made here in the text.

time Menger's book, and especially its preface, freely acknowledged profound indebtedness to earlier writers, particularly to the "foundation laid by previous work that was produced almost entirely by the industry of German scholars."[12] Indeed Streissler has in recent work drawn attention to a mid-nineteenth-century German "protoneoclassical" tradition in which Menger's work should be recognized as a contribution offering continuity of forward development, rather than providing any revolutionary departure.[13] Although Menger emphasized themes central to the marginal utility revolution, Streissler argues, Menger saw himself as a reformer rather than a revolutionary.

Yet this ambiguity concerning possible links between Menger's *Principles* and this German "protoneoclassical" tradition must surely relate strictly to specific features of Menger's system, especially his subjective theory of value. There seems little doubt concerning Menger's awareness that he was, in his *Principles*, offering *a perspective on the economic system* which was entirely new. Menger's emphasis, in his preface, on the need to balance "careful attention to past work in all the fields of our science thus far explored" against criticism, "with full independence of judgment, [of] the opinions of our predecessors, and even [of] doctrines until now considered definitive attainments of our science,"[14] suggests his very clear sense of breaking sharply with the past. Hayek has told us that Menger is said to have "remarked that he wrote the *Grundsätze* in a state of morbid excitement."[15] It seems reasonable to attribute this excitement to Menger's conviction that he was writing a pathbreaking book.

Menger's acknowledgment of debt to German scholars and his dedication of his book to Wilhelm Roscher, the famous leader of the (older) German Historical School, should not be misunderstood. These references are surely to be understood, not as reflecting any failure to perceive the novelty of his own work, but as expressing his meticulous sense of propriety toward earlier scholars whose contributions he valued (as

12. Carl Menger, *Principles of economics*, translated from the original German edition (1871) by B. F. Hoselitz, 1950 (reprinted New York: New York University Press, 1981), 49.

13. E. Streissler, "Menger, Böhm-Bawerk, and Wieser: the origins of the Austrian School," in *Neoclassical economic theory, 1870 to 1900*, ed. K. Hennings and W. J. Samuels (Boston: Kluwer, 1990).

14. Menger, *Principles*, 46.

15. Hayek, "Introduction" to Menger, *Principles*, 16.

well as being prudent strategic policy in seeking to ally himself with the most influential scholars of his time, in his effort to dislodge the classical orthodoxy). This interpretation is entirely consistent with the measured criticism which Menger accorded the work of Roscher himself a dozen years after the *Grundsätze*.[16] The difference in tone (in regard to Roscher and the other pre-Schmoller German economists) that separates Menger's *Untersuchungen* from the *Grundsätze* need not be attributed to a change of heart, or of opinion, on these matters (to be explained perhaps by the coolness with which the *Grundsätze* was received in Germany). Menger still warmly acknowledged (in 1883 as in 1871) the "virtues of the scientific personality of the learned Leipzig scholar; his outstanding merits and his advancement of the historical understanding of a number of important economic phenomena; the incomparable stimulation which his studies in the literature of our science have given to all younger colleagues."[17] The criticisms of Roscher in 1883 may rather be understood as expressing Menger's recent realization that his own success in fashioning his new understanding of the economic system depended crucially on his own theoretical orientation, with which the now-dominant German approach must be sharply contrasted. (Moreover, the cool reception accorded to the *Grundsätze* in Germany may have convinced Menger that no strategic alliance with the German economists could now realistically be anticipated.)

So Menger's work in 1871 is surely to be read as quite deliberately offering an entirely fresh perspective on the economic system as a whole. It is true that important elements (concerning subjectivism, utility, and so on) were drawn from earlier German writers, as Streissler (and Hayek)[18] have pointed out. Yet the overall vision of the economy as a system driven entirely and independently by the choices and valuations of consumers—with these valuations transmitted "upwards" through the system to "goods of higher order," determining how these scarce higher-order goods are allocated among industries and how they are valued

16. Carl Menger, *Investigations into the method of the social sciences with special reference to economics*, translated from the original German edition (1883) by F. J. Nock (New York and London: New York University Press, 1985), a reprint of *Problems of economics and sociology* (Urbana: University of Illinois, 1963), 185–89.

17. Menger, *Investigations*, 189.

18. Hayek, "Introduction" to Menger, *Principles*, 13–14, 17.

and remunerated as part of a single consumer-driven process—was one which Menger surely (and correctly) sensed as being wholly new.

And if this, rather than any technical innovations in marginal utility theory, is to be seen as Menger's self-recognized original contribution, then it seems reasonable to understand Menger as perceiving a correspondingly original implication of his vision for normative economics. This assertion calls for brief elaboration.

MENGER AND THE EFFICIENCY OF THE MARKET ECONOMY

Menger's vision of the economic system as one controlled entirely by consumer preferences, valuations, and choices has significant welfare implications. Against a given background of scarce resources (potential goods of higher order) consumer preferences and choices set in motion an ever-widening ripple series of entrepreneurial productive activities which result in market valuations of factor services, and corresponding allocations of them among industries. From this vision there emerges a clear sense of *consumer sovereignty*—a concept with obviously important normative implications.

This vision of consumer sovereignty offers a normative criterion which differs sharply from the classical basis for laissez faire. Classical economists saw the free market economy producing (under the incentives afforded by the invisible hand) the *greatest possible volume of material wealth*. Menger's view of the market pointed, not so much to a maximization of aggregate output, as to a pattern of *economic governance exercised by consumer preferences*. This aspect of Menger's vision suggests an appreciation for the outcomes of free markets that differs subtly from more standard neoclassical welfare theorems concerning the social optimality of laissez faire. For Marshall and Pigou the sense in which free markets can be argued (in the absence of externalities) to be economically optimal is one which focuses on the *maximization of aggregate welfare*. For Walras and other continental neoclassical welfare economists, markets achieve welfare ideals by achieving *an optimal allocation of resources* (equivalent, in a world of interpersonal utility comparisons, to maximization of aggregate welfare). It is true that such optimality is predicated upon the welfare primacy accorded to the need to respect consumer preferences; but this still-standard mainstream perspective of welfare economics does not focus on the effective control exercised by consumer choices. For mainstream welfare theory what is important is the pattern of allocation achieved by the market (measured against the yardstick of the structure of consumer preferences). But from Menger's vision of the economy appears the insight that it is *in fact* solely the series of choices taken by consumers which create the market values and determine the entrepreneurial valuations which control the actual allocation of resources.

It is difficult to avoid the conjecture that Menger's appreciation for the achievements of the free market economy (as expressed, let us say, in Rudolph's essays) is to be attributed in large measure to this novel Mengerian insight concerning consumer sovereignty. It seems plausible in the extreme that it was in this insight, thoroughly absorbed into the economics of Menger's younger colleagues and followers, Böhm-Bawerk and Wieser, that Marxists saw their principal conflict with Austrian economics. For Bukharin, steeped in the Marxian perception of the capitalist economy as a system of exploitation, the claim that the pure capitalist economy is one in which consumer preferences dictate all, in which the capitalist assignment of income shares is that pattern "required" and imposed by consumers, must have appeared dangerous indeed. No wonder that he saw Austrian economics as the most powerful opponent of Marxism. And there can be no doubt that it was this tenet of consumer sovereignty, so central to Austrian economics, which subsequently inspired Mises's critique of socialism. As Mises was to emphasize throughout his career, the key to economic literacy is the understanding that entrepreneurial decision making is grounded entirely in the incentive to anticipate consumer preferences: "By themselves the producers, as such, are quite unable to order the direction of production. This is as true of the entrepreneur as of the worker; both must bow ultimately to the consumers' wishes. And it could not well be otherwise. People produce, not for the sake of production, but for the goods that may be consumed."[19] It was this thoroughly Mengerian insight which nourished Mises's lifelong polemic against socialist and interventionist misunderstandings of the market economy.

Yet, as we shall see, this insight of Menger's, his pioneering perception of the role of consumer sovereignty, was not by itself sufficient to require him unambiguously to subscribe to a policy of pure laissez faire. Certainly the appreciation for consumer sovereignty carries normative implications. But for a mind as careful, as sensitive to subtle distinctions,

---

19. L. Mises, *Socialism* (London: Jonathan Cape, 1936), 443.

and as thorough as Menger's, his understanding of the paramountcy of consumer valuations in the structure of an economic system can hardly have guaranteed unqualified endorsement of pure laissez faire. Menger's own economic theory left a number of openings for conceivable arguments, economic or social, in favor of specific interventions. Let us see how this must have been the case.

MENGER, CONSUMER SOVEREIGNTY, AND
SCOPE FOR GOVERNMENT INTERVENTION

We wish to identify three circumstances which rendered Menger's vision of the consumer-driven market economy an insufficient basis for *Manchestertum,* for a policy insisting on unblemished laissez faire. There is every reason to assume Menger was alive to these circumstances (and for us to explain the various conflicting strands of evidence concerning his position by reference to these circumstances and the extent to which he articulated the social implications of these circumstances). Streissler has emphasized externalities as a basis for Menger's concessions to interventionism.[20] We wish to suggest three other circumstances that are likely to have been at the basis of Menger's list (cited above from Stephan Boehm's discussion) of legitimate tasks for the state.

First, we have every reason to believe Menger recognized that his vision *assumed* a *given* structure of property rights and property law. When Menger discussed the scarcity-based reasons for the institution of private property, he referred to the arbitrariness of such an institution. A "new social order," he explained, "could indeed ensure that the available quantities of economic goods would be used for the satisfaction of the needs of different persons than at present." But such redistribution would never eliminate scarcity; it would not avoid the need for the institution of property itself. Any "plans of social reform can reasonably be directed only toward an appropriate distribution of economic goods but never to the abolition of the institution of property itself."[21] Nothing in Menger's theory suggested that the status quo, in regard to the distribution of resource ownership, is socially optimal. It seems highly plausible to understand much of Menger's sympathy for "Schmoller's passionate

20. Streissler, "Intellectual and political impact," 201.
21. Menger, *Principles,* 97–98.

concern for the poor and weak"[22] as reflecting this extraeconomic dissatisfaction with the status quo. Menger's vision of consumer sovereignty was, logically speaking, entirely consistent with a social conscience which preferred a different set of effective consumers to be in control.

Second, although Menger emphasized the role of consumer preferences, he was certainly of the opinion that consumers may be "mistaken" as to what is in fact in their own best interest. Menger dwelt explicitly on the possibility that consumers may erroneously assign value to primitive medicines, love potions, and the like.[23] He noticed the weakness which people display for "overestimating the importance of satisfactions that give intense momentary pleasure but contribute only fleetingly to their well-being,"[24] and so on. This paternalistic attitude on his part might easily suggest state policies to correct consumer errors in valuation. It is plausible to read Menger's reference to the need for state action to encourage thrift[25] as expressing his paternalistic urge to counteract the circumstance that "men often esteem passing, intense enjoyments more highly than their permanent welfare, and sometimes even more than their lives."[26]

Third, we must emphasize that Menger distinguished sharply between the "economic prices" explained by his theory of exchange (based, in turn, on marginal utility foundations for consumer valuation and demand) and real-world prices. The former are the prices which would prevail in the absence of error, if economizing individuals acted in their own best mutual interests without the hindrance of incomplete information.[27] In the real world, error clouds human decision making, considerations of goodwill toward others affect the economic character of transactions, and other causes complicate the outcomes: "A definite economic situation brings to light precisely *economic* prices of goods only in the rarest cases. *Real* prices are, rather more or less different from economic."[28] The sense in which Menger's overall view of the economic system saw it

22. See above, note 3.
23. Menger, *Principles*, 53.
24. Ibid., 148.
25. See above, note 2.
26. Menger, *Principles*, 148.
27. On this point see Israel M. Kirzner, "The entrepreneurial role in Menger's system," *Atlantic Economic Journal* (September 1978), reprinted in Kirzner, *Perception, opportunity and profit* (Chicago: University of Chicago Press, 1979), 62–69.
28. Menger, *Investigations*, 69.

as governed entirely by consumer valuations is confined to the model in which the effects of error and similar complications are ignored. Only if economic prices—prices which "correctly" reflect the underlying realities of "correct" consumer valuations—were to prevail, would it be true that resource allocation indeed expresses, faithfully and efficiently, the wishes of the sovereign consumers. I have elsewhere[29] expressed bafflement at the absence, in Menger, of any *analysis* of a market process through which, possibly, errors on the part of market participants might be systematically eliminated. Be this as it may, it can confidently be asserted that while Menger did indeed apparently assume that markets will, sooner or later, tend toward an array of economic prices, he certainly did not claim that at all times such an array can be assumed to be already in place. It is plausible to read his reference to the need for state action to encourage entrepreneurial initiative[30] as expressing a fear that circumstances may arise where entrepreneurial error or otherwise-founded lack of initiative will lead to pathologically uneconomic prices (and allocations of resources) unless state action to spur corrective entrepreneurial initiatives is introduced.

THE MENGERIAN REVOLUTION AND THE CASE
FOR LAISSEZ FAIRE: SUMMARY ASSESSMENT

We are now in a position to sum up discussion thus far. Menger had introduced a revolutionary view of the operation of a market system, in which he saw consumer valuations governing the entire structure of production and rigorously determining the allocation of resources and the corresponding market remunerations of scarce resource services. This perception of consumer sovereignty certainly carried with it important implications for the social assessment of the efficiency of the capitalist system.

There can be little doubt that (as we have seen to be the case for Mises) acceptance of the Mengerian vision carries with it a powerful defense of capitalist results. These results can be seen as rigorously necessary and desirable, *if* we indeed wish to respect the wishes of consumers as they themselves express them, and *if* we wish to treat existing property and other rights and endowments as given and not subject to challenge. What

29. See above, note 27.
30. See above, note 2.

we have seen, however, is that for Menger himself it was not necessarily the case that the expressed wishes of consumers are to be seen as requiring respect; nor was it the case that any given initial pattern of property endowment be invested with title to moral approbation. More to the point, we have seen that Menger's insight into the nature of consumer sovereignty was circumscribed by his awareness that entrepreneurial errors and other aberrations may easily serve as a wedge separating the real-world economy from Menger's consumer-governed "economic" model of that reality.

What we wish now to submit is that these considerations serve adequately to account for the conflicting strands of evidence (concerning Menger's attitude toward state intervention in the market economy) cited at the outset of this paper. We should not be at all surprised to find passages in Menger consistent with pure laissez faire; we should not be surprised to find passages in Menger consistent with thoroughgoing interventionism; we should not be surprised to find passages in Menger consistent (as Gunnar Myrdal read them) with a complete detachment from policy issues. And we should certainly not be surprised to find Marxist writers such as Bukharin perceiving in Mengerian economics a powerful enemy of any exploitation theory of capitalism.

RECONCILING THE CONFLICTING EVIDENCE

There can surely be no mystery concerning the widespread perception (cited by Boehm) of the early Austrians as stout defenders of the free market system. As we have seen, Menger's basic vision of the market economy, a vision never totally lost sight of in the subsequent Austrian tradition, certainly does have to it a strong classical-liberal ring. It shows how, absent error and aberration, markets may faithfully express consumer sovereignty rather than entrepreneurial control. Markets are not only not seen as chaotically discoordinated, they are seen as systematic, efficient servants of the consuming public. It is easy to see how the centrality of this vision could lead subsequent historians of thought (as well as subsequent Austrians themselves) to conclude—without reference to the Mengerian fine print[31]—that Austrian economics vindicates the free market as a requirement for the achievement of consumer sovereignty.

---

31. As we shall argue, this conclusion was, to a significant degree, a justified one. It was legitimate to accept the central Mengerian message while rejecting or ignoring

But as we have seen, the Mengerian fine print is indeed there to be read and taken account of. When we move from the realm of economic theory to that of social policy, the apparently clear message arising out of the Mengerian view becomes cloudy, complex, and ambiguous. Not only may one harbor doubts as to the applicability of the theory to the real world (since in the real world the array of "economic" prices is likely to be absent—with an inefficient, erroneous, array of "noneconomic prices" in place instead); in addition the social policy maker may legitimately question the moral acceptability of the pattern of resource ownership which the economic theory had simply taken for granted. Moreover, once one moves from the value-free desk of the economic theorist to the paternalistic podium of the policy maker, it becomes necessary to consider the extent to which freely made consumer choices may appear mistaken and wrong, not consistent with the "true" well-being of the consumers. All these considerations are amply sufficient to account for the statements adduced by Boehm and others testifying to Menger's willingness to assign important interventionist responsibilities to the state.

And, again, an observer such as Gunnar Myrdal could legitimately cite the Austrians as having no political or ideological axes to grind. Menger's exposition of his central vision of the market did not attempt to articulate any laissez-faire policy implications—and, as we have seen, did not in fact preclude adoption of a moderately interventionist program. So while Bukharin quite correctly read the Austrian theory as a powerful threat to the Marxist vision of the capitalist economy, Myrdal could equally correctly commend the Austrians for pursuing a program of scientific research untainted by any political agenda. A number of further observations need to be made in order to complete our story, reconciling the apparently conflicting strands of evidence concerning Menger and the early Austrians.

CONCLUDING CONSIDERATIONS

Our reconciliation of the conflicting strands of evidence has depended upon being able to distinguish sharply between Menger's central vision of the economic system on the one hand, and complicating considerations

---

the fine print. Even Menger himself, in lecturing to Rudolph, felt that the importance of the central message required that the fine print be almost entirely set aside, at least for introductory purposes.

regarding error and property rights on the other. It is because the context in which Menger articulated his central vision was one into which these latter complicating considerations did not have to be explicitly introduced, that apparently conflicting conclusions concerning Menger's views on economic policy could come to be drawn. Certain additional circumstances combined to create this somewhat confusing situation.

Streissler has pointed out that the tradition in German and Austrian universities was for there to be "two chairs of economics in each university: a chair of economic theory and a chair of economic policy."[32] Menger and the early Austrian economists held chairs of theory; they were not responsible for the teaching of economic policy. Their research and their books dealt almost exclusively with positive theory. This circumstance must have encouraged followers of the early Austrians, as well as historians of thought, to draw their own conclusions concerning the policy direction to which Austrian theory was pointing. This tendency can only have been strengthened by the fact that the centrality of Menger's new vision of the economic system was given so much emphasis in his theoretical work, while the "fine print" acknowledging the legitimacy of state intervention found its way into the more peripheral, even journalistic, contributions of the Austrian founders. It is plausible that Menger himself may have seen his "fine print" as having distinctly less impact on practical policy considerations. This would explain his being able to lecture to Rudolph along lines which, at a first approximation, so to speak, permitted him to avoid emphasis on his own "fine print."

As Boehm has reminded us,[33] the principal frontier of ideological and political conflict in late nineteenth-century Austria was not that which separated proponents of pure laissez faire from those of aggressive state intervention. Rather it was between the champions of the older, entrenched privileges of the clergy, aristocracy, army, and bureaucracy and the exponents of *"Josephinismus,* the Austrian version of enlightened absolutism." The Austrian economists endorsed a "liberalism . . . deeply rooted in Josephinic traditions, whose primary [purpose] was to do away with feudal privileges and guilds."[34] Menger's scientific work did not need to address these concerns. His openness toward state

32. Streissler, "Intellectual and political impact," 200.
33. Boehm, "Political economy," 256–57.
34. Ibid.

interventionism could quite easily be relegated to the fine print. When, in the course of decades, the frontier shifted, so that the principal policy issues among economists revolved around the degree of desirable state intervention, it became easy to focus almost exclusively on Menger's central, consumer-sovereignty vision of the economic system and to draw one's own conclusions.

Moreover, as Austrian economics entered its second and third generations, the focus of public policy inquiry shifted toward the feasibility of socialism. Here Mises was, as noticed above, able to draw on both the Böhm-Bawerkian and Mengerian roots of Austrian economics to restate the case for the free market with a new sharpness of focus. It is not surprising, therefore, that in light of this twentieth-century concern of the Austrians their tradition has come, in the view of historians of thought, to be identified with a consistent support for the free-market economy.

Our conclusions are, therefore, that each of the positions cited at the outset of this paper can be defended but that an understanding of the complexities surrounding the policy positions of the early Austrians permits us to see how this involves no necessary inconsistencies, either in regard to what the Austrians themselves maintained or in regard to what they were perceived to have maintained.

ECONOMIC EDUCATION

THE NATURE AND SIGNIFICANCE OF
ECONOMIC EDUCATION

For many years I have been fascinated by what at first glance seems a paradoxical feature in Ludwig von Mises's attitude to the economics he taught. I believe that this seeming paradox in the life and work of my revered teacher can provide us with the key to understanding the role of economic education (and, I will further propose, to appreciating the special character and philosophy of the Foundation for Economic Education).

On the one hand, even the casual reader of Mises senses the enormous *passion* with which he preached the message of the free society and its dependence upon free markets. (See, for example, the almost dramatic closing paragraph of his magnum opus, *Human Action,* reprinted on the next page [in original].) On the other hand, one of the foundations of economic science was, for Mises, the austere *wertfreiheit* with which, he maintained, the economist must pursue his scientific work. Science, Mises insisted, must never express or reveal the personal preferences, or judgments of value, of the scientist. The economist's work requires objectivity and detachment, in order that its conclusions can be arrived at, and accepted by, persons subscribing to widely divergent sets of personal ideologies. Many superficial readers of Mises have failed to understand the manner in which his life and work showed that these two apparently contradictory attitudes—passion and scientific detachment—can and must be simultaneously maintained, without jeopardizing either the purity of the *wertfreiheit* or the white-hot fervor of the passion.

Economics is a science; the truth of its predictions does not depend on whether or not we find these truths palatable. But this circumstance does not, to be sure, wipe out the palatability or unpalatability of the predicted outcomes. Mises's economic science, in fact, predicts consequences of central planning that are not only unpalatable, but tragically disastrous for human well-being—even for human survival. It was this which ignited Mises's passion, not as a scientist, but as a human being agonizing over what he (so accurately!) foresaw as the inevitably horrible consequences of twentieth-century *dirigisme*. For Mises, economic education is the only tool we have with which to warn mankind of these terrible consequences. The *content* of this education is science. This content must be established and demonstrated with austere, disinterested objectivity. The *purpose* of this education, however, is to further human goals (since, after all, *any* human activity, including scientific activity, must have as its objective, *some* human goal). In the case of economics, that human goal is of such overriding importance for the human race that passionate concern becomes well-nigh inevitable and a morally natural phenomenon. It is this fascinating fusion of austere objectivity with passionate concern that characterized the life and work of Mises—and which, I believe, defines the philosophy of the Foundation for Economic Education.

But why is economic education *needed*? Why can we not rely on the truths of economics being recognized by the intelligent public without deliberate, organized effort at public enlightenment? We may identify two interrelated reasons:

1. The conclusions of economics are, in general, counter-intuitive. Without careful guidance, the intelligent layman is likely to be led to accept as "obvious," policy prescriptions that economics reveals as tending to generate wholly unwanted consequences.

2. The reasoning by which economics reaches its conclusions is not only *not* self-evident, but in fact involves insights the subtlety of which is likely to be completely missed by the untrained. An education in economics does not have to be lengthy or very elaborate—but it *is* needed in order to introduce the intelligent layman to new ways of looking at and understanding the world. Let us take up in turn these two sources for the need for economic education.

THE COUNTER-INTUITIVE CONCLUSIONS OF ECONOMICS

The most significant of the counter-intuitive conclusions can be succinctly presented as follows:

First, despite individual freedom in the making of decisions in the free-market economy, there do emerge "law-like" *regularities* in economic phenomena—regularities that society can ignore or defy only at its own peril.

Second, these regularities appear as powerful *tendencies* in free markets toward the directing of scarce resources:

- into those branches of production which the consuming public values most urgently and most highly;
- into those methods of production which, judged from the consumers' perspective, must be described as the most efficient;
- with market consequences such that the rewards to owners of scarce resources express those resources' respective relative productive values, as judged by consumers, and thus stimulate these owners to place their resources and talents in the efficient service of consumers. Many have identified these conclusions with what the textbooks often call Adam Smith's "invisible hand" doctrine.

These conclusions are counter-intuitive. Very many intelligent, well-meaning persons during the past two centuries have simply assumed exactly the opposite of these conclusions to be the truth—and have concluded that government planning and control of market activities are crucially needed in order to avoid economic chaos, disorder, and social inefficiency. It was, however, true of the heyday of neoclassical economics (between, say, 1890 and 1930), that the overwhelming balance of professional opinion came to endorse the "invisible hand" conclusions. The major schools of economic thought (not including the German Historical School) agreed with these conclusions. And after World War I, with the demise of the German Historical School, it seemed to Mises[1] that economists of all schools were virtually unanimous in their understanding of markets. To deny these conclusions, it appeared, was simply to reveal a gap in one's education.

This unanimity rapidly crumbled away during the central decades of this century. The dominant orthodoxy of the years between, say, 1935 and 1970, was one that urgently endorsed centrally planned intervention in market economies (and, indeed, looked rather favorably upon the possibility of efficiency under socialism even in its purest forms), on both macroeconomic and microeconomic grounds. Such intervention was needed at the macro level, the conventional wisdom ran, in order to avoid the instability predicted by Keynesian economics; it was needed at the micro level in order to avoid the distortions and inefficiencies predicted by the theorists of imperfect competition and/or of externalities.

Austrian economics never gave up the central conclusions of the earlier shared consensus of neoclassical economics. In fact, both Mises and Hayek significantly deepened Austrian economic understanding (of how markets work and of how they set benign, efficiency-enhancing, tendencies into motion) during these decades of eclipse.[2] They demonstrated (in effect if not always quite explicitly) how Austrian insights concerning the entrepreneurial role, the competitive process, and the knowledge-discovery process in fact respond effectively to both the macro and the micro concerns of the new interventionist orthodoxy in the economics profession. And their work and teaching during those lonely decades of the fifties and sixties laid the groundwork for the subsequent modest but important revival of Austrian economics during the past quarter of a century.

Economic education, aiming to enlighten the intelligent lay public to these significant—but still counter-intuitive—implications of economics, surely has a valuable role to play. Let us however now turn to the second of the reasons we have identified (as responsible for the need for economic education).

THE SUBJECTIVISM AND SUBTLETY
OF ECONOMIC REASONING

Economic understanding does not call for sophisticated technical prowess. It does, however, require appreciation for a way of looking at human actions and of social interaction, which many at first find rather strange and unfamiliar. Economic understanding requires one to see the "objects" with which economic activity is concerned—the money, the natural resources, the capital equipment, the flows of half-finished goods, the fully produced goods ready for delivery to the consumer—from a subtly different perspective from that to which the layperson has been accustomed. Take, for example, the simple act of exchange. To the untrained eye, an episode of market exchange is seen as one in which an exchange of objects, presumably of *equal* value, occurs. When I buy a meal for $20, I have given up a $20 bill for food and service having a market value of $20. For the economist this episode is seen in an entirely different light. For me the meal was subjectively valued as being *more* important than the $20 bill that I was asked to surrender for the meal. For the owner of the establishment that sold me the meal, its value was *lower* than that of the prospective $20 he hoped to receive from me. So that this simple episode of exchange must have meant, in the prospective judgments of both the consumer and the vendor, that new, *additional* value was being *created* by this exchange. This elementary insight, so foundational to economic reasoning and understanding, is strange and unfamiliar to the world of commerce and of everyday activity.

In fact, the subtlety of such "subjectivist" insights often eludes analysts equipped with sophisticated mathematical tools. Their training, and the scope of their analytical tools, lead them to focus on the objects exchanged in such episodes, rather than on the human motives expressed in the purposeful actions of which such episodes consist. And it has been this "blind-spot" in modern mathematical economics that has tended to render it, in general, surprisingly insensitive to the role of expectations and of knowledge in economic decision making and in market processes.

Without the subtlety conferred by the subjective perspective, the market process appears to consist of endless sequences of exchanges. From the subjective perspective, however, it becomes possible (if not indeed imperative) to recognize the market process as involving processes of mutual discovery (to use a Hayekian phrase) on the part of market participants. It becomes possible to recognize scope for superior entrepreneurial vision into the future, and for the consequence that such vision can be expected continually to shake up existing patterns of production and of market exchange (in directions inspired by more accurate or, at least, more up-to-date assessments of the underlying realities).

Not only does the subjective perspective taught in economic reasoning offer new and deeper understanding of market phenomena and of market processes, it permits us to *judge* these phenomena and processes from a more comprehensive and all-encompassing vantage point. One of the most pervasive fallacies in public opinion has been that of seeing the gain that one participant derives from a market exchange as having necessarily been extracted and subtracted from his partner in that exchange. After all, if I profit from an exchange with my neighbor, that profit can only have arisen from my neighbor's presumed, corresponding, loss. It is of course an elementary economic insight, yet one often entirely missed, that my profit must, at least prospectively, be in fact accompanied, not by a loss to my exchange partner (as in a "zero-sum game"), but by *profit* to him (a "positive-sum game"). No one, after all, engages in a voluntary act of exchange unless he or she expects to gain from it. This kind of entirely fresh perspective introduced by the subjective foundations of economic reasoning often (correctly) strikes beginners in economics as offering revolutionary new insights. It does not require lengthy training to introduce beginners to this kind of perspective. But economic education clearly has a "revolutionary" role to play in this regard.

ECONOMIC EDUCATION AND ECONOMIC POLICY

An eminent economist once provocatively declared that economists *qua* scientists have no business making normative pronouncements on economic policy (or, in fact, on anything else). To make such pronouncements, George Stigler somewhat impishly asserted, was to engage in "preaching."[3] As a citizen the economist may certainly express dismay at the consequences of economic policies; he may abhor these consequences. But those who initiated and executed these policies, he argued, obviously *desired* these consequences (which others are viewing with abhorrence). We have no reason to presume that those engaged in actions or in executing policy are unaware of the consequences of what they do. To object to these policies is then simply to assert what those with the power to initiate policies refuse to accept, namely, that their consequences are indeed abhorrent. To so object, Stigler maintained, is merely to preach, not to engage in scientific discourse. The position we have been articulating in this lecture (and, I suggest, the position consistently taken by FEE) utterly rejects Stigler's contention.

That contention rested on the premise that we must assume those who take actions or undertake policies to be correctly aware in advance of the likely consequences of those actions or policies. But, as we have argued here, the truth is that, because of sheer economic ignorance, well-meaning policy makers may be completely unaware that what they are doing may in fact generate consequences quite the reverse of what they wish to achieve. Someone once defined the job of an economist as that of warning people when and how they are seeking to run in two opposite directions at the very same time. My teacher, Mises, used to say something like the following in his lectures on price controls: "These laws passed by the legislators are bad not because I, Mises, do not like their consequences. These laws are bad because they produce consequences which *they*, the legislators themselves, would not like and certainly did not aim at." In other words, economic ignorance is rife; it leads voters and politicians to support policies the consequences of which they themselves can only regret. The economist has a role to play in offering policy advice, and this role is *not* one of preaching, but one of pointing out the respective consequences of alternative policies among which voters and legislators must choose. Economic education is vitally and essentially relevant for this role. And this returns us to the paradox with which we began this lecture, the paradox of passion and austere *wertfreiheit* that permeated Mises's life and work.

THE PASSIONATE PURSUIT OF AUSTERELY DEFINED ECONOMIC EDUCATION

If one recognizes, as Mises did, how central planning in all degrees is likely to generate disastrous human consequences, it becomes clear that a passionate urge to spread elementary scientific economic understanding among the public involves no contradiction whatever. The phenomenon of economic ignorance is so widespread, and its consequences so frightening, that the objective of reducing that ignorance becomes a goal invested with independent moral worth. But the economic education needed to reduce such ignorance must be based on austere, objective, scientific content—with no ideological or moral content of its own. Precisely because it is necessary to "persuade" (that is, to educate) the lay public, it is necessary that this public be convinced of the objectivity and ideological impartiality of the insights being transmitted.

If public policies seeking to increase the scale and scope of government intervention in the economy are to be successfully fought at the legislative and executive levels, the economic understanding of the public must certainly and urgently be enhanced. For this to be achieved, the delicate interface between moral passion and scientific detachment must be recognized and respected.

There is, we have insisted, a fundamental difference between economic education (the raison d'être of this Foundation) and "libertarian" ideology or rhetoric. The former is not, and must not be, a mere "public relations" expression of the latter. The legitimate moral, and even passionate, commitment with which the Foundation and its supporters seek to promote its goals need not (in fact, dare not) compromise the detachment and objectivity of the *content* of the economic education, the dissemination of which makes up those goals.

NOTES

1. Ludwig von Mises, *Epistemological Problems of Economics* (Princeton, N.J.: Van Nostrand, 1960 [translation of *Grundprobleme der Nationalökonomie*, 1933]), p. 214.

2. It was in 1949 that these two Austrian economists published major works (unappreciated for a long time) developing these deepened insights: Ludwig von Mises, *Human Action: A Treatise on Economics* (New Haven: Yale University Press, 1949) and F. A. Hayek, *Individualism and Economic Order* (London: Routledge and Kegan Paul, 1949).

3. George J. Stigler, "The Economist as Preacher," in *The Economist as Preacher and Other Essays* (Chicago: University of Chicago Press, 1982).

THE LEGACY
OF AUSTRIAN
ECONOMICS

The birth of the Austrian School of Economics is usually recognized as having occurred with the 1871 publication of Carl Menger's *Grundsätze der Volkwirthschaftslehre*. On the basis of this work Menger (hitherto a civil servant) became a junior faculty member at the University of Vienna. Several years later, after a stint as tutor and travelling companion to Crown Prince Rudolph, he was appointed to a professional chair at the University. Two younger economists, Eugen von Böhm-Bawerk and Friedrich von Wieser (neither of whom had been a student of Menger) became enthusiastic supporters of the new ideas put forward in Menger's book. During the 1880s a vigorous outpouring of literature from these two followers, from several of Menger's students, and in particular a methodological work by Menger himself, brought the ideas of Menger and his followers to the attention of the international community of economists. The Austrian School was now a recognized entity. Several works of Böhm-Bawerk and Wieser were translated into English; and by 1890 the editors of the U.S. journal *Annals of the American Academy of Political and Social Science* were asking Böhm-Bawerk for an expository paper explaining the doctrines of the new school. What follows seeks to provide a concise survey of the history of the Austrian School with special emphasis on (a) the major representatives of the school; (b) the central ideas identified with the school; (c) the relationship between the school and its ideas, and other major schools of thought within economics; (d) the various meanings and perceptions associated today with the term Austrian Economics.

THE FOUNDING AUSTRIANS

Menger's 1871 book is recognized in the history of economic thought (alongside Jevons's 1871 *Theory of Political Economy*, and Walras's 1874 *Eléments d'économie politique pure*) as a central component of the "Marginalist Revolution." For the most part, historians of thought have emphasized the features in Menger's work that parallel those of Jevons and Walras. More recently, following especially the work of W. Jaffé (1976) attention

Reprinted from *The New Palgrave: A Dictionary of Economics*, ed. Peter Newman, Murray Milgate, and John Eatwell, vol. 1 (London, New York, and Tokyo: The Macmillan Press, 1987), 145–51. Reproduced with permission of Palgrave Macmillan.

has come to be paid to those aspects of Menger's ideas which set them apart from those of his contemporaries. A series of recent studies (Grassl and Smith, 1986) have related these unique aspects of Menger and the early Austrian economists to broader currents in the late nineteenth-century intellectual and philosophical scene in Austria.

The central thrust of Menger's book was unmistakable; it was an attempt to rebuild the foundations of economic science in a way which, while retaining the abstract, theoretical character of economics, offered an understanding of value and price which ran sharply counter to classical teachings. For the classical economists value was seen as governed by past resource costs; Menger saw value as expressing judgements concerning future usefulness in meeting consumer wants. Menger's book, offered to the German-speaking scholarly community of Germany and Austria, was thus altogether different, in approach, style and substance, from the work coming from the German universities. That latter work, while also sharply critical of classical economics, was attacking its theoretical character, and appealing for a predominantly historical approach. At the time Menger's book appeared, the "older" German historical school (led by Roscher, Knies and Hildebrand) was beginning to be succeeded by the "younger" historical school, whose leader was to be Gustav Schmoller. Menger, the thirty-one-year-old Austrian civil servant, was careful not to present his work as antagonistic to that of German economic scholarship. In fact he dedicated his book—with "respectful esteem"—to Roscher, and offered it to the community of German scholars "as a friendly greeting from a collaborator in Austria and as a faint echo of the scientific suggestions so abundantly lavished on us Austrians by Germany . . ." (Menger, 1871, Preface). Clearly Menger hoped that his theoretical innovations might be seen as reinforcing the conclusions derived from historical studies of the German scholars, contributing to a new economics to replace a discredited British classical orthodoxy.

Menger was to be bitterly disappointed. The German economists virtually ignored his book; where it was noticed in the German language journals it was grossly misunderstood or otherwise summarily dismissed. For the first decade after the publication of his book, Menger was virtually alone; there was certainly no Austrian "school." And when the enthusiastic work of Böhm-Bawerk and Wieser began to appear in the 1880s, the new literature acquired the appellation "Austrian" more as a pejorative epithet bestowed by disdainful German economists than as an honorific label (Mises,

1969, p. 40). This rift between the Austrian and German scholarly camps deepened most considerably after the appearance of Menger's methodological challenge to the historical approach (Menger, 1883). Menger apparently wrote that work having been convinced by the unfriendly disinterest with which his 1871 book had been received in Germany, that German economics could be rescued only by a frontal attack on the Historical School. The bitter *methodenstreit* that followed is usually (but not invariably, see Bostaph, 1978) seen by historians of economics as constituting a tragic waste of scholarly energy. Certainly this venomous academic conflict helped bring the existence of an Austrian School to the attention of the international economics fraternity—as a group of dedicated economists offering a flood of exciting theoretical ideas reinforcing the new marginalist literature, sharply modifying the hitherto dominant classical theory of value. Works by Böhm-Bawerk (1886), Wieser (1884, 1889), Komorzynski (1889) and Zuckerkandl (1889) offered elaborations or discussions of Menger's central, subjectivist ideas on value, cost, and price. Works on the theory of pure profit, and on such applications as public finance theory, were contributed by writers such as Mataja (1884), Gross (1884), Sax (1887), and R. Meyer (1887). The widely used textbook by Philippovich (1893), who was a professor at the University of Vienna (but more sympathetic toward the contributions of the German school), is credited with an important role in spreading Austrian marginal utility theory among German-language students.

In these early Austrian contributions to the theory of value and price, emphasis was (as in the Jevonsian and Walrasian approaches) placed both on marginalism and on utility. But important differences set the Austrian theory apart from other early marginalist theories. The Austrians made no attempt to present their ideas in mathematical form, and as a consequence the Austrian concept of the margin differs somewhat from that of Jevons and Walras. For the latter, and for subsequent microeconomic theorists, the marginal value of a variable refers to the instantaneous rate of change of the "total" variable. But the Austrians worked, deliberately, with discrete variables (see K. Menger, 1973). More importantly the concept of marginal utility, and the sense in which it decreases, referred for the Austrians not to psychological enjoyments themselves, but to (ordinal) marginal *valuations* of such enjoyments (McCulloch, 1977). In any event, as has been urged by Streissler (1972), what was important for the Austrians in marginal utility was not so much the adjective as the noun. Menger saw his theory as demonstrating the unique and exclusive role played, in the determination of economic value, by subjective, "utility," considerations. Values are not seen (as they are in Marshallian economics) as *jointly* determined by subjective (utility) and objective (physical cost) considerations. Rather values are seen as determined *solely* by the actions of consumers (operating within a given framework of existing commodity and/or production possibilities). Cost is seen (by Menger, and especially by Wieser, whose name came to be associated closely with this insight) merely as prospective utility deliberately sacrificed (in order to command more highly preferred utility). Whereas in the development of the other marginalist theories, it took perhaps two decades for it to be seen that marginal utility value theory points directly to marginal productivity distribution theory, Menger at least glimpsed this insight immediately. His theory of "higher-order" goods emphasizes how both the economic character and the value of factor services, are derived exclusively from the valuations placed by consumers upon the consumer products to whose emergence these higher order goods ultimately contribute. Böhm-Bawerk contributed not only to the exposition and dissemination of Menger's basic subjective value theory, but most prominently also to the theory of capital and interest. Early in his career he published a massive volume (Böhm-Bawerk, 1884) in the history of doctrine, offering an encyclopedic critique of all earlier theories of interest (or "surplus value" or "normal profit"). This he followed up several years later with a volume (Böhm-Bawerk, 1889) presenting his own theory. At least part of the renown of the Austrian School at the turn of the century derived from the fame of these contributions. As we shall note later on, a number of subsequent and modern writers (such as Hicks, 1973; Faber, 1979; and Hausman, 1981) have indeed seen these Böhm-Bawerkian ideas as constituting the enduring element of the Austrian contribution. Others, taking their cue from an oft-repeated critical remark attributed to Menger (Schumpeter, 1954, p. 847, fn. 8), have seen Böhm-Bawerk's theory of capital and interest as separate from, or even as somehow inconsistent with, the core of the Austrian tradition stemming from Menger (Lachmann, 1977, p. 27). Certainly Böhm-Bawerk himself saw his theory of capital and interest as a seamless extension of basic subjectivist value theory. Once the dimension of time has been introduced into the analysis of both consumer and producer decisions, Böhm-Bawerk found it possible to explain the phenomenon of interest. Because production takes time, and because economizing men systematically choose earlier receipts over (physically similar) later receipts, capital-using production processes cannot fail to yield (even after the erosive forces of competition are taken into account) a portion of current output to those who in earlier periods invested inputs into time-consuming, "roundabout" production processes.

Böhm-Bawerk became, indeed, so prominent a representative of the Austrian School prior to World War I that, largely due to his work, the Marxists came to view the Austrians as the quintessential bourgeois, intellectual enemy of Marxist economics (Bukharin, 1914). Not only did Böhm-Bawerk offer his own theory explaining the phenomenon of the interest "surplus" in a manner depriving this capitalist income of any exploitative character, he had emphatically and mercilessly refuted Marxist theories of this surplus. In his 1884 work Böhm-Bawerk had systematically deployed the Austrian subjective theory of value to criticize witheringly the Marxist labour theory underlying the exploitation theory. A decade later (Böhm-Bawerk, 1896) he offered a patient, but relentless and uncompromising elaboration of that critique (in dissecting the claim that Marx's posthumously published Volume III of *Capital* could be reconciled with the simple labour theory forming the basis of Volume I). This tension between the Marxists and the Austrians was to find later echoes in the debate which Mises and Hayek (third- and fourth-generation Austrians) were to conduct, during the 1920–40 interwar period, with socialist economists concerning the possibility of economic calculation in a centrally planned economy.

Menger retired from his University of Vienna professorship in 1903. His chair was assumed by Wieser. Wieser has been justly described as

> the central figure of the Austrian School: central in time, central in the ideas he propounded, central in his intellectual abilities, that is to say neither the most outstanding genius nor one of those also to be mentioned. . . . He had the longest teaching record . . . (Streissler, 1986).

Wieser had been an early and prolific expositor of Menger's theory of value. His general treatise on economics, summing up his life's contributions (Wieser, 1914), has been hailed by some (but certainly not all) commentators as a major achievement. (Hayek, 1968, sees the work as a personal achievement rather than as representative of the Austrian School.) In the decade prior to World War I, it was Böhm-Bawerk's seminar (begun when Böhm-Bawerk rejoined academic life after a number of years as Finance Minister of Austria) that became famous as the intellectual centre of the Austrian School. Among the subsequently famous economists who participated in the seminar were Josef A. Schumpeter and Ludwig von Mises, both of whom published books prior to the war (Schumpeter, 1908, 1912; Mises, 1912).

AFTER WORLD WAR I

The scene in Austrian economics after the war was rather different than it had been before. Böhm-Bawerk had died in 1914. Menger, who even in his long seclusion after retirement, used to receive visits from the young economists at the university, died in 1921. Although Wieser continued to teach until his death in 1926, the focus shifted to younger scholars. These included particularly Mises, the student of Böhm-Bawerk, and Hans Mayer, who succeeded his teacher Wieser, to his chair. Mises, although an "extraordinary" (unsalaried) faculty member at the university, never did obtain a professional chair. Much of his intellectual influence was exercised outside the university framework (Mises, 1978, ch. ix). Other notable (pre-war-trained) scholars during the Twenties included Richard Strigl, Ewald Schams, and Leo Schonfeld (later Illy). In the face of these changes the Austrian tradition thrived. New books were published, and a new crop of younger students came to the fore, many of whom were to become internationally famous economists in later decades. These included particularly Friedrich A. Hayek, Gottfried Haberler, Fritz Machlup, Oskar Morgenstern, and Paul N. Rosenstein-Rodan. Economic discussion among the Austrians was vigorously carried on, during the Twenties and early Thirties, within two partly overlapping groups. One, at the university, was led by Hans Mayer. The other centred around Mises, whose famed *privatseminar* met in his Chamber of Commerce office and drew not only the gifted younger economists, but also such philosophers, sociologists and political scientists as Felix Kaufmann, Alfred Schutz and Erik Voegelin. It was during this period that British economist Lionel Robbins came decisively under the influence of the intellectual ferment going on in Vienna. A distinctly important outcome of this contact was Robbins's highly influential book (Robbins, 1932). It was largely through this work that a number of key Austrian ideas came to be absorbed into the mainstream literature of twentieth-century Anglo-American economics. In 1931 Robbins invited Hayek to lecture at the London School of Economics, and this led to Hayek's appointment to the Tooke chair at that institution.

Hayek's arrival on the British scene contributed especially to the development and widespread awareness of the "Austrian" theory of the business cycle. Mises had sketched such a theory as early as 1912 (Mises, 1912, pp. 396–404). This theory attributed the boom phase of the cycle to intertemporal misallocation stimulated by "too low" interest rates. This intertemporal misallocation consisted of producers initiating processes of production that implicitly anticipated a willingness on the part of the public to postpone consumption to a degree in fact inconsistent with the true pattern of time preferences. The subsequent abandonment of unsustainable projects constitutes the down phase of the cycle. Mises emphasised the roots of this theory in Wicksell, and in earlier insights of the British currency school. Indeed Mises was tempted to challenge the appropriateness of the "Austrian" label widely attached to the theory (Mises, 1943). But, as he recognized, the Austrian label had become firmly attached to the doctrine. Hayek's vigorous exposition and extensive development of the theory (Hayek, 1931, 1933, 1939) and his introduction (through the theory) of Böhm-Bawerkian capital-theoretic insights to the British public, unmistakably left Hayek's imprint on the fully developed theory, and taught the profession to see it as a central contribution of the Austrian School. Given all these developments it is apparent that we must consider the early 1930s as constituting in many ways the period of greatest Austrian School influence upon the economics profession generally. Yet this triumph was to be short-lived indeed.

With the benefit of hindsight it is perhaps possible to understand why and how this same period of the early 1930s constituted, in fact, a decisive, almost fatal, turning point in the fortunes of the School. Within a few short years the idea of a distinct Austrian School—except as an important, but bygone, episode in the history of economics—virtually disappeared from the economics profession. While Hans Mayer continued to occupy his chair in Vienna until after World War II, the group of prominent younger economists who had surrounded Mises soon dispersed (for political or other reasons), many of them to various universities in the U.S. With Mises migrating in 1934 to Geneva and later to New York, with Hayek in London, Vienna ceased to be a centre for the vigorous continuation of the Austrian tradition. Moreover many of the group were convinced that the important ideas of the Austrian School had now been successfully absorbed into mainstream economics. The emerging ascendancy of theoretical economics, and thus the eclipse of historicist and anti-theoretical approaches to economics, no doubt permitted the Austrians to believe that they had finally prevailed, that there was no longer any particular need to cultivate a separate Austrian version of economic theory. A 1932 statement by Mises captures this spirit. Referring to the usual separation of economic theorists into three schools of thought, "the Austrian and the Anglo-American Schools and the School of Lausanne," Mises (citing Morgenstern) emphasized that these groups "differ only in their mode of expressing the same fundamental idea and that they are divided more by their terminology and by peculiarities of presentation than by the substance of their teachings" (Mises, 1933, p. 214). Yet the survival and development of an Austrian tradition during and subsequent to World War II, largely through the work of Mises himself and of Hayek, deserves and requires attention.

Fritz Machlup has, on several occasions (Machlup, 1981, 1982) listed six ideas as central to the Austrian School prior to World War II. There is every reason to agree that it was these six ideas that expressed the Austrian approach as understood, say, in 1932. These ideas were: (a) methodological individualism (not to be confused with political or ideological individualism, but referring to the claim that economic phenomena are to be explained by going back to the actions of individuals); (b) methodological subjectivism (recognizing that the actions of individuals are to be understood only by reference to the knowledge, beliefs, perception and expectations of these individuals); (c) marginalism (emphasizing the significance of prospective *changes* in relevant magnitudes confronting the decision maker); (d) the influence of utility (and diminishing marginal utility) on demand and thus on market prices; (e) opportunity costs (recognizing that the costs that affect decisions are those that express the most important of the alternative opportunities being sacrificed in employing productive services for one purpose rather than for the sacrificed alternatives); (f) time structure of consumption and production (expressing time preferences and the productivity of "roundaboutness").

It seems appropriate, however, to comment further on this list. (1) With varying degrees of emphasis most modern microeconomics incorporates all of these ideas, so that (2) this list supports the cited Morgenstern–Mises statement emphasizing the common ground shared by *all* schools of economic theory. However (3) subsequent developments in the work of Mises and Hayek suggest that the list of six Austrian ideas was not *really* complete. While few Austrians at the time (of the early 1930s) were perhaps able to identify additional Austrian ideas, such additional insights were in fact implicit in the Austrian tradition and were to be articulated explicitly in later work. From this perspective, then, (4) important *differences* separate Austrian economic theory from the mainstream developments in microeconomics, particularly as these latter developments proceeded from the thirties onwards. It was left for Mises and Hayek to articulate these differences and thus preserve a unique Austrian "presence" in the profession.

LATER DEVELOPMENTS IN AUSTRIAN ECONOMICS

One early expression of such differences between the Austrian understanding of economic theory and that of other schools, was Hans Mayer's paper criticizing "functional price theories" and calling for the "genetic-causal" method (Mayer, 1932). Here Mayer was criticizing equilibrium theories of price that neglected to explicate the *sequence* of actions leading to market prices. To understand this sequence one must understand the causal genesis of the component actions in the sequence. In the light of the later writings of Mises and Hayek, it seems reasonable to recognize Mayer as having placed his finger on an important and distinctive element embedded in the Austrian understanding. Yet the Austrians themselves during the 1920s (and such students of their works as Lionel Robbins) seemed to have missed this insight. What appears to have helped Hayek and Mises articulate this hitherto overlooked element, was the well-known interwar debate concerning the possibility of economic calculation under central planning. A careful reading of the contributions to that debate suggests that it was in reaction to the "mainstream" equilibrium arguments of their opponents that Mises and Hayek made explicit the emphasis on process, learning and discovery to be found in the Austrian understanding of markets (Lavoie, 1985).

Mises had argued that economic calculation calls for the guidance supplied by prices; since the centrally planned economy has no market for productive factors, it cannot use factor prices as guides. Oskar Lange and others countered that prices need not be market prices; that guidance could be provided by non-market prices, announced by the central authorities, and treated by socialist managers "parametrically" (just as prices are treated by producers in the theory of the firm, in perfectly competitive factor and product markets). It was in response to this argument that Hayek developed his interpretation of competitive market processes as processes of discovery during which dispersed information comes to be mobilized (Hayek, 1949, chapters 2, 4, 5, 7, 8, 9). An essentially similar characterization of the market process (without the Hayekian emphasis on the role of knowledge, but with an accent on entrepreneurial activity in a world of open-ended, radical uncertainty) was presented by Mises during the same period (Mises, 1940, 1949). In the light of these Mises–Hayek developments in the theory of market process (and recognizing that these developments constituted the articulation of insights taken for granted in the early Austrian tradition: Kirzner, 1985; Jaffé, 1976), it seems reasonable to add the following to Machlup's list of ideas central to the Austrian tradition: (g) markets (and competition) as processes of learning and discovery; (h) the individual decision as an act of choice in an essentially uncertain context (where the identification of the relevant alternatives is part of the decision itself). It is these latter ideas that have come to be developed in, and made central to the revived attention to the Austrian tradition that, stemming from the work of Mises and Hayek, has emerged in the U.S. during the last decades.

AUSTRIAN ECONOMICS TODAY

As a result of these somewhat varied developments in the history of the Austrian School since 1930, the term Austrian Economics has come to evoke a number of different connotations in contemporary professional discussion. Some of these connotations are, at least partly, overlapping; others are, at least partly, mutually inconsistent. It seems useful, in disentangling these various perceptions, to identify a number of different meanings that have come to be attached to the term "Austrian Economics" in the 1980s. The present status of the Austrian School of Economics is, for better or for worse, encapsulated in these current perceptions.

(a) For many economists the term "Austrian Economics" is strictly a historical term. In this perception the existence of the Austrian School did not extend beyond the early Thirties: Austrian Economics was partly absorbed into mainstream microeconomics, and partly displaced by emerging Keynesian macroeconomics. To a considerable extent this view seems to be that held by economists in Austria today. Economists (and other intellectuals) in Austria today are thoroughly cognizant of—and proud of—the earlier Austrian School, as evidenced by several commemorative conferences held in Austria in recent years, and by several related volumes (Hicks and Weber, 1973; Leser, 1986), but see themselves today simply as a part of the general community of professional economists. Erich Streissler, present holder of the chair occupied by Menger, Wieser and Mayer, has written extensively, and with the insights and scholarship of one profoundly influenced by the Austrian tradition, concerning numerous aspects of the Austrian School and its principal representatives (Streissler, 1969, 1972, 1973, 1986).

(b) For a number of economists the adjective "Austrian" has come to mark a revival of interest in Böhm-Bawerkian capital-and-interest theory. This revival has emphasized particularly the time dimension in production and the productivity of roundaboutness. Among the contributors to this literature should be mentioned Hicks (1973), Bernholz (1971, 1973), Faber (1979) and Orosel (1981). In this literature, then, the term "Austrian" has very little to do with the general subjectivist Mengerian tradition (which had, as noted earlier, certain reservations in regard to the Böhm-Bawerkian theory).

(c) For other economists (and non-economists) the term "Austrian Economics" has come to be associated less with a unique methodology, or with specific economic doctrines, as with libertarian ideology in political and social discussion. For these observers, to be an Austrian economist in the 1980s is simply to be in favour of free markets. Machlup (1982) has noted (and partly endorsed) this perception of the term "Austrian." He has ascribed it, particularly, to the impact of the work of Mises. Mises' championship of the market cause was so prominent, and his identification as an Austrian was at the same time so unmistakable, that it is perhaps natural that his strong policy pronouncements in support of unhampered markets, came to be perceived as the core of Austrianism in modern times. This has been reinforced by the work of a leading U.S. follower of Mises, Murray N. Rothbard, who has also been prominent in libertarian scholarship and advocacy. Other observers, however, would question this identification. While, as earlier noted, many of the early contributions of the Austrian School were seen as sharply antagonistic to Marxian thought, the school on the whole maintained an apolitical stance (Myrdal, 1929, p. 128). Among the founders of the school, Wieser was in fact explicit in endorsing the interventionist conclusions of the German Historical School (Wieser, 1914, pp. 490ff). While both Mises and Hayek provocatively challenged the possibility of efficiency under socialism, they too, emphasized the *wertfrei* character of their economics. Both writers would see their free market stance at the policy level as related to, but not as central to, their Austrianism.

(d) For many in the profession the term "Austrian Economics" has come, since about 1970, to refer to a revival of interest in the ideas of Carl Menger and the earlier Austrian School, particularly as these ideas have been developed through the work of Mises and Hayek. This revival has occurred particularly in the US, where a sizeable literature has emerged from a number of economists. This literature includes, in particular, works by Murray N. Rothbard (1962), Israel Kirzner (1973), Gerald P. O'Driscoll (1977, 1985), Mario J. Rizzo (O'Driscoll and Rizzo, 1985), and Roger W. Garrison (1978, 1982, 1985). The thrust of this literature has been to emphasize the differences between the Austrian understanding of markets as processes, and that of the equilibrium theorists whose work has dominated much of modern economic theory. As a result of this emphasis, this sense of the term "Austrian Economics" has often (and only partly accurately; see White, 1977, p. 9) come to be understood as a refusal to adopt modern mathematical and econometric techniques—which standard economics adopted largely as a result of its equilibrium orientation. The economists in this group of modern Austrians (sometimes called neo-Austrian) do see themselves as continuators of an earlier tradition, sharing with mainstream neoclassical economics an appreciation for the systematic outcomes of markets, but differing from it in its understanding of how these outcomes are in fact achieved. Largely as a result of the activity of this group, many classic works of the early Austrians have recently been republished in original or translated form, and have attracted a considerable readership both inside and outside the profession.

(e) Yet another current meaning loosely related to the preceding sense of the term, has come to be associated with the term "Austrian Economics." This meaning refers to an emphasis on the radical uncertainty that surrounds economic decision making, to an extent that implies virtual rejection of much of received microeconomics. Ludwig Lachmann (1976) has identified the work of G. L. S. Shackle as constituting in this regard the most consistent extension of Austrian (and especially of Misesian) subjectivism. Lachmann's own work (1973, 1977, 1986) has, in the same vein, stressed the indeterminacy of both individual choices and market outcomes.

This line of thought has come to imply serious reservations concerning the possibility of systematic theoretical conclusions commanding significant degrees of generality. This connotation of the term "Austrian

Economics" thus associates it with a stance sympathetic, to a degree, toward historical and institutional approaches. Given the prominent opposition of earlier Austrians to these approaches, this association has, as might be expected, been seen as ironic or even paradoxical by many observers (including, especially, modern exponents of the broader tradition of the Austrian School of Economics).

[An earlier article on the Austrian School of Economics was begun and substantially drafted by Professor Friedrich A. Hayek—himself a Nobel laureate in economics whose celebrated contributions are deeply rooted in the Austrian tradition. The present author gratefully acknowledges his indebtness (in the writing of this essay) to the characteristic scholarship and treasure-trove of facts contained in Professor Hayek's unfinished article, as well as to Professor Hayek's other numerous studies that relate to the history of the Austrian School.]

BIBLIOGRAPHY

Bernholz, P. 1971. Superiority of roundabout processes and positive rate of interest. A simple model of capital and growth. *Kyklos* 24(4) 687–721.

Bernholz, P. and Faber, M. 1973. Technical superiority of roundabout processes and positive rate of interest. A capital model with depreciation and n-period horizon. *Zeitschrift für die gesamte Staatswissenschaften* 129(1), February, 46–61.

Bostaph, S. 1978. The methodological debate between Carl Menger and the German Historicists. *Atlantic Economic Journal* 6(3), September, 3–16.

Böhm-Bawerk, E. von. 1884. *Geschichte und Kritik der Kapitalzins-Theorien.* English trans. as Vol. I of *Capital and Interest,* South Holland, Ill.: Libertarian Press, 1959.

Böhm-Bawerk, E. von. 1886. Grundzuge der Theorie des Wirtschaftlichen Guterwerths. *Conrad's Jahrbuch,* 1–88, 477–541.

Böhm-Bawerk, E. von. 1889. *Positive Theorie des Kapitales.* Innsbruck: Wagner.

Böhm-Bawerk, E. von. 1891. The Austrian economists. *Annals of the American Academy of Political and Social Science,* January, 361–84.

Böhm-Bawerk, E. von. 1896. *Zum Abschluss des Marxschen Systems.* Trans. (1898) as *Karl Marx and the Close of his System,* ed. P. Sweezy, New York: Kelley, 1949.

Bukharin, N. 1914. *The Economic Theory of the Leisure Class.* Translated from Russian (1927), London: M. Lawrence; reprinted, New York: Monthly Review Press, 1972.

Faber, M. 1979. *Introduction to Modern Austrian Capital Theory.* Berlin: Springer.

Garrison, R. W. 1978. Austrian macroeconomics: a diagrammatical exposition. In *New Directions in Austrian Economics,* ed. L. M. Spadaro, Kansas City: Sheed, Andrews & McMeel.

Garrison, R. W. 1982. Austrian economics as the middle ground: comment on Loasby. In *Method, Process, and Austrian Economics: Essays in Honor of Ludwig von Mises,* ed. I. M. Kirzner, Lexington, Mass.: Lexington Books.

Garrison, R. W. 1985. Time and money: the universals of macroeconomic theorizing. *Journal of Macroeconomics* 6(2), Spring, 197–213.

Grassl, W. and Smith, B. (eds) 1986. *Austrian Economics, Historical and Philosophical Background.* New York: New York University Press.

Gross, G. 1884. *Die Lehre von Unternehmergewinn.* Leipzig.

Hausman, D. M. 1981. *Capital, Profits, and Prices.* New York: Columbia University Press.

Hayek, F. A. 1931. *Prices and Production.* London: Routledge & Sons.

Hayek, F. A. 1933. *Monetary Theory and the Trade Cycle.* London: Jonathan Cape.

Hayek, F. A. 1939. *Profits, Interest and Investment: and Other Essays on the Theory of Industrial Fluctuations.* London: Routledge & Kegan Paul.

Hayek, F. A. 1949. *Individualism and Economic Order.* London: Routledge & Kegan Paul.

Hayek, F. A. 1968. Economic thought VI: the Austrian School. *International Encyclopedia of the Social Sciences,* ed. D. L. Sills, New York: Macmillan.

Hicks, J. 1973. *Capital and Time: A Neo-Austrian Theory.* Oxford: Clarendon Press.

Hicks, J. R. and Weber, W. 1973. *Carl Menger and the Austrian School of Economics.* Oxford: Clarendon Press.

Jaffé, W. 1976. Menger, Jevons and Walras de-homogenized. *Economic Inquiry* 14(4), December, 511–24.

Jevons, W. S. 1871. *The Theory of Political Economy.* London: Macmillan.

Kauder, E. 1965. *A History of Marginal Utility Theory.* Princeton: Princeton University Press.

Kirzner, I. M. 1973. *Competition and Entrepreneurship.* Chicago: University of Chicago Press.

Kirzner, I. M. 1981. Mises and the renaissance of Austrian Economics. *Homage to Mises, the First Hundred Years,* ed. J. K. Andrews, Jr., Hillsdale: Hillsdale College Press.

Kirzner, I. M. 1985. Comment on R. N. Langlois, "From the knowledge of economics to the economics of knowledge: Fritz Machlup on methodology and on the 'Knowledge Society.' " In *Research in the History of Economic Thought and Methodology,* ed. Warren J. Samuels, Greenwich, CT: JAI.

Komorzynski, J. von 1889. *Der Werth in der isolirten Wirthschaft.* Vienna: Manz.

Lachmann, L. 1973. *Macro-economic Thinking and the Market Economy.* London: Institute of Economic Affairs.

Lachmann, L. 1976. From Mises to Shackle: an essay on Austrian Economics and the Kaleidic Society. *Journal of Economic Literature* 14(10), March, 54–62.

Lachmann, L. 1977. Austrian Economics in the present crisis of economic thought. *Capital, Expectations, and the Market Process.* Kansas City: Sheed, Andrews & McMeel.

Lachmann, L. 1986a. Austrian Economics under fire: the Hayek–Sraffa duel in restrospect. In Grassl and Smith (1986).

Lachmann, L. 1986b. *The Market as a Process.* Oxford: Basic Blackwell.

Lavoie, D. 1985. *Rivalry and Central Planning: The Socialist Calculation Debate Reconsidered.* Cambridge: Cambridge University Press.

Leser, N. (ed.) 1986. *Die Wiener Schule der Nationalökonomie*. Vienna: Hermann Böhlau.

Machlup, F. 1981. Ludwig von Mises: the academic scholar who would not compromise. *Wirtschaftspolitischen Blätter*, No. 4.

Machlup, F. 1982. Austrian Economics. *Encyclopedia of Economics*, ed. Douglas Greenwald, New York: McGraw-Hill.

Mataja, V. 1884. *Der Unternehmergewinn*. Vienna.

Mayer, H. 1932. Der Erkenntniswert der Funktionellen Preistheorien. In *Die Wirtschaftstheorie der Gegenwart*, ed. H. Mayer, Vienna.

McCulloch, J. H. 1977. The Austrian theory of the marginal use and of ordinal marginal utility. *Zeitschrift für Nationalökonomie*, No. 3–4.

Menger, C. 1871. *Grundsätze der Volkwirthschaftslehre*. Translated (1950) as *Principles of Economics*, ed. J. Dingwall and B. F. Hoselitz; reprinted, New York: New York University Press, 1981.

Menger, K., Jr. 1973. Austrian marginalism and mathematical economics. In *Carl Menger and the Austrian School of Economics*, ed. J. R. Hicks and W. Weber, Oxford: Clarendon Press.

Meyer, R. 1887. *Das Wesen des Einkommens: Eine volkswirthschaftliche Untersuchung*. Berlin: Hertz.

Mises, L. von. 1912. *Theorie des Geldes und der Umlaufsmittel*. Translated as *Theory of Money and Credit* (1934), Indianapolis: Liberty Classics, 1980.

Mises, L. von. 1933. *Grundprobleme der Nationalökonomie*. Translated as *Epistemological Problems of Economics*, Princeton: Van Nostrand, 1960.

Mises, L. von. 1940. *Nationalökonomie, Theorie des Handelns und Wirstschaftens*, Geneva, Editions Union.

Mises, L. von. 1943. "Elastic expectations" and the Austrian theory of the trade cycle. *Economica* 10, August, 251–52.

Mises, L. von. 1949. *Human Action, A Treatise on Economics*. New Haven: Yale University Press.

Mises, L. von. 1969. *The Historical Setting of the Austrian School of Economics*. New Rochelle: Arlington House.

Mises, L. von. 1978. *Notes and Recollections*. South Holland: Libertarian Press.

O'Driscoll, G. P., Jr. 1977. *Economics as a Coordination Problem: The Contributions of Friedrich A. Hayek*. Kansas City: Sheed, Andrews & McMeel.

O'Driscoll, G. P., Jr., and Rizzo, M. J. 1985. *The Economics of Time and Ignorance*. Oxford: Basil Blackwell.

Orosel, G. O. 1981. Faber's modern Austrian capital theory: a critical survey. *Zeitschrift für Nationalökonomie*, 141–55.

Philippovich, E. von Philippsberg. 1893. *Grundriss der Politischen Ökonomie*. Freiburg: Mohr.

Robbins, L. 1932. *The Nature and Significance of Economic Science*. London: Macmillan.

Rothbard, M. N. 1962. *Man, Economy, and State: A Treatise on Economic Principles*. Princeton: Van Nostrand.

Sax, E. 1887. *Grundlegung der Theoretischen Staatswirtschaft.* Vienna: Holder.

Schumpeter, J. A. 1908. *Das Wesen und der Hauptinhalt der Theoretischen Nationalökonomie.* Leipzig: Duncker & Humblot.

Schumpeter, J. A. 1912. *Theorie der wirtschaftlichen Entwicklung.* Leipzig: Duncker & Humblot. English translation (1934) *The Theory of Economic Development,* Cambridge, Mass.: Harvard University Press.

Schumpeter, J. A. 1954. *History of Economic Analysis.* New York: Oxford University Press.

Streissler, E. 1969. Structural economic thought: on the significance of the Austrian School today. *Zeitschrift für Nationalökonomie* 29(3–4), December, 237–66.

Streissler, E. 1972. To what extent was the Austrian School marginalist? *History of Political Economy* 4(2), Fall, 426–61.

Streissler, E. 1973. The Mengerian tradition. In *Carl Menger and the Austrian School of Economics,* ed. J. R. Hicks and W. Weber, Oxford: Clarendon Press.

Streissler, E. 1986. Arma virumque cano. Friedrich von Wieser, the bard as economist. In Leser (1986).

Walras, L. 1874. *Eléments d'économie politique pure.* Lausanne: Corbaz.

White, L. H. 1977. *The Methodology of the Austrian School Economists.* Revised edition, Auburn, AL: The Ludwig von Mises Institute of Auburn University, 1984.

Wieser, F. von 1884. *Ursprung des Wirtschaftlichen Wertes.* Vienna: Hölder.

Wieser, F. von 1889. *Der Naturliche Werth.* Vienna: Hölder. Trans. as *Natural Value,* ed. W. Smart, London: Macmillan, 1893; reprinted, New York: Kelley, 1956.

Wieser, F. von 1914. *Theorie der Gesellschaftlichen Wirtschaft.* Tübingen: Mohr. Translated (1927) as *Social Economics,* London: G. Allen & Unwin; reprinted, New York: Kelley, 1967.

Zuckerkandl, R. 1889. *Zur Theorie des Preises.* Leipzig: Stein.

FRIEDRICH AUGUST VON HAYEK

ROGER W. GARRISON AND ISRAEL M. KIRZNER

Friedrich August von Hayek (born 1899), a central figure in twentieth-century economics and foremost representative of the Austrian tradition, 1974 Nobel laureate in economics, a prolific author not only in the field of economics but also in the fields of political philosophy, psychology and epistemology, was born in Vienna on 8 May 1899. Following military service as an artillery officer in World War I, Hayek entered the University of Vienna, where he attended the lectures of Friedrich von Wieser and Othmar Spann and obtained doctorates in law and political science. After spending a year in New York (1923–24), Hayek returned to Vienna where he joined the famous *Privatseminar* conducted by Ludwig von Mises. In 1927 Hayek became the first director of the Austrian Institute for Business Cycle Research. On an invitation from Lionel Robbins, he lectured at the London School of Economics in 1931 and subsequently accepted the Tooke Chair. Hayek soon came to be a vigorous participant in the debates that raged in England during the 1930s concerning monetary, capital, and business-cycle theories and was a major figure in the celebrated controversies with John Maynard Keynes, Piero Sraffa and Frank H. Knight.

During the late 1930s and early 1940s Hayek's research focused on the role of knowledge and discovery in market processes, and on the methodological underpinnings of the Austrian tradition, particularly subjectivism and methodological individualism. His contributions in these areas were an outgrowth of his participation in the debate over the possibility of economic calculation under socialism.

In 1950 Hayek moved to the United States, joining the Committee on Social Thought at the University of Chicago. His research there engaged the broader concerns of social, political and legal philosophy. He returned to Europe in 1962 with appointments at the University of Freiburg, West Germany, and then (1969) at the University of Salzburg, Austria. Since 1977 Hayek has resided in Freiburg.

Reprinted from *The New Palgrave: A Dictionary of Economics*, ed. Peter Newman, Murray Milgate, and John Eatwell, vol. 2 (London, New York, and Tokyo: The Macmillan Press, 1987), 608–15. Reproduced with permission of Palgrave Macmillan.

Hayek's scholarly output spans more than six decades. Still growing in the mid-1980s, his bibliography (Gray, 1984) includes eighteen books, twenty-five pamphlets, sixteen books edited or introduced, and 235 articles. Although these publications have brought Hayek international renown and honours in several disciplines, his contributions to other social sciences emerged, to a significant degree, as extensions of his scholarship in the field of economics and its methodological foundations. The following survey refers rather narrowly to the career and contributions of Hayek the economist.

ECONOMICS AS A COORDINATION PROBLEM

Throughout all of Hayek's writings, both the questions asked and the answers given reflect his general conception of economics as a coordination problem (O'Driscoll, 1977). Thoughtful observation of market economies suggests that they are characterized by order more complex and intricate than can be explained in terms of deliberate efforts to achieve coordination among individual activities. According to Hayek (1952, p. 39), it is precisely the existence of this "spontaneous order" that provides the subject matter for the science of economics.

While market economies are better coordinated than can be accounted for by references to deliberate planning, they are always less than fully coordinated, hence the coordination *problem*. In one important sense, coordination failures are an integral part of an ongoing market process that iterates toward a greater degree of coordination. An oversupply or undersupply of some particular good, for instance, is evidence that the plans of producers and consumers of that good are not well coordinated one with the other. But the discoordination itself provides both an indication of the inconsistency in plans and the incentive for producers and consumers to make the appropriate adjustments.

But market economies do occasionally experience profound economy-wide coordination failures. Much of Hayek's research has been aimed, either directly or indirectly, toward discovering the set of circumstances or, more appropriately, the sequence of events that could cause such failures, i.e. that could cause an economy to collapse into economic depression. The focus of his research is *intertemporal* discoordination. The coordination of activities over time is inherently more difficult, more problematic, than the coordination of activities in a given period. Producers must make decisions now in anticipation of decisions that other producers and, ultimately, consumers will make sometime in the future. The fact that production is time consuming, the more so the more well developed the economy, figures importantly in Hayek's theorizing. This essential time element increases the likelihood of erroneous investment decisions and gives scope for cumulative investment errors. A spate of intertemporally discoordinated investments, whether triggered by a real or a monetary disturbance, can increase employment opportunities producing an artificial boom. But the eventual realization of the discoordination will necessitate a partial liquidation, which constitutes a bust. In this context, the Austrian theory is differentiated from other macroeconomic theories by its attention to the problem of intertemporal coordination *within* the investment sector. The more conventional treatments of macroeconomic coordination problems focus on the general *level* of investment in comparison with the level of saving or the size of the labour force.

Hayek adopted a two-tier approach to the study of business cycles. Prerequisite to the question of how an economywide coordination failure could occur is the question of how any degree of intertemporal coordination can be achieved at all in market economies. In Hayek's words, "before we explain why people commit mistakes, we must first explain why they should ever be right" (1937, p. 34). His account first of how a market economy works to coordinate activities over time and then of what can go wrong draws from several different fields of study within the science of economics. In particular, it draws in fundamental ways from price theory, capital theory and monetary theory.

Each of these fields required further development before becoming part of Hayek's account. Price theory had to be recast so as to emphasize the role of the price system as a communication network and as the most efficient means of making use of economic information. Capital theory had to be detailed so as to give play to the individual elements of the capital structure, which is made up of heterogeneous pieces of capital of various degrees of specificity and durability and related to one another by various degrees of intertemporal substitutability and complementarity. And monetary theory had to be extended in scope so as to allow the identification of systematic relative price effects associated with the process of monetary expansion or contraction.

While Hayek contributed importantly to each of these fields of study, his ultimate achievement consists in the integration of price theory, capital theory and monetary theory. Hayek integrated his own developments in these fields into a cohesive account of a market process that tends toward intertemporal coordination and of central-bank policies that can interfere with that process in such a way as to cause artificial economic booms which are inevitably followed by economic busts. Hayek's business cycle theory provided a basis for interpreting much of nineteenth- and twentieth-century economic history, for evaluating alternative macroeconomic theories—especially those of John Maynard Keynes, and for promoting institutional reform of the kind that will prevent or minimize intertemporal discoordination.

SUBJECTIVISM AND METHODOLOGICAL INDIVIDUALISM

The methodological norms adopted by Hayek are a direct reflection of his perception of the subject matter: economic phenomena as *spontaneous order*. Fundamental institutions in society owe their existence to no identifiable creator. They are the "results of human action but not of human design." The most obvious examples of spontaneous order are the use of language and, among economic phenomena, the use of money. Money, the most commonly accepted medium of exchange, came to be accepted, commonly accepted, and then most commonly accepted as a result of a long sequence of actions on the part of a multitude of individual traders none of whom *intended* to create the institution of money. Other economic phenomena— from the simple division of labour to the more broadly conceived organization of industry—are to be understood as instances of spontaneous order.

If there were no order in society except for what was consciously designed, Hayek argued, there would be no scope and no need for the social sciences. The task of these sciences in a world characterized by spontaneous order is precisely to account for those aspects of social order that were not consciously designed.

A central methodological theme that has consistently pervaded Hayek's investigation of spontaneous order stems from his insistence that it is inappropriate to apply uncritically the methods of the physical sciences to the phenomena of the social sciences. Hayek used the term *scientism* to refer to the slavish imitation of the methods of the physical sciences without regard for the innate differences between physical and non-physical reality. Scientisim, which unavoidably overlooks crucial aspects of social reality, such as perception, intent and anticipation, was the focus of two long and critical articles published by Hayek during World War II. In these articles, which constitute the central core of his 1952 book, *The Counter-Revolution of Science: Studies on the Abuse of Reason*, Hayek spelled out the case for subjectivism and methodological individualism in the social sciences. "It is probably no exaggeration," according to Hayek, "to say that every important advance in economic theory during the last hundred years was a further step in the consistent application of subjectivism" (1952, p. 31).

Classical economists had focused their attention on the *objects* being valued and had looked for common denominators of value in terms of labour input or costs of production. The Austrian economists, particularly Menger, Mises and Hayek, are to be credited with shifting attention from the objects being valued to the subjects engaged in valuation. The value attributed to the various objects of economic actions, Hayek emphasized, can be accounted for only with reference to human purposes and in terms of the views that people hold about those objects.

Hayek's thoroughly subjectivist outlook and his adherence to the strictures of methodological individualism were mutually reinforcing. Methodological individualism is not a prescription of how to engage in economic research but rather a recognition of what counts as an economic explanation. To explain the undesigned aspects of a spontaneous order is to trace those aspects to the consciously taken individual actions that gave rise to that order. In Hayek's own words, "it is the concepts and the views held by individuals which are directly known to us and which form the elements from which we must build up, as it were, the more complex phenomena . . ." (Hayek, 1952, p. 38).

The contention that Hayek's crusade against scientism has consistently informed his substantive work is at least partly in conflict with a recent argument by T. W. Hutchison, who has sought to establish that Hayek's 1937 article "Economics and Knowledge" marked a sharp change in his methodology toward a "falsificationist" approach to economic science (Hutchison, 1981). This argument has been effectively disputed by John Gray (1984, pp. 16–21), who recognizes that the 1937 article was intended to persuade Mises that, contrary to Mises' own "praxeology," there is an essential empirical element in our understanding of economic phenomena. Further, Hayek's (1952) commitment to subjectivism and methodological individualism, and his emphasis on the fallacies of scientism suggest in fact a deepening, rather than an erosion, of his recognition of the extent to which economic theory is independent of—in fact a prerequisite for—empirical economic observation.

THE PRICE SYSTEM AS A COMMUNICATION NETWORK

It is a short step from Hayek's appreciation of the phenomenon of spontaneous order to his understanding of the price system as a communication network. The key contribution of the price system to social well-being consists, Hayek demonstrated, in the system's capacity to transmit information from one part of the market to another. In the event of a natural disaster which has curtailed the availability of a specific raw material, for example, the fact of a reduced supply will be effectively communicated to potential users through the medium of a higher price—which also provides the incentive for the socially desirable economizing of the particular raw material (Hayek, 1945, p. 85–86). The need for such a communication network arises out of the fact that the information to be communicated is dispersed throughout the society. This insight into the nature of prices as *signals* has, during the past decade and a half, come to be fairly widely recognized and expounded in modern textbooks.

In his treatment of the use of knowledge in society, Hayek made a sharp distinction between two kinds of knowledge: (1) scientific, or theoretical, knowledge and (2) the knowledge of the particular circumstances of time and place. The first-mentioned category is the proper concern of the economist; the second-mentioned category is the proper concern of the market participant. Failure to recognize this "division of knowledge" can lead to one of two serious errors. The assumption that *economists* can assimilate both kinds of knowledge leads to the conclusion that "rational planning" can outperform—or at least duplicate—the market itself: the assumption that *market participants* can assimilate both kinds of knowledge leads to the conclusion that "rational expectations" can nullify the systematic effects of monetary manipulation.

Hayek recognized and emphasized that if a fully adjusted system of prices—one corresponding to attained equilibrium—can be held to offer a system of coordinated and mutually reinforcing signals, such a system must depend on some prior groping process of market *discovery*. Hayek saw this process as consisting of market *competition*—which meant for him not the state of affairs consistent with the conditions for so-called perfect competition, but rather the rough-and-tumble process of market agitation kept in motion by complete freedom for competitive entrepreneurial entry. What such a competitive process can accomplish. Hayek argued, is the discovery of possibilities and preferences that no one had realized hitherto (Hayek, 1968).

These insights concerning knowledge and discovery articulated by Hayek in a number of profound papers from the late 1930s to the mid-1940s (Hayek, 1948) were partly responsible for, and partly emergent from, Hayek's participation in the celebrated interwar debate over the possibility of economic calculation under a socialist system. In deepening and widening the case originally presented by Mises in 1920, which challenged the feasibility of such calculation in the absence of market prices for factors of production, Hayek came to perceive the market process itself as crucial for the generation of that very knowledge which it would be necessary for a central planning authority to possess *before* it could hope to achieve a successful and efficient allocation of societal resources.

It was especially this Hayekian appreciation for the market as a discovery process that has significantly contributed to the contemporary revival of interest in the Austrian paradigm. In this context the Austrian contribution is to be distinguished from the more formal, or mathematically tractable, theories by its emphasis on the role of the entrepreneurial discovery in those systematic market processes upon which we must depend, in a world of ignorance and disequilibrium, for any possible tendency toward mutual coordination among the market participants. What Hayek showed was that much modern economics misconstrues the nature of the economic problem facing society by assuming away the problems raised by the fact of dispersed information. To imagine (as earlier critics of Mises and Hayek had proposed) that it would be possible to run a socialist system by simulating the market and promulgating non-market "prices" for the guidance of socialist managers is to ignore the extent to which market prices—both of consumer goods and of the capital goods that constitute the economy's capital structure—*already* express the outcome of an entrepreneurial discovery procedure that draws upon scattered existing knowledge.

THE INTERTEMPORAL STRUCTURE OF CAPITAL

Hayek's contribution to the development of capital theory is commonly regarded as his most fundamental and pathbreaking achievement (Machlup, 1976). His early attention (1928) to "Intertemporal Price Equilibrium and Movements in the Value of Money" (English translation in Hayek, 1984) provided both the basis and inspiration for many subsequent contributions in this area, most notably for those of John Hicks. The widely recognized but rarely understood Hayekian triangles, introduced in his *Prices and Production* (1935), provided a convenient but highly stylized way of describing the changes in the intertemporal pattern of the capital structure. The formal and comprehensive analysis in *The Pure Theory of Capital* (1941) fleshed out the earlier formulations and established the centrality of the "capital problem" in questions about the market's ability to coordinate economic activities over time.

The essential element of time in the economy's production process coupled with the inherent complexities of the capital structure gives special significance to the problem of intertemporal coordination. Individual producers must commit resources in the present on the basis of some production plan. Intertemporal coordination in the strictest sense requires that all such plans be mutually compatible and that they be jointly consistent with resource availabilities. The extent to which such compatibility and consistency actually exists is determined only through the market process in which each producer attempts to carry out his own plan. The individual production plans take shape as non-specific capital (e.g. raw material) is committed to a specific use (e.g. a particular tool or machine); the passage of time and the efforts of each producer to secure the additional capital needed to complete his own production plans reveal the extent to which the capital structure is intertemporally coordinated or discoordinated. The actual availability of some raw material complementary to already-committed capital may be less, for instance, than the amount needed for each producer to carry out his plan. As such discoordination is revealed (by an increase in the price of the raw material), production plans are revised. In Hayek's formulation, the capital goods that make up the production process are neither so specific that such plan revision is impossible nor so non-specific that it is costless.

In his *Pure Theory of Capital* (1941), Hayek provides a detailed treatment of capital goods in terms of reproducibility, durability, specificity, substitutability and complementarity. These multifaceted characteristics of various capital goods and of relationships among them cause the structure of production, taken as a whole, to be characterized by a longer or shorter "period of production," a greater or lesser degree of "roundaboutness." The degree of roundaboutness, the extent to which the production process ties up resources over time, is determined by the market rate of interest—with the "market rate" broadly conceived as the terms of trade between goods available in the present and goods available in the future. The market process works to translate intertemporal preferences into production plans. For instance, a fall in the rate of interest reflecting an increased willingness to forgo present goods for future goods creates incentives for engaging in production processes of greater degrees of roundaboutness. The characteristics, mentioned above, of the individual capital goods and of the relationships among them determine the extent to which the existing capital structure is actually adaptable to changes in intertemporal preferences.

MONEY AND ITS EFFECTS ON PRICES

Hayek's contribution to monetary theory and to trade cycle theory are intertwined, a circumstance that reflects the nature of his contribution in both areas. In summary terms, Hayek's monetary theory consists of integrating the idea of money as a medium of exchange with the idea of the price system as a communication network. His trade-cycle theory consists of integrating monetary theory and capital theory—in which a particular aspect of the price system, namely the system of intertemporal prices, is emphasized.

Both in his *Monetary Theory and the Trade Cycle* (1933) and his *Prices and Production* (1935), Hayek argued against the then-dominant (and still-prevalent) idea that the appropriate focus of monetary theory is on the relationship between the quantity of money and the general level of prices. The kernel of truth in the quantity theory of money was not to be denied, but progress in monetary economics was to be made by moving beyond the simple proportionalities implied by a relatively stable velocity of circulation. According to Hayek (1935, p. 127), the proper task of monetary theory requires a thorough reconsideration of the pure theory of price determination, which is based on the assumption of barter, and a determination of what changes in the conclusions are made necessary by the introduction of indirect exchange.

Hayek introduced the concept of "neutral money" in part as a means to contrast his own view of money with the more aggregative views. By definition, neutral money characterizes a monetary system in which money, while facilitating the coordination of economic activities, is itself never a source of discoordination. According to the aggregative views, money is neutral so long as the value of money (as measured by the general level of prices) remains unchanged. Thus, increases in economic activity require proportionate increases in the quantity of money in circulation. According to Hayek, monetary neutrality requires the absence of "injection effects." When the quantity of money is increased, the new money is injected in some particular way, which temporarily distorts relative prices causing the price system to communicate false information about consumer preferences and resource availabilities.

The contrasting views on the requirements for monetary neutrality had important implications for U.S. monetary policy during the prosperous decade of the 1920s. The rate of monetary growth during that period was roughly equivalent to the rate of real economic growth, a circumstance which resulted in a near-constant price level. The absence of price inflation was taken by most monetary economists to be a sign of monetary stability. Hayek's contrary assessment (1925) that the injection of money through credit markets must result in a misallocation of resources despite the price-level stability was the basis for his prediction that the money-induced boom would eventually lead to a bust.

It should be noted that in other writings, both early and late in his career (e.g. 1933 and 1984), Hayek was ambivalent about the choice between a monetary policy that avoids injection effects (a constant money supply despite a positive real growth rate) and a monetary policy that avoids price deflation (a money growth rate that "accommodates" real growth).

THE TRADE CYCLE AS INTERTEMPORAL DISCOORDINATION

Hayek's contribution to the theory of the trade cycle consists in his developing the idea that monetary injections can have a systematic effect on the intertemporal pattern of prices. The Austrian theory of the trade cycle was first formulated by Mises (1912), who showed that money-induced movements in the interest rate (as identified by Knut Wicksell) have identifiable effects on the capital structure (as conceived by Eugen von Böhm-Bawerk). Hayek's major contribution to the theory (1935), as well as many subsequent developments of it, was based on an extremely stylized portrayal of the economy's time-consuming production process. The relevant characteristics of the "structure of production" were identified with the dimensions of a right triangle. One leg of the triangle represents the time dimension of the structure of production, the degree of roundaboutness; the other leg represents the money value of the consumer goods yielded up by the production process. Slices of the triangle perpendicular to the time leg represent stages of production; the heights of individual slices represent the money value of the yet-to-be-completed production process.

Resources are allocated among the different stages of production as a result of entrepreneurial actions guided by price signals. But because of the distinct temporal dimension of the structure of production, the supplies and demands for resources associated with the different stages are differentially sensitive to changes in the rate of interest: the demand for the output of extraction industries, for example, is more interest-elastic than the demand for the output of service industries. Changes in the rate of interest will have a systematic effect on the pattern of prices that allocates resources among the different stages of production. A fall in the rate of interest, for instance, will strengthen the relatively interest-elastic demands drawing resources into the early stages of production. This modification is represented by a relative lengthening of the temporal dimension of the Hayekian triangle.

A crucial distinction is made between interest-rate changes attributable to changes in the intertemporal preferences of consumers and interest-rate changes attributable to central-bank policy. In the first instance (Hayek, 1935, pp. 49–54), entrepreneurial actions and resulting changes in the pattern of prices allow the structure of production to be modified in accordance with the changed consumer preferences; in the second instance (Hayek, 1935, pp. 54–62), similar changes in the pattern of prices induced by the injecting of new money through credit markets constitute "false signals," which result in a misallocation of resources among the stages of production. The artificially low rate of interest can trigger an unsustainable boom in which too many resources are committed to the early stages of production. The market process triggered by the injection of money through credit markets, Hayek showed, is a self-reversing process. More production projects are initiated than can possibly be completed. Subsequent resource scarcities turn the artificial boom into a bust. Economic recovery must consist of liquidating the "malinvestments" and reallocating resources in accordance with actual intertemporal preferences and resource availabilities.

Hayek (1939) recognized that expectations about future movements in the rate of interest and entrepreneurial interpretations of intertemporal price movements can have an important effect on the course of the trade cycle. That is, prices are signals, not marching orders. But Hayek did not assume, as some modern economists do, that falsified price signals plus "rational" expectations are equivalent to unfalsified price signals. Such an equivalence would require that market participants make use of knowledge of the kind that they cannot plausibly possess; it would require that they have knowledge of the "real" factors independent of the price system that supposedly communicates that knowledge.

CRITIQUE OF KEYNESIANISM

Hayek's critique of Keynesian theory and policy followed directly from his own theories of capital and of money. Hayek argued that by ignoring the intertemporal structure of production and particularly the intertemporal complementarity of the stages of production, Keynes failed to identify the market process that could achieve intertemporal coordination: "Mr Keynes's aggregates conceal the most fundamental mechanisms of change" (Hayek, 1931, p. 227). And by shifting the focus of analysis from money as a medium of exchange to money as a liquid asset, Keynes failed to see the harm caused by policies of injecting newly created money through credit markets or of spending it directly on public projects.

Hayek had emphasized that in functioning as a medium of exchange, money "constitutes a kind of loose joint in a self-equilibrating apparatus of the price mechanism which is bound to impede its working—the more so the greater the play in the loose joint." Keynesian theory and policy were the specific targets of Hayek's criticism when he warned that

> the existence of such a loose joint is no justification for concentrating attention on that loose joint and disregarding the rest of the mechanism, and still less for making the greatest possible use of the short-lived freedom from economic necessity which the existence of this loose joint permits (Hayek, 1941, p. 408).

In the decades that followed the debate between Hayek and Keynes, economic theory was dominated by Keynesianism, and the corresponding macroeconomic policies consisted precisely of those measures that Hayek had warned against: monetary manipulation for political advantage. Monetary injections during the Great Depression, conceived as "pump priming," soon gave way to a more broadly conceived policy of "demand management." The short-run trade-off between inflation and unemployment were treated in the political arena—and in some academic circles—as a societal menu from which elected officials, and hence voters, could choose; deviations of the economy from some conception of full employment or from some long-run growth path were taken as mandates for macroeconomic "fine tuning" to be implemented by the central bank in cooperation with the fiscal authority.

As Hayek clearly recognized in his critique of Keynes's theories and his analysis of the actual effects of Keynesian policies, the political exploitation of the monetary loose joint contains an inherent inflationary bias. Newly created money can be used to hire the unemployed and to finance politically popular spending programmes. Monetary injections through the commercial banking system can stimulate the economy by triggering an artificial economic boom. The undesirable effects of inflating the money supply, the eventual collapse of the artificial boom and the general increase in the level of prices, are removed in time from the initial, politically desirable effects and are less conspicuously identified with the elected officials who engineered the monetary expansion (Hayek, 1960, pp. 324–39). As the political process continues, elected officials face the choice of monetary passivity which would permit the market to undergo the painful adjustments to earlier monetary injections or further monetary injections which would reproduce the desirable effects in the short run while staving-off the eventual adjustment. The cumulative effects of the play-off between political advantage and economic necessity is the theme of Hayek's critique of Keynesianism. Excerpts of "a forty years" running commentary on Keynesianism by Hayek, compiled by Sudha Shenoy, is appropriately entitled *A Tiger by the Tail* (1972).

DENATIONALIZATION OF MONEY

Hayek as a monetary reformer is interested in minimizing the potential for discoordination that is inherent in monetary mechanisms and precluding the manipulation of money for political advantage. He has long doubted that the government has either the will or the ability to manipulate the money supply in the public interest.

In his early writings Hayek took for granted the existence of a central bank and focused his analysis on the consequences of different policy goals, for example, the goal of stimulating economic growth or the goal of stabilizing the general price level. In his later writings, he began to see the monopolization of the money supply as the ultimate cause of monetary disturbances. As early as 1960, though still convinced that modern credit banking as it has developed requires some public institutions such as central banks, [he was] doubtful whether it is necessary or desirable that they (or the government) should have the monopoly of the issue of all kinds of money (1960, p. 520, n.2).

In the mid-1970s Hayek's interest in the denationalization of money (1976) was renewed. Having lost all hope of achieving monetary stability through the instruments of highly politicized monetary institutions, Hayek suggested—by his own account, almost as a "bitter joke"—that the business of issuing money be turned over to private enterprise. Soon taking this suggestion seriously, he began to explore the feasibility and the consequences of competing currencies.

Hayek's proposal for competition in the issue of money is not subject to the standard objection based on the so-called common-pool problem. The proposal is not that private issuers should compete by issuing some generic currency. Clearly, competition on this basis would produce an explosive inflation. The proposal, rather, is that each competitor issue his own trade-marked currency. Under this arrangement, each issuer would have an incentive to maintain a stable value of his own currency and to minimize the difficulties of using this currency in an environment where other currencies are used as well.

In spelling out just how such a system of competing currencies would or could work, Hayek has had to walk the fine line between constructivism on the one hand and blind faith in the market process on the other. His discussions of possible outcomes of the market process should not be taken as prescriptions for the provision of competing currencies, but rather as a basis for believing that competition between private issuers is feasible. Individuals may choose one currency over another on the basis of the issuer's demonstrated ability to achieve purchasing-power stability for that currency. Their choice may be influenced, Hayek has suggested, by what particular price level serves as the issuer's guide for managing the currency. Or it may be that public confidence can be maintained only by a currency that is convertible at a fixed rate into some stipulated commodity or basket of commodities. Hayek does doubt that a gold standard would re-emerge as a result of the competitive process, largely because the confidence and stability of gold was based upon beliefs and attitudes on the part of the public that no longer exist and cannot easily be recreated. But if gold did prevail in a competitive environment, there would be no basis for objection.

More importantly, Hayek's proposal for monetary reform should be seen not as an aberration from but as thoroughly consistent with his view of economics as a spontaneous order. Markets serve to coordinate the activities of individual market participants. The use of money, while greatly facilitating economic coordination, contains an inherent potential for discoordination. Competition in the market for money holds that potential in check and allows market participants to take the fullest advantage of the remaining elements of the spontaneous order.

SELECTED WORKS

1925. (In German.) The monetary policy of the United States after the recovery from the 1920 crisis. In F. A. Hayek, *Money, Capital, and Fluctuations: Early Essays*, ed. R. McCloughry, Chicago: University of Chicago Press, 1984.

1928. (In German.) Intertemporal price equilibrium and movements in the value of money. In F. A. Hayek, *Money, Capital, and Fluctuations: Early Essays*, ed. R. McCloughry, Chicago: University of Chicago Press, 1984.

1931–32. Reflections on the pure theory of money of Mr J. M. Keynes I–II. *Economica*, Pt I, 11, August 1931, 270–95; Pt II, 12, February 1932, 22–44.

1933. (In German.) On "neutral money." In F. A. Hayek, *Money, Capital, and Fluctuations: Early Essays*, ed. R. McCloughry, Chicago: University of Chicago Press, 1984.

1933. *Monetary Theory and the Trade Cycle*. New York: Augustus M. Kelley, 1975.

1935. *Prices and Production*. 2nd edn, New York: Augustus M. Kelley, 1967.

1937. Economics and knowledge. *Economica* NS 4, February, 33–54.

1939. Price expectations, monetary disturbances, and malinvestments. In F. A. Hayek, *Profits, Interest, and Investment*, Clifton, NJ: Augustus M. Kelley, 1975.

1941. *The Pure Theory of Capital*. Chicago: University of Chicago Press.

1945. The use of knowledge in society. *American Economic Review*. 35, September, 519–30. Reprinted in F. A. von Hayek, *Individualism and Economic Order*. London: Routledge & Kegan Paul, 1949.

1949. *Individualism and Economic Order*. London: Routledge & Kegan Paul.

1952. *The Counter-Revolution of Science: Studies on the Abuse of Reason*. Glencoe, Ill.: Free Press.

1960. *The Constitution of Liberty*. Chicago: Henry Regnery & Co., 1972.

1968. Competition as a discovery procedure. In *New Studies in Philosophy, Politics, Economics and the History of Ideas*. Chicago: University of Chicago Press.

1972. *A Tiger by the Tail*. Ed S. Shenoy, London: Institute for Economic Affairs.

1975. *Full Employment at Any Price*. Occasional Paper No. 45, London: Institute of Economic Affairs.

1976. *Denationalization of Money*. London: Institute of Economic Affairs.

1984. The future monetary unit of value. In *Money in Crisis: The Federal Reserve, the Economy, and Monetary Reform*, ed. B. Siegel, Cambridge, Mass.: Ballinger.

BIBLIOGRAPHY

Gray, J. 1984. *Hayek on Liberty.* Oxford: Basil Blackwell.

Hutchison, T. W. 1981. *The Politics and Philosophy of Economics: Marxians, Keynesians, and Austrians.* New York: New York University Press, ch. 7.

Keynes, J. M. 1936. *The General Theory of Employment, Interest, and Money.* New York: Harcourt, Brace.

Machlup, F. 1976. Hayek's contribution to economics. In *Essays on Hayek,* ed. F. Machlup, Hillsdale, Mich.: Hillsdale College Press.

Mises, L. 1912. *The Theory of Money and Credit.* New Haven: Yale University Press, 1953.

O'Driscoll, G. 1977. *Economics as a Coordination Problem: The Contribution of Friedrich A. Hayek.* Kansas City: Sheed, Andrews & McMeel.

LUDWIG M. LACHMANN, 1906–1990 [OBITUARY]

On December 17, 1990, Ludwig M. Lachmann, one of the most important influences in the contemporary revival of Austrian economics, passed away in Johannesburg, South Africa, after a long illness, just weeks short of his eighty-fifth birthday. Ludwig Lachmann spent a long, productive life pursuing the study of the social sciences in general, and of economics in particular, with single-minded dedication, penetrating insight, and utter intellectual honesty.

Born in Berlin in 1906, Lachmann studied in Berlin and Zurich, obtaining the degree of Doctor rerum politicarum from the University of Berlin in 1930. He came to England in 1933, and pursued research under Hayek at the London School of Economics and subsequently at the University of London. A period of service as a faculty member at the University College of Hull was followed by his appointment, in 1949, to the chair of Economics and Economic History at the University of Witwatersrand, Johannesburg, South Africa. In 1972 Lachmann became Professor Emeritus, and spent a substantial part of the subsequent fifteen years (until the spring semester of 1987) as a visiting Research Professor in the Austrian Economics Program at New York University, this having been made possible by far-sighted Moorman Foundation financial support. At a gathering held at New York University celebrating his eightieth birthday in February 1986, Professor Lachmann was presented with a festschrift (*Subjectivism, Intelligibility, and Economic Understanding,* New York University Press, 1986) in which twenty-four scholars from around the world paid him tribute. In the course of more than a full half century of vigorous research activity, Lachmann was author of five books and monographs, and scores of journal articles. (A valuable survey of that work up until 1976 was provided by Walter E. Grinder as the Introduction to Ludwig M. Lachmann [1977] *Capital, Expectations, and the Market Process,* Kansas City: Sheed, Andrews and McMeel.)

From The *Driving Force of the Market: Essays in Austrian Economics* (New York and London: Routledge, 2000), 286–89. Reprinted by permission of the Institute of Humane Studies; the original source is Institute for Humane Studies, *Institute Scholar,* 1991, 10 (2–3): 6–7.

The editor of the *Institute Scholar* has suggested that this obituary dwell more on Professor Lachmann's intellectual contributions than on biographical details. Accordingly, we shall endeavor in what follows to capture (with the desperate brevity required by assigned space constraints) certain central elements in Ludwig Lachmann's rich, lifelong exploration of the social sciences—despite our acute awareness that it is far too early to attempt any full assessment of the emergence, development, and completion of Ludwig Lachmann's work. This writer is abundantly aware of the additional difficulties surrounding this hasty, preliminary statement; his feelings of profound affection and admiration for Ludwig Lachmann, recollecting some thirty years of personal friendship and correspondence, render him a most imperfect judge; to complicate matters even further, this writer had, for twenty out of these thirty years found himself locked in a friendly (but quite insoluble) disagreement with Lachmann on certain fundamental points of economic understanding. It will be for future scholars to provide the full scale, dispassionate historical and critical assessment which the prolific work of Ludwig M. Lachmann so richly deserves and demands.

The central thread running through Lachmann's work is, unquestionably, his radical subjectivism—his conviction that economic understanding calls for recognition, not merely that external events influence human action only as they have been filtered through the human mind, but also that each human mind is active and idiosyncratic in interpreting external events and in thus arriving at what it knows and what it expects. It was this conviction that led him, as early as 1959, to assert that as "soon as we permit time to elapse we must permit knowledge to change, and knowledge cannot be regarded as a function of anything else." In his most recent works, Lachmann pursued the implications of this insight with a consistency undeterred by what some have considered the nihilism toward which he appeared to be gravitating. Lachmann was never one to concern himself with conforming to current intellectual fashions and fads. Even where intellectual honesty led him to question the positions maintained by writers for whom he had enormous regard, he never flinched.

In fact there seems to have occurred a steady deepening, or radicalization, of Lachmann's subjectivism during the last forty years of his life. In 1950, in his inaugural lecture at the University of Witwatersrand, Lachmann was clearly expressing a view of economics largely built upon

Mises (whose recently published *Human Action* he was to review enthusiastically a year later in *Economica*). When, in an act of rare kindness to a lonely young Misesian, Lachmann first wrote to this writer in 1961, he was most explicit in his commitment to "praxeology" and to its Misesian character. Yet, as the years passed, it became clear that for Lachmann the subjectivism of Mises (and even more so, the subjectivism of Hayek) came to seem incomplete. The focus of Lachmann's intellectual attention began to shift from Mises to Shackle. In his letters to me of the 1960s Lachmann had described Shackle as an important writer who should be seen as a potentially valuable ally; but after Shackle's *Epistemics and Economics* (1972) it was clear that Lachmann saw its author as embodying that perfection of subjectivist insight toward which Mises provided only the first approach. (See Ludwig M. Lachmann [1976] "From Mises to Shackle: An Essay," *Journal of Economic Literature*.) The major shortcoming in the Austrian literature, Lachmann maintained, was its failure to extend subjectivism to encompass expectations. It was Shackle's great virtue, in Lachmann's eyes, that, by underscoring the subjectivism of expectations, he decisively unmoored human action from any deterministic constraints imposed by external events.

Despite his differences with the Austrians, it should be emphasized that his enormous personal and professional admiration and respect for both Mises and Hayek were never in question. And it was with the Austrians that Lachmann found the common ground needed to accomplish what he saw as his overriding intellectual and scholarly duty—the nurturing of a younger generation of economists impervious to what he held to be the blight of late twentieth century economics, the distortions wrought by viewing economic phenomena through the spectacles of deterministic, mechanical, general equilibrium models. This he saw as his life's goal. In the 1960s he could have been pardoned for seeing this goal as almost beyond reach. (In a poignant paragraph written to this writer in 1969, Lachmann wrote: "If we two start quarrelling, what becomes of praxeology?") Yet at the time of his death, barely twenty years later, he could (and did!) look with calm satisfaction at the scores of younger Austrian scholars and colleagues in this country and abroad—including especially, Gerald O'Driscoll, Mario Rizzo, Don Lavoie, and Stephan Boehm—whose economic perspective had been profoundly affected by his patient, sparkling teaching and writing. He could point to the revival, in universities around the world, of appreciation for those subtleties in economic understanding which emerge from a recognition of the need to proceed, beyond "subjectivism as the expression of 'human disposition' to subjectivism as a manifestation of spontaneous action."

Ludwig Lachmann was the eternal intellectual optimist. In his voracious and extraordinarily retentive reading, he discovered nuggets of truth in the writings of thinkers with whom he disagreed most vehemently. Out of these, building on the work of his intellectual heroes, Weber, Mises, Hayek, Hicks, and Shackle, Ludwig Lachmann constructed an edifice of economic understanding peculiarly his own. In erecting this edifice and actively nurturing a sympathetic audience for subjectivist economics until only weeks before his passing, Lachmann made his lasting intellectual contribution to the understanding of society and—perhaps in ways in which he did not himself always quite appreciate—to the understanding of how the market society can systematically foster that social coordination upon which human well-being depends.

We have lost a delightful, encyclopedic colleague who told us the truth with white hot passion discreetly clothed in the most elegant old-world courtesy. How we shall miss this stern but beloved teacher, this warm, but ever-honest friend!

FIFTY YEARS OF FEE—FIFTY YEARS OF PROGRESS IN AUSTRIAN ECONOMICS

At this time of FEE's golden jubilee, an Austrian economist's thoughts dwell naturally upon the pivotal role which the Foundation has played in the survival and resurgence of Austrian Economics during the twentieth century. The state of and prospects for Austrian Economics in 1996 are far healthier and more promising than they were fifty years ago. This essay briefly sketches some highlights in the developments that have occurred during these five decades, and draws attention to FEE's important contribution in this regard.

AUSTRIAN ECONOMICS IN 1946

An observer of the intellectual scene in 1946 might have been excused for concluding that the distinguished tradition of Austrian Economics, the tradition that had begun with Carl Menger, Eugen von Böhm-Bawerk, and Friedrich von Wieser, was no longer alive. The Austrian School, which a scarce fifteen years earlier had been perhaps at its peak in professional prestige and had been enjoying widespread attention in the United States and in England, was, by the end of World War II, virtually nonexistent and was thoroughly ignored in the mainstream of the economics profession. History of economic thought textbooks published soon after the war tended to refer to the Austrian School in the past tense. The reason for this is, at a superficial level, not difficult to understand (although the full explanation for the sudden demise of the School would require a detailed study that still awaits its doctoral dissertation). Consider some of the basic facts of the situation:

1. A variety of circumstances (including especially the political unrest in Europe) had, already in the mid-thirties, physically dispersed most of the brightest minds in the interwar Viennese scene. F. A. Hayek had been brought by Lionel Robbins (later Lord Robbins) to London at the beginning of the thirties. Ludwig von Mises had fled to Geneva in

1934; Fritz Machlup, Gottfried Haberler, Oscar Morgenstern, and Paul Rosenstein-Rodan (and, of course, later Mises himself) eventually found their separate ways to the United States. Richard von Strigl had died in Vienna during the war.

2. Mises, who had arrived in New York in 1940, had been cold-shouldered by the U.S. economics profession. Not until 1945 was he able to secure a visiting teaching position at New York University—one hardly commensurate with his international stature. His major work, *Nationalökonomie*, published during the war in Geneva had made virtually no impression—certainly in large part as a result of the place and date of its publication. (The intensely critical tone of Knight's review article in the November 1941 issue of *Economica* cannot have helped, either.) A visiting professorship afforded Mises neither the stimulus nor the opportunity for intellectual influence which had been made possible by his famous *Privatseminar* in Vienna, nor did he have the relaxed, carefree opportunity for teaching and for scholarly work which he had enjoyed in Geneva.

3. Hayek, who had entered the British economics scene with great success in 1931, had, by the outbreak of World War II, seen his professional eminence sharply reduced. In the public perception, at least, he had been decisively defeated by John Maynard Keynes (in regard to business cycle and monetary theory) and by Oskar Lange (in regard to the possibility of efficient socialism). His major recent contribution, *The Pure Theory of Capital* (1941) was, like Mises's 1940 book, virtually ignored by the postwar profession. (A 1948 reference to the work saw it as not much more than a restatement of earlier positions expressed during the 1930s.[1] In any event, the profession was clearly not now interested in those earlier discussions.) Although his 1944 *The Road to Serfdom* was certainly a resounding success, it was (correctly) seen as a primarily political work rather than one in which Hayek was contributing to Austrian Economics. In regard to both Mises and Hayek, the public perceived Austrian Economics in the 1940s as not much more than an unfashionable ideological residue left over from a once vibrant but now defunct intellectual tradition.

4. The scientific methods which Austrian Economics had consistently applied since Menger, were becoming increasingly unfashionable in the profession. Keynesian economics was making its inroads, pushing methodological individualism off center-stage; logical positivism in

philosophy was (with the usual cultural lag) taking a firm hold in economics; advances in the sophistication of mathematical tools used in economics were beginning to threaten the literary tradition. Hayek's brilliant wartime *Economica* articles on method later to be published as *The Counter-Revolution of Science* were early reactions to the shifting tides already being felt in economic methods. But his passionate appeals on behalf of subjectivism and methodological individualism in the social sciences were falling on deaf ears.

5. Paradoxically, a significant element supporting the common impression that the Austrian tradition was no longer alive, was the earlier *success* of that tradition in influencing the British mainstream in economics. A number of Austrians, including Hayek and Machlup (and, to a degree, Mises as well[2]), had come to believe that what was valid and important in Austrian Economics had been successfully absorbed into the mainstream. Robbins's influential 1932 book, *The Nature and Significance of Economic Science*, which is thoroughly steeped in the Austrian perspectives of the late 1920s, was not seen as an attempt to change the substance of British economics. Rather the work was seen (by its author as well as by others) as an attempt to teach British economists that, with relatively minor adjustments in their methodological orientation, they would see that their own economics had for a long time been entirely congruent with the Austrian variety.

This view, that Austrian economics was by now thoroughly integrated into mainstream thinking, undoubtedly helped the sense among younger Austrians that there was no intellectual tragedy to be seen in the physical dispersal of the Vienna group among far-flung British and American universities. Brilliant young Austrian economists, such as Machlup, Morgenstern, and Haberler, felt able to pursue economic research alongside their newfound academic colleagues, without the need to emphasize any uniqueness derived from their Viennese training.

Yet despite all this, Austrian Economics, as we shall see, was certainly *not* dead in 1946. In fact, at that very moment both Mises (in New York) and Hayek (in London) were deepening their own understandings of the economic system in ways, rooted in Austrian insights, that would profoundly influence the subsequent course of the Austrian tradition. Their work would, in the fullness of time, inspire a remarkable resurgence of interest in that very tradition.

THE EXTENSION OF AUSTRIAN SUBJECTIVISM

What was occurring during the 1940s in the works of Mises and Hayek was, it is now apparent in the hindsight of half a century, a most significant extension of Austrian subjectivism. There is a certain drama in the circumstance that, precisely at the time when the Austrian tradition seemed most thoroughly extinct, there were emerging from the pens of Mises and Hayek papers and books that radically deepened the Austrian insights which they had inherited from their intellectual forebears.

To be sure, these advances did not occur in a vacuum. Mises had for many years devoted much thought to the methodological foundations of economics. In 1933 he had published a volume of collected papers as *Grundprobleme der Nationalökonomie* (later to be translated as *Epistemological Problems of Economics*); many of the insights developed in those papers had been welded together to form the basis for the "praxeological" approach Mises explicitly adopted in his 1940 *Nationalökonomie*. Yet his work in developing the latter volume into his magnum opus, *Human Action,* was more than mere translation. Certainly as far as the English-speaking world was concerned, the 1949 book was a major extension of Mises's earlier work.

Hayek's work during the 1940s was also, certainly, rooted in his pioneering contributions of the 1930s involving the role of knowledge and learning in the economic process.[3] Yet it can be argued that his 1948 collection of papers, *Individualism and Economic Order,* offered a fundamentally fresh, integrated approach that had not been placed before the profession until that time. These extensions to Austrian subjectivism by both Mises and Hayek, we now recognize, can plausibly be linked to their experiences during the interwar debate on the possibility of socialist economic calculation.[4] These experiences gradually taught Mises and Hayek that what separated their economics from that of the British/Walrasian neoclassical mainstream was more than language and style. The lessons which these two Austrians respectively learned constituted separate but complementary extensions of the subjectivism which had, already for six decades, characterized Austrian economics.[5]

ACTION AND KNOWLEDGE

Much of Mises's deepened self-awareness is captured in the title of his magisterial work, *Human Action.* Economics was seen and presented as the science of human action—with "action" articulated in a way which sets it decisively apart from the utility- or profit-maximizing decision which forms the analytical building block of mainstream microeconomics. Mises's analysis of action, it can be argued,[6] is unique in its incorporating the *entrepreneurial* element in human choice. This element reflects the open-ended context in which choices are made; that is, it reflects the circumstance that the future consequences of one's actions are never "given" to the prospective agent, but must always be conjectured against a background of absolute uncertainty as described by F. H. Knight. This open-endedness of Misesian economics has subtle but profoundly important implications for one's understanding of the market process. This process now becomes visible, not as a clockwork mechanism grinding out instantaneous solutions to systems of simultaneous equations (made up of the complicated supply and demand functions relevant in a multicommodity universe), but, Mises emphasized, as a process of continually changing entrepreneurial conjectures concerning the open-ended future. In this process, competition plays a role, and is expressed through innovative entrepreneurial entry (and threat of entry).

Mises's science of human action constitutes an extension of Austrian subjectivism in that it sees human action as "choosing," as it were, the very framework within which to engage (simultaneously!) in conventional maximizing decision making. Choices do not merely reflect and express the subjective preferences of the agent among given alternatives; choices reflect also (and, for Mises, more importantly) the agent's subjective judgment concerning the *range* of alternative courses of action in fact available, and concerning the likelihood of their alternative outcomes. It is this additional dimension for subjectivism which definitively shapes the character of the entrepreneurial market process in Mises's perception.

Hayek's contribution to the extension of Austrian subjectivism consisted in his focus upon *knowledge* and its role in the market process. In the course of a remarkable series of papers, culminating in his 1945 *American Economic Review* paper, "The Use of Knowledge in Society," and in his 1946 paper, "The Meaning of Competition," Hayek saw the market process as one of mutual *learning* on the part of market participants. Such learning is required if a disequilibrium set of decisions—i.e., a set of decisions which must to some extent eventually be frustrated because they are based on inadequate mutual awareness—is to be replaced by a better coordinated set of decisions. In focusing on knowledge and learning, Hayek was offering a radically altered view of the market process—a subjectivist view which draws our attention not so much to changing prices or production processes, but rather to the subjective perceptions of market participants concerning the opportunities available to be grasped in the market.

No doubt there are significant differences between the Misesian "entrepreneurial" view of the market process, and the Hayekian focus upon processes of systematic mutual learning. But it seems reasonable to recognize both views as complementary extensions of Austrian sub-jectivism as applied to the understanding of market outcomes. These views emerged, as already mentioned, as a result of painful exposure to mainstream misunderstandings concerning the differences between the socialist economy and the market economy. In the mainstream view there was, at that time at least, virtually no room for entrepreneurial creativity and very little indeed for knowledge and learning. Hence, socialist econo-mists such as Oskar Lange or Abba Lerner might be excused for wildly underestimating the subtlety and complexity with which a market econ-omy spontaneously stimulates entrepreneurial awareness and thus sets in motion the process of systematic, mutual knowledge-enhancement. It was in the course of their being forced to grapple with these mainstream misunderstandings, that Mises and Hayek were led to articulate their respective restatements of the theory of the market process. They not only learned that Austrian Economics had *not* been successfully absorbed into the mainstream, they also learned to appreciate more than they themselves had been hitherto able to do, the full implications of Austrian subjectivism in market theory. This enhanced appreciation deserves to be recognized as a significant advance in Austrian Economics.

POST-1950 DEVELOPMENTS

Despite these important contributions by Mises and Hayek, the extent of research and teaching activity in Austrian Economics in the years immediately after the first half of the century was meager indeed. Mises conducted a seminar (as well as a classroom course) at New York Univer-sity at which he kept the tradition alive. Although the seminar included a number of future leaders in Austrian Economics, including especially Murray Rothbard and Hans Sennholz, it was nonetheless but a pale shadow of Mises's Vienna *Privatseminar*. Both within the university and in the profession generally, Mises was seen as a relic of a bygone era. At best, he and his seemingly archaic views were tolerated; more often he was roughly dismissed as an obscurantist ideologue, out of touch with modern social science techniques and encrusted in unfashionable, rock-ribbed conservatism seen as serving the interests of big business. Although he continued to write a remarkable stream of new books (including particularly *The Ultimate Foundation of Economic Science,* 1962, and *Theory and History,* 1957), Mises's impact upon the profession seemed to be almost invisible.

Hayek had joined the University of Chicago in 1950, not primarily as an economist, but as a member of the interdisciplinary Committee on Social Thought. Indeed his own writing thereafter was to concentrate upon political philosophy rather than upon pure economics. In the world of academic economics, Keynesian doctrines had become the dominant new orthodoxy, with even mainstream neoclassical microeconomics (let alone Austrian Economics) very much on the defensive. Hayek's trade cycle theory of the 1930s seemed to be completely forgotten; his recent new work on knowledge and the economic process was entirely ignored. This writer can (as can many others) attest that Austrian Economics was not rejected or disparaged by the economics profession of the 1950s and '60s; for the profession at that time, Austrian Economics simply did not exist (except, of course, as a chapter in the history of economic thought, to be studied alongside Mercantilism, Classical Economics, or the German Historical School).

At the same time, developments in the mainstream of the profession were pushing and pulling economic thinking in a variety of directions. Important work by the monetarist school was beginning to undermine Keynesian dominance, even as it strengthened the positivist trends toward an economics consisting largely of econometric model building and empirical testing procedures. Advances in mathematical economics were vastly increasing the sophistication of pure theory. These developments were, by the early 1970s, restoring the centrality of neoclassical microeconomic theory, but in a way which seemed, if anything, to widen the gap between that theory and the traditional Austrian approach. These events seemed, moreover, to push economics into two paths: either along a highly abstract theoretical road which appeared to be supremely unconcerned with the real world, concentrating overwhelmingly upon elegance of mathematical technique; or along an empirical road employing powerful econometric techniques to establish functional relationships relating to extremely narrow slices of real world economic history. Both these paths were not just unattractive (to put it mildly) to appreciators of the Austrian tradition; it seems fair now to say with the benefit of hindsight that they drained economics of excitement for subsequent generations of graduate students. Plausibly, all this played a role in laying the ground-work for the resurgence of interest in Austrian Economics that began to manifest itself in the mid-1970s.

THE RESURGENCE OF AUSTRIAN ECONOMICS

The works of Mises and Hayek, although they were indeed ignored dur-ing the 1950s and '60s, had not been written in vain. And the teaching to which Mises dedicated himself for years at New York University, while largely absorbed by graduate business students for whom the study of eco-nomic theory was of distinctly secondary importance, was yet destined to bear fruit. If Mises's contributions were, in those lonely decades, appreci-ated primarily by a handful of stalwart individuals, almost all of whom were not academicians, this was to change, if only gradually. One by one the small number of Mises's U.S. students who obtained their doctorates under his guidance went out into the world to teach and to write. (Some of those inspired in his seminar went on to obtain their degrees at other universities.) And his books, as well as those of Hayek, began to be dis-covered by a small but growing number of students at universities around the country. Farsighted networking, supported by private foundations, was able to identify a number of such individuals thirsting for a more satisfy-ing economics than they were being taught in the classrooms of their own colleges or graduate schools. A good deal of this interest was sparked by growing interest in libertarian thought, to which it was believed Austrian Economics was somehow related. But many of those who discovered Aus-trian Economics in this way were to pursue it subsequently strictly for its own intellectual and scientific worthwhileness, quite apart from any ideo-logical implications that may have been perceived.

The death of Mises in 1973 brought with it a certain amount of atten-tion to his life's work. And, in 1974, all this ferment of activity and interest culminated in a pivotal event, the now-famous South Royalton meeting, at which several lecturers, including especially Ludwig Lach-mann and Murray Rothbard, set forth (in a weeklong series of lectures and discussions) the foundations and main features of a subjectivist way of understanding economics, a way rooted in the work of Carl Menger and articulated in the mid-century contributions of Mises and Hayek.

Following the South Royalton conference (and certainly assisted by the encouragement seen in Hayek's receipt in 1974 of the Nobel award in economics), there ensued years of vigorous growth in the number of graduate students pursuing their doctorates while they were absorbing and exploring further the subtleties of what sets Austrian Economics apart from mainstream economic thinking. By the early 1980s a number of full-fledged faculty members at universities around the country were self-acknowledged "Austrians." Centers of Austrian academic teaching and research crystallized at New York University, George Mason University, Auburn University, and the University of Nevada, Las Vegas. In addition many individual faculty members across the country, in Europe, and around the world met at regularly held summer seminars at which they were introduced to Austrian Economics.

By the mid-1990s the upsurge in interest in Austrian Economics has matured to the point where: (i) very few in the economics profession have not heard, at least, of Austrian Economics; (ii) some of the best publishers of economics books are vigorously competing to publish the steady stream of new Austrian books being written (and indeed the sum total of Austrian work published during the past five years is most impressive in its volume, scope, and quality); (iii) major economics journals, long coldly uninterested in what appeared to them to be an old-fashioned approach, have begun to show a lively interest in publishing Austrian contributions; (iv) a number of professors who were graduate students in the 1980s have since won tenure at universities, based solidly and forthrightly on their scholarly contributions to Austrian Economics. We have every reason to hope that the intellectual momentum of this growth in Austrian Economics will carry it to increased levels of scholarly activity and professional recognition.

FEE'S ROLE IN THE SURVIVAL AND RESURGENCE OF AUSTRIAN ECONOMICS

FEE's identification with Austrian Economics has been unmistakable from its very beginning. The appreciation of how free markets contribute to societal prosperity has been taught by FEE primarily as seen through Austrian lenses. Not only Leonard Read, but in particular farsighted and deeply knowledgeable longtime FEE trustees such as Larry Fertig and Henry Hazlitt, set the intellectual tone for FEE and charted the course of its educational mission. It was their vision which brought Ludwig von

Mises to FEE at a time when he was, to put it mildly, all but ignored on the academic scene. It was through the resources of FEE, its skilled use of the tools of communication and public education, which ensured that Mises's message would survive.

There must be few among today's Austrian academicians who do not look back with profound gratitude for the moral and material support which FEE provided to them, directly or indirectly, in the lonely years prior to the contemporary revival of Austrian Economics. This writer can attest that the very first financial foundation for the New York University doctoral program in Austrian Economics, was laid through the good offices of Leonard Read in the early 1970s. Together with other foundations who have had the vision to support the resurgence in Austrian Economics during recent years, FEE has continued to play a central role. For the past eight years FEE co-sponsored and hosted New York University's annual weeklong summer seminar in Austrian Economics for faculty and graduate students from around the world.

FEE's identification with Austrian Economics has become even more deeply engraved in its philosophy and activities ever since its presidency has been entrusted to the steady hands of Dr. Hans Sennholz, veteran teacher of Austrian Economics to thousands upon thousands of students at Grove City College, ever since his completion of his doctorate under Mises in the 1950s.

If today Austrian Economics has returned to a substantial measure of professional recognition and respect, the Foundation for Economic Education is entitled to a major share of the credit. As we celebrate FEE's anniversary, this element in its half century of achievement, too, deserves our recognition and our appreciation.

NOTES

1. Howard S. Ellis (editor), *A Survey of Contemporary Economics* (Homewood, Illinois: Richard D. Irwin [1948] 1963), volume 1, p. 39.

2. See Ludwig von Mises, *Epistemological Problems of Economics* (Princeton: Van Nostrand, 1960 [translated from the German original, 1933]), p. 214.

3. See especially, "Price Expectations, Monetary Disturbances and Malinvestment" (1935), in F. A. Hayek, *Profits, Interest and Investment* (London: George Routledge, 1939); "Economics and Knowledge," *Economica* IV (new series, 1937), pp. 33–54 (republished in F. A. Hayek, *Individualism and Economic Order* (London: Routledge and Kegan Paul, 1949). For the thesis of continuity in Hayek's work on Knowledge, see Gerald P. O'Driscoll, Jr., *Economics as a Coordination Problem: The Contributions of Friedrich A. Hayek* (Kansas City: Sheed, Andrews & McMeel, 1977).

4. See the writer's "The Economic Calculation Debate: Lessons for Austrians," *Review of Austrian Economics* (1988, vol. 2), republished in Israel M. Kirzner, *The Meaning of Market Process, Essays in the Development of Modern Austrian Economics* (London and New York: Routledge, 1992).

5. For development of this thesis concerning the complementarity between the work of Mises and Hayek, see the writer's *Meaning of Market Process, op. cit.*, chapter 7.

6. For this thesis, see the writer's *Competition and Entrepreneurship* (Chicago: University of Chicago Press, 1973), pp. 32–37.

This term has been introduced frequently into economic discussion, and especially into discussions concerning the history of economic thought. Yet there seems to be a good deal of ambiguity as to what it is to mean. Moreover, there has developed considerable disagreement concerning the centrality of the "harmony" idea to the development of economic thought, and similar disagreement concerning the extent to which the classical economists, in particular, are to be seen as harmony-theorists. We will return a little later to distinguish various different senses that have been attached to the term "harmony" in economics. For each of these different senses, however, acceptance of the harmony thesis has been held to imply a favourable stance toward a policy of laissez-faire. It is thus not surprising that eighteenth-century precursors of the notion of harmony have been discovered in Cantillon and in Quesnay (Schumpeter, 1954, p. 234). And we are not surprised to find some writers emphasizing the harmony ideas they see in the classical economists, especially in Adam Smith (Halévy, 1901–4, p. 89: Heimann, 1945, p. 65), while others vehemently question the unqualified identification of these writers with harmony theories (Robbins, 1952, pp. 22–29; Samuels, 1966, pp. 6–8; Sowell, 1974, pp. 16f). It was in the middle of the nineteenth century that the best-known writings appeared concerning economic harmony. The term appeared in the title of two books by the American economist Henry C. Carey (Carey, 1836, 1852). These works were followed by a general treatise stressing the same theme (Carey, 1858–60). The term also appeared in the title of a book by the French economic writer Frédéric Bastiat (1850). For a (muted) defence of Bastiat against widespread nineteenth-century charges that his work in this respect was a crude plagiarism of Carey, see Teilhac (1936, pp. 100–113), who points to the inspiration that both Carey and Bastiat received from J. B. Say. Subsequent references to harmony theories in economics generally tended to be critical, as economists began to argue (from the latter decades of the nineteenth century into the twentieth century) for greater state intervention in market economies

Reprinted from *The New Palgrave: A Dictionary of Economics*, ed. Peter Newman, Murray Milgate, and John Eatwell, vol. 1 (London, New York, and Tokyo: The Macmillan Press, 1987), 35–38. Reproduced with permission of Palgrave Macmillan.

on perceived grounds of economic efficiency or economic justice. During most of the twentieth century economists, even when they have defended the efficiency and justice of markets, have generally not couched their arguments explicitly in terms of harmony theory. Even Ludwig von Mises who, as we shall see, was an important exception to this last generalization, relegated the notion of harmony to a distinctly subsidiary role in his system. Recent re-awakened attention to eighteenth-century theories of spontaneous order, especially as rediscovered and expanded in the work of Hayek, has not had the effect of reintroducing the term "economic harmony" to current usage. We turn now to take notice of the several different (although certainly interrelated) senses in which this term has been used during the history of economics.

HARMONY AS FLOWING FROM DIVINE PROVIDENCE

A harmony "theory" is not, in this sense, one that flows out of economic science; rather it represents an attitude of (usually religious) optimism and faith, which itself suggests and guides the course of scientific investigation.

> Just as Kepler was inspired by the doctrine of harmony in the spheres to discover the laws which govern the orbits of the planets, so the early economists were inspired by the doctrine that there is a harmony of interests in a society to formulate economic laws (Streeten, 1954, p. 208).

It was from this sense of the term that Lord Robbins vigorously dissociated the classical school. It was this optimistic doctrine that came to be referred to contemptuously by the German term "Harmonielehre." Archbishop Whately, who in 1832 set up a chair of political economy at Trinity College, Dublin, was an influential harmony theorist in this sense. He saw the purpose of the chair as that of combatting the irreligious implications, as he saw them, of Ricardian economics. The early Dublin professors "were under pressure to present an optimistic or harmonious picture of how the market economy operates" and the resulting critical attitude toward Ricardian theory reflected "these extrascientific concerns" (Moss, 1976, p. 153). A variant of this approach to the harmony doctrine was the Enlightenment view, in which Deistic philosophy perceived a natural order as responsible for "predetermined harmony" (Mises, 1949, p. 239; Heimann, 1945, p. 49).

604 THE LEGACY OF AUSTRIAN ECONOMICS

HARMONY THEORY AS THE DOCTRINE
OF MAXIMUM SATISFACTION

When major neoclassical economists such as Marshall (1920, p. 470) and Wicksell (1901, p. 73) referred to harmony theorists, they evidently had in mind those who believed that economic theory demonstrates that free competitive markets generate maximum total satisfaction for society as a whole. "Harmony theory" thus referred to a very specific conclusion of economic science, a conclusion central to welfare economics, but a conclusion whose validity both Marshall and Wicksell were concerned to refute. Of special concern, in this context, was the issue of whether the new marginal utility doctrines had been successfully deployed by Jevons, or by Walras, to arrive at "harmony" conclusions similar to those that had been reached, on other grounds, by Bastiat.

Parallel to this sense of harmony was that which attributed *ethical* virtues to the distributive results of competitive markets. Thus J. B. Clark's demonstration of the justice of marginal-productivity incomes is seen as "harmony doctrine" (Myrdal, 1932, p. 148).

HARMONY DOCTRINE AS THE DENIAL OF CLASS CONFLICT

One sense in which harmony doctrines have been understood throughout the history of economics is that in which it is sought to demonstrate the mutual compatibility of the interests of the various individuals and groups in society. In particular, such doctrines tend to dismiss the notion of inherent class conflict under capitalism. A twentieth-century economist who has himself emphasized this idea of harmony of interests in the market society, put the genesis of this idea as follows:

> When the classical economists [asserted "the theorem of the harmony of the rightly understood interests of all members of the market society" they were stressing] two points: First, that everybody is interested in the preservation of the social division of labour, the system that multiplies the productivity of human efforts. Second, that in the market society consumers' demand ultimately directs all production activities (Mises, 1949, p. 674).

Mises, indeed, saw these ideas as important results of economic science, having wide application. "There is no conflict between the interests of the buyers and those of the sellers, between the interest of the producers and those of the consumers" (Mises, 1949, p. 357). Only in the special case of resource monopoly ownership may it happen that the "emergence of monopoly prices . . . creates a discrepancy between the interests of the monopolist and those of the consumers" (Mises, 1949, p. 680).

HARMONY AND THE SPONTANEOUS ORDER TRADITION

Since the early 1940s F. A. Hayek has succeeded in drawing the attention of economists and others to a line of social analysis since the eighteenth century, an approach often termed the "spontaneous order tradition." The emphasis, in this tradition, is on the evolution of institutions and social outcomes "which are indeed the results of human action, but not the execution of any human design" (Ferguson, 1767, p. 187, cited in Hayek, 1967, p. 96). There is no doubt that the term "economic harmony" has often been applied as an expression of belief in the *possibility and social benignity of undesigned social outcomes*. To some extent, of course, this sense of the term overlaps those listed above, but the emphasis here is not in the denial of conflict, not on any particular welfare theorem, certainly not on any religiously based optimism, but on the counter-intuitive possibility of orderly results emerging without deliberate design from the spontaneous interplay of independently acting individuals. "Order" in this context has come to mean "mutually reinforcing expectations." The following reference to this notion of harmony expresses this usage of the term:

> The great general rule governing human action at the beginning, namely that it must conform to fair expectations, is still the scientific rule. All the forms of conduct complying with this rule are consistent with each other and become the recognized customs. The body of custom therefore tends to become a harmonious system (Carter 1907, p. 331, cited in Hayek, 1973, p. 169).

The above survey has been confined to notions of economic harmony believed to be achieved spontaneously, "naturally," without design. For the sake of completeness it should perhaps be noted that the term "harmony" has occasionally been used to describe the objective of *deliberate* social policy. Thus a well-known debate was initiated by E. Halévy in his claim that Bentham and the philosophical Radicals subscribed to two partly contradictory principles: the "economic" principle of "natural identity" (i.e. harmony) of interests, and the "juristic" principle of the "artificial identification of interests" (Halévy, 1901–4, pp. 15, 17, 489). Lord Robbins, in disputing Halévy concerning any contradiction in the Benthamite position, refers to the juristic principle as contending it to be "the function of the legislator to bring about an artificial harmonization of interest" (Robbins, 1952, pp. 190f). While occasional references may be found to harmony sought to be artificially accomplished, the term has, in general, been associated almost invariably with harmony achieved undeliberately in a decentralized system.

BIBLIOGRAPHY

Bastiat, F. 1850. *Les harmonies économiques*. Paris: Guillaumin.

Carey, H. C. 1836. *The Harmony of Nature*. Philadelphia: Carey, Lea & Blanchard.

Carey, H. C. 1852. *The Harmony of Interests, Agricultural, Manufacturing, and Commercial*. 2nd edn, New York: Myron Finch.

Carey, H. C. 1858–60. *Principles of Social Science*. Philadelphia: J. B. Lippincott.

Carter, J. C. 1907. *Law, Its Origin, Growth and Function*. New York and London: G. P. Putnam's Sons.

Ferguson, A. 1767. *An Essay on the History of Civil Society*. London.

Halévy, E. 1901–4. *The Growth of Philosophic Radicalism*. Translated from the French by M. Morris, 1928, Boston: Beacon, 1955.

Hayek, F. A. 1967. *Studies in Philosophy, Politics and Economics*. Chicago: University of Chicago Press.

Hayek, F. A. 1973. *Law, Legislation and Liberty*. Vol. I: *Rules and Order*, Chicago: University of Chicago Press.

Heimann, E. 1945. *History of Economic Doctrines, An Introduction to Economic Theory*. New York: Oxford University Press.

Marshall, A. 1920. *Principles of Economics*. 8th edn, London: Macmillan, 1936.

Mises, L. von. 1949. *Human Action: A Treatise on Economics*. 3rd edn, Chicago: Regnery, 1966.

Moss, L. S. 1976. *Mountifort Longfield: Ireland's First Professor of Political Economy*. Ottowa, Ill.: Green Hill.

Myrdal, G. 1932. *The Political Element in the Development of Economic Theory*. Translated from the German by P. Streeten, Cambridge, Mass.: Harvard University Press, 1954.

Robbins, L. 1952. *The Theory of Economic Policy in English Classical Political Economy*. London: Macmillan, 1965.

Samuels, W. J. 1966. *The Classical Theory of Economic Policy*. Cleveland and New York: World.

Schumpeter, J. A. 1954. *History of Economic Analysis*. New York: Oxford University Press.

Sowell, T. 1974. *Classical Economics Reconsidered*. Princeton: Princeton University Press.

Streeten, P. 1954. Recent controversies. Appendix to Myrdal (1932).

Teilhac, E. 1936. *Pioneers of American Economic Thought in the Nineteenth Century.* Translated from the French by E. A. J. Johnson (1936), reprinted, New York: Russell and Russell, 1967.

Wicksell, K. 1901. *Lectures on Political Economy.* Vol. I, Translated from the Swedish by E. Classen, London: Routledge and Kegan Paul, 1934.

AUSTRIAN ECONOMICS AND MAINSTREAM
ECONOMICS, 1930–1950
A STUDY IN DOCTRINAL COMPLEMENTARITY
AND SUBSTITUTABILITY

It is well known that, among contemporary Austrian economists, a certain tension is present between (a) those who see Austrian Economics as almost wholly incompatible with and distinct from the dominant ideas of mainstream neoclassical microeconomics, and (b) those who, while critical of many of the central perspectives of neoclassical theory, still believe that significant elements of that theory can be salvaged by infusing them with the understanding provided by Austrian theory. The former group of Austrian economists has charged that the approach of the latter group merely "incorporate[s] Austrian insights within the context of the larger neoclassical paradigm."[1]

The purpose of this paper is to throw some light on this issue by surveying the historical interaction between the mainstream and the Austrians.

Marshallian economics, Walrasian economics, and Austrian economics developed side by side from the 1870s onward; by about 1930 it seemed as if their doctrines were, as in Mises's words of 1932, "divided more by their terminology and by peculiarities of presentation than by the substance of their teachings."[2] As the international communication of ideas expanded from the 1890s to the 1930s, Austrians had come to be seen by mainstream economists (and also by themselves) as merely one among several parallel streams of "modern" economic thought. Yet

This paper draws on ideas (and incorporates several whole sentences) from earlier works by the author, especially his "Introduction" to each of the three volumes of *Classics in Austrian Economics: A Sampling in the History of a Tradition*, which he edited (London: Pickering, 1994).

Reprinted from K. Leube, A. M. Petroni, and J. Sadowsky, eds., *An Austrian in France, Festschrift in Honour of Jacques Garello* (Torino: La Rosa Editrice, 1997), 190–202.

1. Karen I. Vaughn, *Austrian Economics in America: The Migration of a Tradition* (Cambridge: Cambridge University Press, 1994), pp. 140–41.

2. Ludwig von Mises, *Grundprobleme der Nationalökonomie* (1933), as translated in *Epistemological Problems of Economics* (Princeton, NJ: Van Nostrand, 1960), p. 214.

subsequent doctrinal developments, both in the mainstream (Marshallian, or Anglo-American) tradition, and within the Austrian School, after the 1930s, were soon to signal very fundamental differences between the economics of these two schools. There was drastic transition from a mainstream perception of Austrian economics as being one version of a commonly accepted (although variously expounded) set of economic understandings—to one which saw it as an outlying, somewhat idiosyncratic set of doctrines, largely in conflict with mainstream economics. This was paralleled, on the Austrian side, by a gradual realisation that mainstream equilibrium theory raised serious logical difficulties which their own insights escaped. The 1932 statement by Mises was one with which a mainstream economist might at that time readily agree. By the time Mises published *Human Action,* less than two decades later, he and that same hypothetical mainstream of economists would most likely still agree—but this time only to an assertion of irreconcilable differences in economic doctrine. It is this puzzling change which we will try to understand in this paper. What we wish to grasp, then, is not so much the precipitous decline in the international professional standing of the Austrian School which occurred during the 1930s.[3] We wish, more importantly, to understand the equally swift change in perception, which occurred between 1930 and 1950, both among Austrian economists and among mainstream economists, regarding the mutual compatibility of their respective systems of (micro)economic theory.

THE SCENE AROUND 1930: A SIMPLIFIED
SKETCH OF MAINSTREAM PERCEPTIONS

The mainstream we have in mind here is, of course, the British economic establishment. England was still (certainly in England!) seen as the intellectual centre of gravity of the economics profession. Continental influences—in particular Walrasian and Austrian ideas—were seen as possibly interesting, but certainly peripheral. These ideas were not seen as in any way threatening to dislodge the rather comfortable set of

---

3. On this, see Mark Blaug, "Commentary" [on S. Boehm, "Austrian Economics Between the Wars: Some Historiographical Problems"], in Bruce J. Caldwell and S. Boehm (eds), *Austrian Economics: Tensions and New Directions* (Boston/Dordrecht/London: Kluwer Academic Publishers, 1992), pp. 31–34.

doctrines making up the core of dominant Marshallian economics. Both for Marshall and for Edwin Cannan, these mainstream doctrines constituted a framework within which Continental emphasis on marginal utility could easily be incorporated, without radically modifying their vision of economics as essentially concerned, in almost classical fashion, with wealth, or, at least, with the material side of human well-being.

From this British mainstream perspective, the bitterness of earlier debates, both on the Continent and in England, concerning methodology (and in particular concerning the relative importance of abstract-theoretical vis-à-vis concrete-historical considerations) was seen as unfortunate and really unnecessary. Marshall had been careful to pay tribute to the German Historical School and its research. Yet the core of his own work, while presented largely in the *context* of economic history, was certainly theoretical. The British view was thus dominated by a methodological eclecticism (à la John Neville Keynes) and could treat the apparent fading of the German Historical School after World War I with equanimity. There was little in the substantive doctrines of, say, Friedrich Wieser, the Austrian founder who lived the longest (he died in 1926), and the one with perhaps least antagonism to the doctrines of the Historical School, with which a Marshallian need disagree.

Although Marshallian economics did revolve around the notion of equilibrium, this notion was never presented in as stark or uncompromising fashion as was characteristic of Walrasian economics. As is well known, Marshall offered a picture of the economic process that ran, not in terms of precisely attained equilibrium solutions to systems of simultaneous equations, but rather in terms of tendencies and equilibrating forces. As J. M. Keynes once put it, "Marshall knits in wool." In Marshall's economics profession, as Frank Machovec has shown, its "geocentre was still anchored in a process perspective of competition"[4]—not in Knightian perfectly competitive equilibrium models. For a Marshallian, the Austrian discussions of the way in which market competition generates market values, must not have appeared fundamentally uncongenial, even if these discussions used more words and fewer diagrams than the British were perhaps accustomed to.

---

4. Frank M. Machovec, *Perfect Competition and the Transformation of Economics* (London and New York: Routledge, 1995), p. 245.

In brief, a Marshallian economist of around 1930 would indeed see the Austrian economics of the Twenties as basically in agreement with his own microeconomics. He might quibble at what appeared to him to be Austrian overemphasis on the demand side of the supply-demand interactive process. He might note different expository techniques adopted by the Austrians. But he would be unlikely to disagree fundamentally with Mises's 1932 statement, perceiving an underlying common ground of economic understanding for both the Austrians and the British.

THE SCENE AROUND 1930: THE VIEW FROM VIENNA

From the Austrian side, too, the content of the doctrinal core of British mainstream economics did not seem to offer a clear excuse for fundamental disagreement. When Lionel Robbins set out, in his enormously influential 1932 book, *The Nature and Significance of Economic Science,* to introduce British economists to Continental, particularly Austrian, ideas, he did not see himself as calling for the abandonment of Marshallian economics. Most of Marshall's or Cannan's economics could be *appreciated* in a new and more satisfying light, once one makes explicit such subjectivist, Austrian tenets such as the defining centrality of allocative, economising choice, the inescapability of opportunity cost, the utterly individualistic nature of human well-being. But this importation of Austrian ideas into the British mainstream did not constitute a clash of inconsistent substantive economic doctrines. Robbins, in offering Austrian insights to British readers, saw himself as simply stating clearly what was already implicit in British economics. "I venture to hope that in one or two instances I have succeeded in giving expository force to certain principles not always clearly stated. But, in the main, my object has been to state, as simply as I could, propositions which are the common property of most modern economics."[5]

It is undoubtedly true that the Austrians of the 1920s saw themselves as proceeding from a different point of departure than were the British mainstream theorists. Fritz Machlup, one of the brilliant young Austrian economists of that decade, was later to spell out what he saw as

5. Lionel C. Robbins, *The Nature and Significance of Economic Science* [1932] second edition (London: Macmillan, 1935), p. xv; this statement appeared in the Preface to the first edition (1932).

the identifying features of Austrian economics. There is reason to believe that in so doing he was identifying the Austrian economics in which he had been trained in the Twenties. Machlup's list was as follows: (i) *methodological individualism*: the view that in seeking "the explanation of economic phenomena we have to go back to the action (or inaction) of individuals"; (ii) *methodological subjectivism*: in "the explanation of economic phenomena we have to go back to the judgments and choices made by individuals on the basis of whatever knowledge they have or believe to have and whatever expectations they entertain . . ."; (iii) *tastes and preferences*: demand is determined by subjective valuations of goods and services; (iv) *opportunity costs*: the true character of economic costs is that they reflect the alternative opportunities that must be foregone; (v) *marginalism*; (vi) *time structure of production*.[6]

Clearly Machlup believed that Marshallian economics did not take these insights as *its* point of departure. But it is also clear (as Robbins had claimed) that the exposition of Marshallian economics could easily be modified so as to incorporate each of these Austrian insights. To be a good Austrian one need not reject the substance of Marshallian theory.

Moreover, a careful scanning of Machlup's list (which, as mentioned, we believe correctly to represent the Austrian views as held in the 1920s) will reveal two striking omissions in this Austrian view. Nowhere does Machlup draw attention to any Austrian emphasis on the dynamically competitive *market process* (as against, say, the fulfillment of the conditions needed to sustain a state of perfectly competitive equilibrium). Nor does Machlup draw attention to any Austrian recognition that economic choices are made in an open-ended context of Knightian uncertainty (in which the determination of the relevant parameters of constraints and preferences is itself an integral part of the act of choice). These omissions are not accidental; they demonstrate that, for an Austrian trained in the Twenties these two latter central features of (later) Misesian economics were not at all integral to their training (or, at the very least, to the uniqueness of that training). For Machlup and his colleagues in Mises's Vienna Private

6. See Fritz Machlup, "Ludwig von Mises: the Academic Scholar who would not Compromise," *Wirtschaftpolitischen Blätter*, 4 (1981); and also his article, "Austrian Economics," in D. Greenwald (ed.), *Encyclopedia of Economics* (New York: McGraw-Hill, 1982).

seminar of the 1920s, these latter two insights (the need for economic understanding capable of focusing upon market processes as these unfold in a world of Knightian uncertainty) were either not recognized as important at all, or, at any rate, not recognized as being any more characteristic of Austrian economics than of other schools of modern economic thought. (It was apparently not until Hans Mayer's 1932 monograph-length paper, translated as "The Cognitive Value of Functional Theories of Price,"[7] that we find explicit dissociation from the "functionalism" of an equilibrium economics which left no room for market processes set in motion by acting human beings—as against "decision-making" by robots programmed to maximise given objective functions subject to given sets of constraints.) Indeed it is probably fair to say that for younger Vienna economists in the Twenties, such as Hayek and Machlup, little thought had as yet been given to any of the difficulties with equilibrium theorising which later Austrian economics was, particularly in the 1940s, to identify.

Perhaps the most important element which led Mises to make his statement of 1932, was the awareness that the once all-powerful German Historical School had been decisively defeated in the intellectual battlefield of twentieth century economics. For Austrians who, like Mises, could vividly remember the pre–World War I disdain with which the Historical School had treated the Austrians, the awareness that in the new postwar economics profession it was the Historical School that had been swept completely from the centre stage of professional attention, was more than simply a pleasing awareness of a doctrinal victory achieved. It was, in addition, the discovery of powerful allies in the struggle against *historismus*; and this discovery made it appear, indeed, that in regard to the really important theoretical issues, all these allies were speaking, more or less, with the same voice.

THE NINETEEN-THIRTIES: THE
UNRAVELLING OF PERCEIVED CONSENSUS

It was primarily during the 1930s that both the British mainstream and the leading Austrian economists began to realise that they were no longer speaking (if indeed they had ever spoken) with the same voice. The bitter

7. This recent translation is included in Israel M. Kirzner (ed.), *Classics in Austrian Economics* (op. cit.), volume II, pp. 55–168.

debates on monetary and cycle theory in which Hayek had been engaged in the early Thirties with Sraffa and with Keynes formed a fitting background against which developments both in mainstream neoclassicism and in Austrian economic thought, were to shatter the illusion of general consensus among British and Austrian economists. Two developments in particular seem to have played crucial roles in destroying the illusion of unanimity. One development was the increased mainstream preoccupation with equilibrium conditions as the result (i) of the infusion of Walrasian general equilibrium theory into the mainstream, and (ii) increased self-awareness in regard to the model of perfect competition. The second development was the debate concerning the possibility of socialist economic calculation. The first development decisively diverted mainstream microeconomics from a still *possible* process-character, toward the strictly equilibrium-always character which it has maintained throughout the century. The second development clarified for both Mises and Hayek the insight that for their economics it was necessary to focus upon the way in which interacting market decisions themselves systematically *change* the prices which occur in markets *not* yet at or near equilibrium.

The first development, the headlong rush into strictly equilibrium theorising, was seen by mainstream economists as simply a result of their more carefully and rigorously pursuing their existing paradigm. The infusion of Walrasian, and, in particular, mathematical, economics, necessarily focused upon the state of affairs marked out by the solution to the relevant sets of simultaneous equations. Whether in the form of Walrasian general equilibrium theory, or in the form of rigorously worked solutions of Marshallian supply-demand situations, the "answer" to any question concerning markets came to be seen as provided by the relevant equilibrium situations. The formalization of the model of perfect competition reinforced this way of seeing the world (although it was not until Hayek's 1946 paper, "The Meaning of Competition,"[8] that the necessarily equilibrium character of the state of perfect competition was explicitly pointed out.) Somewhat paradoxically, it seems that it was the very challenge to the perfectly competitive model offered by the (separate) theories of imperfect and monopolistic competition of Joan Robinson

---

8. In Friedrich A. Hayek, *Individualism and Economic Order* (London: Routledge and Kegan Paul, 1949).

and Edward Chamberlin which appears to have made the economics profession most familiar with the perfectly competitive model.[9] By the end of the Thirties, the centrality of Knight's set of necessary conditions for perfect competition[10] had become firmly implanted in mainstream textbooks (and had, in addition, generated the Chicago School's insistence that no consideration of imperfection in competition need disturb the economic theorist).[11] It was this crystallisation of mainstream preoccupation with equilibrium states, and its consequent view that economic understanding requires that we see the world as at each moment having *already* attained the relevant equilibrium state, which played a central role in the realisation by Austrians that their economics was *not* telling the same story as mainstream economics.

That this was indeed the case was, it can be argued,[12] brought home to Mises and Hayek by the second of the two developments mentioned earlier (viz. their participation in the debate concerning the possibility of socialist economic calculation). It was in the course of their participation in this important interwar debate that it became apparent to both Mises and Hayek that a large part of the misunderstanding by opponents (in particular by Oskar Lange[13]) of the Misesian assertion that a socialist planning authority could not simulate the results of the market economy, was due to a failure to understand adequately how the market economy in fact works. The defenders of the possibility of socialist economic calculation were devising ingenious ways of simulating the price conditions fulfilled under market equilibrium conditions—as if indeed the market works by being, virtually all the time, in fulfillment of the conditions for perfectly competitive equilibrium. Certainly it was this realisation which

9. On this, see Shorey Peterson, "Antitrust Policy and the Classic Model," *American Economic Review* (March, 1957); Frank M. Machovec, *Perfect Competition and the Transformation of Economics* (op. cit.).

10. As developed in Frank H. Knight, *Risk, Uncertainty and Profit* (Boston: Houghton and Mifflin, 1921), part 2.

11. For an example, see George J. Stigler, *The Theory of Competitive Price* (1942).

12. On this, see the writer's "The Economic Calculation Debate: Lessons for Austrians," in his *The Meaning of Market Process: Essays in the Development of Modern Austrian Economics* (London and New York: Routledge, 1992), ch. 6.

13. See Oskar Lange, "On the Economic Theory of Socialism," in B. E. Lippincott (ed.), *On the Economic Theory of Socialism* (New York: McGraw-Hill, 1964); Lange's paper was originally published in 1936.

led Hayek to his important series of papers concerning the role of knowledge in market processes, and his exposition of the market process as one of mutual learning on the part of market participants (as opposed to a view of the mainstream "competitive" market as necessarily reflecting an *already-attained* state of complete mutual knowledge) and it seems similarly reasonable to explain the dynamic, entrepreneurial character of the Misesian system presented in his *Human Action* (of 1949, it being a translation and revision of Mises's German-language 1940 *Nationalökonomie*), as expressing Mises's similar reaction to mainstream preoccupation with states of equilibrium.

THE SCENE AROUND 1950

By 1950 the sharp divergence of Austrian Economics from the mainstream was abundantly apparent to the Austrians. For mainstream economists it was similarly apparent (to the extent that they paid no attention at all to the work of Mises and Hayek) that a gulf separated Austrian economics from that of the mainstream textbooks. From the mainstream perspective the Austrian expositions of markets seems to have been seen not so much as representing an alternative paradigm to that of the mainstream, but rather as reflecting a non-rigorous, outdated understanding of markets, one not yet attuned to the rigorous mathematics of modern equilibrium economics. To be an economic theorist, it appeared through mainstream spectacles, one had to acquire the knack of seeing beyond the seemingly chaotic series of mutually frustrating actions by real world market participants, and focusing instead upon that pattern of prices and quantities which would, given the underlying patterns of preferences and resource availabilities, be mutually sustaining. To be an applied economic theorist, this view maintained, one must subscribe to the proposition that, whether we understand how this has happened or not, and in spite of how business people themselves perceive their own situations at any given time, the prices and quantities we observe in the real world market do, as a matter of empirical fact, correspond to such equilibrium patterns. To pay central attention to entrepreneurial decisions aimed at grasping profitable opportunities (that is, to pay attention to what are surely the central features of the business world) is, from this perspective, to display an old-fashioned lack of sophistication in economic understanding, a regrettable unfamiliarity with the progress made in modern economic analysis.

By 1950 the term "Austrian" was, indeed, hardly used to refer to any on-going, live tradition in economic thought. What one means, in talking of the Austrian perspective around 1950, is the work of Mises and of Hayek. In one sense an Austrian "school" of economic thought no longer existed at all. Hayek, who moved to the University of Chicago at that time, was to devote almost all of his subsequent (vast) scholarly work to such areas as political philosophy. Mises was a lonely voice during the Fifties, a scholar already in his eighth decade, with very narrow academic influence, generally dismissed within the economic profession as an aged rock-ribbed ideologue surviving from an earlier, rather primitive era in economic thought. For Mises, again, the economics profession had, particularly in regard to microeconomics, simply taken a wrong turning, so that currently trained economists were well-versed in mathematical and econometric techniques which, however, had little to do with the way in which markets in fact work.

Two exceedingly important works, respectively by Mises and by Hayek had, despite all the above, been published in the years just prior to 1950. Mises's magisterial *Human Action* (1949) represented a remarkably complete and clear statement of the Austrian view (including his view of the market process as one of entrepreneurial pure-profit-inspired decision-making) as he saw it after over four decades of economic research in both economic theory and economic policy. In no way could this book be seen as fitting comfortably in the mainstream of mid-century economics. The work was, in the fullness of time, to inspire a new generation of younger scholars to seek economic understanding along lines not available in mainstream programmes of graduate training in economic theory, nor in the related textbooks. This book would inspire them to rediscover the insights and relevance of Carl Menger, and to recognize their own new Mises-inspired economics as simply the further development of a century-old tradition of Austrian economics that had begun with Menger.

At the same time this subsequent rediscovery of the Austrian tradition would also owe a major debt to the second book published just prior to 1950, Hayek's *Individualism and Economic Order* (1949). Hayek's book contains his seminal papers on knowledge, dynamic competition, and the theory of socialism. These very important papers spelled out Hayek's developing insights (which, we have argued above, emerged in response to mainstream arguments in the course of the socialist economic calculation debate) into the market process as one of mutual learning. Precisely in the years when the Austrian tradition seemed to have expired, Mises and Hayek were publishing books which advanced the teachings of that tradition in a way that would eventually become very influential indeed.

A bit of personal history on the part of this writer may be in order here. My own training as an economist began in the mid-fifties when I attended the lectures and seminars of Ludwig von Mises and, at the same time, lectures given by other economists on orthodox, mainstream price theory. The gulf between these two sets of lectures was obvious. It was to take me many years and much intellectual perspiration before I would be able to satisfy myself that I thoroughly understood the relationship between the two paradigms to which I was simultaneously (and confusingly!) subjected. The source of the difficulty was that *both* the Misesian theory of market price and the mainstream theory were derived from that *same* set of broadly defined neoclassical economic doctrines of around 1930 to which both the Austrians and the British mainstream subscribed. What had in 1930 appeared as a common set of economic understandings had, a quarter of a century later, evolved into entirely inconsistent sets of ideas—or so it seemed on the surface.

AUSTRIAN AND MAINSTREAM MICROECONOMICS: COMPLEMENTARITY AND SUBSTITUTABILITY

My own efforts at that time to understand for myself what had happened, led me to explore, in the work of earlier neoclassical economists, for clues to how they might rationalise the importance attached to equilibrium positions. What hypothetical processes (other than such artificial constructs as Walrasian tatonnement processes) might lead us to believe in the plausibility and real-world relevance of such modelled positions? Writers such as Wicksteed, Lindahl, Hayek and Arrow had, at least, to some extent grappled with this problem. It was Hayek's ideas on the competitive process as one of mutual learning which led me to appreciate Mises's entrepreneurial market process as one of continual mutual discovery. While in his earlier work Mises had not articulated this understanding of the market, there is also no reason to believe that he saw himself, in *Human Action,* as offering anything else but a careful exposition of the general perspective which he had already maintained for decades. Whatever the major (earlier) neoclassical economists may have had in mind as being responsible for the equilibrative character of markets in which they clearly believed, it appears that Mises (in his 1932 statement cited earlier) had been prepared to recognise their economics as being, at bottom, entirely consistent with his own understanding of it as an entrepreneurial discovery process.

The central features of mainstream neoclassical economics which Mises, in 1932, found so compatible with his own Austrian understanding were, it seems obvious, the general idea that market prices are the systematic outcomes of forces generated by the interplay of the conditions of supply and demand (that is, of the decisions being made by potential consumers and potential producers), and the related insight that these market prices play a crucial role in guiding individual market participants to make decisions which, taken together, result in the coherency which we observe in market economies. It was these ideas which Mises saw as the common property of all "modern" schools of economic thought, epitomising their rejection of what had been the German Historical School.

It seems abundantly clear that these unifying general ideas were indeed capable of generating two distinct lines of development: the mainstream development toward its mid-century preoccupation with equilibrium positions, and the Mises–Hayek development toward an Austrian understanding of markets as processes of entrepreneurial discovery.

It is not inconceivable that further rigorous development of the ideas of Mises, Shackle, or Lachmann, on decision-making under radical uncertainty, may lead Austrians, at some time in the future, to be skeptical concerning the validity of what we have called the above unifying general ideas. Such a conceivable (although, to this writer, implausible) doctrinal development would certainly wipe away any complementarity between Austrian and mainstream economics. On the other hand, however, demonstration of the fundamentality of these general ideas for Mises's own economics certainly does *not* shrink that economics to merely adding selected insights to be incorporated into the larger corpus of late-twentieth century neoclassical economics. To provide a background for the case on behalf of this latter negative proposition, has been the purpose of this very brief paper.

THE USE OF LABELS IN DOCTRINAL HISTORY: COMMENT ON BAIRD

In his lively and provocative paper, Charles Baird seeks to establish that "the economics of James Buchanan has much in common with modern Austrian economics." I am prepared to agree that Baird has succeeded— almost completely—in proving the validity of his claim. Although one may wish to quibble on matters of detail, there can be little doubt that Baird has learnedly and skillfully demonstrated that Buchanan shares many if not all of the fundamental economic insights generally held to be characteristic of the contemporary Austrian revival. Some questions, however, do remain, especially those pertaining to Baird's section on political economy. In particular, is there really an "Austrian position" on the appropriate constitution for government? And are Hayek's and Buchanan's views on this question part of their economics?

Beyond congratulating Baird on his sensitive and insightful survey of Austrian ideas, the reader must surely be inclined to wonder what the author wishes us to conclude from the demonstrated validity of his claim. Is it intended that one's judgment on who are the modern Austrians be revised to include so eminent a scholar as Buchanan? Or is it rather intended that card-carrying Austrians be persuaded to dissolve what others have seen as an overly self-conscious "priesthood," and even to discontinue using the label "Austrian," (since what was held to be characteristically Austrian has been shown now to be part of the well-understood doctrinal equipment of a prominent non-Austrian)?

At the very least Baird's paper is to be appreciated as a provocation to reconsider the use of traditional labels in doctrinal history. This issue is by no means a new one for Austrian economics. About a half-century ago, Austrians such as Mises, Hayek, and Machlup all maintained that important Austrian insights had been successfully absorbed into the mainstream by the early 1930s, suggesting that a continued separate identity for Austrian economics was no longer required. Nevertheless, Mises and Hayek decisively distanced themselves from such a suggestion, while

From *Cato Journal*, vol. 9, no. 1 (Spring/Summer 1989): 231–35. Cato Institute. Reprinted by permission.

Machlup emphatically affirmed it to the end of his life.[1] What Baird has now done is to force present-day Austrians to reconsider, in the light of the economics of 1989, the legitimacy and expediency of their self-assumed doctrinal label.

THE USES OF DOCTRINAL LABELS

There seem to be several separate justifications for the use of doctrinal labels. First, such labels may have value in terms of the history of ideas. The history of economic thought *has* singled out an Austrian tradition. History does have its claims, and one cannot appreciate the work of Mises, say, without recognizing the provenance of his thought in the Menger–Böhm-Bawerk tradition within which he was trained. Perhaps, then, Baird is suggesting that this history-of-ideas basis for the Austrian label no longer pertains, since what was distinctive in that tradition has now been absorbed into the profession at large. Second, doctrinal labels may have strategic or semantic value in accentuating the uniqueness of a set of scientific insights, in arousing professional interest in them, or in identifying them in easily recognizable fashion to the world at large. Perhaps, then, Baird's paper is to be read as suggesting that such use of the Austrian label is, within today's economics, now confusing and inappropriate.

But clearly, discontinuance of the Austrian label on either of these two grounds would require more than a demonstration that a single prominent economist—even one so eminent as Buchanan—shares basic insights and views with the Austrians. Baird is careful, it appears, not to claim that the public choice school in general shares these Austrian views (although at certain spots he seems perilously close to implying this). When Lionel Robbins (1933, p. xv) noted that Philip Wicksteed's place in the history of economic thought was alongside that occupied by the Austrians, he was not placing Wicksteed in the Austrian School, nor was he declaring the notion of an Austrian School to be meaningless.

---

1. My observations, in part, rest on Mises (1969, p. 41), personal conversations with Hayek, and Machlup (1981, p. 21). It is abundantly clear from Mises's writings since 1940 that he perceived a yawning gulf separating his own Austrian economics from mainstream doctrines. So that his 1969 statement must be read to imply that the fundamental Austrian ideas, absorbed into general economics by the 1920s came, somehow, to be lost from general economics by about 1940.

Yet one senses that Baird does, after all, wish us to draw lessons from his demonstration. It seems plausible, therefore, to read Baird as trying to correct an unfortunate attitude sometimes evident among Austrians, namely, an apparent conviction that there is no point in attempting to debate economists outside the narrow band of the Austrian faithful because non-Austrians simply do not (cannot) understand. Perhaps Baird wishes Austrians to recognize that, as exemplified by so prominent a scholar as Buchanan, Austrian ideas do have appeal to many economists outside the Austrian circle. So that it is time for Austrians to cast off their inward-facing insularity, and to embark with confidence on more open discussions with the rest of the profession. On this point, one can only heartily concur with Baird.

ARE WE ALL AUSTRIANS NOW?

When key Austrian insights are presented to other economists these days, the ideas are, as a matter of fact, unlikely to be rejected outright. Of course, it will often be readily conceded, economics must remain methodologically individualistic, the consequences of ignorance and uncertainty must be explored, the nature of economic processes (as distinct from states of equilibrium) must be studied. But all this, some mainstream economists will contend, can be achieved, if at all, only at the very frontiers of highly technical research. The settled core of economic theory must necessarily—if only provisionally—deal with a more simplified model of reality. Thus, it is not that mainstream theory is today intrinsically inhospitable to Austrian concerns, but rather that it feels compelled to postpone addressing these concerns while comfortably pursuing its settled neoclassical agenda. Non-Austrian critics of mainstream theory (such as post-Keynesians), on the other hand, are likely to contend that Austrian insights are so devastatingly valid as to compel utter rejection of neoclassical conclusions. In effect, this means that rejection of Austrian appreciation for the coordinating capacity of markets may be grounded precisely in those insights on which Austrian dissatisfaction with mainstream theorizing has characteristically been based.

While Buchanan, as ably demonstrated by Baird, is almost unique among economists generally in his appreciation for and depth of understanding of the importance of Austrian insights, he is by no means unique in recognizing the validity of these concerns. What our professional colleagues at large dispute is not the abstract validity of Austrian concerns, but what these concerns must mean for everyday economics. For mainstream neoclassicals these concerns mean that equilibrium theory must eventually grapple with yet higher orders of technical sophistication—without which, they will argue, one must settle provisionally for existing equilibrium theory. For post-Keynesian critics, again, these concerns mean that the traditional appreciation by economic theorists for the benign quality of market institutions must once and for all be given up. But for modern Austrian economists neither of these responses is acceptable.

Contrary to both neoclassical economists and their post-Keynesian or radical critics, the Austrian school's insights concerning process, discovery, and uncertainty provide precisely those elements necessary for understanding the market price system. Austrian economics is therefore ideally suited to uphold the traditional appreciation of economics for the market. It is not that markets work in spite of the open-ended uncertainty surrounding human action, but rather that they work *precisely because* of this quality of human action. The open-ended uncertainty of the environment itself provides the scope and possibility for an entrepreneurial process of competitive discovery. In sum, Austrian insights are central and essential for understanding markets and not merely refinements to our knowledge.

Modern Austrian economics, which is unique among contemporary schools of economic thought, did not spring up overnight. It evolved from the study and elaboration of the ideas of Ludwig von Mises and Friedrich Hayek. Mises emphasized the entrepreneurial nature of market processes; Hayek gave us the understanding of such processes in terms of the discovery and mobilization of hitherto dispersed and useless information. Modern Austrians have articulated and welded these elements into their contemporary formulations. There is every justification, from the perspective of the history of ideas, for retaining the identification of the modern Austrian understanding of markets with the Menger-Mises-Hayek tradition. It is difficult to imagine how contemporary formulations of the Austrian School's understanding of markets could have been forthcoming unless nurtured in the intellectual tradition traced back to Menger. Nor is it the case, by any means, that this understanding of markets—as distinct from the Austrian insights undergirding this understanding—has been absorbed into mainstream economics. Quite the contrary: Mainstream theorists understand the achievements of the market in terms which do *not* incorporate the

Austrian concerns; radical and other critics of mainstream theory deploy Austrian concerns to deny validity to mainstream (and Austrian) appreciation for market coordination.

Buchanan may well be the brilliant exception to the generalizations of the preceding paragraph. It is a tribute to his open-mindedness, clarity, and profundity of thought that—coming from a rather different (Knightian) tradition (which Baird delicately reminds us also generated the most consistently neoclassical of contemporary schools)—Buchanan has independently arrived at so much that is central to modern Austrian economics. But to label Buchanan "Austrian" would be obviously bizarre in terms of the history of ideas (and insulting to the breadth of Buchanan's professional interests and influence). And to use Buchanan's commonality with Austrians as grounds for discontinuance (by Austrians and by others) of the "Austrian" label, as a means to identify the work of the disciples of Mises and Hayek, would appear to be equally unreasonable. The distinctiveness of the Austrian approach is surely still sufficiently significant for the doctrinal label to serve a useful identifying function— besides its justification in doctrinal history.

However, Baird is certainly on safe territory to imply that Austrians be more appreciative of insights shared with economists trained in other traditions. Such greater appreciation might well generate more fruitful interaction between Austrian economists and their colleagues. Such interaction can be expected to sweep away vestiges of the attitude perceived among Austrians that expresses the sense of an impenetrable barrier separating Austrians from their professional colleagues—an attitude to be explained, and perhaps excused, as a natural response to the refusal of the economics profession, as recently as fifteen years ago, to see Misesian economics as anything but crude, obscurantist apologetics for capitalism. Dissolution of such a barrier, real or imagined, can only enhance common economic understanding and scientific progress. The prospect of such enhanced understanding does not, I would maintain, argue against recognizing the distinctiveness of modern Austrian economics, and of its doctrinal roots in a proud intellectual tradition. But, one may perhaps hope, this prospect may eventually point toward a climate of scientific understanding in economics in which continued Austrian distinctiveness may indeed no longer be called for. Baird is to be commended for a fascinating paper directed at that end.

REFERENCES

Machlup, Fritz. "Ludwig von Mises: A Scholar Who Would Not Compromise." In *Homage to Mises, The First Hundred Years.* Edited by J. K. Andrews, Jr. Hillsdale, Ill.: Hillsdale College Press, 1981.

Mises, Ludwig von. *The Historical Setting of the Austrian School of Economics.* New Rochelle, N.Y.: Arlington House, 1969.

Robbins, Lionel. "Introduction." In Philip H. Wicksteed, *The Common Sense of Political Economy.* 1910. Reprint. London: Routledge and Kegan Paul, 1933.

THE AUSTRIAN TRADITION
COMMENTARY BY ISRAEL M. KIRZNER

Dr. Boehm has written a chapter on Schumpeter and Mises with his accustomed perceptiveness and scholarship. He has moreover laced his account with numerous pungent asides on the pretensions and foibles of contemporary commentators on the two economists. All this adds up to a lively, provocative and learned piece. Yet one leaves this chapter with a vague sense of dissatisfaction—for which its author should, in all fairness, probably not be held responsible. Consider the task that he confronted.

This chapter is in a book surveying the varieties of neoclassical economics from 1870 to 1930. The Austrian school has already been discussed in an earlier chapter in the book, a chapter focused on the founding Austrians, Menger, Böhm-Bawerk, and Wieser. Understandably enough, however, the book's editors felt that this earlier chapter was not quite enough. Since the overwhelming bulk of the significant published work of Menger and Böhm-Bawerk dates back to the years before 1900, and since Menger went into virtual seclusion after his retirement in 1903, and Böhm-Bawerk died in 1914, the earlier chapter could hardly be held to cover the period up until 1930. Moreover, although Wieser continued to teach until his death in 1926, the mantle of intellectual leadership within the Austrian tradition had clearly passed on by the 1920s. So an additional chapter on the "younger Austrians" was assigned—and what could be more natural than to ask its author to focus on the most eminent of Böhm-Bawerk's pupils, Schumpeter and Mises, both of whom enjoyed international reputations by the 1920s?

But there were problems associated with this assignment. Writing from the perspective of 1989, it is clear that no discussion of the work of Mises and Schumpeter could avoid taking account of the diverse paths taken by these writers after 1930, nor could any such discussion avoid coming to grips with recently revived interest in their respective works. The task of writing about these two Austrians as a pair representing the

From K. Hennings and W. J. Samuels, eds., *Neoclassical Economic Theory, 1870–1930* (Boston, Dordrecht, London: Kluwer, 1990), 242–49. Reprinted by permission of Springer.

continuity of the Austrian tradition, when each of them was somewhat of a maverick, not only from the perspective of the economics profession generally but from that of the Menger–Böhm-Bawerk tradition, must have seemed a most formidable one indeed.

Boehm has fulfilled his difficult assignment with competence and wisdom, employing a variety of skillful strategies: he has assessed the controversy surrounding Schumpeter's "Austrian" credentials; he has reviewed the recent (separate) resurgences of interest in both Schumpeter and Mises; he has analyzed points of similarity and of contrast in their work; he discourses most learnedly and philosophically about the roller-coaster gyrations in scientific reputation that have attended each of these two writers during the past half-century. He has, in short, written a fascinating chapter, taking account of an enormous array of recent contributions to the literature. Yet, as indicated earlier, one feels a vague sense of incompleteness. We have *not* been given an account of the Austrian strand of neoclassical economics as it developed from Böhm-Bawerk's death up until the 1930s. We have not been given an account of the contributions Schumpeter and Mises made to that strand of economics. Or, to put it somewhat differently, Boehm's erudite discussion somehow has not presented Schumpeter and Mises as the mid-century protagonists and continuators of an "Austrian tradition"—on the one hand, rooted in the ideas of Menger and his colleagues, and on the other hand, capable of generating a late-century resurgence of those ideas. Mises and Schumpeter remain discrete individuals, rather than being seen as complementary role-players in a coherently developing intellectual tradition.

To articulate in this way one's vague dissatisfaction with this chapter is at the same time to exculpate both the editors and the author of any blame for having stimulated that satisfaction. Surely the editors were right in choosing Böhm-Bawerk's most distinguished disciples as the economists upon whom to focus attention for the years after Böhm-Bawerk's death. And surely Stephan Boehm can hardly be faulted for failing to find any major complementary contributions which these two writers, viewed as a pair, made toward the continuation and the development of the Austrian tradition. In fact, from the perspective of the mid-century (say, at the time of Schumpeter's death) one would have been compelled to conclude that (1) the contributions of these two writers were sufficiently divergent in spirit, purpose, and direction, to stamp them as being poles apart; (2) the life's work of neither of them, appeared to have been *both* sufficiently influential *and* sufficiently "Austrian" to contradict the impression, then widespread in the economics profession, that the Austrian school had, in effect, died with Böhm-Bawerk (or, at any rate, with Wieser).

What follows is an attempt—perhaps a not wholly disinterested attempt—to suggest that, viewed from a 1989 perspective, matters might be interpreted rather differently. From this perspective, I shall argue, the writings of Schumpeter and Mises, divergent though these have certainly been, nonetheless jointly constituted vehicles through which key Austrian ideas were preserved and extended, during a period in the history of economics in which these ideas might otherwise well have become completely lost from economics. From the perspective of the late-century resurgence in Austrian economics (to which Boehm refers throughout his paper), then, it can be argued that Schumpeter and Mises—despite their doctrinal differences and despite the coolness with which each assessed the other—in fact jointly contributed to an organic development of the Austrian tradition, a development that should be credited with its subsequent revival and resurgence.[1]

Just as each new generation might be able to reconsider past history in the light of more recent developments, so may later generations of intellectual historians reinterpret and redefine groupings and/or sequences of ideas identified by earlier historians of thought. What seemed important about the early Austrians in 1930—or even in 1950—was their methodological individualism, their subjectivism, their emphasis on consumer demand. In fact, it was largely as a result of this that, at mid-century, the idea of a separate Austrian tradition in economics appeared a matter strictly of the distant past. By mid-century everything considered valid in these identified points of Austrian emphasis had arguably been absorbed into mainstream microeconomics. But from our present 1989 perspective, what appears uniquely important in the Austrian tradition can be seen rather differently. If one is to account for the contemporary, late-century Austrian revival, one must now recognize that the earlier Austrian tradition encompassed important ideas (or pointers toward ideas) that never were absorbed into mainstream economics. These ideas—although easy to overlook in 1950—somehow survived the decades-long, mid-century eclipse of the Austrian tradition and subsequently sparked the present Austrian revival. I shall argue that there were such ideas present, if only in embryonic form, in the writings of Menger and his disciples, and that *it was the work of Schumpeter and Mises that kept these ideas alive*. If this reinterpretation of the essence of the Austrian contribution is valid, then we must recognize Schumpeter and Mises as having maintained and developed the Austrian tradition and—perhaps without recognizing it themselves—as having jointly contributed to the extension and revival of the Austrian school well into the closing decades of this century. To be sure, much of the work of Mises and Schumpeter in this regard came after 1930. Nonetheless both of them had written enough, along the relevant lines, before 1930 to justify our contention that they be now perceived as having, in the post-Bawerkian era, importantly developed the Austrian tradition along new lines (that would reach their fullest development much later). Mises and Schumpeter do make up a chapter in the history of Austrian economics after all.

THE THESIS DEVELOPED

Stated briefly, our thesis is as follows. Neoclassical economics during the first decades of this century *was moving toward a dominantly general equilibrium paradigm*. While this paradigm became firmly installed only after World War II, it is clear that the analytical steps refining earlier marginal analysis toward that paradigm were being taken in the twenties and thirties. We argue here that the Austrian tradition, rooted in Menger's mode of "seeing" economic phenomena, was *not* taking these steps—and would eventually be compelled to rebel vigorously and openly against the subsequently dominant paradigm. During the decades between 1920 and 1950 it was surely the writings of Schumpeter and of Mises that contained the clearest statements of dissociation from an exclusively equilibrium understanding of markets. Moreover, while the late-century Austrian revival took its cue primarily from the work of Mises (and of Hayek), it is not to be denied that it was Schumpeter's writings on the dynamically benign role of *departures* from perfectly competitive equilibrium that kept such ideas from being entirely forgotten in the mainstream of the economics profession.

To be sure, an outside observer of the intellectual scenery in Vienna during the twenties would not have seen much to suggest our thesis. Such an observer would not have found anything really significant separating the economic theory of the Austrians from that of their Marshallian or Walrasian cousins. In fact, the protagonists themselves would not have suggested anything to support our thesis. As late as 1932 we find Mises declaring:

> We usually speak of the Austrian and the Anglo-American Schools and the School of Lausanne. . . . [The fact is] that these three schools of thought differ only in their mode of expressing the same fundamental

idea and that they are divided more by their terminology and by peculiarities of presentation than by the substance of their teachings (Mises, 1933, p. 214).

But such statements, valid though they seemed at the time, do *not* contradict our thesis. It is true that the Austrians of 1932 did not recognize any significant difference between their theory and that of the Marshallians and the Walrasians. In fact there *was* no such significant difference! All economic theorists recognized a role for equilibrium, but all of them also understood the equilibrating process as consisting of entrepreneurial steps of dynamic competition.[2] All recognized the perfectly competitive state as merely the limiting case that models the theoretical state of affairs that might, in principle, be eventually attained if exogenous change were to be indefinitely suspended. The difference between the Austrian version of this commonly understood theory, and the version being refined in Marshallian and Walrasian circles was, we argue, a most subtle one. The refinements occurring in the Marshallian and Walrasian systems were pointing, we can now see, in the direction of the subsequently dominant general equilibrium paradigm. The work taking place in Vienna was, we argue, pointing in a quite different direction—in the direction of the work of Mises and Hayek in the forties, breaking sharply and clearly with the general equilibrium paradigm.

Let us not forget that theorists of all schools had, up until the outbreak of World War I, seen themselves as facing a powerful and common intellectual foe, the German historical school. Although the German historical school did not essentially survive after World War I, nonetheless theorists of the twenties understandably still saw other theorists as their comrades-in-arms. Given the versions of Marshallian and Walrasian economics then being taught, we must not be surprised that the Austrian economists saw their own economics as basically similar to that of their fellow theorists in other schools. It was not until 1940, in fact, that Mises recognized at all clearly how far distant his own economics was from that of the neoclassical mainstream.[3]

In the first decades of this century theorists of all neoclassical varieties saw the market process as a systematic one, *achieving a translation of the underlying realities—resource constraints and consumer preferences—into prices, incomes, and allocation patterns.* This commonly held view differed totally from that of the economists of the historical school (and also of other schools dissenting from the mainstream). To those not accepting economic theory, the prices, the distribution of income, and the allocation of resources among industries do not benignly and rationally reflect the relevant data. So sharply was this contrast felt that the early twentieth century theorists were hardly aware of the differences separating the alternative statements being made of their commonly held central thesis. Yet these differences existed, at least potentially, and in time they would be revealed as being, in fact, highly significant.

Equilibrium theorists saw the translation of underlying realities into appropriate market outcomes as occurring with reasonable smoothness and rapidity. They tended to focus attention not on the process of translation but on its results. As tools of analysis, geometrical and later algebraic, became better formulated, it became possible to articulate these theoretical results with greater and greater rigor and precision. This development was eventually to lead to a special view of the real world— that it represents at all times the equilibrium conditions appropriate to the underlying economic realities. In the early decades of the century this development had not proceeded very far. Equilibrium theorists recognized that the real world presents us with the higgling and haggling, the tentative steps of trial and error, the imaginative but hazardous competitive forays of entrepreneurs, *through which* equilibrium may be thought of as being continually approached. Yet the direction of analytical development was clear, toward the eventual complete dominance of equilibrium analysis over the understanding of process.

The Austrians drew their understanding of markets from a different fount. Menger, it is widely recognized, had a theory of markets in which disequilibrium was never far from the focus of attention.[4] Eventually Wieser's student Hans Mayer (1932) would formulate with emphasis the "causal-genetic" approach followed by the Austrians in contrast to the "functional" approach followed by the equilibrium theorists. In the early decades of the twentieth century this contrast was not clearly perceived by the Austrians. It seemed quite natural to follow through the causal steps of process analysis in order to see where it might, absent exogenous change, eventually lead to. So that it is not difficult to grasp how, for Mises in 1932, the Walrasians were seen as intellectual allies, rather than foes. Yet this perception was eventually bound to change.

As equilibrium theory came to be refined during the twenties and thirties, with mathematical tools of greater rigor, its direction became clearer.

The notion of dynamic competition, integral to much of the earlier neo-classical analysis, came to be replaced almost entirely by that of perfect competition.[5] In other words, analysis of process came to be replaced entirely by analysis of equilibrium results. Austrians came to be wary of this newly apparent thrust of mainstream theory. Despite his own fascination with the Walrasian vision, Schumpeter continued to emphasize his appreciation for the dynamics of markets. He hammered away at the role of entrepreneurial innovation, continually disrupting the placid circular flows of equilibrium. Eventually, in his *Capitalism, Socialism and Democracy*, Schumpeter would rebel against the dominance of the perfectly competitive model as a portrayal of real-world capitalism, and at the uncritical assignment of benign normative significance to the perfectly competitive state of affairs. Mises (who had in 1932 seen equilibrium theorists as allies) came by the end of the decade to distinguish sharply between Austrian economics seen as a science of human action, and the dominant equilibrium paradigms (Mises, 1940, 1949). Hayek (who up until the early thirties had seen no contradiction between the Austrian tradition in which he had been trained and the Walrasian economics that was becoming widely embraced) came, as a result of the debate on socialist economic calculation, to point out the limitations of exclusive preoccupation with states of equilibrium, and of the associated shortcomings of the model of perfect competition (Hayek, 1940, 1945, 1948).

It is true, as cited by Boehm, that Schumpeter did not have the highest regard for Mises as a theorist. It is true that Mises did not view Schumpeter as an Austrian economist (and, as cited by Boehm, indeed saw him as an equilibrium theorist). And it is true that Hayek sharply criticized Schumpeter (in regard to the socialist calculation problem) for taking the entrepreneurial-competitive process for granted (Hayek, 1945). But the fact remains that a student of economics searching, during the central decades of this century, for voices dissenting from the dominant preoccupation with the perfectly competitive equilibrium paradigm, would be bound, sooner or later, to bracket Mises and Schumpeter in this regard.

For each of these two scholars, this attention to the process of dynamic competition must have appeared entirely consistent with the common training they had received in Vienna. During the decades at mid-century, with the Austrian school considered quite dead, and as simply a closed chapter in the history of modern economics, not much significance could have been attached to this attention to the process of dynamic competition shared by Mises and Schumpeter—who were in every other respect so different from each other. But, as the twentieth century draws toward its close and economists are rediscovering the contributions of Schumpeter and are witnessing the revival of the Mengerian tradition as transmitted by Mises and Hayek, things must appear differently. It matters not, for our thesis, whether Schumpeter is to be counted as a "genuine" Austrian. What is important, from our present-day perspective, is that we may surely say that Mises and Schumpeter kept alive those insights and approaches to economic understanding that can now be seen as essential to the ongoing Austrian tradition. In articulating these insights and in making them explicit, Schumpeter and Mises were not just preserving ideas that could subsequently nourish a revival in Austrian economics. In doing so, we can now see, they were jointly contributing to a genuine enrichment and deepening of the Austrian teachings, bringing to the fore of Austrian self-awareness, an understanding of economic process that had been virtually absent in the Austrian economics of the twenties.

The thesis advanced in this comment does not, in this writer's opinion, contradict anything put forward in the lively and learned chapter contributed by Boehm. It does, however, perhaps permit us to see how this chapter properly completes the story of the Austrian contribution to neoclassical economics after World War I.

NOTES

1. To assert this is, of course, not at all to assert that Schumpeter would have been pleased to receive such "credit," or that Mises would have recognized Schumpeter as being in any sense his intellectual ally.

2. On this see the doctoral dissertation of Frank M. Machovec (1986).

3. For an account of how Mises appears to have arrived at this later recognition as a result of the debate on socialist economic calculation, see Kirzner (1988).

4. For a survey of the literature on this aspect of Menger, see Kirzner (1979, pp. 63–75).

5. The development of theories of imperfect or monopolistic competition tended in fact to emphasize the centrality of perfect competition for neoclassical theory. Moreover, these theories, too, were equilibrium theories; see Kirzner (1973, pp. 112–19).

REFERENCES

Hayek, Friedrich A. 1940. "Socialist Calculation: The Competitive 'Solution.'" *Economica* n.s., 7, 125–49. Reprinted in *Individualism and Economic Order*. Chicago: University of Chicago Press, 1948.

Hayek, Friedrich A. 1945. "The Use of Knowledge in Society." *American Economic Review*, 35, 519–30. Reprinted in *Individualism and Economic Order*. Chicago: University of Chicago Press, 1948.

Hayek, Friedrich A. 1948. "The Meaning of Competition." In *Individualism and Economic Order*. Chicago: Unversity of Chicago Press, 1948.

Kirzner, Israel M. 1973. *Competition and Entrepreneurship*. Chicago: University of Chicago Press.

Kirzner, Israel M. 1979. *Perception, Opportunity, and Profit*. Chicago: University of Chicago Press.

Kirzner, Israel M. 1988. "The Economic Calculation Debate: Lessons for Austrians." *The Review of Austrian Economics*, 2, pp. 1–18.

Machovec, Frank M. 1986. "The Destruction of Competition Theory: The Perfectly Competitive Model and Beyond." Ph.D. Dissertation, New York University.

Mayer, Hans. 1932. "Der Erkenntniswert der Funktionellen Preistheorien." In *Die Wirtschaftstheorie der Gegenwart*, Vienna: Julius Springer.

Mises, Ludwig. 1933. *Epistemological Problems of Economics*. Princeton, N.J.: Van Nostrand, 1960. (Translation of *Grundprobleme der Nationalökonomie*, Jena: Gustav Fischer.)

Mises, Ludwig. 1940. *Nationalökonomie: Theories des Handelns und Wirtschaftens*. Munich: Philosophia Verlag, 1980; first edition, Geneva: Editions Union.

Mises, Ludwig. 1949. *Human Action*. New Haven: Yale University Press.

"INTRODUCTION" TO *CLASSICS IN AUSTRIAN ECONOMICS*, VOLUME 1

The three volumes making up this collection of papers in Austrian Economics cover a one-hundred-year span of modern intellectual history, from approximately 1870 to 1970. In the history of economics, the Austrian School is recognized as an important component in the development of contemporary economic thought. The purpose of these volumes is to provide a sampling of the contributions of the major writers in the Austrian tradition, in order to illustrate the nature of that tradition, its development and maturation during its history, and its relation to other contemporaneous varieties of economics. A major focus is thus upon the modifications and changes in Austrian thinking which have occurred over the decades, and consequently upon the changing character of what has constituted the essential characteristics of Austrian thought, at different periods throughout this century of Austrian economic thought. The time period covered commences, naturally enough, with the beginning of the school's existence, as marked by the 1871 publication of Menger's *Grundsätze*. It concludes at about 1970, by which time all the important contributions to economics of both Mises and Hayek had already been made.

It has proved convenient to divide this collection into three chronologically separate volumes. The first volume contains contributions by the early Austrians up until the outbreak of World War I. The founding period between 1871 and 1914 is generally recognized as constituting a single continuous stage of intellectual development in Austrian Economics. The papers selected for this volume express the major contributions of the founders of Austrian Economics, and cover the gamut of topics, from methodology to utility theory, to the theory of value, the theory of capital, the theory of money, and to an exercise in applied economics.

Volume II consists of papers taken from books and journals of the interwar period. This period saw a vigorous spurt of development in Austrian thought, propelling the school to the forefront of professional

From *Classics in Austrian Economics: A Sampling in the History of a Tradition*, vol. 1, edited by Israel M. Kirzner (London: William Pickering, 1994), ix–xxx. Reproduced by permission of Israel M. Kirzner.

attention, and also marking its closest agreement with mainstream economic doctrine. In a narrow sense, it was the period of greatest professional success—but the close of this period also represented the beginning of a long period of eclipse for Austrian Economics.

This period of eclipse beginning in the late 1930s left only two major economists whose on-going work was clearly identified by the profession as being in the Austrian tradition. These economists were, of course, Ludwig von Mises and Friedrich von Hayek. Their work continued vigorously, for each in his own separate mode, for several decades; and, as we shall argue, that work, taken together, represented a decisively important new stage in the history of Austrian Economics. The work of Mises and Hayek (*including* a sampling of their contributions during the interwar years) make up the contents of Volume III. For a variety of reasons this collection of papers does *not* cover the period since 1970, which has been marked by a remarkable rebirth of interest and work in the Austrian tradition (largely building upon the work of Mises and Hayek).

Both Volume II and Volume III open with introductory essays by the editor, providing overviews of the character and significance of the respective periods covered by these volumes. This present introductory essay will, besides providing a similar overview of the contents of Volume I, offer a somewhat idiosyncratic bird's-eye view of the entire history of Austrian Economics, and comment on a variety of fascinating *dogmengeschichtliche* puzzles and ironies that characterise that history.

* * *

THE DISTINCTIVENESS OF THE
AUSTRIAN SCHOOL: PUZZLE AND PARADOX

The founding period in Austrian Economics began with the 1871 publication of Carl Menger's *Grundsätze* (see in this volume, papers 2 and 3). The notion of any such entity as an Austrian *School,* however, certainly had no factual relevance before the 1880s (see Mises, 1969, p. 10). It was in the 1980s that a series of important works by Eugen von Böhm-Bawerk and Friedrich von Wieser reinforced the central innovative doctrines introduced by Menger. Several students of Menger published their books in this period. In addition Menger's 1883 work on methodology, together with Gustav Schmoller's contemptuous review of it (on this see further in this volume, paper 5), ushered in the *Methodenstreit,* the famous (or notorious) dispute over method which raged between the Austrians and the dominant German Historical School. All this focused professional attention on the work of Menger and his younger colleagues, so that by the early 1890s, Menger, Böhm-Bawerk, and Wieser, were writing articles for British and American scholarly journals, for foreign audiences apparently eager to learn about the newly emerging school of thought in Austria (see, in this volume, papers 4, 5, 9). By the turn of the century, such overseas attention to the Austrians had generated translations of their books into English, and (particularly for Böhm-Bawerk) extensive polemical discussion with foreign critics (see e.g. in this volume, paper 6).

Paradoxically, the features of Austrianism which set it apart from other contemporary schools of economics were eventually to undermine its distinctiveness in the eyes of the profession. In these formative, founding decades of the Austrian School, this distinctiveness was perceived (both by its own members and by economists elsewhere) as consisting in two significant features. First, it was identified as the *subjectivist* school (sometimes, for example by Wieser, see in this volume, paper 11, this was expressed by reference to the "psychological method"), in that its theories placed prime emphasis upon the subjective preferences of consumers (rather than upon the objective conditions governing production). Second, the Austrian School was identified as a *theoretical* school, impatient with the narrowly descriptive studies of the Historical School, and eager to demonstrate the validity of economic laws which transcend the particularities of time, place, and institutional circumstance. The first of these two features came, for later historians of economic thought, to mean that the Austrians were perceived as hardly distinctive at all, being seen as merely one element in the marginalist revolution which introduced neoclassical economics and pushed Ricardianism (and classical economics generally) from centre stage in post-1870 economics. The second of the above two features was, again, to mean (especially with the decline of the German Historical School after 1914) that the Austrian methodological stance was seen as basically identical with that adopted by economists generally. To insist on the vindication of pure economic theory, however controversial this may have been in the latter decades of the nineteenth century, was, in the early twentieth century, to push against an open door. So it is not surprising to discover that, by 1930, it was widely held among Austrians and other economists alike, that while the emergence of the Austrian School was indeed an important and benign historical element in the advance of modern economics, there was nonetheless no continuing basis for emphasizing any uniquely distinctive characteristics of Austrian economic thought (as compared to the neoclassical consensus which had crystallized within the profession by that date). When Lionel (later Lord) Robbins wrote his hugely influential 1932 book, *The Nature and Significance of Economic Science,* he did so after having thoroughly absorbed the Austrian ideas of the interwar period, in the works of such Austrians as Mises, Mayer, Schams, Strigl, Schönfeld, Hayek and Morgenstern, but he saw these Austrian ideas as throwing a fresh light on the true character of a commonly shared *mainstream* economics, rather than as representing an alternative theoretical structure. What was valid and important in Austrian economic theory had, by the time Robbins wrote, already been successfully absorbed into the mainstream itself. Or so, at least, ran the conventional wisdom.

And here we have before us the essential puzzle which suffuses the history of the Austrian School—and to the exploration of which much of this *Introduction* will be directed: the subsequent history of Austrian Economics (particularly that reflected in the papers in the third volume of the present collection) would prove this conventional wisdom, which seemed so plausible around 1930, to be quite false. It would become apparent that the Mengerian legacy would generate developments in the theory of the market process which would be thoroughly inconsistent with the central content of the neoclassical orthodoxy (as that orthodoxy developed organically from the mainstream economics of the pre-Keynesian era). These developments would mature in the decades *after* the close of the Mises-Hayek era represented here in the third and final volume of this collection. It is in the contemporary *post*-Misesian revival of Austrian Economics that the distinctiveness of the Austrian tradition has emerged as a natural extension of—or perhaps more accurately, the explicit unpacking of the ideas implicit in— the theoretical contributions pioneered by Menger in his 1871 *Grundsätze.*

A THESIS ASSERTED

In this section we concisely present, as a thesis to be developed and defended in the subsequent sections of this Introduction, an interpretation of the overall history of the Austrian tradition capable, we claim, of accounting for the changes over time in the perception of the distinctiveness (or lack of it) of Austrian Economics.

This thesis is that Menger, already in 1871, glimpsed a radically subjectivist way of understanding the determination of economic phenomena in market economies, which diverged sharply, of course, from that of classical economics. It was a vision, however, which really did differ sharply, in its radical subjectivism, also from the broad understandings of the economic process which came to be encapsulated in Marshallian and in Walrasian economics. Menger, however, was not able to articulate the full implications of what he glimpsed. Nor did his immediate associates and followers fully grasp the complete perspective which their master had, at least in outline, perceived. They proceeded, therefore, to develop certain parts or aspects of Menger's explicitly stated economic doctrines *without* placing their contributions in the context of Menger's wider (but incompletely articulated) subjectivist vision of the economic process. Because the early developments in Austrian economics (certainly up until about 1930) were direct extensions of the work of Böhm-Bawerk and Wieser, rather than of Menger himself, it is not surprising that the Austrian economics of the interwar period failed to reflect those aspects of the Mengerian subjectivist vision which, as stated, really did differ sharply from the understandings of Marshallian and of Walrasian economics. It is for this reason that the economics of the interwar Austrians (represented in this collection in the papers on Volume II) seemed, and still seems, by and large to be closest to the economics of the mainstream of the profession.

Our thesis further maintains that the debate concerning the possibility of rational economic calculation under central planning, a debate which raged in the interwar period and in which Mises and Hayek were the prominent exponents of what came to be seen as the "Austrian" position had, as an unintended side effect, an important influence on the thought of both Mises and Hayek (but not necessarily upon that of other Austrians). The debate forced Mises and Hayek separately to come to grips with aspects of the economic process which called for precisely those radically subjectivist insights which had been implicit, at the very least, in Menger's broad vision. It was their articulation of these newly discovered or rediscovered insights (see e.g. papers 22, 26, 30, 31) which definitively came to mark the Austrian economics of the era of Mises and Hayek as in no way to be considered congruent with mainstream economics. It was, further, these newly articulated insights which inspired the revival of Austrian Economics which we have witnessed in the post-Misesian period. And it is, accordingly, by no means surprising that it has been in the course of this revival (and of reactions to it) that there has occurred in recent years a remarkable volume of fresh research into the economics of Menger and its relation to the economics of his contemporary marginal utility pioneers in other schools. See for example Smith and Grassl (1986), Caldwell (1990), Alter (1990), Streissler (1990), Hayek (1973).

What was it that Menger saw? How did his followers, pursuing Menger's insights, fail to see what Menger had seen? And how did these lost insights come to be rediscovered in the work of Mises, Hayek, and of the subsequent Austrians who were themselves inspired by Mises, or by Hayek, or by both? Let us start from the beginning.

THE MENGERIAN VISION

In order to understand what constituted the essence of Menger's vision, we have to appreciate the revolution which that vision implied in regard to the Ricardian view of the world, which Menger was concerned to displace. In the Ricardian view of the world, the economic phenomena which economic theory can account for (and which therefore mark out the boundaries within which attempts by economists to account for real world observables must be confined) are those rigidly determined, at least in the long run, by objective, physical realities. It is the set of such realities which inexorably determine, for Ricardian economics, the size and rate of growth of aggregate output, and the pattern of distribution of this output among the major classes of productive factors which produce that output. It is true that no Ricardian could *entirely* exorcise the human element from the economic explanations. Wealth must, after all, be defined in terms of human needs and desires. The economic explanations must rely upon the behaviour of "economic men." But the central point is that in the Ricardian view, the nature of wealth and the behaviour of economic men can be treated as physical, or at least biological, constants. The explanations need place no reliance upon human resourcefulness, human valuations, human expectations, human discoveries. The inexorable course of economic history is one which proceeds almost regardless of what mere mortals may wish, desire, believe, or decide. (The circumstance that it is this view of economic history which was to characterize Marxist economics was to have much to do with the dramatic tensions which were later to develop between the Marxists and the Austrians—the heirs to the Mengerian anti-Ricardian legacy.)

As opposed to this Ricardian view of the economy, Menger saw a way to understand economic history in diametrically opposite terms. Economic outcomes, while certainly vitally affected by physical and biological realities, are directly caused only by the actions of human beings. From this Mengerian perspective the physical and biological realities recede into the background; they become the passive material of the world upon which acting man impinges. Admittedly, what acting man can achieve is sharply constrained by the natural scarcities which circumscribe the world and which, indeed, impose the need to economize; but what is achieved, and the entire array of prices, patterns of outputs, and structure of production methods, are achieved through human actions and are vitally affected by man's beliefs, desires, expectations and knowledge.

Understanding Menger's revolutionary perspective upon the economic process in this way rather than as an approach focused narrowly upon the foundations of the theory of economic value permits us, perhaps, to solve a certain puzzle which has been introduced into Mengerian scholarship by the work of Erich Streissler (1990). What we have seen is that Menger's revolutionary perspective consists not in the theory of subjective value which it generated, but in its understanding of the prime causal role of human action in the determination of economic phenomena. It is only in terms of this appreciation of Menger's vision that we can account for the fact that, of the marginal utility pioneers, only Menger perceived the outlines, at least, of a marginal productivity theory of resource prices. For Menger the subjective theory of value was merely an implication of the subjective appreciation of the economic process. Streissler has, in a paper of surpassing scholarship, drawn attention to earlier German economists such as Hermann, Rau, Hufeland, Schäffle, Mischler and Schuz, whose value theories incorporated subjectivist insights long before Menger. He has therefore labelled as "myth" the doctrine that Carl Menger developed his "novel insights quite independently and in actual constrast to German economics" of the time (op. cit., p. 31).

Yet it is difficult to ignore Menger's own apparent conviction of the revolutionary character of his work. Hayek has reported that Menger "is said to have once remarked that he wrote the *Grundsätze* in a state of morbid excitement" (Hayek, 1934). While subsequent historians of economics may perhaps have created something of a myth concerning Menger's supposed independence of predecessors, it seems safe to assert that Menger's revolutionary *overall* perspective owes little to the precursors Streissler has identified. It is one thing to show that subjective theories of value preceded Menger and may well have influenced Menger's own theory of value, either directly or indirectly. It would be quite another thing to claim that Menger's vision of an economy created and shaped by human action was not a totally original one. Streissler's thesis, of course, implies no such claim. And indeed the integration of earlier ideas concerning subjectively determined values into Menger's own subjectivist perspective on how economic phenomena in general are generated, *would* certainly constitute a most revolutionary advance in economic understanding.

Having characterized Menger's innovation as consisting in its vision of economic phenomena as being caused by human action, it is necessary immediately to point out the incompleteness of that vision (see Kirzner, 1992, chapter 4). A critic of the above suggested interpretation of Menger's essential contribution might well draw attention to crucial passages in Menger's writings which appear to contradict that interpretation. In the preface to his *Grundsätze,* for example, Menger was concerned to counter the views of those "who question the existence of laws of economic behaviour by referring to human free will." Menger responded to these views by asserting, *inter alia,* that "whether and under what conditions an *economic exchange* of goods will take place between two economizing individuals, and the limits within which a *price* can be established if an exchange does occur—these and many other matters are fully as independent of my will as any law of chemistry is of the will of the practising chemist." Reference to the freedom of the human will can never justify the "denial of the conformity to definite laws of phenomena that condition the outcome of the economic activity of men and are entirely independent of the human will. It is precisely phenomena of this description, however, which are the objects of study in our sciences" (Menger, 1981, pp. 48ff.).

Although these passages might admit of interpretation not inconsistent with what we have claimed to be Menger's subjectivist perspective, we certainly cannot and do not claim that Menger believed himself to have seen how it is *precisely* the freely exerted wills of human beings which generate powerful tendencies toward definite outcomes. We do not claim that Menger at all clearly understood the entrepreneurial role exercised by alert market participants in achieving a tendency toward market coordination. Our claim is simply that he saw the causal source of market phenomena in the actions of the human participants in the market process; and that it was this vision of Menger's which, consciously or unconsciously, inspired subsequent generations of Austrians toward a more completely subjective theory of the market process.

ON THE DISTINCTIVENESS OF THE
AUSTRIAN SCHOOL: PARADOX CONFRONTED

Our statement of Menger's revolutionary perspective on the entire economic process can perhaps help us resolve some of the paradoxes noted
earlier regarding perceptions of the distinctiveness of the Austrian
School. We noted how the emergence of the Austrian School during the
1880s attracted professional attention in England and the U.S.A. The
methodological and doctrinal characteristics of the school were considered sufficiently novel to confer a certain distinctiveness upon it. And yet,
within a few short decades, it came to be thought that there was little that
set the economics of Vienna apart from that of other neoclassical schools.
No doubt some fraction of this change in perceptions can be attributed to
developments that had occurred, during these decades, in the economics
of other neoclassical schools. (It was during these decades that equilibrium theorizing came to be refined and widely introduced explicitly into
mainstream discussions.) But attention to changes within Austrian Economics itself can, in the light of our statement of Menger's overall vision
of the economy, offer still further insights.

What seems to have occurred is that Menger's subjective view of
the determination of economic phenomena came rather rapidly to be
reduced, in Austrian Economics, to the subjective theory of value. In the
work of both Böhm-Bawerk and Wieser, it was the subjective theory of
value which was emphasized; certainly there is little in their work which
recognizes, let alone expands upon, Menger's groping glimpse of a fully
subjective theory of the market process. Böhm-Bawerk's theory of capital and interest reflected his emphasis upon subjective intertemporal
rankings of value (time-preferences); as such it represented an extension
of marginal utility theory. But the macroeconomics of Böhm-Bawerk's
vision of a capital-using market economy owes very little to subjectivism. Indeed the late Ludwig Lachmann has pronounced Böhm-Bawerk's
vision to be a fundamentally Ricardian one [Lachmann, 1977, p. 253].

After World War I, with both Menger and Böhm-Bawerk no longer
alive (Menger died in 1921), with Menger's book seen as something of a
dated classic work rather than as the basis for current advanced research,
the development of economics in Vienna seems to have been in a direction definitely at variance with that adumbrated, at least, in Menger's
original anti-Ricardian vision. The theory of consumer choice that was

being refined during the 1920s, based on marginal utility theory, was hardly different, on fundamentals, from that which was being developed in Marshallian and in Walrasian economics. (See in this edition [*Classics in Austrian Economics*], Volume II, paper 17.) Human choice was still viewed in rather mechanical terms, with the outcome seen as more or less already implicit in the relevant operative constraints and assumed marginal utility schedules (see Ebeling). There was little in the economics of Vienna in the 1920s that could draw attention to the problems of uncertainty, information and ignorance. Even expectations were hardly in the forefront of Austrian economists' minds at that time. While Austrian Economics could hardly be confused with the Ricardian perspective, the same was after all true also of Marshallian and Walrasian economics. It is true that Marshallian economics did explicitly seek to retain an explanatory role for the physical realities which condition production possibilities, while Austrian economics did not. But this difference (if indeed it was noticed at all) must have appeared as not much more than a matter of detail in the theory of value, rather than as reflecting any deep-seated philosophical differences regarding the nature of economic explanations.

On the surface at least, a certain unanimity among the major theoretical schools of the 1920s must have seemed to prevail. As noted earlier, Robbins's *Nature and Significance* did not seek to improve British economics by introducing Austrian theoretical innovations. Rather he sought to teach British economists how their own Marshallian doctrines could be expressed more tightly and understood more satisfyingly when placed consistently within a continental framework which emphasizes individual allocative decisions and the manner in which they interact in markets. While there *was* a sense that new frontiers were beckoning to be conquered (perhaps by extensions of Austrian capital theory, or monetary theory, for example), the settled territory already well behind the front lines was seen as shared in common by economists of all schools.

For the Austrians themselves, especially those old enough to remember the pre-war dominance of the Historical School in German-language economics, this unanimity was perceived to be reinforced by the shared theoretical and anti-historicist methodological approach. No doubt it was this that led Mises to declare in 1932 that, although it is "customary to distinguish several schools," in modern economics, the fact is "that these three schools of thought differ only in their mode of expressing the same fundamental idea and that they are divided more by their terminology and by peculiarities of presentation than by the substance of their teachings" (Mises [1933], 1960, p. 214).

As we shall see, however, this unanimity was superficial. Although in 1932 it might have *seemed* to Mises that "the substance" of the teachings of the major schools was a commonly shared one, nonetheless it would become apparent in the years ahead that in fact Austrian economic thought pointed in a direction very different from that toward which the confluence of Marshallian and Walrasian thought was to proceed. In fact it would be Mises himself, more than anyone else, who very soon came to emphasize the sharp differences which separated his own economics from that of the neoclassical mainstream. And it seems plausible to claim that it was the Mengerian subjectivist legacy, with all its incompleteness, which was to inspire those subsequent developments in Austrian Economics which would reestablish unmistakably the unfashionable distinctiveness of Austrian Economics. A number of these subsequent developments seemed to have occurred in the course of, and as a result of the celebrated interwar debate on the possibility of rational economic calculation under central planning. (See Kirzner, 1992, chapter 6.) But before we turn to examine the impact of this debate upon the future history of the Austrian School, it may be useful to consider what an eminent Austrian-trained economist, thoroughly steeped in the economics of Vienna circa 1930, was to see years later as the basic tenets of Austrian Economics. This list will be revealing in its confirmation of the fundamental *lack* of distinctiveness in Austrian Economics at that date, ascribed to it by its staunchest adherents.

FRITZ MACHLUP AND THE ESSENTIALS OF AUSTRIAN ECONOMICS

Fritz Machlup was one of the remarkable young economists, educated at the University of Vienna in the 1920s, who were participants in Mises's famous *Privat-seminar* at that time, and who were, in later phases of their careers, to become world famous in their profession. Machlup, whose work on Austrian Economics during the interwar period is represented in the present collection by paper 20 in Volume II was to migrate to the U.S. in the 1930s and establish a brilliant and prolific teaching and research record. On a number of occasions Machlup sought to identify the essential components of Austrian Economics (see Machlup, 1981, 1982).

For Machlup these components were (i) *methodological individualism*: in "the explanation of economic phenomena we have to go back to the actions (or inaction) of individuals"; (ii) *methodological subjectivism*: in "the explanation of economic phenomena we have to go back to the judgments and choices made by individuals on the basis of whatever knowledge they have or believe to have and whatever expectations they entertain . . ."; (iii) *tastes and preferences*: demand is determined by subjective valuations of goods and services; (iv) *opportunity costs*: the true character of economic costs is that they reflect the alternative opportunities that must be foregone; (v) *marginalism*; (vi) *time structure of production*.

A brief glance at this list must confirm the judgment that the Austrian Economics of which Machlup was writing was hardly different from that of the mainstream Anglo-American approach. In the latter, too, (at least insofar as it is expressed in mainstream microeconomics), methodological individualism and subjectivism play a role. Of course the mainstream theory of consumer demand has a place for tastes and preferences. And marginalism and the jargon of opportunity costs are, of course, among the most fundamental elements in the professional vocabulary of all the modern economists.

Two items are strikingly absent from Machlup's list which, from the perspective of late twentieth-century Austrian Economics, would seem utterly essential. These are (vii) the emphasis upon market *process* (rather than upon market equilibrium conditions); and (viii) the recognition that economic choices are made in an open-ended context of Knightian uncertainty, in which the determination of the relevant parameters of the choice context (constraints and preferences) is itself an integral part of the act of choice. That Machlup omitted these elements of the modern Austrian position expresses, certainly, the extent to which the Austrian Economics of 1930 was to develop in the subsequent half-century— the age of Mises and Hayek. At the same time these omissions explain, in part, why an economics which would seem so unfashionable in the 1970s, a half century earlier could be thought to be so close to the mainstream. What we wish to show now is how, partly as a result of the economic calculation debate, the legacy of Mengerian subjectivism was to generate, within the Austrian Economics of the 1920s, a ferment of intellectual development that would eventually produce a variety of Austrian Economics which someone trained in the earlier decades (such as a Fritz Machlup) might find it difficult to comprehend fully.

It will be this ferment of intellectual development which will account for the difference in "flavour" between many of the papers in Volume II of the present collection (covering the interwar period), and many of those in Volume III (covering the decades after World War II, the age of Mises and Hayek).

THE SOCIALIST ECONOMIC CALCULATION DEBATE

It was Mises's famous 1920 article (paper 22 in Volume III of this collection) which set off the debate. Although, as was later established (see Hayek, 1935; Mises [1922], 1936, p. 135 fn.), several turn-of-the-century economists had raised the question of how socialist planners might grapple with the allocative problems of a complex society, it was Mises who placed the calculation problem squarely before the economics profession. He pointed out that rational planning in a complex economy demands that planners distinguish between the values of different resource quantities. Only by reference to such values (reflecting the alternative uses that might be served by these resources elsewhere in the economy) might planners be able efficiently to steer resources away from less important uses toward more valuable purposes. Such indexes of value emerge in capitalist economies, of course, as a result of competitive markets in resource services. But because such resource markets must, by the very definition of socialism, be absent in the centrally planned economy, the central planners necessarily find themselves without the basic tools necessary for economic calculation. It was this Misesian thesis which came to be perceived as the "Austrian" side of the calculation debate.

A flurry of German-language responses in the 1920s sought to defend the possibility of socialist economic calculation. But it was not until the 1930s that a series of more sophisticated responses emerged, and these happened to be in the English language. For the purpose of our brief survey here it is sufficient to focus attention upon the contributions asserting the viability of socialist calculation which were made by Oskar Lange and Abba P. Lerner (see Lange [1936] 1964; Lerner, 1944). It was these contributions which persuaded the mainstream writers (but not the Austrians themselves!) that Mises's critique of socialist planning was, while important and insightful, not necessarily fatal for the possibility of rational central planning.

The Lange-Lerner thesis (it is generally treated as a single thesis, although it was developed in separate contributions by these two economists) acknowledges the force of Mises's basic argument. Mises is certainly correct in drawing attention to the critical need for resource prices, in order for efficient production decisions to be made that should not misallocate scarce social resources. However where Mises erred, in the opinion of Lange and Lerner, is in his assertion that without capitalist markets for the services of productive resources no prices can be imagined for these services. Prices, Lange and Lerner maintain, are simply magnitudes attached to economic goods which govern the decisions being made concerning the utilization of these goods. (The statement by Wicksteed [(1910) 1933, p. 28] is cited, in which a wider sense of the meaning of price is held to be "the terms on which alternatives are offered to us.") There is no reason, in principle, why these magnitudes must be those emerging from the exchanges made in markets. A central planning authority could announce these non-market prices and instruct the managers of socialist enterprises on the manner in which these prices should govern production decisions. By periodically monitoring the aggregate outcomes of these managerial decisions, the central planners can adjust these non-market prices periodically (in a manner not fundamentally different from that in which market prices fluctuate in response to the surpluses and shortages occurring in resource markets). In brief, Lange and Lerner are suggesting an artificial resource "market" in which socialist managers "compete" for scarce resources on the basis of "prices" announced by the central planners. This is not the place to examine critically the substantive content of this Lange-Lerner response to the Austrian challenge to the possibility of socialist efficiency. We are concerned only to trace those developments in Austrian Economics that occurred during the age of Mises and Hayek which, we argue, can be attributed to the impact of the socialist calculation debate.

As has been extensively demonstrated by Professor Don Lavoie (see Lavoie, 1985), the position articulated by Lange and Lerner reflects the mainstream understanding of the nature of price and the centrality of market equilibrium. The position taken by Mises and by Hayek, on the other hand, reflects a different Austrian appreciation of the nature of market prices, and also the Austrian perspective on the centrality of dynamic, entrepreneur-driven market processes (rather than of equilibrium states of affairs). In subsequent literature it was considered that the Lange-Lerner solution had effectively disposed of Mises's challenge to the possibility of socialist efficiency. This must be attributed to the dominance of the mainstream equilibrium paradigm and to the unfamiliarity of that literature with the Austrian market process paradigm. The responses by Mises and by Hayek to the Lange-Lerner literature must, *ex post,* be pronounced to have proven unconvincing. This must be partly attributed, in turn, to the circumstance that both Mises and Hayek were at least in the earlier stages of the calculation debate, not yet completely aware of the paradigmatic contrast between the mainstream and the Austrian perspectives. Indeed, it was only their exposure to the Lange-Lerner arguments which gradually compelled Mises and Hayek to recognize clearly the process character of their own understanding of markets. Understandably their early responses to the Lange-Lerner arguments failed to come to grips with the roots of the disagreement. While both Mises and Hayek certainly sensed the inadequacy of a non-market price system for overcoming the problems of mutual ignorance which beset the disequilibrium economy, at that stage of the development of Austrian Economics, they were not able to spell out the nature of that inadequacy convincingly.

It should be emphasized that our contention is not that the calculation debate taught the Austrians to advance from an equilibrium view to a *different* view—a process view—of markets. We maintain, rather, that for the Austrians, the debate induced a more complete and clear understanding of what was already implicit in their theory of the market. In arguing that the calculation debate was an important catalyst in the development of Austrian Economics we are asserting that the debate led to the crystallization, in the work of Mises and Hayek, of insights which had indeed not been specifically articulated until then, but which were nonetheless deeply embedded in the Mengerian perspective. These insights had, during the interwar period, not been explicitly articulated, which permitted the general view at that time that Austrian Economics differed only in language and style from the Marshallian and Walrasian mainstream. It was the emerging clarity with which these insights came to be perceived and articulated by Mises and Hayek, as the calculation debate faded during the years of World War II, which ushered in an era in which Austrian Economics became unfashionably distinctive and, in fact, professionally marginalized. That era is the period beginning about 1940, covered in Volume III of the present collection.

A superficial reading of Mises's 1920 paper might, we acknowledge, see it as a not particularly sophisticated statement of neoclassical equilibrium theory. It could be said that Mises pointed out the allocative-efficiency properties of an equilibrium set of competitive prices, and claimed that capitalism achieves its efficiency by presenting market participants with a set of prices reasonably approximating the structure of the relevant equilibrium set. The reader might be excused for missing insights concerning the capacity of prices to inspire those processes of entrepreneurial discovery and learning, *in disequilibrium markets,* which were to be so characteristic of later Misesian and Hayekian economics. The explanation for this is, however, not that the 1920 Mises was an equilibrium theorist, but that the importance of the distinction between the equilibrium and the process perspectives had at that time not yet come to be recognized. (Indeed many contemporary statements of neoclassical economics were based similarly on perspectives which relied upon *both* an appreciation of the dynamic character of competitive market processes *and* upon a conviction that market prices are reasonable approximations of equilibrium prices.)

In considering attempts to defend the possibility of socialist efficiency by reference to non-market prices, Mises and Hayek reached a more careful appreciation of the nature and function of market prices in the course of dynamic processes of equilibration, as distinct from the allocative properties of prices in the attained state of equilibrium.

FROM MENGER TO MISES: THE SEARCH FOR SUBJECTIVISM

In his autobiographical sketch (Mises, 1978, p. 33) Mises recounts how he first read Menger's *Grundsätze* as a student in 1903. "It was the reading of this book," he remarks, "that made an 'economist' of me." Certainly the central message which Menger sought to convey was the *subjective* character of the fundamental elements in economic theorizing, such as "goods," "resources," "structure of production." For Menger these ideas are not to be understood as inhering in economic objects themselves, but as emerging from the attitudes toward these economic objects, of valuing and acting human beings. (See particularly in this volume, papers 2 and 3.) If we claim that the age of Mises and Hayek, the age of lowest general professional esteem for the school, represented the most consistent development and deepening of the Mengerian legacy, we do so on the basis of the more fully developed subjectivism which has characterized Misesian and Hayekian economics. It was Hayek who put his finger on the centrality of subjectivism for Mises's life's work. In a footnote (to an oft-quoted remark hailing subjectivism as the fountain of advances in economic theory; see Hayek, 1955, p. 31) Hayek observes that this development of economic theory on the basis of the consistent application of subjectivism "has probably been carried out most consistently by L. V. Mises." He adds his belief "that most peculiarities of [Mises's] views which at first strike many readers as strange and unacceptable are due to the fact that in the consistent development of the subjectivist approach he has for a long time moved ahead of his contemporaries" (Hayek, op. cit. pp. 209–10). Here Hayek has delicately drawn attention to the decided unfashionability, at the middle of the twentieth century, of the Austrian Economics expounded by Mises. If in 1930 the subjectivism of the Viennese School had permitted its adherents to enjoy the comfort and prestige of being close to the gravitational centre of the profession, by 1950 the consistent extension of this subjectivism had expelled the heirs of Mengerian subjectivism to the outer reaches of professional exile. If in 1930 the Austrian School was at the peak of professional recognition, by 1950 the school was considered to have become utterly extinct leaving as vestigial remains only the persons and writings of Mises and Hayek.

Yet (as we shall argue in the Introduction to Volume III) it was precisely during this time of professional eclipse that Mises and Hayek made original contributions that would eventually inspire a modest but significant Austrian revival. This revival would occur after 1970 (the closing date for coverage in these volumes) but it was during the age of Mises and Hayek that the groundwork was being laid. In the course of the rebuilding of Austrian Economics that was to occur in the latter portion of the twentieth century, Mengerian subjectivism was again and again to be the lodestar. What has encouraged younger members of the profession to rediscover the Austrian tradition has been a sense of dissatisfaction with the mechanical quality of a mainstream economics in which human aspirations, human errors, and human discoveries are downplayed, ignored, or simply assumed away. In searching for a mode of economic understanding sensitive to these elements in the human condition, it is the work of Menger which has proven most fertile; and it is the development of the Mengerian tradition spurred by the work of Mises that latter-day Austrians have found most helpful. From the perspective of the closing years of the twentieth century, therefore, it is in the gradual deepening and maturing of Mengerian subjectivism that the history of the Austrian School finds its unity and its *raison d'être*.

AUSTRIAN ECONOMICS AND ECONOMIC IDEOLOGY

No survey of the Austrian School, no matter how cursory, can ignore wide-spread impressions which link it to libertarian ideology in general, and to vigorous (if not virulent) opposition to socialism in particular. Although our story, in the preceding pages, has made little mention of ideological considerations (even in our account of the socialist economic calculation debate), we must certainly confront this issue forthrightly. Briefly, our position can be summarized in the following two propositions.

First, the intellectual content of Austrian Economics, throughout its history, *can* be disengaged from any ideological accompaniments that may have been present. To dismiss any portion of this intellectual history as merely the propagandistic pseudo-academic facade for ideological prejudgments is not only to be grossly unfair to the economists concerned, but also to manufacture shoddy excuses for avoiding to grapple with important theoretical argumentation. Intellectual honesty requires, on these grounds alone, that any ideological disagreements with Austrians be laid aside if Austrian Economics is to be treated with the seriousness it deserves.

Second, the ideological dimension of the Austrian School cannot be denied. Many of its members have in fact been prominently identified with a political position close to classical liberalism (or even, for some, to libertarianism). This appears to have been true of Menger (see on this Boehm, 1985; Kirzner, 1992, chapter 5; Streissler, 1990), of Böhm-Bawerk, and, certainly, of both Mises and Hayek. Although socialism in the twentieth century has usually been viewed as the ideological opposition against which Austrians were doing battle, we should not forget that the original ideological enemy was not socialism *per se,* but rather authoritarian government domination over private activity, as under the Prussian monarchy. (On this see Mises, 1969.) Yet it was the Austrian Böhm-Bawerk who sharply criticized the Marxist labour theory of value and its ideological entailments; it was the Marxist Bukharin, later to be liquidated by Stalin, who pronounced the Austrians the "most powerful opponent" of Marxism (Bukharin, [1914] 1972, p. 9). A recent example of (fearful?) interest on the part of Marxists in Austrian Economics and its current revival is the impressive work of Stavros Ioannides (1992). And, as we have seen, it was Mises and Hayek who denied the viability of socialist planning.

It is not our objective here to explore the precise interrelationship between the pure intellectual content of Austrian Economics and the broadly classical liberal ideological stance of many (or most) of its most prominent exponents. Although we insist on the epistemological independence of the former from the latter, we certainly recognize that the intellectual content of Austrian Economics, and its development during the century covered in these volumes, did not occur in an ideological vacuum. Austrian support for free market policies was, in the view of the Austrians themselves, at least, solidly based on Austrian understanding of the way free markets work. The stimulus to explore the subtle webs of causation which prevail in markets was, for Austrians (as for most economists in the history of the science) strongly related to the overall policy objective of improving the well-being of society in general. We draw attention to these rather obvious aspects of Austrian Economics simply to alert the reader who may have an interest in pursuing the ideological dimension of those changes and developments in Austrian Economics between 1870 and 1970 as reflected, perhaps, in the papers collected in these volumes.

* * *

THE PAPERS IN VOLUME I OF THE PRESENT COLLECTION

Volume I covers that period in the development of the Austrian School which is the best known in the conventional history of economic thought. (Indeed, in much of that history the term "Austrian School" refers strictly and exclusively to this period.) From the perspective of this conventional history, what occurred in Vienna, Innsbruck, and Prague between 1871 and 1914 was the emergence of a separate tributary of ideas that would, however, flow into, merge with and reinforce the mainstream of modern neoclassical economics with its very success in this latter function ensuring its eventual loss of identity. In the preceding sections of this Introduction we have offered a sharply differing view of the historical significance of this early period of Austrian economic thought. For us the work of Menger, Böhm-Bawerk and Wieser was historically significant primarily in that it pointed beyond itself to a more fully subjectivist tradition which that work was to generate. Although the Austrian work sampled in this volume is better known to the profession than that presented in Volumes II and III, we urge that the papers in this first volume, several of them made available in English for the first time, be freshly examined from the perspective of the thesis advanced in this Introduction.

These papers offer methodological statements by each of the three founders of the school (papers 1, 5, 11). They offer expositions of the subjective theory of value (Menger, papers 2, 3; Wieser, papers 8, 9). They include Menger's classic statement of his theory of spontaneous evolution of economic institutions (paper 4); Böhm-Bawerk's elucidations of the Austrian perspectives on the foundations of capital and interest theory (papers 6, 7); and Wieser's application of Austrian theory to the applied area of urban ground rent (paper 10). Finally, these papers include a classic debate between Böhm-Bawerk and his outstanding Czech student Franz Čuhel, on the cardinality or ordinality of the concept of utility (papers 12, 13). We wish to suggest briefly here that much of the work offered in this volume illustrates the extent and force of the subjectivist insights which, we have argued, provided the initial spark which set the Austrian tradition into motion.

The Austrian defences of the deductive method express an epistemological assertion concerning the causal role of human decisions. For economists of the Historical School, human decisions played no such decisive role in the generation of economic regularities; any such regularities were seen as emerging from the welter of observable economic events. The Austrian position, often denigrated as pointless quibbling over trivial matters in scholastic dispute, actually reveals a unique perspective on the nature of economic causation and on what can be known concerning that causation (see Bostaph, 1978). That perspective stemmed from a Mengerian subjectivist understanding of the manner in which economic phenomena express human preferences and decisions.

Menger's theory of spontaneous institutional evolution, central to his view of the nature and scope of social science, relies heavily on subjectivist insights. The dynamics of the emergence of money as an institution is driven by human perceptions of differential marketability among exchangeable goods, generating decisions concerning exchanges which themselves cause further snow-balling effects on marketability. Although the process is not a planned one, it is driven, step by step, by the planned actions of choosing, evaluating human beings.

Čuhel's critique of Böhm-Bawerk's cardinalism illustrates at once both the radical subjectivism implicit in the Mengerian legacy, and the limitations of that subjectivism as it was expressed in the work of Menger's immediate, and most eminent, followers. The Čuhel–Böhm-Bawerk debate represents a fascinating anticipation of the cardinalist-ordinalist debates in British economics three or four decades later. But whereas Hicksian ordinalism stemmed primarily from an application of Occam's Razor (i.e. from the consideration that demand theory can be developed without recourse to a cardinal utility), Čuhel's ordinalism arises from his subjectivist (introspective) appreciation of the nature of human preferences and choices. Admittedly, Čuhel's ordinalism was significantly rooted in psychological (rather than in purely economic) insights. But his rebellion against Böhm-Bawerk's cardinalism, had it been completely successful, would have helped weaken the view that choices (and hence all market phenomena) are somehow "determined" by a law which ensures the achievement of maximum possible total cardinal utility for each market participant. Such a (mainstream) view of microeconomics changes the nature of the choices made by choosing, imagining, dreaming and purposeful human beings. Such a microeconomics makes it appear as if market phenomena emerge without human action, emerging, instead, automatically as it were from the "data" (including individual utility functions in the data), being merely the outcomes of maximization exercises which are inevitably and mechanically fulfilled. Čuhel's ordinalism might have steered economics toward a more consistently Mengerian-subjectivist understanding of how market phenomena emerge through individual acts of conscious valuations and comparisons. The influence which Čuhel's work exercised on the thinking of Ludwig von Mises is a matter of record (see Mises, [1912] 1953, p. 41; 1978, p. 57). It is reasonable to attribute Mises's own radical subjectivism, at least in part, to this influence.

That Austrians were aware of the danger that their "subjective" theory of value might permit itself to become embedded within a mechanical, positivist analytic framework, is clear from Wieser's highly critical review essay on Schumpeter's first (1908) book. (See paper 11 in this volume.) Schumpeter, writing his book under the influence of the emerging positivist perspective associated with the Viennese physicist Ernst Mach, had seen economic phenomena as governed deterministically by the mechanics of utility maximization. Just as physical bodies are held to be located in the cosmos by the rigid operation of gravitational laws, so also the location of "economic quantities" is governed rigidly by the principle of utility maximization. Wieser, apparently sensing the danger of this kind of positivist thinking for subjectivist economics, carefully but effectively criticizes Schumpeter's position.

The papers in this volume thus illustrate the variety of aspects of economics explored by the Austrian founders. They illustrate in particular, we wish to emphasize, both the centrality of Mengerian subjectivism to their work, and the ambiguities in the degree of consistency with which they pursued that subjectivism. As argued earlier, it was the fate of Mengerian Subjectivism which would dictate the course of subsequent intellectual history for the Austrian School.

REFERENCES

Alter, Max, *Carl Menger and the Origins of Austrian Economics* (Boulder: Westview Press, 1990).

Boehm, Stephan, "The Political Economy of the Austrian School," P. Roggi (ed.), *Gli Economisti e la Politica Economica* (Naples: Edizioni Scientifiche Italiene, 1985).

Bostaph, Samuel, "The Methodological Debate Between Carl Menger and the German Historicists," *Atlantic Economic Journal* 6 (3) September 1978, pp. 3–16.

Bukharin, Nikolai, *The Economic Theory of the Leisure Class* (New York: Monthly Review Press, 1927; translated from the Russian original of 1914 by M. Lawrence).

Caldwell, Bruce, (ed.), *Carl Menger and his Legacy in Economics* (Durham, NC: Duke University Press, 1990).

Ebeling, Richard M., "Action Analysis and Economic Science, the Economic Contributions of Ludwig von Mises," unpublished manuscript.

Hayek, Friedrich A., "Introduction," C. Menger, *Principles of Economics* (New York: New York University Press, 1981), originally published as "Introduction," *Collected Works of Carl Menger* (London: London School of Economics, 1934).

———, *Collectivist Economic Planning* (London: Routledge and Kegan Paul, 1935).

———, *The Counter-Revolution of Science. Studies on the Abuse of Reason* (Glencoe, IL: Free Press, 1955).

———, contribution to Hicks, J. R., and Weber, W., *Carl Menger and the Austrian School of Economics* (Oxford: Clarendon Press, 1973).

Ioannides, Stavros, *The Market, Competition and Democracy, A Critique of Neo-Austrian Economics* (Aldershot, Hants, England: Edward Elgar, 1992).

Kirzner, Israel M., "The Economic Calculation Debate: Lessons for Austrians," *The Review of Austrian Economics* (1988).

———, "Carl Menger and The Subjectivist Tradition in Economics," *The Meaning of Market Process, Essays in the Development of Modern Austrian Economics* (London: Routledge, 1992).

———, "Menger, Classical Liberalism and the Austrian School of Economics," *The Meaning of Market Process* (1992).

Lachmann, Ludwig M., *Capital, Expectations, and the Market Process, Essays on the Theory of the Market Economy* (Kansas City: Sheed, Andrews and McMeel, 1977).

Lange, O., "On the Economic Theory of Socialism," B. E. Lippincott (ed.), *On the Economic Theory of Socialism* (New York: McGraw-Hill, 1964).

Lavoie, Don, *Rivalry and Central Planning: The Socialist Calculation Debate Reconsidered* (Cambridge: Cambridge University Press, 1985).

Lerner, Abba P., *The Economics of Control* (New York: Macmillan, 1944).

Leser, N. (ed.), *Die Wiener Schule der Nationalökonomie* (Vienna: Hermann Bohlau, 1986).

Machlup, Fritz, "Ludwig von Mises: the Academic Scholar who would not Compromise," *Wirtschaftspolitischen Blätter*, 4, (1981).

——, "Austrian Economics," D. Greenwald (ed.), *Encyclopedia of Economics* (New York: McGraw-Hill, 1982).

Menger, Carl, *Principles of Economics* (New York: New York University Press, 1981), originally published in 1871 as *Grundsätze der Volkwirthschaftslehre*.

——, *Investigations into the Method of the Social Sciences with Special Reference to Economics*, trans. F. J. Nock (New York: New York University Press, 1985), originally published in 1883 as *Untersuchungen über der Methode der Socialwissenschaften und der Politischen Oekonomie insbesondere*.

Mises, Ludwig von, *The Theory of Money and Credit* (New Haven: Yale University Press, 1953); the original German-language version was published in 1912.

——, *Socialism: An Economic and Sociological Analysis* (London: Jonathan Cape, 1936), translated from the German-language *Die Gemeinwirtschaft*, 1st edn 1922, 2nd edn 1932.

——, *Epistemological Problems of Economics* (Princeton, NJ: Van Nostrand, 1960), translated from the German original, *Grundprobleme der Nationalökonomie*, 1933.

——, *Notes and Recollections* (South Holland, IL: Libertarian Press, 1978).

——, *The Historical Setting of the Austrian School of Economics* (New Rochelle, NY: Arlington House, 1969).

Robbins, Lionel, *The Nature and Significance of Economic Science* (London: Macmillan, 1932; 2nd edn 1935).

Smith, Barry, and Grassl, Wolfgang, *Austrian Economics, Historical and Philosophical Background* (New York: New York University Press, 1986).

Streissler, Erich, "The Intellectual and Political Impact of the Austrian School of Economics," *History of European Ideas*, 92 (1988).

——, [in Caldwell, op. cit.] "The Influence of German Economics on the Work of Menger and Marshall," pp. 31–68 (1990).

——, "Menger, Böhm-Bawerk, and Wieser: The Origins of the Austrian School," K. Hennings and W. J. Samuels, eds, *Neoclassical Economic Theory, 1870 to 1930* (Boston, MA: Kluwer, 1990).

Wicksteed, Philip, *The Common Sense of Political Economy* [1910] (London: Routledge and Kegan Paul, 1933).

"INTRODUCTION" TO *CLASSICS IN AUSTRIAN ECONOMICS,* VOLUME 2

The eight papers in this second volume have been selected to represent the interwar period in the history of Austrian Economics. (Although also several of the papers included in Volume III belong, chronologically, to the interwar period, they have, primarily because of the authorship, been grouped with the other (post-1940) papers representing the "Age of Mises and Hayek." On this see further in the Introduction to Volume III.) It was, it will be recalled, our thesis in the Introduction to Volume I that in the interwar period Austrian Economics came to converge more closely than at any other time throughout its history toward mainstream neoclassical economics. We also argued, in that earlier Introduction, against the mainstream view (in histories of modern economic thought) that the Austrian Economics of the 1871–1914 era was nothing more than a separate tributary of ideas which flowed into, merged with, and reinforced the mainstream of modern neoclassical economics. Nonetheless we must emphatically concur in the conventional judgment to the following extent: much of the economics of interwar Vienna, *taken in isolation from post–World War II developments,* does appear thoroughly consistent with that (here rejected) mainstream view of the history of modern economics. The papers in this volume reflect these ambiguities and complexities which characterize interwar Austrian Economics.

In a recent paper on the interwar period in Austrian Economics, Stephan Boehm ably explored some of these (and other) complexities and ambiguities.[1] His perspective was richly informed by his familiarity with the post-1970 revival of interest in the Austrian tradition. For deploying this perspective he was gently taken to task by Mark Blaug[2] for whom, it appears, the interwar period in Austrian Economics is important not in its constituting a background against which subsequent developments in the tradition were to occur, but rather as consisting of a series of resounding Austrian defeats (in debates with mainstream economics) particularly in the areas of capital theory, business cycle theory, and the

From *Classics in Austrian Economics: A Sampling in the History of a Tradition,* vol. 2, edited by Israel M. Kirzner (London: William Pickering, 1994), vii–xx. Reproduced by permission of Israel M. Kirzner.

theory of socialist economic calculation. For Blaug an adequate survey of this period would offer "a definitive account of how Böhm-Bawerk was vanquished by Frank Knight, how Hayek and Robbins were laid low by Sraffa and Kaldor, and how Mises was buried by Lange."[3] The papers selected for this volume do not quite coincide with Boehm's emphasis on the Mengerian (rather than the Boehm-Bawerkian) roots of interwar Austrian Economics (and his related interest in potential links between the economics of this period and the later Austrian revival); nor do they at all reflect Blaug's perception of this period in Austrian Economics as substantially consisting of a series of major defeats (presumably responsible for the decisive eclipse of the School by the end of the 1930s). Rather the selection of these papers reflects the (not unrelated) judgments (a) that it was the influence of Böhm-Bawerk and of Wieser (rather than that of Menger) which was most predominant in the Vienna of the 1920s and 1930s, (b) that this influence generated a perspective which naturally converged toward mainstream neoclassical thought (so that "defeats," both the real and the imagined, at the hands of mainstream economists, can no longer be seen as having been *necessary* for the eclipse of Austrian Economics by the outset of World War II). If, despite all this, we concur in Boehm's broad conclusion, that seeds of the subsequent revival in Austrian Economics are to be sought in some elements of interwar Austrian work, we must at least modify this concurrence by the observation that such a search is likely to demand both patience and persistence.

THE SCENERY IN VIENNA: SOME RELEVANT HIGHLIGHTS

The intellectual landscape in Austrian Economics after the conclusion of World War I was rather different from the pre-war scene. Böhm-Bawerk had died in 1914; Menger, who died in 1921, had retired from his university professorship many years earlier; only Wieser, who was to die in 1926, remained still active in teaching after the war's end. A younger generation of economists were coming to the fore, particularly represented in the forceful personalities of Ludwig von Mises (a star veteran of Böhm-Bawerk's seminar) and Hans Mayer ("the favourite pupil of Wieser").[4] For our purposes it will suffice to ignore many other fascinating aspects of the scenery in Viennese economics in the 1920s, and to focus on what Boehm[5] has called the "interlocking circles" which formed around these two economists. At the University of Vienna Wieser's chair (once occupied by Menger) was given, after his retirement, to Hans Mayer. Around him at the university there came to be formed an important circle of able young economists including Leo Schönfeld-Illy, Paul Rosenstein-Rodan, and Oskar Morgenstern. Mises never did obtain a chair at the university (despite the judgment of many that his scholarly work and international renown rendered this something of an academic scandal).[6] In Mises's own words, a "university professorship was closed to me inasmuch as the universities were searching for interventionists and socialists."[7] Yet his title of Associate Professor enabled him to conduct a highly successful seminar at the university (despite what Mises has described as Mayer's occupying "his time . . . with mischievous intrigues against me").[8] Mises's main intellectual influence, however, was exercised outside the university, in his famous *Privatseminar*. This met once in two weeks at Mises's office in the Chamber of Commerce (a tax-supported parliamentary entity formed by businessmen) where he earned his livelihood—and from which he exercised considerable influence at the national level—as the Chamber's economist. In this *Privatseminar* there participated a remarkable group of young scholars, not only economists, but also historians, philosophers and sociologists. One important Austrian scholar in the group was Richard Strigl, who had been trained in the pre-war Böhm-Bawerk seminar. His work was to influence, in particular, that of Lionel Robbins. (For a sample of Strigl's work see in this volume paper 14; for a contemporary Austrian critique of Strigl's major book, see paper 18.) Among the group were also several who were later to become internationally famous scholars in their respective fields, including Friedrich Hayek, Gottfried Haberler, Fritz Machlup, Oskar Morgenstern, Paul Rosenstein-Rodan, Felix Kaufman, Alfred Schütz, and Erich Voegelin. Despite the coolness (to express it mildly) between Mayer and Mises, several (such as Morgenstern and Rosenstein-Rodan) participated both in the Mayer seminar and Mises's *Privatseminar* (hence Boehm's reference to "interlocking circles"). Almost all of the more important economists in both of these circles are represented in these volumes, with the work of Mises himself, as well as that of Hayek, being collected separately in Volume III. Let us attempt to identify the general perspective on economics which characterized interwar Vienna.

THE CHARACTER OF INTERWAR VIENNESE ECONOMICS

We have already (in the Introduction to Volume I) drawn attention to Machlup's list of the doctrinal foundations of Austrian Economics as he understood it. There can be little doubt that this list expresses with precision the general perspective which pervaded Austrian Economics in the 1920s, when Machlup began his career, both as student and as scholar. There is also little doubt that this general perspective was broadly shared by economists in both the Mayer and the Mises circles. When Lionel Robbins wrote his 1932 *The Nature and Significance of Economic Science* (which, as we shall see, importantly imported this Austrian perspective into the British scene) his citations were to Austrian scholars both in the Mises circle (including Mises, Haberler, Hayek, Kaufman, Machlup and Strigl) and in the Mayer circle (including Mayer, Schönfeld-Illy, Rosenstein-Rodan and Morgenstern).

It will be recalled that Machlup's list was made up of 1) methodological individualism, 2) methodological subjectivism, 3) the importance of tastes and preferences, 4) the centrality of the opportunity cost concept, 5) marginalism, 6) the time structure of production. In what follows we shall attempt to show how this list, making up the shared perspective of interwar Austrian economists, was distinct from that of the dominant British approach of that time, but was nonetheless sufficiently close to that approach as to appear to justify the standard history-of-thought thesis. In this thesis what is valid in Austrian Economics is seen as becoming benignly absorbed (circa 1930) into the neoclassical mainstream. Yet, on the other hand, this list traced its intellectual ancestry to earlier (especially Mengerian) roots. In the fullness of time, this would generate an expansion in Machlup's "Austrian list" so as to incorporate, especially, explicit attention to the importance of (disequilibrium) *processes* set in motion by entrepreneurial *discovery* in a world of *open-ended ignorance* and *uncertainty*.

This latter development could hardly have been foreseen by an Austrian economist (or any other economist, for that matter) during the 1920s, and was not at all an *obvious* implication of the articulated perspective shared by Austrian economists of the period. This led us to assert earlier that the papers in this volume reflect the influence of Böhm-Bawerk and of Wieser, rather than that of Menger. On the other hand, the fact that the later development (half a century later!) occurred after all permits and compels us, at the same time, to concur with Boehm in recognizing the need to search (in the economics of interwar Vienna) for the seeds of the late twentieth-century Mengerian revival. Boehm suggest that these seeds are likely to be found in the ideas being discussed in the Mayer circle. While we shall certainly recognize, later in this Introduction, the historic significance of Mayer's work in this regard, and will indeed recognize a certain indirect influence exercised by that work upon some late twentieth-century Austrian economists, we find it difficult to attribute the post-1970 Austrian revival, as a whole, to that work. Rather (as will be discussed in the Introduction to Volume III) the post-1970 Austrian revival must, it seems to us, be traced back to seminal insights, discovered and/or articulated by Mises and by Hayek in the 1940s which owed relatively little, it would appear, to Mayer's pioneering work of the early 1930s.[9] Because we have gathered together the relevant work of Mises and of Hayek (including that from the interwar period) in the third Volume of the present work, it follows that the papers in this present Volume can be expected to offer relatively little basis for understanding the subsequent developments in Austrian Economics which were, we have maintained, ultimately to render "Machlup's list" incomplete. Moreover, it can be argued that, despite important anticipative indications, the work of both Mises and Hayek up until 1940 hardly expressed with any clarity those new insights which they would make explicit in the 1940s. With or without the work of Mises and Hayek, therefore the Machlupian perspective correctly captures what was explicit in the economics of interwar Vienna.

THE AUSTRIAN AND THE BRITISH TRADITIONS—
DISTINCT BUT CONVERGENT

Prior to 1930 the mainstream tradition in English economics did not recognize the centrality of the foundation concepts contained in Machlup's list. It was not so much that the substance of Marshallian economics was antithetical to those concepts. (In fact, as we shall see, Robbins was to argue that the Austrian insights were able to illuminate what British and other neoclassical economists had been doing and saying all the time.) Rather the failure, in British neoclassical economics up until the 1930s, to recognize the centrality of such insights as methodological individualism, subjectivism, and the opportunity cost doctrine, must be attributed to Marshall's vision of his economics as being simply the elaboration and completion of the classical perspective inherited from Smith, Ricardo and Mill. To *this* perspective a doctrine of methodological individualism must indeed appear alien, the notion of opportunity cost must indeed appear awkward and confusing.

For Alfred Marshall or for Edwin Cannan the link between economics and material wealth, while not as straightforward as it had been for Ricardo or Mill, was nonetheless difficult to abandon. In defining economics as studying "that part of individual and social action which is most closely connected with the attainment and with the use of the material requisites of well-being,"[10] or "the general causes on which the material welfare of human beings depends,"[11] Marshall and Cannan are continuing a tradition which was rooted in an explicitly objectivist perspective. What identifies the economic side or department of social life is not, in this perspective, allocative choice, or purposefulness in individual decision-making, but the *material* character of the objects of attention. Although neoclassicism had, unquestionably, vastly enriched the corpus of classical theory by introducing utility considerations (alongside the objective circumstances which identify the costs of production) into the theory of the determination of market values, this was achieved without fundamentally altering the way in which economic science and economic processes were understood. In the picturesque words of Wicksteed's well-known critique of Marshallian economics, the "new temple, so to speak, has been built up behind the old walls, and the old shell had been so piously preserved and respected that the very builders have often supposed themselves to be merely repairing and strengthening the ancient works."[12]

So that, while the individual decision was indeed an element in the analytical framework of British neoclassical economics, the *centrality* of that element as capturing the essential, defining character of the entire science—and the subjectivism which must as a consequence surely pervade that analytical framework, were not recognized. It was this which Robbins found frustrating in British economics and which led him to discover, in continental (and, particularly, Austrian) approaches to economics, subjectivist insights which at once simplified and illuminated economic understanding. It was Robbins's genius to distil these insights and articulate them in a manner (and at a moment) which decisively affected the course of mainstream microeconomic thought in Britain and the U.S for decades to come.

Robbins's 1932 book did not require a student of Marshall's *Principles* to *abandon* the substance of his science. Most of Marshall's or Cannan's economics could, for a reader of Robbins, be *appreciated* in a new and satisfying light, once one makes explicit such subjectivist ideas as the defining centrality of allocative, economizing choice, the inescapability of opportunity cost, the utterly individualistic nature of human well-being. To be sure, consistent application of these insights must transform the perspective from which Marshallian or Cannan's economics is understood.

(It was to provoke Robbins himself to question the meaningfulness of economic aggregation in general, and of aggregate economic well-being in particular.) To employ Wicksteed's metaphor, these insights permit one to tear down the ancient shell to reveal that neoclassical economics indeed makes up a hitherto unappreciated new temple. It was the discovery of this transformed perspective which excited Robbins and inspired his book.

This importation of Austrian ideas into the British mainstream did not constitute a clash of inconsistent substantive economic doctrines. In fact Robbins saw himself as simply stating clearly what was already implicit in British economics. "I venture to hope that in one or two instances I have succeeded in giving expository force to certain principles not always clearly stated. But, in the main, my object has been to state, as simply as I could, propositions which are the common property of most modern economics."[13] Clearly, Robbins saw the elements that would later be grouped in Machlup's list of Austrian fundamentals as thoroughly consistent with British economics. All schools of economics since the marginal utility revolution are, in Robbins's view, ultimately saying the same things. "At the present day, as a result of the theoretical developments of the last sixty years, there is no longer any ground for serious differences of opinion on these matters, *once the issues are clearly stated.*"[14] What Robbins found in interwar Austrian economics was a set of insights which enabled one to state clearly what economists of *all* post-1871 schools were already saying with greater or lesser clarity.

It is not our purpose here to pursue the story of how, through Robbins's book and related importation of other continental insights into British economics in the early 1930s, Austrian ideas came to play a key (often overlooked) role in the subsequent crystallization of mainstream mid-twentieth-century microeconomics. Our purpose in this Introduction is to draw attention to the presence of these ideas in the contributions of interwar Austrian economists collected in the present volume, and to identify both their distinctness from the British mainstream (as it was understood up until 1932) and the ease with which Lionel Robbins felt himself able to introduce them into that very same British mainstream. The papers in the present volume do illustrate the degree of convergence with mainstream neoclassicism achieved by interwar Austrian Economics.

If our interest in offering the present collection of papers were confined to those in this volume of interwar Austrians, it might perhaps not be important to go much beyond the fact of this "convergence." However our purpose in these three volumes is to offer a sampling of Austrian work covering an entire century of intellectual development. We cannot eschew the task of understanding interwar Austrian Economics as it appears in the full sweep of that century-long development. From this longer run perspective any convergence to the British mainstream that occurred during this period must (as we argued in the Introduction to Volume I) appear as something of a short-run sub-plot in a more ambitious intellectual multi-generational saga. That long-run saga offers a story which began in 1871 with Menger's *Principles* and was to lead—through the mid-twentieth-century work of Mises and Hayek—to a late-century revival of the Austrian tradition in a form which sets it almost dramatically apart from mainstream microeconomics (as that microeconomics itself, paradoxically enough, evolved as a result of the Robbinsian, Austrian-inspired, influence!). Although that longer-run story will occupy us more substantively in the Introduction to Volume III, we can hardly avoid an attempt to place interwar Austrian Economics in the context, at least, of this longer-run story. Once again a reference to Robbins's book will offer a clue.

SUBJECTIVE VALUE THEORY: MENGER, MAYER AND MISES

Robbins, in his attempt to characterize the central propositions of shared neoclassical theory, found it convenient to refer to the subjective theory of value. "It does not require much knowledge of modern economic analysis to realise that the foundation of the theory of value is the assumption that the different things that the individual wants to do have a different importance to him, and can be arranged therefore in a certain order. This notion can be expressed in various ways and with varying degrees of precision, from the simple want systems of Menger and the early Austrians to the more refined scales of relative valuation of Wicksteed and Schönfeld and the indifference systems of Pareto and Messrs Hicks and Allen."[15] From this elementary insight into the character of individual preference, Robbins points out, economic analysis proceeds to derive the idea "of an equilibrium distribution of goods between different uses, of equilibrium of exchange and of the formation of prices."[16] Now, this way of seeing these central propositions of microeconomics may certainly have correctly expressed the subjective value theory of the interwar Austrians as Robbins encountered them in his visits to Vienna in the late

1920s. But (as will be seen in Mayer's long paper in this volume, paper 16, and as will be briefly pointed out in our Introduction to Volume III) Austrian Economics itself, even that of the interwar period, was *beginning* to evolve toward an entirely different understanding of value theory. And it was to be this evolution which would result in Austrian Economics turning out, by the second half of the twentieth century, to be unmistakeably different from the theory of subjective value as understood by Robbins (and as subsequently developed in mainstream microeconomics).

Hans Mayer (see paper 16 in this volume) put his finger squarely on the sources of the disagreement, two of which happen to be referred to in the passage we have quoted from Robbins. These are (a) the character of Paretian indifference maps, and (b) the centrality of equilibrium patterns of exchange and of prices. Mayer, in his lengthy critique of Pareto's indifference curve analysis, draws critical attention[17] to Pareto's well-known assertion that, for purposes of understanding economic equilibrium the "individual can disappear, provided he leaves us this photograph of his tastes." He also[18] draws attention to a problematic character of equilibrium theory: "there is an immanent, more or less disguised, fiction at the heart of mathematical equilibrium theories: that is, *they bind together, in simultaneous equations, non-simultaneous magnitudes operative in genetic-causal sequence as if these existed together at the same time.*" One prominent late twentieth-century Austrian economist, Ludwig M. Lachmann (who was a student at the time Mayer was writing his paper), was deeply influenced by Mayer's critique of "functional" (rather than genetic causal) theories of price in mainstream microeconomics as it was already presented in its Paretian formulation, and as it was to become even more deeply entrenched as the century was to develop. As we shall see in the Introduction to Volume III, similar objections to mainstream mid-century microeconomics were to be presented by Mises several years after Mayer's pioneering critique.[19] Although Mises's articulation of his theory of *human action* paralleled the objections of Mayer, and appeared subsequently to Mayer's paper, there is no reason to question the subjective originality of Mises's position (especially in the light of his earlier methodological papers, collected in his 1933 *Grundprobleme der Nationalökonomie*). Regardless of questions of priority, we have here definite signs that, despite the convergence of interwar Austrian Economics (both in the Mayer and Mises circles) toward the neoclassical mainstream, there was already movement toward Austrian rebellion against that mainstream.

It was the continuation of that movement that would manifest itself at mid-century in the work of Mises and of Hayek, which would, in turn, nourish the late century revival of the Austrian tradition.

From the perspective of the latter revival, with its emphasis (especially in the work of Lachmann) upon uncertainty and ignorance, the subjectivism of the interwar Austrians, the subjectivism introduced into the mainstream by Robbins, appears severely limited. As will be seen from Rosenstein-Rodan's magisterial survey of the state of utility theory in the 1920s (paper 17 in the present volume) the interwar Austrians saw utility as expressing "a property attributed to a good, namely its effectiveness in fulfilling the purpose of satisfaction of wants." It was briefly recognized that "since only expected anticipated needs are the motive force of economic action, only the expected and not the actually realized utilities are relevant to economic theory." But this subjectivist recognition was immediately sharply modified by the comforting assurance provided that "owing to economic experience" actual utility will "not diverge significantly" from expected utility.[20] Despite the sophistication of the utility analyses surveyed by Rosenstein-Rodan, there is little recognition of human decision-making as grappling with an open-ended future fraught with radical uncertainty. Future wants are treated as given; the capacity of goods to satisfy these wants in the future is treated as given; utility is a property attributed to goods. Given the individual's wants, given the capacity of goods to satisfy these wants, utility analysis can proceed, almost in Paretian fashion, entirely without any decision-making by that individual. For the interwar Austrians, as in mainstream neoclassical microeconomics, individual decisions are assumed actually to maximize utility; the perceived ranked options among which choice is assumed to have been made, turn out to have been exactly those that were in fact available. So that the decision outcome is in fact an outcome which is already implicit in the given situation. In other words, subjective value theory, for interwar Austrians, is achieved by drastically abstracting from precisely those aspects of human action which were, for Mises and later Austrians, to supply the driving force for market processes.

As will be seen from Oskar Morgenstern's paper on the role of time in value theory (paper 21 in the present volume), interwar Austrians, especially those influenced by relevant contributions of Hans Mayer, had a lively awareness of the complexities that must be introduced into economic analysis as soon as we take into account the "dating" of economic events. This will surely come as no surprise in regard to a school of thought steeped in Böhm-Bawerkian doctrines. Yet Morgenstern's paper hardly moves beyond what O'Driscoll and Rizzo have referred to as the "spatialized" treatment of time.[21] (It is true that Morgenstern's 1928 monograph *Wirtschaftsprognose* went some way beyond such a treatment. However what is presented here in paper 21 seems to have accurately captured the general sense in which time was understood in interwar Viennese economics.) For Morgenstern the economic analysis of economizing decisions made in the face of a multi-period future hardly proceeds beyond what he himself describes as "some introduction of time-parameters into some systems of equations and the tagging of all economic processes with time indices."[22] Most perceptively, Morgenstern does, at the very end of his paper, recognize that in order to "penetrate the problem" more thoroughly, it would be necessary to pay special attention to the entrepreneurial role. But this research programme is merely recognized as a most urgent problem facing economic theory; interwar Austrian economics had not yet attended to this unfinished agenda. And clearly the Austrian perspective which Robbins transmitted to economists in the British mainstream went no further in its subjectivism than these comprehensive treatments by Rosenstein-Rodan and by Morgenstern. All this contrasts with the flavour with which Mises was later to endow his economics of human action (in which a radical subjectivism in regard to time was to transform the analysis of human action in a manner entirely missing from twentieth-century mainstream microeconomics).

THE ECLIPSE OF AUSTRIAN ECONOMICS

No survey of interwar Austrian Economics can ignore perhaps the most arresting relevant feature of that period's history, viz. the precipitous decline in the school's professional fortunes which occurred at the end of the 1930s. At the beginning of the decade the school was held in highest international repute; Robbins and Hayek were introducing Austrian ideas, in microeconomics generally, in capital theory, and in business cycle theory, to the British scene with a degree of success which led to London's being puckishly described as a suburb Vienna. By the end of the decade this repute and success had virtually evaporated. We have already noticed Blaug's impression of the interwar period as being one of resounding Austrian defeats, in capital theory, in business cycle theory, and the theory of socialist economic calculation. We have indicated, on the other hand, that at least part of the eclipse of Austrian Economics in the 1930s can be explained, not so much by reference to doctrinal battles lost to formidable mainstream foes, as by reference to the degree of Austrian *success*. In the view of many Austrians, the extent to which, by the early 1930s, Austrian ideas had been absorbed into the British mainstream was a sufficient reason to believe that there was no longer any good reason to maintain a doctrinally distinct Austrian label. Apparently this feeling was also (and relatedly) partly the expression of the view that all neoclassical schools had faced a common doctrinal enemy, the German Historical School. The unifying effect of such a common foe, and the euphoria generated, at the start of the 1930s by widespread recognition of the final defeat of that common foe, was at least partly responsible, it appears, for the feeling among Austrians that one could now, once for all, lay aside narrow national-doctrinal labels, and join in joint international research programs for the advancement of economic science.

Yet doctrinal defeats were indeed suffered by Austrians during this period. Hayek's (and Mises's) "Austrian" theory of the business cycle was unquestionably seen as a casualty of the sudden and extraordinary professional success achieved by John Maynard Keynes's 1936 *General Theory*. Böhm-Bawerkian capital theory, seen, in the eyes of many, as the backbone of the Austrian cycle theory, appeared to be another casualty as a result of (or, at any rate, to be very much on the defensive against) the work of Sraffa, Knight, and Kaldor. It is true that at least the Austrians themselves were far from admitting defeat (see especially in the present volume, paper 20 in which Machlup valiantly defends the Austrian position from the Knightian onslaught). Hayek was, at the end of the 1930s, busily at work on his *Pure Theory of Capital* (which would appear in 1941). Yet Austrian capital theory was not to recover the attention and acceptance of the profession for decades to come. Even in the debate concerning socialist economic calculation, in which Austrians had been so influential and successful in stirring up an extraordinarily vigorous debate during the interwar period, it appeared as if, after the 1936 defenses of socialism by Lange and by Lerner, the pendulum of professional favour was moving decisively away from the Misesian position. Again, it would be many decades before the profession would recognize that Lange and Lerner had by no means provided the last word in this debate.

The papers in the present volume do not provide direct insight into these damaging doctrinal wars in which Austrians were (in the court of professional opinion) suffering so badly. This is no accident and should be explained. It is true that business cycle theories were seen as a most important element in interwar Austrian Economics, at least after Hayek made this field his own around 1930; and it is true that Böhm-Bawerkian capital-theoretic ideas were important for those theories. Yet, from the perspective of 1994, the wounds suffered by the Austrians in these wars do not appear as decisive or as historically significant as they must have appeared at the time. Böhm-Bawerkian capital-theoretic ideas have proven themselves, in the long run, to be surprisingly durable. Even outside the narrower scope of the late twentieth-century Austrian revival, those ideas have retained a remarkable degree of appeal.[23] And, while the current Austrian revival has certainly awakened renewed interest in Hayekian business cycle theory,[24] it seems fair to say that from the perspective of this Austrian revival that theory is seen as not at all so central (and therefore its post-1936 unfashionability as not so disastrous) as it may well have appeared during the years of the Great Depression, and at the time of the appearance of Keynes's *General Theory*. A paper (by Mises) which contains a statement of the Austrian Cycle theory is included in Volume III. In that volume there is also included Mises's classic statement concerning what he strongly maintained to be the impossibility of socialist economic calculation. Our assessment of the significance of the widespread (and in our judgment, wholly erroneous) conclusion in the profession that Mises's position had been decisively refuted by Lange and Lerner, will therefore not be provided in this Introduction. We should perhaps here point out, however, that interwar Austrian understanding of Mises's position on this matter was decidedly less than monolithic. The failure on the part of some Austrian-trained economists to appreciate Mises's thesis seems, in fact, paradoxically to be traceable precisely to the interwar Austrian preoccupation with the Imputation Problem. (On this problem, and its significance in interwar Austrian Economics, see in this volume [*Classics in Austrian Economics*], papers 15 and 19.) This "problem" was a peculiarly Austrian one, in that Austrian economists had been trained to believe that "consumers in evaluating ('demanding') consumer goods *ipso facto* evaluate the means of production which enter into the production of those goods."[25] (Such a belief seems to have been derived from Menger's doctrine of lower- and higher-order goods; the theory of imputation addressed the question of the precise manner in which the prices of resources in fact reflect the values of consumer goods.) Schumpeter at least was tripped up by this Austrian training, to reject Mises's argument as apparently denying a proposition of elementary economics. For this he was properly reproved by Hayek;[26] as we shall see in the Introduction to Volume III, Schumpeter's error arose out of his failure—a failure basically shared by the interwar Austrians in general—to recognize the role of the entrepreneurial market *process* in transmitting consumer valuations of consumer goods to the resources from which these consumer goods are produced.

It is true that the close of the interwar period found the Austrians in eclipse. The story of how the Austrian economic tradition survived and matured in spite of this eclipse is a fascinating one, but belongs to the "Age of Mises and Hayek," covered in Volume III of the present edition. It will be our task in the Introduction to that volume to show how the contributions made by Mises and by Hayek during the decades following 1940 would ultimately inspire a revival in the Austrian tradition, rendering the eclipse of the late 1930s and the related Austrian "defeats" of definitely lesser significance than might then have been thought to be the case.

NOTES

1. Stephan Boehm, "Austrian Economics Between the Wars: Some Historiographical Problems," Bruce J. Caldwell and Stephan Boehm (eds), *Austrian Economics: Tensions and New Directions* (Boston/Dordrecht/London: 1992, Kluwer).

2. Mark Blaug, "Commentary" [on S. Boehm, op. cit.] in Caldwell and Boehm (eds), op. cit.

3. Blaug, op. cit. p. 31. For further observations by Blaug on this topic, see his "Comment on O'Brien's 'Lionel Robbins and the Austrian Connection,'" Bruce J. Caldwell (ed.), *Carl Menger and his Legacy in Economics* (Durham and London: Duke University Press, 1990).

4. L. von Mises, *Notes and Recollections* (South Holland, IL: Libertarian Press, 1978), p. 94.

5. Boehm, op. cit. pp. 6ff.

6. On this point see for example the observations of Felix Kaufman, quoted in Margit Mises, *My Years With Ludwig von Mises,* 2nd edn (Cedar Falls, Iowa: Center for Futures Education, 1984), p. 202. See also that work, pp. 202–10, for additional recollections of the scenery in interwar Viennese economics, by Fritz Machlup, Gottfried Haberler, Paul Rosenstein-Rodan, and others.

7. Mises, op. cit. p. 73.

8. Mises, op. cit. p. 94.

9. On this point see, however, the closing sections of the Introduction to vol. iii, and especially the text there in regard to endnote 16.

10. Alfred Marshall, *Principles of Economics*, 8th edn (London: Macmillan, 1920), p. 1.

11. Edwin Cannan, *Elementary Political Economy*, p. 1. Both this definition, and that of Marshall referenced in the preceding note, are cited by Robbins, in his *The Nature and Significance of Economic Science* [1932], 2nd edn (London: Macmillan, 1935), pp. 1–2n.

12. Philip H. Wicksteed, *The Common Sense of Political Economy* [1910], (London: Routledge and Kegan Paul, 1933), vol. i, p. 2.

13. Robbins, op. cit., p. xv. (This is from the Preface to the 1st edn).

14. Robbins, op. cit., p. xiv (emphasis supplied).

15. Robbins, op. cit., p. 75.

16. Ibid.

17. See in the present volume, p. 111.

18. See in the present volume, p. 92.

19. See Mises, *Nationalökonomie* (1940), which appeared in the English version as *Human Action* (New Haven: Yale University Press, 1949).

20. See in the present volume, p. 173.

21. Gerald P. O'Driscoll and Mario J. Rizzo, *The Economics of Time and Ignorance* (Oxford: Basil Blackwell, 1985), p. 53.

22. See in the present volume, p. 338.

23. See especially J. Hicks, *Capital and Time: A Neo-Austrian Theory* (Oxford: Clarendon Press, 1973); M. Faber, *Introduction to Modern Austrian Capital Theory* (Berlin: Springer, 1979); G. O. Orosel, "Faber's Modern Austrian Capital Theory: A Critical Survey," *Zeitschrift für Nationalökonomie* (1981), pp. 141–55.

24. See for example, Gerald P. O'Driscoll, *Economics as a Coordination Problem: The Contribution of Friedrich A. Hayek* (Kansas City: Sheed, Andrews & McMeel, 1977).

25. Joseph A. Schumpeter, *Capitalism, Socialism and Democracy*, 3rd edn (New York: Harper & Row, 1950), p. 175.

26. See F. A. Hayek, *Individualism and Economic Order* (London: Routledge and Kegan Paul, 1949), pp. 90ff.

The ten papers collected in this volume are described as representing the "Age of Mises and Hayek." We shall indeed argue that the period from 1940 to 1970 does constitute such an "age," an era in the history of the Austrian tradition with a character and an importance of its own. In this Introduction we will explore and defend this proposition, that this period has a character and an importance of its own for the long-run evolution of Austrian Economics. This discussion will thus set forth the general perspective from which these papers by Mises and by Hayek have been selected, and will place them, in particular, in the context of the 120-year-long history of the Austrian School.

We must, of course, acknowledge that several of the papers in this volume, both by Mises and by Hayek, belong chronologically to the interwar period, and might thus have been expected to have been included in Volume II of the present edition. Such an expectation, it should be added, might have appeared all the more plausible in the light of the circumstance (already pointed out in our Introduction to Volume II) that up until about 1940 the work of both Mises and Hayek hardly expressed with any clarity those important insights which their subsequent work would articulate (and upon which we base our identification of the post-1940 decades as making up the age of Mises and Hayek). Our justification for including these pre-1940 papers by Mises and by Hayek in the present volume is twofold. First, it seems convenient, simply on authorship grounds, to keep all the papers of these authors together. Second, there are grounds for maintaining that (although we have asserted that the age of Mises and Hayek did not properly begin before 1940, since their own work prior to 1940 did not yet articulate the key insights with which we shall identify the post-1940 decades), the post-1940 work of Mises and Hayek did not spring forth from a vacuum. There is in fact much in the formidable pre-1940 corpus of Mises's writings which foreshadowed, at least, the character of his later, more maturely subjectivist

From *Classics in Austrian Economics: A Sampling in the History of a Tradition,* vol. 3, edited by Israel M. Kirzner (London: William Pickering, 1994), vii–xviii. Reproduced by permission of Israel M. Kirzner.

contributions.[1] And similarly for Hayek, there is sufficient continuity running through both his earlier work and his post-1940 writings to justify the inclusion of selected pieces of the former work together with those later papers which we see as belonging more unambiguously to the Age of Mises and Hayek.

THE CHARACTER AND SIGNIFICANCE
OF THE AGE OF MISES AND HAYEK

Briefly stated, our position will be that, in the decades between 1940 and 1970, Mises and Hayek were responsible, separately but in complementary fashion, for important extensions of the limited subjectivism which (as we have seen in the Introduction to Volume II) characterized the economics of interwar Vienna.[2] These extensions set post-1940 Austrian economics decisively apart from mainstream neoclassical micro-economics as it was developing during those same decades. The convergence toward the neoclassical mainstream which we saw as apparently characterizing interwar Austrian Economics (and as crystallized in the impact made, under Austrian influence, by Lionel Robbins's 1932 book) would, after 1940, *not* be a feature of the economics of Mises and of Hayek. Austrian economists, such as Machlup, who continued to maintain that what was important in the Austrian tradition had been successfully absorbed into the neoclassical mainstream, were evidently thinking of that tradition in its interwar manifestation, and were simply overlooking, or misreading, the post-1940 developments.

The post-1940 extension of subjectivism by Mises and by Hayek had a significance which went, we shall argue, beyond the substantive contributions of these two Austrian economists. The more radical subjectivism of their post-1940 work was to inspire the revival of interest in the Austrian tradition which has occurred subsequent to 1970 (the date which closes the period covered by the papers included in the present collection). From the perspective of the 120-year history of Austrian economics, therefore, the 1940–1970 period must appear as the era in which, while Austrian Economics was unquestionably in deep professional eclipse, there yet occurred profoundly important extensions of the subjectivist tradition, setting the stage for the late twentieth-century revival of professional interest in this tradition. In the course of this revival, the discovery of these contributions by Mises and by Hayek would stimulate explorations in the earlier history of the Austrian tradition which would lead back beyond the limited subjectivism of the interwar period, back beyond the foundational contributions of Böhm-Bawerk and Wieser (upon which so much of the interwar understanding was based), back to the original pioneering subjectivist insights of Carl Menger. The more radical subjectivism of Mises and of Hayek thus paved the way for a deepened appreciation, within the Austrian tradition, of what we have identified, in the Introduction to Volume I, as Menger's original vision. In this he saw how all economic phenomena and all human history are to be understood as the outcomes of human action, driven by the dreams and expectations, the desires and hopes, of human beings living in an open-ended world of radical uncertainty. We must now provide further details concerning the thesis which we have here outlined.

MISES, HAYEK AND THE EXTENSION OF AUSTRIAN SUBJECTIVISM

In the Introduction to Volume II we have drawn attention to the limited character of interwar Austrian subjectivism. During that period the subjectivism of Austrian Economics consisted in its refusal to see economic phenomena as inexorably determined by physical constraints: it was subjective utility, tastes and preferences which must be invoked in order to account for the arrays of goods produced, methods of production employed, prices of consumer goods and of productive resources arrived at in markets. However, given the tastes and preferences of economizing agents, given the physical circumstances surrounding a known society, these arrays of economic outcomes are seen as emerging as if by themselves "from the data." Although, as we have seen, Hans Mayer expressed his discomfort at Pareto's assertion that economics has no need for individual decision-makers (only for the photographs of their indifference maps), the truth is that for interwar Austrians (as for most twentieth-century mainstream microeconomists) that assertion rather accurately captures their picture of the world.

What is often not noticed, however, is that, for this Paretian picture of the world to hold, it is necessary to confine analytical attention to states of affairs in which individual anticipations concerning the decisions being made by other market participants are in fact correct and mutually sustaining. (In other words, an analytical picture of the world in which the Paretian assertion holds true can never be more than the picture of a world *already* in equilibrium.) For if the prices or availabilities of goods expected by a market participant turn out not to occur, then his decision plan will have been frustrated and the actual outcome can no longer be held to have been implicit in the data (which were believed to define the framework for his decision-making). A more complete subjectivism will have to refer to a disequilibrium world, and will have to recognize that in such a world, in which mutual awareness among market participants must be seriously flawed and incomplete, actual outcomes must depend, not merely on the relevant physical constraints and on tastes and preferences (being expressed at the moment of choice), but, most decisively, also upon the beliefs and expectations of market participants, and upon the way in which these beliefs and expectations change as a result of disappointments suffered and surprises experienced.

A more radical subjectivism must, in this way, if it is to sustain the economists' appreciation for the systematic character of market processes, encompass far more than an understanding of the subjectivity of tastes. It must, in particular, also encompass two distinct further elements. First, it must embrace an understanding of the role of mutual *knowledge* and of the possible ways in which improved mutual knowledge may be *learned*. Second, it must, for its analytical building block, move beyond the notion of pure economizing, toward a more open-ended concept of decision-making (that is, it must focus on the individual decision-maker, not as confronted by correctly and certainly *known* sets of options, among which he simply selects that which ranks highest on his *given* scale of preferences, but rather as somehow encompassing within his decision the determination of which courses of action he may consider as available options, and also determination of the relative preferability to himself of the available alternatives). Our thesis here is that Mises supplied the second of these two elements necessary for a radical extension of Austrian subjectivism, while Hayek supplied the first. The new subjectivism achieved by focusing on open-ended decision-making (going beyond Robbins's *given ends* and *given means*); and on possible processes of systematically improving mutual awareness (going beyond a bland assumption of complete relevant mutual knowledge), offered for the first time the possibility of a meaningful theory of market equilibration. We see in these radical extensions of subjectivism by Mises and by Hayek two complementary advances in Austrian thought which together justify our identifying the 1940–1970 period as the Age of Mises and Hayek.

It was Mises, in his radical conception of the role of *human action*, with its inescapable element (in the world of uncertainty) of entrepreneurial discovery, who refused to confine economic analysis to equilibrium states of perfect mutual information. In so doing he explicitly and decisively rejected the idea that choices are made as if dictated by preference rankings somehow established prior to (or, at any rate, apart from) the acts of choice themselves.[3] In other words Misesian subjectivism, in understanding economic decisions, requires that we focus not on the "state of affairs" (including given preferences) surrounding an act of choice (as if that state of affairs, in and of itself, determines choices made), but, most importantly, on the subjective *perception* by the agent of what the relevant state of affairs actually is. What drives market processes, Mises insisted, is the entrepreneurial function,[4] the drive for pure entrepreneurial profit; what makes the entrepreneurial function possible is the ability of some decision-makers more correctly than others *to anticipate* the course of events (and thus correctly to judge the relevant "state of affairs").[5] It is the entrepreneurial process which enables the market, in an ever-changing world, continually to nudge production decisions toward the equilibrium pattern (that would be consistent with relevant consumer preferences).[6] Mises's view of the dynamic market process is represented in this volume by paper 26.

It was Hayek, in a series of papers beginning in 1937 (most of which are collected in his 1949 book, *Individualism and Economic Order*) who focused on the importance of individual knowledge of market conditions, on the learning process of which the market process consists, and on the market and economic consequences of dispersed information. (Much of this work is to be found in the present volume, particularly in papers 29, 30 and 31). By drawing attention, in this way, to the crucial role of mutual information, Hayek was able to see the competitive, equilibrating market process discussed by economic theorists as a process of systematic learning by market participants of their mutual attitudes. In so doing he was opening up a fresh dimension for subjectivism, viz. the manner in which individuals, through their interpretation of their experiences, arrive at what they believe about the world in which they must make their decisions.

What it is important to notice, in this extension by Mises and by Hayek of Austrian subjectivism, is that the new, more radical, subjectivism did not at all require the abandonment of the notion of systematic, equilibrating market processes (as did the radical subjectivism, for example, of Shackle or Lachmann). The notion of equilibration does not depend, for Mises or for Hayek, upon our freezing the subjective elements in the human agent into sets of given preferences and given perceived physical possibilities and constraints. On the contrary, it is precisely the extended scope for subjectivism (permitting our analytical recognition for the entrepreneurial element, and for learning processes inspired by disequilibrium market experiences) which makes possible, for the Mises-Hayek understanding of markets, those systematic processes of equilibration so central to economic theory. It is all this which supports our reading of the state of Austrian Economics from 1940 to 1970 (by which date virtually all the important contributions to economics by these two writers had been completed) as making up a distinctive and important new era in the history of the Austrian tradition.

MISES AND HAYEK HOMOGENIZED? A DIGRESSION

Our thesis, that the 1940–1970 period in the history of Austrian economics constitutes "the age of Mises and Hayek" (and our identification of the unifying thread which joins together the work of these two Austrians, as consisting in their extensions of Austrian subjectivism) may not command the assent of all historians of economic thought, or even of all contemporary Austrian economists. In particular we wish to take note here of a recent paper by J. T. Salerno, in which he was explicitly concerned to deplore the tendency to "homogenize" Mises and Hayek, and to argue, on the contrary, that Mises and Hayek were responsible for "two very different paradigms," a Hayekian paradigm deriving from Wieser, and a Misesian paradigm representing "a development of Böhm-Bawerk's thought."[7] In Salerno's view, present-day Austrians are, *whether they recognize it or not,* divided into two camps, a "Misesian" camp and a "Hayekian" camp, with each pursuing a wholly distinct path in the understanding of the nature and significance of market processes.[8] Although Salerno does recognize a measure of what he terms "the 'Mengerian overlap' between the Misesian and Hayekian paradigms," he nonetheless insists on the need to rebut a common tendency among present-day Austrian economists "to conflate the views of Mises and Hayek."[9]

This is not the place to dissect Salerno's attempt at establishing the existence of two separate and conflicting "paradigms" in present-day Austrian thought. Despite Salerno's careful scholarship and subtle textual analysis of both Mises's and Hayek's writings, he is by no means convincing in his assertion of a gulf separating their understandings of how the market works (nor, indeed, can this writer claim even to have grasped with clarity the precise basis upon which Salerno makes his assertion). After all, historians of ideas may legitimately differ on whether to regard the differences between figures in intellectual history, as grounds for treating them as contending figures, or whether to see them as offering jointly a single general position, based on the elements which these figures share. However we do feel compelled to insist here, at any rate, that our identification of the 1940–1970 period as constituting a joint "age of Mises and Hayek," based on their complementary extensions of Austrian subjectivism does *not* depend on any "homogenization" of the ideas of Mises and Hayek.

We certainly do not need or wish to deny the existence of significant differences between Mises and Hayek in regard to fundamental methodological issues.[10] Although the economics profession has correctly viewed Hayek as supporting or extending the views of Mises on a number of key substantive issues (e.g. in the "Austrian" malinvestment theory of the business cycle, and in the socialist economic calculation debate), it is certainly true that Hayek's understanding of economics is not based on Misesian epistemological foundations. For Mises economic understanding is grounded in a priori reasoning (on this see in this volume, papers 24, and 25); for Hayek this is, explicitly, not the case.[11] Nor is it our position that, throughout their respective careers (or in fact at any time or times during those careers) Mises and Hayek would each have been willing to accept the other's formulation of the manner in which markets work, without modification. What we do maintain, however, is that during the 1940s insights were (separately) articulated by Mises and by Hayek which, *taken together* must, from the long-run *dogmengeschichtliche* perspective, be seen as *mutually reinforcing* and as most significantly advancing Austrian understanding. To insist on the existence of conflicting Misesian and Hayekian "paradigms" is—quite apart from its being unfortunate and confusing for Austrian research programmes of the 1990s—to divert attention from a highly significant episode in the history of the Austrian tradition. It is to this episode of subjectivist complementarity in the work of Mises and Hayek that we are here drawing attention.

THE END OF CONVERGENCE

We have cited, in the Introduction to Volume I, a statement by Mises from the early 1930s, to the effect that the various schools of economic theory active at that time were not substantially at odds with each other on the core propositions of the science. In the Introduction to Volume II we have further explored the convergence toward the British neoclassical mainstream which was indeed unmistakeably occurring in interwar Austrian Economics. The papers in the present Volume represent the age in which this convergent trend came to a somewhat abrupt halt.

By the end of World War II historians of economic thought were treating Austrian Economics as if it was no longer a live tradition. The eclipse of Austrian Economics which occurred during the late 1930s (and to which we devoted the final section of the Introduction to Volume II) seemed, from that post-war perspective, to be a permanent one. The histories of economic doctrines being written from that perspective tended to make references to Mises and to Hayek as surviving figures, relics of an earlier, but no longer vital, school of thought. What is of interest for our purposes is that such references tended (as we noted in the Introduction to Volume I) to emphasize the unfashionability, during this post-war period, of both the substance and the style of their work. To the extent that their work was identified as "Austrian" (and it was so identified), the age of Austrian convergence toward the mainstream was over.

From the perspective we have set forth in this Introduction, this treatment of Mises and Hayek was (if not for the right reasons, then at least in substance) largely correct. Contemporary historians of economic thought seemed to have placed Mises and Hayek together as being unfashionable largely on such grounds as their shared critical position on the possibility of socialist economic calculation, or their common refusal to accept the validity of Keynesian doctrines. We would prefer to emphasize their distinctiveness from the contemporary Anglo-American mainstream by reference to the radical advances they were making, or enunciating, during the 1940s, in our understanding of the most basic propositions of economic science. What is beyond contention is the recognition that Mises and Hayek could not, by any stretch of imagination, be considered as part of the dominant mainstream of early post-war economics.

There is a certain drama, it seems to us, in the circumstance that the radical advances to which we have drawn attention were being (separately) made by these two Austrian economists, not on Austrian soil, at a time when it was the conventional wisdom in the economics profession that Austrian Economics was no longer alive. These advances were being made after most of the important figures in the "interlocking circles" led in interwar Vienna by Mayer and by Mises had dispersed (for political or other reasons) and were to be found either in England or the United States. Precisely during the years when both the physical presence of an Austrian school and the doctrinal vitality of that school were seen as matters strictly for the history of economics, Mises and Hayek were developing and/or articulating insights which (*dogmengeschichtliche* hindsight now permits us to assert) were not only radically deepening Austrian economic understanding in a way which would stamp it as unmistakeably distinct from mainstream microeconomics, but which, decades later, would inspire a renaissance of interest in the Austrian tradition that would breathe new life into the Mengerian legacy. We can now see that the ideas which Mises and Hayek kept alive during the decades of Austrian eclipse were in fact ideas, adumbrated three-quarters of a century earlier by Carl Menger, which never were "absorbed into the neoclassical mainstream."[12]

THE SOCIALIST CALCULATION DEBATE: ITS
RELEVANCE FOR THE AGE OF MISES AND HAYEK

This volume contains two important papers published in the course of the celebrated interwar debate on the possibility of socialist economic calculation. The first of these papers is the original 1920 paper by Mises (here published as paper 22) in which he challenged the very possibility of central planning. The second of these papers (here paper 29) is Hayek's final (1940) critical assessment of the various attempts by socialist writers during the 1930s, to meet Mises's challenge. Following up on the ideas suggested in a section of the Introduction to Volume I, we wish to draw especial attention to these papers, and to the socialist calculation debate in general, in regard to what we have called the Age of Mises and Hayek.

The socialist calculation debate occurred during the interwar years. It would be possible for a historian of economic thought to treat the Austrian side of the debate (i.e. the side represented most prominently in the contributions of Mises and Hayek) as merely expressing the contemporary economics of interwar Vienna. While not categorically incorrect, such a judgment would, in our view, be misleading and overly narrow. The truth is that it was *in the course of* the socialist calculation debate that Mises and Hayek seem to have become alive to those fresh insights which they articulated only during the 1940s (after the debate had died down, and at a time when, in the contemporary mainstream view, the Austrian position in the debate had been definitively refuted in the work of Lange and of Lerner).[13] During this debate it appears that Mises and Hayek came to appreciate more deeply than before the extent to which their own position depended on understanding the market as an entrepreneurial process of mutual discovery. Our inclusion of these two papers in the present volume illustrates the point made early in this Introduction: with the benefit of hindsight, we can see how the pre-1940 work of these two writers anticipated, at least to some extent, their important post-1940 explicit advances in Austrian understanding. It is no accident that some of the most stimulating work in the late-twentieth-century renaissance of Austrian Economics has been in the revisionist history-of-ideas examination of the interwar debate on socialist economic calculation.[14]

An example of the manner in which the Austrians, in the calculation debate, were being impelled ahead of their fellow interwar Austrians (and without, it should be observed, themselves quite noticing that this was in fact occurring) is the clash between Schumpeter and Hayek (noticed briefly at the end of the Introduction to Volume II) on an aspect of this debate. Schumpeter (in his 1942 *Capitalism, Socialism and Democracy*, see p. 175 in the 3rd [1950] edition) had declared that there was in fact *no* problem for socialist economic calculation, because "consumers in evaluating ('demanding') consumers' goods *ipso facto* also evaluate the means of production which enter into the production of these goods." Hayek expressed his surprise that "an economist of Professor Schumpeter's standing should thus have fallen into a trap which the ambiguity of the term 'datum' sets to the unwary."[15] The sense in which valuation of factors of production is implied in the valuation of consumers' goods is a *logical* one, Hayek pointed out; and such an implication can be asserted only with respect to a mind which knows simultaneously not only all valuations of consumers' goods but also all the conditions of the supply of the various factors of production. While valuations of consumers' goods and the conditions of factor supply may be the "data," without a process through which knowledge of the data is arrived at, such data cannot be presumed immediately and automatically to generate values for the productive factors.

What is noteworthy here is: (a) that Hayek was articulating an insight concerning the role of knowledge and its discovery (in the market process through which factor prices are generated) that was, as far as mainstream microeconomics is concerned, ahead of its time; (b) that he was expressing surprise that an economist of Schumpeter's standing had overlooked this insight. It seems clear that, in enunciating this insight, Hayek did not believe himself to be making an analytical innovation (since, if that were the case, he could hardly have been surprised at Schumpeter's error). Yet, on the other hand, it seems clear that Hayek *had,* in this confrontation with Schumpeter, been impelled to articulate something new, since this insight had *not* been so stated (or at any rate, so clearly stated) before—and since in fact it *had* escaped Schumpeter (as well-trained as any interwar Austrian could have been!).

As Hayek pointed out in his criticism of Schumpeter, the error must be attributed to preoccupation with equilibrium theorizing (in which it is taken for granted that the objective facts embodied in relevant simultaneous equations are, in effect, fully known to market participants). Although the Austrian tradition had, of course, not employed Walrasian simultaneous equation analysis for the understanding of markets, there was little in interwar Austrian Economics apart from the Hans Mayer paper discussed in the Introduction to Volume II (where the paper is included as paper 16), that rendered interwar Austrian Economics inconsistent with equilibrium theory. (In his 1937 paper on "Economics and Knowledge," in which Hayek had begun to develop his critique of equilibrium theory, he had cited Mayer's 1932 paper.)[16] It was the debate concerning socialist economic calculation which appears to have been the catalyst that influenced the Austrians in articulating their non-equilibrium understanding of the systematic character of market processes. And it was certainly blindness to this aspect of the Austrian side of that debate which for so many decades permitted the belief in mainstream economics that Mises's challenge to the possibility of socialist calculation had been successfully met by the work of Lange and Lerner.

CONCLUDING OBSERVATIONS

Not all the papers in this volume can be linked directly to the fresh insights introduced by Mises and by Hayek during the 1940–1970 period, which as we have argued, justify our view of this period as a distinct era in the history of the Austrian tradition. We have also included several other classic papers by these writers, both for their intrinsic importance in the work of these economists, and for their general importance in any survey of Austrian work. Paper 23 provides a statement by Mises of what has come to be known as the Austrian (monetary, or malinvestment) theory of the business cycle. Paper 27 offers a classic work by Hayek concerning the intertemporal economy, which is often cited in advanced work on general equilibrium theory for its pioneering role in the development of that theory in its modern form. Finally, Paper 28 (1935) provides a well-known and important work by Hayek in which he explored some of the subtle problems in capital theory with which he would deal more extensively in his *Pure Theory of Capital* (1941).

Together with the remaining papers in this volume, these contributions offer, it is hoped, a useful introduction to the work of two major figures in the history of Austrian Economics. Taken altogether, the classic papers included in the entire three volumes of the present collection provide a sampling of the major economic contributions of the leading figures during the first century of an important school of modern economic thought. The importance of this school is certainly enhanced by the circumstance that it has, in the final decades of this century (i.e. in the decades immediately following the closing date for the present collection), enjoyed a significant revival within the profession. This development, which contemporary historians of economic thought have treated as rather remarkable, is both a tribute to and evidence of the continued vitality and fascinating quality of the ideas assembled in these volumes. This collection will therefore, it is hoped, contribute not only to a deeper understanding of a historic century in modern economic thought, but also to its continued refinement and progress during the century ahead.

NOTES

1. Besides a number of important passages in *The Theory of Money and Credit* [original German edition, 1912], (New Haven: Yale University Press, 1953), other relevant passages in this regard are to be found in the various papers collected in Mises's *Epistemological Problems of Economics* [original German edition, 1933] (New York: New York University Press, 1981).

2. We have argued this thesis in "Ludwig von Mises and Friedrich von Hayek: The Modern Extension of Austrian Subjectivism," N. Leser, ed., *Die Wiener Schule der Nationalökonomie* (Vienna: Böhlau, 1986), reprinted in Israel M. Kirzner, *The Meaning of Market Process: Essays in the Development of Modern Austrian Economics* (London: Routledge, 1992).

3. L. Mises, *Human Action* (New Haven: Yale University Press, 1949), pp. 102ff.

4. Mises, *Human Action*, op. cit. pp. 249, 297.

5. Mises, *Human Action*, op. cit. p. 288.

6. Mises, *Human Action*, op. cit., p. 335.

7. Joseph T. Salerno, "Mises and Hayek Dehomogenized," *Review of Austrian Economics*, vol. 6, no. 2, pp. 114ff.

8. Salerno, op. cit. p. 145.

9. Salerno, op. cit. ibid.

10. For discussion of some of these differences see Kirzner, *The Meaning of Market Process*, op. cit., pp. 119ff.

11. See F. A. Hayek, "Economics and Knowledge," originally published in *Economica*, February, 1937, reprinted in *Individualism and Economic Order* (London: Routledge and Kegan Paul, 1949); see also *Law, Legislation and Liberty*, vol. 3, *The Political Order of a Free People* (Chicago: University of Chicago Press, 1979), p. 205, n. 51 for Hayek's observation on a basic philosophical disagreement which he has with Mises.

12. On this see further, E. Streissler, "Menger, Böhm-Bawerk, and Wieser: The Origins of the Austrian School," K. Hennings and Warren J. Samuels, eds, *Neoclassical Economic Theory, 1870 to 1930*, pp. 178–81. On the part played by Schumpeter in keeping Mengerian ideas alive during this period, see Stephan Boehm, "The Austrian Tradition: Schumpeter and Mises," Hennings and Samuels, eds, op. cit., and I. M. Kirzner, "Commentary" (to this paper by Boehm), especially p. 244.

13. The writer has elaborated this thesis in *The Meaning of Market Process*, op. cit., ch. 6.

14. See especially Don Lavoie, *Rivalry and Central Planning: Socialist Calculation Debate Reconsidered* (Cambridge: Cambridge University Press, 1985).

15. F. A. Hayek, *Individualism and Economic Order*, op. cit., p. 91.

16. F. A. Hayek, "Economics and Knowledge," *Economica* iv (new series, Feb. 1937), p. 34 fn. I am indebted to M. Rizzo for pointing out this footnote to me (and for noting the absence of this footnote from the version of the paper reprinted in *Individualism and Economic Order*, op. cit).

INTERVIEWS

AUSTRIAN ECONOMICS AND THE
THEORY OF ENTREPRENEURSHIP
ISRAEL M. KIRZNER INTERVIEWED
BY STEPHAN BOEHM ON 2 MAY 1989

BOEHM: Professor Kirzner, may I begin on a personal note? When you started writing *Competition and entrepreneurship* (Kirzner, 1973), did you do this with any view, however dim, to inaugurating an Austrian revival?

KIRZNER: No, certainly not, I had no such presumptuous plans. Although I did hope by writing that book to explain to the economics profession what Mises, particularly, was saying. It always seemed to me that Misesian ideas were ideas which economists in general ought to appreciate, and which for some reason they were not able to appreciate. There was a communication barrier, and I saw my book as a way of somehow piercing that barrier and transmitting these Misesian and Hayekian ideas to the profession at large. I was under no illusion that this would turn around the profession in any way—and of course it hasn't. Nonetheless, I should say that I felt at the time I was writing a certain excitement, in that I sensed that there were a number of economists who would be waiting for such an exposition. I did not interpret that as meaning in any sense an Austrian revival, but nonetheless I had a feeling this was a book whose time had come.

BOEHM: At that time, who were the economists whom you considered to be writing in, or contributing to, the Austrian tradition?

KIRZNER: At the time there were really no writers. Of course, Mises died in 1973; Hayek was still writing, but most of his work was not in economics per se. Murray Rothbard was a prominent disciple of Mises who had written important contributions to Austrian economics, but in the early 1970s, I believe, the focus of his attention was more on libertarian political thought than on economics.

From *Review of Political Economy* 4, no. 1 (1992): 95–110. Interview by Stephan Boehm, reprinted by permission of the publisher, Taylor & Francis Ltd, http://www.tandfonline.com.

BOEHM: What do you think are the greatest achievements within the Austrian resurgence so far?

KIRZNER: I think the Austrian resurgence consists primarily of a small group of writers who have made their own contributions to Austrian economics, including Gerald O'Driscoll, Mario Rizzo, Larry White and Don Lavoie. Beyond this, the influence of the aforementioned group of writers and the renewed literature on Austrian economics have made themselves known to a very significant segment of the economics profession, both in this country and in a number of European countries, and indeed around the world. This has been fostered by a number of conferences that have been held over the past fifteen years or so, in which hundreds of young faculty members, both from the USA and Europe, have been exposed to Austrian ideas and have learned to understand and appreciate some of them. Besides, this has reflected itself in a significant European literature which I know you yourself are thoroughly familiar with.

BOEHM: Pursuing this a little bit further, what about achievements in substantive terms? Which areas of research would you single out?

KIRZNER: There has been particularly good work in the analysis of socialist calculation; there has been a renewal of interest in the theory of entrepreneurship, competition and monopoly; and there has been some exciting new work in the area of the possibility of free markets in banking.

BOEHM: Surely there must have been failures and disappointments as well?

KIRZNER: Certainly. It is somewhat disappointing that, of the hundreds of people whom I have just mentioned as having been exposed to Austrian ideas, so few of them, relatively speaking, have chosen to pursue their own research along Austrian lines. I think what has happened is that many of them do appreciate fundamental Austrian insights; they have acquired an Austrian way of looking at the market economy, but their own research tends to follow more conventional lines. Whether this is because of the incentives of the academic market-place in this country I don't know, but it has been a source of disappointment.

BOEHM: Would you say there is a difference between American and European scholars in this regard?

KIRZNER: I believe the incentive structure in this country is probably such as to discourage independent pursuit of Austrian ideas. This appears to be somewhat different in Europe. I am not entirely familiar with the academic incentive structure there, but I suspect that has something to do with the willingness of Continental (and UK) writers to pursue Austrian ideas more actively than their American counterparts.

BOEHM: There can be no doubt that the revival of interest in Austrian modes of thought has occurred against the background of a worldwide sea change in the political climate, away from a widely held belief in the efficacy of "interventionist" policies toward a "free market" approach, to put it in those crude terms. Many commentators perceive Austrian economics as having been in the vanguard of this reorientation of policies. Do you feel comfortable with the notion, or would you emphatically reject a contamination of Austrian economics with libertarianism?

KIRZNER: This is a good question. It is of course true that for many observers Austrian economics does have a political connotation. I think this view is fundamentally mistaken. I believe that Austrian economics by itself is politically and ideologically neutral. At the same time, however, it would be disingenuous and naïve to deny that Austrian economists have tended to favour a libertarian approach to economic policy. This has to be explained. Let me first pursue the central idea that Austrian economics per se is politically and ideologically neutral. Economics, if it is to maintain its scientific character, must surely be value free. The tradition of value freedom (*Wertfreiheit*) is something that Austrian economists have always respected. While the notion has been questioned by some writers, nonetheless Austrian economists have always believed in the possibility of a value-free approach to social science and have always believed that their economics was consistent with such an attitude. I think if we take Ludwig von Mises as a case in point this will illustrate all of the complexities and subtleties surrounding the issue. Mises believed himself and his economics to be value free. He believed that that value freedom was of tremendous importance in upholding the scientific character of the economics that he developed; and yet there can be no question that Mises was one of the most passionate champions of liberty. The solution to this apparent paradox is that Mises as a citizen was indeed passionately committed to promoting liberty; in order to promote that goal it was necessary in his view to show that economic science demonstrates certain qualities of a free society which are likely to meet the political and emotional approval of citizens at large. To achieve this demonstration it was necessary for economic science to be appreciated as the disinterested, austere, impartial pursuit of truth. Mises believed that Austrian economics met those criteria. I find myself fundamentally in support of this attitude of Mises. I believe that Austrian economics per se should pursue its search for economic understanding without prior political or ideological commitment. I believe as a goal it is of tremendous importance to aim at achieving it. It's certainly not easy, and I sympathize with those like Gunnar Myrdal who have argued that it is impossible. Once that has been said, it has to be recognized that Austrian economics as pursued until now has tended to demonstrate rather persuasively that a free society does achieve certain results that are likely to be widely applauded. For this reason we can understand how Austrian economists have tended to be supportive of the free society, and therefore, we can understand also why in the eyes of the public Austrian economics has tended to be perceived as a politically slanted body of knowledge. I think that judgement is incorrect and in a way unfair, but I can understand it.

BOEHM: This may have to do with the fact that, at least to my knowledge, there isn't any professed socialist economist working in the Austrian tradition. Would you agree?

KIRZNER: Yes, I think so. In fact, that's what I had in mind when I said that Austrian economists have tended to be supporters of a free society. Sometimes, with tongue in cheek, we say we are waiting for the first Austrian socialist to come up, because it's not logically impossible for such a combination to be imagined. Certainly Friedrich von Wieser, one of the great Austrian pioneers, was identified as a far more interventionist social thinker than some of his Austrian colleagues.

BOEHM: To continue in this vein: one of the aspects of modern Austrian economics that many, I suppose, would have some difficulty in comprehending is its outright dismissal—entirely consistent in a purely subjectivist framework—of *any* conception of "social welfare" (whether Paretian or not), while at the same time it makes all sorts of favourable pronouncements on the superiority of market arrangements. This apparent, or real, tension surely calls for some sort of explanation.

KIRZNER: Yes, this is one of the troubles which many critics of Austrian economics have had. In keeping with the now time-honoured rejection of the possibility of interpersonal comparison of utilities going back to Lionel Robbins's work in the 1930s, Austrian economics cannot accept the idea of the possibility of aggregating social well-being. Austrians are fundamentally committed to methodological individualism and do not feel the possibility of treating society as if it were a single mind whose well-being could be discussed in meaningful terms. At the same time, Austrians, as you point out, have been understood to be making all sorts of favourable pronouncements on the superiority of market arrangements. But when one analyses these pronouncements, I think one would find they do not consist of assertions that society will be better off under market rather than under interventionist arrangements. Rather, what is pointed out is that interventions will tend to discourage or to obstruct certain co-ordinative activities which would otherwise tend to emerge spontaneously. So, what is being argued is not that social well-being is increased—we have no clear idea what that might mean—but rather that the possibilities for independent members of society to make arrangements with each other for mutual benefit are likely to be enhanced by a promotion of freedom and are likely to be obstructed and hampered by well-meaning interventionist policies. This does not lead unambiguously to a defence of the free society; rather it points out that co-ordination, if co-ordination is considered to be desirable, does depend on the possibility of spontaneous action being taken by members of society. It is up to citizens to provide value judgements as to whether such co-ordination is a social goal worthy of support. It is not difficult to imagine a society in which the preferences of particular members of the public are such that one would wish to obstruct such co-ordination.

BOEHM: So you would flatly reject as meaningless a statement to the effect that society is better off under some institutions than others?

KIRZNER: We would reject that statement in anything other than a metaphorical sense. One should remember that we do use metaphors of this kind. We say that the USA went to war; we say that Europe emerged from the middle ages. These are statements which we understand as being metaphorical. There was no entity called the USA as such which decided to go to war; there were individual decision makers who participated in the political process. These metaphors do have their merit, and one should not reject them out of hand, but nonetheless, strictly speaking, they would have to be rejected.

BOEHM: Let me now move on to your own theory of entrepreneurship, which has been taken to task on several counts over the years. As far as I am aware, you have rarely responded to your critics. In fact, I can recall only one such occasion—your contribution to the Mises-*Festschrift* (Kirzner, 1982). Perhaps I can succeed in challenging you to respond. One long-standing bone of contention is the charge levelled against you to the effect that, like Schumpeter, you only consider the successful entrepreneur without paying any attention to the consequences of entrepreneurial failure. I wonder, what is your reaction to this?

KIRZNER: Let me first of all recognize that this kind of criticism is quite valid. I am guilty of paying insufficient explicit attention in my writings to unsuccessful entrepreneurs. I have occasionally tried in recent years to redress some of the balance because I think it is important in discussing entrepreneurship to pay explicit attention to the possibility of entrepreneurial errors, entrepreneurial losses and the disco-ordinating effects of such activities. Having said that, let me defend the bias which my writings on entrepreneurship do display toward the successful entrepreneur. Let us, for the moment, focus on the realm of human action in general rather than on commercial entrepreneurship in particular. As human beings we operate in an uncertain world; as human beings we take actions. Human action may be successful, or it may fail. The extent to which human actions may fail depends in large measure on our success in anticipating the conditions upon which our actions will impinge. One can easily imagine a world in which our actions are almost invariably frustrated by unexpected changes which lead us to regret having taken those actions. Were we to live in such a world, the focus of our attention would certainly be not so much on successful as on unsuccessful actions. It is a matter of empirical circumstance, surely, that in a very significant degree we act successfully and expect to act successfully, and that we are surprised and dismayed when our actions turn out to be frustrated. We are not totally shocked when a train fails to show up on time, but we are dismayed when we make an appointment to meet someone and that person fails to appear at the expected time. And this is true in so many different aspects of life. We take actions; these actions depend on anticipations in a world of uncertainty; and we have learnt to expect success. Our approach to entrepreneurship is somewhat similar. It seems to me that there is a strong bias toward successful entrepreneurship. Perhaps I can take as a benchmark the assertion of Frank Knight (an assertion with which I disagree) to the effect that the success or failure of entrepreneurship is largely a matter of pure chance and that there is no systematic tendency for entrepreneurial gains to outweigh entrepreneurial losses. I think this view is mistaken; there is in the world a bias toward successful entrepreneurship. This bias is built into our make-up as human beings. We are on the look-out for the circumstances which will make our actions work, and we are on the look-out for those circumstances which might frustrate our actions, and we tend not to take those actions which we believe will not work out. This means that unsuccessful entrepreneurial actions are likely to be surprises, and relatively infrequent surprises. Now, this is an empirical matter; it is not something that could not have been different. It is easy, as I suggested, to imagine a world in which most of our actions are frustrated. I believe that when we look around us we see this built-in bias toward successful entrepreneurial action. It boils down, I think, to the purposefulness of human beings. We are purposefully on the look-out for profits; we are obviously not purposefully on the look-out to make losses. It's that difference which makes successful entrepreneurship more the norm than unsuccessful entrepreneurship. This is the justification for the bias which my work certainly shows toward successful entrepreneurship, but this, I repeat, does not deny the validity of the criticism that explicit attention should be paid to the possibility of unsuccessful entrepreneurship. It certainly does occur.

BOEHM: Your story seems to rest on what Sir Karl Popper has christened "the bucket theory of knowledge." Arising from a change in some data, new knowledge is injected into the economy. Therefore, some decisions will be based on error, providing in turn profit opportunities for alert entrepreneurs. Your idea seems to be that there is some newly fabricated "objective" truth out there, merely waiting to be discovered by alert people. There doesn't seem to be any need for testing entrepreneurial conjectures in the market-place (as in Popper's "searchlight theory").

KIRZNER: I am not sure I understand your question correctly. Let me try to respond, and correct me if I have missed the point. My theory of entrepreneurship has sometimes been criticized as viewing the future as a kind of tapestry waiting to be unfolded: it is already there; it is simply behind the screen; it only has to be unrolled and then the future will come into the field of vision, whereas the truth surely is, the critics point out, that the future does not "exist" in any philosophically valid sense. It must be created so that the notion of alertness in the sense of seeing what is out there in the future is a mistaken notion. I recognize the philosophical validity of this kind of criticism. But I am not sure that is really relevant to the nature of entrepreneurship in its economic understanding. I think the distinction surely is one between an *ex ante* and an *ex post* perspective. From an *ex ante* perspective it is quite clear that the circumstances on which an entrepreneur's actions will impinge do not exist in any philosophically valid sense. They are going to be created by the actions of others, etc. But from the entrepreneur's perspective, what he is always trying to do, surely, is to project himself into the future and to ask himself: a year from now, when I look back on the history of the intervening twelve months, will I regret the actions I have taken, or will I be able to say that the actions I took were consistent with what will have already emerged? From this perspective, the philosophical validity of the idea of future events is really not the point. *Ex post* we look back and say: if only I had seen this coming. This opportunity was there. Does an opportunity exist? An opportunity is always something in the future; it does not exist. Yet we do talk about an opportunity existing, meaning that *ex post* we can say: well, the action I took was successful; or the action I took missed being a more proximate action that I might have taken. In that sense, I believe, the theory of knowledge about the future required for entrepreneurial understanding does not necessarily conflict with the more profound philosophical issues having to do with the uncertain future.

BOEHM: By definition, an entrepreneur is right while everybody else is wrong. Since in your theory everybody is, to a greater or lesser extent, an entrepreneur, this might pose problems. Consider the case of G. B. Richardson's hesitant investor. Clearly, there is a profit opportunity here, resources to exploit it are available, yet profitable transactions do not occur.

KIRZNER: Let me first demur to the assertion that by definition the entrepreneur is always right. As suggested in my answer to the preceding question, I certainly do recognize the possibility that an entrepreneur is wrong. In fact, there is nothing newsworthy about discovering that people make errors. If one looks at the world in the abstract it seems almost extraordinary that people take successful actions. We live in a world in which the future is unknowable, as Professor Lachmann so often pointed out. If one drives in a deep fog on a dark night without headlights, with one's eyes closed, it would seem remarkable that one would not drive off the road. So there is nothing inherently shocking about the possibility that the profit opportunity does not necessarily induce the transactions that might have occurred. What surely is noteworthy is how, despite the uncertainty, despite this fog regarding the future, so much successful and inspired entrepreneurial activity does take place. So, I don't think there is any problem as to why errors occur. I think, rather, what we need to do is to appreciate the great extent to which entrepreneurial alertness has enabled us to operate in this world of uncertainty with a remarkable degree of success.

BOEHM: Returning to my previous question: in the case envisaged by Richardson there has to be some sort of institutional precaution encouraging entrepreneurs to do their bit and making them feel confident enough that their actions are not thwarted, or impeded, by other entrepreneurs.

KIRZNER: As I recall the Richardson case, he has in mind here a profit opportunity which is clearly out there and which has been widely perceived as such, but precisely because the profit opportunity has equally been perceived by all entrepreneurs, it is no longer profitable for any one of them to pursue that opportunity. Now, I think this is an interesting special case. Obviously, looking at it *ex post*, what each of the entrepreneurs has failed to do is to recognize that the others would indeed succumb to the paralysing effect of the circumstance that the opportunity is seen by all. Each of them has made an entrepreneurial error; each of them was wrong. Now, the precise symmetry of Richardson's case is responsible of course for each of them almost inevitably having to be wrong, but this does not contradict the circumstance that surely each one of them was wrong. Once again, if the world was empirically always of this kind where the opportunity was obviously visible for many, one could imagine how this kind of entrepreneurial error would be much more prevalent than it really is. But I don't think that an inconsistency with the framework of entrepreneurial analysis that I try to pursue presents a problem. The special case of perfect symmetry certainly creates problems. But as Richardson himself recognizes—and this is a critical area for further research—asymmetries, or frictions, are important in providing the motivating power enabling the entrepreneurial market process to proceed. And it's quite true: it's like a friction between one's shoes and the road which makes walking possible. A perfectly smooth road, perfectly smooth shoes would frustrate ambulation entirely. I think something similar is going on here.

BOEHM: I take it you would not agree that Richardson's case reflects something of an institutional failure?

KIRZNER: Well, if all opportunities were obvious to all, one could then certainly suggest that an institutional correction might better grapple with such circumstances. In other words, the circumstance of a symmetry is hardly the empirical background which permits the entrepreneurial process in real markets to operate.

BOEHM: Suppose we have two types of entrepreneurs: those that are successful, that is, those who co-ordinate the market, and those who destabilize the market owing to malinvestment. Is there anything that we can say about a "tendency" toward equilibrium in that market? Obviously, this would turn on the question of which type of entrepreneur prevails, which is not simply a question of numbers but of the scale of capital invested. Can we say anything about the relationship between the co-ordinating forces introduced by one type of entrepreneur and the disruptive forces inaugurated by the other? In that case, the notion of "co-ordination" may take on a different meaning.

KIRZNER: Certainly I would accept the classification that seems to be implicit in your question, namely that the disco-ordinative forces in the market ought to be attributed to incorrect entrepreneurship while the co-ordinative forces ought to be attributed to the correct entrepreneurs. I think that's a useful classification.

BOEHM: Is this not a case of circular reasoning?

KIRZNER: Well, our esteemed colleague, Professor Lachmann, has, as you may know, used a terminology that attributes the set of disruptive forces to those spontaneous exogenous changes which continually impinge on markets. I think we have to recognize the importance of those spontaneous exogenous changes, but I also think we have to keep them quite separate from the disco-ordinative effects of unsuccessful entrepreneurial activity. Having recognized that, yes, unsuccessful entrepreneurial activity will be disco-ordinative. It certainly does boil down to an empirical question as to which are likely to be the more dominant. You are quite right, the scale of capital involved is crucial rather than being mere numbers, and I can only repeat something mentioned earlier in our discussion, namely that empirically disco-ordinative entrepreneurial activity does seem to be outweighed by co-ordinative activity. The old line going back to Bastiat, I suppose, is that Paris does get fed. In other words, when we look around at modern society, we can only be amazed at the extraordinarily intricate degree of division of labour and co-ordination characterizing it. Surely this is the empirical circumstance that has provided economists with the starting-point from which they have sought explanations. They have sought to explain this amazing phenomenon that without central directives such an efficient system of division of labour can emerge. It seems to me that an explanation in terms of a tendency toward successful entrepreneurship is convincing and fruitful.

BOEHM: Pressing this further, is it not inevitable that different types of entrepreneurs trespass on each other's terrain? For instance, when there are speculators who drive prices of commodities through the roof on whose better usage arbitrageurs thrive?

KIRZNER: I am not sure if I have got this question right; correct me if I have not. If the point is that speculators might drive commodity prices significantly above the true equilibrium price, this would have to be understood as an error on the part of the entrepreneurs who are permitting these resources to be bid away from their more valuable current purposes. To say error is inevitable, is going a little bit too far, but it is certainly possible. Wherever there are errors, there are profit opportunities created for others. There is always room for successful entrepreneurship to take off from others' errors, and even relatively successful entrepreneurship may be seen as simply a part of a larger error. That is to say, within its immediate context it is successful, but it is part of a larger trend that may be erroneous. That larger trend itself, precisely because it is erroneous, will tend to attract entrepreneurs who will discover that more serious error. The successful entrepreneurs operating within that larger error are performing a co-ordinative function within the framework of the error. So, I think, the circumstances you draw attention to may of course take place, but they are not fundamentally inconsistent with my point of view.

BOEHM: Another frequently aired criticism of your theory is that it does not take *time* seriously—as devastating a criticism as any that might be directed against any Austrian theory. You seem to assume that during the time an entrepreneur draws up a plan until its implementation "data" remain constant. As Ludwig Lachmann would say, in a world in which there are stock exchanges open round the clock, there will be huge capital gains and losses every minute. The constancy of data could not even serve as a useful piece of fiction.

KIRZNER: Certainly, an economic theory which doesn't take time seriously would be fatally deficient. I would recognize that in its simplest illustrations the theory of entrepreneurship does appear to be operating against a background of unchanging data, but I think that is simply for ease of exposition. There is nothing in the theory of entrepreneurship that requires us to assume that the world stands still while the entrepreneur engages in his activity. Quite the opposite, the essence of entrepreneurship surely is that the entrepreneur is pitting his imagination of what future changes would occur against the corresponding imagination of others. Therefore, the entire theory of entrepreneurship does depend precisely on the dynamics of the real world. Admittedly, the examples that we sometimes give of profit opportunities, particularly in the context of simple arbitrage examples, appear to depend heavily on a given background. But this is not essential to the theory at all, and in more elaborate investigations such a static background is explicitly rejected.

BOEHM: It has always seemed to me that your theory of entrepreneurship is situated most comfortably within a Marshallian partial equilibrium context.

KIRZNER: Well, we sometimes find it convenient to talk about the entrepreneur in a single commodity market. Certainly entrepreneurial activity would be much simpler in such a context; consequently, we use such a context for expositional purposes. But surely the entrepreneur as such, acting as he has always been imagined to do, i.e., buying in input markets and selling in output markets, or buying in wholesale markets and selling in resale markets, is straddling more than one market, and consequently can hardly be seen as potentially tied to a single market partial-equilibrium context. The entrepreneur in the multicommodity world is active in perceiving inconsistencies between markets in all areas of the economy. In the simplest model of a producing economy what the entrepreneur does is to buy resources and sell products; this is hardly partial equilibrium analysis.

BOEHM: It has been suggested that your entrepreneur is really nothing but Marshall's merchant.

KIRZNER: Marshall certainly had a richer perception of what the entrepreneur does than is often understood. I think that Marshall's theory is presented in the textbooks in a way in which the entrepreneur has very little to do, but I would not deny that there is a good deal of overlap between Marshall's merchant and my own entrepreneur except that the function of pure entrepreneurship is never, as I recall, made explicit in Marshall.

BOEHM: According to the "kaleidic" view of the world, as epitomized in the work of Shackle and Lachmann, speculative markets such as asset markets rule the roost. Do you feel there is a need for a special theory of entrepreneurship in such markets?

KIRZNER: No, I don't believe we need a special theory of entrepreneurship; I think that in the case of asset markets we must of course be very much alive to the long-term time dimension in which entrepreneurship is being exercised. When one deals with entrepreneurship in an asset-market context, one must recognize that entrepreneurship does not involve perceiving current profit opportunities but perceiving opportunities that will emerge only in the future, possibly in the long-distance future. There is no immediate discipline which the market can impose on the incorrect entrepreneur, but I still believe that the tendency for successful entrepreneurship is not to be discounted even in the abstract. So, as far as the theory of entrepreneurship is concerned, I don't think there is any fundamental problem.

BOEHM: Would the divergence of expectations characteristic of speculative markets pose any problems for their co-ordinating properties?

KIRZNER: I don't think so. After all, we are talking about divergence of expectations *now* about what the future reality will be. "Divergence" simply means that there are entrepreneurs who are going to be correct and entrepreneurs who are going to be incorrect. There is nothing surprising about that possibility. The mere fact that asset markets make it inevitable for transactions to involve both correct and incorrect entrepreneurs does not by itself change the nature of the forces at work. The realities will sooner or later manifest themselves. Sometimes I have the feeling that the writers who emphasize asset markets as somehow constituting a challenge to the theory of entrepreneurship are perhaps thinking of a world in which reality never catches up with markets—in which everything is simply a matter of beliefs and expectations, as in Keynes's casino view of the market. But surely future reality will always catch up with markets sooner or later, and as the future comes closer and closer, markets will tend to anticipate more and more accurately what those future realities will be. But I don't think there is a fundamental difference in kind between the theory of entrepreneurship in the asset-market case and the current-market case, recognizing as I do that the likelihood of error must be treated much more seriously in the former.

BOEHM: You have frequently been criticized for neglecting the role of entrepreneurship within organizations such as firms. What goes on within firms and in the sphere of production generally does not seem to constitute much of a concern for Austrian analysis. As one critic put it, "As with Keynes, the 'road to freedom' bypasses the shop floor. There is silence about the real processes of production" (Hodgson, 1985: 31). I wonder what is your reaction to this charge?

KIRZNER: Well, this is a criticism that applies not only to Austrian but to a great deal of modern microeconomics. It has always been a technique of exposition to treat the firm as if it were a dimensionless dot in economic space. But, of course, there have been many valuable contributions in organization theory dealing with what goes on within firms, and Austrians should pay attention to and learn from such theorizing. Let me point out that in some of my earlier work, particularly in *Competition and entrepreneurship,* I did draw attention to the possibility of entrepreneurial activities within the organization, the idea being that wherever there was room for discretionary behaviour on the part of an employee that employee might be seen as an independent entrepreneur who uses the employment possibility offered to him by the employer as a means for profiting himself within the assigned limits of discretion. This, I think, is important in today's corporate context where the complexities of the corporate structure may very well leave significant scope for discretionary behaviour within which the individual corporate employee may very well gain pure profit, if not pecuniary profit, perhaps profit in terms of prestige, material comfort and conditions of employment. Such things should not be ruled out, and certainly this could be identified as a possible area of future research.

BOEHM: Now, turning to the inevitable question: many commentators are troubled by the epistemological status of your propositions concerning "the tendency toward equilibrium." Is this a praxeological axiom, part and parcel of your definition of entrepreneurship, or a nomological statement reminiscent of Hayek's prospect held out in "Economics and Knowledge" concerning the "empirical" part of economics?

KIRZNER: This is a fascinating question; I think the answer must be none of the above. I do not see the assertion of a tendency toward equilibrium as a kind of apodictic statement. I do not believe there is a built-in tendency that must under all circumstances emerge for entrepreneurial activities to equilibrate the markets in which they operate. I do not think there is such an inevitable tendency. As mentioned earlier, I can easily perceive market conditions where the degree of change is so kaleidic, so drastic and so unpredictable that successful entrepreneurial activity will always be frustrated. However, the question always has to be, how do we account for the extraordinary degree of co-ordination which has historically been observed in market society? In other words, the problem always is not so much to predict what will happen but to explain what in fact does happen. This is, I can only repeat, something demanding explanation. Insights into entrepreneurial behaviour and what seems to be a net tendency toward successful entrepreneurship offer a practical and plausible explanation for a circumstance which strikes the scientist as a problem to be explained.

BOEHM: As I understand you, the Austrian position on the issue of equilibration is somewhat intermediate between the neoclassical and the post-Keynesian stance?

KIRZNER: I think, that's quite correct. Austrian economics does seem to follow, as Roger Garrison has pointed out, a kind of middle-of-the-road policy on this question, neither affirming the inevitability, nor denying the fundamental possibility, of equilibrium. However, I should point out that what I am saying here should not be represented as an official pronouncement on Austrian economics. My own views may differ in a number of respects from those of my Austrian colleagues.

BOEHM: What is your view of the role of institutions for the operation of market processes? On which institutions does the market process crucially depend? In particular, what is the role you ascribe to social and cultural conditions and institutions for the moulding of entrepreneurial activity and imagination?

KIRZNER: Institutions are certainly important; I think your question properly draws our attention to the different dimensions of institutions which we should be interested in. First of all, given a certain degree of entrepreneurial activity and imagination, what institutions are necessary for a market process to be able to be pursued? I think here we go back to the fundamental institutions of private property and freedom and enforceability of contract, which constitute the definition of a market economy. Certainly the market process does crucially depend on *some* system of private property—not a particular system, but *a* system of private property law must be presumed. The second part of the question very usefully draws attention to the possibility that institutions may be responsible for moulding an entrepreneurial attitude and for inspiring an attitude toward entrepreneurial alertness. I think this is an important question which still offers a very fruitful field of potential research. I can see that perhaps this involves some extraeconomic analysis, perhaps psychological research as to what kinds of institutional frameworks for society are likely to promote an attitude toward risk-taking and challenging uncertainty, and an attitude toward being awake and alert. Of course, some work has already been done by a number of writers on the cultural determinants of entrepreneurial attitudes. I believe this is a most useful field of psychological research in which economists should be vitally interested.

BOEHM: Moving finally away from entrepreneurship, let me point out that in your work you always seem to have had an intense interest in capital theory. In a long paper, still unpublished I believe (Kirzner, 1983), you have addressed yourself to the Cambridge controversy, which by many commentators was perceived to have dealt a deadly blow to the Austrian theory of capital. In your "Postscript to the 'Grand Debate'" you try to make the case that the pure time-preference approach as espoused by Fetter and Mises escapes the strictures of the UK Cantabrigians concerning the reswitching and capital-reversing paradoxes. How would you, on the basis of a pure time-preference approach to interest, defend the claim that a reduction in the rate of interest and the subsequent adoption of a less time-consuming production process would not constitute a puzzle for the theory? I realize that a satisfactory response to this question would cover so much ground that we could easily spend hours on it, but may I nevertheless persist and ask you to convey the essential point in a few minutes?

KIRZNER: The Cambridge (UK) criticism of Austrian capital theory, it seems to me, is largely directed at, and its validity is largely confined to, that version of Böhm-Bawerkian theory that sees time, or waiting, as productive. Time is seen as a factor of production. It seems obvious that different production processes ought to be able to be ranked in terms of the quantity of this factor of production that is required. This presumes that there is a unidimensional way of ranking different production processes as involving more or less time. If so, then one understands how it becomes a damning paradox if it can be shown that a reduction in the cost of using time seems to be associated with a reduction in the quantity of time used. This is the basic paradox involved in the capital-reversal and reswitching problems. The Fetter/Mises approach to Böhm-Bawerkian theory does not attribute interest to the productivity of capital, or to time or waiting. Interest is simply emerging as a matter of evaluation, given a prevalent attitude toward time. Given widely shared positive time preferences, there is in the Fetter/Mises view a strong bias toward positive rates of interest, which has nothing per se to do with the productivity of time. Once one no longer treats time as a factor of production, then it does no longer become necessary to view each production process as involving either more or less time than a second process. Rather, what we would be able to do is to ask ourselves: is it possible for a reduction in the cost of time, a reduction in the rate of interest, to be associated with a reduction in the degree to which one uses time in production processes? This, too, would appear to involve a paradox. Even if time were not productive, surely one would expect a reduction in the cost of waiting to inspire the taking advantage of the possibilities offered by more waiting. But the solution has to be that all of the cases of capital-reversal and reswitching involve production processes exhibiting multidimensional inputs of time so that it seems to be simply incorrect to say that in these cases we have situations where a reduction in the rate of interest involves the use of the less time-consuming production process. Rather, what happens is that the same production process, because it involves time injected at different points in the process, can be seen as calling for more postponement, or calling for less postponement, depending on the rate of interest. Leland Yeager has pursued a somewhat similar defence of the Austrian view. I believe this does depend on rejecting the notion of time as a productive factor. I think that is the essential point.

BOEHM: Let me also conclude on a more personal note. In your work, you always pay generous tribute to Ludwig von Mises. I wonder whether there are any other influences which have profoundly shaped your outlook as an economist?

KIRZNER: Certainly, Ludwig von Mises as my teacher has been a major influence. But I think that I would not have appreciated that influence, had I not learnt a great deal from neoclassical writers. The major neoclassical economists influenced me a great deal, partly because they explicated the universe from which the more profound Austrian insights that I learnt from Mises could be derived. Philip Wicksteed was another important influence in my early days. Let me say a few words about Professor Hayek and what I perceive to be the relationship of his work to that of Mises. The work of Mises and Hayek is in many respects fundamentally different. Yet it always seemed to me that their work exhibits a great deal of complementarity which has helped me reach whatever understanding I have of the market process. Mises was superbly clear on the entrepreneurial character of the market process, whereas one finds very little explicit recognition in Hayek. Conversely, in Mises you will find very little explicit attention to the role of knowledge, whereas of course it is precisely knowledge that is most relevant to Austrian economics. I think that by bringing together the entrepreneurial perspective of Mises and the recognition that Hayek has made clear to all of us—viz. that economic processes are processes of communicating knowledge—it becomes possible to perceive the kind of processes involving the pure discovery of knowledge (as opposed to the mere communication of existing knowledge) which I see as the essence of entrepreneurship. So I think that the confluence of the teaching of Mises and Hayek had a tremendous influence on my understanding of the market process.

BOEHM: Thank you very much indeed, Professor Kirzner.

REFERENCES

Hodgson, G. M. 1985: Persuasion, expectations and the limits to Keynes. In Lawson, T., and Pesaran, H., editors, *Keynes' economics: methodological issues*, London: Croom Helm, 10–45.

Kirzner, I. M. 1973: *Competition and entrepreneurship*, Chicago: The University of Chicago Press.

———— 1982: Uncertainty, discovery, and human action: A study of the entrepreneurial profile in the Misesian system. In Kirzner, I. M., editor, *Method, process, and Austrian economics: essays in honor of Ludwig von Mises*, Lexington, Mass.: D. C. Heath, 139–68.

———— 1983: Pure time-preference theory: a post script to the "Grand Debate." Research Report no. 83–23, C. V. Starr Center for Applied Economics, New York University.

THE KIRZNERIAN WAY: AN INTERVIEW
WITH ISRAEL M. KIRZNER

AUSTRIAN ECONOMICS NEWSLETTER: You were Mises's assistant for some years.

KIRZNER: Yes, and in addition to attending his weekly lectures, I spent time in his office downtown being available for his students. He used to read my manuscripts, and I was honored to have him write the introduction to *The Economic Point of View* (1960). Otherwise, he didn't comment very much on my work, and we didn't have extensive discussions on the details.

It was not easy to discuss matters of theory with Mises. He was always gracious, polite, and kind, but at the same time reserved. There was also a bit of a language barrier. He spoke English perfectly, but I think he still *thought* in German.

I would never claim that my interpretations of Mises were given his personal approval. Most of what I understood of Mises was attained from diligently studying and thinking about passages in *Human Action* again and again.

AEN: Any other insights on Mises the man?

KIRZNER: He was a man of great integrity. I remember an episode after completing my master's degree in 1955. I was studying with Mises and was strongly under his influence. But I also applied for fellowships at other schools. I received an offer from Johns Hopkins. I went to ask Mises's advice on whether I should go. Even though he had very few students, he told me to accept the offer. He pointed out that Fritz Machlup teaches there, and that Johns Hopkins is a prestigious school. As it happens, I did not take his advice, but this says something about his concern for his students' interests. It was an extraordinary gesture on his part.

AEN: How were you first attracted to Mises?

From *Austrian Economics Newsletter*, Spring 1997, volume 17, number 1, 1–8. Reprinted by permission of the Ludwig von Mises Institute.

KIRZNER: At first, I did not know who he was. But as I was looking around for programs and professors, I *did* happen to notice that Mises seemed to have more books than anyone else. I found that impressive, so began my studies with him. Eventually I was hooked.

AEN: Did you know you were getting involved in a school of thought that most of the profession regarded as old-fashioned?

KIRZNER: Not at first. But I eventually came to realize that the mainstream of the profession was headed in a different direction. In 1954, there was no Austrian movement. There was no Austrian School. There was Mises, and there was Hayek. They must have been seen as the last of their generation, and not too much of a threat.

Now, I don't regard my choice as heroic by any means. True, I was isolated as far as the profession was concerned. But I received my PhD, taught at New York University, did my work, and published my books. I was content with this, and had no great difficulties. Gradually, as the sixties wore on, I began to think I had an idea that might even have an impact on the profession. Indeed, *Competition and Entrepreneurship* interested some reviewers at the University of Chicago Press, which pleased me very much.

AEN: When you look at the Austrian School today, what do you think?

KIRZNER: Its sheer size is very pleasing, of course. To some extent, the fact that the profession at large has moved even further along in the technical-mathematical direction created an opening for the Austrian School among younger scholars. They began to see the sterility and aridity of the way the mainstream has gone. The Austrian School appears as a whole different way of approaching the discipline. And today, there is room out there for Austrians in the profession—however, not yet at the *top* of the profession.

AEN: In today's colloquium, and in your writings, you seem to be increasingly occupying what's sometimes called Austrian "middle ground."

KIRZNER: No question. This has been true ever since people have begun to take more extreme positions on the question of the uses of the equilibrium construct in economics. When they began to deny its relevance altogether, I began to realize that my position is not as extreme as theirs. The phrase "middle ground" was first used by Roger Garrison to describe a theoretical position that neither entirely spurns nor fully embraces a construct like equilibrium that is most often associated with neoclassical economic thought.

AEN: Is it excessive subjectivism that troubles you?

KIRZNER: I wouldn't say so. The argument that says we can't use equilibrium constructs at all is not a valid use of subjectivism. It takes economic theory in an entirely different direction.

AEN: What is the middle ground on the question of equilibrium?

KIRZNER: The two extremes, simply stated, are "equilibrium always" and "equilibrium never." The "equilibrium always" view is the strict neoclassical/Chicago perspective which never permits us to consider a world in which everything is not completely adjusted. The other extreme is one in which there are no systematic, overriding tendencies that could lead to regularity. I don't think an Austrian economist can be satisfied with either of these positions.

Austrian economics cannot be "equilibrium always," but neither can it be "anything goes." As Mises used to say, it was the great contribution of the classical economists to enunciate the concept of economic law. There are, indeed, systematic consequences to our actions. If one accepts that economics is the study of those systematic consequences, one cannot live with a perspective that sees the world as so open-ended that anything is possible. That's why I would disagree with the characterization of economics as essentially the study of the unfolding of an uncertain future.

AEN: Is Professor Mario Rizzo correct that Austrians must think in terms of non-equilibrium "real time" as versus some static variant?

KIRZNER: I think it is highly useful to think in non-equilibrium terms, to be open to the possibility of change and surprise. You certainly cannot do good economics without understanding the role of surprise. But if one pursues this to the point where the surprises tend to overwhelm the regularities, then I don't believe you have a science that reflects existing realities.

AEN: There's an impression out there that you believe entrepreneurship is always equilibrating. Is this a mischaracterization of your position?

KIRZNER: Yes. Entrepreneurship is not always equilibrating. The equilibrating features of the real world ought to be ascribed to entrepreneurship; it doesn't follow that all entrepreneurship is always equilibrating. Entrepreneurs make losses, and losses are not equilibrating.

The idea I reject is this: there is successful entrepreneurship, there is unsuccessful entrepreneurship, and it's a toss-up which is going to outweigh which in the end. That was Frank Knight's position, by the way, and I think that is a mistake.

The fundamental Misesian insight into human action is that it involves a tendency to be right rather than to be wrong. People have an interest in being right. They do not have an interest in being wrong. This definitely, distinctively weights the tendency of human action in the direction of being right.

This does not guarantee "equilibration always." And certainly a permanent equilibrium is out of the question. It would be incorrect even to *imply* that in any given time period, the changes we observe are necessarily equilibrating. But there are tendencies which tend to overwhelm disequilibrating forces in the market, most of the time.

AEN: Are there times when disequilibrium is a sure thing?

KIRZNER: Much depends on the nature of the exogenous changes we are experiencing. In a world in which change is of such a volatility that entrepreneurial activity and action are continually frustrated, we will find continual non-equilibration. There are historical circumstances in which chaos, violence, and uprisings do indeed overwhelm orderliness and evolution. Perhaps we can even point to such occasions. For equilibrium to be the regular tendency, we do need, empirically, a certain environment of stability.

AEN: Can you give an example of such volatility?

KIRZNER: Suppose people's tastes change every day, *drastically*. Sometimes they like the temperature inside to be 32 degrees; other times, they like it very hot. Sometimes people eat three times a day; sometimes only one. Sometimes they like to wear shoes; other times, they insist on going barefoot. Suppose that technology were to change *drastically* and in unexpected ways. This is extreme volatility. In these times, we have no guarantee whatsoever that a market theory can really provide a systematic understanding of change. In such a world there would be so little that is stable, I don't believe an economic theory would be of much help.

AEN: In these times, does economic law cease to exist?

KIRZNER: Not at all. It only becomes more difficult to take account of the pattern of change. For example, we can always predict that an increase in demand will increase the price. But under extreme volatility, demand changes and wobbles so quickly that the forces that would otherwise cause prices to rise will be swamped temporarily by forces that cause them to fall. We can't rule it out. But economic law still continues to be the underlying reality.

AEN: Do you regard Joseph Schumpeter's theory of entrepreneurship as an Austrian theory?

KIRZNER: There's a good deal of controversy about that. There was personal tension between Mises and Schumpeter, and most of what we would currently identify as key Austrian features were not accepted by Schumpeter. Walrasianism did dominate his thinking.

Yet I have defended Schumpeter as an Austrian in a very special way. He never really bought into the neoclassical view of "equilibrium always." Certainly his emphasis on the entrepreneur is consistent with that. He never forgot the lessons he learned from Austrians, even if he *tried* to forget them. The Austrian revival owes something to Schumpeter.

AEN: What is the relationship between his theory and yours?

KIRZNER: Let me recognize that in my 1973 book I was perhaps overeager to draw a distinction between Schumpeter and myself. In later writings I have pulled back somewhat from that. I have recognized that you can subsume the Schumpeterian entrepreneur under my own theory, if you like.

For Schumpeter, the entrepreneur was a disrupter. He breaks an existing, evenly rotating system. Paul Samuelson has a metaphor for Schumpeter's view of the world. He said it's like a violin string. You pluck it, it vibrates, and finally settles down. I would say that Schumpeter saw the entrepreneur as the person who is doing the plucking from a taut position, generating the change. All the vibrations are attributed to his action.

Originally, I emphasized the other side of the issue. The entrepreneur generates a tendency to restore the evenly rotating system to a new level or a new pattern. But it is the restoration, not the disruption, that is brought about by the entrepreneur.

AEN: How would his, and your, theory apply to a specific technological change?

KIRZNER: Imagine Victorian England, where everything is calm and still, with horse carriages and trains carrying people here and there. Along comes the entrepreneur who invents the automobile. The stillness is utterly shattered. People lose jobs and physical resources are shifted to new lines of production. All of this is to be ascribed to the entrepreneur in Schumpeter's view.

In one sense this is correct. But my 1973 book emphasizes a different point. We have to recognize that when the entrepreneur discovers the automobile, he is not simply disrupting the calm. He is identifying what was in fact waiting to be introduced. Technological knowledge was being misapplied. Resources were being wasted on trains, carriages, and bicycles, when, in fact, what was waiting to be put together was this new gadget called the automobile. A person who recognizes this is responding to a preexisting, gaping hole in the market.

Of course, the role of the entrepreneur can be understood as disrupting in a very down-to-earth sense. People had jobs and their jobs are destroyed. People had careers, and they are now gone. Granted. But what appear to be disruptions aren't disruptions at all. They are simply the revealing of misallocations that were there before.

Very often people object. "You say entrepreneurship is coordinating, but surely an entrepreneur who discovers new ways of doing things is putting people out of work and disrupting people's expectations."

Yes, he is, but in a more fundamental sense, he is correcting an already existing discoordination. He is redirecting resources that are already misplaced. People do not have to go on for years and years behaving in ways that are socially inefficient. The person who abruptly draws their attention to this inefficiency is assisting in the process of economic coordination. However, this does not reduce, in any way, the importance of Schumpeter's focus on the innovation of the entrepreneur. Nothing I have said should be interpreted to do so.

AEN: What do you mean in saying something is "waiting" to be discovered?

KIRZNER: Philosophically, people have objected to that. I do not mean to convey the idea that the future is a rolled-up tapestry, and we need only to be patient as the picture progressively unrolls itself before our eyes. In fact, the future may be a void. There may be nothing around the corner or in the tapestry. The future has to be created. Philosophically, all this may be so. But it doesn't matter for the sake of the metaphor I have chosen.

Ex post we have to recognize that when an innovator has discovered something new, that something was metaphorically waiting to be discovered. But from an everyday point-of-view, when a new gadget is invented, we all say, gee, I can see we needed that. It was just *waiting* to be discovered.

AEN: Consumer demand was there, resources were there, and the technology was there . . .

KIRZNER: Yes, so there was no reason why it wasn't being done. The entrepreneur is alert to this reality, to the profit opportunity it represents, and responds creatively to it.

AEN: Some have said your careful definition of the "pure" entrepreneur is excessively abstracted from that of the capitalist, and that in this respect your theory departs from Mises.

KIRZNER: I know that Murray Rothbard and Joe Salerno have suggested this, but I don't think it is correct. Frankly, I've always thought I picked up the idea of the "pure entrepreneur" from Mises. I've written a comment on this view in a book edited by Bruce Caldwell and Stephen Boehm [*Austrian Economics: Tensions and New Directions*, Boston: Kluwer, 1992]. I argue that it depends on your analytical purposes. We recognize that in the real world the pure entrepreneur never exists. A pure laborer never exists. A pure capitalist never exists. Yet it remains highly useful to speak of the pure entrepreneur.

AEN: In theory, then, if not in reality.

KIRZNER: Yes, but I have no difficulty in recognizing the theoretical meaning of the pure entrepreneur. The more difficult question is: can you have a capitalist who is not an entrepreneur? In a world of uncertainty, I don't believe so. If there is no pure capitalist, because every capitalist must also be an entrepreneur, then what does one gain by talking about the pure entrepreneur? It helps us to understand the precise nature of his contribution to the process of economic change.

Let's assume that all the uncertainty in the world is subsumed within the entrepreneur, and nobody else has any element of uncertainty. The actions of everyone else are not human actions; they are the movements of robots. Neither the laborers, nor the capitalists, nor the consumers are entrepreneurs. They are Robbinsian maximizers. In this world, the pure entrepreneur buys resources at prices which are known to the resource sellers, sells them at prices which are known to the buyers, and he's the one who sees the difference between the two.

In the real world, of course, no one performs a purely non-entrepreneurial function. The consumer is an entrepreneur, the capitalist is, and the laborer is too. They are all taking risks, taking leaps. They are all forgoing some opportunities for others. Granted. But that doesn't by itself preclude us from talking about the central entrepreneurial function of being alert to new opportunities, of discovering something that others have not seen.

AEN: And this understanding is consistent with your 1973 book?

KIRZNER: I don't believe I've made substantial revisions. I've made revisions from my earlier books. My *Economic Point of View* [1960], *Market Theory and the Price System* [1963], and *Essay on Capital* [1966] were not informed by the entrepreneurial insights, which I only gained later.

AEN: *Market Theory and the Price System* is said to have made a contribution to the Austrian view of efficiency.

KIRZNER: I sweated a great deal over that book. I put a tremendous amount of thought into trying to translate Misesian economics, as I understood it then, into terms that would be understandable to the profession at large and usable at the undergraduate level. It wasn't easy. It is probably the winner in a contest over having sold the least copies.

AEN: Do you regard your entrepreneurial insight as a bridge between the Austrian and neoclassical worlds?

KIRZNER: The word "bridge" is a diplomatic word. I've been accused of turning Austrian economics into a footnote of neoclassical economics. I think that is incorrect. But I would accept the word "bridge." It is a bridge in the best sense of the term.

Neoclassical economics in its modern version is an "equilibrium always" theory. It didn't use to be that way. Frank M. Machovec has written a book in which he points out that the great neoclassical thinkers from 1880 to 1930 did not really believe in a world built on equilibrium theory. They thought about the price system as a competitive process. It's the modern version of neoclassical economics that has been Walrasian—and Machovec goes further to argue that not even Walras believed in "equilibrium always." I don't think I would go that far, but I see his main point.

The idea of the entrepreneur enables us to see how there might conceivably be an equilibrium system, or why an equilibrium system might be of any interest to us. Even if we deny that equilibrium is ever attained, we can look at neoclassical theory and understand it in relationship with Austrian theory.

When Mises talked about the evenly rotating economy as a model against which to understand equilibrating processes, he is doing exactly what should be done. We can understand market process theory by *contrasting* it with equilibrium states. How can a contrast be a bridge? It can by drawing attention to the role of equilibrium models in understanding the process. But I strongly disagree with those who have said that this theory of the entrepreneur merely restores neoclassical economics to its pristine glory.

AEN: But if a neoclassical economist told his class about Kirzner's theory of entrepreneurship, that would be an improvement.

KIRZNER: Certainly, given today's rigid environment. Once, however, I gave a talk on the Austrian view of the market process, and the late Abba

Lerner was there. He said that what I was calling the Austrian view is precisely what he had been taught in school and had long accepted. I'm sure it's true. The perfectly competitive model was never dominant in neoclassical economics until E. H. Chamberlin and Joan Robinson brought us imperfect competition. Then, they retroactively attributed *perfect* competition to those that preceded them.

AEN: Prior to this, Mises even thought of himself as within the mainstream of thought.

KIRZNER: That's right. There's a passage which I've often quoted from a 1932 piece where Mises is saying that all modern schools of economics are basically saying the same thing. That is very revealing. What did he mean? He was noting that all schools have abandoned the German historical school. In short, *vis-a-vis* the common enemy, they are all saying the same thing.

Later on, the differences between the schools—Walrasian, Marshallian, Austrian—began to widen. Think of them like three parallel runners who start off close to each other but move progressively further apart as they proceed.

By the time I came to study under Mises in 1957, I don't believe he would have subscribed to the view that all schools taught the same thing.

AEN: What in particular changed Mises's mind?

KIRZNER: I've made the argument, in *The Review of Austrian Economics*, that it was partly a result of the socialist calculation debate in the 1930s. This debate exposed deep differences between Austrians and others in the very conception of what the market is and how it works, I think it's true of Hayek too.

AEN: Congratulations on the new edition of *An Essay on Capital,* along with two additional essays, just out from Edward Elgar. How did that earlier book come about?

KIRZNER: When I wrote *An Essay on Capital* in 1966, I didn't believe I was breaking any new ground. After completing my 1963 book, I spent several years hoping to write a history of capital theory since the 1880s. I found myself getting deeper and deeper in what I found to be an endless muddle of ideas, confusion of purposes, and definitional ambiguities. I finally gave up. I found instead that it would be useful for me to write down in clear and simple terms a summary of what I got out of my research, in light of the Misesian framework.

AEN: Can you summarize the argument of this work?

KIRZNER: Usually, people look at capital as objects, usually highly valued objects. That tempts us to think that physical capital is itself the source of the flow of income. The view of capital I present relates directly to the purposes of individuals. I insist that Austrians see capital as the intermediate form in which plans are brought about.

I like to use the metaphor of the half-baked cake in an oven. This is a desk, and the person who made it was planning that I would use it to write on, put papers on, and so on. By itself, the desk is a half-baked cake, just as are cars, buildings, and machines.

It goes back to Eugen von Böhm-Bawerk's view of inchoate output. We must look at capital, not in objective terms, but as representing the plans of individuals and their forecasts of the future. There are overlapping, multiperiod plans, of course, so that new cakes are going into the oven before old ones come out.

AEN: It is said sometimes that Hayek should not have spent so much time writing the treatise on capital that appeared in 1941.

KIRZNER: He expected that book to be followed by a subsequent volume, I believe. He stuck it out, and produced a very difficult book that is largely ignored today. I have some criticisms of that book too, and it is good that he moved on, but it was an honest and grand effort.

AEN: In those early years, did you have a goal of doing more macro-oriented work?

KIRZNER: No. I have never really seen myself as a macroeconomist. Of course I've taught macro for many years, yet I felt I never *understood* Keynesian economics. It assumes that decision making doesn't matter. All that matters are the relationships between totals. While I often pointed out what seemed to me gaping holes, I had no great desire to counter this with a separate macroeconomic theory of some sort.

AEN: You've never thought of providing a systematic critique of the Austrian business cycle theory, for instance?

KIRZNER: No, I've never had too much interest in the Austrian business cycle theory. I've never felt that the Hayekian business cycle theory was essentially Austrian. In fact, Mises, who was the originator of this whole idea in 1912, didn't see it as particularly Austrian either. There are passages where he notes that people call it the Austrian theory, but he says it's not really Austrian. It goes back to the Currency School and Knut Wicksell. It's certainly not historically Austrian. Further, I would claim that, as developed by Hayek, there are many aspects of it that are non-Austrian. I don't believe that to be an Austrian you have to buy into the Hayekian view of business cycles.

AEN: Are there any aspects of Hayek's business cycle theory that you regard as Austrian?

KIRZNER: I recently wrote a paper to accompany the facsimile German edition of *Prices and Production*. I identified what seemed to me to be elements of Hayek's later work on coordination, miscoordination, and knowledge. I argued that the germs of his later ideas can be traced to this volume, especially his description of the upswing stage of the cycle. This is a phase during which some decisions are out of sync with other decisions. Current investors are making decisions which anticipate the decisions of others down the road, which are in fact not there. Leaving the exact mechanism aside, that is the kind of thing Hayek taught us to look for in analyzing the market process. In that respect, it's Austrian.

AEN: And the rest of the theory?

KIRZNER: Otherwise, the Austrian theory of the business cycle is a macro theory. It's an equilibrium theory. And it treats capital in an objective sense rather than a subjective sense. It treats time as somehow embedded in the capital goods themselves. So I've always had a certain reserve about that particular theory, however brilliant it may be. I think the way Hayek developed it was not quite consistent with the way Mises laid it out in 1912.

AEN: Do you accept the idea that interest-rate manipulation by the central bank can cause distortions in the structure of production?

KIRZNER: Certainly the Austrian cycle theory showed brilliantly how this can happen. But it's one thing to develop a theory which could explain a downturn. It's quite another to claim that historically every downturn is to be attributed to that particular theory. That does not necessarily follow. If one were asked, does this theory necessarily explain each and every cycle, I would say no.

Mises used to poke fun at those who criticize the Austrian theory of the business cycle as being too simple. He said that still doesn't tell what's wrong with it. That's correct, as far as it goes. Perhaps many market aberrations are of this kind. But that can only be a question of historical understanding. We must be able to look at every case to see just what is happening.

AEN: Should Austrians insist that the scope of Austrian theory be limited to only praxeologically valid theorems?

KIRZNER: No, I'm not saying that Austrian economics should not deal with applications of praxeology. But it's one thing to explain what must necessarily follow under certain assumptions. It's another to take this and claim, without justification, that this therefore is *the* explanation for a particular empirical phenomenon. There's a danger in doing that.

AEN: In recent years, you've written about the implications of entrepreneurial discovery for matters of ethics and justice, and particularly the idea of "finders keepers."

KIRZNER: Let me be clear. Finders keepers is not necessarily my preferred ethical teaching. I am not proclaiming it should be followed. I'm not an ethicist; I'm an economist. I'm merely suggesting ways that people's own ethical conceptions can be applied to economic categories. I picked up the phrase "finders keepers" from Murray Rothbard, who got it from a book by Henry Oliver. I then linked the finders-keepers ethic to the idea of entrepreneurial discovery, which I discuss as a new kind of finding.

By "finding," I do not mean that someone is walking along the street and sees something in the gutter. I mean finding a new way of producing something, coming up with a new gadget, discovering some way of meeting an unmet need. Once you broaden the concept of finding, the finders-keepers ethic becomes immediately relevant. A theory of justice that considers the role of entrepreneurship will have a place for the finders-keepers ethic, an ethic that would not come into play in an equilibrium view of markets.

AEN: What is the most direct application of this concept?

KIRZNER: To the morality and justice of profits. People have great difficulty with justifying how someone can pocket money that is over and above what it costs to produce it. If someone buys something for $10, and sells it for $17, why does he get to keep the $7? It seems to many people that it's pure luck that you can sell it for a higher price, and the products of luck should probably belong to all mankind. Or it might seem to be a fraud or a con job.

Those are the obvious ethical problems. But those problems appear only insofar as we assume that everyone begins with potentially full and equal knowledge. In that case, this $7 profit might represent an attempt to deceive. But if people lack knowledge that someone else has, does taking advantage of that constitute fraud? I don't take a position qua ethicist. I am simply pointing out that the finders-keepers ethic may throw light on this problem. The entrepreneur, after all, found value in something.

AEN: And this is different from merely paying for expertise?

KIRZNER: I don't believe in defenses of profit that say we have to pay for people's know-how and skills. These items will have their own independent price on the market. Pure entrepreneurial profit rises above all of these costs, and it needs a separate defense. It is not a payment for some-*thing* for which a price can be established; the entrepreneur is paid for overcoming ignorance through alertness. A person might say, you have no right to cash in on somebody else's ignorance. Now is everybody who makes a pure profit cashing in on somebody else's ignorance? In fact, yes. Full and equal knowledge is not a reality. If people could not cash in on other people's ignorance, there would be no such thing as pure profit.

AEN: Among the items integral or incidental to Austrian economics, where does the pure-time-preference theory of interest stand?

KIRZNER: I can imagine an Austrian economist who might not fully accept this theory of the origination of interest. I myself have never understood exactly what Mises meant by giving pure time preference an *a priori* basis. When I say I don't understand it, I mean literally that, and not that it's wrong. It is a very difficult chapter in Mises.

The pure-time-preference theory I've written about is not based on *a priori* reasoning. I've merely concluded that time preference is a reasonably universal empirical phenomenon. I ask my students: do you know anybody who is indifferent between receiving a paycheck now and receiving it in ten years? The answer is no. To me, that is enough to provide the basis of the theory.

AEN: You don't rule out the possible existence of negative rate of time preference?

KIRZNER: I would be surprised, but I don't rule it out apodictically. If there is a tax on bank balances that is sufficiently high, it would pay people to lend money at negative interest, provided the interest is less than the tax rate. Is that negative time preference? Probably not, but it does show that a positive rate of time preference can coexist with a negative rate of interest. That seems to be what Mises is denying, so my theory cannot claim to present the Misesian view.

AEN: Is it right to say you have adopted a Misesian rather than Rothbardian view of monopoly?

KIRZNER: That is correct. Mises had a view of monopoly in which he said that under certain exceptional circumstances, the pattern of resource ownership may fly in the face of the interest of consumers.

Ordinarily, the ownership of a resource provides value to its owner only to the extent he is prepared to put that resource to use in the service of the consuming public. The only possible exception is where the entire supply of a scarce resource, for which there are no substitutes, happens to be in the hands of a single seller. It *may* indeed be the case that the interests of the resource owner may be counter to that of consumers. In other words, the resource owner may discover an advantage in producing less of a product for consumers than consumers themselves desire.

This is a possible conflict of interest, and, for Mises, an extraordinary phenomenon. Here we see Mises's integrity. He was willing to recognize that it's not always true that a private-property system conduces to the well-being of the consuming public. He didn't think it was an important case, but he did draw attention to it. He did *not* use this exceptional case to argue for controls over monopolies.

I too think this point is interesting. I don't believe it is empirically important. It doesn't provide justification for monopoly regulation, or breaking companies, or anything like that. It simply points to a theoretical implication of certain patterns of resource ownership.

Others have disagreed. Rothbard used to say you can never really know if a producer is storing up resources in order to gain more profits or whether his doing so is even contrary to the interest of consumers. That's true. You never will know. But the theoretical possibility is still there.

AEN: A recent controversy has centered on the attempt to "de-homogenize" Mises and Hayek. Do you think this debate has been constructive?

KIRZNER: The short answer is no. Most definitely no. Such thinkers as complex as Mises and Hayek are not going to be identical at every point. There were differences between them, and these differences should be studied, developed, and their roots identified. Certainly. But for what I believe to be the major agenda of Austrian economics, the points of commonality between Mises and Hayek are far, far more important than what I consider to be the marginal differences. To draw a division between them is a major mistake, and possibly a tragic one.

AEN: Why do you say tragic?

KIRZNER: Tragic from the standpoint of the influence of Austrian economics on the profession in general. Moreover, if people believe they must choose between being Hayekians and being Misesians, they are going to say, well, Hayek was the Nobel Prize winner, so he must have done the better work; Mises will be neglected.

KIRZNER: How do you regard Ludwig Lachmann's contributions to the Austrian School?

AEN: Lachmann played a vital role in the revival of Austrian economics. He was a gadfly. He kept us honest. He had a personal link with Mises and Hayek that nobody else had. He was a bridge between the generations. He had deep respect for Mises and Hayek, even where he disagreed with them. He showed young students that you could be a respected economist even if you thought Mises was a great thinker.

Doctrinally, Lachmann was much closer to the extreme Shackelian position on choice, uncertainty, and time, and went much further than I am willing to go. At the same time, he was a circumspect scholar. He was careful to keep a lot of his ideas to himself. But I believe he was trying to steer Austrian economics in a more subjectivist direction.

AEN: And Murray Rothbard?

KIRZNER: Rothbard was unquestionably a genius. His *History of Thought* exemplifies his life-long ability to absorb an enormous amount of literature and write clearly. He played an important role in inspiring young scholars to take a careful look at the Austrian body of thought. Just as I have had disagreements with Lachmann, I've had them with Rothbard, in matters of style and in matters of substance. Some of his impact was deepened, and some of it qualified, by his ideological work in libertarian political theory.

AEN: What about Frank Fetter of Princeton?

KIRZNER: Yes, he too made valuable contributions. Rothbard did a fine job in drawing together his essays on interest. I don't believe that Fetter can be considered an Austrian except in this one narrow area, however.

AEN: What is your most overlooked contribution to Austrian economics?

KIRZNER: Chapter seven in my 1963 book, which I've often cited to students and colleagues. It's where I provide a scenario of the spread of knowledge in the market process, starting with a nonequilibrium state and building to a systematic process of learning. It provides, I think, a very useful framework.

AEN: Are you generally optimistic about the prospect for the Austrian School?

KIRZNER: Austrians never make forecasts in their role as scientists, but I will venture this. There is work for us to do. There is a generation open to these ideas. The developments of the last twenty years demonstrate this. So, yes, I am optimistic. That's a frame of mind, not a forecast.

A CONVERSATION WITH ISRAEL KIRZNER,
JULY 2006, BY PETER J. BOETTKE AND
FRÉDÉRIC SAUTET

EDITORS: Professor Kirzner, we are very happy and honored to be putting together this edition of your *Collected Works*. All of your stand-alone books will be republished on their own while all of your other papers will be published thematically. Our goal with this interview is not to gather information about your personal life but to discuss different aspects of your work to help your readers better understand your contribution to economics by providing them some sort of intellectual biography. Let's start with *The Economic Point of View*, which was your doctoral thesis and is reprinted as the first volume of your *Collected Works*. Can you tell us more about this book?

ISRAEL KIRZNER: It grew out of my doctoral thesis. The history is simple. I was applying for a Volker fellowship. Mises encouraged me to apply for it. It was soon after my first year of graduate study at NYU, and I had been a fairly active member of Mises's seminar. In the meantime, I had applied to go to Johns Hopkins to study with a fellowship there. I went to talk to Mises to ask his advice, and he said, "Go to Johns Hopkins because Machlup is a good teacher," which I always thought was sort of a self-negating piece of advice, because Mises had very few students at that time, and I was interested, of course, in his work. But I didn't go. I stayed and Mises arranged for me a Volker fellowship. He told me to write a paper, which, later on, became his suggestion for my dissertation. That's how it started. The dissertation itself was chronological, and it got so long that I cut it off at 1900. In other words, it includes the conceptions of economic thought until 1900. I didn't really deal with Mises at all in the dissertation. Subsequently it was expanded into a book and that's how it came about.

EDS: So, the discussion of praxeology was not in the dissertation?

KIRZNER: It is not in the dissertation. The dissertation covered the history until 1900. I cut it off almost arbitrarily. It was becoming too long,

Interview © 2018 by Liberty Fund, Inc.

and Mises didn't mind. It went all the way up to the concepts of welfare economics; some of the German works from the late nineteenth century, Wicksell, etc. Most of the conceptions that I have in the book were there. In other words, a good deal of the content of the book was in the dissertation but I don't believe that the Croce-Pareto debate was there, as it was past 1900.

EDS: You were asked once what was your most overlooked contribution to Austrian economics and you pointed out chapter seven of *Market Theory and the Price System*. It is the chapter on pure exchange.

KIRZNER: I worked very hard on the book, and on that chapter, in the early 1960s (especially in 1961 and 1962). I had emerged from Mises's graduate classes sort of mixed up. I knew all about modern neoclassical microeconomics, and I thought I knew Mises's economics and they both seemed right—yet they were contradictory. In *Market Theory and the Price System* I tried to write a textbook that could make sense of these two views and to distill what I thought was the Misesian-Hayekian perspective on price. I found that I had very little to work with. Mises was talking more in generalities. Hayek did also, but it was a different type of generalities. Both were enormously wise and helpful, but when you get down to the nitty-gritty of a textbook for undergraduates, I had to work it out myself. I found that Wicksteed was more helpful than Mises and Hayek. It is clear to me now, in retrospect, that I had not fully understood Mises yet; that was to come later. But I did understand that there is such a thing as a market process, and that is the essence of the difference between the Misesian and the standard point of view. I wanted to articulate that in the textbook. But what exactly was that process that I had to articulate? The process that I articulated was very Hayekian, defined in knowledge terms, without bringing in entrepreneurship and entrepreneurial alertness in an explicit way. I think it was really an original contribution. That's what I may have meant when I mentioned chapter 7. More recently I have come to the conclusion that probably my most neglected book is my 1989 book *Discovery, Capitalism, and Distributive Justice*. At the time, I was hoping it might just take off, because I really thought it was a contribution to a lot of discussions on economic justice and I think it had some new ideas. So that's why there is a certain amount of repetition in later papers, as I have gone over some of that material because I felt it needed to be repeated.

EDS: One of the things that struck us in your textbook, and we don't want to be guilty of reading your later works back into your early book, was the way you describe the essence of competition as rivalry between alternatives. Given the times, it is amazing to read this.

KIRZNER: It was Mises who sent me back to read Hayek's *Meaning of Competition*. That didn't change subsequently. What came later was the realization that competition is simply the other side of the coin of entrepreneurship. Alertness wasn't there at the time. I hadn't grasped that yet. It came in 1967 with the *Methodological Individualism* paper. But I think the textbook was an honest attempt to translate Mises, Hayek, and Wicksteed into terms that the profession could understand.

EDS: Do you think one can see a unity in the development of your first three books? In the *Economic Point of View* you laid the groundwork for the purposefulness perspective. This is the way we are going to approach economics now: purposeful human action. Once we do that, we look at the price theory that emerges out of the implication of the fact that people have purposes and act on them. This gives birth to the *Essay on Capital*, which is the transformation from physical objects to the notion of the plan, and this comes back to the notion of purpose. And of course, your 1967 paper on the entrepreneurial perspective explicitly brings the human element back into the market process through the focus on alertness.

KIRZNER: Certainly this connection was explicit in my mind, I can assure you. I remember now that when I wrote the manuscript for *Market Theory and the Price System*, Murray Rothbard was the reviewer. In his review he complained, perhaps with some justification, that I was carrying water on both shoulders, that I was not Austrian enough. I was trying to have it both ways. I was trying to make a bridge between Austrian and neoclassical microeconomics. And I tried to do the same in *Competition and Entrepreneurship*, as well. So, I have no regrets about chapter 7. I have some regrets about the chapter on monopoly, which I think may have some analytical flaws, but I think I tried my best to translate the very difficult ideas of Mises.

EDS: When you worked on the concepts of purpose, plan, capital, and so on, it seems like the notion of entrepreneurship was really not far from development. Indeed, entrepreneurship was part of Misesian economics. Do you think there was a bridge in your mind between a Misesian understanding of entrepreneurship and these views that you were developing?

KIRZNER: Mises talked about entrepreneurship—he talked about it a lot. His discussion of the market process is very subtle, extremely subtle in fact, and easy to misunderstand. I am proud of the fact that for a number of years, I grappled with *Human Action*. I really did. Having a neoclassical background on the one hand and yet having a feel that Mises was seeing things that others hadn't seen; I tried to come to grips with it. I really worked very hard at clearing up my confusions, especially since I was writing that market theory book. I had to translate Mises's almost poetic work into a technical volume to teach undergraduates.

EDS: You had to elaborate a body of analytics.

KIRZNER: Right. To focus on the idea of entrepreneurship and to identify something that Mises had in mind, which others didn't, was not obvious. Back in the 1890s and early twentieth century, there was a lot of work on entrepreneurship, but none of those writers, absolutely none of them, grasped what Mises had in mind. Entrepreneurship is such a subtle concept that it was really missed entirely. So, when you say, "Well, wasn't it obvious that this was entrepreneurship?" I don't think this was obvious at all; I don't think so.

EDS: It seems to us that the focus at that time would have been on entrepreneurship on the production side, and since you treat production as given in chapter 7, it's really just the exchange process and the idea of gains from trade that dominate your analysis. In chapter 7, we deal with a pure exchange economy; it is a catallactic perspective, which made Mises unique.

KIRZNER: The focus on pure exchange was almost Walrasian. Walras's first book was about pure exchange, not production. This was an analytical device. If you want to understand the full market, you first have to focus on the simple context, that is to say, the pure exchange economy.

EDS: We agree with you, but then in Walras's system, the auctioneer does all the heavy lifting. There is no plan to be reconciled, as it's all done from the outset. Instead, in your work, there is a reconciliation process. Chapter 7 helps us understand the contrast between the two views.

KIRZNER: Yes that was the contribution of chapter 7. There is no process in Walras, by contrast to Mises. What I tried to do in chapter 7 is to pin down that process. But then I missed the entrepreneurial angle almost completely, while I emphasized the knowledge aspect. That's why that book is more Hayekian than Misesian. Looking at it in retrospect, the focus on purpose was certainly there, but rereading my chapter 7, I am almost amazed at the over-subtlety. When I say over-subtlety, I am not saying this in praise of the chapter, quite the opposite actually. I think I was splitting hairs. I was trying to flesh out the difference between Robbins and Mises; I felt it and I was working very hard to articulate it, but I don't think I succeeded.

EDS: So was there a defining moment that brought your attention to the entrepreneurial role? Was it in 1967?

KIRZNER: I do remember the moment—the "aha moment"—I do remember that. It was in my parents' house and I was walking on the porch. I had been invited to give a paper at the 1967 Mont Pelerin Society meeting in Vichy. It was at that point that it hit me what the difference was between the Misesian and the neoclassical view: the idea of determining the framework within which allocation is taking place, the determination of context. I do remember that episode. I look back at that 1967 paper as extremely important, it was the foundation for much of my subsequent work.

EDS: Because of the Volker fund, you were professionally engaged with various free market economists at that time, such as James Buchanan, Armen Alchian, and Harold Demsetz. Was that important to your thinking?

KIRZNER: I believe you are referring to the mid 1960s when I went to a couple of conferences and met Alchian and Demsetz. (At least one conference was supported by Pierre Goodrich, whose funding subsequently created Liberty Fund.) I am not sure whether I met Buchanan on those occasions. I began to meet other economists at that time. But I was very lonely, no question about it. I was extremely lonely at New York University where there was nobody to talk to in the early 1960s, absolutely nobody. And one always had a very strange feeling that maybe it's not that I am right and the rest of the world is wrong; maybe the rest of the world is right. Mises in those years was in his eighties and not able to communicate all that well. I used to attend his seminar, in which we would mostly discuss the more practical policy stuff. One could not engage him on the subtleties of his pure theory that he had developed in the 1930s, when he developed his system. Unfortunately, there was no way I could engage him on that. I was his assistant. I used to sit in his office to help students who were attending Mises's seminar. We'd discuss what we didn't understand in the seminar and so forth, and it was clear that many students didn't "get it."

EDS: Did Mises read your 1967 piece?

KIRZNER: I am sure I sent it to him. By that time, however, he was in his upper eighties. The last seminar he gave was in 1969. I think I mention in *Competition and Entrepreneurship* that he read the manuscript, but I don't think he was in a position to comment subsequently on that. I don't recall any specific feedback that he gave me on the 1967 paper.

EDS: Talking about that period, would you consider your most fertile time of research between 1967 and 1975? Is that when you think that you were making the most progress in your ideas?

KIRZNER: Well, the most exciting time was when I was writing *Competition and Entrepreneurship*. That was extremely exciting. Writing the 1989 ethics book was also exciting. As I look back over these books, I still find myself nodding with approval, you know.

EDS: When you were working on these ideas for the first time, Machlup was still doing economics, and Hayek might not have been doing much economics anymore, but there was a time in the 1960s when Hayek thought he was going to return to economics with *Competition as the Discovery Procedure*, et cetera. He did those Volker Fund lectures at the University of Virginia. Did you communicate with Machlup much?

KIRZNER: I am not sure what year Machlup came to NYU. Machlup didn't come to NYU, I believe, until about 1970. So, until then I had had no contact at all with Machlup. Machlup was extremely loyal to Mises on a personal level, but careful not to be embraced by Austrians, and we were careful—I was careful—not to claim him as one of ours. But he was extremely helpful in getting the department to agree to bring Ludwig Lachmann. Yet he was certainly *not* part of our "Austrian" group. I think you heard this from me before: Machlup was on Don Lavoie's doctoral dissertation committee, and he said this was one of the best dissertations he had ever seen. I am convinced he didn't understand it. However if he said so, he meant it. He saw something there, but he didn't understand it (in my view). Machlup was trained in an earlier milieu of Austrian economics.

EDS: When you were talking about your loneliness before, had you found any professional allies in say Alchian and Demsetz, who were at least groping toward some notion of an exchange economy that would be similar to yours?

KIRZNER: It was Harold Demsetz who was the reader for *Competition and Entrepreneurship* and he approved it. I found this out later, as he told me. He was the one who convinced the University of Chicago Press to accept the book, so a lot depended on Harold. He is a friend. Although he is on a different wavelength, he is intellectually honest, and he saw merit in the book. I have had some good contact with him over the years. For instance, he reacted to my exchange with Gary Becker and felt that I was right.

EDS: We were just wondering, because you said at one time that Ludwig Lachmann was the only person that you could have an intellectual exchange with.

KIRZNER: I have had this long and extensive correspondence with Lachmann beginning in 1960 or '61. He was lonely in Johannesburg; I was lonely in New York. The correspondence was very helpful to me.

EDS: Everyone who was attracted to Mises in the 1950s and 1960s in America was attracted for ideological reasons primarily, and technical reasons secondarily, including Murray Rothbard. You don't fit that profile. You say that you don't see yourself as heroic, but one could view you as a heroic figure because, as a scholar, you were trying to maintain a unique position.

KIRZNER: I was trying to maintain a certain level of intellectual integrity. I wouldn't call that heroic. I was trying to be honest to myself, being faithful to what I thought Mises was saying. When I say faithful, I mean in the sense that I felt that he has got something right that hasn't been appreciated. And it was my duty to bring that out.

EDS: Once, when Peter Boettke was a graduate student and Lachmann used to spend a week at George Mason University every spring with Don Lavoie, the students were reading your *Essay on Capital* and Lachmann's work on capital. Lachmann was very excited that GMU students were studying his stuff and yours. He explained that it was always such a lonely time working on capital theory. His example of being lonely was when you and Donald Dewey met once at Columbia University and the two of you didn't really talk about capital. So Lachmann said that not only working on capital theory was a lonely area but also it was lonely to work on Austrian capital theory. Even when capital theorists met in the same city, they didn't talk about it.

KIRZNER: You are right. Lachmann wrote back to me once: "Don't people in New York ever talk to each other?" He liked Dewey's book; but I wasn't so enthusiastic about it.

EDS: In those days, did you have much to do with Murray Rothbard?

KIRZNER: I wasn't one of the youngsters who were around Murray all the time. I went to his apartment one time, but I wasn't one of those who used to go regularly, as I was extremely wary of his anarchism and radical libertarianism. I frankly didn't want to have anything to do with that. I certainly used to read his Libertarian Forum; I used to follow his writings quite a bit. Murray was a genius; there is no doubt about it. I don't believe that he fully understood Mises. I believe that he struggled honestly to do so, but he didn't provide a satisfactory Misesian economics, as far as I am concerned. There were bright people at Mises's seminar such as George

Reisman, Ralph Raico, and Larry Moss. But I didn't feel that they were able to help me reformulate Austrian economics in a way that should command respect within academia.

EDS: It is fair to say that Rothbard, after *Man, Economy, and State,* becomes involved in politics. He is involved in the anti-war protest, etc. He pretty much thought that economics had been worked out in his book. In some of your past interviews, you mention a frustration with the tension that you see in the works of Mises and Hayek that others don't see. There is a communication gap. And you see yourself in this role of trying to communicate this tension.

KIRZNER: It is a work of translation. Mises's grand vision had to be somehow brought down to earth in a simple analytical fashion. That was the real challenge.

EDS: Do you think this is why some of your critics have said that your work is just a footnote to neoclassical economics?

KIRZNER: Let me give you my understanding of that. At that time there was no question, among the Austrians and others, that economic theory in its microform meant the theory of equilibration. There was no question—that wasn't a matter of dispute. It wasn't until about twenty years after I had been corresponding with Lachmann that I realized he had absolutely no use for the equilibrium concept in any possible sense of the word. What I tried to do in chapter 7 [of *Market Theory and the Price System*] was to figure out where in economics does it explain how equilibration comes about. Chapter 7 presented a theory that would explain how, along Hayekian lines at least, equilibration could occur. Later on, when I developed the ideas about the entrepreneurial function, the idea of market process changed in my own mind. The market process came to be seen not primarily as an equilibration process but as a "governing" process—meaning that the market is not random, as Shackle and Lachmann might maintain it is. "Economic laws" govern the market. At that time, what seemed important to me was to understand how economics explains causation, that is, the idea of economic law. It was the idea of cause and effect. If there is a sudden shortage of a good and its price goes up, how does it happen? Why is there a systematic relationship between supply changes and prices? There is no question in my mind that the objective of economics in general, and price theory, micro theory, and entrepreneurial theory in particular, must be to explain those chains of cause and effect. Now if that's a footnote to neoclassical economics, so be it. I have never seen *this* research as focusing on the equilibrative properties of the market. I see it as pointing to why, at any given point in time, there are systematic changes taking place in the social system. Equilibrium is a foil that explains to us what happens when you are not in equilibrium. I think people have misunderstood my research to some extent and they have assumed that what I'm trying to do is to explain equilibration. This is not accurate. I think this is the explanation of the footnote story. Of course, I will certainly accept the charge that, yes, I am not a Shackelian and I am a not a Lachmannian.

EDS: Your explanation is very compelling when you think about it in terms of applied economics. One useful distinction when you think in terms of applied theory is the one made by Böhm-Bawerk between pure theory, the application of theory, and economic history. The realm of applied theory is when you allow the systematic tendencies to be examined in light of different contexts. Think about the horse-trading market: if we change the rules of horse-trading, the systematic tendencies are still there but they manifest themselves in different directions. You actually make this point about Austrian Business Cycle theory, which you see as being an applied theory that may only explain certain events. In other words, the systematic tendencies manifest themselves in some historical episodes but not in all. One should be very careful about the application of theory because one of the things Austrians often get criticized for is that we don't do enough applied work, but a large part of that is because of the extreme difficulty of sorting out those systematic cause and effect relationships in actual real world phenomena.

KIRZNER: I stand in admiration and awe for people who do applied economics. I do not know exactly where you draw the line between pure theory and applied theory. Buchanan has done some work on this for Hayek's festschrift. That's a difference between the apodictic system of Mises and the less apodictic applications.

EDS: In Hayek's 1937 *Economics and Knowledge* paper, which all the people take as his departure, including his own self-description of a departure, he says that pure logic of choice is a necessary but not sufficient component of the explanation of the market. In order to have a fuller explanation, we have to have some empirical subsidiary assumptions about the way in which people learn. Hayek said that Mises's reaction to his paper was unusual because Mises said, yes, this is what we talk about.

KIRZNER: You know I've heard Hayek say that when he told Mises about the paper, he was trembling. He was afraid of Mises's reaction. He was afraid of an explosion. But what Mises said about the paper was great. I suggested an explanation of this episode in my book *Perception, Opportunity and Profit*. I think the explanation was that Mises took for granted the link between the pure and the applied. Mises took that for granted and said, "yes of course." It's possible that Mises may not have fully grasped that Hayek was saying: "careful, we cannot spell out the relationship between the pure and the applied too blatantly."

EDS: Do you think your own knowledge of what you have developed in your dissertation work, your own knowledge of the history of entrepreneurship in economic doctrines, was helpful for you to realize the role of the entrepreneurial function?

KIRZNER: That would be indirectly, I would say. I don't think that the particular line of history of economic thought that I was pursuing in the dissertation or in the *Economic Point of View* was directly related to it. But I am fully aware that everything I know in economics is against the background of history of thought.

EDS: You view economics as a scholarly enterprise as opposed to the self-description of a lot of economists from your generation forward, which states that economics is a subject that becomes more and more complex over time. This latter view means that the more we look to the past, the less developed the science was. Thus knowing the history of ideas in economics is not important.

KIRZNER: In the graduate course in history of thought, we used to have an introductory lecture to present those different ways of seeing the subject. I saw history of thought not as an antiquarian enterprise. It is really the perception that ideas renew themselves in different ways, in different languages, and in different frameworks but they're basically the same ideas. There is a fascination there. But I don't think there is any direct linkage through history to entrepreneurship.

EDS: There is a broader question here, which is about the decline of the history of economics in our discipline. What are the consequences of that? There is a great article by Jacob Viner called *A Plea for Scholarship in Economics,* which was his address to the graduating class at Brown. Reading this paper, one realizes how far back this battle actually goes. You, Dr. Kirzner, sort of grew up in this battle. They won: there is no history of thought systematically taught in PhD programs anymore, even at George Mason. We killed the history of thought requirement. George Mason has classes in it and Duke has classes in it, but most schools don't, when it used to be part of the training for a PhD.

KIRZNER: When I taught the history of thought course, I used it to develop current ideas and to present how they were rooted in older debates.

EDS: Let's now move on to the subject of entrepreneurship per se. There is something about the notion of "alertness" that has somewhat puzzled people over the years. It's the idea that alertness is not a factor of production and yet is somehow part of human capacity.

KIRZNER: I would not deny that alertness is a datum in the sense of a "resource." You have it or you don't have it, I grant that. But the word resource in economics has a very special meaning. It has a meaning that makes it the subject of a resource market, where resources are bought and sold and the resource prices are the result of a balance between supply and demand. You cannot apply that kind of analysis to alertness. In that sense alertness is not a factor, you don't deploy it, as I often say. If I want to bake a cake, I need flour, sugar, eggs, butter, and salt. All this is what I need, but I don't need alertness as an ingredient. Now, I may need to be alert, but I don't find this on my list to pick up from the supermarket. You can't pick up alertness. If you pick it up, then it's a resource, then it's a research capability. You can hire somebody because he sells himself to be a sharp researcher. But it's not his *alertness* that you have. It is the employer who has evinced alertness; *he* noticed the researcher's ability to do the research. What the researcher provides is a factor, but that's not the alertness we're talking about. You can call it whatever you want: the knowledge, or the capacity to get knowledge, or the sense of smell. But at the end of the day, he is selling his sense of smell. He advertises: I am a great researcher, I've got it, you need it, this is my price. And the employer says, well, you've got it, I need it, and this is what it's worth to me. I am the employer, and it's my alertness to what I think he is worth to me. So in that sense, it's not a factor, which tends toward equality of return. We may ask the question: is profit a return on alertness? It's *not* a return on alertness in the sense that there is a tendency for alertness's rate of return to equalize throughout the market. There is no such tendency; there cannot be such a tendency with regard to pure alertness because it's not bought and sold in the factor market.

EDS: So, does this mean that you introduced a new category in economics? There are factors of production and there is also alertness?

KIRZNER: Well, in a way, if you go back to the earlier literature on entrepreneurship at the end of the nineteenth century, there was this idea: besides the three factors, we've got entrepreneurship. Sometimes entrepreneurship was lumped as a fourth factor, sometimes it wasn't. Now, this I think is the way to understand why entrepreneurship is not really a fourth factor.

EDS: It's an element but not a factor for production.

KIRZNER: Absolutely, and you can consider it the most important element if you like.

EDS: This is where we run into trouble in our dialog with those who see entrepreneurship as a factor of production. What they want to do most of the time is to understand the determinants of the supply curve of entrepreneurship (since it is a factor) and the role of startups, R&D, et cetera. Although they have shifted their focus toward institutions as of late, they still maintain a very neoclassical view. Another important actor is

William Baumol and his work on why some countries are rich and others are poor, and the role of entrepreneurship.

KIRZNER: Baumol has done important work indeed. There is also an article by Theodore Schultz on this in which he talks about profit as the equilibrium point between the supply and demand for entrepreneurship.

EDS: It is difficult to find a common ground even though everyone is talking about entrepreneurship. It's a bridging exercise but it's a difficult one. "How do we communicate with a community of entrepreneurship scholars?" is an important question. We don't want to ignore their conversation, because it's a great opportunity for us to take the ideas that we have and bring it to them, but we're having a hard time figuring out how to do it. When you realize that even among Austrians, some people discuss whether alertness is the most crucial concept or if it is judgment or something else. How would you yourself communicate the notion of alertness to a crowd influenced by Baumol's work for instance?

KIRZNER: There is a line that Baumol uses sometimes, which I think is absolutely true, but I don't think he's altogether consistent on that: "If it is something that you can teach, it isn't entrepreneurship." I have often used that myself. If there is something that can be systematized, it is not entrepreneurship. There are courses in business administration in which one can learn to run a business. Someone can say, well that's entrepreneurship, right? They are teaching you how to manage a business. Clearly an entrepreneur who runs a business has to know about business administration, but he also has to do more than that. So you're dealing with a very subtle separation between entrepreneurship and management. But there is a crucial difference. You have to filter out those parts that can be systemized from those parts that cannot. To the extent that you can put your finger on it, it melts away. That's where the difficulty comes in. One may try to find a measurement analog or a statistic for alertness, but if you can put your finger on it then it isn't alertness anymore. It's something that has become part of the system; it has become a factor of production.

EDS: A major theme of your work is that entrepreneurial discoveries are undeliberate but they are also not accidental. They are inspired by the prospect of gain. This is why your notion of alertness is so crucial. But there is another side to that coin that you seem to have underplayed in your work, and it's the notion of prior knowledge. In the *Primacy of Entrepreneurial Discovery* you state that "human beings tend to notice that which it is in their interest to notice." In other words, entrepreneurial activity is stirred by pure profit. But another and complementary interpretation of your statement relates to the knowledge human beings possess at the time they act. The noticing of opportunities not only depends on the entrepreneur's interest (pure profit), but also on his prior knowledge (i.e., his interest in the situation discovered). Entrepreneurs make entrepreneurial discoveries that are neither random nor determined; they are somewhere in between. But if choices are neither random nor accidental, can one say that alertness depends, to some limited extent, upon the prior knowledge possessed by the entrepreneur?

KIRZNER: The question asks whether a potential entrepreneur's "prior knowledge" (which you—somewhat puzzlingly—appear to equate with that person's "interest in the situation discovered") plays a role in generating that person's alertness. Now, of course, what it is that a human being notices depends significantly on that person's past history (including his "prior knowledge"). Someone on a beach will tend to notice seashells; someone in a shopping mall will tend to notice bargains. However, I sense that, in your question, you are after something else. You seem to wish to suggest that alertness itself is a function of prior knowledge (not merely that what one is alert to is shaped by prior knowledge.) You seem to suggest that one's "noticing-potential" is itself a function of prior knowledge. On this I have little to say. No doubt future cognitive psychologists may one day explore this suggestion. I do recognize your point that if one accepts the (rather crude) generalization that one tends to notice what it is in one's interest to notice, then it follows that what one tends to notice depends on one's interest. And I recognize that one who is "uninterested" in just about everything, is likely not to notice anything. However, I would not myself equate one's "interests" with one's "prior knowledge." I believe that one tends to notice also opportunities, which one has not hitherto known to be of advantage. A barefoot primitive man (who has never known of "shoes") who accidentally places his feet into a pair of comfortable shoes will tend to "notice" their comfort, et cetera.

EDS: Another topic of interest is that of the relationship between preferences and discovery. Are preferences given as it is usually assumed in economics and, if so, what does this mean for entrepreneurial discovery?

KIRZNER: One can reformulate the question as, "Are preferences autonomous or are they molded by the entrepreneur?" This relates to the old debate about capitalism as the manipulation of people's minds. That gets us into the pure economics of advertising, and I have always followed Mises in this. Mises asked: "why should it ever be profitable to me to mold people's taste and then sell them a product that I produced, when I can sell them a product that they want in the first place?" There is an economic fallacy involved in the standard understanding of advertising. Why should I spend resources changing their minds and then produce the product that fits what I have made them want? Now, admittedly, this has to be qualified. Supposing I have got an enormous amount of investment, fixed investment, in producing cigarettes. Then it might be in my interest to persuade people that smoking is good for them, that smoking is healthy, that smoking is pleasant, and pleasurable. I do grant that. So you cannot rule out a priori the possibility that entrepreneurs may find it profitable to try to mold people's tastes. You can't rule that out categorically. But this means that there have been entrepreneurial errors. If I got into the business of selling cigarettes but people don't really want cigarettes, I have to try to recoup my investment by persuading them. But in the long run, entrepreneurs are not going to make mistakes like that and certainly are not *looking* to make mistakes like that. So when one says that advertising shows that the *essence* of capitalism is the manipulation of people's minds, this is not true at all. I did write about it in *Competition and Entrepreneurship*. There is a chapter there on selling costs, which I think Mises got absolutely right. The whole distinction between selling costs and production costs is absolutely fallacious. What does this mean as far as preferences are concerned? I am not saying that preferences are static; there is nothing, no requirement, to say that they are static. And sure, people's preferences respond to stimuli; they respond to what's out there. But the idea that the essence of capitalism is the manipulation of people's minds is wrong.

EDS: In your tobacco example, if I persuade you that smoking is good for you, and you eventually buy my product, would you say that you came to discover that truly you like cigarettes, so, it's truly your taste, or would you say that your taste has been manipulated?

KIRZNER: That's a slightly different issue, which relates to what happens if I educate you to *realize* what it is that you really want (of course what you really want may not "really" be "good" for you). Now, there is a subtle distinction between changing your mind and educating you to what is good for you. For example, I come into a primitive country where they have never heard of shoes, and I bring them a pair of shoes and I say: "try them on." And they walk around and say, "great, wonderful." Have I changed their tastes, or have I educated them to an advantage of something that was really there all the time, something they would have wanted but they didn't realize it until I came along? Now here again it might be argued that, before, they did *not* want them; I have barraged them with selling costs, given them free pairs of shoes, and *now* they want shoes. However, once you accept the premise that there cannot be a long-run interest on the part of entrepreneurs to change people's tastes from what they are right now, then there is no reason to question that selling costs are likely to be educational costs. In which case this is part of production. To produce shoes, which are good for you, really good for you, and then not to teach you that they are good for you means that one has not served the consumer.

EDS: Some economists have said that a difficulty with the Austrian view is that it introduces philosophical discussions in the realm of economics, which are probably too cumbersome to be dealt with, and we're better off without them. In the closed model of neoclassical economics, these issues don't arise. Would you say that the notion of the entrepreneur as you have developed it opens the door to some philosophical questions such as the problem of free will, or would you say not at all, that's nothing to do with economics?

KIRZNER: I don't think free will is an issue in my view of entrepreneurship. I sometimes used to suspect that Lachmann's position was based on the importance of freedom of will. Personally I certainly do believe in free will, but I don't believe that anything that I have written on entrepreneurship depends on that. I may be wrong—maybe some presuppositions may have entered. I don't think alertness requires freedom of the will in a philosophical sense. It can be seen as a product of nurture or nature.

EDS: Beyond the question of free will, there are also thorny issues such as "open-endedness" and its counterpart "novelty." Knight famously rejected the possibility of analysis in a situation of open-endedness. Mises, Hayek, and yourself have embraced it as a building block of economic analysis. Do you think "open-endedness" is only found in Austrian literature because of its philosophical implications?

KIRZNER: The notion of "open-endedness" relates to the economists' standard attempts to fit the world into a model made up entirely of strictly economizing individuals. These individuals are seen as, at all times, confronting *given* ends-means frameworks. Knight recognized that the entrepreneurial role can*not* be constrained into such a model. But, because he adopted the economists' standard assumption that it is *only* the given-ends-means framework that can generate systematic outcomes—he treated open-endedness as unable to be reconciled with any analysis capable of leading to systematic outcomes. But casual observation should surely convince us that, while we certainly do live in an open-ended world, we *are* nonetheless able to conduct our lives—while depending on interpersonal exchanges—in fairly systematic fashion. *This* casual empirical observation leads us to focus on "entrepreneurial alertness" as the source for systematic outcomes (*despite* the open-endedness of our environment). I would *not* characterize this disagreement with Knight as a "philosophical" disagreement.

EDS: You state clearly on page 74 of *Competition and Entrepreneurship* that entrepreneurship is a "responding agency" rather than a source of innovative ideas ex-nihilo. Many critics took this to mean that you do not pay attention to creativity and innovation in your view of entrepreneurship. In other words, the Kirznerian entrepreneur only "discovers what's already there" as opposed to "innovates," the way the Schumpeterian entrepreneur supposedly does. Others have said that your theory enables innovation, but innovation constrained by the future state of the market. Could you clarify your position?

KIRZNER: I have, more than once, tried to clear up the confusions, which have arisen on this point. *Of course* innovation and creativity are typical expressions of entrepreneurship. When I insist that entrepreneurship is to be seen as a "responding" agency, this is in order to dissociate myself from Schumpeter's view of the entrepreneur as an essentially *disruptive* (albeit often benignly disruptive) force. When we see the entrepreneur as "responding," we mean that he is responding to an opportunity (with the notion of "opportunity" understood as including, importantly, "pure profit opportunity"), which is "out there waiting" to be exploited. Such an opportunity may certainly be the opportunity to create, to innovate, to venture where no one has hitherto ventured. Now the notion of an opportunity "waiting" to be discovered certainly raises philosophical puzzles: how can we describe an opportunity available only in the *future,* as "waiting" to be discovered? Nevertheless, I believe, once the innovation *has* been introduced, once the creative idea *has* been hatched, it becomes obvious to all that, indeed, that innovation, that idea, *was* waiting to be noticed. To emphasize that the entrepreneur is responding to a given situation (including the future course of events as that future presents itself to today's entrepreneur) permits us to see the sequence of entrepreneurial discoveries as, in a sense, emerging out of the earlier entrepreneurial failures (to have made those discoveries up until now)—rather than as a random series of exogenous disruptions.

EDS: We have heard you say often times that resolving the deep methodological debates (such as that of the neo-Kantian foundations of a priorism) wasn't for you, as an economist, an important issue. The implication of the fact that men act, on the other hand, is crucial.

KIRZNER: Well, I felt that what Mises referred to as a priorism didn't make all that much of a difference to substantive Misesian economic theory.

EDS: You do mention in your book on Mises that you asked him once and his reply was somewhat surprising.

KIRZNER: I asked him: "How do we know that other people act?" He replied: "By observation." So, that means that economics is not totally a prioristic. I recall Mario Rizzo showing me a passage once in *Human Action* in which Mises virtually says that our conviction that others act is based on observation.

EDS: There is little doubt that when compared to other books of that era, Mises's *Human Action* possesses a sort of philosophical sophistication that other economists were starting to move away from. Obviously, if you read Frank Knight, it's there and certainly when you go back to the nineteenth century, it's clearly there as well. The issue space for most economists today is the Price and Quantity (P&Q) space, while for Mises and Hayek and subsequently yourself, it is the philosophical underpinnings of the P&Q space. Another one who also wrote with a clear vision of the philosophical underpinnings of the discipline is Shackle's book on *Epistemics and Economics,* which is almost a philosophical reflection. It is a book in economic poetics. There are really very few books in economics that are written in that vein in the twentieth century.

KIRZNER: Many of us became technicians in the twentieth century, which is why this aspect disappeared. I talked about the definition of human action and other economic phenomena in the first chapter of *The Economic Point of View.*

EDS: Let's move to equilibration, another issue that has been debated in the 1980s and 1990s among Austrian economists. What do you think the whole debate amounted to? Do you think your view of entrepreneurship has been clarified as a result?

KIRZNER: The main critique of my position in this debate on equilibration is the Buchanan-Vanberg paper. That paper was, I thought, the most important critique and the one that I did try to respond to (the papers were published in my 2000 book *The Driving Force of the Market*). Buchanan and Vanberg are very close to the Lachmann position. So in a way we are back to the Lachmann issue, to the Lachmann-Kirzner debate, if you want, the one that Karen Vaughn had written about in her book *Austrian Economics in America: the Migration of a Tradition.* I'm comfortable with my defense of what I think is the Misesian position. I am comfortable in the sense that I do believe that I articulated correctly, validly, that there is no contradiction between the valid insights that are in the Buchanan-Vanberg piece and the idea that there are systematic chains of cause and effect. Roger Garrison has called this position the "middle ground." I think it is extremely important. I stand in the middle between those like Shackle and Lachmann and perhaps Buchanan and Vanberg on the one hand and an equilibrium-always view on the other. I don't know if Buchanan and Vanberg are really consistent with their own position, however. In their critique of the teleological view, they explain that there is no point toward which we are going, and I say that's correct. But that does not mean that there are no systematic chains of cause and effect, which *would* create such a point if exogenous changes wouldn't occur. The other extreme is the neoclassical position that equilibration is so dominant that you can in effect treat it as having been attained at any given point in time. I don't accept that at all. The middle ground remains valid in that there are systematic chains of cause and effect. These systematic changes are driven by entrepreneurial alertness to opportunities that have been created by earlier ignorance. That's my position. Having gone through that decade of the 1990s, I don't think that I have been shown to be wrong.

EDS: Your paper "The Meaning of Market Process" had a big influence on the debate on the nature of market process. It is perhaps just another variation of the "middle ground" position, but it has been seen as a more subtle way to describe it, at least by us. Has the approach in terms of underlying and induced variables always been in your mind?

KIRZNER: I think so. The paper was written in response to a specific situation. I presented my own ideas in a slightly different way. It's possible that this particular way of expositing the idea associated with market process theory was particularly compelling at that moment. But I don't think there was anything really new there.

EDS: There have been comments of your thin treatment of the notion of entrepreneurial error in your work. Some believe that your theory is mostly one of entrepreneurial success and leaves little scope for entrepreneurial error. Entrepreneurs do not seem to make any loss in the entrepreneurial discovery process. Could you comment on this?

KIRZNER: Entrepreneurs make errors. The whole theory of entrepreneurship depends on entrepreneurial error. The opportunities that entrepreneurs discover are a manifestation of earlier entrepreneurial errors. So there is no question that, yes, in theory, entrepreneurship depends on error. In Frank Knight's work, the world is radically uncertain: the cookie could crumble in many different ways, we just don't know. There are some individuals who stick their necks out, willing to beat that uncertainty. They're the entrepreneurs. Knight makes it clear that he believes entrepreneurial losses quantitatively outweigh entrepreneurial profits. The likelihood of entrepreneurial error is higher than the likelihood of entrepreneurial success in Knight's view. And I think that's a mistake, an empirical mistake. Why? Because human beings act. Action is an empirical phenomenon and the whole science of economics depends on that. Included in that fact (that humans act) is that people act in a way that makes sense to them, otherwise we wouldn't have met here today. Many things could have gone wrong, and yet we acted in a way that made sense to us. Human beings have a certain degree of control. We have a degree of control over our future. I am pretty confident I will be getting home tonight. A lot of things could happen that might frustrate that objective of getting home tonight, but we act in a way that reflects our conviction that we have a very high degree of control. That's an empirical fact. Does this mean that we have empirical evidence that entrepreneurship is more likely to be successful? No. What it means is that all action is entrepreneurial as Mises explained, and the purposeful alertness of acting human beings has a systematic bias in favor of success as opposed to failure. If it were true that in general action would lead to losses—if that would be really the case, then we wouldn't be acting. Knight famously said that in absolute certainty, we would be frozen, as everything would already be known. Action would be unnecessary. The same context of action convinces us that, subjectively and objectively, we do discover opportunities to succeed. Now, I'll be first to concede that I pay too little attention to entrepreneurial error and entrepreneurial loss in my work. I grant that much, and I have pointed that out a few times and in a few places. But we are trying to understand human society and you cannot build your analysis on the Knightian or Shacklean view that human beings are floating around as if they were pushed by winds. That's what I mean when I say there is bias in favor of success. The explanation for that is Misesian purposefulness. This notion of purposefulness includes (and *this* is what I realized in 1967) *the powerful motivation to see what's around the corner.* When Mises uses the word "rationality" of course, he uses it to mean "purposefulness." In other words, people are noticing things that haven't been noticed before. Knight by contrast says that losses outweigh gains, in other words, that people do not act with the idea of succeeding. In

Knight's work, there is nothing systematic that links results to the purposes from which they proceed.

EDS: In other words, if you start out from a world in which people get it more wrong than right, you couldn't have Bastiat's observation that "Paris gets fed." So you have the recognition of an empirical pattern of behavior (Paris gets fed) and you have purposefulness to help explain the mechanism by which that occurs.

KIRZNER: That's right.

EDS: And what about the case where an entrepreneur sees an opportunity, but by the time she seizes it, it's gone. Was she seeing around the corner?

KIRZNER: Suppose there is a five-dollar bill on the floor and I just noticed it. I dive for it. But a few instants before I dove for it, somebody else dove for it. That person gets it before me. Now, was I wrong? Yes, I was wrong. I was wrong to underestimate the likelihood that other people would notice the bill. My entrepreneurial discovery was incorrect, so to speak. The five-dollar bill in fact wasn't there. I anticipated that it would be there by the time I reached the floor but I was wrong.

EDS: Economists have always had difficulties with the economics of error. That's why Stigler eliminated error, as it doesn't sit comfortably in the rational choice mechanics. In *Market Theory and the Price System,* you make the distinction between type 1 and type 2 errors. In that book, you make the connection between error and how error-correction drives markets. If we lived in a world where there weren't any of those errors being committed we wouldn't have any process to describe.

KIRZNER: I was at a conference outside Vienna once, and they put us up in some kind of conference center. I had a room on the top floor with a sloped ceiling above my bed. When I got up the first morning I bumped my head on the ceiling. I didn't bump my head on the second morning. In other words I learned from my error the first day. That is a type of error where I thought I could get up without banging myself but I couldn't. I realized I couldn't and I learned that I couldn't. Of course, there is also the other error of noticing something that you didn't know existed at all.

EDS: Would you say that these errors are errors of perception? Somehow the perception is wrong? There was no five-dollar bill when you thought there was one?

KIRZNER: Entrepreneurial prescience is about the future, always about the future. Not so much about whether there is a five-dollar bill on the floor now. Entrepreneurial activity is about the result of my action in five minutes, five months, or five years, so it is about prediction. It is not a question of, "Did I see it or didn't I see it?" It is only about seeing the future, about what is around the corner.

EDS: Another important issue regarding the notion of error relates to ownership and monetary losses. In a comment Jack High said, "If entrepreneurship is completely separate from ownership, is it meaningful to speak of entrepreneurial loss? Can losses fall on the entrepreneur or must they fall on the resource owner?" In the example of the five-dollar bill, you expend resources to dive to get the bill and you miss it, thus you incur losses. Do you incur them as an entrepreneur or a capitalist? Do entrepreneurial losses exist in your system?

KIRZNER: It is true that the disembodied, purely entrepreneurial function cannot be observed in the real world. Usually the real-world entrepreneur is also a capitalist (and a laborer). So that indeed entrepreneurial losses will, in the real world, be suffered by owners of assets. But this does not mean that the phenomenon of pure entrepreneurial loss is *intrinsically* associated with the purely capitalist function. A skilled artisan may be seen as a capitalist (in the sense that he invested in the acquisition of his skills); nonetheless, insofar as his salary tends to be determined by competitive market evaluation of his marginal productivity, that salary (although it is a return invested capital) must certainly also be seen as a *pure* wage. Entrepreneurial profit and loss is to be traced to the purely entrepreneurial function.

EDS: Another aspect of your work that has led to debates is the role of the entrepreneurial function vis-à-vis risk and risk taking. Does risk play a role in your framework? Is the entrepreneur a risk taker?

KIRZNER: Insofar as risk bearing is a necessary "ingredient" in the production process (and some market participants are willing to provide risk-bearing services), these services are no different from other services bought and sold in the market. Knight, of course, saw uncertainty bearing (for which insurance principles are utterly irrelevant) as the *residual* function associated with the pure entrepreneurial role. Our disagreement with Knight on this point (explained earlier) will account for our unwillingness to see uncertainty bearing as *nothing more* than this residual function.

EDS: Mises uses the notion of the "promoter" in *Human Action*. You have never used it. Do you understand the difference Mises was trying to get at by using the "promoter" as opposed to the "entrepreneur"?

KIRZNER: I have never understood this distinction. Maybe in those years when I was grappling with Mises, maybe I should have tried harder. But I don't think those particular pages are all that crucial.

EDS: There are more and more social scientists interested in entrepreneurship. To some extent, your influence has grown. Do you think this will help in the translation work that we were talking about before?

KIRZNER: I must say that I saw one of Edward Elgar's recent brochures, and I said, "Good gracious, hundreds of books on Entrepreneurship. Entrepreneurship has become a buzzword!" But then a lot of the authors were not economists.

EDS: It is true that a lot of the work that is being done doesn't really get the essence of your ideas. But the fact that they are talking about it creates an opportunity for us to try to help them get it. Take the book *Strategizing Disequilibrium and Profit*, which was recently published by Stanford University Press and written by John Mathews, a business professional. It relies heavily on your work. His main point is that, unless we recognize that we are living in a world of disequilibrium, there is no need for managerial strategizing, because it only makes sense within a world of disequilibrium. So that is his wedge to get into the debate and talk about these issues.

KIRZNER: It's been the case for quite a number of years now that there are people in business who like that theoretical angle and are interested in Austrian economics. It has been found that business students could not relate to standard economics, but they like Austrian economics. Remember that for economists, the notion of entrepreneur, as I have pointed out many times, is an analytical pest. It is an analytical nuisance, from which the scientist must abstract. Those in the business world know how unrealistic such observations must be.

EDS: But so is error, and that's why they are flipped together. You have used this analogy between, on the one hand, frictions in an economy and, on the other, frictions between the sole of your shoes and the ground. It is the friction between the soles and the ground that enable you to walk. In the economic system, the frictions, which many other economists assume away, are in fact the very driver of the market.

KIRZNER: I should say, I don't think that was an original analogy of mine. I think that metaphor is in the literature. I was using it, but I wouldn't claim to be the originator of that analogy.

EDS: But think of the difference with Joseph Stiglitz's work in which it's these very frictions that make markets fail. You flipped that around: it's the very frictions that, in fact, make markets work. But to finish on the topic of error, among modern economists, whom else would you put in the camp that recognized the essential role of error? Shackle and Lachmann perhaps?

KIRZNER: Well, it's Frank Knight, of course, who talked about it in part three of his book, but the Chicagoans never read part three. They stopped at perfect competition. I can't claim to really understand Knight's picture of the world, but he was, of course, the one who brought in error.

EDS: Let's move to the topic of monopoly pricing. You have famously credited Mises for holding the view that monopoly pricing could emerge in an unhampered market. But you may be saying two things in your writings. On the one hand, you're saying, "Unless you have extra-market privileges, the competitive process is always at work. There will always be entrepreneurial activity taking place within the boundaries of the market." But then, when it comes to monopoly, you suddenly say, "We could imagine the way Mises did, monopoly pricing emerging in the free market. If you imagine someone who owns every resource needed in some production process, he could derive from this monopoly some sort of rent and therefore, there would be suddenly a disjoint between the consumer's welfare and the producer's interest." Are these two views entirely compatible?

KIRZNER: Let me make two points. The number one is, as you said, that I would argue that there is always a competitive process at work. You are absolutely right. The monopolist emerges *within* the competitive process. It's the competitive process, which teaches the monopolist what he is able to charge. He doesn't know his demand curve. It's the competitive process that teaches him what his demand curve is. So markets are *always* competitive, that's the core of the Misesian position. To the extent that markets are not competitive, they are not markets. All markets are competitive, so to the extent that there is a market process that determines the monopoly pricing, that's a competitive process. The idea that you have a spectrum beginning with monopoly at one end and competition at the other is wrong. That's not the Misesian view. The second point you made is also right. I always like to use oranges as an example. If a producer has sole control over all the oranges in the world, he can become a monopolist of orange juice. Of course, sooner or later somebody else is going to discover grapefruits, and enter the market. That's why Mises thought that empirically monopoly pricing was not a problem. But having said that, it still remains that to the extent that there is a lack of perfect substitutability among resources (grapefruits are not a perfect substitute for orange juice); to that extent, there may be a scope for motivation by the owner of the oranges *to destroy some oranges*. This is where theoretically we could see "monopoly pricing" (in Mises's sense of this term) emerging. Nothing that you said disagrees with that as a theoretical possibility. I don't believe that as an empirical matter Mises thought monopoly pricing amounted to anything at all. But the possibility is still there. Now, I have a paper, "The Driving Force of the Market" that I wrote in response to Jerry O'Driscoll who had published a paper in which he accused Mises of having a neoclassical position on monopoly theory. The position that O'Driscoll took is that if there is such a thing as monopoly rent then competition will grind it down. But this fails to grasp Mises's point. To the extent that there are substitutes, yes, O'Driscoll would be correct. But the definition of a Misesian monopoly position is that you are dealing with something for which there are *no* perfect substitutes.

But realize that the word *curiosum* applies here. The monopoly case is a curiosum, meaning it's a strange and very special narrow case in market process theory.

EDS: Let's assume there is a coffee shop right downstairs from here where we can get coffee. We also know that if we walk three blocks from here, there is another coffee shop. Going from one to the other is not costless. We have to walk or take a cab or something so the two are not perfect substitutes. If someone were to say that the first coffee shop has a monopoly on making coffee within this street, one can always reply that there is that other coffee shop, three blocks from here. You have to incur some cost to go there, but you can still go there. There always are costs attached to pretty much all the alternatives we can find in the market. So why in some cases, do we just say, "Well, this could lead to a situation of monopoly pricing"?

KIRZNER: All these cases that we are talking about (oranges, grapefruits, coffee shops, etc.) they mean that the monopolist faces a downward sloping demand curve. There is a local situation where the coffee shop three blocks away is not a perfect substitute to the one on this block. So to that extent this means that even if the prices were raised, there would still be some people who would buy in this street. Now, Mises says that *under certain circumstances* (e.g. there's no empty store here for another coffee shop), it *may be* that the money I can get by raising my price will be the result of exploiting a monopoly position. I may be able to get more by deliberately withholding or destroying some of my coffee. Whereas market forces ordinarily "compel" owners of resources to place those resources at the service of consumers—the "monopoly price" curiosum motivates resource owners to *destroy* some of their resources.

EDS: Given your own analytical framework where we are always talking about markets in which people are price makers not price takers, aren't we always going to have, at least to some degree, a downward sloping demand curve?

KIRZNER: Downward sloping demand curves are a necessary but not sufficient condition for monopoly pricing. So, wherever the possibility exists, producers will attempt to restrict supply in order to raise the price and total revenue. You have to understand that monopoly in Mises's framework is totally different from monopoly in the standard neoclassical framework. It's a resource phenomenon. It may pay the owner of a resource to restrict its availability to the public. This is extremely unlikely. However, I am convinced that Mises believed that you wouldn't find an empirical case exemplifying this. It is just a theoretical curiosum; you cannot rule it out.

EDS: In the situation of the evenly rotating economy, monopoly rents would continue to exist, right?

KIRZNER: It's conceivable that rents will continue to exist, that they would never be competed away, to the extent that this is possible. You might have a situation where these monopoly rents are obtainable only by destroying or limiting the supply—actually destroying some of the resources. This is what Mises would consider to be an extraordinary phenomenon: that ownership of a resource yields benefits to its owner by removing it from availability to the consumers. That was his position and I think there is nothing that I have seen that refutes the possibility.

EDS: But monopoly rents are impossible to identify empirically.

KIRZNER: Well, of course. You know, Rothbard said that even if I am burning some oil, that may simply show that I like bonfires. And of course, he is right. You can't prove empirically that a resource is being deliberately destroyed. But the theoretical possibility (of what Mises called "monopoly pricing") nonetheless exists.

EDS: You said that downward sloping demand curves are necessary but not sufficient to have monopoly pricing. And we know that entrepreneurs are price makers and thus in general face downward sloping demand curves for their new products. So what here would distinguish monopoly rents from entrepreneurial profits? Is the former the result of reduced supply while the latter is not (and the latter is, moreover, transient)?

KIRZNER: The notion of "monopoly rents" in the Misesian system is inseparable from unique asset ownership. It is only because the owner of the unique resource finds that his revenues are increased by deliberate withholding (of the services) of this resource from the market that his "additional" resource-revenues are to be labeled monopoly rents (since they cannot be competed away). So these rents can certainly not be seen as pure entrepreneurial profit (which is a theoretical category unrelated to resource *ownership*).

EDS: Moving on to the broader topic of institutions and economic systems, we have an introductory question on Mises. Mises emphasizes capital accumulation and the division of labor as the main factors that lead to prosperity and growth. In some ways he is quite classical in his understanding of that process. He seems to underestimate entrepreneurship, especially the discovery of gains from trade and new technology. What is your view of his analysis?

KIRZNER: If you would ask Mises, which is more important for the historical phenomenal success of capitalism, is it capital accumulation or freedom? He would say you are talking about two different realms of discourse. If you are talking institutional framework, freedom is more important. It is the free market. If you are talking at the practical level of resource availability, then Mises would focus on capital goods as being determinative (within a given level of freedom of course). This has to do with the insight that entrepreneurship is not a factor of production. Mises used to emphasize capital. One example he often used was that of ancient Greeks who could have had the technology to build steam engines, as they knew the science. Mises said the reason why they didn't build steam engines is because they didn't have the capital. So, at the practical level, at the nitty-gritty level, he believed that capital was extremely important. It was more important than technological knowledge. He used to say that the engineers from developing countries can come to the United States and study at engineering schools, but they don't have the capital back home to use it. Now, that wouldn't have in any way been inconsistent with his pointing out that many of these developing countries don't have a free market within which to operate.

EDS: Another related difficult issue with Mises is his view that you can tell how rich a country is by its per capita capital level. This requires our ability to aggregate capital and then divide it by the population. But this is difficult to reconcile with Mises's skepticism concerning aggregate measurements.

KIRZNER: This is indeed a puzzle. I addressed this puzzle in my work on Austrian capital theory.

EDS: One question we have often debated is the role of institutions and entrepreneurship. Do you see, for instance, economics as taking place only against an already defined set of institutions? Do you think people can create institutional rules but only because there exists an already agreed upon moral stance about the desirability and legitimacy of certain rules such as property rights? The big question is what is the role of institutions in your work?

KIRZNER: What I have said on this subject is that the market process occurs within an institutional framework. The market process is an entrepreneurial process. The way in which the entrepreneurial process operates depends on and is framed within the institutional framework. It cannot *embrace* the institutional framework. Now, obviously, the institutional framework is evolving and is changing. Human action is involved in modifying institutions, in modifying laws, and so forth, but that's not the market process. Is it part of economics? It *might* be part of economics, suitably defined; but I would insist that this process of institutional modification is not part of the *market* process. I argue that it's not just analytically useful to keep that perspective; it's also ethically and morally relevant. I have quoted Charles Fried who points out that Harold Demsetz's theory of property rights makes the economic process responsible for the institutions. I grant that Demsetz's work is extremely interesting and extremely valuable, but I don't think that institutional development can be assimilated within the analysis of market process. The market process has to take the institutional framework for granted. It is true that over history the market process is accompanied by an evolving set of institutions. I don't deny that but to the extent that the market process is entrepreneurial; to that extent, entrepreneurship has to take those institutions as a datum, which is given. My argument for that is similar to my argument against Gary Becker's "economic imperialism" view. My fundamental point is that there is no entrepreneurial *market process* involved in institutional modification. There could be entrepreneurship in the sense that people are acting, people are grasping political profits, etc., but that's not the market process.

EDS: How far would you push that view? Take the development of free banking theories in the last two or three decades. It claims that the monetary framework, which is traditionally viewed as exogenous, can in fact be endogenized through market mechanisms. Would you have the same reservations with that work?

KIRZNER: Hayek saw Menger's theory of the emergence of money as a typical economic process. This is inconsistent with what I have just been saying. The problem is that it may seem to be an entrepreneurial process because entrepreneurs use money. As people use these commodities more and more, it eventually becomes money. People want the item itself more and they feel confident that it's going to be easy to download the commodity onto somebody else. So it's a snowballing effect, which generates the emergence of money. That's fine. I accept Menger's theory absolutely, but that is not an entrepreneurial process. No one is inventing money because it is profitable to do so. It's a snowballing effect, but these effects can be perverse you know, like say the escalation of a conflict or an arms race. I am afraid of you so I get a gun; you see that I've got a gun and you get a bigger gun. I get an even bigger one and that escalates. That's a snowballing effect. In the entrepreneurial process in contrast, where errors have been made, they will tend to be discovered if it is mutually beneficial to do so. This corrective process is not what happens in a snowballing effect. Hayek was wrong. The same thing applies in regard to free banking. This is not a criticism at all of the work itself. People used to ask me, "Do you believe in free banking?" and I would reply, "I don't know. I am not an expert on that." All I know is that the monetary system is part of the *framework*. I've always thought of the monetary system as part of the *framework* within which the market operates. I have no problem with the State being in charge of the law. I am not an anarchist by any means. Now, it *could* be that what I believe to be part of the framework is in fact something, which is part of the process emerging *within* the framework. I don't know, I think that work on these issues is most interesting.

EDS: So much of what goes on in Eastern and Central Europe but also in Africa and in other developing countries is failed and weak states that are not doing a very good job with the institutional framework. The key question is one of finding a system, which eliminates error in the institutional framework, the way the market process does it. But then do you see the political process as potentially a market process, the way public choice theory does?

KIRZNER: I don't know. I keep an open mind. I am willing to hear what results from the political process. It could be that there exists a political framework within which political entrepreneurship may be socially benign. I just don't know how it would work. I wouldn't say categorically that there couldn't be an analog to market process in political institutions; I am not saying that. But we would need one to obtain a process. My critique of Becker runs along similar lines. Therein I said that, in general, you don't find analogs to the market process. When Becker assumes a marriage market in equilibrium (everybody has found the ideal mate), it is not just unrealistic; it also assumes a process at work that would *lead* toward such an ideal state. If there were only marriage brokers profiting from marrying people, you could perhaps think of a possibility of such an analog, but there isn't such a process. The same is true in the political area I assume, but I really don't know.

EDS: The crucial difference, then, is between the notion of entrepreneurship on the one hand and the entrepreneurial process on the other. One can have the former without having the latter.

KIRZNER: Absolutely. Entrepreneurship does not imply market process, but the entrepreneurial process does. There is always entrepreneurship everywhere, including in politics and institutional activity. Every human action is entrepreneurial.

EDS: So while there is entrepreneurship in politics, there is not necessarily a systematic political entrepreneurial process.

KIRZNER: That's right.

EDS: Would you treat institutions and ethical mores as part of the framework within which people act, and not as factors of production?

KIRZNER: Yes, absolutely.

EDS: You are always careful when comparing the results of different institutional systems. Can you explain why?

KIRZNER: Coordination can only be defined against the background of given rights. The market tends to coordinate. But then you say: "Look at the Soviet Union. Was that coordination or not?" Well, you can only talk about coordination against a framework of given rights. An example I gave in one of my papers is where I like beef and you like chicken, and you've got the beef and I've got the chicken. In such a case, coordination requires that we exchange. But suppose I've got the beef *and* the chicken—then we have a fully coordinated situation even though you remain hungry. So coordination can only be defined against a background of given rights. It is perhaps a purist point, but it is crucial.

EDS: You made important contributions to the ethics of capitalism. You always emphasize that a thorough understanding of economics is necessary to make ethical statements about the market system. The introduction of entrepreneurial discovery in the debate is a very important achievement in the field of economic justice and ethics. One of the most difficult questions is that of the role of sheer luck in entrepreneurship. Can you comment on this?

KIRZNER: As you point out, this is a difficult question. Many scholars concerned with the ethics of capitalism find room in principle for only two kinds of "winnings": (a) those attributable to asset ownership (e.g., the fruit of my tree is held to be mine) with a broad interpretation of "asset" (so that the fruit of my hard work, my ingenuity, and my integrity, is mine); [and] (b) those winnings attributable to pure luck. These scholars may or may not accept the ethical legitimacy of my title to the first of these two kinds of winnings (often they may challenge the legitimacy of my title to the "tree" from which these winnings sprang); but they tend to unanimity in finding almost *no* justification for the second kind of winnings. (Why should *I* be the sole beneficiary of circumstances, which are in no way of my making?) My position has not been to challenge the *ethics* of this latter position. (In fact, qua economist, I claim no expertise at all in the field of pure ethics.) My contribution has been to point out that besides the above two kinds of "winnings" is a third kind of "winnings." (Many winnings, which the ethical scholars attribute to pure luck, can be seen, I maintain, as in fact constituting this "third kind" of winnings.) This "third kind" of winnings can be attributed neither to my owned assets (including my labor power) nor to pure luck. Such winnings are, of course, pure entrepreneurial profits. The pure arbitrage profit available to the alert entrepreneur was not *created* by his alertness (it was "waiting" for someone to notice it) nor was it the result of pure luck. It was *discovered* by the entrepreneur. No one seeks to deny the possibility that luck *may* play a greater role in entrepreneurial discovery than in the emergence of other kinds of winnings. But I have seen no demonstration of this. (After all, is it not possible that what is considered "pure luck" may affect the quantity of fruit grown by different trees, and so on?)

EDS: Do you have any opinion on the role of intellectual property?

KIRZNER: No. I have struggled with things like these before. Mises struggled too. It was one of the very few issues for which he had no definite opinion.

EDS: You have often mentioned that psychological research could help develop an understanding of alertness. Some economists are interested in using cognitive science to better understand consumer behavior, et cetera. What is your opinion of these developments?

KIRZNER: I used to have disagreements with Mario Rizzo on these types of issues. Mario has been very eager to make common ground with other disciplines and other approaches. I, on the other hand, always felt that we would be threatened, that we'd be absorbed and that the integrity of Austrian ideas could be lost. It is perhaps not inevitable, as one can maintain for instance the distinction between pure and applied economics. But I would favor an interdisciplinary approach, rather than a merger of different views.

EDS: Especially as you realize that some economists are looking to overturn the systematic tendencies that are at the core of Austrian ideas. Cognitive sciences can always be used to show that demand curves slope upwards, arguing that economics is built on the wrong psychological foundations. It goes back to the reasons why studying the history of economic thought is crucial. Most modern debates are in fact reenactments of older ones. As Veblen remarked, Austrians were the most value-free thinkers. But, as you mentioned somewhere, Austrian reputation reached its lowest point at the time it was making its most original contributions.

KIRZNER: Indeed, it's a dramatic circumstance that at the time when Austrian reputation was at its lowest level, Mises and Hayek were in fact revolutionizing Austrian economics. This was around 1948.

EDS: What do you tell people who ask: "What difference does it make to look at individuals as entrepreneurs because you cannot really prove the existence of the entrepreneurial function?" Moreover, you can explain the consequences of the minimum wage without having recourse to entrepreneurship.

KIRZNER: It is true. That's simply saying that there's nothing wrong with neoclassical price theory at a certain level of analysis. When Mises used to lecture about rent control, he was talking about simple supply and demand curves. This is simple partial equilibrium analysis, which does not depend on entrepreneurship. When you get behind supply and demand theory and explore its validity then you have to get into the entrepreneurial approach, dynamic competition, et cetera. So there is a level of practicality where you do not need entrepreneurial analysis. I have always insisted that's why we should not throw out supply and demand analysis and should understand its practical usefulness.

EDS: As far as intellectual missed opportunities are concerned and in reflecting back on your career, do you view any intellectual missed opportunities that you should have used or organizational missed opportunities to advance Austrian economics that you should have seized but didn't?

KIRZNER: What's in the forefront of my mind right now (and as one gets older, less and less things are in the forefront of one's mind) is the missed opportunity of capital theory in the 1960s. Austrians really had an opportunity, which we missed, which I certainly missed. I've drawn attention to this when I published the *Essays on Capital and Interest*. Remember Austrian economists always had a certain comparative advantage in capital theory. It was recognized, so that Austrians could have exploited that particular avenue; we didn't do it. When I wrote my *Essay on Capital*, I don't think I was even aware of this debate. I discovered it in 1966, the year my book was published. I don't think I was aware of it at the time I was writing my book. There may have been other lost opportunities, but I can't identify them.

EDS: An important issue for the development of Austrian ideas in the 1960s was whether there were opportunities for alliances with other economists that we missed or others that we mistakenly tried to exploit. For example, much of the Lachmann agenda to align with post-Keynesianism was a mistake intellectually because post-Keynesians could never get over the fundamental vision of the way the system worked. Despite how much we might have shared with them, in terms of criticisms of the late neo-Ricardianism of Chicago economics, there was an aspect of the basic vision (what you refer to as the systematic tendencies) that we didn't share.

KIRZNER: I am convinced that if you, Peter Boettke, had been sitting in my chair in the 1960s, *you* would have found allies, but I didn't. This is a question of personality and intellectual entrepreneurship in the sense of finding linkages. I didn't have that. I was lonely, and I stayed lonely. I grabbed the opportunity that I saw, but I didn't see all the opportunities, and I don't even see them in retrospect. Sure, they were there. I had a correspondence on monopoly theory with an economist from Harvard named Bishop, but I didn't pursue this very far. I sort of saw myself in a backwater corner. I believe my basic stance was valid. The whole profession out there looked down on Mises and Hayek. Before the 1970s Hayek was in the pits. When Jerry O'Driscoll wrote his book in 1977, he was investing in something that had no future. And yet Hayek's Nobel Prize turned things around. Not so much for Mises. As a student, when I told a member of our department that I was doing my dissertation under Mises, he replied to me that Mises hadn't had a new idea in thirty years. Mises wasn't a sophisticated economist in the modern sense; somehow along the way, his reputation went down and has never recovered. What I have tried to do is not to lift up Mises's reputation directly but to lift up his ideas and to communicate, hoping indirectly that this will lift up his reputation. But it hasn't been easy. Hayek's reputation of the 1930s was restored by the 1980s. Mises's profound contribution is still widely unrecognized.

EDS: Last question. You use the Hebrew words "B'EZRAS HASHEM" at the beginning of your books. What do they signify?

KIRZNER: These words represent my invocation and acknowledgment of Divine help.

EDS: Well, Israel, thank you so much for taking the time to talk to us about your work.

KIRZNER: It was a real pleasure to discuss with you both.

This book is set in Scala and Scala Sans, created
by the Dutch designer Martin Majoor in the 1990s.

This book is printed on paper that is acid-free and
meets the requirements of the American National
Standard for Permanence of Paper for Printed Library
Materials, z39.48-1992. ⊗

Book design by Richard Hendel, Chapel Hill, North Carolina
Typography by Apex CoVantage, Madison, Wisconsin
Index by Mary Mortensen, Lawrence, Kansas
Printed and bound by Thomson-Shore, Inc., Dexter, Michigan